Engaging Theories in Interpersonal Communication

Multiple Perspectives

Second Edition

Engaging Theories in Interpersonal Communication

Multiple Perspectives

Second Edition

Dawn O. Braithwaite
University of Nebraska–Lincoln

Paul Schrodt
Texas Christian University

Editors

Los Angeles | London | New Delhi
Singapore | Washington DC

Los Angeles | London | New Delhi
Singapore | Washington DC

FOR INFORMATION:

SAGE Publications, Inc.
2455 Teller Road
Thousand Oaks, California 91320
E-mail: order@sagepub.com

SAGE Publications Ltd.
1 Oliver's Yard
55 City Road
London EC1Y 1SP
United Kingdom

SAGE Publications India Pvt. Ltd.
B 1/I 1 Mohan Cooperative Industrial Area
Mathura Road, New Delhi 110 044
India

SAGE Publications Asia-Pacific Pte. Ltd.
3 Church Street
#10-04 Samsung Hub
Singapore 049483

Acquisitions Editor: Matthew Byrnie
Editorial Assistant: Janae Masnovi
Production Editor: Kelly DeRosa
Copy Editor: Terri Lee Paulsen
Typesetter: C&M Digitals (P) Ltd.
Proofreader: Alison Syring
Indexer: Joan Shapiro
Cover Designer: Candice Harman
Marketing Manager: Liz Thornton

Printed in the United States of America

Library of Congress Cataloging-in-Publication Data

Engaging theories in interpersonal communication: multiple perspectives / [edited by] Dawn O. Braithwaite, University of Nebraska, Lincoln, Paul Schrodt, Texas Christian University. — Second edition.

pages cm
Includes bibliographical references and index.

ISBN 978-1-4522-6140-9 (pbk. : alk. paper)
1. Interpersonal communication—Philosophy. I. Braithwaite, Dawn O. II. Schrodt, Paul.

P94.7.E54 2015
153.6—dc23   2014019041

This book is printed on acid-free paper.

MIX
Paper from
responsible sources

FSC
www.fsc.org

FSC® C014174

14 15 16 17 18 10 9 8 7 6 5 4 3 2 1

Contents

Foreword

Growing Interpersonal Communication Theory

Interpersonal communication matters. To those who adopt a constitutive approach to communication, it matters because interpersonal communication constructs the everyday social world as we know it. To those who adopt an effects approach to communication, it matters because interpersonal communication affects the hearts, minds, and actions of individuals as they function in the everyday social world. Although it is difficult to imagine that anyone in the social sciences would not agree that communication is important, scholars in our sister disciplines tend to take communication for granted, positioning it as a neutral conduit or carrier of psychological phenomena such as speaker beliefs and motivation, or sociological phenomena such as roles. Unfortunately, such a conduit view situates communication as the handmaiden, secondary to what are widely accepted as the more important psychological or sociological drivers of the social experience. Scholars in communication studies think otherwise, presuming that communication is a force in its own right and deserving of attention as such.

It is difficult to understand interpersonal communication on its own terms if scholars simply adopt theories from other social scientific fields, because communication typically is not their central concern. For too long, communication scholars suffered from what Berger (2005) has described as the import-export problem: communication scholars have for too long imported their theories from other disciplines and have not generated enough "homegrown" theories to export outward to other disciplines in order to promote the constitutive and effects perspectives that are central to our disciplinary mission. Fortunately, the second edition of this book continues a pattern documented in the first edition: the development and maturation of homegrown theories of communication. Not only are communication scholars increasingly grounding their research in theory, but they also are developing a rich theoretical toolkit of homegrown theories from which to choose in understanding or explaining interpersonal communication.

Growing theory is a complicated business for a field and for an individual scholar. At the level of a disciplinary field, theories wax and wane in popularity and influence contingent on any number of factors. Society is in flux with emergent social problems that merit scholarly attention and require new theories. Existing theories are differentially successful over time in winning loyal followings. Sometimes theories are so provocative that they motivate theorists to develop new theoretical offshoots. Academic institutional needs for different types of research vary depending on needs for external fundability and stakeholders who demand research of both local and global significance. Research, in short, is a fluid business. Theories fit the times. This second edition shows turnover in theories that reflects this fluidity: Some theories present in the first edition are not represented in this second edition, and several new theories have been added to the volume. In fact, the Introduction chapter to this volume indicates that only three theories have continued in the "top 10" most frequently used theories across both editions to this book: uncertainty reduction/management (a cluster of theories), politeness theory, and relational dialectics theory.

Growing theory is also a dynamic business for the theorist(s) identified with its creation. Theory building is not unlike raising a child. There is a pre-theory stage of gestational development in which a theorist doesn't yet have a fully coherent theory but an emergent research program with preliminary theoretical glimmers. Gestation is followed by birth, the first formal articulation of the theory. Birthing a theory then enters a long period of nurturance and adaptation. A theorist nurtures and adapts his or her theory, just as a parent nurtures a child and adapts to the child's development. Theorists promote their theories, educating fellow scholars to their benefits. They use their theories in research, learning what facets of the theory work best and which need revision. A good theory goes through several iterations and articulations as it changes and grows, requiring volumes such as this one to produce new editions to reflect those changes over time in existing theories. Finally, just as parenting is a gradual process of "letting go" of a child as they broaden their bases of relating, so a theorist lets go of his or her theory, hoping that it is taken up by others to produce an intellectual life beyond that authored by the original theorist associated with the theory.

Theories come in a variety of forms. I have long been attracted to Turner's (1986) distinction between three theoretical forms: analytical schemes, modeling schemes, and propositional schemes. Analytical schemes are typologies or classification schemes intended to describe the properties of the phenomena under study. Understanding comes through the development of an exhaustive set of mutually exclusive categories that create order for the social world of interest. A given datum is explained by locating its place in the classification system. Typologies provide understanding of *what* a given phenomenon is. A classic typological theory in interpersonal communication is relational communication theory (Rogers & Escudero, 2004), in which interpersonal behaviors of control were typologized as one up, one down, and one across in nature, tied to one another in a larger transaction unit that was typologized as symmetrical, complementary, or transitional.

By contrast, Turner's modeling scheme is a diagrammatic representation of some process of interest. Models are often oriented toward distal and proximal causal explanations of processes. They focus on *how* a given phenomenon happens, examining antecedent variables that function through mediating variables to result in a variety of possible outcomes. Models often present a set of key concepts and a set of symbols (e.g., lines, arrows) by which those concepts are connected. Early stage-based models of relationship development (and decay) illustrate modeling theories (see Mongeau & Henningsen, Chapter 29, this volume).

A propositional scheme (Turner, 1986) specifies the connection between two or more concepts. Propositional schemes address questions of *why*, either in a causal manner of how independent and dependent variables function in a patterned way or in a reason-based manner of understanding how cultural rules and systems of meaning account for patterned regularities. These schemes vary in their level of abstraction and the logical tightness of their organization and usually take one of two forms: axiomatic theory and formal theory. In interpersonal communication, the most famous axiomatic theory is uncertainty reduction theory (Berger & Calabrese, 1975). Formal theories, more common in interpersonal communication, are less hierarchical in their deductive reasoning, consisting of a set of abstract principles that are then deployed in "rather loose deductions to explain empirical events" (Turner, 1986, p. 15), in contrast to the axiom/theorem structure of axiomatic theories. This second edition has many exemplars of formal theories.

Some scholars are inclined to frame these three forms of theory in a hierarchy, with propositional schemes (and axiomatic theory in particular) viewed as superior to either typologies or models. But I urge communication scholars to resist such a framing. So long as a theory does well what it is designed to do, it merits respect. Typologies, models, axiomatic theories, and formal theories do different kinds of analytic work and must be judged against different criteria. Hierarchies of theory form inevitably function to belittle some theories and empower others. All good theories—whether typological, diagrammatic, or propositional—deserve an equal voice at the theoretical table. This second edition has examples of all three forms of theories, and I am pleased that the editors do not privilege one kind of theory above others.

Although I am excited to see this second edition, I must admit to one disappointment, not in the volume but with the current state of interpersonal communication scholarship that the volume represents. The Introduction in Chapter 1 reveals that interpersonal scholars made no progress from the time of the first edition in adding to the diversity of meta-theoretical perspectives represented in their research. Post-positivistic work still holds the dominant position (stable at around 85% of all empirical, theory-based research), and interpretive and critical perspectives combined occupy a more marginalized footing (15%). Perhaps I have been a scholar of Bakhtin's dialogism (for discussion, see Baxter & Norwood, Chapter 21, this volume) for too long, but I find myself suspicious of any monologic inclinations. Put simply, monologue produces calcification of thinking. To be sure, post-positivism is not an absolute monologue because of the presence of its 15% minority, but it is too close to monologue status for my comfort zone. I do not intend to be critical of post-positivistic work, for much of it is excellent. I myself continue to conduct research in this tradition, although over the past two decades it is fair to argue that I have shifted to interpretive and critical traditions. What I am critical of is the absence of the enriched intellectual conversation that would undoubtedly ensue if interpretive and critical voices could be as easily heard as the post-positivistic voice. Good things happen when difference is respected and taken seriously. In order to realize the dialogic potential of difference, interpersonal scholars need to develop more theories in the interpretive and critical tradition. Such theories are in short supply in this second edition, not because the editors haven't worked diligently to present them, but because very few such theories currently exist. I hope to see a different profile should there be a third edition of this volume.

One future change that might result from a heavier infusion of a critical perspective, in particular, as a fourth organizational section to the volume—a set of theories that focus on identity, social justice, and social change. I think the current organization of the book captures well the current landscape of interpersonal communication (and in fact, as a co-editor of the first edition of this book, I was partially responsible for the initial articulation of this tri-partite organizational structure). To the extent that interpersonal communication scholars focus on social structure, we privilege the micro-structures of everyday life: patterned interactions within daily encounters and dyadic relationships between parties. But people do more with their interpersonal communication practices than accomplishing seamless encounters with others and building/ sustaining social and personal relationships with those others over time. Our interpersonal words and actions contribute to a larger social order, one in which identities are negotiated through structural lenses of race, class, gender, age, and sexual orientation, among other bases of identity. It is through interpersonal communication that neighbors accomplish such feats as forming and sustaining

Neighborhood Watch associations. It is through interpersonal communication that community members reach decisions about the kinds of educational experiences their children have in local schools. It is through interpersonal communication that people mobilize in myriad ways to impact local, national, and global decisions. I do not wish to belittle research that concentrates on dyadic relationships. A wealth of research documents the benefits to individual well-being that are associated with having a social network populated with healthy, functioning relationships. But interpersonal communication scholars should seek to broaden our scholarly agenda to consider the important work in the larger world that is accomplished by interpersonal communication. Interpersonal communication is political, not just personal.

I was proud to be a co-editor for the first edition of this volume. Unfortunately, other commitments, including a book project whose production deadline coincided with the schedule for this volume, precluded me from serving as a worthy co-editor of the second edition. I am proud nonetheless to be a part of this volume in contributing two of its chapters and in being asked to write this Foreword. A good read is in store for all who use this second edition, whether an advanced student or an established scholar. Long live the growing of theory.

Leslie A. Baxter

References

Berger, C. R. (2005). Interpersonal communication: Theoretical perspectives, future prospects. *Journal of Communication, 55,* 415–447.

Berger, C. R., & Calabrese, R. J. (1975). Some explorations in initial interaction and beyond: Toward a developmental theory of interpersonal communication. *Human Communication Research, 1,* 99–112.

Rogers, L. E., & Escudero, V. (Ed.). (2004). *Relational communication: An interactional perspective to the study of process and form.* Mahwah, NJ: Erlbaum.

Turner, J. H. (1986). *The structure of sociological theory* (4th ed.). Chicago, IL: The Dorsey Press.

Preface

This second edition of *Engaging Theories in Interpersonal Communication: Multiple Perspectives* springs from an updated analysis of the current state and scope of interpersonal communication theory and scholarship. Paul Schrodt joins Dawn O. Braithwaite on the editorial team for this edition. We are in many ways a perfect match as editors as we are both teachers of interpersonal communication with 40 years of faculty experience between us, we are active researchers who work together and separately, and we earned our doctoral degrees 15 years apart, deepening our collective insights. In addition, most of our research projects grow from different meta-theoretical perspectives—Dawn's work is largely interpretive and Paul's is post-positive. These differences provide opportunities for fruitful discussions and open up avenues of research and insight that we would never achieve alone. We do not always agree, yet at all times we share a deep respect for the breadth of perspectives and understanding in our chosen field.

We'll briefly discuss four reasons for publishing a book of interpersonal communication theories. First, while there are some fine books available about interpersonal communication, most take the approach of examining communication at the different stages of relationships or are focused on the different interpersonal communication processes in play. In most books, theories play a supporting role and most often receive brief coverage at best. Our goal with this book is to make a unique contribution where interpersonal communication theories take center stage.

A second motivation for a book focused on theories is that it helps us understand and enlighten the current state of interpersonal communication theories. Tracing its roots in the college classroom back to 1970 (with research starting well before that), the first volume of the book was intended take to stock of the field. Here in the second edition, we update that work for new generations of scholars and students. We have often heard communication scholars lament that we borrow theories from other disciplines more than we create our own. Thus we wanted to examine the state of interpersonal communication theory, particularly theories that are *homegrown* (that is, constructed by scholars whose primary professional affiliation is in communication), as well as those from other disciplines. We note in Chapter 1 that we have seen the number of home-grown theories increase in this second edition. This is important because while communication is part of research in many disciplines, one of our primary goals in this book is to focus on the unique contributions of communication scholars and theorists in furthering our understanding of communication in the constitution and enactment of our close relationships.

Third, both of us share concerns when we read research that lacks a theoretical foundation or contribution. As we will discuss in Chapter 1, we both are fans of theory-based research whenever it is feasible. We believe that we can best understand the breadth and strength of the study of interpersonal communication and move the field ahead by centering research in the broader theoretical conversation of the discipline.

Fourth, our continuing sense is that, as a whole, interpersonal communication scholarship is not as inclusive or broad as it could or should be. This second edition was an opportunity to better understand the current landscape of the field and to track new developments. We continue to believe that interpersonal communication will be at its best when the field is open to different ways of studying and understanding social interaction (i.e., different paradigmatic approaches).

Chapter 1 presents our interpretation of the landscape of interpersonal communication. In preparation for the first edition, Dawn and Leslie Baxter analyzed a study of 15 years of scholarship beginning in 1990 to track what theories were being used most in interpersonal communication and what meta-theoretical discourses or paradigmatic perspectives scholars were using. In preparation for the second edition, we updated that study through 2013 and report the results in the first chapter. We are grateful to Dr. Jill Tyler at the University of South Dakota, who completed the initial study of interpersonal communication scholarship from 1990–2005, and to Chapter 1 co-author Dr. Kristen Carr, who expanded the data through 2013. Their careful and thoughtful work helped lay the groundwork for us to understand the state of interpersonal communication theory, and it helped Dawn and Paul choose what theories should be represented in this second edition. In this book, you will find theories that you would expect to see as they have been employed widely by interpersonal communication scholars. The book also includes some of the newer, up-and-coming theories, as well as some theories that you may have not seen explicitly connected to interpersonal communication in the past.

In Chapter 1, we trace the development of interpersonal communication theory from its beginnings, and we organize theory and research within the larger discussion of meta-theory, or paradigms. We asked the different authors to talk about the roots and paradigmatic homes of their individual theories in each of their chapters. While this task appears simple at first glance, it is often challenging, as there were times when authors had different perspectives on meta-theory and we discovered that some of the theories do not fit neatly into one category.

Following the first chapter are 30 theory chapters written by outstanding interpersonal communication scholars. We begin each of the three main sections of the book with a description of what binds the theories in that section together and the meta-theoretical discourses represented by the theories in the particular section. Each chapter follows the same structure to help readers easily find and compare information across theories.

We have many people to thank for their contributions to this project. We both express deep gratitude to our friend and colleague Leslie A. Baxter, who co-edited the first edition of the book. We are so pleased that she wrote the foreword for the book, updated one chapter, and wrote a new one for this volume. Clearly, the book would not exist without the expertise and dedication of this outstanding group of authors, many of whom created the theories about which they wrote. Every new or returning author we invited agreed to be part of the book. All of the authors have been active as theorists and researchers, challenging and refining the theories as they use them to enlighten us about interpersonal communication. We thank our colleagues for sharing their excellent work and being so easy to work with.

We also appreciate the contributions of Matthew Byrnie, senior acquisitions editor of Communication, Media, and Cultural Studies at SAGE Publications, along with the excellent work of Sage Editorial Assistant Gabrielle Piccininni. We acknowledge the contributions of Todd Armstrong, who served as editor on the first edition of the book, and his continuing encouragement and insight. We thank University of Nebraska–Lincoln doctoral student Katie Brockhage for proofreading some of the chapters. We are very grateful to several book adopters who gave us excellent advice on the second edition, particularly Clark Olson at Arizona State University; Colleen Colaner, University of Missouri; Leanne Knobloch, University of Illinois; Haley Kranstuber Horstman, University of Missouri; Erin Sahlstein Parcell, University of Wisconsin–Milwaukee; Jennifer Samp, University of Georgia; and Allison Thorson, University of San Francisco.

Paul and Dawn have been co-travelers on this and other projects, starting the journey as professor and doctoral student, and quickly becoming close friends, research collaborators, and co-editors. Our own interpersonal communication and relationship make working together productive and enjoyable. Dawn is grateful to Paul for his commitment, friendship, and support. She dedicates this book to Betsy, Leslie, Sandra, Steve, Clark, and Laura for being dearest friends; to Jordan and Jody for being wonderful colleagues; to Chris for being Mom; to Walt Hoffman for being a central influence and inspiration; and to Chuck Braithwaite for being the love of her life for over 30 years. Paul thanks Dawn for the opportunity to work together on this important project, as well as for her professional wisdom, guidance, and friendship. He dedicates this book to his beautiful wife and best friend, Danielle, to his two sons, Isaac and Eli, and to Andrew, Kristen, Adam, Mark, Kory, Paul, Matt, Tammy, and Wes for being friends.

Dawn O. Braithwaite and Paul Schrodt

1

Introduction

Meta-Theory and Theory in Interpersonal Communication Research

Dawn O. Braithwaite,
Paul Schrodt, and Kristen Carr

O ur goal for this book was to create a helpful resource for researchers and students who are interested in studying interpersonal communication. Some readers of the book will be researchers designing studies of interpersonal communication and looking for a theory to guide their project. Others will be students or instructors who want to better understand the breadth of interpersonal communication theory or are looking for a concise discussion of a particular theory. Still others will be studying interpersonal communication to better understand their own relationships, for example, looking to address challenges in a friendship, romantic, or close workplace relationship. They may need help tackling a particular problem related to interpersonal communication and need to make choices about what information to reveal or conceal via social media or the best way to communicate support and concern.

Most textbooks or handbooks of interpersonal communication contain summaries of research programs on different topics, for instance, conflict communication, deception, or relational maintenance (e.g., Greene & Burleson, 2003; Knapp & Daly, 2011; Knapp, Vangelisti, & Caughlin, 2014). Our goal for this book is different in that we provide a collection and overview of important theories that are, or have the potential to be, useful for studying interpersonal communication. Our goal is a very practical one as we see theories as useful tools for addressing choices and concerns people encounter. For students and scholars alike, this collection of theories becomes a toolbox to help you approach and understand interpersonal communication from a variety of perspectives.

1

In this chapter, we first present a brief background on the study of interpersonal communication, explain our approach to interpersonal communication, and discuss meta-theoretical perspectives for research on interpersonal communication. Second, we present findings from our own analysis of 492 data-based studies of interpersonal communication published from 2006 to 2013 by scholars affiliated with the discipline of communication. This study is a follow-up of the analysis included in the first edition of 958 studies published from 1990 to 2005. Third, we present some of our own conclusions about the state of interpersonal communication theory today and where we wish to see the field move in the future. Finally, we overview the sections in this book, organizing more than 30 different theories, authored by top experts in the interpersonal communication field.

Roots of Interpersonal Communication

Today's students likely think that the study of interpersonal communication has been around forever. Although people have been communicating interpersonally since the beginning of human existence, the academic study of interpersonal communication is relatively recent. In fact, many of the senior authors writing our chapters were students at its early stages. To help you understand how and why interpersonal communication theories have developed, we provide a brief history of the study of interpersonal communication in the larger context of the discipline of communication.

Those of us from the discipline of communication trace our roots back to ancient Greece and Rome, and most believe earlier than that, to Africa and China. The study of communication has always been a very practical one. The earliest work came from teachers and scholars of rhetoric and persuasion to help people create effective arguments and speeches (Ehninger, 1968).

Moving forward to the twentieth century, there were no communication departments in universities like we have today, but courses in public speaking, performance of literature, debate, and persuasion were taught most often in English or theater departments under the title of "speech." In 1914, a group of speech professors broke off from English and formed their own professional organization (Cohen, 1994). Soon thereafter, two main approaches to the study of speech emerged. The Cornell School included those who approached the study of speech from a humanities perspective, and the Midwestern School included those who thought it best to study speech as a science (Pearce & Foss, 1990). These schools represented the two main approaches of rhetoric and speech (subsequently, communication) and these scholars later formed speech departments, breaking off from English and theater departments. As many of you recognize from your own campuses, communication departments have different configurations, for example, some include mass communication and other specialties.

After World War II, speech teachers also began teaching courses in small group discussion as a way of promoting democracy, and scholars began studying interaction within groups. Social scientists, especially in psychology, began studying persuasion and obedience to authority, trying to understand the process of interpersonal influence to help explain some of the atrocities that happened during that war. While they were interested in the psychology of persuasion, many also recognized the need to study how people communicate to persuade. Into the 1950s, scholars of communication who took a social scientific approach were focusing on persuasion and social influence in mass media, on models of information transmission, and on systems thinking about relationships (to better understand these developments, see Berger, 2005; Bormann, 1980; Delia, 1987; Knapp & Daly, 2011).

As the 1960s began, cultural shifts like the civil rights and women's movements, as well as changes in families and relationships, were in full swing. The practical reasons for wanting to understand communication persisted and, as Gerald Miller (1976) explained, "students themselves began to demand answers about how to relate communicatively with their acquaintances and close friends, and romantic partners" (p. 10). Some scholars whose research had originated in social psychology and sociology began moving to speech departments, as they realized the centrality of the communication process to what they were studying. These scholars brought with them a social scientific and post-positivist orientation to research, focusing largely on cognitive approaches to understanding communication behavior (Delia, 1987; Miller, 1983). They were studying topics such as interpersonal persuasion, nonverbal message transmission, interpersonal attraction, self-disclosure, and deception, to name a few. They joined the rhetoricians, and departments were a blend of humanistic and social scientific approaches to understanding human communication. This blend of humanities and social sciences remains in most of our departments today.

The research interests of these social scientists in the 1960s had an effect: Interpersonal communication courses began to appear in college curricula in the early 1970s and spread rapidly throughout the United States in the next 10 years. There was much excitement and momentum among those studying interpersonal communication during this time, and the Interpersonal and Small Group Interaction Division formed in the national association and quickly became one of the largest divisions. On college campuses, departments of speech were starting to change their names to "speech communication" and later to "communication." Interpersonal communication scholars were importing theories from other disciplines and beginning to develop their own theories.

Interpersonal communication was joined in the 1970s and 1980s by research and by new college classes in nonverbal communication, conflict communication, gender communication, workplace communication, and intercultural communication, followed in the late 1980s and into the 1990s by family communication and health communication classes. Some of the scholars studying in these contexts began to use qualitative data and interpretive methods, although most of the research employed quantitative methods. At this point, the national association also changed its name from the Speech Communication Association to the National Communication Association. Research and college courses in relational communication sprung up as the interdisciplinary field of close relationships was developed, as scholars in communication, family, psychology, and sociology joined forces (Guerrero, Andersen, & Afifi, 2014). Most of these new topics (e.g., health, family, nonverbal) were initially thought of as part of interpersonal communication. Slowly, they have developed into their own specializations, leaving us to wonder at times, "What is the center of interpersonal communication?"

Over the years, colleagues stressing humanistic and social scientific approaches to communication have gotten along well at times and less well at other times, largely because they do not speak the same research language, nor do they share the same perspectives on how communication works and how we should study it (Braithwaite, in press). Since the 1990s and into the 21st century, communication departments are also home to scholars who take a critical perspective on communication, which we will discuss below. While these groups of scholars pursue different approaches to understanding interpersonal communication, we contend that, ultimately, it will be in this diversity of perspectives that our discipline creates strength.

Defining Interpersonal Communication

Before we define interpersonal communication, we need to focus on our definition of communication, as our perspective on interpersonal communication grows out of that. Early definitions of communication focused quite simply on the exchange of messages. For example, in one of the early interpersonal communication textbooks, Giffin and Patton (1971) defined communication as "a process involving the sending and receiving of messages" (p. 5), and interpersonal communication was thought about as communication in dyads. As theorizing about interpersonal communication developed, scholars began to focus on interpersonal communication as a symbolic process humans use to create meaning. For example, as he developed this perspective, Stewart (1999) stressed:

> Communication is the way humans build our reality. Human worlds are not made up of objects but of peoples' responses to objects, or their meanings. And these meanings are negotiated in communication. Try not to think of communication as simply a way to share ideas, because it's much more than that. It's the process humans use to define reality itself. (p. 25)

From this perspective, interpersonal communication is more than information transmission between two people. Instead, it becomes the way that humans create and negotiate meanings, identity, and relationships through social interaction—how we constitute selves and relationships (Baxter, 2004; Craig, 1999).

In terms of interpersonal communication, different approaches to understanding it and studying it abound. A complete discussion is impossible here; we recommend sources dedicated to giving a more detailed history and overview (e.g., Berger, 2005; Knapp & Daly, 2011). Authors often divide interpersonal communication into processes (e.g., social support), developmental stages (e.g., initiating, disengaging), contexts (e.g., family, workplace), or types or channels (e.g., nonverbal, computer mediated). For our purposes, we will talk about three broad approaches to interpersonal communication that form our organization of theories in this book: interpersonal communication as (a) *individually* centered, (b) *discourse or interaction* centered, and (c) *relationship* centered.

The first focus of interpersonal communication theory is what we are calling individually centered theories of interpersonal communication. This perspective is centered on understanding how individuals plan, produce, and process interpersonal communication messages—theories that envision communication as an individually centered cognitive activity. This work began with Gerald Miller and others who argued that interpersonal communication occurs when people make predictions about the other interactants based on perceiving the person as an individual rather than based on a social role—for example, a teacher or store clerk (see Miller, 1976; Miller & Steinberg, 1975). Those taking this perspective on interpersonal communication focus on mental representations that influence how people interpret information and how they behave (e.g., Berger, 2005; Knapp & Daly, 2011; Vangelisti, 2011). These approaches have been prominent in interpersonal communication research and theory, as we will see.

A second focus of interpersonal communication theory is what we are calling discourse- or interaction-centered theories of interpersonal communication. The central focus of this perspective is on understanding interpersonal communication as a message or a joint action behaviorally enacted between persons. The focus in this perspective moves from a focus on the individual and his or her dispositions or cognitive states to a wide variety of theories that share a focus on the content, forms, and functions of messages, and the behavioral interactions between interacting parties. Scholars focused on discourse are interested in "the ways our understandings, meanings, norms, roles, and rules are worked out interactively in communication" (Littlejohn & Foss, 2005, p. 45). Work in this second tradition has many origins, including the classic volume by Watzlawick, Bavelas, and

Jackson (1967) on behavioral patterns of joint actions, scholarship by language philosophers such as Wittgenstein (1953) and Austin (1962), and social construction (Berger & Luckmann, 1967).

The third focus of interpersonal communication theory is what we are labeling relationship-centered theories of interpersonal communication. Scholars taking this perspective on interpersonal communication focus on understanding the role of communication in developing, sustaining, and terminating social and personal relationships, including friendships, dating relationships, romantic relationships, and cohabiting relationships. Important classics in this third approach were two 1973 volumes, one by Murray Davis and the second by Irwin Altman and Dalmas Taylor. Beginning in the 1980s, scholars interested in personal relationships across psychology, communication, sociology, and family studies began meeting to present their research to each other, and creating interdisciplinary journals. In fact, the initial goal of the founders of these associations was to create a separate interdisciplinary field devoted to studying personal relationships. While there are diverse approaches to studying relational communication, scholars taking a relational perspective on interpersonal communication focus on messages within close relationships that influence (Guerrero et al., 2014) or constitute (Baxter, 2004) those relationships.

Each of these three broad approaches to understanding and studying interpersonal communication is distinct in how it helps us understand what interpersonal communication is and how it functions in human life. To define interpersonal communication, we will need to concentrate on what these approaches have in common. As we examined books and articles on interpersonal communication, we found that all authors seem to agree that there are many different definitions and that defining interpersonal communication will be problematic, as it will highlight some dimensions and leave others out. Most scholars agree that interpersonal communication is a process; it involves a dyad or normally a small number of people; it involves creating and negotiating meanings; and it is enacted through verbal and nonverbal message behaviors. Because our purpose in this book is to represent the breadth of interpersonal communication, we are best served by viewing interpersonal communication in the most broad and inclusive way we can. Thus, our definition of interpersonal communication is the production and processing of verbal and nonverbal messages between two or a few persons. This definition includes elements that speak to each of the three broad approaches to interpersonal communication that organize this book: (a) "the production and processing of . . . messages" emphasizes the first approach, (b) "verbal and nonverbal messages between . . . persons" emphasizes the second approach, and (c) "two or a few persons" emphasizes the relational orientation of the third approach.

Meta-Theory and Theory in Interpersonal Communication

As we seek to explore the theories of interpersonal communication, it is important to know that scholars do differ (greatly, at times) on how to study and develop interpersonal communication theory. Scholars use different meta-theoretical discourses, which are schools of thought or paradigms that scholars use to think about and talk about a phenomenon of interest (Deetz, 2001). These discourses are points of view that help us to understand and appreciate the different approaches to asking questions about interpersonal communication, to choose research methods to answer these questions, and to provide the criteria by which to evaluate research findings and conclusions (Baxter & Babbie, 2004). Each paradigm carries a different set of assumptions about the nature of truth and reality, the relationship between the researcher and the phenomenon under investigation, the role of values in theory and research, and how best to write up and present one's scholarship. Rather than argue for one of the discourses (or paradigms) as superior, our goal here is to value them equally. Thus, we have organized our thinking around three very general discourses of interpersonal communication that have been identified by many scholars (e.g., Baxter & Babbie, 2004; Bochner, 1985; Habermas, 1971; Miller, 2002): post-positivist, interpretive, and critical. We do recognize that there are specific schools of thought within each of these broad discourses, which is more than we can take into account here.

POST-POSITIVIST PERSPECTIVE

Researchers adopting a post-positivist discourse take a scientific approach to research. This approach is often also called the "logical-empirical tradition." These scholars believe in an objective reality that can be discovered through appropriate research methods. That is, they believe in a knowable reality apart from the researcher. The goal of post-positivist theory and research is to advance predictions and to offer generalized, law-like cause and effect explanations or functional explanations about how variables or structures are interdependent with one another. Causal explanations view the social world as webs of variables, some of which function as independent variables in causing outcomes or effects on other variables known as dependent variables. Functional explanations are organized around the presumption that the social world is a system of interdependent parts: The functioning of one part depends on its patterns of interdependence with other parts of the system. Researchers committed to the discourse of post-positivism favor an a priori process in which they initially identify a theory relevant to the phenomenon they wish to explain and predict. Theories should consist of law-like statements, which apply across situations, about how variables or structures relate, causally or functionally. Post-positivists are committed to value-neutral theorizing in which researcher subjectivity should be controlled or neutralized. According to the post-positivist perspective, a good theory is one that is accurate (i.e., in agreement with observations), testable (i.e., capable of being verified and falsified or proven wrong), logically consistent, parsimonious (or appropriately simple), appropriate in scope, and useful in generating predictions and explanations about interpersonal communication.

In its idealized form, the researcher's task is to deduce testable hypotheses from a theory. For example, a researcher adopting this perspective might be interested in explaining how talk about one's occupation functions in self-presentation and impression management. Beginning with a relevant theory in which variables have been logically linked causally or functionally, the post-positivist researcher would derive testable hypotheses. For instance, a researcher might adopt one of the theories discussed in Part III of this book, social penetration theory (Chapter 29), because it focuses on the process of self-disclosure of personal information as people become acquainted. Based on this theory, the researcher might argue that there are various kinds of information that a person can reveal about his or her occupation, and that this information can vary in its superficiality or depth. Because social penetration theory argues that we disclose relatively superficial information early in a forming relationship and more in-depth information later in a relationship's development, our researcher might hypothesize that superficial disclosures about one's occupation (e.g., "I'm a professor of communication studies," "A professor's job has three components—teaching, research, and service") are more likely with strangers than are more in-depth disclosures about one's occupation (e.g., "I earn about half of what a physician earns," or "The worst part of my job is grading papers"). Additionally, more in-depth disclosures about occupation would be more characteristic of communication among acquaintances than among strangers. In this example, depth of disclosure about one's occupation is the dependent variable because it is the consequence of the independent variable, the closeness of the relationship with the other person (stranger versus acquaintance). The assumption of the researcher is that both relationship closeness and depth of disclosure can be objectively measured.

INTERPRETIVE PERSPECTIVE

The meta-theoretical discourse of interpretivism rejects a single objective view of reality that can be discovered. From the interpretive perspective, the social world consists of multiple realities according to the subjective position of the person or group. Humans are agents who act on their world in light of their subjective positions. Although humans often act to reproduce existing patterns, they can choose also to change those patterns. Interpretive researchers are committed to a detailed understanding of how particular social realities are produced and maintained through the everyday practices of individuals, relational parties, families, and so on. Researchers committed to the discourse of interpretivism value the "native's point of view": the perspectives and language choices of the individuals being studied. In addition, they tend to value context or situation-specific research. Because the interpretive project is committed to local meanings and rule-governed meaning-making processes, the theories valued by interpretive researchers are those focused on meanings and meaning-making, looking for common patterns of meaning among members of a particular group or context being studied.

Contrary to the hypothetico-deductive theories of post-positivism, interpretive theories might be used by researchers as *sensitizing devices* or guides to getting started in a research study, and subsequently put into conversation with locally emergent meanings. For interpretive researchers, the goal is not to test a theory in a specific situation, but rather to engage the theory in conversation with the emergent observations and interpretations that flow from the natives' experiences. Thus, from an interpretive perspective, a theory can be a heuristic device, useful in sensitizing a researcher; it is a conversational partner, if you will; it is open to transformation when put into play with the native's point of view and the interpretations of the researcher.

For example, an interpretive researcher might be interested in how members of a local community—let's say neighbors in a given neighborhood populated with middle-class Euro-Americans—construct their identities in interaction with one another and the role that one's occupation holds in such identity work. That is, the researcher is interested in how the natives— members of the neighborhood—make sense of one another as persons and how occupation figures into the meaning-making process. There might be a local theory available in existing scholarship that examines the code of communication among middle-class Euro-Americans more generally. However, it does not directly address the question of interest to our researcher—the role of occupation talk in identity constructions. Nonetheless, our researcher could use this theory as a sensitizing device, which is perhaps helpful in guiding preliminary interview questions or in making findings intelligible at the analysis stage of the study. For example, the communication code for middle-class Euro-Americans might emphasize concepts of "self," "achievement," and "independence." These concepts might be helpful in rendering intelligible the observation by our researcher that neighbors appear to value more positively occupations that appear to have a great deal of autonomy of action. The interpretive researcher would not test hypotheses derived from the theory. Rather, the researcher would conclude that the theory was more or less useful in illuminating the natives' experiences in the particular neighborhood group under observation.

Alternatively, an interpretive researcher might prefer to operate entirely inductively, developing a theory from the "bottom up" from observations. This process is often referred to as "grounded-theory construction." Returning to our example, our researcher might discover that no scholarship exists on how middle-class, Euro-American neighbors interact more generally, or in the neighborhood of interest more specifically. Our interpretive researcher would of necessity adopt an inductive approach, with the goal of developing a grounded theory of the role of occupation talk in constructing the identity of persons.

Whether the researcher uses a general interpretive theory or constructs a grounded theory, common criteria apply in evaluating an interpretive theory. The theory needs to be heuristic—that is, it must shed fruitful insights into the meanings and meaning-making process of the "native" group of individuals under study. A heuristic theory moves beyond mere description: It does more than summarize the "native's point of view." Specifically, it provides an interpretation of observations that renders them intelligible or understandable. This goal of understanding or intelligibility differs from the prediction and explanation goals of post-positivist theories. Furthermore, the emphasis is on the local, not the general, which is (again) unlike post-positivist theories. However, like post-positivist theory, interpretive theory should be logically consistent and parsimonious.

CRITICAL PERSPECTIVE

In contrast to both post-positivist and interpretive researchers, a critical scholar would view identity work in general, and occupation talk in particular, as social constructions that serve some interests more than others. A critical researcher would rely on a theory of institutional or ideological power to provide the analytical guide that would uncover marginalized or silenced voices, and to inform his or her explanation or understanding of the process by which other voices become dominant. Key to this analysis would probably be the role of various societal structures and ideologies—for example, the ideology of individualism or the ideology of patriarchy, in personal identity. Critical researchers often focus on the interests of predetermined, identifiable groups, such as women, people of color, or non-elite social groups, such as people with disabilities. The work of critical researchers is often characterized by a goal of emancipation or enlightenment and an agenda that is activist and that supports social change. As Baxter and Asbury note in Chapter 14, critical theorists come from both critical modern and critical postmodern traditions, both centered on the goal of understanding "how power functions in communicative life with the twin scholarly goals of emancipation and empowerment (p. 186). While the methods of critical scholars may align more closely with the interpretive tradition than with post-positivism, they depart from the goals of interpretive scholarship that seek to identify patterns or consensus and rather focus on contradictions, dissension, or inequities. A good critical theory is evaluated by its capacity to accomplish social change, thereby emancipating disempowered groups from oppressive social structures or ideologies.

Returning to our example one final time, a critical researcher might be interested in examining whose interests are served (and whose are not served) when, for example, the media marks a person's occupation as the central feature of his or her identity. Such marking clearly privileges persons who are employed outside of the home, for example. One critical consequence of such marking might be that people whose occupation is relatively invisible (for example, homemakers and parents who work in the home without pay) might have reduced status in the society because their occupation is not formally legitimated.

Researchers rarely articulate explicitly their meta-theoretical commitments (and perhaps they should do so more than they do). Rather, scholars' philosophical alignments often float at a latent level, between the lines of their prose. The sophisticated reader needs to know how to interpret a given researcher's choices in order to infer what his or her meta-theoretical commitments are in a given study. Once one knows what key signs to look for, it is possible to locate a given researcher's commitments. Why is this helpful and important? Because it tells the reader what the researcher values about theory and how theory should be used and evaluated in the given study. Thus, we have asked each of the authors in the book to locate their theory, or cluster of theories, within its appropriate meta-theoretical discourse. As you read each chapter, we encourage you to work through the intellectual exercise of identifying the specific ways in which a meta-theoretical discourse seeps through in the articulation of that chapter's theory (or theories).

But let's bring down the level of abstraction a bit, and turn our attention to interpersonal communication research. In doing so, we will note some interesting patterns and trends with respect to both theories and the meta-theoretical discourses in which they are embedded.

Interpersonal Communication Research, 2006–2013

As in the first edition of this book, we needed to map the current state of research and theory in interpersonal communication before choosing which theories to include in this book. In their previous summary of interpersonal communication research from 1990 to 2005, Braithwaite and Baxter (2008) identified 958 interpersonal communication citations, accounting for approximately 60 per year. For the second edition of this book, we updated this summary to include the 492 interpersonal communication articles published from 2006 to 2013. In this eight-year span, the number of data-based articles on interpersonal communication increased slightly to an average of 62 per year.

In our analysis, we included all empirical/data-based studies published by interpersonal communication researchers who professionally identify with the communication discipline. Our goal was to analyze all interpersonal communication studies published during this period. Our approach to interpersonal communication was intentionally broad, encompassing all studies of person-to-person communication (face-to-face or mediated). We included studies of dyadic interpersonal communication (e.g., communication in dating, committed, cohabiting, friendship, or marital relationships), and we excluded studies situated in role-based relationships (e.g., manager-employee, doctor-patient—what Miller and Steinberg [1975] would have categorized as "sociological"). Given a separate analysis available on family communication research (see Baxter & Braithwaite, 2006), the only familial form of interaction we included was marital communication, because partners relate to one another as intimates, and not only in their respective roles as "husband" and "wife." We chose to include interpersonal communication research that is located at the level of the individual (e.g., studies of message planning, production, and processing), and we included persuasion research when the focus was interpersonal (e.g., compliance-gaining or planning and processing of persuasive messages in a person-to-person context). We also included research on language and social interaction in interpersonal contexts and data-based critical studies of interpersonal communication. Finally, we included only data-based studies (rather than conceptual essays) in this analysis because our goal was to assess the role of meta-theory and theory in qualitatively or quantitatively oriented research.

For this study of the literature, we identified 19 journals that would be most likely to contain the published research of interpersonal communication scholars. We included in our search 14 communication journals sponsored by the International Communication Association (ICA), the National Communication Association (NCA), or the four NCA-affiliated regional communication associations: *Communication Monographs, Communication Quarterly, Communication Reports, Communication Research Reports, Communication Studies, Human Communication Research, Journal of Applied Communication Research, Journal of Communication, Qualitative Research Reports in Communication, Quarterly Journal of Speech, Southern Communication Journal, Text and Performance Quarterly, Western Journal of Communication,* and the Western States Communication Association affiliate organization's *Women's Studies in*

Communication. In addition, we included five journals that regularly publish articles authored by interpersonal communication scholars: *Communication Research, Journal of Language and Social Psychology, Research on Language and Social Interaction,* and the two interdisciplinary journals on social and personal relationships: *Journal of Social and Personal Relationships* and *Personal Relationships.*

It is important for us to note that we understand that researchers in other disciplines undertake studies on interpersonal communication. We certainly value the work on communication by scholars from outside the communication discipline, and there are excellent volumes of work that take an interdisciplinary approach. However, our goal in the present project was to focus on work by the community of scholars whose primary intellectual affiliation is the discipline of communication.

Thus, for this second edition, a total of 492 research-based articles on interpersonal communication were included in our analysis. For each study analyzed, we determined the meta-theoretical commitment (paradigm) of the researchers, and the theory (or theories), if any, engaged by the researcher.

META-THEORETICAL COMMITMENTS

We studied each research article to determine the meta-theoretical approaches taken by interpersonal communication researchers. From our analysis, we determined that 85% of the interpersonal communication research articles from 2006 to 2013 were embedded in a post-positivist discourse (up slightly from the 83.2% reported by Braithwaite and Baxter, 2008), 13% were interpretive in nature (down slightly from 13.9%), and just 2% displayed a critical perspective (down from 2.9%). Clearly, interpersonal communication research continues to emanate largely from the discourse of post-positivism, with some presence of interpretive research. Critical studies are rarely found in interpersonal communication, although we understand that there may be relevant critical manuscripts published in journals not included in our analysis.

THEORETICAL COMMITMENTS

We also wanted to know how much of the published interpersonal communication research displays theoretical presence and which specific theory (or theories) were engaged. Determining theoretical presence is not as easy as it sounds. What does one count as a theory? Must the theory be used a priori, or may it be imposed post hoc after the data are analyzed, or both? How prominent must the use of theory in a study be to be counted as theory-based research? In the end, our choice was to be very generous in our approach to theory-based research. Thus, we included articles in which the author mentioned at least one theory in the introductory warrant or argument for the study, used at least one theory as a framework to analyze data, developed a grounded theory, or discussed at least one theory in the conclusions of the research report as a way to make post hoc sense of their findings or to address their implications. We thought about it this way: "If the author waved the hot dog over the fire of theory, we counted it." While our approach to identifying theoretical presence departs little from the idealized use of theory among interpretive or critical theorists, we took a more generous approach to post-positivist work. As in the last edition of this volume, we acknowledge there may be theoretical presence in many post-positivist studies that did not deduce testable hypotheses from an identified theory. In the end, using our criteria, 75% ($n = 370$) of the interpersonal communication studies published from 2006 to 2013 had a theoretical presence of some sort, reflecting an increase of nearly 10% from studies published in 1990 to 2005 when 66.5% reflected theoretical presence.

Many different theories were cited in the studies we examined. The top 10 most frequently cited theories, in descending order of frequency, were:

Uncertainty Reduction/Management Theory/Relational Uncertainty (cited 34 times)

Supportive Communication Theory/Social Support (28)

Attachment Theory (19)

Face/Politeness Theory (19)

Interpersonal Deception Theory (18)

Relational Dialectics/Dialectical Theory (17)

Theory of Motivated Information Management/Self-Efficacy (14)

Communication Privacy Management Theory (14)

Affection Exchange Theory (14)

Communiobiological/Evolutionary Theories (13)

As a point of comparison with Braithwaite and Baxter's (2008) analysis, only uncertainty reduction/management theories, politeness theory, and relational dialectics theory remained within the top 10 most frequently cited theories. Obviously, we made a decision to include all of these theories in this revised edition of the book, given their salience in the research. Of these 10 most frequently cited theories, over half are homegrown in the communication discipline. However, many other theories were cited with some frequency as well, and we tried to include as many of those in the book as was feasible.

In the end, all but seven of the theories in this book are homegrown in the communication discipline. We take this as evidence of the continued growth and maturity of the field of interpersonal communication. As we noted above, in the early years of scholarship on interpersonal communication, researchers relied heavily on importing theories from allied disciplines of psychology and sociology, and while researchers continue to find great value in these theories, they do not dominate the landscape.

In addition to these frequently cited theories, we also note that there are a number of constructs often referenced in interpersonal communication research that do not have corresponding theories. These include constructs such as social support, relational maintenance, topic avoidance, and memorable messages. Because of the discrepancy between their use and lack of developed theory, we refer to these constructs as "undertheorized." Historically, undertheorized but frequently used constructs often serve as a catalyst for developing new theory, and we note how important these areas of research are in interpersonal communication. This is the case with several newer homegrown theories such as the dual-process theory of supportive communication, advice response theory, and the relational turbulence model, all now appearing for the first time in this edition.

IMPLICATIONS FOR INTERPERSONAL COMMUNICATION RESEARCH

We see at least three implications of our study of the landscape of interpersonal communication research. The first implication is that we are encouraged to maintain and even strengthen our argument for theory-based scholarship. As editors of a book devoted to theories of interpersonal communication, it is likely not surprising that we hold this position. Indeed, it is important to note that not all scholars will agree with us on this point. Some believe it is enough to embed a study within the conversation of accumulated findings from others' studies, and of course, individual studies may form the building blocks of theory. Some scholars believe that centering studies theoretically carries a risk of making observations to support what one expected to see. While we appreciate all good research, we favor and recommend theoretically centered research for two reasons. First, we believe that theory helps researchers bring both intelligibility and coherence to their research findings. We understand that several atheoretical studies can produce a common finding, and we argue that theory makes these findings intelligible and useful. We are also well aware that what we see and what we learn will be different depending on the theory guiding our attention, just as putting a different lens on a camera changes how we see and record our world. Given that theories operate out of different meta-theoretical discourses, we can change the discourse or the theories to enable us to take a different view of communication phenomena. Not only does changing the lens of theory alter our view, but when we pay attention to theory, we also have a heightened awareness that we are indeed seeing the world through a particular lens, focusing on certain things and not engaging others.

Second, we favor theory-based research because theory helps us launch new research, either by providing the basis of testable hypotheses (post-positivist) or by providing us with a heuristic sensitizing device (interpretive), or highlighting marginalization that calls us to action (critical). In addition, we believe that in the best of circumstances, each study should also question and advance our body of theoretical knowledge. Thus, while we are heartened to see the percentage of theory-based research in interpersonal communication increase to 75%, our desire is to see this number grow as the years go on. We hope this book project continues to encourage and facilitate theory-based research.

The second implication of our review of interpersonal communication theory is to highlight the continuing disparity among the meta-theoretical discourses, with the vast majority of research on interpersonal communication representing the post-positivist tradition. This is not a critique of the excellent research coming out of that paradigm, and in fact, the work of one of the co-editors comes largely from this tradition. Post-positivist scholars are doing important and high-quality work. In the end, what we want to see is openness to the different perspectives at all stages of the research enterprise, from methodological education to reviewing research reports for presentation and publication. We contend that our capacity as a field to shed light on some of the most important issues in the lives of humans rests in our ability to embrace and apply multiple perspectives and methods to capture the complexity that is interpersonal communication.

Our third implication leads us to reflect on what a greater diversity of meta-theoretical perspectives might bring to interpersonal communication. The scope of interpersonal communication opportunities and challenges facing us in the 21st century is endless. For example, consider choices on how to interact via social media, manage the effects of economic downturn or unemployment, navigate multiethnic or interfaith relationships, or maintain relationships across increasingly long lifespans. We believe interpersonal communication will be strongest when scholars examine the important issues of the day from a variety of perspectives. In addition, we encourage the study of a broad range of contexts, populations, and topics. The call to focus on nontraditional and understudied relationships has been strong (e.g., Wood & Duck, 1995) and the discursive burden of legitimacy faced by these persons cannot be discounted (e.g., Baxter, in press).

We note that much of the research on person-to-person communication in underrepresented groups is not appearing in interpersonal communication, but rather in intercultural communication, family communication, or language and social interaction. Some of this research is centered in the critical and interpretive paradigms. Historically, interpretive and critical scholars have struggled about whether their work will be welcome in interpersonal communication (Braithwaite, in press). In addition, we have also observed too little diversity within the ranks of interpersonal scholars themselves. We are less concerned about trying to achieve a balance of the research across paradigms. We are committed to see that the interpersonal communication field is open and welcoming to scholars and scholarship on diverse topics and from across the meta-theoretical spectrum. We are encouraged that many young scholars appreciate openness to a variety of ways of answering the important questions that face us. In short, we want all voices present and heard. To facilitate this goal, in this book we have intentionally included selected theories that interpretive and critical scholars will find relevant to and facilitative of their work, in addition to those theories important to scholars with post-positivist meta-theoretical commitments.

The Organization of the Book

Analyzing such a large number of studies confirmed what we already knew: There are many interpersonal communication theories to choose from, and it would be difficult to make choices about which ones we could include in the second edition of this book. We began by reviewing the theories covered in the first edition and comparing those theories with the ones most frequently cited in our updated review of the interpersonal communication literature. Although we invited authors to update many of the chapters that were included in the first edition, we decided also to showcase newer theories of interpersonal communication in lieu of some of the more classic theories. For example, rather than include an updated chapter on uncertainty reduction theory, we invited leading theorists to write new chapters on the relational turbulence model, the theory of motivation information management, problematic integration theory, and uncertainty management theory. Likewise, in place of constructivism theory, we invited scholars who study supportive communication to write a chapter on the dual-process theory of supportive communication and advice response theory. If you compare the first and second editions, you'll see that we added chapters such as evolutionary theory and critical approaches to interpersonal communication, as well as theories that continue to make their mark in the field, for example, the communication theory of identity. In the end, our editorial decisions are in no way meant to diminish the value and utility of classic theories on which the field was built, and we owe an intellectual debt of gratitude to their authors.

Our goal in this second edition remains to promote theoretical advancement within the field by offering current and new theories that we believe hold tremendous promise for current and future researchers. Ultimately, we applied three criteria when choosing the theories to include in this second edition. First, as noted above, we chose theories that represent the most frequent presence in the interpersonal communication literature. Second, we chose theories that we believe hold the greatest promise for researchers and students to use.

Third, we chose a group of theories that produce a presence for all three meta-theoretical perspectives. This meant that we had to make some difficult choices and were not able to include all theories in one book.

We invited an outstanding group of researchers and theorists as first authors to write chapters for the book. We received enthusiastic responses from them and were delighted they wanted to be part of the project. Some invited coauthors to work with them, including scholars of equal senior status and some promising new scholars. We are pleased to welcome all of these colleagues and appreciate their contributions to interpersonal communication theory. In order to present this comprehensive set of theories, the chapters had to be written in brief and very concise ways. The authors certainly would have had more to say about the theories, and readers of the chapters will find the references lead them to some fuller treatments of the theories, as well as their application in research.

After we chose the chapters we wanted to include in the second edition of this book, we needed to think about how to organize them. Consistent with the first edition, we knew that we did not want to divide the theories into the three meta-theoretical discourses because we wanted, as much as possible, to continue focusing on how these discourses integrate (Deetz, 2001). In the end, we chose to retain the organization of the book into three sections, modeled after the three broad approaches to interpersonal communication we discussed earlier in this chapter: interpersonal communication theories that are individually centered, those that are discourse or interaction centered, and those that are relationship centered. We organized the theories alphabetically in each of the three sections. Of course, we understand that some might quibble with our placement of chapters into one section or another. After deciding to retain the original structure for organizing the theories in the second edition of this book, we found that they divided fairly evenly between the three parts.

Part I of the book presents individually centered theories of interpersonal communication. As we described above, these theories are centered in how individuals plan, produce, and process interpersonal communication messages. Theories in this section of the book primarily envision communication as an individually centered, cognitive activity. Of the three parts in the book, this first part has the most meta-theoretical similarity—the post-positivist paradigm.

Part II of the book includes theories with a focus on discourse or interaction. These theories share an understanding of interpersonal communication as a message, a discourse (i.e., a system of meaning), or a joint action behaviorally enacted between persons. Meta-theoretical commitments are more diverse in this second section of the book, drawing across meta-theoretical traditions, with the fullest representation of interpretive and critical theories.

Part III includes relationship-centered theories of interpersonal communication. This group of theories focuses on understanding the role of communication in developing, sustaining, and terminating social and personal relationships.

Theories in this part tend to mirror the first part, with greater representation from the post-positivist paradigm.

As you read the theory chapters in the book, you will see that each chapter is structured around the same set of issues: (1) intellectual tradition of the theory, (2) main goals and features of the theory, (3) how communication is conceptualized in the theory, (4) research and practical applications of the theory, (5) evaluation of the theory, and (6) continuing the conversation about the theory. We hope this common structure will help readers easily understand and compare what each theory has to offer.

While we highlighted some of our concerns about the state of interpersonal communication theory above, we want to stress that we are very positive about the field and appreciate the advances and strengths of the study of interpersonal communication. It is our belief that the collection of theories by this superior set of scholars demonstrates the advances and contributions of this important area of study. As the 21st century is well underway, we can imagine few undertakings more important than understanding and improving interpersonal communication. We trust that the readers of this book will find the work of these scholars engaging and enlightening.

References

Altman, I., & Taylor, D. (1973). *Social penetration: The development of interpersonal relationships.* New York, NY: Holt, Rinehart & Winston.

Austin, J. L. (1962). *How to do things with words.* Oxford, UK: Clarendon.

Baxter, L. A. (2004). Relationships as dialogues. *Personal Relationships, 11,* 1–22.

Baxter, L. A. (in press). *Remaking "family" communicatively.* New York, NY: Peter Lang.

Baxter, L. A., & Babbie, E. R. (2004). *The basics of communication research.* Belmont, CA: Wadsworth.

Baxter, L. A., & Braithwaite, D. O. (2006). Introduction: Meta-theory and theory in family communication research. In D. O. Braithwaite & L. A. Baxter (Eds.), *Engaging theories in family communication: Multiple perspectives* (pp. 1–15). Thousand Oaks CA: Sage.

Berger, C. R. (2005). Interpersonal communication: Theoretical perspectives, future prospects. *Journal of Communication, 55,* 415–447.

Berger, P. L., & Luckmann, T. (1967). *The social construction of reality: A treatise in the sociology of knowledge.* New York, NY: Anchor.

Bochner, A. P. (1985). Perspectives on inquiry: Representation, conversation, and reflection. In M. L. Knapp & G. R. Miller (Eds.), *Handbook of interpersonal communication* (pp. 27–58). Beverly Hills, CA: Sage.

Bormann, E. G. (1980). *Communication theory.* Salem, WI: Sheffield.

Braithwaite, D. O. (in press). "Opening the door": The history and future of qualitative scholarship in interpersonal communication. *Communication Studies.*

Braithwaite, D. O., & Baxter, L. A. (2008). Introduction: Meta-theory and theory in interpersonal communication research. In L. A. Baxter & D. O. Braithwaite (Eds.),

Engaging theories in interpersonal communication: Multiple perspectives (pp. 1–22). Thousand Oaks, CA: Sage.

Cohen, H. (1994). The history of speech communication: The emergence of a discipline, 1914–1945. Washington, DC: National Communication Association.

Craig, R. T. (1999). Communication theory as a field. *Communication Theory, 9,* 119–161.

Davis, M. (1973). *Intimate relations.* New York, NY: Free Press.

Deetz, S. (2001). Conceptual foundations. In F. M. Jablin & L. L. Putnam (Eds.), *The new handbook of organizational communication: Advances in theory, research, and methods* (pp. 3–46). Thousand Oaks, CA: Sage.

Delia, J. K. (1987). Communication research: A history. In C. R. Berger & S. H. Chafee (Eds.), *Handbook of communication science* (pp. 20–98). Newbury Park, CA: Sage.

Ehninger, D. (1968). On systems of rhetoric. *Philosophy and Rhetoric, 1,* 131–144.

Giffin, K., & Patton, B. R. (1971). *Fundamentals of interpersonal communication.* New York, NY: Harper & Row.

Greene, J. O., & Burleson, B. R. (2003). *Handbook of communication and social interaction skills.* Mahwah, NJ: Erlbaum.

Guerrero, L. K., Andersen, P. A., & Afifi, W. A. (2014). *Close encounters: Communicating in relationships* (4th ed.). Thousand Oaks, CA: Sage.

Habermas, J. (1971). *Knowledge and human interest.* Boston, MA: Beacon.

Knapp, M. L., & Daly, J. A. (2011). Background and current trends in the study of interpersonal communication. In M. L. Knapp & J. A. Daly (Eds.), *The SAGE handbook of interpersonal communication* (4th ed., pp. 3–22). Thousand Oaks, CA: Sage.

Knapp, M. L., Vangelisti, A., & Caughlin, J. P. (2014). *Interpersonal communication and human relationships* (7th ed.). Boston, MA: Pearson.

Littlejohn, S. W., & Foss, K. A. (2005). *Theories of human communication* (8th ed.). Belmont, CA: Wadsworth.

Miller, G. R. (1976). Foreword. In G. R. Miller (Ed.), *Explorations in interpersonal communication* (pp. 9–16). Beverly Hills, CA: Sage.

Miller, G. R., (1983). Taking stock of a discipline. *Journal of Communication, 33,* 31–41.

Miller, G. R., & Steinberg M. (1975). *Between people.* Chicago, IL: Science Research Associates.

Miller, K. I. (2002). *Communication theories.* New York, NY: McGraw-Hill.

Pearce, W. B., & Foss, K. A. (1990). The historical context of communication as a science. In G. L. Dahnke & G. W. Clatterbuck (Eds.), *Human communication: Theory and research* (pp. 1–19). Belmont, CA: Wadsworth.

Stewart, J. (1999). Introduction to interpersonal communication. In J. Stewart (Ed.), *Bridges not walls* (7th ed., pp. 15–65). New York, NY: Random House.

Vangelisti, A. L. (2011). Interpersonal processes in romantic relationships. In M. L. Knapp & J. A. Daly (Eds.), *The SAGE handbook of interpersonal communication* (4th ed., pp. 597–631). Thousand Oaks, CA: Sage.

Watzlawick, P., Bavelas, J. B., & Jackson, D. D. (1967). *Pragmatics of human communication: A study of interactional patterns, pathologies, and paradoxes.* New York, NY: W. W. Norton.

Wittgenstein, L. (1953). *Philosophical investigations (Philosophische Untersuchungen;* G. E. M. Anscombe, Trans.). New York, NY: Macmillan.

Wood, J. T., & Duck. S. (Eds.). (1995). *Understudied relationships: Off the beaten path.* Thousand Oaks, CA: Sage.

PART I

Individually-Centered Theories of Interpersonal Communication

C onsistent with the first edition of this book, the contributors to Part I of this edition address theories that hold prominence in understanding how individuals plan, produce, and process interpersonal communication messages. Theories in this section of the book are based on the basic assumption that individual cognitive activity is the heart of the communication process—both in producing and in processing messages. All but two of the theories are homegrown—that is, developed by scholars who identify professionally with the communication studies discipline. The two exceptions include the family of attribution theories, developed in the discipline of psychology, and evolutionary theories of interpersonal communication.

The majority of theories in this section are positioned in the post-positivistic meta-theoretical tradition. The contributors flag this tradition using many terms, including

- logical-empirical,
- scientific,
- realism,
- prediction,
- causal explanation, and
- generalization.

In general, the theories examined in this section are based on the assumption that there is an objective reality organized by patterned regularities that researchers seek to predict and to explain by identifying basic cause-effect relationships. Although the chapters in this section focus on individual cognitive activity, the theoretical assumption is that regularities exist across individuals in how and why this activity takes place that can be objectively studied through sound scientific observation. Most of this observational work is quantitatively based.

Two of the theories examined in this section have been variously placed as either post-positivistic or interpretive: the uncertainty management theories of Problematic Integration Theory and Uncertainty Management Theory. Basically, the assumptions of these theories include an appreciation of meaning as locally organized and ultimately indeterminate, while the theories hold to a belief that fundamental regularities can still be identified.

The chapters in this section are organized alphabetically. In this second edition, we made several notable changes to Part I in an effort to advance new theories of interpersonal communication that we believe hold tremendous promise for future research. First, we opted not to include revised chapters on Uncertainty Reduction Theory and Constructivism Theory. Historically, these two theories represent two of the oldest homegrown members of this theoretical family, both originating with work by communication scholars in the 1970s. Consequently, we did not make this decision lightly given that these two theories helped to shape two of the major intellectual problems addressed by scholars of interpersonal communication over the past three decades: uncertainty management and communicator effectiveness.

Uncertainty Reduction Theory (URT) was formulated with a goal of explaining communicative activity organized around the goal of reducing uncertainty in initial interactions between strangers. Uncertainty management has emerged as a core intellectual problem for theorists of interpersonal communication, and several of the chapters in this part of the book illustrate different approaches to the problem of uncertainty. In place of a revised chapter on URT, for instance, we included new chapters on Problematic Integration Theory and Uncertainty Management Theory, as well as a new chapter on the Theory of Motivated Information Management. Each of these theories challenge URT's commitment to uncertainty reduction, instead focusing more broadly on how uncertainty is managed. Uncertainty management can involve the reduction of uncertainty, but does not necessarily do so. Scholarship in uncertainty reduction and uncertainty management has branched out well beyond the context of initial interactions between strangers, as becomes clear in reading the chapters authored by Babrow and Striley, W. Afifi and Robbins, and the chapter authored by Knobloch (on the Relational Turbulence Model in Part III).

One way that communicators cope with uncertainty as they produce messages is to engage in a variety of mental planning activities or rehearsal work. Several of the chapters in this section focus on planning-related activity: in particular, the chapters devoted to Planning Theory, Action Assembly Theory, Goals-Plans-Action Theory, and Imagined Interaction Theory. All four of these chapters are committed to explaining how communicators produce messages through cognitive planning work. Planning Theory concentrates on characteristics of cognitive plans in general, whereas Goals-Plans-Action Theory focuses more narrowly on plans related to the goal of social influence, with particular attention on the role that goals play in the process of producing social influence acts. Action Assembly Theory takes a process approach, examining the general process by which messages are produced—that is, assembled—by communicators. And Imagined Interaction Theory attempts to explain how people use internal dialogues within their minds to test out the various possible scenarios of an event in advance of the act. For example, this theory is currently being used to examine the ways in which effective conflict management is related to how we construct in our minds both past and anticipated conflicts with others.

The intellectual problem of uncertainty management is one faced when we produce communication messages. In addition, we face the challenge of uncertainty when we undertake the processing of others' messages. Two of the theories in this section of the book focus directly on the processing of messages. The family of attribution theories, older in fact than either Uncertainty Reduction Theory or Constructivism Theory, has its origins in psychology. Nonetheless, it has proven its value to communication scholars, shedding light on the question of how people make sense of what causes others' actions. In the context of our relationships, we also must determine what another's communication means with respect to the underlying nature of our relationship. Was that comment a criticism (implying dominance) or a teasing joke (implying a relationship based on intimacy or affiliation)? When we make judgments like this one, we are engaged in a framing activity, attempting to understand the message in light of the underlying relationship between the parties. Such framing work is the topic of Relational Framing Theory.

Along with Uncertainty Reduction Theory, Constructivism Theory is the second homegrown theory that has origins in the 1970s. This theory focuses on message production with an eye toward communicator effectiveness or competence, asking what distinguishes more from less skilled communicative messages. Paying homage to Constructivism Theory in this second edition, Bodie and MacGeorge's chapter examines both a Dual-Process Theory of Supportive Message Outcomes and Advice Response Theory. These theories highlight the second major intellectual problem of message production for scholars of interpersonal communication—effectiveness or competence. Both theories suggest that features of the message, its source, the recipient, and the situational context influence how people think about the supportive messages they receive. Of course, how individuals produce and process messages requires a more comprehensive understanding of social interaction than what can be gleaned by analyzing the senders, the receivers, and the situational contexts in which they interact. Physiology plays an equally meaningful role in explaining how individuals produce and process messages competently, and there is a growing body of interpersonal communication research that examines the links between biology and interpersonal communication. Consequently, T. Afifi, Davis, and Denes's chapter on Evolutionary Theories examines three bio-social approaches to interpersonal communication, approaches that advance our understanding of how communication enables human beings to acquire resources, adapt to stressful situations, protect themselves and close others, and prolong their lives.

In summary, the chapters in this section examine several core issues of interest to scholars of interpersonal communication: coping with uncertainty, communicating effectively, and improving physical and mental health. They focus on the individual as the centerpiece of study, especially the role of individual cognitive activity in the production and processing of messages.

2

Action Assembly Theory

Forces of Creation

John O. Greene

T his is a sentence I have never written before.

Now *you* try it. No, don't copy my sentence (or anyone else's, for that matter). Keep your eyes on your own page and write your own never-before-written sentence:

How did you do? Okay, I'm betting it's not the quote you'd want to pass on to your descendents as the essence of the wisdom you've acquired over your lifetime (although it might make the next person who reads this book snicker), but you were able to do it, weren't you?

This chapter is about the creative character of human behavior—about how it is possible for us to say, think, and do things that we've never heard, said, thought, or done before. When you and I wrote our sentences, we did something that is remarkable in many ways. It is remarkable that we have this capacity to create—to write (and say, and think) new things. And it is also remarkable that it is often relatively easy for us to do—so much so that we tend to take this marvelous capacity for granted. In fact, it turns out that the property of creativity is always present in our behavior, even if we don't recognize it. It is rather like breathing, in that it comes so naturally to us.

But these characteristics are only part of what makes this topic so fascinating. Two other aspects of our behavior might at first appear to be distinct from, or even opposed to, processes of creation, but in fact, they turn out to be essential for understanding the forces of creation that shape thought and action. First, it is true that novelty is an inherent and ubiquitous property of our behavior, but it is also true that we all experience situations where our creative genius fails us—times when we stutter, and stammer, and just can't think of the right things to say to help a friend feel better, tell a convincing lie, make a good impression in a job interview, or ask someone for a date. Second, just as behavior is always "new," it is also always "old." Go back and look at your novel sentence. Sure, you never wrote that particular sentence before, but you've written sentences that followed the same rules of grammar (e.g., "singular subjects require singular verbs"), and you've used each one of those words in other sentences. It's as if we have a set of established building blocks that we use to make new structures. And the same applies to all our behavior. You may not know this, but your friends do: You have facial expressions and gestures and ways of moving that they would recognize in a second as being "you," and, just like the words you own, these are building blocks that you combine and morph to produce something unique.

Intellectual Tradition of Action Assembly Theory

Theorists make pretty crummy deities. They do not survey the void and speak their creations into being out of nothingness. Rather, theorists always work from and in a complex landscape of assumptions and biases that plays a key role in shaping what they do. Consequently, it is easier to understand a theory and appreciate its nuances when we have some insight about the influences that helped to shape that theory.

We can make some headway in charting these influences if we remind ourselves of the simple fact that theory building is just another sort of human activity—like walking a dog or reading a book—and, as a result, reflects an underlying what-why-how logical structure. In other words, even though the landscape is complex, we can get some sense of the lay of the land if we ask, "What was the theorist trying to do, why was he or she trying to do this, and how did he or she seek to go about it?" Thinking about the process of theory building in what-why-how terms provides a convenient way of addressing the issues that are the focus of this section. That is, we learn about the theorist's purpose when we explore the "what" and "why" questions, and we gain insight about a theory's underlying meta-theoretical assumptions when we examine "how" the theorist went about the business of constructing the theory.

WHAT WAS THE THEORIST TRYING TO DO?

A good place to start in seeking to understand a theory is to determine what phenomena the theory seeks to address or illuminate. Action assembly theory (AAT; Greene, 1984) was developed within the Communication discipline, and over the last thirty-plus years, has served to crystallize and define a number of phenomena and research agendas that have become central to the field.

At the most general level, the focus of AAT is on two broad sets of phenomena. The first of these is people's overt behavior, and especially those aspects of behavior that are of interest to students of communication and social interaction. Although AAT pertains to all the various activities that you engage in every day (e.g., driving a car, playing video games), the theory is particularly concerned with why and how it is that you produce the verbal and nonverbal behaviors you exhibit when interacting with others—the things you say, the way you say them, your facial expressions, your gestures, and so on.

The second major focus of AAT follows directly from the first. The basic idea is that if you want to understand why and how people say and do what they do, you need to take into account how and what they think. Thus, AAT addresses the thought processes that make it possible for us to speak and move. In other words, the theory is concerned with what transpires in our minds when we formulate and produce our verbal and nonverbal messages: How are you able to tell your roommate about your vacation, explain to your little brother where the stars go during the day, or find the right words and actions to tell someone that you love her? And the thought processes of interest in AAT aren't limited to those involved in formulating and producing messages on the fly—they also include processes such as advance planning and rehearsing that may occur hours or even days before an interaction. Finally, it is worth noting that the thought processes that are the focus of AAT also include those related to what we do not say, processes such as "editing" (i.e., deciding not to say something we are thinking) and "encoding failures" (i.e., being unable to put our thoughts into words).

WHY WAS THE THEORIST TRYING TO DO THIS?

We can turn next to the question of "why" one might want to understand the processes involved in formulating and producing messages. There are many reasons that might be given in response to this question, but I'll mention just two here. We all recognize that communication can be done well or poorly. There are times when our message behavior seems right on target—when we are able to express ourselves clearly (and cleverly!), and our messages have precisely the impact that we hoped they would. Nevertheless, every one of us is also all too familiar with those times when things just don't come out right, or when what we say only seems to make matters worse. One advantage of understanding the processes involved in formulating and producing messages is that we gain insights about how to enhance the quality of our message behavior. The situation is much like the advantage that comes from knowing how your car engine works. If you don't understand much about the way that engine works, then you're probably not going to be able to do much to improve things when it's not running well.

A second response to the "why" question is, to my way of thinking, even more compelling than the first. Simply put, the processes of formulating and producing messages are inherently fascinating. Think about just a few of the many manifestations of these processes that you experience on a daily basis: You have a self-conception that plays a role in guiding how you treat other people; you can carry on a conversation with another person while thinking about something else; you can mask your facial expression so as not to reveal that another's comment hurt. And the list goes on and on, all of them examples of the workings of the system that produces thought and action.

HOW DID THE THEORIST SEEK TO GO ABOUT IT?

As I noted above, addressing the "what" and "why" questions informs us about the purpose of a theory; pursuing the "how" question involves an examination of the theorist's approach (i.e., the "meta-theoretical assumptions" underlying a theory). Of the three general meta-theoretical perspectives described in Chapter 1, the meta-theoretical foundations of AAT are most similar to the authors' characterization of the "post-positivist view." For our purposes, we can think about the approach reflected in AAT as a hierarchy consisting of three levels. At the most basic level of the hierarchy, AAT reflects a commitment to science as a way of knowing. Numerous lists of the characteristics of science are available, and we need not delve deeply into those characteristics here, but they include the notions that science rests on data rather than appeals to authority or tradition, that science attempts to minimize the error and bias inherent in human sense-making, and that science is public in the sense that researchers should be able to confirm or disconfirm one another's results and conclusions.

Moving up to the second level of our hierarchy, the particular brand of science reflected in AAT is that of "realism" (see Pavitt, 2001). Scientists who are also realists (and almost all of them are) believe that there is a "real world" of causal mechanisms that exists independent of people's understanding of those mechanisms. For example, regardless of whether scientists understand them, there are processes that cause children to be autistic. The goal of theory building, then, is to describe the causal mechanisms at work in producing the phenomena of interest. The terms of the theory are taken to refer to real-world entities and events, but of course the theorist recognizes that these descriptions will correspond only to some degree to the nature of the actual mechanisms at work in the world. The task of science is to continually refine our understanding of those mechanisms.

At the third and highest level of our hierarchy, AAT reflects the stance of "generative realism" (Greene, 1994). If, as realism suggests, the task of theory building is to describe the processes that give rise to some phenomenon, then generative realism is concerned with the kinds of theoretical terms that are likely to be required in those descriptions. In essence, generative realism says that people are simultaneously three things: (a) social beings, (b) psychological beings, and (c) physical beings. Theories of human behavior should incorporate all three of these elements. Theories that try to treat people as if they are only social beings (or only psychological beings, or only physical beings) and that ignore either or both of the other two components can only provide an incomplete description of the causal processes responsible for the things people say and do.

Main Goals and Features of Action Assembly Theory

THE CONCEPT OF ACTION FEATURES

I certainly would not do it, and I would not advise you to do it either, but you could express the basic idea of AAT by getting a small tattoo that reads "action is assembled." By that I mean that our thoughts and overt behaviors are built up out of smaller parts, just as a child builds a tower out of Legos, or as a composer "builds" a melody out of individual notes. Instead of Lego pieces or musical notes, though, in the case of human behavior the individual parts are "action features"—tiny snippets of thought and action that each of us has acquired over the course of our lives. When you finish reading this paragraph, put your book down and go to a mirror. Try to maintain a blank expression and examine your face for a few moments. You will be looking at dozens and dozens of action features corresponding to the positioning of your brows, eyelids, lips, and so on. Behind your eyes, countless other action features will make up each thought that runs through your mind as you stare into that mirror.

According to AAT, you have an enormous number of action features stored in your memory. The theory tells us a lot about the memory system where action features are held, but the only point that we really need to be concerned with here is the idea that action features are represented in multiple formats. For example, some action features are represented in memory in low-level codes that correspond to motor behaviors (e.g., the features involved in well-practiced skills such as hitting a tennis ball); others correspond to the routines you've acquired for pronouncing various word sounds; others reflect rules of grammar for combining words to make sentences; and still others reflect lessons from your parents, teachers, and friends about how to get along in life (e.g., "be kind to others" and "never give a sucker an even break").

THE ACTIVATION AND ASSEMBLY PROCESSES

AAT says that people have thousands and thousands of action features stored in memory. This is an important concept to grasp, but by itself it doesn't take us far toward understanding how it is that we are able to think and move (or how you were able to write your original sentence at the beginning of this chapter). The theory goes on, then, to specify two processes involved in using action features to produce behavior.

The first of these processes, *activation,* is basically a selection process. It accounts for how, from the huge storehouse of action features one has acquired, only certain ones are involved in shaping our behavior at any given time. For example, it's probably a pretty safe bet that your action features for swimming weren't activated until you read this sentence. They are there in memory (assuming, of course, that you know at least a little about how to swim!), but they weren't activated. Stripped to the bare essentials, AAT says that action features are activated when they are relevant to our ongoing activities. For example, when you pick up a Sudoku puzzle, all of the action features related to strategies and shortcuts you've learned for solving Sudokus will become activated (although, according to the theory, some will be more highly activated than others).

Once a feature is activated, things really get interesting. On the one hand, an activated feature is in a race against time—activation decays quickly. You could think about activating a feature as being similar to striking a match—it will blaze for a short time and gradually burn out—but the truth is that for most features, the burn time of their activation level is closer to that of a camera flash than that of a match.

But it is also the case that once an action feature is activated, a second process, *assembly,* kicks in, and that changes the entire dynamic. Assembly occurs when two or more complementary action features are fit together, something like a key fitting in a lock or puzzle pieces fitting together. For example, when you lift a cold beer to your lips, the action features for moving your shoulder, elbow, and wrist mesh to produce a smooth, coordinated movement. The action features for what to say when introducing yourself (e.g., "Hi, my name is _____") complement the features for actually pronouncing your name. When attempting to express your perception that Dr. Phil takes advantage of troubled people, the words "he," "is," "a," and "bully" might lock in with that idea, with features representing the rules governing word order that you learned as a child, and with each other. And, when you are sitting through a boring lecture, an abstract action feature such as "try to look interested" may fit with lower-level features coding facial expression and direction of eye gaze to create a convincing package of an alert listener.

COALITIONS, OVERT BEHAVIOR, AND CONSCIOUSNESS

The entity that results from fitting together action features is termed a *coalition.* Coalitions have several important properties. Remember that activation doesn't last long. However, when two features are fit together, they reinforce each other, and that coalition will remain activated longer than either feature alone (just as simultaneously striking middle C and upper C on a piano will cause the notes to reverberate longer than if you hit just one of those keys). This same idea applies as more and more features are added to a coalition; you get something of a snowball effect where coalitions that are able to recruit new features last longer, and, because they last longer, they are able to recruit more new features.

The view of human behavior portrayed in AAT, then, is of an ever-evolving constellation of coalitions, some big, others small, emerging into existence and decaying. Nevertheless, most of these coalitions never show up in our overt behavior or enter our conscious awareness of what we're thinking and doing. How is it, then, that of all these coalitions, some actually do become manifested in conscious thought, or overt action, or both?

There is more to what AAT has to say about these phenomena than can be unpacked here (see Greene, 2006), but the basic ideas are pretty simple. Regarding the question of how it is that some coalitions become manifested in overt behavior, recall that action features are represented in a number of different code systems that vary in level of abstraction. As a general principle, abstract action features will be manifested in overt behavior when they coalesce with lower level, motor-code features. If a person isn't able to translate some higher-level conception of what he or she wants to do into motor codes via the assembly process, that higher-order conception isn't going to show up in his or her overt behavior. The situation is analogous to those times when you've got some understanding in mind, but you just can't come up with words to express that emotion or understanding.

Then there is the question of why only a small subset of coalitions ever enters conscious awareness. Think for a moment about what consciousness is like—it flits over the landscape of your mind, lingering here and there, hovering as a succession of thoughts unfolding, and sometimes abruptly shifting to something seemingly unrelated to what came before. In AAT, though, consciousness isn't simply a passive observer. To be sure, it is a slower player in the rapid-fire world of activation and assembly, but it serves some important functions.

According to AAT (Greene, 1997), we become conscious of coalitions that are highly activated for longer periods of time (say, for seconds rather than for fractions of a second). As a result, we tend to be aware of abstract action specifications, which change slowly, rather than being aware of coalitions of low-level features, which tend to change rapidly. Moreover, when we run into assembly problems (as, for example, when we don't know how to say something without hurting someone's feelings), becoming conscious of the incompatible action specifications helps us to hold them in mind while we search for ways to solve the assembly problem.

FORCES OF CREATION

Because it is static and linear, Figure 2.1 is somewhat misleading, but it does give a rudimentary depiction of the features of AAT presented in this section. As we have seen, action features stored in memory are brought to bear in behavioral production via the activation process. The assembly process then serves to combine complementary action features to form coalitions. Some of these coalitions will be manifested in overt behavior because they are able to recruit low-level motor programs. Finally, some coalitions, because they are highly activated for extended periods of time, will enter conscious awareness.

With this basic model in place, we're in a position to take a fresh look at the issues introduced at the beginning of this chapter. Recall that the overarching focus here is the creative character of behavior (i.e., how it is possible for people to think, say, or do things that they've never heard, thought, said, or done before). And one important key in addressing the creative nature of behavior is recognizing that, although it is true that unfolding behavior is always new and unique, it is also always old in the sense that it reflects established elements and ways of doing things.

AAT addresses the simultaneous old and new character of behavior in a relatively straightforward way. The established elements of your behavior are those that are represented in memory as action features—all your characteristic (or *old*) ways of saying and doing things. The creative nature of your behavior comes from combining these action features in *new* sequences and configurations. An analogy I often invoke, although it is grossly oversimplified, is a tune played on a piano (see Greene, 2007). The piano has just 88 keys (reflecting a single level of abstraction, and none are likely to be added); from those limited keys, though, an infinite number of unique compositions can be constructed by combining these 88 features in new ways. Imagine, then, what you can do with tens of thousands of action features (reflecting many levels of abstraction, coupled with the fact that, unlike the finite number of piano keys, you can acquire new action features every day).

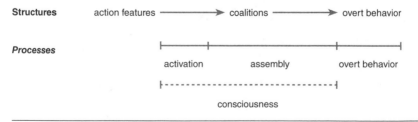

Figure 2.1 The Features of AAT

The simultaneous old-and-new character of behavior is only one of the paradoxes introduced earlier. There we also saw that while creativity comes effortlessly and naturally, there are also situations when our creative capacity fails us—situations where we stutter and stammer; where we just can't come up with the right thing to say; where we fail to think, say, and move as we want. A key precept of the intellectual tradition that fostered AAT is the notion that instances where a system fails to function optimally are just as important for understanding that system as the occasions where it runs smoothly. Breakdowns are not viewed as something to be ignored or passed off as insignificant; instead, they are prized as opportunities for deeper understanding. In keeping with this perspective, AAT encourages scrutiny of our lapses and awkwardness, and explains them in terms of the properties of the activation and assembly processes (see below).

One other key point merits mention here as well. Models of message production typically are top-down, in the sense that they assume that people formulate an abstract idea or understanding that then passes through a series of successively more concrete levels, terminating with verbal and nonverbal cues. AAT, however, tells a slightly different story about the creation of messages (Greene, 2006). AAT holds that message behavior, especially verbal behavior, *tends* to be top-down, but is not necessarily so. The nature of the coalition-building process is such that lower-level codes can actually drive the formation of higher-level thoughts. Thus, in AAT, a "just-right" word can drive the crystallization of a previously nebulous idea and a hand gesture, the formulation of a sentence.

How Communication Is Conceptualized in Action Assembly Theory

There are a number of properties of communication highlighted by AAT, some of which we've already touched on in this chapter. From the perspective of AAT, communication involves the interaction of two or more individuals, each of whom is, fundamentally, a physical, psychological, and social being. The presence of one's interlocutors and their behavior in such social contexts both poses assembly problems for the individual, and also affords solutions to assembly problems. Such interactions, then, are inevitably characterized by mutual influence—and mutually driven creation, both intra- and inter-individually. Moreover, each individual, via overt verbal and nonverbal behavior, expresses less than he or she "means" (i.e., the constellation of current coalitions) and more than he or she "knows" (i.e., that he or she is consciously aware of)—and all of this unfolds at speeds faster than the individual is able to apprehend.

Research and Practical Applications of Action Assembly Theory

Because it is a general theory of behavioral production, AAT is relevant to virtually any behavioral phenomenon one might wish to investigate. As a result of its broad applicability, the theory has provided a foundation for addressing such diverse topics as the *behaviors that distinguish liars from truth-tellers*, processes underlying the experience of *social anxiety*, the nature of our *self-concept*, and people's *behavioral consistency* (or lack thereof) from one situation to another (see Greene, 1995a).

Beyond these applications, others merit a little more discussion. One of these other applications is the topic of *social skill* and why we sometimes fail to communicate with others as we would like. We typically think of performance failures as stemming from a lack of either ability or motivation (or both). But Greene and Geddes (1993) noted that sometimes we have the necessary ability, and the motivation, but still are not able to produce a socially skilled response. For example, did you ever think of a great comeback to something someone said—but only after that person had left—or gotten into an argument with your "special someone" where you said things you knew you shouldn't have said? Greene and Geddes attempted to show how we can understand these sorts of situations in terms of the properties of the activation and assembly processes. A related series of studies based on AAT has explored the dynamics of *communication skill acquisition*—that is, understanding how communication skills can be improved (and why a lot of what we do in our classes on public speaking, group discussion, and so on is misguided or inadequate; see Greene, 2003).

Another realm in which AAT has found application is examining the factors that affect *speech fluency.* When we think about message behavior, we typically focus on the content of what people say, but all of us have an intuitive understanding that the temporal properties of a message are important as well (for example, we notice when a person pauses a long time before responding to a question). From the perspective of AAT, temporal features of a message, such as pauses and speech rate, are particularly fascinating. On one hand, they have social significance, and on the other, they provide a window on activation and assembly. According to AAT, many instances of disfluency and hesitation stem from difficulties in meshing (i.e., assembling) incompatible message features. This aspect of the theory has led to a number of studies exploring the effects of *advance planning* on speech fluency, and the impact of trying to accomplish *multiple goals* (e.g., to be kind while delivering bad news) in a single message (Greene, 1995b).

Evaluation of Action Assembly Theory

There are standard lists of criteria for evaluating scientific theories (utility, range, heurism, falsifiability, etc.), and you are encouraged to apply these criteria in evaluating AAT. But for present purposes, let us consider just one limitation and one strength of the theory. One of the former is that it may sometimes be difficult to take it all in—that is, to keep in mind all the details and at the same time to see the big picture of how they function together, and on top of this to apprehend the implications of the speed with which these processes unfold. The flip side of this same coin is one of the strengths of the theory. Science gives considerable weight to the "aesthetic value" of theories—that is, their elegance and the pleasure afforded by their contemplation. AAT is filled with puzzles and surprises that, like an undiscovered code, have always been embedded in the theory, and that emerge unexpectedly as you turn it over in your mind.

Continuing the Conversation

The fact that AAT is a general model of behavioral production means that it can be applied to virtually anything that happens when people come together. If you've got some issue or phenomenon you've been pondering, try casting it in AAT terms to see what implications the theory has for understanding that process in a new way. To illustrate what I have in mind, I'll mention just two areas of application of AAT that my colleagues, students, and I are currently pursuing. The first of these concerns what we call *transcendent interactions*— those wonderful conversations where we just seem totally connected and in sync with our interlocutor. We've used AAT as a way of understanding these exceptional experiences of interpersonal "sharedness" and engagement (Greene & Herbers, 2011). A second issue that my colleagues and I have focused on lately is why some people seem better than others at creating messages on the fly. You probably know people who are quick witted, who can think on their feet. We call this phenomenon *creative facility,* and we're trying to understand why some people have more of it than others. As for you, you've already proven that you can create a novel sentence; now where are you going to apply your creative message genius?

References

Greene, J. O. (1984). A cognitive approach to human communication: An action assembly theory. *Communication Monographs, 51,* 289–306.

Greene, J. O. (1994). What sort of terms ought theories of human action incorporate? *Communication Studies, 45,* 187–211.

Greene, J. O. (1995a). An action-assembly perspective on verbal and nonverbal message production: A dancer's message unveiled. In D. E. Hewes (Ed.), *The cognitive bases of interpersonal communication* (pp. 51–85). Hillsdale, NJ: Erlbaum.

Greene, J. O. (1995b). Production of messages in pursuit of multiple social goals: Action assembly theory contributions to the study of cognitive encoding processes. In B. R. Burleson (Ed.), *Communication yearbook 18* (pp. 26–53). Thousand Oaks, CA: Sage.

Greene, J. O. (1997). A second generation action assembly theory. In J. O. Greene (Ed.), *Message production: Advances in communication theory* (pp. 151–170). Mahwah, NJ: Erlbaum.

Greene, J. O. (2003). Models of adult communication skill acquisition: Practice and the course of performance improvement. In J. O. Greene & B. R. Burleson (Eds.), *Handbook of communication and social interaction skills* (pp. 51–91). Mahwah, NJ: Erlbaum.

Greene, J. O. (2006). Have I got something to tell you: Ideational dynamics and message production. *Journal of Language and Social Psychology, 25,* 64–75.

Greene, J. O. (2007). Formulating and producing verbal and nonverbal messages: An action assembly theory. In B. B. Whaley & W. Samter (Eds.), *Explaining communication: Contemporary theories and exemplars* (pp. 165–180). Mahwah, NJ: Erlbaum.

Greene, J. O., & Geddes, D. (1993). An action assembly perspective on social skill. *Communication Theory, 3,* 26–49.

Greene, J. O., & Herbers, L. E. (2011). Conditions of interpersonal transcendence. *The International Journal of Listening, 25,* 66–84.

Pavitt, C. (2001). *The philosophy of science and communication theory.* Huntington, NY: Nova Science Publishers.

3

Attribution Theory

Finding Good Cause in the Search for Theory

Brian H. Spitzberg and Valerie Manusov

Humans are an inquisitive species: We wonder why and how things occur, and we develop religions, philosophies, and sciences as ways of answering our questions. Such curiosity intricately influences our cultural, societal, interpersonal, and personal lives. We ask ourselves why another person looks so lonely, we wonder why we did not get a job, and we talk to others to try to figure out why the person we went out with on Saturday has not contacted us since then. After all, it's Tuesday!

The process of asking and answering "why" questions is a basic human activity (Heider, 1958). The family of theories that answer how and why we try to answer "how and why" questions is referred to as attribution theory. This set of interrelated theories attempts to describe and explain the mental and communicative processes involved in everyday explanations, most typically explanations of individual and social events. In this chapter, we describe select parts of these theories and their related scholarship, and we offer critiques of its usefulness for understanding interpersonal communication processes.

Intellectual Tradition of Attribution Theory

Attribution theory arose primarily in the Psychology discipline, although it has been applied across many disciplines. Given this origin, attribution theories lean heavily toward a logical-empirical view of the world. Although there are important cultural and personal differences in attribution making (e.g., Maddux & Yuki, 2006), the underlying process of attempting to understand the world around us is considered universal and predictable (Mezulis, Abramson, Hyde, & Hankin, 2004).

Fritz Heider is generally recognized as the originator of attribution theory. He argued that people naturally behave like naïve scientists as they attempt to make sense of their larger social worlds. For Heider (1958), people are active interpreters of the events that occur in their lives, and they use consistent and logical modes of sense-making in their interpretations. The more important or unexpected the event, the more likely people are to seek an explanation to make sense of that outcome. We make sense of such events primarily by determining what the cause is.

Main Goals and Features of Attribution Theory

Attribution theory has generally been applied in two related but distinct ways: as event causation or as trait inference. With *event causation,* we understand actions or events by attributing cause(s) to behavior (e.g., she smiled at him because she thinks he's attractive). With *trait inference,* we make an inference or judgment about a person's characteristics that makes sense of that person's behavior (e.g., she smiles a lot—she must be a very friendly person).

Within either application of attribution theory, we tend to use four dimensions when making attributions (Weiner, 1986): (1) *locus,* or whether the cause is internal or external to the person; (2) *stability,* or the extent to which the cause is temporary or enduring; (3) *specificity,* or the degree to which a cause is unique to an individual or event versus a cause that is more universal or global; and (4) *responsibility,* or the extent to which a person can be held as responsible or blameworthy for an event. A decision underlying most of these dimensions, in one way or another, is the perception of the intentionality of the act (Bazarova & Hancock, 2010; Malle, Knobe, & Nelson, 2007).

For example, in regard to the event causation approach to attributions, if you receive a bad grade on a paper, you have four possible sources to attribute this outcome: your ability (e.g., you are not smart enough), your effort (e.g., you did not study enough), task (e.g., the assignment was too hard), or (bad) luck (e.g., the professor was not paying attention, or entered the wrong grade by mistake). In regard to the trait inference approach, if a classmate receives a bad grade, you might conclude that it was due to the student's lack of effort (e.g., "She's lazy") or ability (e.g., "He's not very bright").

These attributional processes occur in everyday encounters, such as in the following conversation, where three friends are trying to explain one of their professor's facial expressions:

Sheryl:	Hey, did you see how Professor Smythe looked at me when I asked him that question?
Theo:	Yeah, he looked like he was really confused!
Sheryl:	Really? I thought he looked like he thought I was the dumbest student ever.
Theo:	No way. I'm sure he was just trying to figure out the answer.
Kyle:	I thought he was coming down with the flu.

Any behavior can be viewed as an effect that has some cause, and the cause we attribute (e.g., confusion, opinion, flu) is likely to influence the meaning of the action and how we might respond to it.

Four primary theoretical currents have emerged since Heider (1958) introduced the concept of attributions. Most research relies on just one of these currents, but, collectively, they make up the primary features of attributional scholarship.

A FOCUS ON CORRESPONDENCE

When attributions are informative of a person's nature or personality, they are considered "correspondent"; that is, we perceive that another's behavior corresponds to some underlying characteristic of who that person is. Jones and Davis (1965) developed this line of theorizing, and it has since been studied in a wide variety of disciplines and contexts. For example, Stamp and Sabourin (1995) found that relationally abusive or aggressive men tend to attribute their violence to things that were external to them, such as a wife's behavior or jealousy. Most of these external factors are considered correspondent, because abusive men tend to attribute such causes to intentional and negative factors in their partners. Importantly, such attributions reflected the men's thinking, rather than what may actually have prompted the behavior.

A FOCUS ON COVARIATION

In order to understand the underlying structure of attributing causes to effects, Kelley (1967, 1971) proposed a normative model that came to be known as the ANOVA (an acronym for "analysis of variance") cube. In general, events are attributed to causes with which they co-vary or co-occur. Causes are attributed to factors that are present when an event or effect is observed, and not present when the event or effect is absent. If you find that your relationships tend to get more complicated and are more likely to dissolve only after one of you says "I love you," you might attribute the utterance or state of love as the cause of relationship problems. For you, these events co-vary.

A FOCUS ON RESPONSIBILITY

Not all attributions are about the cause of an action, however. When we are making sense of things, we often focus instead on who or what was responsible for that behavior or outcome (Weiner, 2004). The potential consequences of responsibility attributions can be significant. In general, the more we view someone's behavior as internal, intentional, and controllable, the more we hold that person responsible for those actions, and their consequences (Weiner, 1995). For example, according to Badahdah and Alkhder (2006), people are more likely to feel sympathetic for a person with AIDS if that person is viewed as not responsible for his or her own plight (e.g., if AIDS was contracted through blood transfusion) as opposed to intentional risky conduct (e.g., unprotected sex). This example shows not only an example of a responsibility attribution, but also how profound those attributions may be for our judgments of others.

A FOCUS ON BIAS

Whereas we may behave like scientists, Heider (1958) considered us naïve and fallible ones. Researchers have predicted systematic biases in how we make attributions, consistent with Heider's contention. The most well-known bias is the *fundamental attribution bias,* which is a tendency to make more internal attributions than external attributions for other people's behaviors (Ross, 1977). A related bias is the *self-serving bias,* which predicts that people generally make more internal, stable, and global attributions for positive events than for negative events, and more external attributions for negative events than for positive events (Malle, 2006; Mezulis et al., 2004; Robbennolt, 2000). Thus, students generally over-report their GPA (Kuncel, Credé, & Thomas, 2005) and consider themselves above average on a variety of positive characteristics (Alicke & Govorun, 2005). Likewise, employees think more highly of themselves than their bosses see those same employees (Jaramillo, Carrillat, & Locander, 2005). Canary and Spitzberg (1990) found that actors in conflicts tend to view their own behavior as significantly more appropriate than the behavior of their partners. We protect our self-image by absorbing responsibility for positive outcomes and externalizing negative outcomes to things other than ourselves.

SUMMARY

Every comment a person makes and every action a person performs can be subject to attributional analysis, by self and by others. The outcome of this analysis has potentially significant implications for how people think about one another and for the nature of how we respond to another's actions. Whether it is an achievement failure, a stigmatizing condition, a need for help, or an aggressive act, if these are attributed to controllable and intentional causes, for instance, responses of anger and reprimand or neglect are more likely, whereas uncontrollable and unintentional attributions are more likely to lead to sympathy and offers of assistance (Weiner, 2004).

How Communication Is Conceptualized in Attribution Theory

The past 30 years have seen particular attention to attributions by communication scholars. Two early chapters (Seibold & Spitzberg, 1982; Sillars, 1982) encouraged communication researchers to address the nature of attributions, and the term "attribution" now shows up as a key word across a broad array of studies, including: developing trust in online relationships (Bekmeier-Feuerhahn & Eichenlaub, 2010), student attributions for their public speaking performance (Luo, Bippus, & Dunbar, 2005), the persuasiveness of two-sided messages (Eisend, 2007), children's views of their parents' communication competence and the resulting outcomes of parental divorce (McManus & Donovan, 2012), reactions to profanity use and emotion expression in conflicts (Bippus & Young, 2005; Young, 2004), student judgments of teacher misbehavior (Kelsey, Kearney, Plax, Allen, & Ritter, 2004) and teacher judgments of student misbehavior (Kauppi & Pörhölä, 2012), workplace harassment (Hershcovis & Barling, 2010), and crisis communication (Coombs, 2007). This body of attribution research in communication is undergirded by three main currents.

ATTRIBUTIONS AS EXPLANATIONS UNDERLYING SOCIAL COMMUNICATIVE ACTIONS

Communication behaviors can be seen as occurring for different reasons, and we provide attributions to explain those communicative actions. For instance, Bippus (2003) demonstrated the conceptualization of attributions as "explanations for communicative behavior" by asking people why a person used humor in an actual conflict situation. She also asked how they interpreted the cause and repercussions. Bippus found that more internal attributions for humor use were associated with more negative outcomes (e.g., conflict escalation, progress, and face loss). Humor thought to be bad and humor that was attributed to the speaker's personality was particularly damaging to the relationship.

ATTRIBUTIONS AS LEADING TO COMMUNICATIVE ACTIONS AND OUTCOMES

When we provide attributions for others' communication (or other behavior), it may affect how we view the other person and his or her behavior. Even more notably, it may also affect our communication toward them. For example, MacGeorge (2001) investigated the ways in which people offer social support to one another in times of crisis and found that when the crisis was attributed as more stable, more a product of the person's effort, and the person as more responsible, it induced greater anger and reduced sympathy for the affected person's plight.

ATTRIBUTIONS AS THE ACTUAL MEANINGS GIVEN TO A BEHAVIOR

Some communication researchers have looked at dialogue—like the dialogue between Sheryl, Theo, and Kyle or at "dialogues" with ourselves—to investigate how attributions reflect the meaning that people give to a communication act. That is, we can also look at attributions to see what a behavior means—what message value it has—for someone. For example, the determination of whether or not a person is being deceptive in communicating is an attributional problem (Bazarova & Hancock, 2010)—and the conclusion that a lie is self-serving ("He lied because he needed the money") as opposed to relationally motivated ("He didn't want to hurt my feelings") can become the meaning attributed to the communication act itself.

Research and Practical Applications of Attribution Theory

These three conceptualizations reflect a strong interconnectedness between attributions and communication. They arise from a large body of context-based scholarship conducted by researchers interested in the interpersonal nature of attributions. Two commonly studied contexts are (a) marriage and (b) the ways in which attributions are involved in some of the darker sides of communication. To follow, we discuss these sometimes overlapping areas of research.

ATTRIBUTIONS IN MARRIAGE

Researchers have looked at the ways in which one spouse's feelings about the relationship (i.e., marital satisfaction) influences, or is influenced by, the kind of attributions the spouse makes for his or her own and his or her partner's behaviors. In general, people in distressed marriages, compared to those in satisfied marriages, tend to overemphasize attributions of negative characteristics or responsibility to their partners rather than to themselves (Fincham & Bradbury, 1992). The tendency for satisfied couples to make low-impact attributions for negative behaviors (and, conversely, to allow positive events more influence) has been termed *relationship-enhancing*; the type of attributions more common for distressed or dissatisfied couples is called *distress-maintaining* (Holtzworth-Munroe & Jacobson, 1988). Satisfied couples also tend to see their own and their spouse's behavior as caused by similar factors (Manusov, Floyd, & Kerssen-Griep, 1997).

The occurrence and impact of distress-maintaining attributions appears augmented when couples are categorized as aggressive. For example, Sillars, Leonard, Roberts, and Dun (2002) concluded that aggressive couples tend to have negative styles of communication and that their communication tends to get even more negative when the husbands drink alcohol. Thus, one spouse may state that he engaged in certain conflict behavior because, "I'm trying to get her to talk about it," yet assert that his spouse engaged in the same behavior for a very different reason: "She's always got to have her way" (see Sillars et al., 2002, p. 97).

In one study, Manusov (2002) reported evidence that attributions made by one spouse for his or her spouse's nonverbal cues may also influence the behaviors the attributor expresses toward the other. That is, when one spouse attributed greater control to his or her partner's emotional expressions, the attributor was more likely to be facially pleasant, gaze more, and use a more upright posture when talking to his or her spouse. The links between attributions and other affective and behavioral outcomes show the extent to which attribution-making may permeate intimate relationships in both positive and negative ways.

THE DARKER SIDE OF ATTRIBUTIONS

The role of attribution processes has been the subject of increasing attention in the explanation of, among other things, aggression and violence. For example, when victims of childhood bullying attribute such actions to the bully's intentionally hostile reasons, the victims are more likely to engage in aggression themselves (de Castro, Veerman, Koops, Bosch, & Monshouwer, 2002). Byrne and Arias (1997) found that there was a substantial negative correlation between marital satisfaction and marital aggression among wives who attributed their husbands as responsible for negative behavior in the relationship. Olson and Lloyd's (2005) detailed interviews with a small sample of women who had experienced aggressive behaviors in their relationships revealed a "glaring pattern" in which "the women explained that aggression was the only way to get their partners' attention or to get the men to listen or acknowledge the women" (p. 615).

In contrast, however, and more consistent with the self-serving bias, Taylor and Sorenson (2005) discovered that spouses were more likely to blame their partners rather than themselves for domestic violence. It appears that abusive men not only demonstrate these attribution biases in their own relationships but in their perception of others, as well. When asked to interpret the thoughts of videotaped interactions, Schweinle and Ickes (2002) learned that abusive men reveal an over-attribution bias in which husbands assume that their wives' thoughts are more critical and rejecting than wives interpret their husbands' thoughts.

Evaluation of Attribution Theory

Despite the expansive and diverse domains and questions to which attribution theory has been applied, the theory is not without its problems, and attribution theory has received its share of critical review (e.g., Bradbury & Fincham, 1990). There are many criteria by which theories can be evaluated. We focus here on (a) explanatory power, (b) scope and generality, (c) conditionship specification, and (d) verifiability or falsifiability to show some of the strengths and limitations of attribution theory *qua* theory (Spitzberg, 2001).

Explanatory power refers to the most essential requirement of any theory: How well does it explain, or make sense of, phenomena? It is a near paradox that a theory explaining how people explain is itself required to be a good explanation. Attribution theories have the advantage of making intuitive sense, developed as they were to account for laypersons as naïve scientists (Heider, 1958). Most of the dimensions and principles of attribution theories are recognizable immediately in everyday interactions. In Sheryl, Theo, and Kyle's conversation, for example, we see a process of negotiating attributions working together in conversation to determine why something occurred and what it meant.

Scope and generality refer to the breadth of phenomena and contexts in which a theory applies. A theory that only applies to a particular time, place, or behavior is narrow in scope and not very generalizable. Attribution theory was developed originally as a universal theory of human sense-making, but research has limited its scope. Most research investigates contexts in which conscious attributional efforts are most likely: contexts involving actual or potential negative consequences and violations of expectations. For example, researchers have centered on shyness, loneliness, conflict, accounts, abuse, anger, shame, achievement motivation, moral responsibility, and relationship breakups. Attributions may or may not work the same way in contexts where the importance of making attributions is less necessary.

Conditionship specification refers to the extent to which a theory clearly articulates the nature of the relationship among its concepts. Even some of the original theorists claim some strict parameters for the theory. For example, Heider's (1958) original propositions were quite formulaic, along the lines of the following: Personal causation is attributed as a multiplicative function of power (can) and trying (effort) plus environmental facilitation (or minus environmental obstruction). Weiner (2004) claimed boldly that "there are three, and indeed only three, underlying causal properties that have cross-situational generality . . . locus, stability, and controllability" (p. 17). Bradbury and Fincham (1990) claimed that "the dimensions of locus, stability, control, and globality are necessary and sufficient for assessing causal attributions in marriage" (p. 17), even though their own review indicated that many studies find little or no support for these dimensions. Despite the intuitive and widely accepted nature of the fundamental attribution bias, research indicates it is often relatively insubstantial and inconsequential (Malle, 2006). On the other hand, the self-serving bias has been extensively verified in research (Malle, 2006; Mezulis et al., 2004). Clearly, attribution theory is open to revision and is receiving significant reconceptualization by scholars explicitly interested in communication processes (e.g., Basarova & Hancock, 2010; Malle et al., 2007).

Such mixed findings raise a significant question of the verifiability and falsifiability of this theory. *Verifiability* is the extent to which evidence in support of a theory can be generated through observation and investigation. *Falsifiability* is the degree to which evidence that contradicts a theory can be generated through observation and investigation. Consider the following proposition: All conflicts are blamed on the partner more than on the self. A verification strategy would take any evidence that conflicts tend to be blamed on the partner more than on the self as evidence in support of the proposition. In contrast, a falsification strategy would take any evidence that it sometimes does *not* happen as evidence that the proposition is incorrect and must be modified or replaced. To date, it is easy to find researchers claiming to have supported or verified attribution theory. Even though lack or only partial support is often reported, only a few scholars argue that attribution theory is fundamentally flawed and that some of its premises need to be replaced.

Continuing the Conversation

Despite such concerns, attribution processes have great potential for additional study and application by scholars interested in interpersonal communication and relationships. There is little doubt that the types of attributions people make can influence important social and relational processes and outcomes. For example, a relatively recent study (Stewart, Keel, & Schiavo, 2006) examined attributions people gave for others who had been diagnosed with an eating disorder. Compared to the attributions made about people without the eating disorder, attributions about people with anorexia nervosa are more likely to blame the affected person for his or her condition. That is, people implicated those with anorexia in their own disorder; such attributions could affect others' treatment of and communication with that person and may, therefore, worsen the people's condition.

The ubiquitous nature of attributions is relatively easy to discover. The next time you and a fellow student or roommate or friend are in a position to observe a person display a facial emotion, compare each other's interpretation of a plausible attribution for that emotional expression (McArthur, 2011). It is likely that you will arrive at different attributions. Consider scenarios that might reveal the importance of such attributions. For example, in passing a person asking for a handout of money or food, consider your behavior and reactions if your attribution is that the person was laid off due to the recession, traumatized as a veteran of two wars, or disabled due to an accident with a drunk driver or genetic disease. In contrast, consider how different your behavior or reactions might be if you attribute the person's behavior to a desire to avoid working, preferring instead to "mooch off" of society.

In closing, we believe that attributional processes are a vital—and conse-quential—set of practices for interpersonal communication scholars to inves-tigate. Their ubiquity in our everyday sense-making means that attributions are ripe for study by people in their everyday lives. Our hope is that this chapter energizes that curiosity in readers.

References

Alicke, M. D., & Govorun, O. (2005). The better-than-average effect. In M. D. Alicke, D. A. Dunning, & J. I. Krueger (Eds.), *The self in social judgment* (pp. 85–106). New York, NY: Psychology Press.

Badahdah, A. M., & Alkhder, O. H. (2006). Helping a friend with AIDS: A test of Weiner's attributional theory in Kuwait. *Illness, Crisis, & Loss, 14,* 43–54.

Bazarova, N. N., & Hancock, J. T. (2010). From dispositional attributions to behavior motives: The folk-conceptual theory and implications for communication. In C. T. Salmon (Ed.), *Communication yearbook 34* (pp. 63–92). New York, NY: Routledge.

Bekmeier-Feuerhahn, S., & Eichenlaub, A. (2010). What makes for trusting relationships in online communication? *Journal of Communication Management, 14,* 337–355.

Bippus, A. M. (2003). Humor motives, qualities, and reactions in recalled conflict epi-sodes. *Western Journal of Communication, 67,* 13–27.

Bippus, A. M., & Young, S. L. (2005). Owning your emotions: Reactions to expressions of self- versus other-attributed positive and negative emotions. *Journal of Applied Communication Research, 33,* 26–45.

Bradbury, T. N., & Fincham, F. D. (1990). Attributions in marriage: Review and critique. *Psychological Bulletin, 107,* 3–33.

Byrne, C. A., & Arias, I. (1997). Marital satisfaction and marital violence: Moderating effects of attributional processes. *Journal of Family Violence, 11,* 188–195.

Canary, D. J., & Spitzberg, B. H. (1990). Attribution biases and associations between conflict strategies and competence outcomes. *Communication Monographs, 57,* 139–151.

Coombs, W. T. (2007). Attribution theory as a guide for post-crisis communication research. *Public Relations Review, 33,* 135–139.

de Castro, B. O., Veerman, J. W., Koops, W., Bosch, J. D., & Monshouwer, H. J. (2002). Hostile attribution of intent and aggressive behavior: A meta-analysis. *Child Development, 73,* 916–934.

Eisend, M. (2007). Understanding two-sided persuasion: An empirical assessment of theoretical approaches. *Psychology & Marketing, 24,* 615–640.

Fincham, F. D., & Bradbury, T. N. (1992). Assessing attributions in marriage: The Relationship Attribution Measure. *Journal of Personality and Social Psychology, 62,* 457–468.

Heider, F. (1958). *The psychology of interpersonal relations.* New York, NY: Wiley.

Hershcovis, M., & Barling, J. (2010). Comparing victim attributions and outcomes for workplace aggression and sexual harassment. *Journal of Applied Psychology, 95,* 874–888.

Holtzworth-Munroe, A., & Jacobson, N. S. (1988). Toward a methodology for coding spontaneous causal attributions: Preliminary results with married couples. *Journal of Social and Clinical Psychology, 7,* 101–112.

Jaramillo, F., Carrillat, F. A., & Locander, W. B. (2005). A meta-analytic comparison of managerial ratings and self-evaluations. *Journal of Personal Selling & Sales Management, 25,* 315–328.

Jones, E. E., & Davis, K. E. (1965). From acts to dispositions: The attribution process in person perception. In L. Berkowitz (Ed.), *Advances in experimental social psychology* (vol. 2, pp. 219–266). New York, NY: Academic Press.

Kauppi, T., & Pörhölä, M. (2012). School teachers bullied by their students: Teachers' attributions and how they share their experiences. *Teaching and Teacher Education, 28,* 1059–1068.

Kelley, H. H. (1967). Attribution theory in social psychology. *Nebraska Symposium on Motivation, 14,* 192–241.

Kelley, H. H. (1971). *Attribution in social interaction.* Morristown, NJ: General Learning Press.

Kelsey, D. M., Kearney, P., Plax, T. G., Allen, T. H., & Ritter, K. J. (2004). College students' attributions of teacher misbehaviors. *Communication Education, 53,* 40–55.

Kuncel, N. R., Credé, M., & Thomas, L. L. (2005). The validity of self-reported grade point averages, class ranks, and test scores: A meta-analysis and review of the literature. *Review of Educational Research, 75,* 63–82.

Luo, L., Bippus, A. M., & Dunbar, N. E. (2005). Causal attributions for collaborative public speaking presentations in college classes. *Communication Reports, 18,* 65–73.

MacGeorge, E. L. (2001). Support providers' interaction goals: The influence of attributions and emotions. *Communication Monographs, 68,* 28–48.

Maddux, W. W., & Yuki, M. (2006). The "ripple effect": Cultural differences in perceptions of the consequences of events. *Personality & Social Psychology Bulletin, 32,* 669–684.

Malle, B. F. (2006). The actor-observer asymmetry in attribution: A (surprising) meta-analysis. *Psychological Bulletin, 132,* 895–919.

Malle, B. F., Knobe, J. M., & Nelson, S. E. (2007). Actor-observer asymmetries in explanations of behavior: New answers to an old question. *Journal of Personality and Social Psychology, 93,* 491–514.

Manusov, V. (2002). Thought and action: Connecting attributions to behaviors in married couples' interactions. In P. Noller & J. A. Feeney (Eds.), *Understanding marriage: Developments in the study of couple interaction* (pp. 14–31). Cambridge, UK: Cambridge University Press.

Manusov, V., Floyd, K., & Kerssen-Griep, J. (1997). Yours, mine, and ours: Mutual attributions for nonverbal behaviors in couples' interactions. *Communication Research, 24,* 234–260.

McArthur, J. (2011). "What happened?" Teaching attribution theory through ambiguous prompts. *Communication Teacher, 25,* 32–36.

McManus, T. G., & Donovan, S. (2012). Communication competence and feeling caught: Explaining perceived ambiguity in divorce-related communication. *Communication Quarterly, 60,* 255–277.

Mezulis, A. H., Abramson, L. Y., Hyde, J. S., & Hankin, B. L. (2004). Is there a universal positivity bias in attributions? A meta-analytic review of individual, developmental, and cultural differences in the self-serving attributional bias. *Psychological Bulletin, 130,* 711–747.

Olson, L. N., & Lloyd, S. A. (2005). "It depends on what you mean by starting": An exploration of how women define initiation of aggression and their motives for behaving aggressively. *Sex Roles, 53,* 603–617.

Robbennolt, J. K. (2000). Outcome severity and judgments of 'responsibility': A meta-analytic review. *Journal of Applied Social Psychology, 30,* 2575–2609.

Ross, L. (1977). The intuitive psychologist and his shortcomings. Distortions in the attribution process. In L. Berkowitz (Ed.), *Advances in experimental social psychology* (vol. 10, pp. 174–177). New York, NY: Academic Press.

Schweinle, W. E., & Ickes, W. (2002). On empathic accuracy and husbands' abusiveness. In P. Noller & J. A. Feeney (Eds.), *Understanding marriage: Developments in the study of couple interaction* (pp. 228–250). Cambridge, UK: Cambridge University Press.

Seibold, D. R., & Spitzberg, B. H. (1982). Attribution theory and research: Review and implications for communication. In B. Dervin & M. J. Voight (Eds.), *Progress in communication sciences* (pp. 85–125). Norwood, NJ: Ablex.

Sillars, A. L. (1982). Attribution and communication: Are people "naïve scientists" or just naïve? In M. E. Roloff & C. R. Berger (Eds.), *Social cognition and communication* (pp. 73–106). Beverly Hills, CA: Sage.

Sillars, A. L., Leonard, K. E., Roberts, L. J., & Dun, T. (2002). Cognition and communication during marital conflict: How alcohol affects subjective coding of interaction in aggressive and nonaggressive couples. In P. Noller & J. A. Feeney (Eds.), *Understanding marriage: Developments in the study of couple interaction* (pp. 85–112). Cambridge, UK: Cambridge University Press.

Spitzberg, B. H. (2001). The status of attribution theory *qua* theory in personal relationships. In V. Manusov & J. H. Harvey (Eds.), *Attribution, communication behavior, and close relationships* (pp. 353–371). Cambridge, UK: Cambridge University Press.

Stamp, G. H., & Sabourin, T. C. (1995). Accounting for violence: An analysis of male spousal abuse narratives. *Journal of Applied Communication Research, 23,* 284–308.

Stewart, M. C., Keel, P. K., & Schiavo, S. (2006). Stigmatization of anorexia nervosa. *International Journal of Eating Disorders, 39,* 320–325.

Taylor, C. A., & Sorenson, S. B. (2005). Community-based norms about intimate partner violence: Putting attributions of fault and responsibility into context. *Sex Roles, 53,* 573–589.

Weiner, B. (1986). *An attributional theory of motivation and emotion.* New York, NY: Springer-Verlag.

Weiner, B. (1995). *Judgments of responsibility: A foundation for a theory of social conduct.* New York, NY: Guilford.

Weiner, B. (2004). Attribution theory revisited: Transforming cultural plurality into theoretical unity. In D. M. McInerney & S. V. Etten (Eds.), *Big theories revisited* (pp. 13–29). Greenwich, CT: Information Age Publishing.

Young, S. L. (2004). What the _ _ _ _ is your problem?: Attribution theory and perceived reasons for profanity usage during conflict. *Communication Research Reports, 21,* 338–347.

4

Evolutionary Theories

Explaining the Links Between Biology and Interpersonal Communication

Tamara Afifi, Shardé Davis, and Amanda Denes

Biology has played an increasingly important role in interpersonal communication research. Scholars (e.g., Beatty & McCroskey, 1997; Floyd & Afifi, 2011; Knapp, Miller, & Fudge, 1994) have long argued that taking a "biosocial approach" to interpersonal communication is the wave of the future. In fact, if researchers want to study stress, it is imperative that they examine the research that uses hormones to assess people's stress levels. Biological approaches are often a more accurate determinant of people's stress levels than self-reports. But, what is meant by a biosocial approach? A biosocial approach involves integrating the social sciences with biology or physiology, particularly examining how one's biology and one's social environment mutually influence each other.

Evolutionary theory is a primary theoretical approach researchers use to study biology and interpersonal communication. Evolutionary theory tends to be an overarching theoretical framework that informs different theories that use a "biosocial approach." Three theories, in particular, tend to assume an evolutionary stance and have been used to explain interpersonal behavior and physiological stress responses: affection exchange theory (Floyd, 2001), tend and befriend theory (Taylor et al., 2000), and attachment theory (Bowlby, 1982). We provide an overview of evolutionary theory and then discuss how these three theories take an evolutionary stance to biosocial research. We then provide some critiques and future directions for studying biological stress responses from an evolutionary approach.

51

Intellectual Tradition of Evolutionary Theory

Evolution is the change in the inherited traits of biological populations over generations. Contemporary evolutionary theory has its origins in evolutionary biology and most of it is based on essentialism or the idea that every species has certain traits that remain relatively stable (Darwin, 1859). Charles Darwin is often considered to be the founder of evolutionary theory, but the idea of evolution is a relatively old antiquity, pre-dating Darwin's most famous 1859 book advancing his theory, *On the Origin of Species by Means of Natural Selection*. Ancient Greek, Roman, and Chinese philosophers advanced the notion of evolutionary decent of life from non-life, and these intellectuals heavily debated these ideas for centuries. Nevertheless, Darwin advanced the most well-known argument for evolutionary change.

Main Goals and Features of Evolutionary Theory

Contemporary scholar Ernst Mayr (1991) summarized Darwin's arguments regarding evolutionary theory into five principles: (1) basic theory of evolution, (2) common decent, (3) multiplication of species, (4) gradualism, and (5) natural selection. The basic theory of evolution is that there is perpetual change in the living world where nothing is constant or repeated exactly. It is said that the other parts are based on this major premise. Darwin's "common decent" states that all living organisms on earth emerged from a common ancestral lineage. Third, the evolutionary process produces new species by splitting old species and transforming them into new ones. Fourth, the aforementioned changes of population occur gradually, rather than at a rapid rate. Darwin believed that the process of evolution could take place over an extensive period of time and after innumerable small steps.

Darwin's (1859) notion of natural selection is considered chief among notions of evolutionary theory because it was so revolutionary. Natural selection rests on four primary assumptions that collectively provide a reason why species succeed or become extinct (Darwin, 1859). First, Darwin argued that individuals are variable. Variation among organisms consists of anatomical, behavioral, and physiological traits. Human species, for example, vary considerably according to their height, hair color, body symmetry, physical aptitude, and more. Even those from the same familial lineage carry a different combination of traits, resulting in noticeable differences among them. Accordingly, the second postulate states that a number of these traits are heritable or passed onto offspring. These genetic traits are reproductively advantageous for an individual (i.e., help acquire more food, help to be more physically adept, protect one's family), and his or her lineage are preferentially chosen to be passed down and retained throughout the generations. Traits that do not prove to be advantageous are not passed down, and therefore are less likely to exist in future generations. Third, individuals produce more offspring than the environment can support. Individuals struggle to acquire and retain resources (i.e., mates, food, water, safe places to sleep) that assist longevity on earth, and so the few individuals possessing traits well suited for acquiring resources will mature long enough to reproduce more offspring, while the large majority of the offspring lacking the proper genetic traits for survival do not survive to maturity. The scarcity of resources favors individuals with the combination of traits that prove to be advantageous for successfully acquiring resources. Over generations, favorable new traits will be passed onto offspring to increase their chance of survival and reproduction. Gradually, the accumulation of changes in species leads to the production of new species in the population.

This dynamic evolutionary process of selecting characteristics that promote survival is called *adaptation,* and it is a key component to the process of natural selection. Adaptation can be thought of as a solution to environmental problems; pressing issues related to the earth and the need for survival increase the likelihood that adaptive strategies will be enacted. It is important to note that adaptation does not operate at the individual level, but at the genetic level. That is, selection and adaptation take place to benefit offspring and future generations and not the individual. This explains why families invest time, money, and resources into children, grandchildren, and other young generations, even at their own expense.

How Communication Is Conceptualized in Evolutionary Theory

Contemporary scholars in the social sciences, such as those in communication and psychology, have readily adopted evolutionary perspectives in their research. It has been used to revolutionize social science research by understanding the evolutionary adaptations of behaviors and traits that occur in *all* human beings, like emotional reactions (Tooby & Cosmides, 1990), selecting attractive and healthy mating partners (Buss, 1995), and identifying kin from strangers (Park & Schaller, 2005). Scholars have shown that the body is organized to serve various functions, most of which assist survival and reproduction. For example, the heart organ pumps blood so that humans can remain alive, and the liver removes harmful substances from a person's bloodstream. Natural scientists agree that the functional structure of the human body is a result of natural selection (see Tooby & Cosmides, 2005).

Psychologists apply this adaptationist perspective of physiology to psychology, making the claim that cognition is a structure that has been created to serve survival and reproductive purposes (e.g., Barkow, Cosmides, & Tooby, 1992). Evolutionary psychology argues that the different parts of the evolved brain function to address qualitatively distinct problems (Cosmides & Tooby, 1997). For instance, the part of the brain that evolved for finding water sources is not the same part that identities a viable mate (Confer et al., 2010). Similar to the process of natural selection among individuals, evolutionary psychology refers to brain functions as *psychological adaptations,* where human behavior is the output of psychological adaptations that evolve by means of natural selection to solve recurrent problems in human ancestral environments (Tooby & Cosmides, 2005).

Evolutionary biology and evolutionary psychology are particularly relevant frameworks for communication scholars because the list of adaptive problems extends beyond those commonly mentioned in evolutionary research (e.g., scouring the environment for food, locating a fertile mate, and avoiding dangerous creatures; Confer et al., 2010). There are other adaptive problems, many of which are communication related, for which the body and mind should adapt. For example, conflict management (i.e., developing violent and nonviolent conflict patterns), investing in relationships (i.e., parents investing time, energy, money, and other resources into their children), and trust in close others (i.e., severing ties with a cheating partner or disloyal friend), are often evolutionary in nature. Communication is a primary way in which human beings acquire resources, adapt to stressful situations, protect themselves and close others, and prolong their lives. In the next section, we review theories that examine biosocial aspects of communicative behaviors that are steeped in evolutionary theory.

Research and Practical Applications of Evolutionary Theory

AFFECTION EXCHANGE THEORY

A theory that was developed in communication and is rooted in evolutionary theory and physiological response systems is affection exchange theory (AET; Floyd, 2001; see also Chapter 23, Part III of this volume). Floyd developed AET to explain how and why people give and receive affection and its implications for people's health (Floyd, 2001). It is based on Darwin's notion of natural selection in that people give and receive affection in ways that are adaptive or evolutionarily advantageous for their relationships. Affection allows people to present themselves as viable parents and mates (Floyd, Judd, & Hesse,

2008). Parents' selective affection with their children also helps further the family's genetic lineage (see Floyd, Hesse, and Generous's chapter).

At a basic level, AET states that humans have an inborn tendency to give and receive affection (Floyd, 2001). However, some people are more comfortable giving and receiving affection than others. AET also suggests that affection and physiological stress response systems are interdependent or influence each other. For instance, if someone has more traces of "trait-like" affection, they may have less stress than others. In fact, trait levels of expressed affection predict lower glycated hemoglobin (Floyd, Hesse, & Haynes, 2007) and higher natural killer cell toxicity (Floyd et al., 2010). Likewise, when people are stressed, it most likely affects their ability to give affection and their willingness to receive it.

In particular, Floyd has found support for the assumption that the amount of affection people give and receive serves an important stress reduction function (Floyd, Hesse, & Haynes, 2007; Floyd et al., 2009). Expressing and receiving affection helps mobilize people to fight the stressors that come their way, as well as protect them from the negative effects of stress on their health. According to AET, the more people give and receive affection, the more their body is able to adapt to the stress of its surroundings, which ultimately promotes better health.

While giving and receiving affection both serve important stress reduction functions, they may have independent effects on one's health (e.g., Floyd & Riforgiate, 2009). For example, Floyd (2006) took four saliva samples throughout the course of a normal workday of 20 healthy individuals. He found that the amount of affection the participants expressed to others throughout the day was positively associated with waking cortisol levels, average cortisol levels, and how steeply the cortisol declined from morning to evening. These associations were significant even after controlling for the amount of affection received by others that day. When the body is stressed, the brain tells the body to release cortisol to combat the stress. A certain amount of cortisol is normal and healthy because it helps people energize, adapt, and fight against impending threats. Cortisol also tends to follow a diurnal rhythm, where it is at its highest point approximately thirty minutes upon waking and slowly declines throughout the day and reaches its lowest point at midnight (see Floyd & Afifi, 2011).

Some of Floyd's tests of AET have also shown that people only need to imagine the level of affection in their relationship, without the other person even being physically present, for it to have a positive effect on their physical and physiological health (see Floyd, Mikkelson, Hesse, & Pauley, 2007). Floyd and others' work testing AET has shown that affection can help mobilize people to fight the stressors they encounter, as well as buffer them from the negative effects of stress on their physical health.

TEND AND BEFRIEND THEORY

Much of the biosocial research focuses on people's "fight or flight" responses or the tendency to aggressively fight against a stressor or retreat from it. One theory that addresses this fight or flight approach to stress is Taylor et al.'s (2000, 2002) tend and befriend theory. Tend and befriend theory suggests that people tend to affiliate with others when they are stressed (Taylor, 2012; Taylor et al., 2002). Under times of threat, human beings often tend to offspring and affiliate with others for joint protection and security (Taylor, 2012). In particular, the theory argues that when women are faced with an impending threat, their bodies release hormones that increase "tending" behaviors. Oxytocin (a hormone that facilities social bonding), in conjunction with the opioid system, counteracts the effects of physiological stress responses (e.g., cortisol, testosterone) that normally arise when faced with a stressor. While men may also have these tending behaviors, women's hormones and mothering tendencies make these behaviors more likely for women than men (Taylor, 2012).

Taylor (2012) argued that women and men may have different fight or flight tendencies, largely because of different hormones and evolutionary tendencies. According to tend and befriend theory, women's most important goal is to protect their offspring and the future of their family (Taylor et al., 2000). As Taylor et al. (2000) noted, sometimes this involves aggression if they are protecting their children from an imminent threat. Most of the time, however, it involves tending and befriending behaviors. When a threat from the environment presents itself, women's instinct is to protect their children by soothing and reassuring them through social support and affectionate communication (tending), and aligning themselves with others who can help preserve these family bonds (Taylor et al., 2000). From an evolutionary standpoint, displaying an aggressive or "fight" response could put women's lives in danger (e.g., if they get in a fight and are killed or injured), which could leave their children and the future of their family in a compromising position (Taylor, 2012). Instead of a fight or flight response, women tend to communicate in ways that "befriend" other people, particularly other women, to reduce social threats and help increase their access to others who could help protect their family in times of need (Taylor et al., 2000; Zwolinski, 2008).

Because women often do not have the same physical strength as men, they may rely on their social resources with other women as a source of resilience. Tend and befriend theory also suggests that when women perceive a gap in their close social networks, it poses an interpersonal threat (Zwolinski, 2008). Women are aware of these social cues and tend to respond by affiliating with others in an attempt to lessen that social gap and minimize their physiological stress response (Zwolinski, 2008). For example, Zwolinski found that women who were previously victimized were particularly sensitive to social cues of rejection from other women, which heightened their cortisol levels, and produced stronger tendencies to affiliate with them. Women, in general, have this same tendency but it may be exacerbated depending upon their past experiences with being marginalized or victimized.

ATTACHMENT THEORY

Attachment theory is also commonly used to explain the connection between physiology and interpersonal communication, and when it is applied in this manner, it links back to an evolutionary perspective (see Chapter 24 in Part III for an additional explanation of this theory). According to attachment theory (Bowlby, 1982), children form bonds or attachments with their parents as a result of parenting practices. These attachments affect how people perceive and approach relationships. Children develop internal working models of how to approach relationships that can affect the nature and quality of their future relationships (Collins & Feeney, 2004).

Most of the biosocial research on attachment has focused on mothers, infants, and oxytocin. Oxytocin is the biosocial marker most closely linked to attachment theory because it is a hormone that has been shown to facilitate social bonds (Campbell, 2010). People with higher oxytocin levels tend to become more social, more attracted to others, and more affectionate (Feldman, Gordon, & Zagoory-Sharon, 2011). Oxytocin has been shown to buffer or reduce some of the effect of stress on people's physiological stress responses (Taylor, 2012). A primary finding is that oxytocin facilitates attachments between primary caregivers and infants. Most of this research has focused on mothers because of their biological connections to their infants during and after pregnancy, as well as their role as primary caregivers. For example, the mother and child have a strong biological connection automatically because of pregnancy. They are sharing oxytocin and other hormones while the baby is developing in the womb. Oxytocin induces contractions during pregnancy and enlarges the uterus so that the baby can be delivered. It also promotes mother-infant attachments after the infant is born. When infants nuzzle against their mothers, it signals the release of oxytocin and subsequent milk flow (Campbell, 2010). Not only does oxytocin help the mother produce milk for the baby to survive, but the touch that occurs during breastfeeding also increases oxytocin levels, which reduces cortisol levels and enhances the attachment between the mother and infant. Evolutionarily, this attachment, in turn, should help promote strong family ties.

These social bonds also develop between fathers and infants, as well as a vast array of other social relationships. Oxytocin is referred to as the prosocial hormone because it makes people feel less inhibited in new social situations, reduces the risk involved with getting to know someone, and allows emotional bonds to form more easily (Feldman et al., 2011). In addition, oxytocin has long been associated with increased bonding during and after sexual activity. Oxytocin is released during foreplay, sexual activities, and in the touching and disclosures that occur between couples after sexual activity, which can enhance the attachments that couples feel toward each other (Afifi & Denes, 2013). In essence, then, the release of oxytocin into the body can enhance people's attachments with others, keeping their relationships strong and evolutionarily advantageous.

Evaluation of Evolutionary Theory

SEX DIFFERENCES IN EVOLUTIONARY THEORY

Despite the many advances being made in communication research on biosocial processes using evolutionary theory, there are limitations of the theory that should be noted, one of which is the assumption of innate differences between sexes. Though not all studies investigating sex differences in communication employ evolutionary theory, many of these studies can be traced back to evolutionary assumptions about men's and women's physical make-up and how individuals' biology and physiology link to psychological behavior. Critics of sex differences research have pointed out that such studies rely on dated stereotypes about male and female behavior, which are often used to guide both predictions and interpretations of findings (Deaux & Major, 1987). Despite the plethora of research using a sex differences framework, many researchers have argued that the differences within sexes are greater than the differences between sexes and that the effect sizes (or statistical size of the differences) for sex are extremely small (see Canary & Hause, 1993). As sex differences research continues to reinforce the idea that men and women are different, so too will men and women be viewed as *unequal* (Rosser, 1992).

When considering the limitations of evolutionary theory in relation to sex differences research, it is necessary to address competing theories of how sex differences evolved. In their biosocial theory, Wood and Eagly (2002) claimed that psychological sex differences are a result of the social expectations that go along with certain physical (or biological) differences between men and women. This viewpoint is in opposition to evolutionary psychologists' assertion that, like evolved biological differences, psychological differences are also evolved. Wood and Eagly's (2002) theory does not deny the role of evolution, but instead proposes that differences in male and female physical characteristics influence the development of social roles for males and females and the psychological differences that go with assuming those roles.

The critique of sex differences in evolutionary theory is an especially important point, as it speaks to a major criticism of early communibiological research (e.g., McCroskey, 1997): the notion of biological determinism. While a strict evolutionary and/or biological approach might suggest that individuals' genetic and biological composition guide all behavior, more recent research focuses on the bi-directional nature of hormonal responses and the fact that individuals' communication can influence their physiological responses and vice versa (e.g., Afifi, Granger, Denes, Joseph, & Aldeis, 2011). Such approaches contend that hormones not only guide behavior, but that behavior can also result in changes in hormones and biology.

CULTURE AND INDIVIDUAL DIFFERENCES

Wood and Eagly's (2002) biosocial theory points to another important limitation of evolutionary theory, which is a lack of recognition for the role of culture in individuals' behavior. For example, from a communication perspective, several studies have found that individuals invest affection differently in those with whom they share increased genetic relatedness and/or those who are most likely to pass on their genes (e.g., Floyd, 2001; Floyd & Morman, 2003). Although these studies focus more on the role of kin in passing on one's genes than on an individual's own reproductive success, they nonetheless speak to the underlying principles of evolutionary theory, which focus on how organisms evolve and pass their genes onto future generations. While strong support was found across this line of research that individuals are more affectionate with those who have the best odds of continuing their genetic lines, the potential role of both culture and individual differences is overlooked.

It is possible that individuals' affection toward kin relates more to rules of cultural appropriateness than to evolutionary drives. For instance, expressing affection between family members, especially in public, may not be perceived as appropriate, compared to other cultures where open displays of affection are more commonplace. It is also possible that a family's unique culture determines the affectionate behavior amongst its members, or that a specific family member's beliefs or personality characteristics may underlie his or her behavior. For example, the relationship between fathers' affectionate behavior and their sons' sexual orientation (as found in Floyd, Sargent, & DiCorcia, 2004) may be more related to fathers' rejection or acceptance of LGBTQ lifestyles than to a child's reproductive ability. These expectations for appropriate levels of affection most likely influence whether affection serves as a physiological stress buffer or stress magnifier.

Continuing the Conversation

An important future direction for communication researchers involves moving beyond a sex differences framework and seeking more complex understandings of variability. One way to increase such complexity is to consider biological and physiological factors associated with male and female bodies. For example, Denes (2013) suggested that the hormone testosterone may be a better predictor of differences in individuals' communication than the categorical distinctions of "male" and "female." In her study, she found that males' and females' communication after sexual activity was better predicted by how much they varied from the mean for their group than whether they identified as male or female. More specifically, Denes found that the higher individuals' testosterone levels were relative to their group mean, the less likely they were to disclose positive feelings for their partners after sexual activity. Such approaches offer one way of extending current research from an evolutionary perspective by suggesting more unique ways of examining sex and individual biological differences.

Future researchers could also use Wood and Eagly's (2002) theory to investigate the ways evolutionary theory operates within a specific culture and context. In correspondence with biosocial theory, such an approach would allow scholars to understand how biological differences play a role in certain social roles within the specific culture being investigated, and how these factors interact to influence communication. It would also be worthwhile for investigators to take a critical approach to understanding male and female societal expectations, as well as gender norms for a given culture. Examining the social roles of individuals in a specific context may offer additional insights on how these roles are both linked to evolved physical differences, as well as psychological, behavioral, and physiological outcomes.

Within this framework, there is also the possibility of considering individual differences. Although biosocial theory focuses on evolution and culture, a more complete understanding of individual differences in communication might consider an individual's communication efficacy, communication apprehension (see McCroskey, 1997), and communication competence, to name a few. Taken together, studies using evolutionary theory would benefit from also considering the cultural, contextual, and individual factors that influence psychological, physiological, and behavioral responses to social interaction.

References

Afifi, T. D., & Denes, A. (2013). Feedback processes and physiological responding. In M. Knapp (Ed.), *The handbook of nonverbal communication* (pp. 333–368). Thousand Oaks, CA: Sage.

Afifi, T. D., Granger, D., Denes, A., Joseph, A., & Aldeis, M. D. (2011). Parents' communication skills and adolescents' salivary α-amylase and cortisol response patterns. *Communication Monographs, 78,* 273–295.

Barkow, J. H., Cosmides, L., & Tooby, J. (1992). *The adapted mind: Evolutionary psychology and the generation of culture.* Oxford, UK: Oxford University Press.

Beatty, M., & McCroskey, J. (1997). It's in our nature: Verbal aggressiveness as temperamental expression. *Communication Quarterly, 45,* 446–460.

Bowlby, J. (1982). Attachment theory and its therapeutic implications. *Adolescent Psychiatry, 6,* 5–33.

Buss, D. M. (1995). Evolutionary psychology: A new paradigm for psychological science. *Psychological Inquiry, 6,* 1–49.

Campbell, A. (2010). Oxytocin and human social behavior. *Personality and Social Psychology Review, 14,* 281–285.

Canary, D. J., & Hause, K. S. (1993). Is there any reason to research sex differences in communication? *Communication Quarterly, 41,* 129–144.

Collins, N. L., & Feeney, B. C. (2004). Working models of attachment shape perceptions of social support: Evidence from experimental and observational studies. *Journal of Personality and Social Psychology, 87,* 363–383.

Confer, J., Easton, J., Fleischman, D., Goetz, C., Lewis, D., Perilloux, C., & Buss, D. M. (2010). Evolutionary psychology: Controversies, questions, prospects, and limitations. *American Psychologist, 65,* 110–126.

Cosmides, L., & Tooby, J. (1997). Dissecting the computational architecture of social inference mechanisms. In T. D. Eells (Ed.), *Characterizing human psychological adaptations* (pp. 132–161). Chichester, England: Wiley.

Darwin, C. (1859). *On the origins of species by means of natural selection.* London, UK: Murray.

Deaux, K., & Major, B. (1987). Putting gender into context: An interactive model of gender-related behavior. *Psychology Bulletin, 94,* 369–389.

Denes, A. (2013). *Beyond sex differences: Using testosterone to investigate communication during the post-coital time interval.* Manuscript submitted for publication.

Feldman, R., Gordon, I., & Zagoory-Sharon, O. (2011). Maternal and paternal plasma, salivary, and urinary oxytocin and parent–infant synchrony: Considering stress and affiliation components of human bonding. *Developmental Science, 14,* 752–761.

Floyd, K. (2001). Human affection exchange: I. Reproductive probability as a predictor of men's affection with their sons. *The Journal of Men's Studies, 10,* 39–50.

Floyd, K. (2006). Human affection exchange XII. Affectionate communication is associated with diurnal variation in salivary free cortisol. *Western Journal of Communication, 70,* 47–63.

Floyd, K., & Afifi, T. D. (2011). *Biological and physiological perspectives on interpersonal communication.* In M. L. Knapp & J. A. Daly (Eds.), *The SAGE handbook of interpersonal communication* (4th ed., pp. 87–130). Thousand Oaks, CA: Sage.

Floyd, K., Boren, J. P., Hannawa, A. F., Hesse, C., McEwan, B., & Veksler, A. E. (2009). Kissing in marital and cohabiting relationships: Effects on blood lipids, stress, and relationship satisfaction. *Western Journal of Communication, 73,* 113–133.

Floyd, K., Hesse, C., & Haynes, M. T. (2007). Human affection exchange: XV. Metabolic and cardiovascular correlates of trait expressed affection. *Communication Quarterly, 55,* 79–94.

Floyd, K., Judd, J., & Hesse, C. (2008). Affection exchange theory: A bio-evolutionary look at affectionate communication. In L. A. Baxter & D. O. Braithwaite (Eds.), *Engaging theories in interpersonal communication: Multiple perspectives* (pp. 285–293). Thousand Oaks, CA: Sage.

Floyd, K., Mikkelson, A. C., Hesse, C., & Pauley, P. M. (2007). Affectionate writing reduces total cholesterol: Two randomized, controlled studies. *Human Communication Research, 33,* 119–142.

Floyd, K., & Morman, M. T. (2003). Human affection exchange: II. Affectionate communication in father-son relationships. *The Journal of Social Psychology, 143,* 599–612.

Floyd, K., Pauley, P. M., Hesse, C., Veksler, A. E., Eden, J., & Mikkelson, A. C. (2010). *Affectionate communication predicts natural killer cell strength in healthy adults.* Manuscript submitted for publication.

Floyd, K., & Riforgiate, S. (2009). Affectionate communication received from spouses predicts stress hormone levels in healthy adults. *Communication Monographs, 75,* 351–368.

Floyd, K., Sargent, J. E., & DiCorcia, M. (2004). Human affection exchange: VI. Further tests of reproductive probability as a predictor of men's affection with their adult sons. *The Journal of Social Psychology, 144,* 191–206.

Knapp, M., Miller, G., & Fudge, K. (1994). Background and current trends in the study of interpersonal communication. In M. L. Knapp & G. R. Miller (Eds.), *Handbook of interpersonal communication* (2nd ed., pp. 3–20). Thousand Oaks, CA: Sage.

Mayr, E. (1991). *One long argument: Charles Darwin and the genesis of modern evolutionary thought.* Cambridge, MA: Harvard University Press.

McCroskey, J. (1997, November). *Why we communicate the ways we do: A communibiological perspective.* The Carroll C. Arnold Distinguished Lecture presented at the annual meeting of the National Communication Association, Chicago, IL.

Park, J. H., & Schaller, M. (2005). Does attitude similarity serve as a heuristic cue for kinship? Evidence of an implicit cognitive association. *Evolution and Human Behavior, 26,* 158–170.

Rosser, S. V. (1992). Are there feminist methodologies appropriate for the natural sciences and do they make a difference? *Women's Studies International Forum, 15,* 535–550.

Taylor, S. (2012). *Tend and befriend theory.* In P. A. M. Van Lange, A. W. Kruglanski, & T. E. Higgins (Eds.), *Handbook of theories of social psychology* (pp. 32–42). Thousand Oaks, CA: Sage.

Taylor, S., Klein, L. C., Lewis, B. P., Gruenewald, T. L., Gurung, R. A. R., & Updegraff, J. A. (2000). Biobehavioral responses to stress in females: Tend-and-befriend, not fight-or-flight. *Psychological Review, 107,* 411–429.

Taylor, S., Lewis, B., Gruenewald, T. L., Gugung, R. A. R., Updegraff, J. A., & Kline, L. C. (2002). Sex differences in biobehavioral responses to threat: Reply to Geary and Flinn. *Psychological Review, 109,* 751–753.

Tooby, J., & Cosmides, L. (1990). The past explains the present: Emotional adaptations and the structure of ancestral environments. *Ethology and Sociobiology, 11,* 375–424.

Tooby, J., & Cosmides, L. (2005). Conceptual foundations of evolutionary psychology. In D. M. Buss (Ed.), *The handbook of evolutionary psychology* (pp. 5–67). New York, NY: Wiley.

Wood, W., & Eagly, A. H. (2002). A cross-cultural analysis of the behavior of women and men: Implications for the origins of sex differences. *Psychological Bulletin, 128,* 699–727.

Zwolinski, J. (2008). Biopsychosocial responses to social rejection in targets of relational aggression. *Biological Psychology, 79,* 260–267.

5

Goals-Plans-Action Theory of Message Production

Making Influence Messages

James Price Dillard

I t is a fact of life that people often use communication in efforts to change the attitudes and behavior of others. Consider the following:

"Could you drop me by campus on your way to work?"

"He's not good for you. You should dump him."

"Let's get together and just hang out."

"You're not pulling your weight on the group assignment. You need to do more."

Goals-plans-action (GPA) theory was developed to explain the process by which people produce messages like these—messages that are intended to change or maintain the attitudes or behavior of others. Although the basic principles of the theory can be used to understand any type of communication behavior, it is helpful to see where GPA theory started before looking at it more broadly.

Intellectual Tradition of GPA Theory

In the mid-1970s, the field of communication began to ask how people produce messages that are intended to influence others. Some researchers sought an answer in personality variables as they developed explanations along the lines of "This kind of person tends to produce this kind of message." Others thought that aspects of the situation might provide a better explanation, such as "When put in this kind of situation, then people produce this kind of message." But, neither approach proved to be very informative. Consequently, researchers began to wonder whether more could be learned by focusing on what individuals were trying to do in the conversation itself. In other words, what is it that people are trying to achieve via interaction?

GPA theory, which was developed by Dillard (1990), is one attempt to address this issue. The theory has elements of scientific realism and of social construction. As with scientific realism (Pavitt, 2001), GPA theory embraces the assumption that much of the world is patterned, knowable, and objective. Certain features of social interaction and the cognitive processes that undergird interaction are objectively real. For instance, knowledge of influence strategies resides in long-term memory, which is a physical-electrical record of behavior. But GPA theory also assumes that many aspects of interaction are socially constructed. For instance, one student might say to another "Hey, I missed the last class. Could I borrow your notes?" This could be seen as just a self-interested attempt to acquire information. But, it might be an opportunity to help someone out too. And, asking for help usually implies that the help-seeker is willing to reciprocate in the future. Thus, the request might be the first step in building a friendship. It's hard to know which of these interpretations is correct. And, it is possible that one is right at the moment, but is replaced with another interpretation later once the two people know more about each other. Not only do people negotiate the meaning of conversations in the moment, but they often engage in revisionist constructions of social reality.

GPA is a theory of purposeful behavior. It assumes that individuals make choices about the messages that they create and that they do so with some degree of awareness. This does not mean that individuals are knowledgeable about all available options, nor does it mean that they are aware of every part of the message production process. It does mean that the theory holds that people usually know what they are doing. This may seem obvious, but it has important implications for theory and research strategy. For example, if people are acting purposefully, then their intentions are valid explanations of their actions. Furthermore, because they are aware of their intentions, truthful answers to the question "Why did you say that?" are invaluable data. Of course, sometimes people lack self-insight or they are knowingly deceitful. But, for most people most of the time, information about their goals can reveal a great deal about their behavior.

Main Goals and Features of GPA Theory

From the perspective of any given individual, GPA theory views message production as a three-step sequence. The first step involves *goals,* which are future states of affairs that an individual is committed to achieving or maintaining (Dillard, 1997). Goals are what people are trying to do. They motivate plans, which is the second component in the model. *Plans* are mental representations of messages and message sequences that are intended to enable goal attainment (see Chapter 7 in this volume). The final step includes *actions,* or the messages that people actually utter in their efforts to realize a goal. So when someone forms a goal of borrowing class notes, that desire prompts a plan (e.g., "I could just ask Bill") and, possibly, an action: "Could I borrow your notes?" One aim of the GPA model has been to elaborate the nature of goals, plans, and actions. Another aim has been to understand the relationships among those three basic elements of the theory.

INFLUENCE/PRIMARY GOALS

It is possible that people try to persuade others for an infinite variety of reasons. However, research suggests otherwise. In fact, in several studies in which people were asked about why they tried to influence others, a relatively small set of goals emerged (Dillard, Anderson, & Knobloch, 2002). They are listed in Table 5.1, along with a description and an example of each.

In the language of the GPA theory, the goals listed in Table 5.1 are influence goals, but they are also known as *primary goals.* They were given this name because the theory views them as special in several respects. For one, primary goals lie at the beginning of the goals-plans-action sequence. They are primary in the sense that they initiate the processes that result in message production. Without a primary goal, there would be no need for a plan or its corresponding action. Thus, primary goals motivate the GPA sequence.

Second, it is possible to think of human behavior as a stream. Primary goals allow individuals to segment that stream into meaningful units. In this sense, they serve a function similar to that of bracketing the interaction—that is, to identifying its beginning and ending points. Such segmentation is surely valuable for making sense of what might otherwise be viewed as an undifferentiated outpouring of behavior. Bracketing is possible because the primary goal imbues the interaction with meaning. Knowledge of the primary goal allows the interactants to say what the exchange is about. Hence, primary goals are culturally viable explanations of the discourse produced by two or more speakers. This is the "social meaning function" of primary goals.

Finally, primary goals direct a number of mental operations. By providing an understanding of the purpose of an interaction, goals determine which aspects of a situation are perceived and which are not. For example, a person who is on the receiving end of a threat may pay close attention to the speaker's size and emotional state while devoting little thought to evaluating the aesthetic qualities of the threatening person's wardrobe. Thus, primary goals serve a "guidance

Table 5.1 Most Common Reasons for Influencing Others

Influence Goals		
Type	*Description*	*Example*
Gain assistance	Obtain material or nonmaterial resources	Can I use your car to go shopping?
Give advice	Provide counsel (often about health and relationships)	I'm worried about you because you've been drinking a lot lately. Do you think you should take a break from it?
Share activity	Promote joint endeavors between source and target	Let's do something together tonight. How about going to see that new band?
Change orientation	Engage target on a sociopolitical issue	I'm going to do my class project on medical marijuana. There are some good reasons to legalize it.
Change relationship	Alter the nature of the source-target relationship	I'm not sure we should see each other anymore. I think we need to take a break.
Obtain permission	Secure the consent of the (more powerful) target	Would it be OK if I handed in the assignment one day late?
Enforce rights and obligations	Compel target to fulfill commitment or role requirement	I'm still trying to study. You promised that you would keep the music down. So, how about it?

function" that results in some perceptions, memories, and thoughts becoming more salient and others becoming part of the background of interaction.

Secondary Goals

When pursuing or planning to pursue a primary goal, other concerns may arise. For example, one college student who hopes to initiate a romantic relationship with another (Goal 1) might recognize the risk of rejection and wish to avoid feeling hurt (Goal 2). Such concerns are called *secondary goals* because they follow from the adoption of a primary goal. You don't have to worry about being rejected or being hurt unless you are taking a chance on the relationship goal in the first place. More formally, the source holds a secondary goal only because he or she is attempting to influence someone else. Thus, it is the desire to achieve the primary goal that brings about consideration of one or more secondary goals.

Research using GPA theory supports the existence of five secondary goals (Dillard, Segrin, & Harden, 1989), though not every goal will be relevant to every situation. *Identity goals* focus on ethical, moral, and personal standards for behavior. They arise from individuals' principles and values and, at the broadest level, individuals' conceptions of self. For instance, a child who wants a piece of chocolate cake might think nothing of knocking down a sibling and taking the piece of cake away. Most adults would reject that strategy on ethical grounds. In this way, the secondary goal of behaving ethically limits the array of possible influence strategies.

Conversation management goals involve concerns about impression management and face. Although there are exceptions, individuals usually prefer that interactions proceed smoothly, rather than awkwardly, and that neither interactant threaten the identity of the other. Thus, while conversation management goals may have implications that extend beyond the conversation, they also have a relatively short time horizon (i.e., typically the duration of the conversation). In this vein, when one person asks, "What did you mean by that?" the other person usually offers some explanation of his or her behavior rather than simply ignoring the question. By playing by the rules of conversation, interactants create a mutual understanding of what is occurring. This is true even when they disagree about the issues under discussion. For instance, both parties agree that they had a fight and both are aware of what the fight was about.

Relational resource goals focus on relationship management. These goals are manifestations of the value that individuals have for social and personal relationships. Hence, it is most often the case that people try to maintain or improve their relationships with others. Of course, relationship resource goals do not really come into play unless one has a preexisting relationship with the hearer or hopes to establish one. Relational resource goals focus on the benefits that flow to the source because of the relationship itself (e.g., I feel good when I'm with her; he can do a lot to advance my career; I need to get along with him because he is part of our group). When they are relevant to the situation, relational resource goals have a longer time horizon than conversation management goals.

Personal resource goals reflect the physical, temporal, and material concerns of the communicator. More specifically, they arise from the desires to maintain or enhance one's physical well-being, temporal resources, finances, and material possessions. The statement, "I cut the conversation short because I realized that I was wasting my time," illustrates concern for the temporal aspect of personal resources. The desire to behave efficiently can be seen as a personal resource goal, although GPA theory does not suppose that individuals always prefer a high level of efficiency. In fact, some people take pleasure in going with the flow rather than having everything organized. These different approaches to life result in different goals in specific conversations. As with any of the secondary goals, personal resource goals will not be relevant to every interaction, but when they are relevant, they can be important to determining how messages are created and uttered.

Finally, by identifying *affect management goals,* the theory posits that individuals try to create or maintain preferred affective states. This is not as simple as wishing to enjoy positive feelings and avoid negative ones. Sometimes people try to increase their level of anxiety because it motivates them to perform well on an exam or speech. Creating that little uptick in anxiety can mean more energy and focus. But, people who are naturally prone to anxiety may have the opposite goal. They need to work hard to tamp down feelings of nervousness, especially prior to a public speech.

RELATIONSHIPS AMONG PRIMARY GOALS AND SECONDARY GOALS

The most basic decision that one can make about communication is whether or not to engage another person in interaction. The interplay of primary and secondary goals can help to understand this choice point in the message production process. To simplify, assume a primary goal and just one secondary goal, then evaluate the degree of compatibility between the two. There are just three possibilities, the first of which being that the two goals are *incompatible.* Imagine someone who intends to end a long-term romantic relationship but not hurt the other person's feelings.

Second, the secondary goal may be *irrelevant* to the primary goal. For example, concern for one's physical well-being is not often an issue when asking a friend to see a film. In this circumstance, some of the secondary goals may not even come to mind. There are some situations, probably very few, in which none of the secondary goals are relevant. Emergencies are one example. Imagine that you are crossing the street when you see an out-of-control car speeding toward a friend in the crosswalk who is lost in the music of his iPhone. You need to warn him and to do so quickly. You probably won't be too concerned about, for example, how to be polite (conversation management) or how saving his life might make you late to class (personal resource goal), or how the situation might create anxiety for you (affect management). Instead, you'll be focusing on just one goal, the primary/influence goal, which is how to create immediate behavior change in your friend.

The third possibility is that the primary and secondary goals are *compatible.* This is akin to "killing two birds with one stone." Although desirable, it occurs less frequently than one might hope. Initiating a relationship illustrates one context in which this might occur. The norm of reciprocity demands that individuals repay favors provided to them by others. When one person asks another for help that he or she cannot immediately repay (e.g., a ride to the grocery store), the message source is signaling a willingness to enter into a relationship in which reciprocity will occur over time. This willingness is a defining feature of friendships. Thus, the speaker may obtain a ride and, in so doing, also enhance a budding relationship.

The concept of secondary goals has at least one major implication for how we conceive of interpersonal influence. Namely, it suggests that most interactions involve multiple goals that individuals try to achieve more or less simultaneously. Every interaction has a primary goal, and most interactions have one or more secondary goals. Because people are rarely trying to achieve one goal in a conversation, interpersonal influence is often a complicated task. On the other hand, it is worth emphasizing that not every influence attempt will activate consideration of all five secondary goals. If secondary goals are to shape message production, however, they must be at least minimally relevant. After passing that threshold, the more important they are, the greater their impact.

PLANS AND PLANNING

Influence plans are mental guidelines for the production of verbal and nonverbal behaviors. Presumably, most people understand that there are a variety of ways to influence others: threats, warnings, rewards, promises, explanation, social pressure, liking, and so on. But, GPA theory suggests that these plans exist at two levels of abstraction. Whereas *strategy-level plans* are concerned with lines of action and sequences of behavior, *tactic plans* are more concrete. They are instructions for producing smaller units of behavior such as individual utterances. For example, although one might approach an influence attempt with the intention of implementing a liking strategy, there are many different ways to do so at the tactical level. The first move might consist of utterances such as, "You look great!" or "That was a really smart thing that you said in our discussion group. I was impressed." That could be followed up with "You and I seem alike in some ways. We make some of the same choices."

Action: Message Behaviors

Research on the perception of message tactics suggests that four dimensions are particularly important to understanding influence plans (Dillard, Wilson, Tusing, & Kinney, 1997). The first of these dimensions, *explicitness*, is the degree to which the source makes her or his intentions transparent in the message itself. Explicit messages require little or no guesswork regarding the speaker's wants, but implicit messages necessitate more interpretation. When one roommate says to another, "I would like for you to come to the gym with me," the speaker's desire is clear. But, if the same person were to say, "Hey, I'm going to the gym," the other roommate has to read between the lines to interpret the speaker's intention. Is the roommate just providing information or is he or she issuing an invitation? Knowing something about the relationship between the two roommates probably makes the two statements not very difficult to understand. Independent of that background knowledge, however, the messages are constructed differently.

Dominance, the second dimension, refers to power of the source compared to the target as expressed in the message. Consider the following requests: "You said that you wanted to work out. So, get off your butt and do it" and "I would really, really appreciate it if you worked out with me." Depending on the source-target relationship, the first message might be seen as a little aggressive. It seems as if the source is implicitly saying that he or she has the right to boss the target around. In contrast, the second message is beseeching. It leaves the decision up to the target and puts the source in a more submissive position. Of course, messages that convey equality are possible too: "I'm thinking about working out later today. Wanna come?"

The third dimension is *argument,* which references the extent to which some rationale for the sought-after action is present (versus absent) in the message. The utterance "I sleep a lot better when I work out. I'll bet that you would too" suggests implicitly what the source wants the target to do, and it provides a reason for the source's wants. In contrast, the message "We should go work out" is clear, but it lacks any sort of justification. In other words, the source's argument is absent. A key thing to keep in mind about argument is that it refers to whether the message *includes* a reason, not whether you think the reason is a good one.

Control over outcomes is the final dimension that characterizes influence plans. This message feature refers to the extent to which the source has control over the reasons for compliance. This distinction makes clear the difference between a threat (e.g., I will hurt you if . . .) and a warning (e.g., You could be harmed if . . .). Reward messages vary in control too. Note the difference between "I will pay you to vote for Smith" versus "Smith will help you. You should vote for him."

When the desire to influence another person arises, individuals will initially search their memory for boilerplate plans that are likely to achieve the primary goal. If the available plans are seen as likely to succeed, then the individual moves toward translating the ideas into action. Of course, this involves a great many lower-level processes that must work in unison if a plan is to be successfully instantiated as behavior; these processes could fail to work together, leading to failure. For example, a plan that depends on flattering the target might fail because the speaker cannot find a way to deliver a compliment that does not sound transparently insincere. In this instance, the plan works at the level of strategy, but not at the level of tactic.

To the extent that the preexisting plans are judged to be less than satisfactory and the primary goal is viewed as important, individuals will try to

(a) make existing plans more complete or more complex, or (b) create new plans. This kind of planning is constrained by the fact that successful interaction depends on the other person. If the message producer sees the other person as unpredictable, he or she will be less likely to go to the effort of plan development. Although there may be many different ways to achieve a primary goal if none of the secondary goals are activated, it is more challenging to devise a plan that will satisfy the competing desires that are present when the set of primary and secondary goals is complex. Students working in group projects may find themselves needing to tell one of the group members that he or she is not making a fair contribution to the workload. This becomes more complicated when the so-called slacker is a roommate or good friend. Achieving two goals simultaneously (i.e., changing behavior and not damaging the relationship) is much harder than achieving either goal alone.

When multiple plans are available, the source must choose among them. The theory assumes that people do this by assessing the degree to which each plan satisfies the combination of primary and secondary goals. This can happen very quickly and often does, as the GPA process typically moves at the speed of conversation. At other times, people will carefully weigh the message options available to them, vacillate about whether or not to engage, perhaps settle on an influence strategy, then rehearse delivery of the message, all in advance of actually saying anything.

How Communication Is Conceptualized in GPA Theory

At the most general level, GPA theory views communication as an interactive process in which each actor adjusts his or her message behavior to the other actor. The adjustments are made as messages that vary in terms of explicitness, dominance, argument, and control. A slightly deeper perspective prompts the question of, "What is communication for?" GPA theory replies that "communication is for getting things done." Communication is one means by which goals are achieved. This should not be confused with simple self-interest because goals can be egoistic or altruistic, self-serving or philanthropic. As the existence of the "Give advice" goal implies (Table 5.1), influence goals might arise for the purpose of benefiting specific others (Dillard & Schrader, 1998). In addition, influence goals may aim to improve the public good, as when one individual attempts to persuade another about some social issue ("Change orientation goal," Table 5.1). Finally, even when an individual's actions are the result of self-interest, they are often mundane, such as when we ask someone to pass the salt ("Gain assistance goal," Table 5.1). In short, GPA theory views communication as instrumental. Of course, communication is more than just that, but understanding how goals are achieved via interaction is not a small thing.

Research and Practical Applications of the Theory

Although GPA theory was first designed to address influence episodes, it is applicable to many other types of social episodes. Some of the research conducted on communication in educational settings reveals basic features of the conceptual framework. In one study, Sabee and Wilson (2005) directed undergraduate students to recall and write about an instance in which they had a conversation with one of their instructors about a grade that was lower than desired. Participants in the study were also asked to describe their goals in the situation and to identify the main goal that characterized the situation for them. From these data, the researchers identified four distinct primary goals. Students motivated by a (a) learning goal wanted to discuss study habits and to go over the test to see what they had missed. Others were moved to speak because they wanted to (b) persuade the instructor to change their grade or give them a chance to redo the assignment. A third group of students reported that their primary goal was (c) to fight, that is, to vent frustration and criticize the instructor, whereas a final group said that their primary motivation was (d) to impress the instructor by showing that they really were good students. Overall, their study was an intriguing application of GPA theory because it showed how situations that are superficially similar—all were about disappointing grades—can be conceived of very differently with regard to primary goals. It also illustrated the potential breadth of the theory. In a narrow sense, only one of the primary goals is concerned with influence, that is, the persuasion/change grade goal. In reality, all of the goals are efforts to create change in another person.

Another study focused more on the process of message production. As with the previous study, Henningsen, Valde, Russell, and Russell (2011) recruited participants by asking them to recall a recent, disappointing grade. Each of these students completed a survey that asked about different features of the GPA process. For example, they were asked a series of questions that measured importance of the primary and secondary goals, the degree to which they planned out what they would say to the instructor, and the likelihood that they would actually engage the instructor in a conversation about grades. Their results underscored several points that are compatible with GPA theory. For one, only two of the five secondary goals (i.e., conversational management and relational resources) were seen as relevant to the situation. This is consistent with the earlier assertion that not all secondary goals are meaningful to every situation. A second point was that planning has multiple causes. As the theory says, the more important the primary goal, the more effort that people put into planning what they might say. But, planning was also influenced by the two secondary goals of conversational management and relational resources. The students were planning communication that would achieve more than one end. Here we see clear evidence of message producers juggling multiple goals in an effort to shape an effective utterance. Finally, more planning led to a stronger commitment to engage the instructor. The more thought that students devoted to the situation, the more options they saw for how to handle it, and the more confident they felt about carrying off the episode successfully.

Evaluation of GPA Theory

One of the assumptions of GPA theory is that of human agency. In other words, the theory is grounded in the idea that humans have at least some control over their own behavior. One limitation mentioned already is that the theory attempts to explain, not all behavior, but only purposeful actions. Whether or not human beings have any control over their own behavior is a question that has occupied philosophers and laypeople for millennia. To the extent that it is incorrect, the theory is limited.

It is often said that theories should be parsimonious, but this is not quite right. Instead, theories should be as parsimonious as we can make them given the complexity of what they are trying to explain. GPA theory attempts to strike the right balance between parsimony and complexity, but readers will have to judge for themselves. Are there too many parts and processes? Too few? Thought experiments in which readers try to apply the theory to their own message production behavior may help to provide an answer.

The theory also has considerable practical value. Readers of this chapter might use the theory to reflect on their own goals, plans, and actions. For instance, trying to fit your own aims into one of the seven goals in Table 5.1 may provide insight into what you are aiming for and how others might view it. Careful consideration of a list of secondary goals could reveal implications of your behavior that you hadn't foreseen. And, knowing how to analyze your plan in terms of influence message features might suggest ways to phrase your message more (or less) clearly, less aggressively (unless you hope to be aggressive), or to recognize that you haven't yet developed an argument. The ideas contained in GPA theory are tools for planning and behavior that have the potential to produce more effective communication.

Continuing the Conversation

Communication theories are only beginning points for understanding the infinitely complex phenomena that is human interaction. GPA theory is no different. It was created to fill a gap in the influence literature, but it has developed into something that can be applied more widely. For instance, goals theory has helped us to understand how students confront other students who have committed academic misconduct (Henningsen, Valde, & Denbow, 2013). Applications of the theory to the health domain illuminates how we think about nurse practitioners interacting with patients (Babler-Schrader & Schrader, 2011) and the way in which goals shape doctor-patient communication online (Sabee, Bylund, Weber, & Sonet, 2012). Although there is little research on applications of GPA to political behavior, this is an area of opportunity. From a purely theoretical perspective, work on GPA theory would benefit from greater emphasis on how goals are understood by speakers/hearers and how they use plans to coordinate their interaction.

References

Babler-Schrader, E. L., & Schrader, D. C. (2011). Interaction goals in the primary care medical interview. *Journal of the American Academy of Nurse Practitioners, 2,* 370–375.

Dillard, J. P. (1990). A goal-driven model of interpersonal influence. In J. P. Dillard (Ed.), *Seeking compliance: The production of interpersonal influence messages* (pp. 41–56). Scottsdale, AZ: Gorsuch Scarisbrick.

Dillard, J. P. (1997). Explicating the goal construct: Tools for theorists. In J. O. Greene (Ed.), *Message production: Advances in communication theory* (pp. 47–69). Mahwah, NJ: Erlbaum.

Dillard, J. P., Anderson, J. W., & Knobloch, L. K. (2002). Interpersonal influence. In M. Knapp & J. Daly (Eds.), *The handbook of interpersonal communication* (pp. 423–474). Thousand Oaks, CA: Sage.

Dillard, J. P., & Schrader, D. C. (1998). Reply: On the utility of the goals-plans-action sequence. *Communication Studies, 49,* 300–304.

Dillard, J. P., Segrin, C., & Harden, J. M. (1989). Primary and secondary goals in the interpersonal influence process. *Communication Monographs, 56,* 19–38.

Dillard, J. P., Wilson, S. R., Tusing, K. J., & Kinney, T. A. (1997). Politeness judgments in personal relationships. *Journal of Language and Social Psychology, 16,* 297–325.

Henningsen, M. L. M., Valde, K. S., & Denbow, J. (2013). Academic misconduct: A goals-plans-action approach to peer confrontation and whistle-blowing. *Communication Education, 62,* 148–168.

Henningsen, M. L. M., Valde, K. S., Russell, G. A., & Russell, G. R. (2011). Student-faculty interactions about disappointing grades: Application of the goals-plans-actions model and the theory of planned behavior. *Communication Education, 60,* 174–190.

Pavitt, C. (2001). *Philosophy of science and communication theory.* Huntington, NY: Nova Science Publishers.

Sabee, C. M., Bylund, C. L., Weber, J. G., & Sonet, E. (2012). The association of patients' primary interaction goals with attributions for their doctors' responses in conversations about online health research. *Journal of Applied Communication Research, 40,* 271–288.

Sabee, C. M., & Wilson, S. R. (2005). Students' primary goals, attributions, and facework during conversations about disappointing grades. *Communication Education, 54,* 185–204.

6

Imagined Interaction Theory

Mental Representations of Interpersonal Communication

James M. Honeycutt

I t is very common in everyday living to anticipate meetings with people that we know we are going to interact with. For example, you may imagine some of the questions that a job interviewer will ask you and how you might respond. Furthermore, after seeing people, we sometimes relive the encounter in our minds as we reflect on what was said or how we could have said things differently. These examples reflect *imagined interactions* (IIs), which are part of daydreaming and which reflect internal talk. They refer to a process of social cognition in which individuals imagine and therefore indirectly experience themselves in anticipated or past communicative encounters with others (Honeycutt, 2003). IIs focus and organize individuals' thoughts on communication, on the actors involved in specific acts of communication, and on the communicative context. IIs possess many of the same characteristics as real conversations in that they may be fragmentary, extended, rambling, repetitive, or coherent.

IIs serve multiple functions, including maintaining relationships and managing conflict. Individuals may feel anger as they relive old conflicts in their minds, or may feel happiness while imagining positive encounters. Our expectancies for interpersonal communication encounters emanate from IIs through replaying images from the electronic media, as well as conversations with parents, siblings, peers, or novels. Furthermore, IIs can help form expectations or relational schemata for how individuals will perform in a variety of roles. They are a means of problem solving by allowing an individual to think through a problem. IIs have been used as a tool in therapy, allowing patients to visualize interaction with others who were not emotionally or physically available to them (Rosenblatt & Meyer, 1986). They can help people in planning messages and in enhancing communication effectiveness.

Intellectual Tradition of II Theory

Post-positivists believe that human knowledge is based on conjectures, assumptions, or premises. These are commonly referred to as basic beliefs (e.g., a person believes that long-term anxiety is detrimental to health). A variety of methods are triangulated in testing the theory out of the recognition that observations and measurements are inherently imperfect. IIs are measured through surveys, journals, and even through the use of a "talk-out-loud" procedure, in which individuals role-play their imaginary dialogues with interaction partners prior to talking with them (see Honeycutt, 2003, 2010). Numerous studies have tested hypotheses and theorems devoted to functions of IIs (see Honeycutt, 2003, for a review).

Imagined interaction theory is based in the work of symbolic interactionism derived from sociology and cognitive scripts derived from cognitive psychology, including Mead (1934), Dewey (1922), Schutz (1962), and Abelson (1976). Mead discussed the internalized conversation of gestures in which individual actors are able consciously to monitor social action by reviewing alternative endings of any given act in which they are involved. II theory presumes that people use internal dialogues within their minds to test out the various possible scenarios of an event in advance of the act.

IIs also have their foundations in cognitive scripts (Zagacki, Edwards, & Honeycutt, 1992). For example, relational scripts are often partly formed through the process of mental imagery and daydreaming, in which individuals think about conversations with significant others. Cognitive researchers argue that much information is stored (sometimes unconsciously) in propositional form, such as "In order to accomplish X, I will Y." Propositional thinking can be done through IIs. Thus, when people experience IIs, they may be experiencing a representation of scripted or partially scripted knowledge, with the information being brought directly into explicit awareness for review. Hence, activating the script through an II may help to reconstitute the existing script. Our memories about relationships form later scripts or expectancies for appropriate behaviors in relationships. For instance, Honeycutt and Bryan (2011) discussed how scripts are a type of automatic pilot, providing guidelines on how to act when one encounters new situations. Thus, scripts are activated mindlessly and created through IIs as people envision contingency plans for actions.

Main Goals and Features of II Theory

It should be noted that the term "imagined interaction" is strategically used instead of "imaginary conversation" or "internal dialogue," because imagined interaction is a broader term that takes into account nonverbal and verbal imagery. *Visual imagery* reflects the scene of the interaction (e.g., office, den, or car). *Verbal imagery* reflects lines of dialogue imagined by the self and by others (e.g., I recall speaking to my sister on my cell phone when she told me that she had just been promoted in the state treasurer's office. I congratulated her with a pun saying, "They invested wisely in you.").

There are six basic functions that IIs serve: (a) maintaining relationships, (b) linking or managing conflict, (c) rehearsing messages, (d) aiding people in self-understanding through clarifying thoughts and feelings, (e) providing emotional catharsis by relieving tension, and (f) compensating for lack of real interaction (Honeycutt, 2003; Honeycutt & Ford, 2001). These functions are used in a variety of contexts, and any combination of these functions can occur simultaneously. For example, the person may experience catharsis while thinking about how to manage conflict for an upcoming conversation. Simultaneously, the II may provide the opportunity to rehearse along with relational maintenance. An example is a female who, in a journal account, reported how she was rehearsing how to tell her boyfriend that she accepted a job offer in another city after telling him the week before that she was thinking about accepting a position in the city that he was living in. She felt tension release and the release of anxiety as she was rehearsing the anticipated encounter.

Researchers have spent considerable time examining the attributes or characteristics of IIs and their association with personality characteristics, gender differences, marriage types, and relational quality (for a review, see Honeycutt, 2003, 2010). The attributes of IIs include

- frequency (how often people experience IIs),
- emotional valence (how enjoyable or uncomfortable they are),
- discrepancy (the degree to which IIs are different from actual communication),
- dominance (the amount that the self or other dominates the talk),
- proactivity (whether IIs precede anticipated encounters),
- retroactivity (whether IIs follow encounters),
- specificity (the amount of detail in IIs), and
- variety (the number of different topics and partners experienced).

Recently, Honeycutt, Pence, and Gearhart (2012–13) examined the associations between II attributes and the Big Five personality traits. In terms of personality, IIs have trait characteristics to the extent they are enduring and stable across similar conditions. Conversely, they can also be measured in terms of state attributes in which their usage would be higher or lower depending on the particular context. The Big Five personality traits include neuroticism, extraversion, openness, agreeableness, and conscientiousness. Honeycutt and his associates found that that the frequency and proactivity attributes of IIs are correlated with lack of neuroticism and openness. Neuroticism increases egocentrism, depression, and anxiety (Hamilton, Buck, Chory, Beatty, & Patrylak, 2009). Highly anxious people have fewer IIs available to them to "predict" their perceived (or believed) unstable environment. They also found that having non-discrepant, pleasant IIs (with the self talking more in the II) is moderately associated with the personality dimensions of extraversion and conscientiousness. Extraverts by nature interact with more individuals than do introverts, so extraverts would therefore imagine themselves having these interactions more often than those who are not extraverted. Likewise, they discovered that extraverts have more pleasant IIs, which may be explained through another relationship between extraversion and narcissism. Extraverts think highly of themselves, and most likely portray themselves in a pleasant manner in their imagined interactions.

How Communication Is Conceptualized in II Theory

Because it concerns individual processing of information, a core feature of II theory is its reliance on intrapersonal communication as the foundation upon which other types of communication rest. Intrapersonal communication involves all of the physiological and psychological processing of messages that happens within individuals as they attempt to understand themselves and their environment (Cunningham, 1989). Regardless if one speaks of dyadic, interpersonal, small group, organizational, societal, cultural, or mass communication, the individual processing of information is nested within all hierarchies of communication systems (Fisher, 1987). Case in point, IIs have been examined in dyadic, family, instructional, political, and organizational communication contexts (Honeycutt, 2010).

Research and Practical Applications of II Theory

Research strategies to test hypotheses derived from II theory include the administration of the Survey of Imagined Interaction, as well as interviews that include individuals discussing recent conversations that reflect retroactive IIs (Honeycutt, 2010). Additional measures include a "talk-out-loud" procedure in which individuals role-play what they might say in a conversation and how they envision the partner responding.

In a practical sense, IIs help sustain relationships. Researchers have revealed that relational happiness is associated with having pleasant IIs (Honeycutt & Wiemann, 1999). IIs help maintain relationships as people think about their relational partners outside of their physical presence. Compared to married couples, engaged couples who live apart use IIs to compensate for the absence of their partner. In addition, functions of talk that reflect enjoying serious discussion of topics, talking about events in the day, and equality of talk are associated with frequent, pleasant, and non-discrepant IIs with partners. Likewise, Honeycutt and Keaton (2012–13) found that having more specific, frequent, and pleasant IIs was positively associated with relational satisfaction. They discovered that increased uses of proactive and retroactive IIs aided the ability of imagined interactions to predict relational quality.

The conflict management function of IIs explains pervasive conflict in personal relationships and the difficulties in managing conflict in constructive ways. This function has resulted in the development of a secondary, axiomatic theory consisting of three axioms and nine theorems that explain the persistence and management of daily conflict (Honeycutt, 2010). The axioms are concerned with how relationships are conceptualized in terms of thinking about relational partners outside of their physical presence. Hence, IIs occur with important people in our lives including loved ones, work associates, and rivals. This secondary theory assumes that a major theme of relationships is concern with balancing cooperation and competition (Honeycutt & Bryan, 2011).

The conflict management function of IIs also highlights the role of rumination in which people have recurring thoughts about conflict and arguing that make it difficult to focus on other things. This has resulted in a supplemental theory of conflict-linkage containing three axioms and nine theorems explaining why it is hard to forgive and forget (Honeycutt, 2010). Honeycutt and Bryan (2011) tested a model in which IIs mediated the relationship between verbal aggression and physical coercion or abuse. Essentially, this means the abuser is thinking about his or her actions and verbal taunts. To the extent IIs partially mediate the association between verbal aggression and physical coercion, communication interventions may be used for the abuser who plans their violence. Indeed, communication intervention may foster forgiveness, which has been shown to be negatively associated with rumination about seeking revenge (Honeycutt, Keaton, Hatcher, & Hample, 2014).

In addition to conflict management, II researchers have spent considerable time examining planning and message rehearsal. For example, Honeycutt (1998–99) demonstrated that a secure attachment style is predicted by rehearsal as compared to other attachment types. Perhaps strategic planning for various encounters may enhance security in romantic relationships. This use of IIs seems also to be linked to cognitive editing, which allows adjustments to messages after their potential effects on a given relationship have been assessed (Meyer, 1997). The implication here is that individuals rehearse messages, presumably through the use of IIs, and make changes as necessary for achieving desired outcomes.

Proactive IIs are a means by which to plan anticipated encounters. Plans are broader than IIs because rehearsal is just one function (see Berger, Chapter 7, in this volume, for a discussion of plans). Plans may be nonverbal in the pursuit of actions or goals (e.g., realizing it's your anniversary and coming up with and buying a gift for your partner). When used for rehearsal, IIs allow for a decrease in the number of silent pauses, shorter speech onset latencies during actual encounters, and an increase in message strategy variety (Allen & Honeycutt, 1997).

The self-understanding function of IIs emphasizes how IIs are used to understand ourselves better. IIs can help to uncover opposing or differing aspects of the self. Zagacki and his associates (1992) indicated that those IIs involving conflict increased understanding of the self. Self-understanding involved more verbal imagery with the self playing a greater role in the II, or being more dominant.

The catharsis function of IIs has to do with their ability to relieve tension and reduce uncertainty about another's actions (Honeycutt, Zagacki, & Edwards, 1989). Rosenblatt and Meyer (1986) proposed IIs as a means of emotional catharsis in counseling sessions, having found that IIs served as an outlet for their patients to release unresolved tension. Patients noted feeling less relational tension after having experienced IIs. In fact, the use of IIs is associated with a reduction in anxiety (Allen & Honeycutt, 1997). When planning for an interaction, making use of IIs results in a lower occurrence of object adaptors. This seems to suggest that when one uses IIs, one experiences anxiety relief, perhaps experiencing a release of certain emotions in the form of catharsis. Honeycutt (2003) provided numerous accounts of individuals reporting how their IIs made them feel better and allowed them to release anxiety.

The final function of IIs is compensating for the lack of real communication. From their early development, IIs have been purported to serve in the place of real interaction when it is not possible to actually communicate with a given individual. In their discussion of IIs used for counseling, Rosenblatt and Meyer (1986) indicated that an individual may choose to use IIs in place of actually confronting a loved one because of fear that the loved one would be hurt by the message. Boldness has been identified as a possible function of IIs, but it appears to reflect compensation. McCann and Honeycutt (2006) discussed how individuals may feel emboldened in situations where there are sanctions for voicing opinion. They found that the Japanese, when compared to Thais and Americans, were more likely to use

IIs to suppress communication and as a means of voicing disagreement because they felt empowered in their imaginary conflicts, which eliminated the possibility of repercussions. Indeed, scholars have described the highly elaborate rules of manners and conduct in Japan that include compliance to others, self-restraint (passivity), suppression of inner feelings, and observance of formal greetings, speech, and appropriate gestures (Rothbaum, Pott, Azuma, Miyake, & Weisz, 2000). McCann and Honeycutt concluded that IIs might have served as a safe, punitive-free outlet for self-expression for their Japanese participants. To the Thais and Americans, who perhaps operate under comparatively less rigid norms for individual expression (Triandis, 1995), this safe II outlet may not have been as necessary.

With the advent of social media, Facebook, and instant gratification, the current generation has been perceived by some as narcissistic (Trzesniewski, Donnellan, & Robins, 2008). *Covert narcissism,* defined as a hypersensitivity to criticism and overcompensating with inflated self-exaggeration, has been ignored in communication and in psychology. Narcissism is associated with frequent IIs that (a) are self-dominant, (b) involve ruminating about conflict, and (c) are negatively associated with compensation and relational maintenance (Honeycutt et al., 2012–13). Relational maintenance and compensation have similar functions in II theory. For instance, relational maintenance IIs can be used to keep a relationship alive in the absence of interaction (e.g., in long-distance relationships), whereas compensation can be used for the specific purpose of substituting real interaction. A sense of entitlement that most narcissists have can lead to a certain obsessive quality. If a narcissist feeds off of others in order to feel superior, needing to fill voids of real interaction with imagined interactions makes sense.

Recently, Bodie, Honeycutt, and Vickery (2013) conducted two studies exploring the multidimensional nature of functions and attributes in IIs. Their first study revealed both corroborative and counter evidence for II theory. In line with the internal structure of II theory, they found that conflict linkage and catharsis IIs are more negatively valenced than those used for compensation and relational maintenance. Rehearsal IIs are more likely to be discrepant than all functions, except relational maintenance, and they are the most proactive. When compared to all other functions, compensatory IIs contained references to more people and were more frequent. They also reported that compensatory and relational maintenance functions were similar insofar as both were equally directed to others and highly specific, providing support for the role of each in close interpersonal relationships (Honeycutt, 2003). Relational maintenance and conflict IIs were used just as frequently as those for catharsis, and relational maintenance IIs were directed toward others in an equivalent manner as those used for conflict.

PHYSIOLOGY AND IIS

In addition to the six functions of IIs, Honeycutt (2010) discussed the importance of physiological variables in order to measure imaging. For instance, Honeycutt (2006) measured change in adrenalin and anxiety levels in terms of imagined interaction and emotion as automobile drivers are "venting" at offending drivers in heavy traffic conditions when they are late for an important meeting with business clients. After controlling for an individual's baseline heart rate (in beats per minute, or BPM) and baseline heart rate variability, Honeycutt found that while driving a car in heavy traffic conditions in which a person is late for an important meeting and being boxed in by an offending driver who is using a cell phone, a person's heart rate BPM is negatively correlated with using IIs to vent at other drivers. Venting at other drivers is associated with tailgating distance in which the driver in heavy traffic pulls up to the vehicle that is immediately in front of them. Consequently, Honeycutt found that using IIs to vent at other drivers is associated with being physiologically aroused.

USING IIS TO ALLEVIATE COMMUNICATION APPREHENSION

Finally, researchers have applied II theory to the study of communication apprehension (CA). According to McCroskey (1977), CA can be defined as "an individual's level of fear or anxiety with either real or anticipated communication with another person or persons" (p. 78). A critical word in this definition is "anticipated," and it is important to note that the anxiety regarding a future communicative encounter can be as powerful as the real interaction itself. The transitive verb, anticipated, implies foresight, which implies proactive IIs. Recall that a major attribute of IIs is proactivity in which individuals envision encounters beforehand in order to rehearse messages. Consistent with this line of reasoning, Honeycutt, Choi, and Deberry (2009) examined how the catharsis and rehearsal functions of IIs facilitate or reduce an individual's level of CA in conversations, groups, meetings, and public speaking. Honeycutt and his associates (2009) found that II catharsis was negatively associated with CA only within the public speaking context. Their study also revealed that discrepancy with communication performance was a significant predictor of CA. This finding is contrary to prior research that suggested that individuals with high CA levels focused on non-communicative rehearsal methods, such as note-taking (cf. Ayers, Keereetaweep, Chen, & Edwards, 1998). Yet, Ayers et al.'s findings suggest that although individuals high in CA might focus more on note-taking, the note-taking is accompanied by mental rehearsal. The implication is that regardless of their levels of CA, individuals rehearse for interactions at similar levels, which are often discrepant. Therefore, discrepant IIs have the potential to act as "catastrophizing" agents when individuals imagine the worst-case scenario, and the II becomes a self-fulfilling prophecy (Honeycutt & Ford, 2001).

Evaluation of II Theory

Since intrapersonal communication is the foundation of all other forms of human communication, the scope of II theory is transcendent across contexts and reflects a general theory of social cognition in terms of message production (rehearsal) and self-awareness. Even in mass media situations, communicators are often being introspective as they think. Indeed, an old maxim reflects the power of II: Think before you speak.

The theory has been tested in over 30 studies and six dissertations across the United States and other countries, including Thailand and Japan, in the areas of instructional, political, intercultural, family, relational, and organizational communication. Imagined interaction conflict-linkage theory is a secondary theory that has been examined in the context of serial arguments, with results providing further support for the theorems derived from II theory (e.g., a person's IIs influence the goals that initiate a serial argument; see Hample, Richards, & Na, 2012). Thus, the theory fares well on testability.

Despite these strengths, one criticism of II theory concerns the ability of cognitive researchers to identify or infer the existence of internal cognitive states from external behavior (Ericsson & Simon, 1980). Even though certain physiological measures allow researchers to document the occurrence of mental states, they tell us very little about these states beyond the physiological level. If one's interest is in the content of mental states or, in this case, the content of IIs, we must rely on individual self-reports. This criticism has been addressed by Ericsson and Simon and by Pelose (1989), who offer guidelines about the validity of retrospective reports. They indicated that providing contextual information and prompts to subjects can aid recall from long-term memory. The Survey of Imagined Interaction (SII) is designed to contextualize subjects through examples of IIs, and a new shorter version of the SII is available (Honeycutt, 2010). Relatedly, Van Kelegom and Wright (2012–13) reported positive correlations between episodic and partner-specific imagined interactions among romantic partners, and Honeycutt (2010) noted how the SII can be modified depending on the researcher's needs, such as contextualizing items to refer to the specific context.

Caughey (1984) argued that by rehearsing anticipated conversations, "we also bind ourselves tightly within a given culturally constructed framework. These inner conversations may be just as important as actual conversations" in managing our sense of social reality (p. 146). IIs provide a mechanism for managing and living on the edge of chaos and complexity. In some cases, IIs might prevent the sudden reorganizing of a complex system into a wholly new and possibly undesirable system. Furthermore, once a system has achieved its new pattern of organization, it does not spontaneously disorganize. The system may become inflexible or stagnant, as in numerous marketing cases where one product gains a permanent economic edge. Analogies with inter-personal communication abound. An example is the spouse whose spontane-ous outburst precipitates a divorce, or who does not confine his or her interactions with alternative partners to the realm of the imaginary. Any complete explanation of communication must ultimately be concerned with three components:

- input (preexisting attitudes, beliefs, experiences, or personality brought into an interaction),
- throughput (the process or actual unfolding of communication as evidenced in behaviors, messages, statements), and
- output (outcomes that emerge from the communication, including post-event attitudes, satisfaction, emotional ratings).

Many communication studies are simple input-output designs in which surveys and hypothetical scenarios are used in lieu of actual coding of verbal and nonverbal behaviors that are costly and time consuming. IIs are primarily focused on input and output. Indeed, a proactive II represents expectations about what may happen during a conversation. It resides within the individual, while ignoring group processes. However, it is possible to link IIs with process or throughput. For example, my colleagues and I code discrepancy in which individuals think about messages that they are going to discuss with their part-ner about some issue in their relationship (e.g., managing finances, social life, how they argue). After the discussion, the individuals watch themselves on DVD and discuss how discrepant the actual conversation was to what they had proactively imagined. Hence, discrepancy is reflected through self-reports and behavioral observation.

Continuing the (Internal) Conversation

Future research in imagined interaction theory is limitless. Because IIs are a pervasive part of daily existence that occur across the lifespan, it is worth examining how they can be facilitated for maximizing outcomes. Indeed, sports imagists use mental imagery in which athletes are taught to imagine successful outcomes using the rehearsal function (e.g., imagining a success-ful kick before kicking a field goal, making free throws, stopping a team from making a first-down on "4th and inches," hitting a baseball or a straight golf drive, and so on). My colleagues and I are currently testing cardiovascular and electrodermal correlates of having IIs about pleasant topics (e.g., sharing news of success) and areas of disagreement in interpersonal relationships. For example, individuals imagine discussing a topic of concern about which they have had prior discussions or arguments with a relational partner. Blood pressure, galvanic skin response, and heart-rate variability are measured while they are imagining the conflict, as well as during a time period in which the partners actually discuss the topic. We are also examining third-party IIs in which people imagine what others are saying about them. During the "heat" of an argument, we are investigating the relationship between taking conflict personally and their association with the functions of IIs. Indeed, through these lines of research, my colleagues and I imagine great insights into the relationship between individual differences and productive communicative outcomes.

References

Abelson, R. P. (1976). Script processing in attitude formation and decision-making. In J. S. Carroll & J. W. Payne (Eds.), *Cognition and social behavior* (pp. 33–45). Hillsdale, NJ: Erlbaum.

Allen, T. H., & Honeycutt, J. M. (1997). Planning, imagined interaction, and the non-verbal display of anxiety. *Communication Research, 24,* 64–82.

Ayers, J., Keereetaweep, T., Chen, P. E., & Edwards, P. A. (1998). Communication apprehension and employment interviews. *Communication Education, 47,* 1–17.

Bodie, G. D., Honeycutt, J. M., & Vickery, A. J. (2013). An analysis of the correspondence between imagined interaction attributes and functions. *Human Communication Research 39,* 157–183.

Caughey, J. (1984). *Imaginary social worlds.* Lincoln: University of Nebraska Press.

Cunningham, S. B. (1989). Defining intrapersonal communication. In C. V. Roberts & K. W. Watson (Eds.), *Intrapersonal communication processes* (pp. 82–94). Scottsdale, AZ: Gorsuch Scarisbrick.

Dewey, J. (1922). *Human nature and conduct: An introduction to social psychology.* New York, NY: Henry Holt.

Ericsson, K. A., & Simon, H. A. (1980). Verbal reports as data. *Psychological Review, 87,* 215–251.

Fisher, B. A. (1987). *Interpersonal communication: Pragmatics of human relationships.* New York, NY: Random House.

Hamilton, M. A., Buck, R. W., Chory, R. M., Beatty, M. J., & Patrylak, L. A. (2009). In M. J. Beatty, J. C. McCroskey, & K. Floyd (Eds.), *Biological dimensions of communication* (pp. 227–250). Cresskill, NJ: Hampton Press.

Hample, D., Richards, A. S., & Na, L. (2012). A test of the conflict linkage model in the context of serial arguments. *Western Journal of Communication, 76,* 459–479.

Honeycutt, J. M. (1998–99). Differences in imagined interactions as a consequence of marital ideology and attachment. *Imagination, Cognition, and Personality, 18,* 269–283.

Honeycutt, J. M. (2003). *Imagined interactions.* Cresskill, NJ: Hampton.

Honeycutt, J. M. (2006). Enhancing EI intervention through imagined interactions. *Issues and Recent Developments in Emotional Intelligence* [Online serial], *1*(1), 1–4. Available at http://www.eiconsortium.org.

Honeycutt, J. M. (2010). *Imagine that: Studies in imagined interaction.* Cresskill, NJ: Hampton.

Honeycutt, J. M., & Bryan, S. P. (2011). *Scripts and communication for relationships.* New York, NY: Peter Lang.

Honeycutt, J. M., Choi, C. W., & Deberry, R. D. (2009). Communication apprehension and imagined interactions. *Communication Research Reports, 26,* 228–236.

Honeycutt, J. M., & Ford, S. G. (2001). Mental imagery and intrapersonal communication: A review of research on imagined interactions (IIs) and current developments. In W. B. Gudykunst (Ed.), *Communication yearbook 25* (pp. 315–445). Mahwah, NJ: Erlbaum.

Honeycutt, J. M., & Keaton, S. A. (2012–13). Imagined interactions and personality preferences as predictors of relationship quality. *Imagination, Cognition, and Personality, 32,* 3–21.

Honeycutt, J. M., Keaton, S. A., Hatcher, L. C., & Hample, D. (2014). Effects of rumination and observing marital conflict on observers' heart rates as they advise and predict the use of conflict tactics. In J. M. Honeycutt, C. R. Sawyer, & S. A. Keaton (Eds.), *The influence of communication on physiology and health* (pp. 71–91). New York, NY: Peter Lang.

Honeycutt, J. M., Pence, M. E., & Gearhart, C. C. (2012–13). Associations between imagined interactions and the "Big Five" personality traits. *Imagination, Cognition, and Personality, 32,* 273–289.

Honeycutt, J. M., & Wiemann, J. M. (1999). Analysis of functions of talk and reports of imagined interactions (IIs) during engagement and marriage. *Human Communication Research, 25,* 399–419.

Honeycutt, J. M., Zagacki, K. S., & Edwards, R. (1989). Intrapersonal communication, social cognition, and imagined interactions. In C. V. Roberts & K. W. Watson (Eds.), *Intrapersonal communication processes* (pp. 166–184). Scottsdale, AZ: Gorsuch Scarisbrick.

McCann, R. M., & Honeycutt, J. M. (2006). An intercultural analysis of imagined interaction. *Human Communication Research, 32,* 274–301.

McCroskey, J. C. (1977). Oral communication apprehension: A summary of recent theory and research. *Human Communication Research, 4,* 78–96.

Mead, G. H. (1934). *Mind, self and society.* Chicago, IL: University of Chicago Press.

Meyer, J. R. (1997). Cognitive influences on the ability to address interaction goals. In J. O. Greene (Ed.), *Message production: Advances in communication theory* (pp. 71–90). Mahwah, NJ: Erlbaum.

Pelose, G. C. (1989). Metacognition as an intrapersonal communication process: The purposes of cognitive monitoring and methodology for its assessment. In C. V. Roberts & K. W. Watson (Eds.), *Intrapersonal communication processes* (pp. 135–165). Scottsdale, AZ: Gorsuch Scarisbrick.

Rosenblatt, P. C., & Meyer, C. (1986). Imagined interactions in the family. *Family Relations, 35,* 319–324.

Rothbaum, F., Pott, M., Azuma, H., Miyake, K., & Weisz, J. (2000). The development of close relationships in Japan and the United States: Paths of symbiotic harmony and generative tension. *Child Development, 71,* 1121–1142.

Schutz, A. (1962). Choosing among projects of action. In M. Natanson (Ed.), *Collected papers, Volume I: The problem of social reality* (pp. 67–96). The Hague, Netherlands: Martinus Nijhoff.

Triandis, H. C. (1995). *Individualism and collectivism.* Boulder, CO: Westview.

Trzesniewski, K. H., Donnellan, M. B., & Robins, R. W. (2008). Do today's young people really think they are so extraordinary? An examination of secular trends in narcissism and self-enhancement. *Psychological Science, 19*(2), 181–188.

Van Kelegom, M. J., & Wright, C. (2012–13). An investigation of episodic and partner-specific imagined interaction use. *Imagination, Cognition, and Personality, 32,* 319–338.

Zagacki, K. S., Edwards, R., & Honeycutt, J. M. (1992). The role of mental imagery and emotion in imagined interaction. *Communication Quarterly, 40,* 56–68.

7

Planning Theory of Communication

Goal Attainment Through Communicative Action

Charles R. Berger

C ommunication is purposive; it is a powerful tool for achieving everyday goals. Even when people talk with someone for the sake of talking, they are probably using communication to achieve a goal. Just talking with someone could be part of a plan to achieve the goal of relieving boredom. In their everyday lives, people use both words and actions to accomplish such goals as persuading, entertaining, informing, and relating to others. The planning theory of communication seeks to explain how individuals produce actions and discourse that enable them to attain their everyday goals, and how individuals arrive at understandings of each other's goal-directed actions and discourse.

Intellectual Tradition of Planning Theory

Planning theory is a social-cognitive theory that identifies and describes the cognitive structures and processes that enable both the generation of purposive, goal-directed action, including verbal discourse, and the understanding of others' actions and discourse. The theory's aim is to explain how mental plans play a role in these communication processes. Although Berger's theory has been developed and tested within face-to-face interaction situations, its scope ranges far beyond these contexts. The theory also has relevance to explaining message production and message processing in print and electronic mass media, as well as communication mediated by such technologies as computers and mobile devices. Whenever people communicate with each other, plans and planning processes are in play.

Planning theory's orientation is post-positivist and represents the tradition of scientific realism. It seeks to describe fundamental cognitive structures and processes that enable communication processes, as well as the mechanisms that prevent communication processes from taking place (Pavitt, 2001). The realist approach represented in planning theory entails the assumption that the cognitive structures and processes that enable the production and understanding of human action and discourse are not merely hypothetical theoretical constructs; they are real.

Main Goals and Features of Planning Theory

This plan-based approach to interpersonal communication can be characterized by the following seven propositions:

Proposition 1. Organisms, including humans, seek to satisfy goals in order to survive. Goal satisfaction is an ongoing activity that gives rise to goal-directed, purposive actions.

Proposition 2. The human's ability to think has grown out of the need to satisfy goals (Bogdan, 1994, 1997, 2000). Cognitive capabilities that enable people to anticipate and recognize opportunities to satisfy goals and to remember successful plans for achieving goals promote more effective and more efficient goal satisfaction.

Proposition 3. People use language to achieve goals, and not merely for the sake of using it. Language is used to accomplish such goals as persuading, informing, problem solving, and relating. Language is a tool or an instrument people use to attain these goals (Clark, 1994; Wittgenstein, 1953).

Proposition 4. *Goals* are mental representations of desired end states toward which people strive; *plans* are cognitive representations of action sequences that enable people to achieve goals. Goals motivate action; plans guide action.

Proposition 5. Knowledge about goals is represented hierarchically in long-term memory, with abstract goals at the tops of hierarchies and subgoals nested below them. Nested below the abstract goal of "happiness" might be the subgoal "wealth" or "serving others," implying that the satisfaction of these subgoals will lead to the satisfaction of the more abstract goal. Achieving subgoals enables achievement of superordinate goals.

Proposition 6. Plans are hierarchically organized and are cognitive representations of action sequences that enable people to reach goals. In the preceding example, individuals might develop or have available to them in long-term memory plans for becoming wealthy or for serving others. Plans can be consciously formulated and used to achieve goals, and previously used plans can be stored in long-term memory, and retrieved and used unconsciously to achieve recurring goals. The ability to store and reuse successful plans increases people's efficiency and effectiveness in satisfying many goals that re-occur in everyday life—obtaining food, exchanging money for goods and services, greeting others, and gathering information.

Proposition 7. Knowledge of goals and plans also plays a vital role in understanding the discourse and actions of other people. When people ask why other people have said or done what they have, their answers to these questions are couched in terms of the goals they infer others to be pursuing and the plans they believe others to be following to achieve their goals. Answering the question "Why did she say that?" may involve statements about both plans and goals, as in the answer "She was trying to get him to stop talking [inferred goal], so she asked him to brush his teeth [inferred plan]."

To take another example, observers watching a person speak with great intensity in a two-person conversation might infer that the speaker's goal is to persuade the other person and that the message plan the speaker is following includes using certain arguments and appeals delivered with high verbal intensity, animated gestures, and other persuasion-related nonverbal behaviors. In order to understand others' discourse and actions in this example, observers must draw on their knowledge of what pursing a persuasion goal typically looks and sounds like, and the plans people usually use to attain that goal. Without such goal-plan knowledge, it would be difficult for communicators to infer others' intentions that, in turn, would make it difficult for people to respond to others in meaningful or effective ways (Berger & Palomares, 2011).

PLANS VS. PLANNING

Although the terms "plan" and "planning" are sometimes used interchangeably, they are not the same. *Plans* are hierarchical knowledge structures that represent goal-directed action sequences, but *planning* is a process that produces a plan or plans as its product. Planning includes assessing the situation, deciding what goal or goals to pursue, creating or retrieving plans, and then executing them (Berger, 1995, 1997). Most of the research motivated by planning theory has focused on characteristics of plans and how these characteristics influence communication effectiveness, rather than focusing on the processes involved in planning.

PLAN COMPLEXITY

A key aspect of communication plans is their complexity (Berger, 1997; Waldron, 1997). Plans can be more or less complex depending on at least two factors. First, plans can be made more complex by including contingencies in them. Communicators' initial planned actions may fail to achieve goals; however, plans can be constructed to anticipate potential action failures by including alternative actions that might be pursued if failures occur.

Contingencies can be built into the plan at different levels of abstraction. In the example shown in Figure 7.1, a persuader might begin an attempt to achieve a compliance goal by using various arguments. If these arguments fail, the persuader could then offer rewards. If rewards fail, the persuader could then resort to verbal threats and, in the extreme, physical force to gain compliance. Such a progression from rational and prosocial persuasion strategies to threatening and coercive strategies has been observed in studies in which individuals' persuasion attempts have been repeatedly thwarted (Berger, 1997). Within each of the abstract action types (arguments-appeals, offer rewards, verbal threats, and physical force), more specific actions that a persuader could enact could be nested. Usually, persuaders have several arguments, rewards, or threats that they could potentially use to achieve their goal. Thus, if a given argument fails to bring about compliance, a persuader might deploy a second argument rather than switch to a new action type such as rewards. As the action contingencies represented in conditional "if-then" statements are added to plans ("If action X fails, then use action Y"), plans exhibit a branching structure that reflects their increased complexity.

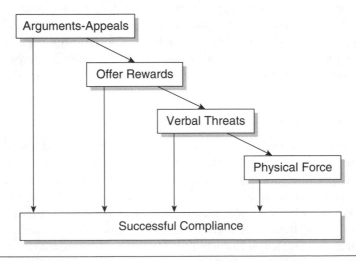

Figure 7.1   An Abstract Compliance-Gaining Message Plan Hierarchy

Second, plans can also vary with respect to their specificity. An abstract persuasion plan lacking specificity might simply include the abstract action category of offering rewards for compliance. By contrast, as shown in Figure 7.2, a detailed, more concrete plan might go on to specify the characteristics of the reward—material (money, goods, services) versus emotional (praise). Monetary rewards could be further specified in terms of their monetary value and their form (cash versus check), and goods and services could be differentiated with respect to their type (jewelry, toaster oven) or form (a free backrub [worth $100]).

As the plan hierarchy shown in Figure 7.2 demonstrates, the plan might further specify the words and actions that would be used to offer the reward to the other person—for example, "If you do 'X,' I will give you this check for $10,000 . . ." said in a sincere voice while smiling and touching the person's arm.

THE HIERARCHY PRINCIPLE

Planning theory predicts, and evidence supports, the proposition that when individuals encounter action failure, their first tendency is to alter plans at more concrete levels than at more abstract levels. This tendency is known as the *hierarchy principle* (Berger, 1997). The hierarchy principle is based on

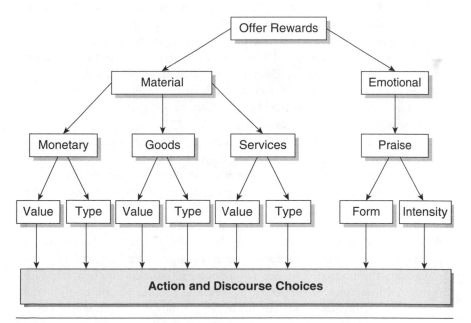

Figure 7.2   A Hypothetical Offer Rewards Plan

the idea that changing plans at more specific levels requires less cognitive effort than changing plans at more abstract levels. In the persuasion examples, it is easier to use another argument or appeal for compliance in the event of failure than it is to switch categories from arguments and appeals to rewards. When more abstract plan elements are altered, the communicator must figure out the specific actions that will be used to represent the new, abstract plan category. By contrast, minor adjustments to specific, concrete actions require much less thought.

Several studies have tested the hierarchy principle and have shown that when communicators are not understood by others, thus thwarting communicators' plans, communicators tend to repeat what they said previously but in a louder voice (a low-level plan alteration), even though the source of the communication failure may have nothing to do with others' failing to hear what was said (Berger, 1997). Moreover, when individuals are asked to alter message plans at higher levels—for example, trying another argument while persuading someone—they take longer to do so than when they are asked to make lower-level adjustments such as repeating what they said previously, but saying it more slowly the second time (Berger, 1997). Because high-level plan alterations are cognitively more demanding, communicators usually try to avoid making such changes, if possible. Consistent with this idea, when people verbalized routine plans that required no modifications, the level of activity in the dorsolateral prefrontal cortex region of their brains was found to be lower than when they verbalized plans that required modifications (Beatty & Heisel, 2007). This brain region is associated with a system dedicated to the regulation of intellectual function and action, and it becomes more active when individuals must consciously sequence actions. Of course, when communicative stakes are high and goals must be attained—for example, divorcing parents negotiating child visitations—communicators may be willing to expend greater cognitive effort to make high-level plan alterations.

Although action plans that include contingencies have obvious advantages by providing communicators with the ability to respond quickly to failures, increased plan complexity may come at a cost, depending on the number of alternative actions or plans a message producer might have available. On the one hand, communicators who pursue goals with no plan alternatives may not be able to respond rapidly if their sole plan or planned action fails. On the other hand, message producers who have many alternative plans available or who have many action contingencies in a plan may have difficulty choosing among the alternatives when failure occurs, thus slowing their response times. A communicator preparing to persuade another person might come up with 15 arguments to support his or her position. However, when one of these arguments fails to be persuasive during an interaction, the communicator has the problem of quickly choosing among the 14 remaining arguments.

A communicator with fewer alternative arguments would face a less difficult decision-making task. Several experiments have shown that individuals with no alternative plans or actions, or as many as six alternative plans or actions, responded equally less rapidly when their current plan or action failed. By contrast, individuals who had three alternative plans or actions responded to the same failure significantly more rapidly than did both of these groups (Berger, 1997). Having alternative plans or actions available in the event of failure pays off in terms of circumventing failure, but too many alternatives may slow down a communicator's ability to respond to failure. The inability to respond quickly in the event of plan failure could be costly in terms of others' perceptions of the slowly responding communicator. It is well established that others judge people who show longer pauses in their speech to be less credible; thus, how quickly individuals recover from plan failures may become an important determinant of how credible others judge them to be (Berger, 1997).

PLANS AND COMMUNICATION EFFECTIVENESS

People can consciously devise plans before they engage in communication—for example, thinking up an excuse for being late for a date—and plans can be retrieved, modified, or constructed on the fly as people communicate. Using planning theory, researchers have shown that planning while interacting with others helps to determine the degree to which communicators are effective in reaching their goals (Waldron, 1997). This research examined the plans individuals recalled using while pursuing such goals as obtaining sensitive information from conversational partners or trying to succeed in a job interview.

In general, Waldron (1997) demonstrated that individuals whose plans look ahead in the conversation and anticipate their partners' future conversational moves, in much the same way as expert chess players anticipate their opponents' future moves, are more effective than those whose plans do not anticipate partners' future actions. Because plans that anticipate conversational partners' future actions are more complex than those that do not, increasingly more complex plans are increasingly more effective. His research also showed that individuals whose plans took into account their partners' goals were generally more effective than were those whose plans did not. The ability of individuals to integrate their partners' goals into their own plans implies that effective message producers have more flexible plans than do less effective communicators. Finally, Waldron's research revealed that plans that included concrete actions were more effective than were highly abstract or vague plans. A plan for trying to persuade another person might include the abstract action of being pleasant, whereas, a more specific plan would detail the actions involved in being pleasant such as smiling and complimenting the other person.

Consequently, those whose message plans are more concrete are generally more effective at achieving their interaction goals.

How Communication Is Conceptualized in Planning Theory

As the planning theory propositions suggest, verbal and nonverbal messages are instruments that individuals use to achieve goals in their everyday lives. Message exchanges between people enable them to achieve their goals. Over human history, people have developed progressively more sophisticated communication systems to make goal attainment more efficient and to make it possible to pursue multiple goals simultaneously. Individual human action and social interaction are hierarchically organized around goal pursuit, thus reflecting the role cognitive plans play in guiding human action and social interaction toward goals (Berger, 2002, 2003). Planning theory suggests that social interaction and mediated communication are instruments or tools that enable individuals to achieve their desired goals by enacting plans. Goal-plan knowledge, in turn, provides meaning to others' discourse and actions.

Research and Practical Applications of Planning Theory

Everyday observation suggests that individuals vary with respect to their ability to achieve their communication goals effectively and efficiently. Some individuals cannot succeed, even in the absence of direct resistance from others, or the unfortunate circumstances that may sometimes interfere with the execution of their planned actions. By contrast, others can succeed in spite of substantial roadblocks that other people and situational factors put in their paths. Among those who succeed, some do so quickly and with apparent ease while others struggle for long periods of time to arrive at the same successful outcome. Planning theory provides a partial explanation for these performance differences. Specifically, because of differences in prior experience and knowledge, some individuals have developed more effective plans for achieving the goal or goals in question than have others. Moreover, to the degree that these plans anticipate potential resistance or unfavorable circumstances and include contingencies for overcoming these sources of interference, these individuals will experience higher levels of success with greater levels of efficiency.

However, planning theory includes an important caution (Berger, 1997): No matter how effective plans may be, if communicators do not have the requisite performance skills to carry out the plan, effective plans may not be successful. This distinction between plan effectiveness and performance skills is reflected in the division of labor between those who plan messages—speech writers, script writers, and news writers—and the politicians, actors, and news anchors who ultimately perform or deliver the messages. This division of labor in these formal communication contexts suggests that the same individual may not necessarily possess both the ability to formulate effective communication plans and the skills to perform them effectively. An extremely effective message planner may lack the necessary physical attributes and verbal and nonverbal skills to implement highly effective plans. The ineffective performer may have odd vocal characteristics or a limited range of nonverbal behaviors. For example, deep, resonant voices are preferred for radio and television announcers because people with these vocal characteristics are generally judged to be more persuasive than are those with high-pitched, nasal voices. Consequently, no matter how effective planners might be, certain communication characteristics may interfere with goal achievement. Conversely, an individual with excellent performance skills may lack the cognitive skills and knowledge necessary to devise effective message plans. Some very successful actors and politicians with very strong performance skills are incapable of performing well unless they are provided with a script (or plan) to follow.

Although this division of labor between plans and performance may be somewhat less obvious during informal, everyday social encounters, sometimes advice givers such as friends and relatives—acting in the role of planners—provide their peers and relatives (the performers) with information about actions they might take to achieve their goals that involve interactions with others. This possibility notwithstanding, the problem that many people face when engaging in everyday social interaction is that they must at once have effective plans for achieving their goals and the performance skills necessary to carry out their plans effectively in discourse and action. Thus, when people fail to reach their social interaction goals, the problem may lie in faulty plans, inadequate performance skills, or both.

Planning theory is also sensitive to the dynamic nature of social interaction and social relationships. This dynamism may render plans that have worked well in the past relatively ineffective at a later time (Berger, 1997). Spouses who use the same gift-giving plan (for example, a piece of jewelry) to determine what anniversary gift they will give their spouse, may, after several repetitions of the same plan, find it to be an ineffective one in reaching the goal of making the spouse happy. However, formerly effective plans may be rendered ineffective by more than their mindless, automatic repetition. A plan that was successful when first implemented, if used on a second occasion may prove to be ineffective because of changes that have occurred in the person or persons on whom the plan is being implemented, or the environment in which the plan is being carried out, or both. Thus, effective communicators must be sensitive to these changes and not be lulled into the potentially false belief that a plan that has worked well in the past will necessarily work well again. Recognizing the possibility that an old, reliable plan may not work in a current social situation is an important social skill.

Closely related to the problem of reusing plans is that of the "success bias" in planning. Research has found that when individuals devise plans to reach goals and they are then asked to estimate the likelihood that they will actually reach their goal, their estimated likelihood of success is significantly higher than that of individuals who have not devised a plan to reach the same goal (Berger, 1997). On logical grounds, the higher likelihood of success estimates of those who have generated plans are unwarranted. After all, these individuals have no idea whether or not their plans will be successful in attaining goals until they use the plans. By itself, the act of devising a plan should not induce planners to become more confident of success. In fact, effective planners explicitly consider the possibility of failure and develop contingencies to meet these potential failures.

Evaluation of Planning Theory

Planning theory provides a way of explaining why some individuals are better than others at achieving their social interaction goals. In addition to sensitizing those interested in improving communication skills to the difference between plan effectiveness and performance skills, planning theory explicitly identifies a knowledge structure (plan) and a set of cognitive processes that are amenable to improvement through instruction. The theory suggests that when groups are devising plans, it is important for the groups to include individuals who may be skeptical of the potential effectiveness of the plans being developed rather than to include only like-minded "team players" who mindlessly agree with each other. Although potentially unpopular, such skeptics may spot potential problems with planned actions that might lead to failure. Including skeptics in groups engaged in planning helps counter the success bias and the negative consequences of "groupthink" (Berger, 1997).

By differentiating between plan and performance effectiveness, strategies for increasing communication effectiveness can be more accurately identified and finely tuned. Problems stemming from ineffective plans are not necessarily solved by focusing on improving presentational skills (gesturing effectively and increasing eye gaze). In order to improve plan effectiveness, individuals may have to be encouraged to incorporate others' goals into their own plans, anticipate their partners' future conversational moves, plan at more detailed and concrete levels, consider the possibility of plan failure, and devise contingencies to meet anticipated failures. Similarly, presentation skill problems may not be solved by honing these cognitive planning skills. The important point is that these cognitive and presentational skill sets can be learned.

One potential limitation to planning theory is its bias toward the individual as the unit of analysis. Planning theorists have recognized that when individuals participate in social interaction, they engage in interactive planning (Waldron, 1997). That is, individuals may base their own plans on the goals and plans they infer others to be following in the interaction. This is most clearly the case in adversarial interactions in which parties attempt to anticipate each other's next attacks and devise plans to protect themselves against them, for example, in military battles and political campaigns. However, even when parties are engaged in cooperative interactions, they must coordinate their efforts through interactive planning. When participating in cooperative endeavors, individuals cannot fully articulate their goals and plans to each other. To do so would require large amounts of time and energy. Thus, there may be uncertainty and room left for partners to fill in these gaps by inferring each other's goals and the plans they are using to pursue their goals. Even among individuals who know each other well, the inferences that fill these gaps may be erroneous, thus leading to communication failures and misunderstandings. Except for noting that interactive planning occurs continuously during everyday social interaction, planning theory does not provide the details of how individuals go about accomplishing interactive planning (Berger, 1997; Waldron, 1997).

Because the theory has focused intensely on the role plans play in guiding message production, almost no attention has been paid to how people make inferences about each other's goals and plans. Those interested in understanding discourse and text comprehension have argued that inferences about goals and plans enable people to provide meaning to each other's words and actions (Berger, 1997). That is, people interpret each other's utterances and actions in terms of the goals they believe their co-interlocutors are trying to achieve, and the plans they think others are using to pursue their goals. The theory has not addressed such questions as how individuals are able to detect each other's goals and plans when they engage in social interaction, although the vital importance of goal detection in social interaction has been discussed (Berger & Palomares, 2011). The theory has also ignored the issue of how inferences about others' goals and plans are integrated into ongoing message production processes. Communicators may base their own message plans and decisions about what to say and how and when to say it on the goals and plans they believe co-interlocutors are following.

Because planning theory addresses a fundamental interpersonal communication process, its scope is quite wide and germane to most social interactions in most contexts. Moreover, the theory has demonstrated its heuristic value by encouraging innovative research in such areas as goal detection (Berger & Palomares, 2011). However, because the theory deals with a set of complex processes, it is not highly parsimonious. Although theoretical parsimony is highly prized in scientific inquiry, pretzel-shaped theories may be necessary to explain pretzel-shaped mechanisms and processes. The fact that creative communicators can generate social interaction plans containing contingent actions that can be altered as their interactions unfold presents a distinct challenge to the ideal of theoretical parsimony. In order to provide useful predictions and explanations of dynamic social interaction processes, the complexity of interpersonal communication theories must match the complexity of the mechanisms that enable these processes.

Continuing the Conversation

There are at least two potential avenues for further research on plans and planning. First, because goal-plan inferences made during social interaction are frequently made quickly and outside of conscious awareness, and because individuals engage in dynamic, interactive planning while conversing with each other, effective methods for measuring these processes must be developed. This is an extremely difficult task because measurement methods that interrupt the flow of social interaction may artificially change its course. Likewise, methods that do not interrupt conversational flow and rely on people's memory for what they were thinking during a just-completed conversation may be inaccurate and distorted, even when people try their best to recall what they were thinking during a conversation. It is difficult to measure automatic processes using methods that require individuals to make verbal reports. Perhaps advances in brain imaging techniques, such as functional magnetic resonance imagining (fMRI), may enable researchers to gain insights into these automatic processes. At this time, however, using such techniques to study individuals during their interactions is difficult. There is widespread recognition that inferences about goals and plans enable individuals to understand each other's actions and discourse and to guide decisions about what to do and say in social encounters. Thus, the difficulties involved in measuring these complex, dynamic, fundamental processes are particularly frustrating.

Second, future research should address in more detail the relationships between plan effectiveness and performance skills. In many social interaction situations, the optimal condition might be for communicators to have highly effective plans implemented by equally high levels of performance skills. Unfortunately, however, individuals may not function at high levels simultaneously in both of these areas. In fact, it is doubtful that most individuals are capable of functioning at high levels in both areas in a given situation. When there is a discrepancy between the two dimensions, as there may often be, which discrepancy is more damaging to goal attainment? Can a highly effective plan overcome mediocre performance skills? Can high performance skill levels compensate for deficient plans? Another way to think about this question is to ask whether substance tends to trump style, or vice versa. The most probable answer to either question is, "It depends." What "it" depends on represents an opportunity for future research.

Almost 70 years ago the psychologist Kurt Lewin, founder of the study of group dynamics, observed that nothing is more practical than a good theory. What Lewin meant is that because theories provide explanations for phenomena we observe every day, practical application based on good theory is more likely to succeed than application based merely on intuition and trial and error. Many individuals would like to be more effective in their everyday social commerce with other people. As I hope this chapter has made evident, planning theory provides one potential avenue for understanding and improving social interaction skills and the skills necessary for communicating effectively with mass audiences. At least, that was one of my goals in planning this chapter.

References

Beatty, M. J., & Heisel, A. D. (2007). Spectrum analysis of cortical activity during verbal planning: Physical evidence for the formation of social interaction routines. *Human Communication Research, 33*, 48–63.

Berger, C. R. (1995). A plan-based approach to strategic communication. In D. E. Hewes (Ed.), *Cognitive bases of interpersonal communication* (pp. 141–179). Hillsdale, NJ: Erlbaum.

Berger, C. R. (1997). *Planning strategic interaction: Attaining goals through communicative action.* Mahwah, NJ: Erlbaum.

Berger, C. R. (2002). Goals and knowledge structures in social interaction. In M. L. Knapp & J. A. Daly (Eds.), *Handbook of interpersonal communication* (3rd ed., pp. 181–212). Thousand Oaks, CA: Sage.

Berger, C. R. (2003). Skillful message production. In J. O. Greene & B. R. Burleson (Eds.), *Handbook of communication and social interaction skills* (pp. 257–289). Mahwah, NJ: Erlbaum.

Berger, C. R., & Palomares, N. A. (2011). Knowledge structures and social interaction. In M. L. Knapp & J. A. Daly (Eds.), *The SAGE handbook of interpersonal communication* (4th ed., pp. 169–200). Thousand Oaks, CA: Sage.

Bogdan, R. J. (1994). *Grounds for cognition: How goal-directed behavior shapes the mind.* Hillsdale, NJ: Erlbaum.

Bogdan, R. J. (1997). *Interpreting minds: The evolution of a practice.* Cambridge, MA: MIT Press.

Bogdan, R. J. (2000). *Minding minds: Evolving a reflexive mind by interpreting others.* Cambridge, MA: MIT Press.

Clark, H. H. (1994). Discourse in production. In M. A. Gernsbacher (Ed.), *Handbook of psycholinguistics* (pp. 985–1021). San Diego, CA: Academic Press.

Pavitt, C. (2001). *The philosophy of science and communication theory.* Huntington, NY: Nova Science.

Waldron, V. R. (1997). Toward a theory of interactive conversational planning. In J. O. Greene (Ed.), *Message production: Advances in theory and research* (pp. 195–220). Mahwah, NJ: Erlbaum.

Wittgenstein, L. (1953). *Philosophical investigations.* Oxford, UK: Basil Blackwell.

8

Problematic Integration Theory and Uncertainty Management Theory

Learning to Hear and Speak to Different Forms of Uncertainty

Austin S. Babrow and Katie M. Striley

Problematic integration (PI) theory and uncertainty management (UM) theory are often invoked together as perspectives sharing a common interest in uncertainty (e.g., Afifi & Matsunaga, 2008). While UM theory focuses on the communicative *management* of uncertainty, PI theory describes the communicative *creation and experience* of uncertainty as part of a broader perspective on challenges of belief and desire. This chapter will explain not only the central tenets of each theory and their overlap, but also how the theories differ in terms of their roots, substance, and range of application.

Intellectual Traditions

Babrow (1992) presented PI theory as a comprehensive framework for understanding communication, not just that occurring in interpersonal contexts or dealing with uncertainty. His ideas grew out of dissatisfaction with post-positivist rational choice models, particularly expectancy-value perspectives, such as the theories of planned behavior and reasoned action (Ajzen, 1985; Fishbein & Ajzen, 1975). These models emphasize the human inclination to anticipate consequences of action in terms of both their likelihood of occurrence and their desirability. When behavior is under our conscious, willful control, we choose those actions believed to be more likely to result in positively, rather than negatively, valued outcomes. For example, in choosing which of two attractive acquaintances to ask on a date, you would be predicted to ask out the person with whom you would expect to have the best time (e.g., more likely to be fun, interesting, and romantic, and less likely to be critical or bossy). Communication constructs belief content and influences belief strength and evaluation.

Babrow (1992) appreciated the elegance of expectancy-value theories but criticized their paradoxically static and dispassionate view of communication and motivation. In particular, these theories say nothing about human struggles with uncertainty, inconsistent expectations and desires, impossible dreams, and painful ambivalence. For example, consider how hard it would be to deal with someone who is, in most ways, powerfully attractive but has worrisome attributes, such as apparent emotional frailty or an unreasonable need for control. In these experiences, beliefs and evaluations are expected to be unstable and sensitive to context, making static models of action less relevant, and prediction and measurement difficult, if not meaningless. In such situations, thick description of emerging, situated meanings is the preferred approach to inquiry (Babrow, 2001). Therefore, as we will soon elaborate, in certain specifiable contexts, meanings and associated behaviors are emergent products of ongoing, situated sense-making, and hence best studied from an interpretive perspective.

Brashers developed UM theory out of two post-positivist primary sources. One was uncertainty reduction theory (Berger & Calabrese, 1975). Around the same time that PI researchers critiqued the idea that social support is mainly a matter of reducing uncertainty (cf. Albrecht & Adelman, 1987; Ford, Babrow, & Stohl, 1996), Brashers independently concluded that the axioms and theorems of uncertainty reduction theory over-emphasize the process named in its title, to the neglect of other ways of *managing* uncertainty.[1] Brashers bolstered this critique by drawing on a second source, Mishel's (1990) cognitive theory of uncertainty in illness. Mishel argued that illness-related uncertainty is neither inherently bad nor good; rather, uncertainty is good or bad depending on context, and so must be appraised. For instance, one pregnant woman might find uncertainty about the sex of her child unpleasant, whereas another woman would find this same uncertainty part of the joyful anticipation of birth. Uncertainty appraisal determines how uncertainty is "managed": whether by sustaining, increasing, or decreasing it. Although his initial work and most subsequent use of the theory was in the context of interpersonal communication related to illness, such as social support in the context of HIV/AIDS, Brashers (2001) emphasized that these ideas applied in many contexts. In addition, despite sharing with PI theory the interpretivist tenet that meanings (e.g., of uncertainty) depend on situation, and relying almost exclusively on interpretive methods in empirical work, Brashers conceived of the theory as post-positivist (Afifi & Matsunaga, 2008).

Main Goals and Features of the Theories

The goals of PI theory are to (a) illuminate an important and ubiquitous communication process, (b) enhance communicator sophistication, (c) provoke alternative ways of understanding and acting, and (d) foster empathy and compassion. What is this ubiquitous process? As in expectancy-value models, PI theory recognizes that people are continually forming beliefs ("probabilistic orientations") and evaluations ("evaluative orientations"). When the world is as we want it to be, our beliefs and desires merge or *integrate* smoothly into effortless and relatively mindless decisions and communicative and other actions. Think, for example, of how easy it is to decide to date someone who is uniformly appealing or how easy it is to decline a date with someone uniformly unappealing. However, when we want the world to be different than it appears to be, when it is difficult to *integrate beliefs and desires,* we become more thoughtful and our communication becomes more challenging. In other words, we experience *problematic integration* when beliefs and desires do not combine readily in forming understandings, motivations, and lines of action. For instance, we might face a more difficult decision, perhaps becoming more pensive or seeking advice from friends, if deciding between dating a less physically attractive individual with a fun personality, or a beautiful individual with a boring personality.

Babrow (2007a) identified four common forms of *problematic integration.* You might experience *uncertainty*[2] about something very good or bad, for instance, not knowing if a job opportunity will be as good as it appears. Perhaps you have inconsistent or *diverging expectations and desires,* such as thinking it unlikely that you will be hired for a very desirable job. Alternatively, you might feel *ambivalence* about what you want, for example, having to move far away from loved ones if you accept an appealing job. Or, you might have *impossible desires,* like learning that you simply do not have the aptitude or connections to obtain a dream career. Babrow (1992) also noted shades of meaning distinguishing different forms of mixed feelings or ambivalence, as well as impossibility (e.g., theoretical vs. practical impossibility). In addition, researchers have differentiated *many different forms of uncertainty* (summarized in Babrow, 2007a). For example, we communicate very differently about uncertainty that we believe is universal compared to that which we think is simply a matter of our own ignorance. Still other forms of problematic integration are emerging as researchers identify distinctive phenomena. For instance, in an ongoing dissertation project, Teresa Keeler's research on sibling communication in caring for elderly parents is exploring what it means to resign oneself to unpleasant apparent realities, like a sibling who simply will not help. Future work will surely illuminate other forms of PI.

At the heart of all of these experiences are our constant efforts to understand and evaluate the world around us and integrate our beliefs and desires. Life is often hard to understand and different than we would like it to be, so PI is ubiquitous in human experience. We gain sophistication when we not only learn to see the underlying PI that is so much a part of our communication, but also when we come to understand some basic guidelines for communicating in these challenging situations (detailed below). In turn, as we learn more about PI's dynamics and communicative implications, we frequently come to realize our thoughts, feelings, and actions have far greater scope than we realized; we feel less constrained or stuck as we notice alternative constructions.[3] Finally, greater awareness of PI's ubiquity and insight into its challenges can foster empathy and compassion. We realize that struggles with beliefs and desires have been characteristic of human beings since the moment we emerged as entities capable of thinking beyond the moment of sensory stimulation. These struggles largely define our humanity, which is why so many of the world's great spiritual and religious wisdom traditions hold compassion as a central value (see Babrow, 2007b).

While PI theory's goals reflect a broad conception of communication, UM theory's goals reflect its titular process. Brashers's characterization of UM theory as post-positivist (Afifi & Matsunaga, 2008) suggests that its goals are understanding, prediction, and control of communication in uncertainty management processes. However, by far the most frequent thrust of research guided by the theory is developing descriptions of the ways in which people actively manage uncertainty, typically in the context of substantial illness. For instance, Brashers et al. (2003) described HIV patients' medical, personal, and social uncertainty and their subsequent management.

Another constant aim in UM theory is its emphasis that uncertainty is not only managed by its reduction. Again, following Mishel, uncertainty is neither inherently good nor bad but must be appraised and managed accordingly. Consider, for instance, the uncertainty that might arise when moving to a new city. One individual might experience the uncertainty about life in the city as dangerous, thus seeking to reduce uncertainty by learning more about what it would be like to live there. However, another individual might view her uncertainty as an exciting opportunity and actually increase uncertainty by imagining myriad possible scenarios. UM researchers aim to increase repertoires of both researchers and natural actors dealing with uncertainty by expanding conceptions of uncertainty management strategies. This goal is consistent with interpretive scholars' insistence that meanings are situationally emergent rather than determined by stable psycho-social structures or processes.

How Communication Is Conceptualized in the Theories

PI theory is consistent with the social constructionist idea that communication creates and recreates reality (Pearce, 1989). Although much communication is relatively mindless recreation of non-problematic routine, communication is also a source of PI and a resource for dealing with its challenges (Babrow, 1992, 2007a). Simply deciding whether to speak and what to say, about one's own PI or to someone else beset by powerful PI, can be deeply unsettling and challenging. Speaking about one's own PI raises identity and relational issues (e.g., vulnerability, dependence, appropriateness, privacy), making self-disclosure risky (see Petronio & Durham, Chapter 25, in this volume). Managed well, these discussions deepen our humanity, intimacy, and connection. Managed poorly, discussion of PI can hurt identity and relationships or become pathological (Albrecht & Adelman, 1987). When encountering another person experiencing PI, we must decide whether to show concern or quietly respect the other's private anguish. Goffman (1967) discussed this in his analysis of presentational and avoidance rituals. We convey our respect and appreciation for another person by showing interest in that person's well-being, but also by avoiding painful topics. As Goffman explained, "it should be plain that there is an inherent opposition and conflict between these two forms of deference" (p. 73). Such conflict is likely to be high when person A believes that interactional partner B is experiencing substantial PI; person A is likely to experience uncertainty about the consequences of engaging in one or the other form of respect, or ambivalence if person A believes that person B will take offense at whatever A does (also see Brown & Levinson's [1987] discussion of positive and negative face; see Goldsmith & Normand, Chapter 20, in this volume). More generally, the push and pull of relational dialectics (see Babrow, 1993; Baxter & Norwood, Chapter 21, in this volume) and relational turbulence (see Knobloch, Chapter 28, in this volume) give rise to PI. So in these and other ways (e.g., interpersonal and broader conflict), communication can be a source of PI.

Communication is also a resource for experiences with PI. Indeed, the theory suggests various ideas about how we can communicate more effectively. Consider, for example, some of the theory's implications for communicating about uncertainty. PI theory defines uncertainty as *difficulty forming a mental association* (Babrow & Matthias, 2009) and contends that this difficulty can take many different forms (Babrow, 2001, 2007a). This differentiation of forms gives rise to two important insights about communication as a resource for dealing with uncertainty. One is the importance of *form-specific adaptation of messages.*[4] Babrow (2001, 2007a) has repeatedly insisted on the need for systematic attention to particular forms of uncertainty. People may say they are "uncertain" (or a synonym), but this can mean many different things. Each specific form of uncertainty has its own distinctive meaning; communication adapted to that specific meaning or form is likely to most effectively foster shared meaning and adaptive interaction.

Babrow and Matthias (2009) offered an extensive discussion of adapting communication to forms of uncertainty, so we offer only a few examples here. For instance, when a person's uncertainty is rooted in personal rather than universal ignorance, the most sensible responses are information seeking on that person's part or another person providing information. By contrast, if our ignorance is universal (nobody knows what we want to know), but the ignorance is thought to be surmountable, responses like hope, patience, or active promotion of research are appropriate responses. As one further contrast, irreducible universal ignorance, such as ignorance of the future or of God's will, requires still other understandings and actions such as faith or acceptance. In all of these examples, we experience uncertainty about what to believe. *Form-specific adaption of messages* means communicating in ways that speak to the precise dilemma rather than to its first, second, or more distant cousin (again, see Babrow & Matthias, 2009). PI theory offers a systematic analysis of, and practical responses to, different forms of dilemma, such as different forms of uncertainty.

A second insight into communication as a resource for dealing with PI also flows from the differentiation of forms of uncertainty. Both PI and UM theory recognize that, when a person is certain that her or his situation is bad, communication creating or sustaining uncertainty can offer hope (Brashers et al., 2000; Ford et al., 1996). PI theory goes further in suggesting that each form of uncertainty represents a potential line of argument in these circumstances. For example, one can undermine (a hopeless) certainty by casting doubt on the extensiveness, credibility, consistency, and/or relevance of available information (again, see Babrow [2007a] for a more extensive list of forms). Hence, systematic attention to different forms of uncertainty is valuable in several ways.

Following PI theory, UM theory recognizes different forms of uncertainty (Brashers, 2001, 2007; Hogan & Brashers, 2009), but unlike PI theory, it does not provide a systematic accounting for these differences or their implications. Rather, as noted above, UM theory emphasizes uncertainty management in quite general terms. The main idea is that uncertainty must be appraised. This in turn explains the theory's treatment of communication. To begin, communication can be an instrument of appraisal. For instance, we might talk to family or friends when we feel uncertain about how to deal with a difficult situation at work. Whether or not these conversations produce explicit evaluations of our uncertainty, they are likely to imply that it is good or bad. When individuals appraise uncertainty negatively, as emphasized in uncertainty reduction theories, effective communication seeks and provides uncertainty reducing information. Acquisition "of new information in turn fuels reappraisal of uncertainty" (Hogan & Brashers, 2009, p. 48).

By contrast, when uncertainty is appraised positively (e.g., as a source of hope), effective communication creates, sustains, or increases uncertainty. Researchers aim to identify uncertainty reducing, maintaining, and increasing strategies within particular study contexts.[5] For example, Brashers et al. (2000) found that people living with HIV/AIDS maintain uncertainty by avoiding information and increase it by perceiving alternatives or blurring distinctions among alternatives (e.g., treatments). Numerous studies have replicated the finding that people create, sustain, or increase positively appraised uncertainty (e.g., Brashers, Neidig, & Goldsmith, 2004; Ford et al., 1996; for reviews, see Brashers, 2007; Hogan & Brashers, 2009).

One other way of communicatively managing uncertainty in UM theory is "adapting to chronic uncertainty" (Brashers, 2007, p. 209). Here, Brashers noted that many uncertainties remain with us for long periods of time. Chronic health problems and the uncertainties of aging are classic examples. Other uncertainties rise and fall with physical and social circumstances. When uncertainty persists, people can adapt by accepting it as natural. Another possibility, Brashers noted, is to alter perception of challenges. For example, his research on HIV/AIDS revealed that its sufferers managed ongoing uncertainty by setting short-term rather than long-term goals, and by creating routines that provide a realm of certainty within a more broadly unsure existence.

Research and Practical Applications of the Theories

Both PI and UM theories have a wide range of practical applications (see below). Here we note a few recent examples. Katie, the second author of this chapter, is currently using PI theory to understand intellectually gifted adolescents' experiences of ostracism. Middle school and high school students with IQs above 130 are participating in online journaling about their social experiences for 12 weeks. Peer acceptance is highly desirable to adolescents, but gifted adolescents might be prone to social rejection (Williams & Gerber, 2005), giving rise to PI as they struggle to cope. For example, they might experience uncertainty about acceptance or diverging expectation and desire if they believe acceptance is unlikely. Gifted students also must come to terms with their PI, perhaps by changing their evaluation of being "popular," or changing their appearance or behavior to increase chances of achieving popularity. Her project is attempting to describe forms of PI and coping, as well as developing new communicative resources.

In a recently launched project, Austin, the first author of this chapter, is studying interpersonal and public communication about climate destabilization. His project focuses on PI related to identity, the emergence of an activist orientation, and barriers to involvement. Austin will use project insights to foster citizen decision-making, interpersonal discussion, and political organizing.

Recent applications of UM theory have expanded its topical reach by analyzing sources of uncertainty in new domains, such as breast cancer risk revealed by genetic testing (Bylund et al., 2012) and online information and social support related to clubfoot (Oprescu, Campo, Lowe, Andsager, & Morcuende, 2013). In a paper examining health information avoidance, Barbour, Rintamaki, Ramsey, and Brashers (2012) identified both reasons for avoidance (e.g., maintaining hope, accepting limits of action, managing flawed information) and strategies for avoidance (e.g., avoiding information sources, controlling conversations).

Finally, in a conceptually rich study, Scott, Martin, Stone, and Brashers (2011) attempted to synthesize UM theory with normative theory. Although UM and PI researchers have long recognized that challenges involve not only instrumental actions but also identity and relational issues, Scott et al. made the useful argument that coping requires messages that deal simultaneously with multiple goals.[6]

Evaluation of the Theories

If we view PI and UM merely as theories of communication and uncertainty, surely a benefit of both perspectives is recognition that we do not always aim to reduce uncertainty.[7] Rather, uncertainty is also a requirement of hope and, some argue, a source of wisdom (Babrow, 2007a; Bradac, 2001; Watts, 1951). The theories are also broadly applicable because uncertainty is pervasive in human experience. Because PI theory extends beyond uncertainty to other dilemmas, its scope is broader than UM theory. However, this may not be advantageous. We say this is in view of the adage that a theory purporting to explain everything actually explains nothing.

The precautionary adage above is justified when a theory achieves breadth by imprecision. This is worrisome for post-positivists, who insist on conceptualizations clear enough to permit demonstrably reliable and valid measurement, and relational statements precise enough to support empirical predictions. To date, neither theory has achieved this level of precision (Afifi & Matsunaga, 2008).

From an interpretive perspective, the question of precision is more complex. While theoretical terms must be sufficiently clear to allow meaningful study and discussion, the post-positivist ideal of maximal clarity is, for interpretivists, an unachievable, unworthy, and misleading goal. Interpretivists prefer to think in terms of sensitizing concepts (Charmaz, 2006) that orient researchers to phenomena, understanding that meaning is contextual and emergent rather than fixed in some absolute sense. From this standpoint, the generality of PI and UM theory and any imprecision is less troublesome.

Still, the theories can be differentiated by their treatment of central terms. UM theory has developed in rather general ways. As noted above, while

Brashers recognized distinctions in forms of uncertainty, he did not make them central concerns that are systematically analyzed in the theory. Instead, he allowed room for specificity to arise in grounded analyses of specific contexts. By contrast, differentiating and clarifying forms of uncertainty and other types of PI has been central to PI theory and research. This leaves PI open to charges of over-theorizing, or creating theoretical concepts without meaning in lived experience (see Bradac, 2001).

Although these theories can be evaluated on other points, a constellation of concerns signified by the theories' names is highly pertinent, especially given the scope of this chapter. UM theory's name is immediately meaningful. Indeed, particularly for those tending to over-emphasize uncertainty reduction processes, the theory's name instantly teaches an important lesson. By contrast, PI theory's name has no immediately clear meaning; it sounds obscure and abstruse. So from the very first words, PI theory requires more explanation. Babrow (2007a) said that the name was chosen purposefully to encourage reflection on meanings of taken-for-granted ideas. Notably, although UM theory recognizes that we sometimes deal with uncertainty by acceptance, the very concept of *management* connotes *control*, and being in control is quite different from the *yielding that constitutes acceptance* (Babrow & Kline, 2000). Unsurprisingly, UM applications have tended to emphasize control. One example is Brashers's (2001) notion of "managing uncertainty management" (p. 485), or meta-control. Babrow and Matthias (2009) argued that over-emphasizing control inhibits theoretical attention to, and practical development of, the acceptance of uncertainty.

Continuing the Conversation

Early PI and UM research aimed to establish that we do not always reduce relational and other uncertainties. This is now well established. Both theories recognize that relational and other uncertainties are ubiquitous, and that uncertainty is often reasonable and healthy, and very often, simply irreducible. We should not, however, conclude that uncertainty reduction is unimportant. Both theories recognize that uncertainty reduction is a powerful motive. PI theory, in particular, asserts that a basic reason for communication and sense-making is forming probabilistic orientations, or beliefs.

A second phase of PI and UM research has entailed cataloging forms of PI (e.g., different meanings of uncertainty) and forms or strategies for managing or coping with these challenges. In PI theory's future development, we encourage and anticipate two major paths. One should be continuing development of the perspective's nuances. For example, it will be useful to differentiate meanings of evaluation, just as meanings of uncertainty have been teased out. The challenge here will be avoiding over-complication. The second path should be developing the theory's practical value by clarifying how its ideas can be used in relationally challenging situations, such as ostracism and other forms of exclusion and conflicts about environmental threats.

For UM theory, paths forward are more difficult to anticipate because of the untimely passing of its champion, Dale Brashers. As Anderson (1996) has said, theories are put in place and held there by the efforts of their advocates. Dale was not only an energetic and talented theorist and researcher, but also a gifted mentor. Surely many of his students and colleagues will continue to develop UM theory. The challenge for them is developing the theory in ways that do not merely replicate PI within the limited domain of uncertainty (see Bradac, 2001). One way forward might be to continue the commitment to building grounded UM theories within specific domains of application. For example, we could see grounded UM theories of social support in additional illness contexts, or of friendship uncertainty in an age of computer-mediated hyper-relationships. More generally, UM researchers will enhance the perspective by sorting out its connections to post-positivism and interpretivism.

In whatever direction researchers take us, we are confident that future studies will continue to find that communicative construction of uncertainty, diverging expectations and desires, ambivalence, (im)possibility, and other forms of PI are at the heart of meaningful and challenging moments of interpersonal communication.

Notes

1. Brashers and Babrow met on a panel at an International Communication Association conference in 1995, where they realized their common dissatisfaction with uncertainty reduction theory. One result was a collaborative essay applying their respective views to health communication (Brashers & Babrow, 1996).

2. Originally, Babrow (1992) described ambiguity as one of four cardinal forms of PI. Subsequent research categorized ambiguity as one of many forms of uncertainty.

3. Expanding the range of alternative constructions is an important goal of interpretive research.

4. It is important to note that we focus here on form-specific adaptation of communication in relation to uncertainty simply to highlight how PI theory differs from UM theory in its treatment of the latter's main concept. PI theory emphasizes the importance of adapting messages not only to different forms of uncertainty but to other forms of PI (discussed earlier), as well.

5. In these practices, UM researchers typically wed the formal theory with the interpretivist, social constructionist methods of grounded theory (Charmaz, 2006).

6. See Jordan and Babrow (2013) for a similar argument related to sustaining uncertainty in creative collaborative problem-solving.

7. Babrow (2001, 2007b) discussed a more extensive set of corrections to oversimplified views of uncertainty.

References

Afifi, W. A., & Matsunaga, M. (2008). Uncertainty management theories: Three approaches to a multifarious process. In L.A. Baxter & D. O. Braithwaite (Eds.), *Engaging theories of interpersonal communication: Multiple perspectives* (pp. 117–144). Thousand Oaks, CA: Sage.

Ajzen, I. (1985). From intentions to actions: A theory of planned behavior. In J. Kuhl & J. Beckman (Eds.), *Action control: From cognition to behavior* (pp. 11–39). Heidelberg: Springer.

Albrecht, T. L., & Adelman, M. B. (1987). *Communicating social support.* Beverly Hills, CA: Sage.

Anderson, J. A. (1996). *Communication theory: Epistemological foundations.* New York, NY: Guilford.

Babrow, A. S. (1992). Communication and problematic integration: Understanding diverging probability and value, ambiguity, ambivalence, and impossibility. *Communication Theory, 2,* 95–130.

Babrow, A. S. (1993). The advent of multiple process theories of communication. *Journal of Communication, 43,* 110–118.

Babrow, A. S. (2001). Uncertainty, value, communication, and problematic integration. *Journal of Communication, 51,* 553–573.

Babrow, A. S. (2007a). Problematic integration theory. In B. B. Whaley & W. Samter (Eds.), *Explaining communication: Contemporary theories and exemplars* (pp. 181–200). Mahwah, NJ: Erlbaum.

Babrow, A. S. (2007b). *Using problematic integration theory, a perspective on communication and human suffering, to promote dialogue across spiritual and other world views.* Paper presented at the annual meeting of the National Communication Association, Chicago, IL.

Babrow, A. S., & Kline, K. N. (2000). From "reducing" to "coping with" uncertainty: Reconceptualizing the central challenge in breast self-exams. *Social Science & Medicine, 51,* 1805–1816.

Babrow, A. S., & Matthias, M. S. (2009). Generally unseen challenges in uncertainty management: An application of problematic integration theory. In T. Afifi &. W. Afifi (Eds.), *Uncertainty, information management and disclosure decisions: Theories and applications* (pp. 9–25). London, UK: Routledge.

Barbour, J. B., Rintamaki, L. S., Ramsey, J. A., & Brashers, D. E. (2012). Avoiding health information. *Journal of Health Communication, 17,* 212–229.

Berger, C. R., & Calabrese, R. J. (1975). Some explorations in initial interaction and beyond: Toward a developmental theory of interpersonal interaction. *Human Communication Research, 1,* 99–112.

Bradac, J. J. (2001). Theory comparison: Uncertainty reduction, problematic integration, uncertainty management, and other curious constructs. *Journal of Communication, 51,* 456–476.

Brashers, D. E. (2001). Communication and uncertainty management. *Journal of Communication, 51,* 477–497.

Brashers, D. E. (2007). A theory of communication and uncertainty management. In B. Whaley & W. Samter (Eds.), *Explaining communication theory* (pp. 201–218). Mahwah, NJ: Erlbaum.

Brashers, D. E., & Babrow, A. S. (1996). Theorizing health communication. *Communication Studies, 47,* 243–251.

Brashers, D. E., Neidig, J. L., & Goldsmith, D. J. (2004). Social support and the management of uncertainty for people living with HIV or AIDS. *Health Communication, 16,* 305–331.

Brashers, D. E., Neidig, J. L., Haas, S. M., Dobbs, L. K., Cardillo, L. W., & Russell, J. A. (2000). Communication in the management of uncertainty: The case of persons living with HIV or AIDS. *Communication Monographs, 67,* 63–84.

Brashers, D., Neidig, J., Russell, J., Cardillo, L., Haas, S., Dobbs, L., Garland, M., McCartney, B., & Nemeth, S. (2003). The medical, personal, and social causes of uncertainty in HIV illness. *Issues in Mental Health Nursing, 24,* 497–522.

Brown, P., & Levinson, S. C. (1987). *Politeness: Some universals in language usage.* Cambridge, UK: Cambridge University Press.

Bylund, C. L., Fisher, C. L., Brashers, D., Edgerson, S., Glogowski, E. A., Boyar, S. R., ... Kissane, D. (2012). Sources of uncertainty about daughters' breast cancer risk that emerge during genetic counseling consultations. *Journal of Genetic Counseling, 21,* 292–304.

Charmaz, K. (2006). *Constructing grounded theory.* London, UK: Sage.

Fishbein, M., & Ajzen, I. (1975). *Belief, attitude, intention, and behavior: An introduction to theory and research.* Reading, MA: Addison-Wesley.

Ford, L. A., Babrow, A. S., & Stohl, C. (1996). Social support messages and the management of uncertainty in the experience of breast cancer: An application of problematic integration theory. *Communication Monographs, 63,* 189–207.

Goffman, E. (1967). *Interaction ritual: Essays in face-to-face behavior.* Chicago, IL: Aldine.

Hogan, T. P., & Brashers, D. E. (2009). The theory of communication and uncertainty management: Implications from the wider realm of information behavior. In T. D. Afifi & W. A. Afifi (Eds.), *Uncertainty, information management, and disclosure decisions: Theories and applications* (pp. 45–66). New York, NY: Routledge.

Jordan, M. E., & Babrow, A. S. (2013). Communication in creative collaborations: The challenges of uncertainty and desire related to task, identity, and relational goals. *Communication Education, 62,* 210–232.

Mishel, M. H. (1990). Reconceptualization of the uncertainty in illness theory. *Image: Journal of Nursing Scholarship, 22,* 256–262.

Oprescu, F., Campo, S., Lowe, J., Andsager, J., & Morcuende, J. A. (2013). Online information exchanges for parents of children with a rare health condition: Key findings from an online support community. *Journal of Medical Internet Research, 15*(1), e16.

Pearce, W. B. (1989). *Communication and the human condition.* Carbondale: Southern Illinois University.

Scott, A. M., Martin, S. C., Stone, A. M., & Brashers, D. E. (2011). Managing multiple goals in supportive interactions: Using a normative theoretical approach to explain social support as uncertainty management for organ transplant patients. *Health Communication, 26,* 393–403.

Watts, A. W. (1951). *The wisdom of insecurity: A message for an age of anxiety.* New York, NY: Vintage.

Williams, K. D. & Gerber, J. (2005). Ostracism: The making of the ignored and excluded mind. *Interaction Studies, 6,* 359–374.

9

Relational Framing Theory

Drawing Inferences About Relationships From Interpersonal Interactions

Rachel M. McLaren and
Denise Haunani Solomon

I magine yourself in a professional work environment, when your boss says, "I'm so glad you have been transferred to our office. You are always so friendly, and you're much better looking than our last analyst!" Or a friend comments, "I'd really like you to come with me to Matt's party. I don't want to go alone." Or imagine your parent says, "You remind me so much of your grandfather when you argue for your beliefs." Or an instructor returns your paper to you and tells you, "Although you did well on the paper, I know you have the potential to do much better." What do these messages mean? Are these comments friendly or unfriendly? Are you being coerced or admired? Situations such as these call for a response, but our reply depends on how we understand these messages. In this chapter, you'll learn about relational framing theory, which explains how we make sense of ambiguous messages about our relationships with others.

Intellectual Tradition of Relational Framing Theory

Relational framing theory (RFT) was developed by communication scholars Jim Dillard, Denise Solomon, and Jennifer Samp to describe how people organize interpersonal messages to support inferences about the relationship between communicators (Dillard, Solomon, & Samp, 1996). According to the theory, people make sense of relational messages by interpreting them as indicators of either dominance-submissiveness or affiliation-disaffiliation, and they evaluate how much people are engaged in the interaction to infer the intensity of the relational messages. *Dominance-submissiveness* refers to the degree to which one person controls, influences, or has status over the other. For example, when a parent directs a child to clean his room, the parent is relying upon status and authority to influence the child. *Affiliation-disaffiliation* captures the appreciation, esteem, or solidarity one person has for the other. As an example, consider how a love letter conveys affection and positive regard to the recipient. *Involvement* captures the extent to which people are absorbed in the interaction. If the parent uses a loud voice and pronounced nonverbal cues, he or she expresses more dominance than if directions were conveyed quietly and calmly, and a letter with intense, emotional words and lots of exclamation points suggests more passion than a brief, descriptive note. Although these three concepts are not new, RFT positions them in an innovative way. In particular, the theory views dominance-submissiveness and affiliation-disaffiliation as functional frames that help people process social messages, resolve ambiguities, make sense of involvement cues, and draw relational inferences (Dillard & Solomon, 2005).

In advancing RFT, Dillard and colleagues (1996) drew on the long history of research on relational communication (e.g., Bateson, 1935, 1958; Kemper, 1973). One important contribution to this body of literature was Burgoon and Hale's (1984) proposal that relational messages address as many as 12 facets of interpersonal associations. While recognizing the utility of the nuances revealed in Burgoon and Hale's perspective, Dillard and his colleagues (Dillard et al., 1996; Dillard, Solomon, & Palmer, 1999) argued that the domain of relational messages could be organized into the three primary dimensions of dominance-submissiveness, affiliation-disaffiliation, and involvement.

RFT emerged from the post-positivist paradigm. It offers a framework that is both rationally deduced and informed by observable facts, and it theorizes about the causes of relational message processing at multiple levels. At the most precise level, RFT locates the immediate source of relational inferences in the contents of utterances, the goals of interactions, and features of the context. RFT also explains message processing in terms of the functions accomplished when people can efficiently resolve ambiguities. At yet another level, the theory recognizes that an ability to draw relational inferences is a human skill that is subject to both cognitive development and socialization. At the broadest level, RFT is rooted in assumptions about human evolution (see Chapter 4 in this volume), namely, our ancestors' abilities to decipher relational information that influences both survival and opportunities to reproduce. Thus, the theory links the dynamics of interaction to the evolution of the human species.

Main Goals and Features of Relational Framing Theory

RFT contains two sets of claims. The first set addresses the nature of relational judgments. In other words, what evaluations are made when people draw inferences about their relationships? The second set focuses on the processes that guide relational inferences. This part of the theory describes how characteristics of the interaction context and cognitive processes jointly contribute to relational judgments. Two of the three dimensions in RFT encompass the substance of relational messages—or, in other words, the topic of the judgments people make about interpersonal associations. Recall that *dominance-submissiveness* captures the degree of status, power, or control between people, and *affiliation-disaffiliation* involves the degree of positive regard, liking, or admiration between communicators. Beyond knowing the substance of interpersonal relationships, people make judgments about the intensity of their associations. The differences between positive regard and unmitigated devotion, authority and subjugation, and between mild dislike and outright hatred are nontrivial distinctions within interpersonal relationships. Thus, RFT positions *involvement* as a third dimension of relational judgments that addresses the degree of coordination, engagement, and immediacy present in the interaction (see also Andersen & Andersen, 2005; Cegala, Savage, Brunner, & Conrad, 1982).

Consider interactions you might observe between two couples at a restaurant. As you glance at one pair, you see that they are maintaining direct eye contact, gesturing actively, and leaning forward. The other couple, in contrast, is talking quietly as they look at their plates. If you learned that both couples were celebrating a wedding anniversary, which pair would you conclude has the more loving relationship? If you learned that the dyads were involved in business meetings, which pair would you think was trying harder to exert control? Odds are you would choose the same couple to answer both questions. In other words, partners that are more involved and active communicate both more liking for each other and more effort to influence each other. In this way, involvement is a modifier of the two substantive dimensions and does not have its own experiential component (Dillard et al., 1996). The theory implies that involvement can polarize judgments toward either extreme of the substantive dimensions (e.g., intense dislike, passionate love, obsequious submission, or total domination).

The concept of relational frames integrates the three dimensions of relational messages. *Relational frames* are mental structures that consist of organized knowledge about social relationships. They are similar to relationship schemas or mental models of relationships (Baldwin, 1995; Planalp, 1985) in that they contain assumptions about interpersonal associations derived from prior experience. RFT suggests that people use knowledge and assumptions about relationships to connect information that they get from dominance-submissiveness, affiliation-disaffiliation, and involvement cues.

To understand how frames work, consider the classic image depicted in Figure 9.1. If you've seen this image before, you know that it is possible to see either a young woman with a feather in her hat or an older woman wearing a scarf. By instructing yourself to focus on one or the other, you can detect the image you're looking for, but you cannot see both images at once. The way you frame the picture mentally determines what you perceive and how you organize the components of the drawing.

According to RFT, dominance-submissiveness and affiliation-disaffiliation constitute frames that guide the interpretation of interaction cues. As in our example, these mental structures direct what you pay attention to, how you organize information, and what you perceive. Because involvement can convey either dominance or affiliation, it is especially influenced by the relational frame through which it is viewed. Thus, relational frames both focus attention on particular cues and guide the meanings that people attach to more ambiguous messages.

THE PROCESS OF RELATIONAL JUDGMENTS

By taking a position with regard to the number and substance of relational judgments, RFT mirrors previous efforts to clarify how people organize their

Figure 9.1   The Old Woman and the Young Girl

social experiences (e.g., Burgoon & Hale, 1984; Kemper, 1973). RFT extends this tradition, however, by specifying the interface among cognitive structures, interaction cues, and relational judgments. Although other theoretical perspectives speak to the information processing patterns set in motion by violated expectations (Burgoon, 1983) or excessive or insufficient arousal (Cappella & Greene, 1982), RFT explains how relational inferences arise from both ordinary and extraordinary interactions.

The process of relational framing commences with the activation of the dominance-submissiveness or affiliation-disaffiliation frame. RFT proposes five overarching factors or sources of relational information that can activate relational frames, ranging from specific to abstract and from temporally brief to long-lasting (see Solomon, Dillard, & Anderson, 2002; Solomon, 2006): features of an utterance, the episodic goal, the relational context, personal qualities, and societal or cultural norms. At the most specific level, the *features of utterances* themselves can clarify whether interactions are about social control ("If you don't follow my rules, I'll demote you") or social closeness ("I'm so glad that I have a friend like you at work"). At a higher level of abstraction, *the episodic goal,* or function of the social interaction, can focus attention on issues of power (e.g., a performance review) or liking (e.g., a birthday greeting). If partners have a *relational context* or history of interactions that focus on dominance or affiliation, that pattern would direct attention within a particular exchange. Likewise, people might have *personal qualities* or dispositional tendencies to focus on dominance-submissiveness or affiliation-disaffiliation when they interact with others. At the most general level, *societal or cultural norms* direct people's attention to the dominance-submissiveness or affiliation-disaffiliation features of an interaction.

The information provided by the interaction, present in the context, and brought to bear by the participants, combines to activate the dominance-submissiveness or affiliation-disaffiliation frames. An important assumption of RFT is that frames are often in competition (Dillard et al., 1996). In other words, the frames tend to displace each other as lenses for making sense of interaction. To develop this point, Dillard and colleagues argued that the simultaneous operation of both frames would undermine efficient processing. This is not to say that it is impossible for both frames to be activated, but that doing so consumes cognitive capacity and is subjectively uncomfortable. Thus, the cognitive system tilts toward one frame or the other. This proposition is the *differential-salience hypothesis.*

For example, consider what happens when you read hastily scrawled text. When you encounter a word you cannot decipher, you look to surrounding cues to guess what it is. Although you might be able to narrow down the options, you'll have trouble moving on in the text until you make a decision about what the word means. Moreover, maintaining alternative interpretations of the word will compromise your understanding of the text that follows. Because confusion about the meaning of ambiguous involvement cues undermines social functioning, human evolution may have promoted cognitive systems that facilitate sense-making. In other words, the activation of the dominance-submissiveness frame suppresses the affiliation-disaffiliation frame (and vice versa) to facilitate efficient and fluid processing of otherwise ambiguous involvement cues.

The forces that influence frame activation, coupled with the tendency toward frame displacement, result in the primary activation of the dominance-submissiveness frame or the affiliation-disaffiliation frame. In turn, the salient relational frame directs attention to features of the interaction that inform relational judgments. When the content of interaction cues aligns with the activated relational frame, relational inferences are straightforward. In the case of more ambiguous involvement cues, the salient relational frame conveys meaning to the messages. Those involvement cues also inform the extremity of the relational judgment, such that involvement can lead to perceptions of either greater dominance or greater affiliation, depending on the salient relational frame. This proposition is the *general-intensifier hypothesis*.

How Communication Is Conceptualized in Relational Framing Theory

As the previous description of RFT reveals, the theory relies on two important assumptions about the nature of communication. First, RFT takes to heart the long-standing axiom that communication has both content and relational components (Watzlawick, Bavelas, & Jackson, 1967). "Content messages" encompass the semantic or denotative meaning of the symbols exchanged; "relational messages" address assumptions about or preferences for the relationship that are implied by symbolic actions. For example, the ways in which your mom might ask you to do chores ("Honey, could you please make your bed?" "Make your bed." "I said make your bed now or else you're grounded!") all convey the content of her goal, but the particular form of her request speaks volumes about how she sees your relationship. RFT centralizes the distinction between content and relational messages, and seeks to explain how people decipher the oftentimes ambiguous relationship component of messages. Specifically, the theory positions both particular utterances and the communicative context as factors that have relational information embedded in them. In that way, communication is a source of relational information that activates the salience or relevance of one relational frame over the other.

Second, RFT highlights the polysemic nature of communication—in other words, the way in which communication supports multiple interpretations and multiple meanings. Of course, RFT is not the first perspective to recognize that meaning is subjective, but RFT suggests that the same cues can support very different inferences, depending on whether they are viewed through a dominance-submissiveness frame or an affiliation-disaffiliation frame. Whether a loud voice is passionate or patronizing, whether mutual eye contact is intimate or intimidating, and whether a hand on a shoulder is comforting or controlling all depend on message interpretations. Consequently, RFT highlights the polysemic nature of communication and elucidates the process by which people reach a variety of conclusions from the same cues.

Research and Practical Applications of Relational Framing Theory

RFT can help us to understand interpersonal communication on many levels, all of which reveal different nuances of the theory. Much of the extant research explores how different sources of relational information activate frame salience. For example, McLaren, Dillard, Tusing, and Solomon (in press) examined two sources of relational information, the form of utterances and the relational context, as sources of relational information. They found that the directness of request messages affected the salience of the dominance-submissiveness frame. Furthermore, requests made in the context of competitive friendships were more relevant to the dominance-submissiveness frame, whereas requests made in the context of cooperative friendships were more salient to the affiliation-disaffiliation frame. In terms of episodic goals, Dillard and colleagues (1996) observed that people rated the dominance-submissiveness frame as more relevant to compliance goals and the affiliation-disaffiliation frame as more relevant to affinity goals. This pattern was replicated in a study that included both same-sex and cross-sex dyads (Solomon et al., 2002).

Tests of the theory have also shown how personal characteristics can influence the framing process. For example, Solomon and colleagues (2002) demonstrated that a dispositional tendency to be anxious about relationships was positively associated with the relevance of both frames as people evaluated strategic messages from peers. Although speculative, Solomon and colleagues reasoned that paying attention to both relational dimensions at the same time could compromise a person's ability to draw relational inferences and might, in turn, perpetuate relational anxiety. Relatedly, Knobloch and Solomon (2005) found that relational uncertainty was positively associated with perceptions of the difficulty of an interaction, and that it corresponded with more conservative (i.e., less extreme) relational inferences. An RFT perspective on these findings suggests that relational uncertainty hinders a person's ability to frame an interaction and, in turn, to draw clear relational inferences.

RFT has been applied to a number of socially significant issues, such as interpretations of sexual advances. Because social-sexual communication is often ambiguous, it can lead to judgments of either liking or sexual harassment. For instance, Solomon (2006) examined how structural power differences influenced framing of social-sexual messages in the workplace. In previous research, Solomon and Williams (1997a, 1997b) found that perceptions of sexual harassment are affected by the formality of the context, the sex of the perceiver, the sex of the message initiator, and the explicitness of the message. By applying an RFT perspective, Solomon demonstrated that the effects of situational, personal, and message features are mediated by perceptions of dominance or affiliation.

Furthermore, Lannutti and Monahan (2002) examined the effect of alcohol on people's interpretations of scenarios involving sexual escalation and coercion. Their results indicated that when people are intoxicated, they perceive affiliation-disaffiliation as the relational frame most relevant to consensual sexual episodes, and they tend to see dominance-submissiveness as more relevant to situations that involve both consensual and coercive activities. Perceptions of involvement, likewise, were correlated with judgments of affiliation in the consensual scenarios. However, involvement contributed to evaluations of both affiliation and dominance in the mixed cue interactions, especially when respondents in the study were intoxicated. Although these results are not wholly in line with RFT predictions, they shed light on relational information processing within sexual episodes.

In addition to sexual advances, RFT has also been applied to understand hurt feelings, which occur frequently in close relationships. For example, McLaren, Solomon, and Priem (2012) found that messages in dating relationships were hurtful to the extent that people framed them as dominant and disaffiliative. Likewise, McLaren and Pederson (2014) examined conversations about hurtful messages between parents and adolescents and found that dyadic discrepancies in relational framing can hinder family members' abilities to understand one another. In other words, to the extent that people framed their conversations in different ways, they had a tendency to perceive less joint understanding following the conversation.

This review of how RFT has been used to understand different aspects of interpersonal communication highlights two more central issues that the theory addresses. First, RFT provides a conceptual tool for representing interpersonal communication as a process. Although communication scholarship privileges the exchange of messages and the co-construction of meaning as an important window on human behavior, few theoretical frameworks clarify how social norms, individual differences, and contextual features are woven together to influence message processing. Thus, RFT provides a framework for embracing interpersonal communication as a dynamic and context-embedded social phenomenon.

In addition, the studies previously reviewed illustrate the particular applicability of RFT to ambiguous relational messages. When confronted with an explicit message—perhaps an expression of devotion or a threatening influence message—a person may be challenged to form a response to that message. But when the message itself is ambiguous, as in the case with hurtful messages or sexual advances, this challenge is two-fold. Not only must recipients form a response to the message, but they must first decipher its relational implications. Whether a person frames a potentially hurtful message as supportive or hostile will affect their feelings and response to that message. Similarly, framing a romantic advance in the workplace as dominating could lead to perceptions of sexual harassment. In contexts such as ongoing relationships, families, the workplace, and first dates, misinterpreting cues and responding inappropriately can have serious consequences. Although the framing processes outlined in the theory are generally applicable to any interpersonal communication encounter, RFT is especially useful for understanding ambiguous and difficult communication experiences.

Evaluations of Relational Framing Theory

As RFT has developed, both strengths and limitations of the theory and corresponding research have emerged. Perhaps the main strength of the theory is its heuristic value. RFT focuses on basic interpersonal communication processes that can shed light on a variety of interaction situations. Moreover, because the theory highlights the potential for confusing distinct relational judgments, it may be especially useful for understanding socially meaningful communication problems such as sexual harassment or hurtful messages. RFT also provides a framework that integrates cultural, personal, relational, and episodic forces that affect interpersonal communication. Thus, this perspective helps us advance specific hypotheses about the effects of the interaction context on relational information processing within a variety of social interactions.

Despite these strengths, the primary limitation of RFT is the lack of clarity about the extent to which frame displacement occurs and under what conditions. Whereas the theory states that the dominance-submissiveness and affiliation-disaffiliation frames are differentially salient, empirical research suggests only a tendency toward frame displacement. These observed patterns could reflect both theoretical and methodological ambiguities. At the conceptual level, the theory is unclear about how quickly a relevant frame can be activated and then replaced by the alternative frame. In fact, the factors that influence frame activation that are specified within the theory suggest that frames can fluctuate based on utterances, episodes, relationship contexts, interaction participants, or social contexts. Thus, the theory leaves ample room for ambiguity about the duration of an activated relational frame.

In addition, conceptual ambiguity about the activation and deactivation of relational frames is compounded by the reliance on imprecise measures of frame activation in research to date. In particular, self-reports of frame relevance are, at best, indirect indicators of underlying cognitive processes. Moreover, because people can infer relational judgments from other evaluations they have made (Dillard, Palmer, & Kinney, 1995), they may perceive both frames as relevant to their perceptions of an interaction. At present, then, tests of RFT are limited by the methods used to assess frame activation.

The limitations noted thus far suggest a potentially more troublesome flaw in the theory. Namely, we wonder whether RFT is sufficiently falsifiable—in other words, are there any experiences or outcomes that RFT couldn't explain after the fact (for further discussion of falsifiability, see Chaffee & Berger, 1987). As long as the details about frame activation and displacement are unspecified, any empirical data could be argued to fit the theory. Likewise, a lack of clarity about how the forces that affect frame activation work in concert invites alternative explanations for empirical observations that are all theoretically viable. Although these loopholes are not fatal flaws for a theory at this stage in its development, the falsifiability of RFT relies on the resolution of these ambiguities in the future.

As a final criticism, research on RFT is limited by the predominant use of hypothetical scenarios to operationalize interpersonal interaction (but see Dillard et al., 1999; McLaren et al., 2012). On the one hand, constructing scenarios that describe specific and consistent interaction goals has allowed researchers to examine the role of involvement in situations that are clearly about issues of dominance or affiliation. On the other hand, those scenarios fail to capture the dynamics and complexities people confront when they must make sense of real-time interactions. Thus, support for the theory remains tentative until its claims can be evaluated in more ecologically valid research designs.

Continuing the Conversation

RFT's strengths and limitations point to directions for improving and expanding the theory. First, RFT would benefit from empirical tests that use diverse research designs and tools. For example, response time measures that index cognitive processes could provide more precise tests of frame activation, frame duration, and frame displacement. Likewise, investigations of more real-time interactions would enhance the external validity of RFT research. Relatedly, research on the theory needs to expand beyond its current focus on verbal messages to consider how people process nonverbal cues. Because nonverbal indicators of involvement (e.g., eye contact, animated gestures) often convey especially ambiguous relational information, the effects of relational frames on interpretations of nonverbal messages may be particularly pronounced.

Another avenue for future research is suggested by evidence that the degree of frame displacement can vary. What are the conditions that make it more or less easy for people to discern the relevance of dominance-submissiveness and affiliation-disaffiliation? Prior research implies that anxiety about relationships (Solomon et al., 2002), intoxication (Lannutti & Monahan, 2002), and relational uncertainty (Knobloch & Solomon, 2005) might make it difficult for people to privilege one frame over the other. And what are the consequences of paying attention to both relational frames simultaneously? RFT was founded on the assumption that frame displacement allows people to quickly process ambiguous social information, and Solomon and colleagues speculated that people who are unable to commit to one or the other relational frame will have difficulty drawing relational inferences.

Still other directions for future research stem from the applicability of RFT to diverse social contexts. For example, we wonder how relational framing might influence how parents and children make sense of interactions about sensitive topics such as drug and alcohol use. Whereas conversations that are viewed through a dominance-submissiveness frame might invite psychological reactance, the same conversations viewed through an affiliative parent-child interaction might have a dramatically different effect. Furthermore, applying RFT to research on interpersonal conflict could help uncover the sources of conflict and differences in people's subjective understanding of relational messages. As McLaren and Pederson (2014) demonstrated, people's competing interpretations of hurtful messages can hinder understanding. By applying RFT to processes of relational deterioration and dissolution, scholars could highlight patterns in the ways that partners are framing relational messages. Perhaps the tendency to interpret interactions in pessimistic ways is a sign that the relationship is in distress.

In this chapter, we have examined RFT's account of the processes by which people draw relational inferences from interpersonal interaction. Because the theory is relatively young and the empirical base is limited, further research is needed to explore core assumptions and clarify conceptual ambiguities. At the same time, we are encouraged that the theory has heuristic value as a framework for making sense of communication—and miscommunication—within a variety of socially significant communication contexts.

References

Andersen, P. A., & Andersen, J. F. (2005). Measurements of perceived nonverbal immediacy. In V. Manusov (Ed.), *The sourcebook of nonverbal measures: Going beyond words* (pp. 113–126). Mahwah, NJ: Erlbaum.

Baldwin, M. W. (1995). Relational schemas and cognition in close relationships. *Journal of Social and Personal Relationships, 12,* 547–552.

Bateson, G. (1935). Culture and contact with schismogenesis. *Man, 35,* 178–183.

Bateson, G. (1958). *Naven* (2nd ed.). Stanford, CA: Stanford University Press.

Burgoon, J. K. (1983). Nonverbal violations of expectations. In J. M. Wiemann & R. P. Harrison (Eds.), *Nonverbal interaction* (pp. 77–111). Beverly Hills, CA: Sage.

Burgoon, J. K., & Hale, J. L. (1984). The fundamental topoi of relational communication. *Communication Monographs, 51,* 193–214.

Cappella, J. N., & Greene, J. O. (1982). A discrepancy-arousal explanation of mutual influence in expressive behavior for adult and infant-adult interaction. *Communication Monographs, 49,* 89–114.

Cegala, D. J., Savage, G. T., Brunner, C. C., & Conrad, A. B. (1982). An elaboration of the meaning of interaction involvement: Toward the development of a theoretical concept. *Communication Monographs, 49,* 229–248.

Chaffee, S. H., & Berger, C. R. (1987). What communication scientists do. In C. R. Berger & S. H. Chaffee (Eds.), *Handbook of communication science* (pp. 99–122). Newbury Park, CA: Sage.

Dillard, J. P., Palmer, M. T., & Kinney, T. (1995). Relational judgments in an influence context. *Human Communication Research, 21,* 331–353.

Dillard, J. P., & Solomon, D. H. (2005). Measuring the relevance of relational frames: A relational framing theory perspective. In V. Manusov (Ed.), *The sourcebook of nonverbal measures: Going beyond words* (pp. 325–334). Mahwah, NJ: Erlbaum.

Dillard, J. P., Solomon, D. H., & Palmer, M. T. (1999). Structuring the concept of relational communication. *Communication Monographs, 66,* 49–65.

Dillard, J. P., Solomon, D. H., & Samp, J. A. (1996). Framing social reality: The relevance of relational judgments. *Communication Research, 23,* 703–723.

Kemper, T. D. (1973). The fundamental dimensions of social relationship: A theoretical statement. *Acta Sociologica, 16,* 41–58.

Knobloch, L. K., & Solomon, D. H. (2005). Relational uncertainty and relational information processing: Questions without answers? *Communication Research, 32,* 349–388.

Lannutti, P. J., & Monahan, J. L. (2002). When the frame paints the picture: Alcohol consumption, relational framing, and sexual communication. *Communication Research, 29,* 390–421.

McLaren, R. M., Dillard, J. P., Tusing, K. J., & Solomon, D. H. (in press). Relational framing theory: Utterance form and relational context as antecedents of frame salience. *Communication Quarterly.*

McLaren, R. M., & Pederson, J. R. (2014). Relational communication and understanding in conversations about hurtful events between parents and adolescents. *Journal of Communication.* Advance online publication. doi:10.1111/jcom.12072

McLaren, R. M., Solomon, D. H., & Priem, J. S. (2012). The effect of relationship characteristics on reactions to hurtful messages from romantic partners. *Journal of Communication, 62,* 950–971.

Planalp, S. (1985). Relational schemata: A test of alternative forms of relational knowledge as guides to communication. *Human Communication Research, 1,* 222–239.

Solomon, D. H. (2006). A relational framing perspective on perceptions of social-sexual communication at work. In B. A. LePoire & R. M. Dailey (Eds.), *Applied research in interpersonal communication: Family communication, health communication, and communicating across social boundaries* (pp. 271–298). New York, NY: Peter Lang.

Solomon, D. H., Dillard, J. P., & Anderson, J. W. (2002). Episode type, attachment orientation, and frame salience: Evidence for a theory of relational framing. *Human Communication Research, 28,* 136–152.

Solomon, D. H., & Williams, M. L. (1997a). Perceptions of social-sexual communication at work as sexually harassing. *Management Communication Quarterly, 11,* 147–184.

Solomon, D. H., & Williams, M. L. (1997b). Perceptions of social-sexual communication at work: The effects of message, situation, and observer characteristics on judgments of sexual harassment. *Journal of Applied Communication Research, 25,* 196–216.

Watzlawick, P., Bavelas, J. B., & Jackson, D. D. (1967). *Pragmatics of human communication: A study of interactional patterns, pathologies, and paradoxes.* New York, NY: W. W. Norton & Co.

10

Supportive Communication Theories

Dual-Process Theory of Supportive Message Outcomes and Advice Response Theory

Graham D. Bodie and Erina L. MacGeorge

S uppose your best friend comes to you with the following problem:

> Okay so, I had an exam two days ago. I don't think I did as well as I would have liked. The reason I didn't do as well was, well, I waited until the weekend to study for it, and I guess by the end of those two days, I guess I didn't feel like I was ready for it.

What do you say? Should you change the subject, analyze the problem, offer advice, try to lift your friend's spirits, or enact some combination of these goals? Once you select a goal, what should you say to accomplish it? These are not trivial choices. Your response could help your friend feel better, think differently about the situation, and successfully cope with the problem, but it could also fail to help; you could even add to his or her distress!

These issues are the focus of scholars interested in *supportive communication*—"verbal and nonverbal behavior produced with the intention of providing assistance to others perceived as needing that aid" (MacGeorge, Feng, & Burleson, 2011, p. 317). Importantly, this work shows that (a) there are better and worse ways to assist others in need of aid and (b) when support recipients receive high-quality support, they experience a wealth of positive benefits, including greater well-being and physical health. This chapter focuses on two theories that emphasize how individuals interpret and evaluate (i.e., process) supportive communication: the dual-process theory of supportive message outcomes and advice response theory. These theories help to explain how your friend might think about and respond to what you say and do when trying to make her feel better. Both theories suggest that features of the message, its source, the recipient, and the situational context influence how people think about the supportive messages they receive, and consequently affect the outcomes of supportive interactions and the relationships within which these interactions take place. By solving a bit of the mystery of how and why supportive messages succeed or fail, these theories will provide you with a better understanding of how your responses to others in need are likely to be interpreted and evaluated.

The Dual-Process Theory of Supportive Message Outcomes

INTELLECTUAL TRADITION

The dual-process theory of supportive message outcomes is a social cognitive theory rooted in the larger approach to human communication known as constructivism. It shares with constructivism a focus on explaining "individual differences in the ability to communicate skillfully" (Burleson, 2007, p. 108) by concentrating on the "causes, origins, and outcomes" of message processing in the domain of supportive communication (Burleson & Rack, 2008, p. 52). The theory's name comes from the larger dual-process framework developed in the field of psychology. This framework includes several "dual process models" (Moskowitz, Skurnik, & Galinsky, 1999) which posit, in line with constructivism, that "people's actions (including their responses to messages) are a function of the ways in which they interpret or make sense of events" (Burleson, 2010, p. 166). As such, the theory is most aptly classified as scientific in nature with its focus on explanation, prediction, and control, although it shares commitments grounded in strands of interpretive theory as well.

Communication scholars are probably most familiar with dual-process approaches to human information processing in the context of persuasion. These approaches were formally introduced in the early 1980s in an effort to resolve several problems in the attitude change literature. In particular, the dual-process framework offered testable explanations for such puzzling phenomena as the varied (and even contradictory) effects of message, source, receiver, and contextual factors on attitude change; the variable strength and persistence of the attitude change achieved through persuasion; and the variable extent to which attitude change predicted behavioral change. The dual-process theory of supportive message outcomes was born out of similar concerns. Although many features of comforting messages have predictable effects on outcomes (MacGeorge et al., 2011), these effects still vary with the message source, recipient, and situation. This fact requires theoretical explanation.

MAIN GOALS AND FEATURES

When you and your friend sit down to talk over her exam experience, what is it about that interaction that influences how she thinks and feels? Intuitively, you might answer, "What I say," and you would be right. In particular, recipients experience statements by helpers that provide legitimacy for feelings (and sometimes actions) as quite helpful, especially when helpers embed such statements in highly person-centered (HPC) messages that also encourage the articulation, elaboration, and exploration of those feelings. Not surprisingly, low person-centered (LPC) comforting messages, which explicitly deny or criticize feeling states, are typically viewed as unhelpful and can even exacerbate stress reactivity (Bodie, 2012). The effects of message features like person centeredness, however, vary; sometimes these messages have a larger impact, and sometimes they have a smaller impact on outcomes. The goal of the dual-process theory is to explain this variability. In particular, it suggests that the impact of messages varies as a function of how those messages are processed, and it provides a detailed analysis of the processing modes that can be applied to supportive messages, the determinants of consequences that follow from particular processing modes, and the varied processes through which changes in affect may occur. Figure 10.1 provides a graphic summary of the essential components of the theory.

Processing modes. *Elaboration* refers to the extent to which an individual thinks with respect to message content. People process supportive messages on an elaboration continuum that ranges from the highly systematic and thoughtful processing of messages to a very low level of thought. Thus, when processing messages systematically, recipients carefully reflect on the content of the message and the information contained within it, thoughtfully consider this information in relation to prior ideas, and give close attention to the full content of a message. In contrast, when engaged in a low level of elaboration, recipients of supportive messages pay comparatively little attention to the content of the message. Instead, environmental cues, like qualities of the message source (e.g., closeness), largely influence communication outcomes.

Determinants of processing mode. Systematic processing of messages is most likely to occur (and occurs most extensively) when recipients are motivated to attend to a message and possess the ability to consider its content thoughtfully. Qualities of both the individual and the situation influence the motivation and ability to carefully consider message content. In the example that opened this chapter, your friend may be highly motivated to attend to your supportive attempt due to distress about the exam result. When faced with a situation eliciting negative affect, people are motivated by the desire to feel better. As negative affect states become more severe, so should the desire

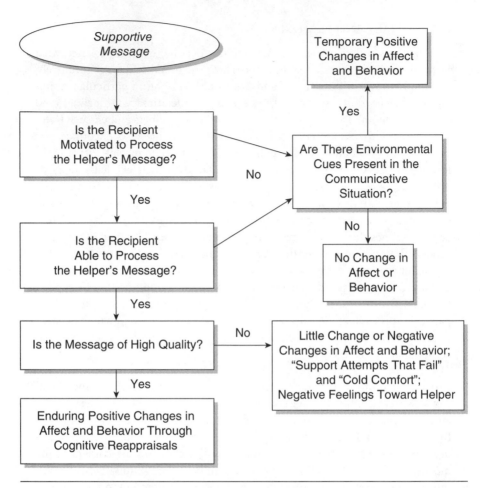

Figure 10.1 A Dual-Process Model for the Processing and Outcomes of Supportive Messages

to do something about it, motivating careful attention to comforting messages. Of course, negative affect could reach a point where it begins to obstruct your friend's ability to process your supportive attempts. Indeed, emotional distress seems to have a dual function, motivating increased processing of supportive messages at moderate levels of distress, but diminishing the ability to process these messages at high levels of distress (Bodie, Burleson, Holmstrom, et al., 2011).

When either the motivation or ability to process supportive messages is low, responses to supportive behavior are likely to be determined by environmental cues that activate low-elaboration processes. For example, relationship status has the potential (under low motivation and/or ability conditions) to trigger a decisional heuristic for processing messages in support situations (e.g., "close friends provide helpful support in times of need") (Holmstrom et al., in press). In other words, your friend may feel better simply because you were there in a time of need; what you say may play a lesser role in the comforting process.

Consequences of processing mode. Importantly, both low and high elaboration of supportive messages can produce desirable outcomes, especially in the short term; yet, their duration and stability differ. When an environmental cue stimulates a cognitive heuristic (e.g., the presence of your friend triggers the rule "support from friends is helpful"), message recipients can feel better as a consequence, regardless of what was actually said. However, the changes in affect and coping generated by such heuristics (and other low-elaboration mechanisms of affect change such as distraction) are likely to be short-lived. In contrast, when recipients extensively process supportive messages, the content of these messages will have a considerable and lasting effect on outcomes.

Operative mechanisms. Supportive communication is posited to "work" (i.e., have its effects) through a variety of mechanisms, some of which involve extensive thinking and some of which take little thought. For instance, cognitive reappraisal has been identified as a high thinking affect change mechanism; reappraisal involves changing judgments about the meaning and personal significance of events and most likely occurs when recipients elaborately process high-quality supportive messages (Bodie, 2013). Other mechanisms of affect change are more "intuitive, automatic, and unconscious" (Lazarus, 2001, p. 51) and do not require much thought to operate. These mechanisms, which include heuristic thinking, distraction, and disengagement, are more likely to operate when individuals are not primed to think much about explicit message content.

HOW COMMUNICATION IS CONCEPTUALIZED

Because it derives from constructivism, the dual-process theory defines communication as "a process in which a person (the source) seeks to convey or make public some internal state to another (the recipient) through the use of signals and symbols (the message) in the effort to accomplish some pragmatic end (the goal)" (Burleson & Rack, 2008, p. 55). Communication is viewed as a goal-directed activity, and thus, message processing is directed by a set of goals that (whether consciously or unconsciously) direct how comforting messages affect outcomes. Finally, similar to theories in other functional domains of communication (e.g., message production), this theory positions message processing as a skill—something that develops over time, especially during a person's formative years, and something that can be trained.

RESEARCH AND PRACTICAL APPLICATIONS

The dual-process theory of supportive message outcomes applies the general logic of dual-process models to the processing and outcomes of varied forms of support, focusing mainly on everyday emotional support (Bodie, Burleson, Gill-Rosier et al., 2011) and grief management (Rack, Burleson, Bodie, Holmstrom, & Servaty, 2008). Most work to date has focused on testing key theoretical claims and establishing the theory as a viable framework for organizing prior findings that indicate variation in the effects of supportive messages. But the theory also provides an empirically sound basis for the practice of effective comforting: It indicates what types of support strategies are likely to be effective in different situations. For example, the theory suggests that simple, brief support messages may be just as effective (and perhaps, more effective) than longer, more complex messages if recipients are unlikely to think carefully about what is said. In fact, under conditions of minimal message processing, simply "being there" may be most effective (Bodie, 2012). Likewise, the theory indicates that when recipients are processing messages extensively, longer, more complex support messages are needed and simple, brief messages are likely to be ineffective. In general, helpers guided by the dual-process theory will take a recipient-centered and contextually sensitive approach to providing support.

EVALUATION OF THE DUAL-PROCESS THEORY

The dual-process theory of supportive message outcomes comprises the first comprehensive synthesis of research findings regarding moderators of the relationship between message features and outcomes. It also provides the first unified explanation for their effects. Application of this theory has enabled an explanation of why numerous demographic, personality, cognitive, and situational factors moderate the effects of supportive messages in the ways that they do. Thus, what was before a diverse and fragmented set of findings, mostly explained through a host of unconnected mechanisms, is now bolstered by a more parsimonious, integrated theory that enhances our understanding of why support strategies affect particular people as they do on particular occasions. In addition, the dual-process framework generates a rich set of predictions about other potential moderators of supportive message outcomes, and it provides justification for positing the underlying mechanisms driving the effects of supportive interactions. Finally, the theory has the potential to inform people as they assist their loved ones in coping with distressing events.

Of course, like all theories, it remains a work in progress. Importantly, the dual-process framework maintains that the same construct can serve different functions in different circumstances, typically through distinct mechanisms.

This feature of the framework is simultaneously one of its greatest strengths and weaknesses. As critics of other dual-process theories have noted, specifying in advance the particular ways in which constructs operate has been the proverbial thorn in the dual-process side. Presently, we are unable to specify whether certain factors that moderate the effects of supportive messages (e.g., recipient sex, recipient depression) do so by affecting processing ability, processing motivation, or both, though some headway on this issue is being made (Burleson et al., 2011). In addition, tests of the theory to date have focused on the analysis of individual messages, ultimately studying the operation of support outside of its interactive context. Clearly, the processing of support attempts within the messiness of conversation operates in some ways similar to processing of single-shot messages, although there are clear differences that should be theorized and tested (see Jones & Bodie, in press).

CONTINUING THE CONVERSATION

Perhaps the most notable critique of the theory is that it is new and thus has limited empirical backing. Future researchers need to pinpoint the precise role served by particular variables in particular sets of circumstances. Researchers could accomplish this task by designing studies that incorporate variables hypothesized to impact the ability and motivation to process support messages; they should also test proposed mediators (e.g., elaboration) through the use of advanced modeling techniques. Without careful tests of the theory, the promising dual-process framework will quickly devolve into a morass of non-falsifiable propositions. In addition, yet to be researched are the various short- and long-term consequences for processing supportive messages of various types.

In the next section, we turn from dual-process theory to advice response theory. Although both theories explain how recipients respond to supportive messages, the dual-process theory has been primarily focused on explaining the effects of comforting messages, whereas advice response theory is specifically concerned with *advice,* or recommendations about what to do, think, or feel in response to a problem.

Advice Response Theory

INTELLECTUAL TRADITION

Advice response theory (ART; MacGeorge, Guntzviller, Hanasono, & Feng, 2013) is a social cognitive theory that was developed to explain how advice outcomes are influenced by qualities of messages, advisors, situations, and recipients. ART's development over the past decade has been stimulated and facilitated by theory and research from several sources, including theories of facework and politeness, and the concept of "stock issues" from argumentation theory (MacGeorge, Feng, Butler, & Budarz, 2004). Recent articulations of ART have integrated insights from research in psychology utilizing the Judge-Advisor paradigm (Bonaccio & Dalal, 2006) and from dual-process models (described above). Like other scientific theories, ART is intended to describe, explain, and predict the processes by which advice recipients evaluate and respond to advice—and consequently to assist advice givers' efforts to "control" their messages in ways that promote positive outcomes.

MAIN GOALS AND FEATURES

Imagine that you try to support your friend who has failed an exam by giving some advice. You might suggest going to the professor's office hours, forming a study group for the next exam, or even dropping the class. How will your friend respond to your advice, and why? ART provides a framework for predicting how your friend is likely to respond, based on your friend's perceptions of (1) the features of the advice message itself, including content and style; (2) your characteristics as an advisor; (3) aspects of the problematic situation; and (4) your friend's traits or enduring characteristics. Beyond identifying key variables in each of these four categories, the theory specifies how they operate collectively and interactively to influence multiple outcomes of advice interactions.

In ART, message features are qualities of the advice message. The theory distinguishes between *content* features, or qualities of the action being advised in the message, and *stylistic* features, or how the message is phrased. According to ART, advice recipients evaluate message content for its *efficacy* (whether the action will work to resolve the problem), *feasibility* (capacity to accomplish the action), *limitations* (drawbacks of taking the advised action), and *confirmation* (whether the advised action is consistent with the recipient's intended plans). They also assess message style for its *politeness,* including the extent to which the advice conveys liking, connection (between advisor and recipient), and respect. To the extent that advice is perceived as more efficacious, feasible, confirming, polite, and not having limitations, the response to the advice will be more positive.

ART asserts that in addition to message features, advice recipients are attentive to characteristics of the advisor that have implications for the value of the advice. These include *expertise* with regard to the problem, *trustworthiness, likeability,* and *similarity* (to your friend). However, ART claims that advisor characteristics are typically weaker influences on advice outcomes than are message features and that advisor characteristics affect advice outcomes primarily by influencing evaluations of message features. In other words, as your friend considers your advice, she will be most influenced by the content and style of the advice message itself, and to a lesser extent by your qualities as an advisor. Further, your expertise, trustworthiness, and so forth will not directly determine how your friend responds to the advice, but instead influence the extent to which your friend sees the advice as efficacious, feasible, polite, and so forth, which will in turn determine how your friend responds. One way to describe this relationship is that message features "mediate" the influence of advisor characteristics on advice outcomes.

ART also predicts that message features and advisor characteristics will exhibit stronger or weaker effects, depending on which of several advice outcomes is being predicted. The theory identifies three related but distinctive outcomes for advice (MacGeorge et al., 2004): *implementation intention* (the intention to do the advised action), *facilitation of coping* (the perception that the advice is helpful in coping with the situation), and *message quality* (an evaluation of the message itself as supportive, effective, etc.). According to the theory, implementation intention is most strongly influenced by message content, because qualities of the advised action are logically relevant to deciding whether to perform it, whereas the politeness of the message and the characteristics of the advisor are less relevant to this decision. On the other hand, message politeness and advisor characteristics are argued to be stronger influences on facilitation of coping and perceived message quality than on implementation intention, because the politeness of the message and the characteristics of the advisor affect how the recipient feels about the advice and the problem situation.

Whereas ART describes message features as having direct effects, and advisor characteristics as having indirect effects, on the evaluation of advice, the theory indicates that situational factors and recipient traits play a different role in determining advice outcomes. Situational factors are aspects of the problematic situation as perceived by the advice recipient, and consequently vary from situation to situation, even if the advisor and recipient are the same. Two important situational factors identified by ART are *problem seriousness*, or the severity of the problem as perceived by the recipient, and *solution uncertainty*, defined as the recipient's level of certainty about how to resolve the problem. Recipient traits are qualities of the recipient that remain relatively constant across situations, including personality traits such as thinking style, abilities such as cognitive complexity, and demographic features such as culture and gender.

ART identifies both situational factors and recipient traits as moderators that alter how message features and advisor characteristics affect advice outcomes. Specifically, drawing from dual-process theories of message reception, ART proposes that certain situational features predispose advice recipients to pay greater or lesser attention to the details of advice message content, and consequently increase or decrease the influence of message content on advice outcomes. Thus, ART suggests that advice recipients with more serious problems will be motivated to pay more attention to the specific content of advice than recipients whose problems are less serious, such that greater problem seriousness results in a stronger influence of message content on advice outcomes. Similarly, the theory suggests that recipients' traits affect how much their responses to advice are driven by advisor characteristics versus message features. For example, people from collectivist cultures such as China tend to be more relationship oriented and rely more heavily on relational cues when communicating than people from individualistic cultures such as the United States. Consequently, ART predicts that advice outcomes for individuals from collectivistic cultures will be more strongly influenced by advisor characteristics than individuals from individualistic cultures (Feng & Feng, 2013).

CONCEPTUALIZATION OF COMMUNICATION IN ART

ART does not explicitly define communication. Because the theory focuses on advice recipients' evaluations, it could be applied to any behavior that someone perceives as advice. In this respect, the theory is arguably consistent with recipient-oriented definitions of communication in which behavior is communication to the extent that someone perceives it as meaningful. However, in research testing ART, and more generally in research on the evaluation of advice, advice is typically operationalized as behavior (predominantly verbal) produced by the advice-giver in response to the recipient's problem disclosure or decision-making dilemma. In this respect, ART implicitly adopts a narrower definition of communication, in which behavior is communication to the extent that it is interpreted as meaningful by a receiver, *and* produced to represent the intentions of a sender.

RESEARCH AND PRACTICAL APPLICATIONS OF ART

The development of ART as a theory has proceeded in tandem with research testing its claims (MacGeorge et al., 2013) and is now stimulating scholarship at an increasing rate. Currently, ART is informing analysis of more than 350 transcripts of supportive interactions between college student friends, a multicountry study of cultural similarities and differences in the meanings and consequences of advice funded by the National Science Foundation, and work examining sources, evaluation, and outcomes of relationship advice given to young adults. This scholarship will enhance the validity and extend the scope of the theory. The theory also has practical application for anyone who gives advice in personal or professional interactions. MacGeorge and colleagues began including "Advice for the Advice Giver" sections in early research articles that drew on preliminary versions of the theory (e.g., MacGeorge et al., 2004). One general insight from the theory is the value of carefully assessing the actions you advise before you advise them, with specific attention to the likely perspective of your advice recipient. For example, if your friend who has failed an exam cannot drop the class without jeopardizing financial aid, such advice from you is unlikely to be implemented—or appreciated. You can also improve your knowledge of the recipient's perspective by asking questions to elicit his or her thoughts and plans before giving your own recommendations. That way, you might find out that your friend hates studying in groups before you offer that as your best advice.

EVALUATION OF ART

ART has synthesized and extended prior theory and research into a comprehensive framework for understanding responses to advice messages, supported by work from multiple scholars who have implemented a range of empirical methods. It is relevant to explaining advice outcomes across relationships and contexts and provides practical guidance for advisors. However, like all theories, it has its limitations. One concern has to do with the accuracy of the theory's description of situational factors as moderating influences, specifically with the idea that greater problem seriousness heightens the influence of message features on advice outcomes. Although this contention based on dual-process theory has been robustly supported in one study (Feng & MacGeorge, 2010), it was not supported in a recent study that utilized a more naturalistic method (MacGeorge et al., 2013). The contradictory findings may indicate that the influence of problem seriousness varies depending on when the advice is evaluated—shortly after the interaction versus days or even weeks later. This theoretical issue will need to be addressed in subsequent studies, as will the role of other situational features. A broader issue for the theory is the need to address how interactional behavior and sequencing influence message evaluations. Recipients evaluate advice more positively when they solicit it and when the advice is preceded by other types of supportive behavior, such as emotional support (Feng, 2009); such findings need to be explained within the ART framework.

CONTINUING THE CONVERSATION

Incorporating recipients' perceptions of interaction into ART is consistent with the theory's broader future. MacGeorge and colleagues have launched work tracing relationships between the perspective and behavior of advisors (e.g., their goals for advice giving) and recipients' evaluations, outcomes, and behaviors (Guntzviller & MacGeorge, 2013). This work is intended to culminate in the development of advice exchange theory, in which the outcomes of advice are explained as a function of cognition and behavior from both parties.

This work is being complemented by efforts to test ART in specific contexts, including the evaluation of advice with regard to major health decisions (e.g., treatment for breast cancer) and the solicitation and evaluation of advice via social media.

Dual-process theory and advice response theory offer complementary explanations for the effectiveness (and ineffectiveness) of supportive communication. Although dual-process theory has focused primarily on comforting and ART on advice, both are social scientific theories with growing research support, and both are sources of guidance for support providers. We are excited by the potential of future work testing these theories and hope the noted limitations can spark creative thinking about how and why supportive communication has its effects.

References

Bodie, G. D. (2012). Task stressfulness moderates the effects of verbal person centeredness on cardiovascular reactivity: A dual-process account of the reactivity hypothesis. *Health Communication, 27,* 569–580.

Bodie, G. D. (2013). The role of thinking in the comforting process: An empirical test of a dual-process framework. *Communication Research, 40,* 533–558.

Bodie, G. D., Burleson, B. R., Gill-Rosier, J., McCullough, J. D., Holmstrom, A. J., Rack, J. J., . . . Mincy, J. R. (2011). Explaining the impact of attachment style on evaluations of supportive messages: A dual-process framework. *Communication Research, 38,* 228–247.

Bodie, G. D., Burleson, B. R., Holmstrom, A. J., Rack, J. J., McCullough, J. D., Hanasono, L., & Rosier, J. G. (2011). Effects of cognitive complexity and emotional upset on processing supportive messages: Two tests of a dual-process theory of supportive communication outcomes. *Human Communication Research, 37,* 350–376.

Bonaccio, S., & Dalal, R. S. (2006). Advice taking and decision-making: An integrative review of the literature. *Organizational Behavior and Human Decision Processes, 101,* 127–151.

Burleson, B. R. (2007). Constructivism: A general theory of communication skill. In B. B. Whaley & W. Samter (Eds.), *Explaining communication: Contemporary theories and exemplars* (pp. 105–128). Mahwah, NJ: Erlbaum.

Burleson, B. R. (2010). Explaining recipient responses to supportive messages: Development and tests of a dual-process theory. In S. W. Smith & S. R. Wilson (Eds.), *New directions in interpersonal communication* (pp. 159–179). Thousand Oaks, CA: Sage.

Burleson, B. R., Hanasono, L. K., Bodie, G. D., Holmstrom, A. J., Rack, J. J., Gill Rosier, J., & McCullough, J. D. (2011). Are gender differences in responses to supportive communication a matter of ability, motivation, or both?: Reading patterns of situational responses through the lens of a dual-process theory. *Communication Quarterly, 59,* 37–60.

Burleson, B. R., & Rack, J. J. (2008). Constructivism: Explaining individual differences in communication skill. In L. A. Baxter & D. O. Braithwaite (Eds.), *Engaging theories in interpersonal communication* (pp. 51–63). Thousand Oaks, CA: Sage.

Feng, B. (2009). Testing an integrated model of advice-giving in supportive interactions. *Human Communication Research, 35,* 115–129.

Feng, B., & Feng, H. (2013). Examining cultural similarities and differences in responses to advice: A comparison of American and Chinese college students. *Communication Research, 40,* 623–644.

Feng, B., & MacGeorge, E. L. (2010). The influences of message and source factors on advice outcomes. *Communication Research, 37,* 576–598.

Guntzviller, L. M., & MacGeorge, E. L. (2013). Modeling interactional influence in advice exchanges: Advice giver goals and recipient evaluations. *Communication Monographs, 80,* 83–100.

Holmstrom, A. J., Bodie, G. D., Burleson, B. R., McCullough, J. D., Rack, J. J., Hanasono, L. K., & Rosier, J. G. (in press). Testing a dual-process theory of supportive communication outcomes: How multiple factors influence outcomes in support situations. *Communication Research.*

Jones, S. M., & Bodie, G. D. (in press). Supportive communication. In C. R. Berger (Ed.), *De Gruyter Mouton handbooks of communication science* (vol. 6, Interpersonal Communication). Berlin: De Gruyter Mouton.

Lazarus, R. S. (2001). Relational meaning and discrete emotions. In K. R. Scherer, A. Schorr & T. Johnstone (Eds.), *Appraisal processes in emotion: Theory, methods, research* (pp. 37–67). Oxford: Oxford University Press.

MacGeorge, E. L., Feng, B., & Burleson, B. R. (2011). Supportive communication. In M. L. Knapp & J. A. Daly (Eds.), *The SAGE Handbook of interpersonal communication* (4th ed.) (pp. 317–354). Thousand Oaks, CA: Sage.

MacGeorge, E. L., Feng, B., Butler, G. L., & Budarz, S. K. (2004). Understanding advice in supportive interactions: Beyond the facework and message evaluation paradigm. *Human Communication Research, 30,* 42–70.

MacGeorge, E. L., Guntzviller, L. M., Hanasono, L. K., & Feng, B. (2013). Testing advice response theory in interactions with friends. *Communication Research.* Advance online publication.

Moskowitz, G. B., Skurnik, I., & Galinsky, A. D. (1999). The history of dual-process notions, and the future of preconscious control. In S. Chaiken & Y. Trope (Eds.), *Dual-process theories in social psychology* (pp. 12–36). New York, NY: Guilford.

Rack, J. J., Burleson, B. R., Bodie, G. D., Holmstrom, A. J., & Servaty, H. L. (2008). Bereaved adults' evaluations of grief management messages: Effects of message person centeredness, recipient individual differences, and contextual factors. *Death Studies, 32,* 399–427.

11

Theory of Motivated Information Management

Struggles With Uncertainty and Its Outcomes

Walid A. Afifi and Stephanie Robbins

The history of research on uncertainty and its management is very long, with a particular spike in activity in the past two decades. The theory of motivated information management (TMIM) was introduced in 2004 (Afifi & Weiner, 2004) as another effort to move our knowledge of uncertainty and its management forward. Since then, the theory has been revised once (Afifi & Morse, 2009) and tested numerous times. Soon after the theory's publication, Afifi, Morse, Dillow, and Weiner (2005)—those primarily responsible for the theory's development—gave a presentation at the National Communication Association conference entitled: "Caring for a Newborn in the Land of Theory: The Theory of Motivated Information Management." Now, nearly a decade later, we review and assess the theory in its adolescence, with important lessons now a part of its intellectual tradition and with considerable growth and change yet to go.

Intellectual Tradition of the TMIM

TMIM was born out of many conversations that Afifi had with friends and colleagues during and shortly after graduate school in the Department of Communication at the University of Arizona, where he was a student and an office mate of Dale Brashers. Brashers was developing uncertainty management theory (UMT) at the time (for review, see Brashers & Hogan, 2013; see also Chapter 8 in this volume), so conversations would sometimes veer formally or informally into questions of uncertainty and its management, especially as it related to individuals' management of illness-related uncertainty (the emphasis of UMT). Austin Babrow's thinking on uncertainty, as it was expressed through problematic integration theory (PIT; Babrow, 2001; see also Chapter 8 in this volume) and through personal conversations with him, also played an important role in shaping TMIM's foundations. Both enthusiasm and frustration emerged from those conversations: enthusiasm for a vision of uncertainty and related processes that was more nuanced than those proposed by uncertainty reduction theory (URT; Berger & Calabrese, 1975)—one of the first interpersonal communication theories and the dominant uncertainty paradigm for two decades—and frustration with UMT and PIT's relatively interpretivist orientation to the process. In other words, Afifi felt that a theory could be developed that both recognized the greater complexity of individuals' experiences with uncertainty and offered predictive specificity. The former would extend URT's thinking and the latter would move beyond the bounds within which UMT and PIT were comfortable.

The TMIM is post-positivist in its orientation (more specifically, out of the tradition of scientific realism, see Pavitt, 2001). In fact, a philosophical commitment to that orientation is what pushed Afifi to find factors that he thought could predict individuals' information management decisions. That search led to two distinct but related social cognitive approaches—subjective expected utility theory (Fischhoff, Goitein, & Shapira, 1981; for review, see Kirsch, 1999) and social cognitive theory (Bandura, 1986, 1997)—that ultimately served as the backbone of TMIM's predictive framework (for review of both approaches and their linkages, see Maddux, 1999). Given that Afifi's graduate advisor was Judee Burgoon, author of expectancy violations theory (Burgoon, 1978) and interaction adaptation theory (Burgoon, Stern, & Dillman, 1995; see also Chapter 16 in this volume), his attraction to the construct of expectations as motivators of the behavioral decisions we make to manage uncertainty should come as no surprise. Finally, TMIM's assumptions about human decision making generally follow those laid out by theories of bounded rationality (e.g., Kahneman, 2003; Simon, 1972). Specifically, TMIM assumes that individuals make decisions based on an assessment of costs, benefits, and feasibilities associated with a particular action, but acknowledges that those perceptions are impacted by emotions and other biasing factors that ultimately limit the degree to which choices are objectively "rational" or ideal.

Main Goals and Features of TMIM

Although the development of TMIM originally began to increase predictive precision in accounting for individuals' varied responses to uncertainty, the theory ultimately addressed two other limitations of the literature at the time: (a) a failure to adequately address the role of efficacy in the uncertainty and information management process; and (b) a failure to recognize the dyadic, transactional nature of the uncertainty management process within interpersonal interactions. In addition, Afifi and Weiner (2004) expressly noted the failure of past theories to restrict the range of contexts to which they applied, thereby limiting their ability to capture context-specific aspects of uncertainty management decisions. As such, the authors cautioned that TMIM is limited to understanding uncertainty management within *interpersonal* encounters and only applies to important issues that motivate uncertainty management action. TMIM's restriction to issues that are perceived as important to the individual in question is critical because it recognizes that only a small fraction of our experiences with uncertainty are sufficiently motivating to have us go through a cognitively laborious process of decision making. So, for example, uncertainty about a partner's attire plans is unlikely to be sufficiently important to initiate the process proposed in TMIM . . . unless it is for an event that has significant implications for personal or relational goals, which then may make it sufficiently important to initiate the proposed information management process.

TMIM envisions a three-phased process that repeats itself (see Figure 11.1). The first step is called the interpretation phase. This begins with the person noticing a difference between the amount of uncertainty he or she has and the amount that he or she wants. The difference is labeled *uncertainty discrepancy* and is what starts the process of uncertainty management.

Any difference between the uncertainty one has and the amount one wants (whether more than he or she has or less) is said to initiate efforts to manage that discrepancy. In that way, TMIM shares Babrow and Brashers's ideas (see Chapter 8) that people sometimes want *more* uncertainty than they have, but Afifi identifies the disjunction between haves and wants as the engine that starts the process (a notion that was adopted from Chaiken, Giner-Sorolla, & Chen, 1996). So, someone might have very high uncertainty, but be comfortable with that level. In that case, he or she has no discrepancy and TMIM would not apply. The next claim of the original theory is that the discrepancy causes anxiety. It is important to note that the theory does not argue that uncertainty causes anxiety, since both Babrow and Brashers show that it sometimes does not. Rather, Afifi and Weiner (2004) argued that it is the *difference* between wants and needs that is anxiety-producing. However, questions from students about the failure of TMIM to recognize emotional experiences of uncertainty other than anxiety (as noted, again, by both Babrow & Brashers, see Chapter 8, in this volume) led Afifi and Morse (2009) to offer a revised version of TMIM, this time proposing that uncertainty discrepancy generally produces anxiety but may sometimes instead be experienced as hope, anticipation, anger, or other emotions (see Figure 11.2). Either way, the emotional

INFORMATION SEEKER

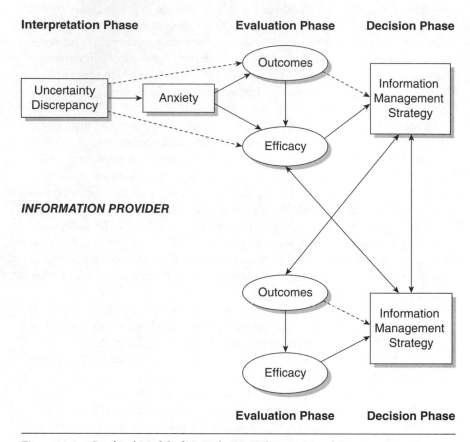

Figure 11.1 Graphical Model of TMIM's *Original* Propositional Structure

Note: The dashed paths reflect paths that are partly mediated by other variables with which the relevant variable has associations. The figure is intended as a visual simplification of the general theoretical framework.

appraisal of uncertainty discrepancy about an important issue pushes people into the next phase of the process, the evaluation phase. TMIM argues that the appraisal of uncertainty impacts assessments made in the evaluation phase.

The evaluation phase is where people think about (a) the possible outcomes of an information search (i.e., *outcome expectancy*), and (b) whether they have the ability to gather the information and cope with it (i.e., *efficacy*). Outcome expectancies involve perceptions about the positive and negative results of information seeking about the issue. In other words, this concept reflects all of the benefits and all of the costs that individuals think will occur if they were to seek information. For instance, suppose some parents are trying to decide

INFORMATION SEEKER

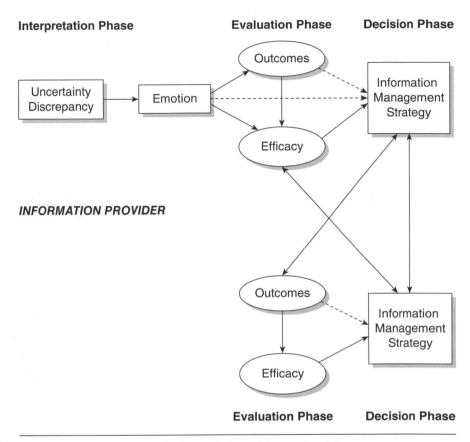

Figure 11.2   Graphical Model of TMIM's *Revised* Propositional Structure

Note: The dashed paths reflect paths that are partly mediated by other variables with which the relevant variable has associations. The figure is intended as a visual simplification of the general theoretical framework.

whether to ask their child about drug use. A benefit they expect may be that they will finally learn whether their child is using drugs, but they may also expect that the answer will be a bad one (that he or she is using drugs) and they perceive that as a significant cost. Another benefit may be that the parents learn more about the people with whom their child is hanging out, but a cost may be that it may produce conflict about those choices. Those are examples of expected outcomes of the conversation itself (i.e., what occurs as a result of information exchanged in the conversation), but other costs and benefits may come from the mere act of initiating a conversation, regardless of the conversational content. For instance, some parents may see the mere act of approaching their child about these issues (regardless of what they learn during the conversation) as benefiting the parent-child relationship, while other parents may see such an act as an intrusion on the child's privacy or as an indication that the child has shown disrespect by not initiating the conversation him- or herself. In another context, the cost of meeting with the boss about your performance may include negative gossip from other coworkers about your visit, while a reward may include credits from your boss for taking initiative to gain feedback—again, regardless of the actual content of the conversation. TMIM argues that people consider all sorts of costs and rewards, both about the content of the conversation (what they expect to be revealed) and about the process of information seeking itself.

Once the costs and benefits are considered, Afifi and Weiner (2004) proposed that people then decide whether they have the ability to both gather the information and cope with it. This process is still part of the evaluation phase and is what scholars call "efficacy" assessments. Importantly, the theory predicts that the more negative the expectations about the outcome of the information search, the less able the person will feel to successfully seek that information (i.e., the less efficacious he or she will be). TMIM discusses three types of efficacy: communication efficacy, target efficacy, and coping efficacy. *Communication efficacy* involves a determination by the person about whether he or she has the skill to seek information about the issue at hand. For example, some people avoid seeking information from their boss about an issue because they know that they freeze in those situations (i.e., they don't have the skill to talk to their boss about those things). *Target efficacy* is an assessment about whether the target of the information search (the person you're considering going to for the information) actually has the information and would be willing to share it. So, parents might not ask their child about a grade in a course because they think that he or she either doesn't have the information yet, or wouldn't be honest about it even if he or she did. Finally, *coping efficacy* reflects a determination about whether one could emotionally, relationally, or financially deal with what he or she expects to learn from the search for information. For instance, people sometimes avoid asking their partner if they are cheating because they don't feel that they have the emotional resources or friendship support to psychologically cope with such a discovery.

TMIM argues that all three of these assessments go into the strategy that individuals ultimately use to manage their uncertainty discrepancy, labeled the decision phase (see Figure 11.2). The theory predicts that people are likely to seek information to the extent that they expect positive outcomes and have high levels of efficacy, and are likely to avoid it to the extent that outcome expectancies are negative and efficacies are low.

In addition to a three-phase process to describe how potential information seekers make information-related decisions, one of the important features of

TMIM is an explicit recognition of the information *provider* in the uncertainty management process. The theory argues that the provider goes through a similar process, though limited to the evaluation and decision phases. Specifically, once asked a question by the information seeker, the provider makes a judgment about whether he or she has the skills to respond to the information request (communication efficacy), has the ability to cope with the result that comes from providing the information sought (coping efficacy), and believes that the information seeker is able and willing to manage the information given (target efficacy). Afifi and Weiner (2004) see this process as extremely fluid, such that these assessments are changed during the interaction and immediately affect assessments. For example, after going through the cognitive process proposed in TMIM, a young woman decides to approach someone to whom she is attracted, with the intent of seeing whether he would be interested in a lunch date. However, his negative demeanor in the initial seconds of the conversation changes her assessments of the likely outcome of a question about a lunch date, negatively impacting her perceived efficacy, and making her decide to abort the information-seeking effort. She ends the conversation without asking him about getting together for lunch. That sort of example reflects the dance between information seeker and provider that TMIM believes is central to understanding the uncertainty management process.

How Communication Is Conceptualized in TMIM

The final phase, according to TMIM, is the decision phase, where the various uncertainty management strategies (and related communication strategies) are housed. In other words, once people pass through the interpretation and evaluation phases, they come to a decision about what to do. That decision could involve direct information seeking (asking the person directly), indirect information seeking ("beating around the bush" with the person or asking a mutual friend), active avoidance (going out of their way to avoid any information on the topic), or passive avoidance (not doing much either way—not seeking information but not actively avoiding it, either).

Although TMIM is, in large part, a psychological framework, communication is the key ingredient that moves the engine. First, the decisions that are being made during the proposed process are entirely communication focused (e.g., to avoid information, to seek information, to provide information). Second, it is in the interaction itself where uncertainty management decisions are adjusted based on the feedback individuals receive. In other words, the transactional process of exchanging messages that emerges between the information seeker and provider is an important component of TMIM and is purely communication focused in its approach.

Research and Practical Applications of TMIM

Several studies have tested the predictive utility of TMIM since its publication in 2004. The first of these was Afifi, Dillow, and Morse's (2004) study of college students' general search for information from their romantic partner. Two investigations followed in 2006, one focusing on information seeking about partners' sexual health (Afifi & Weiner, 2006) and the other examining TMIM's ability to predict individuals' willingness to discuss their organ donation decision with their next-of-kin (Afifi et al., 2006). Research since then has applied TMIM in the context of parent-child discussions about sensitive topics (Afifi & Afifi, 2009), adult children's decision to seek information about their elder parents' caregiving wishes (Fowler & Afifi, 2011), and college students' interest in discussing issues related to sexual assault with their friends (Potocki, 2013). In addition, several studies have tested part of the theory, often with particular focus on the role played by the evaluation phase assessments. For instance, Jang (2006) applied these assessments to the context of deception from a romantic partner, Ohs (2008) to older adults' searches for information about their health care, Morse and colleagues (2013) to college students' information seeking about their friends' illicit drug use, McCurry, Schrodt, and Ledbetter (2012) to discussing religious topics in romantic relationships, Jang and Tian (2012) to the pursuit of knowledge about uncertainty-increasing events in close relationships, and Carter, Moles, White, and Chen (2012) to Australian patients' willingness to use a health information service.

In sum, TMIM is a useful framework for studying a wide range of issues for which individuals seek information. It is especially worth noting that many of the contexts in which it is studied offer socially meaningful implications, including organ donation, sexual assault, eldercare, and sexual health, among others. Moreover, many of the authors have included recommendations for ways in which their findings can be used by health professionals to improve the lives of community members. For example, Afifi et al. (2006) recommended that the importance of conversations regarding organ donation be emphasized to the African American community, who seemed to be less likely to engage in these discussions because of lower importance given to the issue, as compared to individuals of Caucasian ethnicity. Additionally, Fowler and Afifi (2011) showed a need to increase efficacy among adult children so that they might initiate discussions with their parents about eldercare desires, thereby improving their well-being, and Potocki (2013) suggested that public health campaigns give individuals communication scripts for discussions of sexual assault as a strategy to reduce the incidence of such crimes.

Evaluation of TMIM

The TMIM has proven to be relatively successful in predicting information seeking decisions, although some aspects of the theory have been stronger than others. Indeed, the TMIM is still in its adolescent stages of development and requires further research, even though the theory seems to explain and predict people's decisions to seek or avoid information rather well. Consequently, what are its strengths and weaknesses to date?

One of its primary contributions has been bringing attention to the role of communication efficacy in studies of uncertainty management and information seeking. In fact, communication efficacy has been the most consistent and strongest predictor of information seeking across most TMIM studies (see Afifi, 2009). Second, Afifi and Weiner (2004) seemed to have had it right by including both outcome expectancies and efficacy as factors in the assessment phase. Most studies have shown that both assessments impact information seeking tendencies. Third, preliminary evidence suggests that Afifi and Morse's (2009) decision to broaden the theory to include wider appraisals of uncertainty (i.e., emotion possibilities other than anxiety) was the correct one. Fowler and Afifi (2011), for example, supported the benefits of that revised notion of uncertainty discrepancy's emotional labeling. In a broader sense, the theory has shown itself to pass the common criteria used to evaluate theory. It has clearly delineated its scope condition (that it is restricted to interpersonal information management and to issues that are perceived to be important), it is testable (the measures have been consistently found to be reliable, and the framework has been shown to be a relatively good fit with the data across populations and contexts), it is heuristic (it has been successfully applied by scholars across a wide range of issues), and it is parsimonious (it arguably offers the smallest number of variables that account for the greatest amount of variance in information management behavior; indeed, scholars are often testing additions to the framework, but none, to our knowledge, argue for greater simplicity).

On the other hand, there are ways in which TMIM could be extended and refined. Most glaringly, outcome expectancy seems to be primarily relevant when expectations are negative. Afifi and Weiner (2004) forecasted that possibility in their original articulation of the theory. Specifically, they argued that the strength of that mediating relationship is likely to depend on the valence of those expectancies:

> Individuals are likely to place considerable weight on their efficacy assessments if they expect negative outcomes from information searches. In such cases, the decision to pursue an information-management strategy through interpersonal

means ultimately rests not on the expected outcomes, but on a belief in the ability to successfully enact the strategy and manage the associated outcomes, and a determination that a target has access to the information and is willing to provide it. . . . In contrast, efficacy's strength as a mediator is likely quite small when the expected outcomes are positive. (p. 180)

Indeed, that is mostly what has been found (for review, see Afifi, 2009). When people expect positive outcomes, outcome expectancies have little influence on efficacy, but when they expect negative outcomes, the impact is relatively large. That makes sense. Assuming that we generally think positively about our ability to seek information, expectations that information seeking will go well should have little effect on that perception. It's only when we expect negative outcomes that those assessments impact our efficacy judgments. Thus, the theory may need to more explicitly propose that the relationship between outcome expectancies and efficacy, and between outcome expectancies and information seeking, depends on the positivity or negativity of those expectations.

But even in the case of negative expectations, the theory may need some adjustment to more fully capture individuals' decisions to seek information despite negative evaluation-phase assessments. As it stands, the theory predicts that increases in uncertainty discrepancy (i.e., a desire for a different level of knowledge than one currently has) generally leads to information *avoidance*. In other words, the more individuals want to reduce their uncertainty, the more they avoid direct searches for information that might do so. How so? Because the theory predicts that increases in uncertainty lead (most often) to anxiety about that discrepancy which, in turn, leads to more negative outcome expectancies and lower efficacy. Negative outcome expectancies and lower efficacy, in turn, lead to a decreased likelihood of direct information seeking. What might be most impressive is that most studies show the theory to predict information seeking quite well, suggesting that the pattern generally captures our decision-making process. That is quite a departure from what most of us believe, namely, that people who want to know more about an important issue are likely to do things to gain that knowledge. Instead, our fears and lack of confidence or trust often seem to lead us to do quite the opposite. The problem with the theory as it stands now, however, is that it doesn't allow for cases when individuals directly seek information despite negative expectations and/or low efficacy. Undoubtedly, there are times when we do so. For example, individuals may ask their romantic partner about his or her relationship satisfaction despite fears that they are unhappy and knowledge that the conversation might lead to the breakup of the relationship, something that would devastate them. Or older adults have difficult conversations with their elderly parents, despite having negative expectancies and low efficacies. The theory may need further adjustment to better capture similar occasions.

Continuing the Conversation

Given the utility of the theory and its continued need for development (i.e., its relative youth), current research in Afifi and colleagues' lab, and that of others, is trending in four directions: (a) testing the TMIM's supposed causal structure, (b) giving increased attention to the role of emotions in the information management process, (c) focusing on the role of the information provider and the transactional nature of information seeking/providing process, and (d) focusing more attention on what happens after the search for information ends, with a particular focus on health and well-being. Each of these directions will undoubtedly improve the theory in important ways in the coming years.

Afifi and his colleagues (Afifi & Morse, 2009; Afifi & Weiner, 2004) have advanced strong arguments for the direction of influence among the variables embedded within the TMIM, but there have yet to be studies explicitly designed to test those causal claims. Take, for example, the theory's suggestion that outcome expectancies change efficacies (as opposed to the other way around). To date, no studies of TMIM have tested that causal direction in the lab to confirm that expectancies change efficacy levels, instead of efficacy impacting outcome expectancies. The same can be said about all of the directional associations posited by the theory. Research obviously needs to be conducted to answer those questions. In a similar vein, scholars have begun to examine the role of emotion in the information seeking process, but a lot more needs to be done. The theory acknowledges that emotions impact information seeking beyond just the appraisal of uncertainty discrepancy, but further research is needed to improve our understanding of the specific ways in which those effects take shape.

More importantly, although Afifi and Weiner (2004) identified the theory's transactional nature as one of its primary strengths, all studies to date have focused on the information seeker, to the exclusion of the information provider. That must change for the theory to meet its potential as a contributor to our knowledge of uncertainty management. Finally, the theory ignores what ultimately may be the most important and interesting aspect of the information seeking process, namely, how the collection of information (or its avoidance) impacts the well-being of the information seeker and provider alike. Afifi and his colleagues are currently undertaking a program of research that seeks to answer that question (e.g., Afifi, Felix, & Afifi, 2012), but, as it stands, it falls out of the direct purview of TMIM. Future revisions to TMIM—or new theoretical efforts than spawn from TMIM—must address what is ultimately the critically applied question: How does uncertainty discrepancy and the eventual collection or avoidance of information impact our well-being over time?

In sum, the TMIM contributes to our understanding of the uncertainty management process in important ways and offers promise as a framework to guide studies in this area. That being said, there is still a lot yet to be done before we can judge the utility of the theory as a framework of uncertainty and information management. It has come a long way since its infancy, but it is still adjusting to its growth spurt. As it continues to develop and other people have an opportunity to join the "information management" conversation, our hope is that it will continue to mature and someday realize the promise that we see in it.

References

Afifi, W. A. (2009). Uncertainty and information management in interpersonal contexts. In S. Smith & S. Wilson (Eds.), *New directions in interpersonal communication research* (pp. 94–114). Thousand Oaks, CA: Sage.

Afifi, W. A., & Afifi, T. D. (2009). Avoidance among adolescents in conversations about their parents' relationship: Applying the theory of motivated information management. *Journal of Social and Personal Relationships, 26,* 488–511.

Afifi, W. A., Dillow, M., & Morse, C. (2004). Seeking information in relational contexts: A test of the theory of motivated information management. *Personal Relationships, 11,* 429–450.

Afifi, W. A., Felix, E. D., & Afifi, T. A. (2012). The impact of uncertainty and communal coping on mental health following natural disasters. *Anxiety, Stress, & Coping, 25,* 329–347.

Afifi, W. A., Morgan, S. E., Stephenson, M., Morse, C., Harrison, T., Reichert, T., & Long, S. D. (2006). Examining the decision to talk with family about organ donation: Applying the theory of motivated information management. *Communication Monographs, 73,* 188–215.

Afifi, W. A., & Morse, C. R. (2009). Expanding the role of emotion in the theory of motivated information management. In T. D. Afifi & W. A. Afifi (Eds.), *Uncertainty, information management, and disclosure decisions: Theories and applications* (pp. 87–105). New York, NY: Routledge.

Afifi, W. A., Morse, C., Dillow, M., & Weiner, J. (2005, May). *Caring for a newborn in the land of theory: The theory of motivated information management.* Paper presented at the annual conference of the International Communication Association, New York, NY.

Afifi, W. A., & Weiner, J. L. (2004). Toward a theory of motivated information management. *Communication Theory, 14,* 167–190.

Afifi, W. A., & Weiner, J. L. (2006). Seeking information about sexual health: Applying the theory of motivated information management. *Human Communication Research, 32,* 35–57.

Babrow, A. S. (2001). Uncertainty, value, communication, and problematic integration. *Journal of Communication, 51,* 553–573.

Bandura, A. (1986). *Social foundations of thought and action: A social cognitive theory.* Englewood Cliffs, NJ: Prentice-Hall.

Bandura, A. (1997). *Self-efficacy: The exercise of control.* New York, NY: Freeman.

Berger, C. R., & Calabrese, R. J. (1975). Some exploration in initial interactions and beyond: Toward a developmental theory of interpersonal communication. *Human Communication Research, 1,* 99–112.

Brashers, D. E., & Hogan, T. P. (2013). The appraisal and management of uncertainty: Implications for information-retrieval systems. *Information Processing and Management, 49,* 1241–1249.

Burgoon, J. K. (1978). A communication model of personal space violations: Explication and an initial test. *Human Communication Research, 4,* 129–142.

Burgoon, J. K., Stern, L. A., & Dillman, L. (1995). *Interpersonal adaptation: Dyadic interaction patterns.* New York, NY: Cambridge University Press.

Carter, S. R., Moles, R., White, L., & Chen, T. F. (2012). Patients' willingness to use a pharmacist-provided medication management service: The influence of outcome expectancies and communication efficacy. *Research in Social and Administrative Pharmacy, 8,* 487–198.

Chaiken, S., Giner-Sorolla, R., & Chen, S. (1996). Beyond accuracy: Defense and impression motives in heuristic and systematic information processing. In P. M. Gollwitzer & J. A. Bargh (Eds.), *The psychology of action: Linking cognition and motivation to behavior* (pp. 553–578). New York, NY: Guilford.

Fischhoff, B., Goitein, B., & Shapira, Z. (1981). Subjective expected utility: A model of decision-making. *Journal of the American Society for Information Science, 32,* 391–399.

Fowler, C., & Afifi, W. A. (2011). Applying the theory of motivated information management to adult children's discussions of caregiving with aging parents. *Journal of Social and Personal Relationships, 28,* 507–535.

Jang, S. A. (2006). *Understanding uncertainty, communication efficacy, and avoidance following the discovery of a relational partner's deception: The mediating role of communication efficacy* (Unpublished doctoral dissertation). The University of Texas at Austin: Austin, TX.

Jang, S. A., & Tian, Y. (2012). The effects of communication efficacy on information-seeking following events that increase uncertainty: A cross-lagged panel analysis. *Communication Quarterly, 60,* 234–254.

Kahneman, D. (2003). Maps of bounded rationality: Psychology for behavioral economics. *The American Economic Review, 93,* 1449–75.

Kirsch, I. (Ed.). (1999). *How expectancies shape experiences.* Washington, DC: American Psychological Association.

Maddux, J. E. (1999). Expectancies and the social-cognitive perspective: Basic principles, processes and variables. In I. Kirsch (Ed.), *How expectancies shape experiences* (pp. 17–40). Washington, DC: American Psychological Association.

McCurry, A. L., Schrodt, P., & Ledbetter, A. M. (2012). Relational uncertainty and communication efficacy as predictors of religious conversations in romantic relationships. *Journal of Social and Personal Relationships, 29,* 1085–1108.

Morse, C. R., Volkman, J. E., Samter, W., Trunzo, J., McClure, K., Kohn, C., & Logue, J. C. (2013). The influence of uncertainty and social support on information seeking concerning illicit stimulant use among young adults. *Health Communication, 28,* 366–377.

Ohs, J. E. (2008). *Health-care decision making at the latter end of the lifespan* (Unpublished doctoral dissertation). The Pennsylvania State University: University Park, PA.

Pavitt, C. (2001). *Philosophy of science and communication theory.* Huntington, NY: Nova Science Publishers.

Potocki, B. L. (2013, November). *Preventing sexual assault: Applying the theory of motivated information management.* Paper presented at the annual convention of the National Communication Association, Washington, DC.

Simon, H. (1972). Theories of bounded rationality. In C. B. McGuire & R. Radner (Eds.), *Decision and organization* (pp. 161–176). Amsterdam: North-Holland Publishing Co.

PART II

Discourse/Interaction-Centered
Theories of Interpersonal
Communication

The contributors to this part of the book address theories that hold prominence in understanding interpersonal communication as an interaction process that unfolds between persons. Theories in Part II are focused on the content, forms, and functions of messages and the behavioral interaction patterns between people. In contrast to the theories in Part I that emphasize what transpires in individual minds to produce or interpret messages, the theories in this part take a decidedly more social turn to study communication as it is enacted between persons. Six of the chapters reflect homegrown theories—that is, theories that were developed within the discipline of communication. The other five theories originate in allied disciplines, but certainly communication scholars have made their own unique contributions to the theories. For example, Sociology is the discipline of origin for Goffman's Face Theory and the theory has been applied widely in Communication. Politeness Theory originated in Sociolinguistics. In addition, as Koenig Kellas makes evident, many narrative theories have been developed, only some of which originate from communication scholars, as is the case for critical and feminist theories.

In contrast to the post-positivistic orientation that prevails in Part I, the theories in Part II are more eclectic with respect to meta-theoretical inclinations. Two of the chapters—representing Communication Accommodation Theory and Expectancy Violations Theory—are straightforward exemplars of the post-positivistic project. These theories were developed with a goal of predicting and explaining patterned regularities among key communication variables. Theorists who developed these theories presume an objective reality whose underlying cause-and-effect patterns can be discovered through scientific observation.

Speech Codes theory is best categorized as interpretive, privileging understanding from the so-called native's point of view, and appreciate that meaning making is a highly contextualized affair. Two of the chapters are decidedly critical—Baxter and Asbury's chapter on critical approaches, which is new to the book, and Wood's chapter on Critical Feminist Theories—and spring from disciplines including women's studies, philosophy, law, cultural studies, and English.

Readers should note that both of these chapters present a compilation of theories that all focus on power and marginalized perspectives. Two of the chapters, Relational Dialectics Theory and Grounded Practical Theory, also cross meta-theoretical borders; Tracy places GPT as a critical-interpretive theory and Baxter and Norwood point out that RDT has been applied across perspectives—most of the work has been interpretive and the most recent rendition of the theory takes a critical bent.

Four of the chapters present theories that are more complicated to categorize. Goffman's Face Theory has roots in the interpretive tradition, yet it has been used productively by both interpretive and post-positivistic researchers, as Metts and Cupach make evident. Similarly, most narrative theories have roots in interpretive or critical traditions, yet Koenig Kellas usefully calls attention to the value of post-positivistic narrative research and her own work has been applying the theory that way. Hecht's Communication Theory of Identity is rooted the goals of post-positivism, but Hecht points out that he integrates the other approaches as well. Last, as Goldsmith and Normand discuss, Politeness Theory has appealed to both post-positivistic and interpretive traditions.

The theories in this part of the book can be productively mapped in ways other than meta-theoretical orientation. Many of the theories share a common focus on the role of communication in giving us our sense of reality. Several theories adopt a constitutive view, presuming that social reality is constructed through communicative action: Conversation Analysis Theory, Face Theory, several of the narrative theories, and Speech Codes Theory. Politeness Theory presumes that "face" is a socially enacted phenomenon, and the performance of facework holds implications for the meaning of the relationship between parties.

Several of the theories represented in Part II recognize that interpersonal communication is a complicated business, fraught with problems and challenges of one kind or another. Grounded Practical theory focuses most explicitly on the dilemmatic nature of a variety of communication practices.

Expectancy Violations Theory examines what happens when a person's expectations are violated, and Interaction Adaptation Theory examines the complexities of how a person responds to such violations in light of other factors. Politeness Theory captures the face-threat implications of speaking directly and efficiently, and why speakers might opt instead for less direct forms of expression. Communication Accommodation Theory concentrates on the problem of coordination between speakers—whether they respond with similar or different behavioral responses. Narrative theories address the challenge of how narrative coherence is rendered from the less coherent, and more chaotic, experiences of living.

Identity, including face, is the focus of several of the theories in Part II. Communication Accommodation Theory, Face Theory, several narrative theories, Politeness Theory, and Speech Codes Theory address, in different ways, the matter of who we are when we communicate interpersonally. Communication Accommodation Theory emphasizes identity as social group identity—for example, whether we are socially positioned as a member of the older or the younger generation. Speech Codes Theory emphasizes identity as cultural membership—for example, whether we are American or Norwegian. Several narrative theories emphasize how our identities are storied phenomena. Whereas Goffman's Face Theory focuses at a general level on face as a Dramatistic performance in which we are always on stage playing a role, Brown and Levinson's Politeness Theory affords a more micro-oriented examination of how interlocutors enact facework on the other's behalf. Although not directly addressing issues of face, Expectancy Violations Theory holds relevance to face threat as a specific form of expectancy violation. Communication Theory of Identity focuses on the ever-changing nature of identity as enacted through communication. The theories centered in the critical paradigm remind us of the presence of power and position in interactions and relationships and ask us to pay attention to which voices are centered and marginalized in our culture.

Three of the theories in Part II remind us that culture is important in interpersonal communication. Communication Accommodation Theory has been examined in diverse cultural contexts and has proven especially useful in addressing intergroup communication encounters. Politeness Theory explicitly notes that not all cultures are alike in the details of facework, despite sharing more abstract principles of facework. Speech Codes Theory is explicitly a theory oriented toward an understanding of how cultures differ in their codes of communication.

Taken as a whole, the contrast between the theories in Parts I and II is somewhat stark. Whereas the theories in Part I are more psychologically and individualistically centered, the theories in Part II have moved beyond the individual to examine interpersonal communication as messages between speakers.

12

Communication Accommodation Theory

A Situated Framework for Relational, Family, and Intergroup Dynamics

Howard Giles and Jordan Soliz

P eople can vary their communicative styles and strategies in ways that reflect their personalities and temperaments, roles and relationships, and social identities. These varying verbal and nonverbal behaviors have significant social meanings: some, such as British Standard English, are lauded, and others, such as so-called "gayspeak," are often stigmatized. Indeed, the same communicative act will be appreciated by some, yet abhorred by others. Such differences in interpersonal communicative styles (and corresponding evaluation of such styles) are abundant and varying by such factors as ethnicity, occupational status, gender, and age.

Intellectual Tradition of Communication Accommodation Theory

Recent attention has been paid to the growth of new language forms especially among young people, particularly regarding new media technologies (e.g., text messaging or tweeting). Not only can these language forms invoke the wrath of older adults, but they also are often viewed as inappropriate and ridiculed when adopted by this latter age group. These types of intergenerational differences in language choice demonstrate how interpersonal tensions are often tied to our modes and styles of communication. Throughout our lives, we are not only faced with ever-changing and evolving language and communication norms but these norms also vary across our relational and social contexts.

How then do we communicatively manage such evolving interpersonal diversity in language preferences of and attitudes toward the varying communicative styles and behaviors across our linguistic landscape? Communication accommodation theory (CAT) is a theory that helps us understand the motivations for why we communicate the way we do with others, the nature of our communication choices, and the relational, identity, and evaluative outcomes of these choices. As such, CAT has been characterized as "one of the most influential behavioral theories of communication" (Littlejohn & Foss, 2005, p. 147). CAT emerged originally as a sociopsychological account of how our dialects and words change depending on to whom we are speaking and the evaluation of such shifts in dialects and word (Giles & Powesland, 1975). For instance, dialects representing social groups typically viewed with less social prestige in society (e.g., ethnic-racial minorities in the United States) are often evaluated more negatively than "standard" dialects. As such, individuals from these groups may code-switch to a more prestigious dialect in order to gain favor and/or establish credibility with others. Conversely, a speaker may maintain their dialect to demonstrate authenticity and the importance of his or her ethnic-racial ingroup. Over the years, the theory has been refined to include other verbal and nonverbal communication adjustments and contextual considerations (see McGlone & Giles, 2011). For instance, younger adults vary the topics of conversation with peers compared to older adults based on the perceived appropriateness of the topic to the relational context. Beyond communication, the theory has been welcomed in other social science disciplinary handbooks, texts, and encyclopedias and, while originating in the post-positivist tradition, has served as an interpretive resource in various traditions. Further, CAT has been invoked (see Dragojevic, Gasiorek, & Giles, in press, for a recent review) across a range of between-group comparisons (e.g., interethnic communication) and applied to various relational and social contexts (e.g., family, health, law enforcement, intercultural interactions).

Main Goals and Features of Communication Accommodation Theory

ACCOMMODATIVENESS

Although notions of "accommodation" have separate meanings in different theoretical terrains, in CAT accommodation is a process concerned with how we can reduce (and, in some cases, even magnify) communicative differences between people in interaction. For example, a common experience for many readers would be traveling abroad and seeing the delight of your waitperson when saying "Hello," "Thank you," "Please," and "Good-bye" in the waitperson's language. Accommodation is considered one of the main routes to reducing social or relational distance as it enhances interpersonal similarities and thereby reduces uncertainties about the other. The effect of converging toward or "approximating" another has been shown to increase liking for convergers, enabling them to be seen as more competent and credible (e.g., Aune & Kikuchi, 1993).

Convergence can occur across a wide range of communicative dimensions. These include switching to the other's language or dialect (as above); assuming the same level of the other's interruptions, speech rate, posture, and so forth (e.g., Li, 2001); or managing discourse to discuss topics of interest to conversational partners. These adjustments can be labeled as upward or downward when the communicative features have value connotations. As we alluded to in the preceding section, "upward convergence" is when a speaker adopts another's more socially acceptable communication style or preference—for example, shifting toward a more prestigious accent. Conversely, "downward convergence" is when a speaker adapts to match another's more parochial, colloquial, or stigmatized speech pattern—for example, when physicians replace medical jargon with lay words and explanations when speaking with their patients. Accommodation can manifest in ways other than convergence, as we take into account the other's conversational needs and goals (see Jones, Gallois, Callan, & Barker, 1999). Important here would be the ability to accommodate what is called another's "interpretive competence," that is, the other's ability to comprehend, or whether the other has had any experience with the topic or event being discussed. For example, a Briton (who has some knowledge of baseball) slowly explains to an American (who has no knowledge of the sport) the game of cricket, using their shared knowledge of baseball as a foundation (e.g., "In cricket, the wicket is somewhat similar to the strike zone in baseball."). Further, individuals accommodate through discourse management (e.g., checking understanding and explicit perspective taking, adhering to conversational turn-taking norms) based on the perceived needs or desires of others in the interactions (e.g., Watson & Gallois, 1998).

Indeed, convergence plays a crucial role in CAT to the extent that accommodative acts are often a function of the social power a target-other is perceived to possess. Others with low power are accommodated less frequently than others with high social power. For example in male-female encounters, women, in general, will accommodate males more than vice versa (Namy, Nygaard, & Saureteig, 2002), while vendors in a market will accommodate more to their clientele than shoppers will to them (e.g., van den Berg, 1986). More generally, people will converge to others they find socially rewarding and respected. Another important feature of CAT is that people will accommodate subjectively to where they believe others to be communicatively rather than where they actually are in any objective, measurable sense (Thakerar, Giles, & Cheshire, 1982). Common instances of this are where social stereotypes associated with another's apparent or presumed group memberships (e.g., elderliness) may lead to faulty expectations about the other's competence and characteristics. In this instance, a younger adult may overaccommodate an older person by becoming extremely deferential and polite, or by touching them, slowing down speech rate, and enunciating loudly. However, the subjective and objective are not always in accord, leading to the potential for miscommunication as an individual may converge inappropriately to a relational partner's communicative needs and/or preferences based on what they believe is appropriate rather that what is actually necessary. For those elders who do not resonate to being so characterized, such miscarried accommodations can be perceived as patronizing and demeaning. However, for more frail elders, this kind of accommodation can be construed as empathic and being helpful. Thus, the evaluation (i.e., positive or negative) of accommodation may vary for conversational partners based on perceived appropriateness of accommodation.

NONACCOMMODATIVENESS

Given the benefits of accommodating to others, this communicative process can almost be regarded as a conversational rule and an integral component of communicative competence and social skills. Indeed, scholars who have studied mimicry have found that "when people interact with each other, there is a nonconscious tendency to match each other's behavior" (van Baaren, Horgan, Chatrand, & Dijkmans, 2004, p. 453). That said, CAT's attention has also been drawn to conditions where not only does this matching not emerge, but where the complete converse also is embraced. For example, if a teenager sends a text message to his mother in the same way he would text a friend, it would likely be indecipherable to her or, at the minimum, viewed as inappropriate or unexpected. As implied above, *non*accommodation from a socially significant other does not usually excite a recipient's affection! Such nonaccommodativeness can message that one's respect and liking is not being sought, thereby rendering some damage to self-esteem, with unfavorable evaluations following for the nonaccommodator.

Nonaccommodation, however, is not necessarily intentional. As alluded to above, accommodation is often based on subjective perceptions of conversational need and, thus, while one may believe they are appropriately accommodating or converging toward another, this behavior may not be perceived as such. One could argue that accommodation or nonaccommodation is in the eye (or ear) of the beholder. The negative consequences attending lack of accommodation can, however, be reduced under extenuating circumstances, such as a presumed inability to speak the other's language, to understand their slang, and so on.

Again, nonaccommodative practices come in different forms. It can be manifest in "speech maintenance" where the speaker sustains a consistent communicative stance from person to person, irrespective of who the latter may be, so as to maintain an aura of authenticity. On other occasions, people can be *under*accommodative in that they do not attend or listen to another's needs (Gasiorek & Giles, 2012) as they may have their own egocentric agendas. Among the most nonaccommodative positions would be where a speaker diverges by using a more or less prestigious accent (upward and downward divergence, respectively) or even switches languages. It, too, can vary from partial to full divergence, and can be triggered by dislike for or mistrust of another—and is usually met with negative and even derogatory responses. In a research experiment in South Africa, Dixon, Tredoux, Durrheim, and Foster (1994) found that so-called colored suspects (that is, suspects of mixed racial heritage) who diverged from a white interrogator by use of a Cape Afrikaans accent were judged guilty of a crime more often than those who converged toward the interrogator's accent.

Divergence has been considered most in interpersonal encounters where interactants feel they are representing different groups, cultures, and communities with which they strongly affiliate, and where their ingroup language or communication style is a fundamental dimension of their social identity. For instance, given the importance of speaking French to a Quebecois's identity, a separatist from this Canadian province might emphasize his or her French accent when talking to a monolingual English-Canadian. To this point, CAT has drawn from social identity theory (Tajfel, 1978). Members of different social groups often accentuate their identities by diverging from one another—not only in dialect or language, but also in their distinctive nonverbal and dress styles—in pursuit of a positive social identity. This divergence can be particularly intense if people feel their identity is threatened and that the other group has historically and illegitimately discriminated against them. Indeed, if a person accommodates an outgroup member in such situations, observers could attribute that person as being a cultural traitor. For example, hearing a colleague from your oppressed minority group converge toward someone of the dominant group can be attributed with disdain, embarrassment, and feelings of betrayal.

From all this, it should be clear that while accommodation is often positively received, it need not always be so. Some members of certain national groups believe their language is so unique to their culture and impossible to learn by outsiders that they may not take kindly to foreigners' use of their own tongues, even if done with native-like proficiency (Ross & Shortreed, 1990). By the same token, divergences are not always negatively perceived: indeed, they made be deemed mandatory and valued (as above) by ingroup peers. In other situations, divergence may be adopted strategically in order to correct a communicative stance in another such as by slowing down in order to recalibrate an overly fast talker who is providing new information at such a fast pace that the hearer cannot absorb it comfortably. In yet other situations, objectively coded divergence could be positively perceived as appropriately meeting the needs and/or desires of another. An example would be when a romantically inclined male accentuates his manliness by adopting a deeper pitch and when a female, in tandem, accentuates her femininity by adopting a softer voice.

SYMMETRICALITY

Note that across all these outcomes, accommodation and nonaccommodation can be mutual, reciprocated, symmetrical, or asymmetrical (see Gallois & Giles, 1998). When they are symmetrical and accommodative, interpersonal relations should be particularly strengthened, but when they are mutually nonaccommodative, interpersonal relations are likely to become hostile and conflicted. An interesting feature of CAT is that communicators can adopt both accommodative and nonaccommodative stances with the same person in an attempt to convey contrastive personas. For example, a speaker can use simple terms and syntax convergently yet, simultaneously, also accentuate their ethnic accent so as to divergently authenticate and honor their cultural heritage.

How Communication Is Conceptualized in the Theory

In the 1980s CAT began to take propositional forms that became increasingly more complex and, arguably, more demanding on readers (e.g., Thakerar et al., 1982). To help clarify the thrust and essence of the theory, Giles, Willemyns, Gallois, and Anderson (2007) crafted four key principles of accommodation that convey how communication is conceptualized within CAT. Given that the theory is supported in naturalistic, experimental laboratory, and mediated settings, the authors believe that the four principles apply equally well to interpersonal communication even in modern technology settings such as how we attune our communication in e-mail messages (e.g., Bunz & Campbell, 2004). These principles are:

- I: Speakers will, up to an optimal level, increasingly accommodate the communicative patterns believed characteristic of their interactants the more they wish to
  - o Signal positive face and empathy;
  - o Elicit the other's approval, respect, understanding, trust, compliance, and cooperation;

- o Develop a closer relationship;
- o Defuse a potentially volatile situation; or
- o Signal common social identities.

- II: When attributed (typically) with positive intent, patterns of perceived accommodation increasingly and cumulatively enhance recipients'

- o Self-esteem;
- o Task, interactional, and job satisfaction;
- o Favorable images of the speaker's group, fostering the potential for partnerships to achieve common goals;
- o Mutual understanding, felt supportiveness, and life satisfaction; and
- o Attributions of speaker politeness, empathy, competence, benevolence, and trust.

- III: Speakers will (other interactional motives notwithstanding) increasingly nonaccommodate (e.g., diverge from) the communicative patterns believed characteristic of their interactants, the more they wish to signal (or promote)

- o Relational dissatisfaction or disaffection with and disrespect for the others' traits, demeanor, actions, or social identities.

- IV: When attributed with (usually) harmful intent, patterns of perceived *non*accommodation (e.g., divergence) will be

- o Evaluated unfavorably as unfriendly, impolite, or communicatively incompetent; and
- o Reacted to negatively by recipients (e.g., recipients will perceive speaker to be lacking in empathy and trust).

These principles are readily converted into testable hypotheses in concrete situations. Moreover, we must consider the transactive cycle of accommodation. By this, we mean that, whereas accommodation can be driven by interpersonal motives of gaining social acceptance and building social connections, ultimately leading to positive outcomes, the converse flow of these communicative, cognitive, and affective mechanisms can exist. Hence, perceptions of accommodation from coworkers likely lead to increased job satisfaction. But, it may be the case that positive job satisfaction leads one to perceive others as accommodating.

Research and Practical Applications of Communication Accommodation Theory

INTERPERSONAL AS INTERGROUP COMMUNICATION

A feature of CAT is its capacity to account for compelling processes not usually considered under the rubric of interpersonal communication, yet which are fundamental to it. Many years ago, Tajfel and Turner (1979) introduced the distinction between encounters (even dyadic ones) that were either "interindividual" or "intergroup." The former were interactions that are based solely on the personal characteristics of the parties involved (e.g., their personalities and moods) and not at all dependent on their respective social category memberships. Hence, accommodation-nonaccommodation in these cases would be toward or away from the idiosyncratic communication attributes of the other. Intergroup encounters were the converse, and so accommodation-nonaccommodation would be pitched vis-à-vis the other's social category memberships (sexual orientation, gang, religion, political membership, and so on). Tajfel and Turner regarded this class of interactions as constituting and actually defining a major proportion of all the interpersonal situations we encounter (see Dragojevic & Giles, in press, for a discussion of much interpersonal communication actually being intergroup). Even intimate communication between married couples—in the context of this gendered institution—can be usefully understood in intergroup terms as in talk about domestic labor (Blain, 1994). Likewise, a friend confiding openly and privately about contrasting sororities, professors, or engineering majors would also constitute intergroup talk as the target of this intimate conversation is to pillory "them" or "the other." Rather than construe these as opposite poles of a single interactional continuum, a number of scholars (e.g., Giles & Hewstone, 1982) felt it prudent to represent conversational possibilities as located along two orthogonal continua: interindividual (high or low) and intergroup (high or low). This lends the possibility of encounters being construed as high on both dimensions, or as a movement within the same conversation from, for example, interindividual to intergroup. An illustration of this would be the occasion when a man discloses to his mother that he is gay. Their relational history dictates that interindividual salience would be high, with the mother dealing with her son as the unique person she has known and loved since birth. At the same time, however, her son's sexual identity will be pertinent, potentially shaping the encounter in many important ways. In fact, many of what we consider our most intimate and personal relationships such as family are infused with interpersonal and intergroup dimensions that are manifested in the relational communication (Soliz & Rittenour, 2012). In sum, interpersonal communication that is triggered by social identities is fashioned by different processes (e.g., stereotyping and social differentiation) and message strategies from the processes molded by interindividual (i.e., interpersonal) processes. Unlike most other theories of interpersonal communication, CAT absorbs and blends interpersonal and intergroup processes into intimate and non-intimate relational encounters (Giles & Giles, 2012).

PHASES OF RELATIONAL DEVELOPMENT

Accommodative processes have never been systematically explored in terms of the stages of relational development and dissolution. Most research on CAT has focused on initial interactions between strangers during the acquainting process, or in role-related situations where accommodation regularly occurs for all the beneficial reasons specified above. But what of more developed relationships, where such functions have already largely been met? Extant research has largely focused on underscoring the value of sustaining accommodative practices for relational solidarity. In the family context, Harwood (2000) showed that closeness in and satisfaction with the grandparent-grandchild relationship from the perspectives of both participants was predicted by the extent to which they perceived the other to be accommodative (e.g., by listening to and talking about topics the other enjoys). Recent studies have demonstrated how accommodative processes are associated with formative processes (i.e., family solidarity and closeness) in stepfamilies (DiVerniero, 2013; Speer, Giles, & Denes, 2013) and in-law relationships (Rittenour & Soliz, 2009) as well as managing differences in interfaith (Colaner, Soliz, & Nelson, in press) and multiethnic families (Soliz, Thorson, & Rittenour, 2009).

Focusing on dyadic interactions, Fitzpatrick, Mulac, and Dindia (1995) examined implicit relational development by videotaping people talking with those of the same sex and opposite sex, as well as people talking with their spouse. Both men and women shift from their own gender-preferential styles of language to that of the other when they move from same-sex to opposite-sex strangers, and shift again when they converse with their spouses. The authors commented that "the magnitude of this shift is striking" and that "for women, the initial leap from the extremes of the female-preferential style occurs when speaking to any man, husband, or stranger" (p. 35). Whereas the participants in this study were happily married, Robertson and Murachver (2006) interviewed victims and perpetrators who were involved in abusive relationships, some of whom had been incarcerated. They found that those who had been psychologically abusive with their partners were much more likely to accommodate an interviewer who adopted negative language forms such as disagreeing and swearing, but less likely to reciprocate an interviewer who assumed more facilitative language forms (e.g., expressed empathy and compliments). It is a common adage— and one often heard at marital ceremonies—that relationships have to be continually worked on. CAT operates on the assumption that managing accommodative practices and dilemmas per se, and especially when one's partner is perceived to veer in nonaccommodative directions, might be an important ingredient in long-term relational satisfaction-dissatisfaction. Further applying CAT to our personal relationship by identifying the nature, motives, and evaluation of (non)accommodative processes provides a novel and perhaps more nuanced way of understanding relational development, maintenance, and dissolution.

Evaluation of Communication Accommodation Theory

For the most part, critiques of CAT have been favorable, empirical support for many facets of it have emerged (e.g., Soliz & Giles, in press), and quantitative as well as qualitative work spawned by CAT has appeared in many journals across different disciplines (Giles, Gasiorek, & Soliz, in press). Indeed, West and Turner (2007) stated that "there is no doubt that the theory is heuristic and has lasting scholastic value" (p. 547), noting that it has not been subject to much scholarly criticism. Many of CAT's strengths have been alluded to already: CAT's capacity to interface micro-linguistic and macro-societal boundaries; interpersonal, family, and intergroup tensions; and short-term and long-term outcomes.

Four of CAT's limitations are pinpointed here. First, we have little understanding regarding which particular communicative feature(s) will be accommodated to or differentiated from, or when and why that would happen. Second, we do not yet understand the dynamics of how accommodative-nonaccommodative practices are adopted throughout the history of interpersonal relationships. Third, we are limited in our understanding of when accommodation directly causes certain interpersonal outcomes, and when it works indirectly. As CAT stands currently (see Principles I and II above), it favors direct paths, yet Hajek et al. (2006) found that people's perceptions of police officers' accommodative practices promote trust in them that, itself (and not accommodation directly), predicts compliance with their instructions. Clearly, more sophisticated mediational models of CAT are begging to be conceptualized and tested. Fourth, the thorny issue of when accommodation and nonaccommodation strategies are consciously versus nonconsciously invoked (i.e., when they are automatic or ritualized) has yet to be studied within CAT.

Continuing the Conversation

The limitations just outlined necessarily segue into and drive future empirical directions and, clearly, other theoretical questions can be raised, only one of which can be ignited here. Recent years have seen an increase in biophysiological underpinnings of interpersonal and intergroup communication (see Floyd & Afifi, 2011, and Chapter 23 in this volume, for an overview). Research has shown that certain communicative acts, such as affection and social support, are associated with a neuroendocrine activity (e.g., cortisol and oxytocin levels) that actually physiologically protects the body from stress (Floyd & Riforgiate, 2009). Hence, it is conceivable that an interpersonal history of expressing and receiving accommodative practices leads not only to mutual trust (Nettle &

Dunbar, 1997) and relational health, but also to similar physiological benefits. The bi-directional effects of biophysiological and neurological activities (e.g., neural synchrony; Weber, Popovam, & Mangus, 2012; see also, Fiske, 2012), in relation to interpersonal accommodation-nonaccommodation along with evolutionary explanations for behaviors (see Reid et al., 2012) holds exciting prospects for the further innovative development of CAT.

References

Aune, R. K., & Kikuchi, T. (1993). Effects of language intensity similarity on perceptions of credibility, relational attributions, and persuasion. *Journal of Language and Social Psychology, 12,* 224–237.

Blain, J. (1994). Discourses of agency and domestic labor: Family discourse and gendered practice in dual-earner families. *Journal of Family Issues, 15,* 515–549.

Bunz, U., & Campbell, S. W. (2004). Politeness accommodation in electronic mail. *Communication Research Reports, 21,* 11–25.

Colaner, C. W., Soliz, J., & Nelson, L. R. (in press). Communicatively managing religious identity difference in parent-child relationships: The role of accommodative and nonaccommodative communication. *Journal of Family Communication.*

DiVerniero, R. (2013). Children of divorce and their nonresidential parent's family: Examining perceptions of communication accommodation. *Journal of Family Communication, 13,* 301–320.

Dixon, J. A., Tredoux, C. G., Durrheim, K., & Foster, D. H. (1994). The role of speech accommodation and crime type in attribution of guilt. *Journal of Social Psychology, 134,* 465–473.

Dragojevic, M., Gasiorek, J., & Giles, H. (in press). Communication accommodation theory. In C. R. Berger & M. L. Roloff (Eds.), *Encyclopedia of interpersonal communication* (pp. 29–51). New York, NY: Wiley Blackwell.

Dragojevic, M., & Giles, H. (in press). Language and interpersonal communication: Their intergroup dynamics. In C. R. Berger (Ed.), *Handbook of interpersonal communication.* Berlin: De Gruyter Mouton.

Fiske, S. T. (2012). Journey to the edges: Social structures and neural maps of intergroup processes. *British Journal of Social Psychology, 51,* 1–12.

Fitzpatrick, M. A., Mulac, A., & Dindia, K. (1995). Gender-preferential language use in spouse and stranger interaction. *Journal of Language and Social Psychology, 14,* 18–39.

Floyd, K., & Afifi, T. D. (2011). Biological and physiological perspectives on interpersonal communication. In M. L. Knapp & J. A. Daly (Eds.), *The SAGE Handbook of interpersonal communication* (4th ed., pp. 87–130). Thousand Oaks, CA: Sage.

Floyd, K., & Riforgiate, S. (2009). Affectionate communication received from spouse predicts stress hormone levels in healthy adults. *Communication Monographs, 75,* 351–368.

Gallois, C., & Giles, H. (1998). Accommodating mutual influence in intergroup encounters. In M. Palmer & G.A. Barnett (Eds.), *Progress in communication sciences* (pp. 135–162). Stanford, CA: Ablex.

Gasiorek, J., & Giles, H. (2012). Effects of inferred motive on evaluations of nonaccom-modative communication. *Human Communication Research, 38,* 309–332.

Giles, H., Gasiorek, J., & Soliz, J. (Eds.). (in press). Recent developments in communica-tion accommodation theory: Innovative contexts and applications. *Language and Communication.*

Giles, H., & Giles, J. L. (2012). Ingroups and outgroups communicating. In A. Kuyulo (Ed.), *Inter/cultural communication: Representation and construction of culture in everyday interaction* (pp. 141–162). Thousand Oaks, CA: Sage.

Giles, H., & Hewstone, M. (1982). Cognitive structures, speech, and social situations. *Language Sciences, 4,* 187–219.

Giles, H., & Powesland, P. F. (1975). *Speech style and social evaluation.* London: Academic Press.

Giles, H., Willemyns, M., Gallois, C., & Anderson, M. C. (2007). Accommodating a new frontier: The context of law enforcement. In K. Fiedler (Ed.), *Social communication* (pp. 129–162). New York, NY: Psychology Press.

Hajek, C., Barker, V., Giles, H., Louw, J., Pecchioni, L., Makoni, S., & Myers, P. (2006). Perceptions of police-civilian encounters: African and American interethnic data. *Journal of Intercultural Communication Research, 35,* 161–182.

Harwood, J. (2000). Communicative predictors of solidarity in the grandparent-grandchild relationship. *Journal of Social and Personal Relationships, 17,* 743–766.

Jones, E. S., Gallois, C., Callan, V. J., & Barker, M. (1999). Strategies of accommodation: Development of a coding system for conversational interaction. *Journal of Language and Social Psychology, 18,* 123–152.

Li, H. (2001). Cooperative and intrusive interruptions in inter- and intracultural dyadic discourse. *Journal of Language and Social Psychology, 20,* 259–284.

Littlejohn, S. W., & Foss, K. A. (2005). *Theories of communication* (8th ed.). Belmont, CA: Wadsworth.

McGlone, M. S., & Giles, H. (2011). Language and interpersonal communication. In M. L. Knapp & J. A. Daly (Eds.), *The SAGE Handbook of interpersonal communication* (4th ed., pp. 201–237). Thousand Oaks, CA: Sage.

Namy, L. L., Nygaard, L. C., & Saureteig, D. (2002). Gender differences in vocal accom-modation: The role of perception. *Journal of Language and Social Psychology, 21,* 422–432.

Nettle, D., & Dunbar, R. I. M. (1997). Social markers and the evolution of reciprocal exchange. *Current Anthropology, 38,* 93–99.

Reid, S. A., Zhang, J., Anderson, G. L., Gasiorek, J., Bonilla, D., & Peinado, S. (2012). Parasite primes make foreign-accented English sound more distant to people who are disgusted by pathogens (but not by sex or morality). *Evolution and Human Behavior, 33,* 471–478.

Rittenour, C. E., & Soliz, J. (2009). Communicative and relational dimensions of shared fam-ily identity and relational intentions in mother-in-law/daughter-in-law relationships: Developing a conceptual model for mother-in-law/daughter-in-law research. *Western Journal of Communication, 73,* 67–90.

Robertson, K., & Murachver, T. (2006). Intimate partner violence, linguistic features and accommodation behavior of perpetrators and victims. *Journal of Language and Social Psychology, 25,* 406–422.

Ross, S., & Shortreed, I. M. (1990). Japanese foreigner talk: Convergence or divergence? *Journal of Asian Pacific Communication, 1,* 135–145.

Soliz, J., & Giles, H. (in press). Relational and identity processes in communication: A contextual and meta-analytical review of communication accommodation theory. In E. Cohen (Ed.), *Communication yearbook 38*. Thousand Oaks, CA: Sage.

Soliz, J., & Rittenour, C. E. (2012). Family as an intergroup arena. In H. Giles (Ed.), *The handbook of intergroup communication* (pp. 331–343). New York, NY: Routledge.

Soliz, J., Thorson, A., & Rittenour, C. E. (2009). Communicative correlates of satisfaction, family identity, and group salience in multiracial/ethnic families. *Journal of Marriage and Family, 71*, 819–832.

Speer, R. B., Giles, H., & Denes, A. (2013). Investigating stepparent-stepchild interactions: The role of communication accommodation. *Journal of Family Communication, 13*, 1–24.

Tajfel, H. (Ed.). (1978). *Differentiation between social groups*. London: Academic Press.

Tajfel, H., & Turner, J. C. (1979). An integrative theory of intergroup conflict. In W. C. Austin & S. Worchel (Eds.), *The social psychology of intergroup relations* (pp. 33–53). Monterey, CA: Brooks/Cole.

Thakerar, J., Giles, H., & Cheshire, J. (1982). Psychological and linguistic parameters of speech accommodation theory. In C. Fraser & K. R. Scherer (Eds.), *Advances in the social psychology of language* (pp. 205–255). Cambridge, UK: Cambridge University Press.

van Baaren, R. B., Horgan, T. G., Chatrand, T. L., & Dijkmans, M. (2004). The forest, the trees, and the chameleon: Context dependence and mimicry. *Journal of Personality and Social Psychology, 86*, 453–459.

van den Berg, M. E. (1986). *Language planning and language use in Taiwan: A study of language choice behavior in public settings*. Taipei, Taiwan: Crane.

Watson, B., & Gallois, C. (1998). Nurturing communication by health professionals toward patients: A communication accommodation theory approach. *Health Communication, 10*, 343–355.

Weber, R., Popovam L., & Mangus, M. (2012). Universal morality, medicated narratives, and neural synchrony. In R. Tamborini (Ed.), *Media and the moral mind* (pp. 26–42). London: Routledge.

West, R., & Turner, L. H. (2007). *Introducing communication theory: Analysis and application* (3rd ed.). New York, NY: McGraw-Hill.

13

Communication Theory of Identity

Multilayered Understandings of Performed Identities

Michael L. Hecht

I dentity is something that has concerned people for as long as recorded history (Sorabji, 2006). Questions like, "who am I" and "how do others see me" are not just teenage concerns but pervasive throughout the lifetime. Why is this? How can we understand identity and use it to communicate more effectively? What is identity, and why do we have theories about it? These are questions that the communication theory of identity (CTI) seeks to answer; but, to answer those questions, we start at the beginning.

Intellectual Tradition of Communication Theory of Identity

The study of "self" is found in literature and philosophy, but our modern social scientific understanding of self and communication finds its historical home in psychology (James, 1891) and sociology (Cooley, 1902; Mead, 1913). In the 1950s and 1960s, as people began to express more individualism (some would say narcissism), scholars, too, came to focus on individuals. They asked themselves what the self was and articulated the constructs of self-concept (how you think about yourself) and self-esteem (how you feel about yourself) (Gergen, 1971). This helped us understand a bit about how people communicated—if you see yourself clearly as a certain type of person and are happy about it you are likely to be more confident and accurate in your communication. However, talking about self in the singular (we have one self) also included the assumption that people had a core or genuine self. From this perspective, does it mean that the police officer who is strong and assertive at work but warm and flexible at home is insincere? How about the nurse who focuses on the needs of others at work but wants his or her own needs met at home? Or someone who is outgoing and joking with one friend but serious and intellectual with another? These examples all question the notion of one core or genuine self.

In the discipline of sociology, the development and popularization of symbolic interactionism (Blumer, 1969; McCall & Simmons, 1978) lead to a conceptualization of the self as emerging out of one's social interactions as well as the perceptions of others. The development of the self through significant others (particular people who were important in shaping the self) and generalized others (a general or communal definition of self) further elaborated the construct. Questions remained about how the individual and the social aspects of symbolic interactionism are merged, and ultimately the theory relies on an individualistic notion of meaning or interpretation. Similar to the psychological tradition, the self was still most often discussed in unitary terms with social roles reserved for the various different manifestations. For example, one might try to understand what influences a child through social constructions but it still comes down to parenting, key adults such as teachers, coaches, and/or religious leaders. Thus, the self, though more complex, remained somewhat problematic.

As people grappled with these problems and scholars in other disciplines began to involve themselves in seeking answers, the term *identity* came into use. An identity approach does not imply a single, unified or core self but that we have multiple identities, as the example of the police officer at home and work demonstrated. This approach drew on "social role theory" from sociology (looking at the various roles people play), realizing that sometimes we come to see and define ourselves through these roles (Burke & Reitzes, 1981; Stryker, 1980). Adopting an identity approach provided a more complex and yet also more accurate picture of people and their communication. However, this complexity was, itself, a problem. Thus, the conundrum: Simple theories of identity do not capture its richness, and overly obtuse or complex theories are not very useful guides for research and behavior.

My own entry into the identity dialogue occurred in response to my research on inter-ethnic communication with Sidney Ribeau at a time when I "was becoming single" in Los Angeles, which I considered almost a foreign culture after growing up in New York and living in Illinois and Montana. I was confronted in my personal life as well as in my scholarly pursuit of theory and research with a very complex web of people, relationships, and messages. I did not want to "essentialize" people as single identities, particularly group-based ones, and miss the nuances in people who went to clubs some nights but watched art films and read novels on others. In our research, we did not want to treat members of ethnic groups as homogeneous and stereotype them. Moreover, we found the theories we were using could not explain our empirical findings. Based on more traditional identity theories we tested a model that predicted that identity would influence inter-ethnic communication that, in turn, would influence outcomes such as communication satisfaction (Hecht, Larkey, & Johnson, 1992):

Identity ⇒ Communication ⇒ Communication Satisfaction

However, when we did more studies we found that our statistical analyses did not support the overall model. On the other hand, we found that a new model in which identity was coupled with communication provided an excellent explanation of communication satisfaction:

Identity/Communication ⇒ Communication Satisfaction

That is, we learned that together identity and communication influence outcomes. I reasoned that this meant that identity was not separate from communication. As Hecht and Hopfer (2010) note, this was a turning point in CTI thinking.

In response, we migrated toward the post-positivist "intergroup" approach of Tajfel and Turner (1979), with Giles and Gudykunst as their leading communication disciples, but also influenced by the interpretive theory and method of Ethnography of Communication (Carbaugh, 1988; Philipsen, 1992) and Critical/Cultural Studies/Post-Modernism[1] (Grossberg, Nelson, & Treichler, 1992) that were becoming a central part of the intercultural communication conversation. It seemed like there must be a way to involve these diverse yet insightful perspectives to help us understand the delightfully complex and paradoxical construct/process known as identity. Thus, the goal was to integrate post-positivist, interpretive, and critical approaches to explain identity and communication. The dilemma was how to use all of these perspectives and still get published in a discipline that often required a single, unified theoretical approach. At the same time, I was migrating my research into the domain of public health and studying substance abuse, and I was concerned about how this direction could be represented to an empiricist, post-positivist community. Thus, while the roots of CTI are in communication as a discipline, its articulation truly emerged from interdisciplinary thought and exposure.

An idea came to me from my reading of Eastern philosophy, particularly Taoism (Bynner, 1944; Huff, 1982) and books attempting to merge Western physics with Eastern philosophy (Capra, 1977; Zukav, 1979) that talk about the "multi-layered" nature of reality. In other words, our lives are experienced at a number of levels or layers. The metaphor that emerged in my mind was the tides in the ocean. Tides are recognizable as distinct but are clearly part of the overall ocean. We can talk about tides as separate entities, but they are a layer in the ocean's reality. OK, that may be a little abstract, but going back to the dilemmas of self we discussed earlier—the police officer, nurse, friend—we can see these as layers of identity. As luck with have it, Charles Bantz, a friend and colleague, had just begun to edit the journal *Communication Monographs* and decided to begin his editorship with essays focused on looking ahead to what communication theory and research might become in the next decade. He invited me to look forward and write about my emerging view, and the original formulation of the communication theory of identity was articulated in my essay "2002—A Research Odyssey: Toward the Development of a Communication Theory of Identity" (Hecht, 1993). Putting aside how long ago 2002 now seems (it was the future then), what did CTI try to accomplish?

Main Goals and Features of Communication Theory of Identity

The overall goal of CTI is to capture the complex and fluid nature of identity by articulating a "layered" perspective of identity in which communication is conceptualized as identity enactment or performance rather than merely a cause or result/effect of communication. CTI adopts a dialectic or paradoxical view of layers, conceptualizing the layers of identity as both changing and stable as well as both subjective and ascribed.

CTI helps us understand that identity is layered in a number of ways. First, layering means that identity is experienced in multiple ways. We can experience ourselves through emotional, behavioral, cognitive, and/or spiritual ways of knowing. In other words, your identity can be known by what you and others feel, do, think, or through mystical means. CTI also emphasizes that we have more than one identity. We might identify with an aspect of our personality (agreeable or conscientious), a relationship (friend or student), or group membership (gender or ethnicity). Typically, our identity at any one moment would consist of many, perhaps all, of these layers.

Based on these premises, CTI points to four identity layers: personal, relational, enacted, and communal. Personal identity denotes how an individual defines him- or herself. Derived from psychology's work on self and personality (Gergen, 1971), this is probably the layer most closely identified with self in Western culture: one that privileges the individual. At the same time, as originally conceptualized, this layer includes group-based identities including ethnic/racial and gender identities (Tajfel & Turner, 1979).

The next layer, relational identity, is more complex. Here, symbolic interaction's looking-glass self and role theory come into play (Blumer, 1969; McCall & Simmons, 1978). The assumption of these theories is that there is a counter-identity for each identity (Burke & Reitzes, 1981). This layer, then, captures identities that are defined in terms of particular relationships (e.g., parent, friend, and boss), in relation to other identities (e.g., leader/follower) as well as identities that are ascribed by others (how others see us).

Next, we have the enacted identity that is the performance of identity—how our behavior expresses who we are. This layer is derived from sociology's role theory as well as the cultural studies and ethnography of communication notion that identity is performed or enacted. This layer is discussed in greater depth in the next section because it articulates a conceptualization of communication (Burke & Reitzes, 1981).

Finally, there is communal identity that is intended as the broadest layer, articulating how society defines identity and identities. Here, the individualism of Western culture (and the resulting limitations of the English language) often interferes with articulation. In talking about CTI, this is the layer that is hardest to explain. Derived from Ethnography of Communication (Carbaugh, 1988; Philipsen, 1992) and Cultural Studies (Grossberg et al. 1992), communal identities transcend the individuals and describe cultures or societies. We learn about this layer from media representations, organizations, religion, education, politics, and so on. One might, for example, ask what our religions say about what we value and how what is taught in our schools tells us about what we believe. If we look at popular websites or the videos viewed most frequently on YouTube, what would we conclude is of interest to us?

As indicated above, the theory does not conceptualize these layers as independent, but rather as interdependent. While I can talk about the personal and relational layers as separate, clearly we learn about our individual identities through our relationships, and our personal identities influence the types of relational identities we form. For example, people who are highly individualistic in their personal identities are less likely to become very dependent on a relationship. To reflect this, the construct of "interpenetration" was borrowed from cultural studies to discuss how layers form amalgamations or as the processes of combining or uniting elements of identity. In other words, layering was seen as an analytical device or a way of describing the theory. But when we use the theory we typically consider more than one layer at a time, and interpenetration is the metaphor for articulating how layers inter-relate.

One of the ways identities interpenetrate is through the individual and social nature of reality. CTI points out that identity, while a subjective or individual experience of self, also involves how others see us. In other words, how we perceive that others "ascribe" identities to us. For example, an individual may view themselves as caring but their peer group labels them as the "mother" or "protector" of the group. While these two identities certainly complement one another, the individual may see the "mother" identity as being a pressure to be more caring than they actually are and/or be uncritical in their support. This individual may then become more caring and mothering as a result of this group identity and perceived pressures. Our best relationships are typically those in which others see us the way we want to be seen. On the other hand, stereotypes are examples of ascriptions that are group- rather than individual-based and rigidly applied. As result, we may want to choose relationships where people see us in a positive way or even as we hope or want to be.

How Communication Is Conceptualized in Communication Theory of Identity

As indicated above, one of the key theoretical "moves" made by CTI is to see communication *as* identity and identity *as* communication. Previously, scholars were concerned with the role of communication in developing identity or how identity might cause people to communicate. They might, for example, study how parents' communication with children influences identity development. Others were concerned with how identity influences communication. As indicated above, originally, Ribeau and I were pursuing this path. We had the idea that people with different types of African American identities would communicate differently in inter-ethnic relationships. For example, we speculated that less salient African American identities would have less influence on communication than more salient versions of the identity. In other words, people of African descent whose gender, work, and other identities were more important to them than their ethnicity would communicate differently than those for whom African American identity was paramount. As noted earlier, our research showed that this model did not fit our data well. Instead, identity salience and communication jointly influenced outcomes. We interpreted this to mean that communication *was* identity and identity *was* communication. Thus was born CTI and the enacted layer of identity.

The idea that identity is performed is not unique to CTI or the communication field. Goffman (1959), for example, a leading interpretivist, wrote extensively about communication as a performance of identity. Goffman viewed communication as more than just something identity causes but, rather, an element of identity itself. Others in communication have followed on in this tradition (e.g., Bergen & Braithwaite, 2009). CTI agrees with Goffman that even though all communication does not enact identity and identity is more than just communication, when we talk we *are* our identities. While this may sound obtuse to some, think about the times you are most self-conscious. The reason you are concerned about how you express yourself in those situations is because others will make assumptions about the kind of person you are. Also think about what you do that communicates your identity (e.g., tell jokes because you are "funny"; work on computers because you are a "geek"). So, you are your communication because the very act of expression is the identity. On the other hand, sometimes we just want information so we ask a question. In this case, the communication is not an identity enactment; rather, it serves other functions.

Research and Practical Applications of Communication Theory of Identity

CTI is guiding a number of lines of research, some of which are mentioned in the previous section. However, perhaps one of the more fruitful lines of work was developed by Jung, who studied "interpenetration" (Jung & Hecht, 2004). Jung argued that two interpenetrating layers could be cognitively consistent or inconsistent, and this poses a dilemma. For example, I might see myself as assertive (personal layer) but others might ascribe aggressiveness to me (relational identity). People with less power often suppress an expression of their identities, creating a gap between personal and enacted identities. Others may have a personal or enacted role-based identity that is inconsistent with how society defines that role (i.e., communal identity). Jung and colleagues labeled these as "identity gaps" and reasoned that this problematic situation should cause ineffective communication and personal discomfort (Jung & Hecht, 2004, 2008; Jung, Hecht, & Wadsworth, 2007; Wadsworth, Hecht, & Jung, 2008). In a series of studies, we were able to demonstrate that identity gaps cause dissatisfying communication and lead to negative psychological outcomes such as depression.

On the other hand, one might speculate that identity gaps may prove useful in promoting health (Hecht & Choi, 2012). If gaps cause dissonance, research suggests that people will try to bring resolution to the situation by changing something about themselves, their thoughts, or their behaviors. By invoking or creating a gap, you may be able to motivate someone to change. Think about a medical doctor who is trying to motivate a patient to follow a prescribed treatment. This turns out to be one of the main challenges people in public health have, as many people, perhaps most, do not do follow the prescribed treatment regimen. This is particularly problematic for diseases that require daily management such as diabetes. It may be that creating identity gaps will create a kind of "cognitive dissonance" that occurs when someone holds two competing beliefs. So, a patient may see themselves as responsible (personal identity) but not see violating the treatment regimen as a problem. If the health practitioner can get the patient to see the violation as an enacted identity (i.e., what kind of person they are) this may create an identity gap that motivates compliance with the treatment. Of course, if the gap is too large the patient may just become depressed and do even less to help him- or herself. We can see potential uses of CTI for communication between parents and adolescents, for example, or supervisors and subordinates.

CTI also can be useful in helping people understand each other. Think of a manager, for example, who is exposed to a very limited part of an employee's identity. It will be difficult to motivate that employee without a fuller picture of who they are—a picture that emerges if they apply CTI. The work-home life conflict that many people experience can be seen as emerging out of the competing identities of, on the one hand, being a good, hardworking employee and, on the other, being devoted to one's family. These competing identities can result in an identity gap.

Similarly, understanding CTI can improve relationships. Remembering that ascriptions can become part of the relationship identity, people in romantic relationships want their partner's view of them to be both positive and valued. One of the insights from my early work on communication satisfaction was that it is not only important for someone to view you positively, but it is even better if the things they like about you are things you like or value about yourself. This also was apparent in work I did on romantic love with Marston (Marston & Hecht, 1994), when we argued that it was more important that the way one partner expresses love needs to be received or complement the other than it is that it match the other's expressions. Thus, we want our romantic partners to value and like things about us that we like and value about ourselves.

Evaluation of Communication Theory of Identity

There have not, as yet, been formal or traditional evaluations of CTI per se. This is, perhaps, reflective of the complexity of the theory. However, a number of scholars have used CTI to frame their research. These studies become practical tests of the theory. Most basic textbooks will tell you that among the criteria for judging theory are its practical utility and heurism. I have argued that the ability to use a theory in practice is one of its strongest tests (Miller-Day & Hecht, 2010). We should not just test our theories by setting up laboratory experiments or administering surveys involving college students; rather, when messages based on those theories have the intended effect in practice or when research using the theory leads to rich and powerful findings it is a testament to the strength of the theory.

Using these criteria, CTI has been tested. For example, both Warren (Warren, Hecht, Jung, Kvasny, & Henderson, 2010; Warren et al., 2010) and

Witteborn (2007) used it to guide their qualitative studies of online health seeking and the identities of Arab women, respectively. Maeda applied CTI to help describe the identities of Japanese single women (Maeda, 2008; Maeda & Hecht, 2012). Others have used CTI to study first-generation college students (Orbe, 2004), bicultural bilingual speakers (Heinz, 2001), and grandchild-grandparent communication (Kam & Hecht, 2009). CTI has informed my work on substance use and cultural identity (Ndiaye, Hecht, Wagstaff, & Elek, 2009) that underlies a drug prevention curriculum called *Keepin' it REAL.* The curriculum has proved effective in reducing adolescent substance use (Hecht, Graham, & Elek, 2006) and now is the most widely disseminated school drug prevention curriculum in the world. We also have used CTI in a series of studies to explicate Jewish American identity and communication (Faulkner & Hecht, 2011; Golden, Niles, & Hecht, 1998; Hecht & Faulkner, 2000; Hecht et al., 2002).

These studies suggest that CTI is effective in guiding thinking about identity and communication. At the same time, they suggest a potential revision of the theory that adds another level of complexity. Warren (2006), for example, developed an ecological model of identity in which she argued that there are both individual and communal levels of the layers. Witteborn (2007) reached similar conclusions, suggesting we think about the layers as indicated in Table 13.1.

One of the key elements of this move is to consider an individual's group-based identities at both the individual level and the communal level. Given the prominence of these identities in theory, research, and practice, this may be a fruitful revision.

Continuing the Conversation

The communication environment I sought to explain when I first started working on CTI in the later part of the 20th century was, in many ways, less complex than what we face in the current millennium. The explosion of social media creates infinite intersections of communal identities as well as vehicles

Table 13.1   Reconceptualizing CTI

Individual Level	Communal Level
Personal Identity	Personal Identity
Relational Identity	Relational Identity
Enacted Identity	Enacted Identity
Communal Identity	Communal Identity

for enacting identities. Just think, if you will, of the proliferation of cat videos on YouTube. Does this invite the following CTI analysis?

- Personal identity—cat person (and maybe even crazy cat ladies)
- Enacted identity—posting and sharing pictures of cats
- Relational identity—pets as friends; ascribed identity—being a cat or dog person
- Communal identity—media constructions of these identities

And when there are intersecting enactments on websites, Twitter, and interpersonal conversations, might there be enacted gaps? It is hard enough to remember the stories you've told your friends, but when you have to remember what you tweet or post on Facebook the task of managing and negotiating identity is even more complex.

We would also ask whether certain identities are themselves inherently problematic. For example, I offered examples of illness identities earlier in this essay (Hecht & Hopfer, 2010; Hecht, Warren, Jung, & Krieger, 2004). Someone who comes to identify as someone with a fatal disease (e.g., cancer patient) is harder to motivate to maintain treatment. One also might ask if highly risky behavior is an unhealthy enactment of identity, does this change how we try to reduce it?

Conversely, we may be able to use CTI to promote healthy behaviors. Elsewhere Choi and I (Hecht & Choi, 2012) suggested that identity layers might prove useful in health message design. We speculated that we might address different health behaviors with health promotion messages from each layer. For example, we might encourage someone to improve their diet if we could get them to believe they would be a better person if they did this. Below, in Table 13.2, are some messages from each layer that might prove useful.

It is my belief that we have barely scratched the surface in using CTI in our personal and professional lives. It is my hope that this chapter invites you to be part of this discussion. How can you use CTI? What can you do with it?

Table 13.2 CTI and Health Message Design

Identity Layer	Health Behavior	Health Promotion
Personal Layer	Health/disease identity	You will be a better person if . . .
Enacted Layer	Health provider–patient communication	You will be the life of the party if . . .
Relational Layer	Family privacy	You will be a better family member if you . . .
Communal Layer	Indigenous health practices	Your family (work group) will benefit if . . .

Note

1. I use the cultural studies convention of "slashes" to denote that the concepts I "borrowed" from these perspectives transcends their differences. I am not equating critical theory, cultural studies, and post modernism but, rather, drawing on certain central constructs like the dialectic/paradoxical nature of the world the contested nature of identity/ites. In this tradition, a single cite is provided to represent a diverse body of theory.

References

Bergen, K. M., & Braithwaite, D. O. (2009). Identity as constituted in communication. In W. F. Eadie (Ed.), *21st century communication* (pp. 165–173). Thousand Oaks, CA: Sage.

Blumer, H. (1969). *Symbolic interactionism.* Englewood Cliffs, NJ: Prentice-Hall.

Burke, P. J., & Reitzes, D. C. (1981). The link between identity and role performance. *Social Psychology Quarterly, 44,* 83–92.

Bynner, W. (Trans.) (1944). *The way of life according to Lau Tzu.* New York, NY: Perigee Books.

Capra, F. (1977). *The Tao of physics.* New York, NY: Harper Collins.

Carbaugh, D. (1988). *Talking American: Cultural discourses on* Donahue. Norwood, NJ: Ablex.

Cooley, C. H. (1902). *Human nature and social order.* New York, NY: Charles Scribner's Sons.

Faulkner, S., & Hecht, M. L. (2011). The negotiation of closetable identities: A narrative analysis of lesbian, gay, transgendered, queer Jewish identity. *Journal of Social and Personal Relationships, 28,* 829–847.

Gergen, K. (1971). *The concept of self.* New York, NY: Holt, Rinehart & Winston.

Goffman, E. (1959). *The presentation of self in everyday life.* Garden City, NY: Anchor.

Golden, D. R., Niles, T. A., & Hecht, M. L. (1998). Jewish American identity. In J. N. Martin, T. K. Nakayama, & L. A. Flores (Eds.), *Readings in cultural contexts* (pp. 62–69). Mountain View, CA: Mayfield.

Grossberg, L., Nelson, C., & Treichler, P. (Eds.). (1992). *Cultural studies.* New York, NY: Routledge.

Hecht, M. L. (1993). 2002—a research odyssey: Toward the development of a communication theory of identity. *Communication Monographs, 60,* 76–82.

Hecht, M., & Choi, H. J. (2012). The communication theory of identity as a framework for health message design. In H. Cho & M. Byrnie (Ed.), *Health communication message design: Theory, research, and practice* (pp. 137–152). Thousand Oaks, CA: Sage.

Hecht, M. L., & Faulkner, S. L. (2000). Sometimes Jewish, sometimes not: The closeting of Jewish American identity. *Communication Studies, 51,* 372–387.

Hecht, M. L., Faulkner, S. L., Meyer, C. R., Niles, T. A., Golden, D., & Cutler, M. (2002). Looking through *Northern Exposure* at Jewish American identity and the communication theory of identity. *Journal of Communication, 52,* 852–870.

Hecht, M. L., Graham, J. W. & Elek, E. (2006). The drug resistance strategies intervention: Program effects on substance use. *Health Communication, 20,* 267–276.

Hecht, M. L., & Hopfer, S. (2010). The communication theory of identity. In R. L. Jackson (Ed.), *Encyclopedia of identity, 1* (pp. 115–119). Thousand Oaks, CA: Sage.

Hecht, M. L., Larkey, L. K., & Johnson, J. N. (1992). African American and European American perceptions of problematic issues in interethnic communication effectiveness. *Human Communication Research, 19,* 209–236.

Hecht, M. L., Warren, J., Jung, J., & Krieger, J. (2004). Communication theory of identity. In W. B. Gudykunst (Ed.), *Theorizing about intercultural communication* (pp. 257–278). Newbury Park, CA: Sage.

Heinz, B. (2001). Fish in the river: Experiences of bicultural bilingual speakers. *Multilingua, 20*(1), 85–108.

Huff, B. (1982). *The Tao of Pooh.* New York, NY: Penguin Books.

James, W. (1891). *The principles of psychology, V01.1.* Cambridge, MA: Harvard University Press. (Original work published 1890)

Jung, E., & Hecht, M. L. (2004). Elaborating the communication theory of identity: Identity gaps and communication outcomes. *Communication Quarterly, 52,* 265–283.

Jung, E., & Hecht, M. L. (2008). Identity gaps and level of depression among Korean immigrants. *Health Communication, 23,* 313–325.

Jung, E., Hecht, M. L., & Wadsworth, B. C. (2007). The role of identity in international students' psychological well-being in the United States: A model of depression level, identity gaps, discrimination, and acculturation. *International Journal of Intercultural Relations, 31,* 605–624.

Kam, J. A., & Hecht, M. L. (2009). Investigating the role of identity gaps among communicative and relational outcomes within the grandparent-grandchild relationship: The young-adult grandchildren's perspective. *Western Journal of Communication, 73,* 456–480.

Maeda, E. (2008). Relational identities of always-single Japanese women. *Journal of Social and Personal Relationships, 25,* 967–987.

Maeda, E., & Hecht, M. L. (2012). Identity search: Interpersonal relationships and relational identities of always-single Japanese women over time. *Western Journal of Communication, 76,* 44–64.

Marston, P. J., & Hecht, M. L. (1994). Maintaining love in romantic relationships. In D. J. Canary & L. Stafford (Eds.), *Communication and relationship maintenance* (pp. 187–202). San Diego, CA: Academic Press.

McCall, G. J., & Simmons, J. L. (1978). *Identities and interactions.* New York, NY: Free Press.

Mead, G. H. (1913). The social self. *Journal of Philosophy, Psychology and Scientific Methods, 10,* 374–380.

Miller-Day, M. A., & Hecht, M. L. (2010). "Applied" aspects of the Drug Resistance Strategies Project. *Journal of Applied Communication Research, 38,* 215–229.

Ndiaye, K., Hecht, M. L., Wagstaff, D. A., & Elek, E. (2009). Mexican-heritage preadolescents' ethnic identification and perceptions of substance use. *Substance Use and Misuse, 44,* 1160–1183.

Orbe, M. P. (2004). Negotiating multiple identities within multiple frames: An analysis of first-generation college students. *Communication Education, 53,* 131–149.

Philipsen, G. (1992). *Speaking culturally: Explorations in social communication.* Albany, NY: SUNY Press.

Sorabji, R. (2006). *Self: Ancient and modern insights about individuality, life, and death.* Chicago, IL: University of Chicago Press.

Stryker, S. (1980). *Symbolic interactionism: A social structural version.* Menlo Park, CA: Benjamin Cummings.

Tajfel, H., & Turner, J. C. (1979). An integrative theory of intergroup conflict. In W. G. Austin & S. Worchel (Eds.), *The social psychology of intergroup relations* (pp. 33–47). Monterey, CA: Brooks/Cole.

Wadsworth, B. C., Hecht, M. L., & Jung, E. (2008). The role of identity gaps, discrimination, and acculturation in international students' educational satisfaction in American classrooms. *Communication Education, 57,* 64–87.

Warren, J. R. (2006). Communicating identities in health information seeking: Single African American mothers, preadolescent substance use prevention, and the Internet. (Unpublished doctoral dissertation). The Pennsylvania State University.

Warren, J. R., Hecht, M. L., Jung, E., Kvasny, L., & Henderson, M. (2010). African American ethnic and class-based identities on the World Wide Web: Moderating the effects of information self-perceived seeking/finding and internet self efficacy. *Communication Research 37*(5), 674–702.

Warren, J. R., Kvasny, L., Hecht, M. L., Burgess, D., Ahluwalia, J. S., & Okuyemi, K. S. (2010). Barriers, control and identity in health information seeking: Listening to lower income African American women. *Journal of Health Disparities Research and Practice, 3,* 68–90.

Witteborn, S. (2007). The situated expression of Arab collective identities in the United States. *Journal of Communication, 57,* 556–575.

Zukav, G. (1979). *The Dancing Wu Li Masters: An overview of the new physics.* London: Ebury Publishing.

14

Critical Approaches to Interpersonal Communication

Charting a Future

Leslie A. Baxter and Bryan Asbury

A s the Introduction to this volume documents, critical approaches to interpersonal communication occupy a very small percentage of the published research. The list of interpersonal communication theories is a short one: relational dialectics theory (Baxter, 2011; see Chapter 21, in this volume), narrative performance theory (Langellier & Peterson, 2004; see also Chapter 19), and the family of feminist theories (see Chapter 15). Although Tracy (Chapter 18) refers to action implicative discourse analysis theory as critical, she admits that her use of this term departs from how scholars in the critical tradition deploy that term. Rather than using our chapter as an exercise in discussing existing critical theories of interpersonal/family communication, we take a different direction in summarizing two primary strands in the critical project more generally in order to encourage the development of additional critical interpersonal communication theories.

Intellectual Tradition of Critical Approaches

Although it is convenient to work within the traditional tripartite distinction among post-positivistic, interpretive, and critical approaches (e.g., Habermas, 1971), none of these is unitary, and each might better be described as a cluster of approaches that bear a family resemblance to one another. Critical organizational communication scholars Deetz (2001) and Mumby (1997) distinguish the critical modern tradition from the critical postmodern tradition, and we find this division useful for the purposes of this chapter on interpersonal/family communication. What these two perspectives share in common is a practice of critique with respect to how power functions in communicative life with the twin scholarly goals of emancipation and empowerment. They differ in how power is conceptualized, a topic to be elaborated on in the next section of the chapter.

Despite conceptual differences, however, critical scholars of both modernist and postmodernist stripes stand united in moving beyond the approaches to power typically adopted by post-positivistic scholars and by interpretive scholars. The post-positivistic tradition conceptualizes power as an individual-level variable based on the various kinds of resources the individual possesses (e.g., Berger, 1994), for example having a reputation as someone who is credible. From this tradition, power is one of a myriad of individual variables from which a researcher might choose in order to causally explain communicative life understood as an objectively observable phenomenon or process. Considered as a whole, the interpretive project is one in which individual consciousness is centered with the scholarly goal of understanding shared systems of meaning in the form of intersubjective agreement, common codes of communication, and shared culture. Interpretive scholars are committed to rich descriptive understanding rather than critique. In fact, scholars such as Philipsen (1989/1990) have gone so far as to argue that a critical agenda impedes the descriptive agenda because of its imposition of a priori concepts and values (see Cushman, 1989/1990, for alternative opinions). By contrast, critical scholars argue that power is omnipresent in the human condition, and an understanding of how it functions is essential in understanding and changing social reality.

Main Goals and Features of Critical Approaches

Mumby (1997) productively differentiates the critical modern tradition from the critical postmodern tradition by describing it as a shift in scholarly sensibilities: from suspicion to vulnerability. Critical modern scholars are suspicious of the consensual view sought by interpretive scholars, instead viewing such surface-level shared meanings as a veil that obscures deeply structured inequities, conflicts, and contradictions. In unmasking such oppressive systems as capitalism, institutional/structural inequities, and ideologies in which the interests of some are advanced over the interests of others, critical modern scholars hope to emancipate socially oppressed persons in the interests of more fully realizing the Enlightenment goals of reason and rationality in a democracy of open exchange.

By contrast, critical postmodern scholars adopt a less finalized stance, one in which faith in the Enlightenment ideal of rational consciousness has been abandoned, along with the a priori view of omnipresent oppressive structural/ideological systems that constrain the unfettered exchange of views. Instead, postmodern scholars adopt a more locally emergent and contingent view of power in which discourses—language-based systems of knowledge claims about what is and what ought to be—supplant individual consciousness as the focus of scholarly attention. In contrast to their critical modern cousins, postmodern critical scholars view the social world as an inherently unstable struggle of competing discourses as dominant discourses are ongoingly vulnerable to resistant discursive voices in the micropractices of everyday life. With the basic distinction in mind between critical modern and critical postmodern projects, each merits elaboration with respect to goals and major characteristics.

THE CRITICAL MODERN TRADITION

Modern critical theory views power as a systemic construct that exists external to the individuals who operate within those systems. The first major wave of critical theory is most closely aligned with the works of German philosopher and economist Karl Marx in the mid-1800s (1988) but can be traced back to earlier works by Hegel and even Aristotle (Pine, 1993). Modern critical theory operates on the belief that the self, presumed to be an autonomous being, is unknowingly operating in larger social systems in ways that are predetermined by those systems, most traditionally economic determinism (Kincheloe & McLaren, 2011). This lack of awareness of constraints on the part of the subordinate person is termed *false consciousness* (Pine, 1993) and allows the individual to participate in and support these broad social systems, which are the true locations of power from the modern critical perspective. These broad social systems are largely taken for granted or misunderstood, including race, class, sexuality, and sex/gender. It is largely the goal of modern critical theories to crack false consciousness and reveal the otherwise invisible systems (McKerrow, 1989) in an attempt to dismantle those oppressive social systems and emancipate people.

Modern critical theory can be difficult in its abstraction. A research exemplar can make these distant concepts more tangible. Park (2009) offers an analysis of interpersonal interactions between urban Black and rural White participants on the reality television show *Real World*. The textual analysis of several episodes explores the ways in which interracial relationships are always attached to broader cultural systems. After several common events occur to both the urban Black and rural White participants of season 15, Park identifies a tension that permeates their relationships. Ultimately, Park deploys critical race theory to identify that these events (e.g., police searching for a gun on one urban Black participant in front of his castmates) are not occurring in social isolation but remain connected to the historical and social systems that predetermine them (such as the racism that has historically plagued Black/White relations, particularly within the American legal system). Although the cast of *Real World* is unable to articulate it in their respective personal interviews, the events on the television show illustrate the ways in which interpersonal interactions are determined and constrained by broader social systems (and also perpetuate those systems). For Park, the interracial relationships are always different for each participant because each race has a different place (with different value, constraints, and privileges) in the system of race in America. We can see the ways in which modern critical theories illuminate the communicative behaviors by pointing to interaction practices that would otherwise go ignored through false consciousness, or inarticulation in this case, about what is occurring. By placing interpersonal behaviors within the larger systems in which they are embedded, researchers are able to articulate the disparate outcomes for different individuals, such as minority races' feelings of isolation in interracial, interpersonal interactions. Without a modern critical perspective, the cycles produced by the broad social systems, such as race, would be ignored and thereby perpetuated.

THE POSTMODERN TRADITION

Postmodern critical scholars resist a view of power as a totalizing, stable phenomenon located in overarching systems of domination such as capitalism and its institutionalized structures. Influenced by the works of the French philosopher Foucault (1979, 1980a, 1980b), power is conceived less as a top-down phenomenon that constrains micropractices of everyday life and more as a bottom-up-and-out dynamic, one that permeates the social world in multiple, dispersed, and decentered everyday sites. Discourses construct power through their knowledge claims: taken-for-granted assertions about what is and what ought to be. The presumptions we have about the world (that is, our knowledge claims in which phenomena are distinguished from one another linguistically, differentially valued, and naturalized) constitute power. The vulnerability of the postmodern stance comes with an appreciation that power (i.e., discourses) is inextricably linked to counterdiscursive resistance (Foucault, 1980b), and thus is unstable and altered in moment-to-moment enactments. The postmodern project is less about understanding how stable institutional and ideological structures constrain the everyday world and more about critically resisting seemingly stable systems of meaning and taken-for-granted constructions of the world. As Deetz (2001, p. 17) so aptly expresses it, the project is to resist "discursive closure" and to "reclaim conflict" by "claim[ing] a space for lost voices" of resistance to dominant discourses.

These ideas are quite abstract, and in an effort to concretize them, let's turn to a representative study in order to understand its postmodern sensibilities: Goltz and Zingsheim's (2010) critical auto-ethnography of their efforts to supplant a heterosexual wedding with a gay Gayla. The study is locally situated in its focus on the coauthors' efforts to resist the heteronormative wedding ritual in executing the alternative commitment ceremony that they refer to as a Gayla to honor their gay partnership. In focusing on one locally enacted ritual event, the authors display a bottom-up-and-out sensibility as opposed to a top-down focus one might find in a modern critical approach, for example, a critique of weddings as a capitalist enterprise that perpetuates the heteronormative model as natural. The essay is centrally about practices of resistance enacted in the Gayla event. It affords a rich description of how the partners organized their Gayla in ways that challenge the taken-for-granted views that their 90 family and friend guests had about what a commitment ceremony should be like, views grounded in the cultural model of the heteronormative wedding ritual. In addition to renaming the event as a "Gayla" instead of a "wedding," the pair enacted practices at every turn to shake up beliefs about what was "normal," including invitations to a weekend celebration of family, community, and love in which the couple was not centered, and the execution of the Gayla event itself through a series of celebrations that continued to de-center the couple in a larger focus on the community of guests. Throughout the study, the authors repeatedly underscore how challenging it is to accomplish resistance, as their guests, who were steeped in the discourse of heteronormativity, ongoingly acted in ways that reframed the Gayla events through a wedding lens. The study affords a rich sense of the discursive push-and-pull as competing discourses of love jockey in constructing the meaning of this weekend event for the partners and for their family and friends. The study challenges readers' taken-for-granted conceptions of heterosexual love and thereby resists discursive closure on what a public commitment ceremony can and should be.

How Communication Is Conceptualized in the Critical Approaches to Interpersonal Communication

Modern and postmodern critical projects have different conceptions of communication. To modern critical scholars, communication is conceptualized as perpetually constrained by the systems within which an individual is operating, such as race, class, and gender. The very rules of grammar, on which oral and written communication traditions are based, are products of class (Schatzman & Strauss, 1955) that reflect power relations. From the modern critical perspective, the way an individual communicates is indicative of that person's social position (i.e., lower classes speak in simple vernaculars and upper classes speak more proficiently as products of class but not producers of that class; e.g., Willis, 1981). Communication is bound by and reflective of the rules and power of the larger social systems. Communication functions to perpetuate systemic constraints, thereby reproducing those very systems.

Postmodern sensibilities are sympathetic to a social constructionist view, albeit with a power overlay: The social world is constituted in communication but not all constructions are equally possible or valued. Communication does not mirror or reflect a preexisting world of objects and phenomena independent from it; rather, communication is that world. That world is biased as some discourses are privileged over others; knowledge is not neutral but favors some worldviews over others.

Research and Practical Applications of Critical Approaches to Interpersonal Communication

Both modern and postmodern critical projects hold potential to bring fresh insights to interpersonal communication scholarship. Two examples, gender and labor, will serve as sites for the application of modern critical theory. Two additional examples, uncertainty and self-disclosure, will serve as sites for the application of postmodern critical theory. By reworking the conceptualization of these phenomena, we seek to open up our scholarship to new possibilities.

GENDER AS A SOCIAL SYSTEM

A modern critical perspective approaches gender as a predetermined system that dictates much of our actions. The modern critical approach to gender does not treat the constraints on behavior and communication by gender or sex as merely a function of biology; the constraints are products of power relations at the systemic level of society. This particular approach to gender has been appropriated in theories of feminist communication (see Chapter 15, in this volume) but can be more fully appreciated in interpersonal scholarship. The modern critical perspective on gender offers additional insights in the ways gender is conceptualized. Instead of the binary of men and women, the modern critical perspective treats gender as a complex system with multiple categorical levels. For example, the category of "man" gets replaced with a system of gender that contains multiple layers of masculinity (Kimmel, 1994). Hegemonic masculinity is the ideal set of behaviors (Connell, 1995) that dictate work, relations, and a myriad of practices from hygiene to sexuality (Trujillo, 1991). In the system of gender, other forms of masculinity, termed *subordinate variants,* exist below hegemonic masculinity, but are still acknowledged (Cornwall & Lindisfarne, 1994). From the modern critical perspective, multiple masculinities exist but are not created equally. In addition to categorical expansion of gender, the treatment of gender as a system by modern critical theories gives interpersonal scholars better access to the influences of that system on relating. Spender (1980) argues that social science fails to approach explanations of gender as it impacts behavior because "research procedures have been so embedded with sexist assumptions that investigators have been blinded to empirical reality" (p. 32). In fact, the very language of relationships and research are entrenched in a language, English, frequently described as inherently masculine in construction and use (Vetterling-Braggin, 1981). Any attempt to describe or analyze using that language will inherently privilege the masculine because the language was constructed in a system set on that end. Appreciating that gender is a broad, complex system beyond the local behaviors or communication investigated within a specific study, we are able to better understand what is occurring and what is at stake in interpersonal interactions.

RELATIONAL LABOR AS A SOCIAL SYSTEM

Given the Marxist roots of modern critical theory, the labor of interpersonal relations would certainly be fertile ground for exploration. In fact, the foundation for such a consideration has strong roots in the work of social exchange theories (see Chapter 30, in this volume) in which the effects of being in a relationship are already riddled with the language of capitalism: costs, benefits, and value. The body of work engaging social exchange theories relies on a metaphor of economy (Chibucos, Leite, & Weis, 2005) but with the assumption that the process occurs within the relational economy at the level of individuals (Kelley, 1979). Modern critical theory can be used to see the economy metaphor through to its end in identifying the ways in which relationships are parts of broader systems with implications for those relational economies. Modern critical theory has been useful in examining the ways in which the types, value, and control of an individual's work is limited or enabled by race (e.g., Royster, 2003), class (e.g., Willis, 1981), and gender (e.g., Howe, 1977); modern critical theory could point to similar insights in relational work. The inclusion of the modern critical perspective would identify the ways in which much of that labor is predetermined without relational negotiations. This reconceptualization of relational work could point to greater systemic consistencies and injustices about the ways in which the work of relationships is actually negotiated and to what ends.

UNCERTAINTY AS A POSITIVE PRECONDITION FOR CHANGE

Because the postmodern sensibility is to view fluidity and flux as inherent in the meaning-making enterprise, uncertainty is the marker of change rather than a problem to be managed, which is the dominant discourse of certainty that grounds existing interpersonal communication research. As Baxter and Braithwaite (2009) note,

> Language use is not without tendency, thus it is significant to note that PIT [Problematic Integration Theory], UMT [Uncertainty Management Theory], and TMIM [Theory of Motivated Information Management] are theories of uncertainty management, not theories of certainty management. Thus, the presumption is that it is uncertainty that requires management.... The prospect that certainty requires management—including the prospect of reducing it—goes unconsidered. (pp. 28–29)

From a postmodern perspective, researchers could productively ask how it is that relating parties resist certainties—discursive closures—for such resistance is the key to opening up new possibilities for meaning. Included in this scholarly agenda is work that examines how it is that uncertainty is discursively constructed as a negative whereas certainty is positively valenced. In a recent study, for example, Baxter and her colleagues (Baxter, Norwood, Asbury, & Scharp, 2013) discuss how adoptive parents' adoption narratives reframe uncertainty in the adoption process from its presumed negative valence to a more positive experience, one which constructs adoption as a profoundly positive experience of redemption (McAdams, 2006).

SELF-MAKING INSTEAD OF SELF-DISCLOSURE

Self-disclosure is among the most researched, if not the most researched, concept in interpersonal communication. But from a postmodern perspective, the concept is predicated on the presumption of an intact, monadic self: an autonomous entity consisting either of a set of cognitive and emotional variables (to the post-positivists) or a subjective consciousness (to interpretivists) that preexists language (e.g., Sampson, 1993). This self functions with intent either to disclose or to keep private information about who the person "really is." Self-disclosure (and its opposite of privacy) is a foundational concept in several popular theories in interpersonal communication (see, for example, Chapters 29 and 25, in this volume—the stage theories and privacy management). A postmodern sensibility shifts the focus away from a presumed intact individual to focus instead on discourses. As such, the "self" invoked in the concept of self-disclosure is a social construct that is produced from within a discourse of individualism. As Baxter (2011) notes, self "is a narrative that feels comfortable in mainstream U.S. society, but it is a narrative nonetheless" (p. 13). Scholars interested in pursuing a postmodern agenda could productively ask not how self is disclosed but rather how the notion of a "self" is discursively constructed through language use with others. Consistent with postmodern vulnerabilities, the postmodern "self" is always in motion or flux rather than the stable, consistent inner rock it is positioned to be in mainstream interpersonal communication research. On its face, this floating self appears similar to the symbolic interactionist (e.g., Blumer, 1969) or social constructionist argument that the self is multiple and emergent (e.g., Gergen, 1994). But these positions tend to ignore the power dynamics that accompany discourses and thus can be considered as more interpretivist than critical in orientation. Postmodern interpersonal communication research is interested in the making of selves would join forces with those critical scholars in other subdisciplinary areas interested in the processes of identity construction (e.g., Mokros, 2003). What interpersonal communication scholars can add to the scholarly conversation is a focus on relating: how our identities as relating beings (e.g., "friend," "significant other," "sister") embedded in organizing units known as relationships (e.g., "friendship," "marriage," "family") are communicatively and ongoingly constructed, again with attention to the reality that not all discourses are equally valued. Although interpersonal communication scholars often opine that relationships are not preexisting context-containers in which communication is situated, research practices persist in positioning relationships as preexisting contexts; hence our research is permeated with research about communication *in* friendships, *in* marriage, *in* gay/lesbian couples, *in* families, rather than a more postmodern inclination to study the performance or construction of "friendship" through talk, and so on. From a postmodern sensibility, however, not all relationship discourses are equally valued, and thus some constructions are more challenging than others to legitimate in the culture. This attention to power is key in differentiating an interpretive approach to social constructionism from a postmodern sensibility in the discursive enterprise of constructing social reality.

Evaluation of Critical Approaches to Interpersonal Communication

Modern and postmodern critical theories are evaluated in other disciplines and within communication along two primary dimensions: ethics and change. Modern and postmodern scholarship, and more broadly all critical work, has a heavy ethical burden. First, the boundaries between the measured and the measurer are always blurry (Minh-ha, 2004). Because we can never be fully removed from our work when engaging critical theories, Code (2008) argues that we must take into account our own positionalities. Second, we must not work to improve conditions within one system or from one perspective at the cost of another. Black feminist critique of White feminism and Black (masculine) scholarship taught critical theorists the difficult lesson that the contributions of any work can only be measured by the damage it does to any other groups of people (Crenshaw, 2008). To measure the ethics of scholarship engaging modern and/or postmodern critical theory, the presence of self-reflexivity is heavily weighted (Visweswaran, 1994) in an attempt to identify one's position as it impacts what is identifiable (the first ethical consideration) and that which is beneficial (the second ethical consideration).

The second category for evaluation is the ability to create change. The goal of both modern and postmodern critical theory is to disrupt the status quo in an attempt to emancipate the marginalized and oppressed (Forrester, 1985). The primary difference between the modern critical approaches and postmodern critical approaches is how that change is envisioned and enacted. For modern critical scholars, change exists at systemic ruptures, such as major shifts in social policy (e.g., Crenshaw, 2008) or the complete dismantling of the system (e.g., Lorde, 2008). For postmodern critical scholars, change exists locally in the discursive (re)negotiation of meaning and practice, such as expanding categories (e.g., Fausto-Sterling, 2008) or possibilities (e.g., Butler, 2008). Across both perspectives, the change must not just simply occur; hooks (2003) contends that all critical scholars must work proactively toward positive change in the lives and conditions of those about whom the work is speaking. Critical theories, modern or postmodern, should be improving the lives of the marginalized, oppressed, and disenfranchised subjects of that scholarship. The final step of evaluating critical scholarship is the extent to which the work meets, or gains ground toward, that end.

Continuing the Conversation

Our argument should not be taken as an argument for the superiority of a critical perspective over post-positivist or interpretive approaches; rather, our argument is that the scholarly conversation could be enhanced with the addition of the critical voice. When scholars of interpersonal communication accept a public-private sphere binary, in which interpersonal relationships are regarded as separate from broader societal and cultural systems and discourses, interpersonal communication can be too easily trivialized, as the public sphere often is valued as somehow more significant or important than the less valued private sphere of the mundane everyday business of relating (Hawes, 1998). Ignoring top-down institutions and ideologies and bottom-up-and-out discourses leads to a peculiar scholarly isolation of interpersonal communication research, as well, which makes it problematic to partake in disciplinary cross-fertilizations with our colleagues in such areas as organizational communication, rhetorical studies, communication ethics, and cross/intercultural communication. Interpersonal communication scholars have much to contribute to the conversation of how society and culture work at the micro-level, complementing more macro-oriented scholarship. A critical turn in interpersonal communication will encourage the continued growth of methodological diversity in our published research, in particular supporting more qualitative work. A critical turn will also encourage more self-reflexivity among researchers, encouraging them to question taken-for-granted assumptions and thereby open new research questions for consideration. We invite you to join us in expanding the scholarly conversation in interpersonal communication!

References

Baxter, L. A. (2011). *Voicing relationships: A dialogic perspective.* Los Angeles, CA: Sage.

Baxter, L. A., & Braithwaite, D. O. (2009). Reclaiming uncertainty: The formation of new meanings in relationships. In W. Afifi & T. Afifi (Eds.), *Handbook of uncertainty and information regulation* (pp. 26–44). New York, NY: Routledge.

Baxter, L. A., Norwood, K., Asbury, B., & Scharp, K. (2013). *Narrating adoption: Resisting adoption as "second best" in online stories of domestic adoption told by adoptive parents.* Manuscript under review.

Berger, C. R. (1994). Power, dominance, and social interaction. In M. L. Knapp & G. R. Miller (Eds.), *Handbook of interpersonal communication* (2nd ed., pp. 450–507). Thousand Oaks, CA: Sage.

Blumer, H. (1969). *Symbolic interactionism: Perspective and method.* Berkeley, CA: University of California Press.

Butler, J. (2008). Performative acts and gender constitution: An essay in phenomenology and feminist theory. In A. Bailey & C. Cuomo (Eds.), *The feminist philosophy reader* (pp. 97–107). Boston, MA: McGraw-Hill.

Chibucos, T. R., Leite, R. W., & Weis, D. L. (2005). *Readings in family theory.* Los Angeles, CA: Sage.

Code, L. (2008). Taking subjectivity into account. In A. Bailey & C. Cuomo (Eds.), *The feminist philosophy reader* (pp. 718–741). Boston, MA: McGraw-Hill.

Connell, R. W. (1995). *Masculinities.* Cambridge, MA: Polity.

Cornwall, A., & Lindisfarne, N. (1994). *Dislocating masculinity: Comparative ethnographies.* London: Routledge.

Crenshaw, K. W. (2008). Mapping the margins: Intersectionality, identity politics, and violence against women of color. In A. Bailey & C. Cuomo (Eds.), *The feminist philosophy reader* (pp. 265–278). Boston, MA: McGraw-Hill.

Cushman, D. P. (1989/1990). The role of critique in the ethnographic study of human communication practices. *Research on Language and Social Interaction, 23,* 243–250.

Deetz, S. (2001). Conceptual foundations. In F. M. Jablin & L. L. Putnam (Eds.), *The new handbook of organizational communication: Advances in theory, research, and methods* (pp. 3–46). Thousand Oaks, CA: Sage.

Fausto-Sterling, A. (2008). Should there be only two sexes? In A. Bailey & C. Cuomo (Eds.), *The feminist philosophy reader* (pp. 124–144). Boston, MA: McGraw-Hill.

Forrester, J. F. (1985). *Critical theory and public life.* Cambridge, MA: MIT Press.

Foucault, M. (1979). *Discipline and punish: The birth of the prison* (A. Sheridan, Trans.). New York, NY: Vintage.

Foucault, M. (1980a). *Power/knowledge: Selected interviews and other writings 1972–1977* (C. Gordon, L. Marshall, J. Mepham, & K. Soper, Trans.). New York, NY: Pantheon.

Foucault, M. (1980b). *The history of sexuality, Volume 1: An introduction* (R. Hurley, Trans.). New York, NY: Vintage.

Gergen, K. J. (1994). *Realities and relationships: Soundings in social construction.* Cambridge, MA: Harvard University Press.

Goltz, D. B., & Zingsheim, J. (2010). It's not a wedding, it's a gayla: Queer resistance and normative recuperation. *Text and Performance Quarterly, 30,* 290–312.

Habermas, J. (1971). *Knowledge and human interests* (J. Shapiro, Trans.). Boston, MA: Beacon Press.

Hawes, L. C. (1998). Becoming-other-wise: Conversational performance and the politics of experience. *Text and Performance Quarterly, 18,* 273–299.

hooks, b. (2003). *Teaching community: A pedagogy of hope.* New York: Routledge.

Howe, K. L. (1977). *Pink collar workers: Inside the world of women's work.* New York, NY: Avon.

Kelley, H. H. (1979). *Personal relationships: Their structures and processes.* Hillsdale, NJ: Lawrence Erlbaum.

Kimmel, M. S. (1994). Masculinity as homophobia: Fear, shame and silence in the construction of gender identity. In H. Brod & M. Kaufman (Eds.), *Theorizing masculinities* (pp. 119–141). Thousand Oaks, CA: Sage.

Kincheloe, J. L., & McLaren, P. (2011). Rethinking critical theory and qualitative research. *Bold Visions in Educational Research, 32,* 285–326.

Langellier, K. M., & Peterson, E. E. (2004). *Storytelling in daily life: Performing narrative.* Philadelphia, PA: Temple University Press.

Lorde, A. (2008). The master's tools will never dismantle the master's house. In A. Bailey & C. Cuomo (Eds.), *The feminist philosophy reader* (pp. 49–51). Boston, MA: McGraw-Hill.

Marx, K. H. (1988). *The Communist manifesto: Annotated text* (F. L. Bender, Ed.). New York, NY: W. W. Norton & Co. (Original work published 1848)

McAdams, D. P. (2006). *The redemptive self: Stories Americans live by.* New York, NY: Oxford University Press.

McKerrow, R. E. (1989). Critical rhetoric: Theory and praxis. *Communication Monographs, 56,* 91–111.

Minh-ha, T. T. (2004). Not you/like you: Post-colonial women and the interlocking questions of identity and difference. In K. A. Foss, S. K. Foss, & C. L. Griffin (Eds.), *Readings in feminist rhetorical theory* (pp. 215–219). Thousand Oaks, CA: Sage.

Mokros, H. B. (2003). *Identity matters: Communication-based explorations and explanations.* Cresswell, NJ: Hampton Press.

Mumby, D. K. (1997). Modernism, postmodernism, and communication studies: A rereading of an ongoing debate. *Communication Theory, 7,* 1–28.

Park, J. H. (2009). The uncomfortable encounter between an urban Black and a rural White: The ideological implications of racial conflict on MTV's *The Real World. Journal of Communication, 59,* 152–171.

Philipsen, G. (1989/1990). Some initial thoughts on the perils of "critique" in the ethnographic study of communicative practices. *Research on Language and Social Interaction, 23,* 251–260.

Pine, C. L. (1993). *Ideology and false consciousness: Marx and his historical progenitors.* Albany, NY: SUNY Press.

Royster, D. A. (2003). *Race and the invisible hand: How white networks exclude black men from blue-collar jobs.* Berkley, CA: University of California Press.

Sampson, E. E. (1993). *Celebrating the other: A dialogic account of human nature.* Boulder, CO: Westview Press.

Schatzman, L., & Strauss, A. (1955). Social class and modes of communication. *The American Journal of Sociology, 60,* 329–338.

Spender, D. (1980). *Man made language.* Boston, MA: Routledge & Kegan Paul.

Trujillo, N. (1991). Hegemonic masculinity on the mound: Media representations of Nolan Ryan and American sports culture. *Critical Studies in Mass Communication, 8,* 290–308.

Vetterling-Braggin, M. (1981). *Sexist language: A modern philosophical analysis.* Patterson, NJ: Littlefield, Adams & Co.

Visweswaran, K. (1994). *Fictions of feminist ethnography.* Minneapolis: University of Minnesota Press.

Willis, P. (1981). *Learning to labor: How working class kids get working class jobs.* New York, NY: Columbia University Press.

15

Critical Feminist Theories

Giving Voice and Visibility to Women's Experiences in Interpersonal Relations

Julia T. Wood

In a book that helped launch the mainstream branch of the second wave of feminism in the United States, Betty Friedan (1963) called attention to what she called "the problem that has no name." Friedan noted that this problem had two parts. First, many middle-class, stay-at-home mothers felt frustrated and not completely fulfilled because their lives were restricted to home and family. Second, because the ideology of the time was that being a stay-at-home mom was the American dream, many of these women felt guilty for not feeling fulfilled and grateful.

Friedan (1963) did not leave the problem unnamed. Instead, she labeled it the feminine mystique—the ideology that being a full-time mother and homemaker was the ideal—and the only ideal—for women. That particular act of naming gave validity to something that was common in many women's experience but unmarked in language. In other words, Friedan gave voice to what had not been voiced, and, in so doing, she gave visibility and social significance to what had been invisible and thus had no social legitimacy (Spender, 1984a, 1984b). Friedan was neither the first nor the last to understand the importance of giving voice—not only to women's experiences, but also to the significance and meaning that women themselves attach to their experiences. Acknowledging and naming women's perspectives on their experiences are prerequisites to having those experiences counted in cultural life. For example, until the term "sexual harassment" was coined, the English language had no adequate name for uninvited and unwelcome sexual attention that targeted women in the workplace and in educational contexts. Similarly, introducing the term "marital rape" into our language increased social and legal awareness that nonconsensual sex between spouses is wrong.

In this chapter, I discuss the process of women's voicing of their experiences, which is a key means by which critical feminist theories contribute to interpersonal communication (Ardener, 1978; Rakow & Wackwitz, 2004; Spender, 1984a, 1984b). Specifically, I will focus on the crucial act of naming, which provides a vocabulary that is essential for recognizing, valuing, and—in some cases—challenging taken-for-granted aspects of interpersonal relationships.

Intellectual Traditions of Critical Feminist Theories

Critical feminist theories grow out of two broader groups of theories: feminist theories, not all of which are critical, and critical theories, not all of which are feminist. I will provide an overview of feminist theories and critical theories as a basis for explaining the focus of critical feminist theories and the assumptions that underlie them.

FEMINIST THEORIES

"Feminism" is defined as the belief that men and women are equal and should have equal rights and opportunities in all spheres of life—personal, social, work, and public. Central to feminist theories are two concepts. The first is "gender," which is distinct from "sex." Sex is a biological category—male or female—that is determined genetically. Gender, on the other hand, comprises social definitions of masculinity and femininity at specific historical moments and in specific cultural contexts. Put another way, gender is the social meanings attached to sex by others and ourselves, as well as our ways of embodying—or refusing to embody—those social meanings. We are born with a distinct sex (for most but not all people, that is male or female), but we acquire gender (masculinity and/or femininity) in the process of socialization, which takes place primarily through communication. Gender influences our perceptions, expectations, and evaluations of women and men, as well as the roles, opportunities, and material circumstances of women's and men's lives.

Feminist theories examine women's social roles, history, activities, experiences, perspectives, and interests in order both to value women's lives and to expose gender inequality in society. Judith Butler (1990, 1993), a prominent feminist theorist, argues that gender comes into being as we perform it in everyday life. We simultaneously enact and produce gender through a variety of mundane, performative practices such as dominating or deferring in conversation, offering empathy or solutions when a friend expresses discomfort, wearing dresses and makeup or not, and inviting others into conversations or commanding the center stage in interaction. All of these practices communicate, embody, and confer an illusory naturalness on normative codes of masculinity and femininity. According to Butler, gender exists if and only if people act in ways that compel belief in the reality of masculinity and femininity.

A second key concept for feminist theories is "patriarchy," which is a system that reflects primarily the interests, values, perspectives, and experiences of men, as a group. Feminist theorists note that many cultures, including those in the West, were originally organized predominantly by White, ostensibly heterosexual men, who relied on their experiences, needs, values, preferences, interests, and perspectives to order social life. As a result, our society is set up in ways that do not fully reflect women's or minorities' experiences, needs, values, preferences, interests, and perspectives.

Feminist theorists do not assume that men necessarily organized society in a deliberate effort to subordinate women and minorities. The point is that when Western cultures were established, White men held positions of leadership, and women did not. Men's perspectives did not—in fact, could not—include many experiences typical for women, such as being on call for children 24 hours a day; feeling responsible for monitoring and tending to interpersonal dynamics; engaging in the thankless, repetitive drudgery of keeping a home clean; and doing all of the work to plan, prepare, serve, and clean up after meals (Galvin, 2006). More prominent in males' perspectives would be activities that men routinely enacted—working outside of the home; engaging in competitive activities in the workplace and battlegrounds; and seeing the home as a haven graced by mannerly children, clean clothes, and nourishing meals. Because patriarchy was set up a long time ago, it is a system that predates you, me, and others now living. If today we could organize society from scratch, we might choose a different model. But the patriarchal model is the one that we have inherited—modified in some ways (women are no longer men's property)—but still patriarchal.

CRITICAL THEORIES

Critical theorists aim to identify prevailing structures and practices that create or uphold disadvantage, inequity, or oppression, and to point the way toward alternatives that promote more egalitarian relationships, groups, and societies. Unlike post-positivist theories, critical theories are centrally concerned with social change—with making a difference in how cultures operate and how those operations affect people in material and nonmaterial ways.

Critical theorists ask how cultural structures and practices shape the lives of members of a culture and, conversely, how members' lives and activities shape cultural structures and practices. Critical theorists are particularly interested in analyzing the means by which dominant groups privilege their interests and structure societies to serve their interests. At the same time, critical theorists want to understand how oppressed groups become empowered and how to change dominant patterns and perhaps the ideologies that underlie them.

Critical theorists are intensely attentive to struggles between competing ideologies, which are sets of ideas that organize groups' understandings of reality (Hall, 1986, 1989). For example, they ask how ideology defines the parameters and sites of struggle between dominant and nondominant races, middle-class and working-class people, heterosexuals and nonheterosexuals, and men and women. In each case, there is a dominant group and a less-powerful group or groups, and they participate in what Stuart Hall (1989) called the "theatre of struggle," which is an ongoing battle over whose voices, whose perspectives, and whose values gain a hearing and cultural legitimacy.

In focusing on ideological control, critical theorists trace how power is deployed and resisted. In doing so, many critical theorists pay attention to both formal kinds of power (e.g., laws that define who can marry) and informal kinds of power (e.g., everyday practices that communicate normative understandings of who is and who is not a family). This allows critical theorists to critique not only official forms of power such as laws, but also "tiny, everyday" practices (Foucault, 1984, p. 211) that reproduce and sustain particular ideologies and their attendant inequities. By studying how dominant and marginal groups enact and resist power, critical theorists aim to identify how cultures work and to challenge, disrupt, and remake cultural life so that it better reflects and represents the interests and perspectives of all who comprise it.

THE INTERSECTION OF FEMINIST AND CRITICAL THEORIES

When critical theories and feminist theories intersect, the result is theories that identify, critique, and seek to change inequities and discrimination, particularly those that are based on sex and gender (Dow, 1995; Dow & Wood, 2006; Wood, 1995). In other words, critical feminist theories ask how cultural structures and practices differently and inequitably shape women's and men's lives and communication practices, and conversely how women's and men's lives and communication shape cultural structures and practices. By extension, critical feminist theorists are particularly interested in understanding how women become empowered and, in some cases, how they change dominant practices and ideologies that constrain women's lives.

Critical feminist theories identify, question, and seek to reform patriarchal ideologies that give rise to asymmetrical rights, opportunities, roles, and material circumstances. Note that the critique mounted by critical feminist theorists is not confined to matters of sex or gender inequality. The critique is broad, questioning efforts to devalue and oppress any groups that do not reflect the standpoint and interests of those who hold dominant positions in cultural life. The dominant masculine and heteronormative ideology of Western culture produces a decidedly partial understanding of interpersonal relationships and the communication that generates and sustains them. Critical feminist theories offer a corrective to this bias by attending to neglected facets of interpersonal relationships and by critiquing perspectives that erase or misrepresent women's experiences in relationships.

Within the broad category of critical feminist theories there are many specific theories, such as Foucauldian, socialist and Marxist, performative, postcolonial, and psychoanalytic. These specific theories are not necessarily mutually exclusive. Obviously, a single short chapter cannot describe how all of these contribute to an understanding of interpersonal communication and relationships. For this reason, I will focus on a particular subset of critical feminist theories that highlight the importance of naming experiences from women's perspectives. This subset of theories includes muted group, co-cultural, and standpoint theories.

UNDERLYING ASSUMPTIONS

Although muted group, co-cultural and standpoint theories differ in some ways (see Wood, 2005), all three assume that members of groups defined by sex, race, and other factors occupy distinct positions in a society—those are their social locations. The theories further assert that social location has implications for what members of distinct groups experience and know and for their language and power. The assumption that social locations are distinct and meaningful is elaborated by four more specific assumptions that inform and underlie this group of critical feminist theories.

First, in patriarchal cultures, women make up a subordinate group because they did not participate in defining the society and how it works. Second, because women, as a group, are subordinate in patriarchal cultures, some experiences, knowledge, and activities that are unique to, or more typical of, women are not represented in language or are represented in ways that do not reflect women's meanings for those experiences. For example, men do not carry fetuses and give birth so their ways of defining those phenomena are unlikely to represent how women experience them. Third, women's experiences, knowledge, and activities merit respect and linguistic status, which are prerequisites to women's full inclusion in interpersonal, social, and political lives. And forth, voice, which can be thought of as the ability to define what phenomena mean, is a key way of valuing and including women's experiences, knowledge, and meanings in cultural life. The character and importance of these assumptions will become clearer as we explore the main goals of critical feminist theories.

METHODOLOGICAL IMPLICATIONS

Because critical feminist theorists are keenly interested in how power is deployed and resisted, they tend to analyze both formal kinds of power (for instance, laws that regulate women's reproductive rights) and informal kinds of power (for instance, media portrayals of women's reproductive choices). This allows critical feminist scholars to analyze not only official forms of power such as laws, but also "tiny, everyday" practices (Foucault, 1984, p. 211) that reproduce and sustain inequitable roles and expectations for men's and women's behaviors, including their communication. Among these tiny, everyday practices are names and, equally important, the absence of names for experiences and perspectives that are more typical of women than of men.

The intellectual commitments of critical feminist researchers do not authorize a specific methodology or methodologies. Rather, most feminist critical scholars state that they simply do "good research" (Gelsthorpe, 1990)—that is, they do not point to distinctively feminist methodologies. They do, however, note that the focus of their research is often on spheres of life that have been un- or under-noticed in traditional research and that their work aims to address broad issues related to social justice.

Main Goals and Features of Critical Feminist Theories

The key assumptions discussed above inform critical feminist theories' goals, which include identifying and challenging gender-based inequity, discrimination, devaluation, marginalization, and so forth. In turn, these goals promote two particular foci of analysis.

POWER

Critical feminist theories focus keenly on power relations and linked issues such as the unequal status and privilege accorded to women compared to that accorded to men. Analyses of power relations have demonstrated that, as a group, men—particularly White, heterosexual, able-bodied men—are more likely than women, as a group, to hold positions of power in society, assume dominance in families, and exercise control in everyday interactions (Collins, 1986; Hartsock, 1983; Keller, 1985; Wood, 1994, 2006; also, see Wood, 2014, for a summary of research). According to critical feminist theorists, the greater power generally held by men is a primary reason that women's experiences, perspectives, and knowledge have been devalued, and that women's voices have been suppressed.

WOMEN'S EXPERIENCES, PERSPECTIVES, AND KNOWLEDGE

Arising out of attention to power relations and women's subordinate location within those relations, critical feminist theories seek to raise awareness of women's experiences, perspectives, and knowledge, which historically have been less acknowledged and valued than men's experiences, perspectives, and knowledge. Highlighting the experiences, perspectives, and knowledge that, at least historically, arise from women's location in social life leads to a focus on what Dorothy Smith (1987) called "everyday life." Traditionally, while men were in the boardrooms and on the war fronts, women were in the home and community where they assumed responsibility for the routine, everyday dynamics of life—caring for children, cleaning and maintaining a home, preparing meals, supporting schools, contributing time and effort to civic organizations, and so forth. According to prominent critical feminist theorists (Haraway, 1988; Harding, 1991, 2004, 2006; Hartsock, 1983; Ruddick, 1989), this enmeshment in everyday life cultivates a particular kind of consciousness that is sensitive to nuances of others' communication, responsive to others' feelings and needs, and attentive to process as well as instrumental goals and outcomes. In short, it is a kind of consciousness that is shaped by and attuned to the rhythms of everyday interpersonal life.

How Communication Is Conceptualized in Critical Feminist Theories

Because communication is the principal way that we create identities, relationships, and culture and also the primary way that we represent experiences, perspectives, and knowledge, communication is an important emphasis in critical feminist theories. Often referred to by related terms such as "language" and "voice," communication is recognized as the primary means by which we express ourselves. In turn, communication—specifically, naming—is central to how we humans understand our experiences, thoughts, and feelings; convey those to others; and have those represented in the common language, and thus knowledge, of a culture. It follows that without names for experiences, thoughts, and feelings, we have less full knowledge of them and markedly less ability to share them with others.

Critical feminist theories offer two important views of communication. First, communication is understood as a means of enacting power relations between people. Second, communication is a way to name phenomena and thereby render phenomena subject to notice, reference, and negotiation. By implication, phenomena that are not named are less noticeable, less acknowledged and valued, less available for reference, and less open to challenge and negotiation.

Use of the theories, like the feminist movement that informs them, is not restricted to the "ivory tower" (Dow & Wood, 2006). Instead, theorists aim for practical impact in the everyday world of personal and social relationships. As hinted above, a primary way this happens is through naming what has not been named, noticed, or valued. To illustrate this value of critical feminist theories, I will briefly identify five phenomena common in women's experience of interpersonal life that once were not named, but that now have been named and thus brought into social awareness. With naming and social awareness, it is possible to change what has been accepted as normal.

Research and Practical Applications of Critical Feminist Theories

SEXUAL HARASSMENT

"Sexual harassment" is unwanted and unwelcome conduct of a sexual nature that interferes with performance in work and educational settings. Doubtlessly, sexual harassment has existed for centuries, yet it was not named until the 1970s (Wood, 1992). Until that time, people, primarily women, who endured unwanted sexualized behavior at work and in school had no way to name what happened to them. The language of their culture provided no language that named the practice as illegal, much less immoral. Victims of harassment could only resort to inadequate language such as "going too far," "being pushy," or "flirting," terms that do not begin to describe the character of sexual harassment and, furthermore, that do not mark it as wrong, immoral, and illegal. Without the capacity to name sexual harassment as wrong, women had little resource for doing anything to stop it.

DATE RAPE AND MARITAL RAPE

Like sexual harassment, date rape and marital rape are not new phenomena. However, naming nonconsensual sex with dates and spouses as criminal—that is, defining these acts as rape—is new. Only toward the end of the 20th century did most states adopt laws that specifically recognized nonconsensual sex between dates or spouses as the crime of rape. And only by naming nonconsensual sex in any context as a crime were the grievous violations recognized for what they are (Wriggins, 1998) and perpetrators subject to punishment. Even today, the term *rape* is contested—it's in the "theatre of struggle," to use Hall's phrase—as our society struggles to define what nonconsensual sex means (Harris, 2011).

CONVERSATIONAL MAINTENANCE WORK

In 1978, Pamela Fishman gave a name to a phenomenon familiar to most women but unnamed until then. Her studies of interaction between men and women led Fishman to conclude that women do a lot of work to maintain conversations. They ask questions about others' activities and interests, pull others into conversation, and respond to what others say with comments and follow-up questions. Fishman's research (1978), as well as later research that confirmed her findings (Alexander & Wood, 2000; Dunn, 1999; Mulac, 2006; Taylor, 2002), showed that women do far more of the work to keep a conversation going than do men. In coining the term "conversational maintenance work," Fishman gave a name to an activity that is vital to interpersonal communication and that values women's role in the process.

SECOND SHIFT

Sociologist Arlie Hochschild (2003) coined the term "second shift" to name a phenomenon common in the lives of women who work outside of the home. The second shift is all of the housework, cooking, and child care that women engage in after returning from a shift in the paid labor force. Hochschild reported that roughly 20% of men in dual-worker couples assume half of the work required to run a home and family. More recent studies (Galvin, 2006; Wood, 2011; for a summary, see Duck & Wood, 2006) have confirmed the persistence of inequity in responsibility for work in the domestic sphere. In naming this phenomenon as a form of work, the term second shift gives visibility to what had been invisible. Although the majority of heterosexual families today have two wage earners, the housework and the care of children, parents, and other relatives continue to be done primarily by women (Council on Contemporary Families, 2010; Schiebinger & Gilmartin, 2010; Sheehy, 2010; Wood, 2011).

PSYCHOLOGICAL RESPONSIBILITY

The second shift involves more than concrete tasks such as fixing meals, bathing children, and vacuuming. In addition, it includes "psychological responsibility" (Hochschild, 2003), which is the responsibility to remember, plan, schedule, and so forth. For example, behind a prepared dinner sitting on a table are a number of generally unseen and unnoticed tasks such as considering household members' nutritional needs and dietary preferences, deciding on a menu, and shopping for the necessary ingredients.

Evaluation of Critical Feminist Theories

By most of the criteria routinely used to assess theories, critical feminist theories fare well. They offer broad frameworks for studying and thinking about interpersonal relationships and the ways in which communication both shapes and reflects the dynamics of those relationships. They meet the criterion of utility or of pragmatism by heightening awareness of aspects of relationships that have little or no visibility within alternative theories. In limiting themselves to relatively few concepts (gender, power, dominance, and so forth), they meet the criterion of parsimony.

Finally, on the criterion of heurism critical feminist theories excel. They provoke awareness of issues such as the second shift and psychological responsibility, and they spark critical perspectives on how relationships do and could operate. They challenge conventional ways of thinking and offer us new insights and choices as we go about the business of organizing relationships, thinking about how others organize theirs, and reflecting on the ways in which cultural structures and practices contour our personal and social relationships.

Two primary criticisms of the theories merit our attention. First, some scholars (Putnam, 1982) have expressed concern that the theories have limited ability to explain interpersonal communication because they (over)emphasize sex and gender while underestimating other influences on how people think, act, feel, and communicate. It is true that critical feminist theories highlight gender (and gender inequities), but, advocates of the theories might respond, that is a necessary corrective to the historic neglect of women and women's perspectives in the study of interpersonal relationships. A second concern is that the theories have limited utility because they focus on a small subset of women—middle-class, Caucasian, able-bodied, heterosexual women—and their experiences. This criticism had greater legitimacy 20 or even 10 years ago than it does today. Influenced by postcolonial scholarship, critical feminist theorists increasingly recognize the diversity of women (Fixmer-Oraiz, Dow, & Wood, in press).

Continuing the Conversation

Critical feminist theories question not only normative understandings of the roles of men and women in relationships but also the interests that are and are not served by existing theories of relationships. Among the ways that critical feminist theories have contributed to our understanding of interpersonal communication is the naming of experiences that are more common and relevant to women than to men. Because naming is powerful, it alters both understandings and evaluations of interpersonal relationships and the concrete, lived experiences that people have in their relationships. In turn, consciousness of inequalities and the ability to name and discuss them enhance individuals' opportunities to make their relationships more fair, deliberate, and satisfying.

Awareness of inequities in relationships is a start, but it is not the ultimate goal. The vital aim of critical feminist theories is to point out and challenge inequities so that people participate equally in relationships and invest and benefit equitably from their interpersonal associations. This goal continues to motivate critical feminist theorizing. In the years ahead, theorists in this tradition will persevere in the important work of naming issues, dynamics, and experiences that help us recognize and overcome inequities in interpersonal relationships. This work will need to accommodate the ongoing changes in relationships such as breadwinner and homemaker roles becoming less distinct and less sex-linked and increasingly varied forms of families (Galvin, 2006). These and other changes will usher in new relationship dynamics and the potentials for new forms of inequity that critical feminist theories will need to address if those theories are to have the influence in the future that they have enjoyed to date.

In the future, interpersonal communication scholars may extend the theories' contributions by noticing and naming additional phenomena that are part of the too-often invisible gendered organization of relationships and cultural life. In addition, scholars and all of us who participate in relationships should be asking what kinds of communication reflect and sustain inequities in relationships and what kinds of communication cultivate or are present in equitable relationships.

References

Alexander, M. G., & Wood, W. (2000). Women, men and positive emotions: A social role interpretation. In A. H. Fischer (Ed.), *Gender and emotion: Social psychological perspectives* (pp. 189–210). New York, NY: Cambridge University Press.

Ardener, S. (1978). *Defining females: The nature of women in society.* New York, NY: Wiley.

Butler, J. (1990). Performative acts and gender constitution: An essay in phenomenology and feminist theory. In S. Case (Ed.), *Performing feminisms: Feminist critical theory and theatre* (pp. 270–282). Baltimore, MD: Johns Hopkins University Press.

Butler, J. (1993). *Bodies that matter: On the discursive limits of "sex."* New York, NY: Routledge.

Collins, P. H. (1986). Learning from the outsider within. *Social Problems, 23,* 514–532.

Council on Contemporary Families. (2010). Unconventional wisdom. http://www.contem poraryfamilies.org/all/unconventional-wisdom-issue-3.html?q=unconventional+ wisdom. Accessed April 14, 2010.

Dow, B. J. (1995). Feminism, difference(s), and rhetorical studies. *Communication Studies, 46,* 106–117.

Dow, B. J., & Wood, J. T. (2006). The evolution of gender and communication research: Intersections of theory, politics, and scholarship. In B. J. Dow & J. T. Wood (Eds.), *The handbook of gender and communication* (pp. ix–xxiv). Thousand Oaks, CA: Sage.

Duck, S., & Wood, J. T. (2006). What goes up may come down: Sex and gendered patterns in relational dissolution. In M. Fine & J. Harvey (Eds.), *Handbook of divorce and relationship dissolution* (pp. 169–187). Mahwah, NJ: Erlbaum.

Dunn, J. (1999). Siblings, friends, and the development of social understanding. In W. A. Collins & B. Laursen (Eds.), *Relationships as developmental contexts* (pp. 263–279). Mahwah, NJ: Erlbaum.

Fishman, P. M. (1978). Interaction: The work women do. *Social Problems, 25,* 397–406.

Fixmer-Oraiz, N., Dow, B., & Wood, J. T. (in press). *Feminism: Real and remembered.*

Foucault, M. (1984). *The Foucault reader.* P. Rabinow (Ed.). New York, NY: Pantheon.

Friedan, B. (1963). *The feminine mystique.* New York, NY: W. W. Norton.

Galvin, K. (2006). Gender and family interaction: Dress rehearsal for an improvisation? In B. Dow & J. T. Wood (Eds.). *The SAGE handbook of gender and communication* (pp. 41–55). Thousand Oaks, CA: Sage.

Gelsthorpe, L. (1990). Feminist methodology in criminology: A new approach or old wine in new bottles. In L. Gelsthorpe & A. Morris (Eds.), *Feminist perspectives in criminology* (pp. 89–106). Buckingham, UK: Open University Press.

Hall, S. (1986). The problem of ideology—Marxism without guarantees. *Journal of Communication Inquiry, 10,* 28–44.

Hall, S. (1989). Ideology. In E. Barnouw et al. (Eds.), *International encyclopedia of communication* (vol. 2, pp. 307–311). New York, NY: Oxford University Press.

Haraway, D. (1988). Situated knowledges: The science question in feminism and the privilege of partial perspective. *Signs, 14,* 575–599.

Harding, S. (1991). *Whose science? Whose knowledge? Thinking from women's lives.* Ithaca, NY: Cornell University Press.

Harding, S. (Ed.). (2004). *The feminist standpoint theory reader: Intellectual and political controversies.* New York, NY: Routledge.

Harding, S. (2006). *Science and social inequality: Feminist and postcolonial issues.* Urbana: University of Illinois Press.

Harris, K. L. (2011). The next problem that has no name: The politics and pragmatics of the word *rape. Women's Studies in Communication, 34,* 42–63.

Hartsock, N. (1983). The feminist standpoint: Developing the ground for a specifically feminist historical materialism. In S. Harding & M. B. Hintikka (Eds.), *Discovering reality* (pp. 283–310). Boston, MA: Ridel.

Hochschild, A., with Machung, A. (2003). *The second shift* (rev. ed.). New York, NY: Viking.

Keller, E. (1985). *Reflections on science and gender.* New Haven, CT: Yale University Press.

Mulac, A. (2006). The gender-linked language effect: Do language differences really make a difference? In K. Dindia & D. Canary (Eds.), *Sex differences and similarities in communication* (pp. 219–239). Mahwah, NJ: Erlbaum.

Putnam, L. (1982). In search of gender: A critique of communication and sex-roles research. *Women's Studies in Communication, 5,* 1–9.

Rakow, L., & Wackwitz, L. (Eds.). (2004). *Feminist communication theory: Selections in context.* Thousand Oaks, CA: Sage.

Ruddick, S. (1989). *Maternal thinking: Toward a politics of peace.* Boston, MA: Beacon.

Schiebinger, L., & Gilmartin, S. K. (2010, January–February). Housework is an academic issue. *Academe,* 39–44.

Sheehy, G. (2010). *Passages in caregiving.* New York, NY: William Morrow.

Smith, D. (1987). *The everyday world as problematic.* Boston, MA: Northeastern University Press.

Spender, D. (1984a). *Man made language.* London, UK: Routledge.

Spender, D. (1984b). Defining reality: A powerful tool. In C. Kramarae, M. Schultz, & W. O'Barr (Eds.), *Language and power* (pp. 195–205). Beverly Hills, CA: Sage.

Taylor, S. (2002). *The tending instinct: How nurturing is essential for who we are and how we live.* New York, NY: Times Books.

Wood, J. T. (1992). Telling our stories: Narratives as a basis for theorizing sexual harassment. *Journal of Applied Communication Research, 4,* 349–363.

Wood, J. T. (1994). *Who cares? Women, care and culture.* Carbondale: Southern Illinois University Press.

Wood, J. T. (1995). Feminist scholarship and the study of personal and social relationships. *Journal of Social and Personal Relationships, 12,* 103–120.

Wood, J. T. (2005). Feminist standpoint theory and muted group theory: Commonalities and divergences. *Women & Language, 28,* 61–64.

Wood, J. T. (2006). Gendered power, aggression and violence in heterosexual relationships. In D. Canary & K. Dindia (Eds.), *Sex differences and similarities in communication* (2nd ed., pp. 397–411). Mahwah, NJ: Erlbaum.

Wood, J. T. (2011). Which ruler do we use? Theorizing the division of domestic labor. *Family Communication Journal, 11,* 39–49.

Wood, J. T. (2014). *Gendered lives: Communication, gender, and culture* (11th ed.). Belmont, CA: Thomson Wadsworth.

Wriggins, J. (1998). Rape. In W. Mankiller, G. Mink, M. Navarro, B. Smith, & G. Steinem (Eds.), *The reader's companion to U.S. women's history* (pp. 612–614). New York, NY: Houghton Mifflin.

16

Expectancy Violations Theory and Interaction Adaptation Theory

From Expectations to Adaptation

Cindy H. White

Expectations are important in virtually everything we do. They color how we approach things, what we make of a situation, and how we interact with others. My initial interest in expectancy violations theory was sparked by the following question: When unexpected things happen, what determines if we see the event as a surprise or a disappointment, and what do we do in response? I was initially interested in situations where the outcome was more positive than expected. For instance, if I expected someone I was about to meet to be distant and aloof but found them to be moderately friendly, why did I find myself evaluating them so positively? But I quickly began to wonder about situations that were less positive than expected. For instance, if I anticipated my daughter would be excited about an event we were attending, but she was not, why did I find myself talking about it in a more excited way to try to draw her in?

Two theoretical perspectives, expectancy violations theory (EVT) and interaction adaptation theory (IAT), offer insight into the experiences I just described. They were developed to explain how communicators identify, interpret, and react to situations based on the expectations they have for the interaction. EVT offered the conceptual foundations for understanding how we respond when expectations, primarily about nonverbal behavior and immediacy, are violated. IAT extends some ideas of EVT by focusing heavily on nonverbal behavior.

However, it was developed to examine how partners in interaction respond to one another (for instance, in situations where expectations aren't met) and to articulate what the patterns of interaction that develop between interaction partners signal communicatively.

Intellectual Traditions of Expectancy Violations Theory and Interaction Adaptation Theory

EVT and IAT are post-positivistic theories that seek to explain and predict patterns of interaction. EVT focuses on how communicators assess behavior that deviates from what is expected and how they respond communicatively to such violations. The theory focuses heavily on nonverbal aspects of interaction but has been used to analyze a range of communication behaviors and contexts. Although following norms and conforming to expectations often seems like the best way to make social interaction work smoothly, Judee Burgoon's early work on the theory proposed that there are circumstances where violating norms is advantageous (Burgoon, 1978; Burgoon, Stacks, & Woodall, 1979). Specifically, initial tests of the theory demonstrated that attractive customers who violated personal space expectations were treated more favorably than attractive customers who conformed to expectations because space violations were interpreted as a positive indicator of immediacy or interest in purchase. IAT is similar in its orientation but more directly addresses behavioral responses to a partner's interaction behavior; it seeks to better explain why patterns of interaction develop between communicators and what patterns of interaction reveal about the interaction. Having been applied to situations such as deceptive interactions (White & Burgoon, 2001), IAT suggests that patterns of interaction can be diagnostic. Both theories follow a hypothetico-deductive approach, which means they utilize a set of concepts (such as expectancies, communicator characteristics, violations) to posit specific predictions about the outcomes of interaction. The goal of the theories is to enable researchers to advance hypotheses and to test specific predictions across different interaction contexts. In the next section, I describe the concepts central to EVT and IAT.

Main Goals and Features of EVT and IAT

EXPECTANCY VIOLATIONS THEORY

Expectancies. According to Burgoon (1993), "expectancy in the communication sense denotes an enduring pattern of anticipated behavior" (p. 31). Expectancies may be related to the behaviors that are appropriate for a situation, or they may reflect what we know to be the typical behavior of a specific individual. Burgoon (1993) noted that expectancies can refer to what we anticipate will occur (*predictive* expectancies) or to what is desired or preferred (*prescriptive* expectancies). In many circumstances, these two types of expectancies are aligned, but they are not always synonymous. For instance, if you've ever had an ongoing interaction with someone who is a consistent "close talker" (the type of *Seinfeld* fame) and felt uncomfortable, you've experienced the tension between predictive and prescriptive expectancies. I have experience with this involving a distant relative who I sometimes interact with at large family gatherings. In this case, I wish this person would follow the prescriptions of standing a bit farther away, but given my prior interactions with him, I set my predictive expectancies to fit with my past experiences and acknowledge that this person is likely to stand closer than is normative.

EVT proposes that our expectations are influenced by three key factors: the communicator, the relationship, and the context in which the interaction occurs. Communicator characteristics include salient features of an interaction partner, such as gender, age, personality, and communication style. Relationship factors include things such as the degree of familiarity between partners or the equality of status between interaction partners. Contextual elements include aspects of the environment that might define how individuals should communicate in a particular situation, such as the formality of the setting or the nature of the task. So, in the "close talker" situation, my expectations are shaped by my relationship to this person (someone in my family—which makes it a little bit less disconcerting) and his age (quite a bit older than me), as well as the typical context of a family gathering, which makes this less disconcerting than it might be in a workplace.

Violation valence. EVT proposes that when someone violates our expectations, we are forced to make sense of what is happening, and thus we shift our focus a bit to try to figure out what the behavior means. That is, when an expectancy violation occurs, arousal is heightened. Heightened arousal initiates cognitive appraisals related to (a) the meaning of the violation and (b) the evaluation of the positive or negative value of the violation (violation valence). Initial versions of the theory proposed that violations create physiological arousal, but later work has described arousal as an orienting response that involves "directing some attention away from the topic at hand and toward the violator and violation" (Burgoon, 1993, p. 35).

The evaluation we make of the violation is described in EVT as the *violation valence* and refers to the positivity or negativity of the meaning we assign to the violation. Some interaction behaviors carry clear social meaning, and so their valence, in a given context or relationship, is relatively clear. For instance, the negative meaning of an unexpected obscene gesture from another driver on the roadway is usually not in doubt and would be considered a negative violation.

However, some interaction behaviors, such as the use of conversational distance, may be more ambiguous in meaning. EVT predicts that a violation that is negatively valenced will typically lead to worse interaction outcomes than meeting expectations. A positively valenced violation will typically lead to better interaction outcomes than a non-violation. So, the valence of a violation determines whether it will be better to do what is expected or to deviate from the norm. A key factor that influences the valence of the violation is the reward value of the communicator committing the violation.

Communicator reward value. We find some people more rewarding to interact with than others. Individuals who are physically attractive, powerful, or highly competent are typically seen as more rewarding than those who do not have any (or all) of those characteristics. EVT suggests that our evaluation of a violation depends on our assessments of these positive or negative attributes, particularly when the meaning of a violation is open to interpretation. When a rewarding communicator interacts at a closer than expected distance, for example, we are likely to evaluate the violation positively, but when the same distance is adopted by a communicator who is not rewarding, we are likely to evaluate the violation negatively.

Extension of EVT to patterns of interaction. Many of the predictions from EVT relate to evaluations of an interaction partner or outcome. However, when someone violates our expectations, how do we respond to them in interaction? EVT has attempted to address this question because these responses are communicative and send a message to the violator. For instance, if a communicator negatively violates expectations by speaking in a way that is too loud and animated for the situation, does their communication partner speak more quietly and calmly in an attempt to influence what is happening, or does the partner say just "grin and bear" it? Studies that have used EVT to predict behavior in interaction have generated mixed results (e.g., Burgoon & Hale, 1988). For instance, Floyd and Voloudakis (1999) examined expectancy violations by friends during conversations in the lab. Since friends are expected to be at least moderately involved and pleasant with one another, they predicted that reduced involvement and pleasantness would be a negative violation of expectations, and that in response to this violation, the friend whose expectations had been violated would increase their involvement/pleasantness in an attempt to draw the other back up to more comfortable levels. They found, however, that decreased intimacy was generally reciprocated, with decreased involvement/pleasantness by one partner leading to decreased involvement/pleasantness of the other. Although EVT has been successful in broadening our understanding of the impact of expectancies on perceptions of interaction, it has been limited in its ability to predict behavioral adaptation that occurs in interaction. Consequently, IAT has emerged as a conceptual framework that focuses more fully on behavioral responses in patterns of interaction.

INTERACTION ADAPTATION THEORY

IAT assumes that adaptation in interaction forms the foundation of our relationships with one another, and that adaptation is communicative, signaling to interactants and observers the nature of the relationship between communicators. Similar to EVT, the theory begins by considering the initial factors people bring to interaction as the foundation of how they approach an interaction and how they make sense of another's behavior. IAT goes beyond expectations, however, to consider how biological needs and individual differences in interaction styles shape what people do initially in interaction. The theory focuses strongly on patterns of interaction by considering how people adapt to one another. *Adaptation* refers to nonrandom behavior that occurs in response to the behavior of an interaction (Burgoon, Stern, & Dillman, 1995). Patterns of interaction are often described in terms of whether the response reflects a matching or reciprocal behavior of a partner (called *reciprocity*), or whether the response involves behavior that appears to offset or compensate for the behavior of a partner (called *compensation*). For instance, I was recently talking with a friend who was excited about a job offer she received. Because of her excitement, her speech was quick and animated. I was immediately caught up in her excitement, reciprocating her speech rate and vocal animation. However, when we had talked previously about a job offer that fell through, I had tried to offset her behavior by remaining upbeat nonverbally and talking about future prospects: I tried to compensate for her disappointment (although I do not know how successful I was at the time). IAT proposes that we are predisposed to adapt to others in interaction because adaptation helps to fulfill survival needs by strengthening relational bonds.

Requirements, expectations, and desires. IAT proposes that some aspects of interaction are driven by basic biological needs related to approach-avoidance. These needs may influence our actions in fundamental and relatively unconscious ways, and are referred to as *requirements* (R). Our *expectations* (E) for a situation reflect primarily social factors such as social or situational norms, as well as knowledge we may have of another's behavior based on past interactions. *Desires* (D) are highly personalized and include things such as one's personality and communication style. IAT notes that R, E, and D are interdependent and often cannot be fully distinguished.

Interaction position and actual behavior. The composite of R, E, and D factors reflects what is referred to as an individual's *interaction position* (IP). "The IP represents a net assessment of what is needed, anticipated, and preferred as the dyadic interaction pattern in a situation" (Burgoon, Stern, & Dillard, 1995, p. 266). The IP for a specific individual helps predict how that individual will interpret a specific interaction situation and what that individual is likely to do initially in interaction. The behavior enacted by a partner is referred to in

IAT as *actual behavior* (A). The theory offers two basic predictions about behavioral responses, which are derived from examining the relationship between interaction position and actual behavior. "If IP is more positively valenced than A [actual behavior], then the anticipated interpersonal pattern is divergence, compensation, or maintenance. . . . Conversely, if A [actual behavior] is more positively valenced behavior than IP, then the anticipated interpersonal pattern is convergence, matching, and reciprocity" (Burgoon & Ebesu Hubbard, 2005, p. 163).

To illustrate, as a teacher, I sometimes have conversations with students about poor performance on exams. How I feel about each interaction is influenced by a number of factors, such as my need for affiliation or avoidance that day (R). I also have some general expectations about how students and professors should interact with one another, as well as expectations about specific students based on their prior actions in my class (E). In addition, I have general desires for these interactions, such as a preference for people who are open and those who are willing to take responsibility for their actions (D). One student in particular comes to mind. Her contributions to class led me to believe that she was a serious student capable of very good work, so I was concerned that she would be upset when she came to my office after performing poorly on an exam. My IP predicted that her behavior would be emotionally laden and rather negative; before she arrived, I felt myself bracing for an interaction that might be negative and anxious. However, when she came to my office, she told me that she had been very busy right before the exam for our class and had not studied in the way she typically might for a test. She was disappointed but not upset, and in fact, she was upbeat about her interest in the class and expectation that she would do better. We were quickly able to identify ways she could improve her performance in the class. According to IAT, her actual behavior (A) was clearly more positively valenced than my IP. As a result, I easily reciprocated her positive tone and engaging interaction style.

Another example also readily comes to mind. A student who had not performed well on prior work and often missed class arrived at my office. Although I expected that she would be concerned about her grade, I assumed she realized before the test that she was not doing well in the course. I thought we might strategize ways to ensure that she passed the class. When the student arrived, she quickly became upset, arguing that the test was unfair and that no student could be expected to adequately answer the questions. I had to work hard in this interaction to remain calm with this student (even though I felt frustrated) because I wanted to try to calm down the interaction. According to IAT, although I may not have been consciously aware of it, this was a situation where A was more negatively valenced than the IP from which I began. So, I sought to offset (compensate) her behavior. These examples demonstrate the way that IAT helps us to understand patterns of interaction between communicators.

How Communication Is Conceptualized in EVT and IAT

EVT and IAT both acknowledge that some behaviors have clear social meanings (e.g., certain gestures), whereas others convey different messages depending on the context in which they are displayed and the relationship between partners. For instance, close proximity in conversation can be associated with displays of affection or of dominance. Thus, communication is assumed to involve some interpretation of the actions of another. Early on, EVT focused on cognitive appraisal and communicator reward value, so that communication was centered in the individual's assessment of a situation. Later EVT work has considered communicative responses to expectancy violations. IAT is a theory of interaction that explains how communicators respond to one another and assumes, at some level, that interaction is adaptive and co-constructed. Burgoon, Stern, and Dillman (1995) described EVT and IAT as theories that were conceptualized in order to explain behavior that is communicative in nature, which means they are primarily "mindful, intentional and symbolic" (p. 11).

Research and Practical Applications of EVT and IAT

EVT and IAT have been applied to a number of different interpersonal communication contexts. Three important contexts of application have been (a) the study of nonverbal behavior during conversation, (b) expectations and patterns of interaction in intimate relationships, and (c) the influence of expectations or adaptation on the detection of deception. Perhaps the most developed application of the theory has been to the study of nonverbal behaviors, such as conversational distance, immediacy, and conversational involvement. One reason nonverbal behavior has been of interest is that researchers wanted to better understand how we make sense of nonverbal cues. What determines if we see another person's close proximity as an intrusion into our personal space rather than as a sign of interest or involvement in the conversation? Burgoon (1978) and Burgoon and colleagues (1979) tested the impact of conversational distance violations in the laboratory; Burgoon and Aho (1982) conducted field experiments that examined distance violations in interactions between sales clerks and customers. In these experiments, confederates adopted conversational distances that either met expectations or were closer or farther than would have been expected, given the situation. Generally, these studies demonstrated that high-reward communicators were perceived most positively by their interaction partners when they violated expectations than when they met expectations. Low-reward communicators were perceived most positively when expectations were met. It is important to note that these initial tests, by focusing on conversational distance, created a situation in which the meaning of the violation was ambiguous, particularly in interactions with strangers. Conversational distance, by itself, may be difficult to interpret, so it may be particularly amenable to the influence of communicator reward value.

Burgoon and Hale (1988) examined the impact of immediacy behavior—a set of nonverbal cues that includes distance, lean and body orientation, eye contact, and openness of posture—on interaction between friends and strangers. Their research demonstrated that as sets of nonverbal cues are enacted, the meaning of behavior becomes clearer and the valence of the violation may not be as readily moderated by communicator reward value. Although initial EVT research focused on evaluations of behavior, later work highlighted the fact that expectancies (and expectancy violations) impact what individuals actually "do" during interaction with a partner. To assess this, Burgoon, LePoire, and Rosenthal (1995) considered the relative importance of expectancies and actual behavior in determining assessments of violation behavior and behavioral responses to violations. Their work demonstrated that expectancies influence perceptions of a partner's behavior, but communication behavior during interaction plays a key role in determining how individuals react to violations during conversation. Additional testing of IAT further supports this conclusion— both expectations and interaction behavior matter (Floyd & Burgoon, 1999; LePoire & Yoshimura, 1999).

A second context of application for EVT and IAT has been the study of expectancies and patterns of interaction in intimate relationships. In ongoing relationships, expectancies play a key role in creating a sense of shared perspective and connection between partners. One thing that makes close relationships satisfying is that we can rely on (or expect) our partners to show interest and immediacy in interaction with us. But it is also possible for close relationship partners to develop negative expectations of one another, and those negative expectations play a key role in producing relationship dissatisfaction. The application of EVT to romantic relationships has been important because, as Guerrero, Jones, and Burgoon (2000) explained, understanding patterns of behavior in relationships can provide "insight into the spirals of positive and negative behavior that can either enhance or destroy relationships" (p. 326). In an initial test of EVT in relationships, Kelley and Burgoon (1991) asked marital partners to report on expectations for intimacy in the relationship, and then later assessed whether those expectancies had been met, exceeded (a positive violation), or not met (a negative violation). The highest levels of satisfaction were found in relationships where a positive violation had occurred and the lowest levels of satisfaction involved negative violations. In a different vein, Bevan (2003) examined sexual resistance as an expectancy violation, comparing dating relationships and cross-sex friend-ships. She found that daters saw sexual resistance as more negatively valenced and more unexpected than cross-sex friends, but friends found sexual resistance to be more relationally important because it highlighted the definitional boundaries of cross-sex friendship.

Attachment style, which is thought to reflect an individual's deep-seated understanding of relational processes, can be understood to include expectancies for relational interaction. Guerrero and Burgoon (1996) posited that attachment style would impact how individuals responded to unexpected increases or decreases in nonverbal intimacy from a romantic partner. They found a general pattern of reciprocity for increased intimacy; however, responses to decreased partner intimacy were related to an individual's attachment style. For instance, individuals with a preoccupied attachment style—a style that leads individuals to seek excessive intimacy and validation from others—were found to most strongly reciprocate increased intimacy and to compensate decreased intimacy, as compared to other attachment styles. Guerrero and Burgoon suggested that this reflects preoccupied partners' strong desire for intimacy. Guerrero and colleagues (2000) further examined how romantic partners respond to unexpected changes in intimacy. They found that while partners tended to nonverbally reciprocate decreased intimacy, they also utilized verbal repair strategies designed to find out why the decrease in intimacy had occurred.

Although little work on relational communication has directly utilized IAT, Burgoon, Stern, and Dillman (1995) noted that personal relationships often highlight one of the most interesting questions that IAT could address, namely, why we sometimes do not respond to a partner's communication in ways that align with what is best for the relationship. For instance, Duggan and Bradshaw (2008) applied IAT to physician-patient interaction to determine if patterns of interaction can be used as an indication of relationship-centered care. Patterns of interaction between third-year residents showed a pattern of compensation around discussion of limitations due to illness. As patients increased their talk about the illness, physicians decreased their talk of it; hence, this pattern may reveal a disconnect between patient concerns and physician responsiveness.

A third application of EVT and IAT has focused on deception. Specifically, how do individuals detect deception and what role do expectations (particularly expectations of truthfulness) play in detection? And given that deception is an interactive process, how does behavior during interaction influence what deceivers do and what partners perceive? For example, Aune, Ching, and Levine (1996) examined whether expectations of violations influenced awareness of deception. They found that attributions of deceptive behavior were strongest for communicators low in social or physical attractiveness. Likewise, White and Burgoon (2001) used IAT to predict patterns of reciprocity and compensation in deceptive and truthful interactions. Their results demonstrated that patterns of interaction could be used to distinguish patterns of interaction for truth-tellers and deceivers.

Evaluation of EVT and IAT

Both EVT and IAT demonstrate the value of programmatic research and possess several strengths. EVT addresses one of the most intriguing questions about human interaction: How much do our expectations impact our perceptions of others and our responses to them in interaction? The predictions of EVT have evolved as researchers have demonstrated that expectations are complex. Although they do impact perceptions of interaction, they do not override what occurs in actual interaction. IAT offers a more complete account of patterns of interaction that occur between communicators. The concept of an IP complicates the idea of expectancies by considering how expectancies are influenced by personal preferences and biological responses to interaction. Also, by focusing on patterns of interaction, IAT brings the behavior of communicators squarely into focus, providing a strong imperative for communication researchers to pay attention to what actually transpires in interaction, rather than just relying on perceptions of communicators or impressions of observers.

On the other hand, the limitations of EVT are primarily related to its ability to predict patterns of interaction. Burgoon and colleagues (Burgoon, Stern, & Dillard, 1995; Burgoon & Ebesu Hubbard, 2005) articulated two shortcomings of EVT. First, EVT does not explain what would be expected when communicator reward value and behavior valence are at odds. For example, what happens when a low-reward communicator engages in a positive violation? Second, EVT does not provide a complete framework for understanding behavioral adaptation in interaction. It generally seems to underestimate the reciprocity that occurs in most interactions. For instance, although reduced involvement is dispreferred by most communicators in social situations, it is often reciprocated to some extent. This suggests that there are complex ways in which partners' interaction behaviors influence what occurs in interaction.

Perhaps the biggest limitation of IAT is that there is only limited empirical evidence supporting the predictions of IAT about adaptation in interaction. Determining whether it can assess the relative importance of various components within the IP is necessary. Further research will also be important to identifying the situations under which communicators are able to resist the pull of reduced involvement from a partner, and how communicators manage to handle problematic patterns of interaction, like negative affect, that can spiral out of control.

Continuing the Conversation

EVT and IAT have the potential to help us better understand communication in a range of contexts. Burgoon and Ebesu Hubbard (2005) argued that because expectancies are central to interaction in all cultures, EVT is applicable to cross-cultural interactions, although whether a violation will be positively or negatively valenced must be understood within the cultural frame of the individual experiencing the violation. They noted that both EVT and IAT can provide insight into intercultural communication patterns because they help us understand how expectations influence our willingness to engage in intercultural interaction and our interpretations of behaviors that are likely to be outside of our typical range of experience. This is a fruitful area for future research.

Although EVT has been used to study romantic relationships, it has not been applied to family communication. Research on family functioning indicates that overly rigid patterns of interaction are typically problematic in relationships (Burgoon, Stern, & Dillard, 1995). IAT provides a framework for better understanding why communicators may lapse into problematic patterns of behavior. Recently, Rodriguez, Dunbar, and Cronin (in press) described how IAT might be used to explore patterns of interaction responsiveness, as well as deception, in text messaging. Their extension of IAT into mediated communication highlights the importance of thinking about how responsiveness and patterns of interaction may be evident in communication behaviors other than nonverbal involvement. In the end, EVT and IAT may help researchers understand a wide variety of contexts, ranging from situations where uncertainty is high and expectations are based on stereotypical knowledge, to circumstances where interaction is strongly patterned and based on intimate knowledge of the other.

References

Aune, R. K., Ching, P. U., & Levine, T. R. (1996). Attributions of deception as a function of reward value: A test of two explanations. *Communication Quarterly, 44,* 478–486.

Bevan, J. L. (2003). Expectancy violation theory and sexual resistance in close, cross-sex relationships. *Communication Monographs, 70,* 68–82.

Burgoon, J. K. (1978). A communication model of personal space violations: Explication and an initial test. *Human Communication Research, 4,* 129–142.

Burgoon, J. K. (1993). Interpersonal expectations, expectancy violations, and emotional communication. *Journal of Language and Social Psychology, 12,* 30–48.

Burgoon, J. K., & Aho, L. (1982). Three field experiments of the effects of conversational distance. *Communication Monographs, 49,* 71–88.

Burgoon, J. K., & Ebesu Hubbard, A. S. (2005). Cross-cultural and intercultural applications of expectancy violations theory and interaction adaptation theory. In W. B. Gudykunst (Ed.), *Theorizing about intercultural communication* (pp. 149–171). Thousand Oaks, CA: Sage.

Burgoon, J. K., & Hale, J. L. (1988). Nonverbal expectancy violations: Model elaboration and application to immediacy behaviors. *Communication Monographs, 55,* 58–79.

Burgoon, J. K., LePoire, B. A., & Rosenthal, R. (1995). Effects of preinteraction expectancies and target communication on perceiver reciprocity and compensation in dyadic interaction. *Journal of Experimental Social Psychology, 31,* 287–321.

Burgoon, J. K., Stacks, D. W., & Woodall, G. W. (1979). A communication model of violations of distancing expectations. *Western Journal of Speech Communication, 43,* 153–167.

Burgoon, J. K., Stern, L. A., & Dillman, L. (1995). *Interpersonal adaptation: Dyadic interaction patterns.* New York, NY: Cambridge University Press.

Duggan, A. P., & Bradshaw, Y. S. (2008). Mutual influence processes in physician-patient communication: An interaction adaptation perspective. *Communication Research Reports, 25,* 211–226.

Floyd, K., & Burgoon, J. K. (1999). Reacting to nonverbal expressions of liking: A test of interaction adaptation theory. *Communication Monographs, 66,* 219–239.

Floyd, K., & Voloudakis, M. (1999). Affectionate behavior in adult platonic friendships: Interpreting and evaluation expectancy violations. *Human Communication Research, 25,* 341–369.

Guerrero, L. K., & Burgoon, J. K. (1996). Attachment styles and reactions to nonverbal involvement changes in romantic dyads: Patterns of reciprocity and compensation. *Human Communication Research, 22,* 335–370.

Guerrero, L. K., Jones, S. M., & Burgoon, J. K. (2000). Responses to nonverbal intimacy change in romantic dyads: Effect of behavioral valence and degree of behavioral change in nonverbal and verbal reactions. *Communication Monographs, 67,* 325–346.

Kelley, D. L., & Burgoon, J. K. (1991). Understanding marital satisfaction and couple type as functions of relational expectations. *Human Communication Research, 18,* 40–69.

LePoire, B. A., & Yoshimura, S. M. (1999). The effects of expectancies and actual communication on nonverbal adaptation and communication outcomes: A test of interaction adaptation theory. *Communication Monographs, 66,* 1–30.

Rodriguez, D., Dunbar, N. E., & Cronin, N. A. (in press). Interpersonal adaptation theory: Deceptive communication in text messages. In C. Liberman (Ed.), *Casing persuasive communication.* Dubuque, IA: Kendall-Hunt.

White, C. H., & Burgoon, J. K. (2001). Adaptation and communicative design: Patterns of interaction in truthful and deceptive conversations. *Human Communication Research, 27,* 3–27.

17

Face Theory

Goffman's Dramatistic Approach to Interpersonal Interaction

Sandra Metts and William R. Cupach

E rving Goffman (1922–1982) was an influential and prolific scholar whose work continues to inform contemporary views of social interaction. As a sociologist, Goffman was not so much interested in the psychology of individuals as in the ways that symbolic systems enable them to coordinate interactions. In Goffman's (1967) words, his goal was to understand the answer to this question: "What minimal model of the actor is needed if we are to wind him up, stick him in amongst his fellows, and have an orderly traffic of behavior emerge?" (p. 3). This description of human interaction may seem somewhat unhuman, but Goffman was trying to make it clear that, no matter what unique characteristics people may have in their psychological identity, all people have a social self, a public image, or—as Goffman called it—a "face," that we display during interaction. If you have ever been nervous about a job interview, a speech, or a first date, or if you have ever spilled your coffee, stumbled as you walked down the hall, or said something stupid, you realize that your public self or face is socially constructed, and that losing it is a uniquely human concern.

Intellectual Tradition of Face Theory

Goffman's face theory helps us understand two important aspects of interaction: (a) why and how people construct their public images, and (b) the strategies people use to maintain or to restore their own or others' images if those images are lost or threatened. This goal is consistent with the meta-theoretical assumptions of the interpretivist paradigm. Indeed, the concept of public image, or face, as socially constructed is deeply embedded within the broader interpretivist perspective known as symbolic interactionism.

The fundamental premise of symbolic interactionism is that the routine interactions we engage in every day are not spontaneous creations of our own making. Rather, they are "symbolic enactments" that reflect our knowledge of the cultural rituals that allow people to coordinate their behavior and generate meaning. We all recognize that words and many nonverbal behaviors are symbols that do not resemble their referent, and generate meaning only in context. For example, we can say, "My dog's name is Lady," or, "That lady is a dog." The meaning for the symbols "dog" and "lady" depend on the sequential ordering within the sentence and the interaction context of their expression.

Importantly, for Goffman "expressive elements" beyond words and nonverbal signals are also symbolic. The meanings of these other elements are learned by children through socialization, in much the same way that verbal language is learned. Why do we speak more politely to a person of higher status? Goffman would say we do so because status is a feature of a person's role and role is part of the system that guides our behavior and gives it meaning during interaction. If we chose to speak with a person of higher status just as we speak to a close friend, and the other person accepted that role definition and responded at the same level, his or her status would no longer constrain our behavior. However, Goffman would be quick to add that when the interaction occurs again in a different context (or "frame") we might recognize that showing deference to the other person's status is expected. We see this often among students and faculty who may have engaging and informal interactions outside the classroom but who reassume the student-teacher demeanor within the context of class.

Finally, a key feature of symbolic interactionism, and the basis of Goffman's face theory, is that even the private "self" is to a large degree a symbolic construction. As Goffman (1967) said, "Universal human nature is not a very human thing. By acquiring it, the person becomes a kind of construct built up not from inner psychic propensities but from moral rules that are impressed upon him from without" (p. 45). To illustrate, consider an infant who has not yet been socialized to an understanding of "self." This infant does not experience embarrassment, envy, jealousy, pride, or shame. In other words, a self that emerges from and acts within social structures, existing apart from the physical body, does not yet exist. The only self that exists is a composite of basic drives for food, security, and comfort. Eventually, these drives are embedded within a social framework that guides the infant's expression and gives the drives symbolic meaning. We now turn to a more detailed discussion of face theory with a particular focus on the dramaturgical metaphor that underlies it.

Main Goals and Features of Face Theory

Goffman used the metaphor of interaction as "drama" in order to illustrate how and why face is constructed, maintained, and lost. For Goffman, interaction is like a performance in a play in the sense that people are like actors who deliver their lines, wear costumes, and use props that are appropriate to each scene. Although this may sound manipulative, contrived, or artificial, consider that you dress for class, bring your notebook and pen, and greet other students with pleasant comments even when you would rather be home in your "sweats."

Goffman's most explicit description of the dramaturgical metaphor is found in his book *Presentation of Self in Everyday Life* (1959), in which he described the coordinated interactions found in institutions such as hospitals or mental care facilities, workplaces, and in public contexts such as restaurants. He studied the mechanisms by which "teams" (e.g., hospital staff or restaurant staff) were able to structure their actions in such a way so as to perform their roles. Goffman also applied his insights to "social teams" such as families and groups of friends. Based on his observations, Goffman (1959) argued that the process of social interaction manifests features similar to those found among actors who prepare themselves to perform on stage, deliver their performances, and receive acceptance by the audience. Specifically, he stated that a person's performance is "all the activity of a given participant on a given occasion that serves to influence in any way any of the other participants" (p. 22). In short, a performance is designed, consciously or unconsciously, to create an impression for others of who we are—an idealized self that fits appropriately into the requirements of the context. This pattern of actions that we use to create the impression is called a "part" or "routine." The other people in the situation contribute to the performance by serving as an audience, observers, or coparticipants.

Goffman (1959) referred to a front region (or front stage) and a back region (or back stage). The "front region" is where the performance takes place; it contains the "expressive equipment" that an individual may use during the performance. Thus, it consists of both the "setting" (e.g., living room, classroom, restaurant, and the furniture or items within) and the "personal front" of the performer, including appearance (e.g., clothing, sex, age, hair style, and racial characteristics) and manner (e.g., looks, posture, facial expressions, bodily gestures) that give clues about the role the performer might play (e.g., aggressive, meek, friendly, and so on). The "back region" is the place where the props for performance are stored and where preparation for performance can be conducted. For most of us, the back region in our lives is our home or our office where we prepare ourselves to perform "on stage" in the presence of others at work, in the classroom, or at social events. We are not much concerned when a close friend stops by our house unannounced because he or she is part of the cast, so to speak, but a relative stranger arriving unannounced would evoke the awkwardness that an actor feels when an audience member enters the back stage and sees him or her "out of character."

When he described the practices of ordinary conversation and the normative order within these events, Goffman used the concept of "face," which he defined as the "positive social value a person effectively claims for himself" (1967, p. 6). Our face is a type of performance, in that we present an image of our "self" through our appearance, our messages, and our actions that we believe will give the impression that we are competent and worthy social interactants.

In what Goffman (1967) called an "expressive ritual," interactants generally support each other's face presentation. We do so in part because we realize that if we do not cooperate in the protection of others' face, we cannot expect that they will cooperate in the protection of ours. In addition, we realize at some level that other people, like ourselves, are emotionally attached to their face. When face is accepted and validated, people feel good; when it is called into question, they feel bad. Thus, the general rules of "self-respect" and "considerateness" lead us to act in ways that maintain our own face and to cooperate in the maintenance of others' face. Importantly, this agreement is a working model for any given interaction. We may or may not actually be expressing or accepting some sincere, heart-felt expressions of self, but we give a ritualistic acknowledgement to the proffered images so that we can continue interaction.

Of course, Goffman (1967) also recognized that sometimes "incidents" occur and that the ordinary state of "being in face" could be disrupted, with the interaction becoming awkward or being derailed. He described two general types of "losing face." First, a person may "be in wrong face" when some type of information or some action discredits the image that he or she is putting forth. Examples of being in wrong face are those occasions when people are expected to (and present themselves as able to) demonstrate competence at an activity such as giving a speech, but they fumble for words. Another example is when people are on a date and fail miserably at small talk, humor, and even simple social manners. Second, a person may "be out of face" when he or she is not able to put forth an image that is expected (even required) in a specific interactional context. Examples of being out of face are those occasions when people are at a loss as to how to act or what to say, as when a person who is married is sitting in a bar showing affectionate behaviors to a person other than the spouse, and a coworker who knows the spouse approaches the table.

Whatever the particular situation, when we lose face, we become flustered, embarrassed, or even "shamefaced." We realize that we cannot continue to present the image we had constructed as legitimate or appropriate. When these incidents occur, we use "facework" to maintain the integrity of our own face or support the face display of others. When the incident is relatively minor, we try to remain poised (to not be flustered by our own embarrassment) and might use humor or a self-deprecating remark so that others will realize we are basically competent. Usually, other people laugh and support our face by saying, "Oh, you're not an idiot," or "I do things like that all the time." However, when face loss is more serious and disruptive, people rely on a ritualistic or scripted type of message exchange to restore face and reconstitute the interaction. These "moves," as Goffman (1967) called them, are deeply embedded within a culture's communication practices, and we present them in more detail in the following section.

How Communication Is Conceptualized in Face Theory

To fully appreciate Goffman's (1959) conceptualization of communication, it is helpful to compare it to the prominent views of his time. From the late 1950s through the 1970s, the common view of interpersonal communication stemmed largely from psychology where communication and self-disclosure were virtually synonymous. For example, Jourard's book, *The Transparent Self* (1964), advocated an authentic and uncalculated openness about our feelings, wants, and needs as a vehicle to good physical and psychological health.

Goffman's view of communication is quite different. He stated, "I assume that the proper study of interaction is not the individual and his psychology, but rather the syntactical relations among the acts of different persons mutually present to one another" (1967, p. 2). A syntactical relation is an ordering based on rules for structure. For example, in English the syntax of a sentence refers to word order as in "John hit the ball," rather than "ball the hit John." The first is meaningful as a sentence (apart from the content), whereas the second is not. What Goffman wanted his readers to understand is that communication consists of ordered sequences of messages between people, and that the only way that communication as an activity (apart from meaning) can occur is when these sequences unfold in a coordinated, rule-abiding pattern of exchange. When these conditions are met, interactants carry off their performances and maintain their face.

When these sequences are threatened or disrupted, individuals engage in a "preventive" or "corrective" process that is essentially a "pause" in the interaction to allow participants to realign their message sequence. For example, to prevent a disruption, speakers will avoid certain topics that might threaten their own or another person's face, or they will show respect for another person's position on an issue and offer disagreement in an indirect, face-saving way. We use civil inattention to appear as if we have not noticed something embarrassing, or we use polite deception when someone asks us to join them in a social activity but we don't want to go because we don't enjoy their company (e.g., "Oh, I wish I could go, but I have other plans").

When a disruption cannot be avoided and one or more participants lose face, an incident has occurred and the interaction order is in a state that Goffman (1967) called ritual disequilibrium. When a disruption occurs, efforts must be made to reestablish a satisfactory order. If the incident is a relatively inconsequential matter, then a simple interchange of two symbolic moves will suffice: "Excuse me. I'm sorry," and, "Certainly. No problem." However, when the incident is more complex, a longer sequence is necessary. According to Goffman (1967), interactants will use four ritualistic moves to restore order. These constitute the remedial interchange: (a) a challenge to "call attention to the misconduct" (spoken or implied), (b) an offering to show others that the offending person recognizes that his or her behavior violated expectations for maintaining face of self and others (e.g., by apologizing, downplaying the severity of the offense, or referring to extenuating circumstances), (c) an acceptance of the offering as sufficient to reestablish order and restore face, and (d) a thanks from the offending person that others have accepted and "forgiven" his or her poor performance. Sometimes one pass through the sequence is sufficient; at other times, it might take several passes.

Interestingly, Goffman argued that even the one aspect of human expression that might seem to be exempt from ritual control—the expression of emotion— is functionally very much a part of the ritual or syntactic order. When referring to sadness (at another's face loss) or anger (when our own face has been threatened), Goffman (1967) explained that these emotions function as moves, and fit so precisely into the logic of the ritual game that it would seem difficult to understand them without it.... In fact, spontaneously expressed feelings are likely to fit into the formal pattern of the ritual interchange more elegantly than consciously designed ones (p. 23).

In sum, Goffman viewed communication as strategic in the sense that messages are used to construct, maintain, and restore the organizational system of interaction that allows participants to enact their identities or conduct their performances. This is not to say that people are consciously aware of their intentions to manage interaction at all times or that people do not sometimes abuse the ritual courtesies afforded them by manipulating impressions for their own gain. It is simply to say that communication is the essential element in what Goffman called the "orderly traffic" of social behavior.

Research and Practical Applications of Face Theory

Among the many facets of interpersonal communication to which Goffman's ideas have been applied, the occurrence of embarrassment has received the most systematic treatment. As R. Miller (1996) noted, Goffman's "rich description of flustered actors and audiences trying to regain their poise and reestablish their scripts drew attention to understudied phenomena and helped prompt the first empirical studies of embarrassment in the 1960s" (pp. 111–112). Goffman (1967) did not consider embarrassment to be dysfunctional. Indeed, he realized that the display of embarrassment (blushing, being flustered, and the like) is constructive insofar as it allows actors to convey that they are competent enough to recognize that the moral order has been breached, and that it requires restoration. Indeed, those who show some chagrin after committing a breach are viewed more favorably than those who do not (e.g., Semin & Manstead, 1982). As Goffman (1967) remarked, "the person who can witness another's humiliation and unfeelingly retain a cool countenance himself is said in our society to be 'heartless,' just as he who can unfeelingly participate in his own defacement is thought to be 'shameless'" (pp. 10–11).

Throughout his writings, Goffman illustrated a number of specific remedial moves, both preventive (e.g., tact) and corrective (e.g., accounts and apologies), designed to counteract embarrassing and otherwise offensive incidents. As noted above, he carefully delineated the remedial interchange. He did not, however, systematically categorize the types of "offerings" that actors might employ. Consequently, one focus of subsequent research has been to elaborate the different ways in which embarrassed actors and observers repair embarrassing incidents (for reviews, see Cupach & Metts, 1994; R. Miller 1996). This research indicates that, in addition to offering "apologies," actors and observers provide "accounts" that explain untoward actions. Accounts include excuses, which minimize responsibility (e.g., "It's not your fault," "I was held up in traffic"), and justifications, which minimize seriousness of the offense (e.g., "It's not as bad as you are making it out to be," "I did it to teach you a lesson"). An actor or observer can use "remediation" by attempting to physically repair damage (e.g., cleaning up a spill or replacing a broken vase). "Humor" (e.g., joking about one's ineptness or faux pas) is also common in relatively mild incidents. "Avoidance" is usually thought of as a preventive strategy, but it can be corrective, as well (e.g., ignoring a faux pas so as not to draw more attention to it, or fleeing the scene). Finally, "aggressive actions" (e.g., insult, criticism, or retaliation) are sometimes used by actors who are seriously offended. In such cases they are motivated to defend and repair their own face at the expense of the offender's face.

Because face reflects "situated" identity, the appropriateness of various remedial strategies depends on the nature of the event. Several studies have assessed this connection. Humor and remediation, for example, are more likely to be employed in response to a loss of comportment (Metts & Cupach, 1989), but less likely when experiencing empathic embarrassment (Cupach & Metts, 1992). Aggression, on the other hand, is more likely to be employed by an actor who is the recipient of teasing, ridicule, or criticism (Cupach & Metts, 1992).

Goffman clearly recognized that embarrassment was not the only consequence of an incident; participants can also feel annoyed, angered, and offended, among other things. Accordingly, some researchers have studied social predicaments more generally, without focusing on the element of embarrassment. Hodgins, Liebeskind, and Schwartz (1996) solicited participant accounts to hypothetical victims of face-threatening predicaments. They found that perpetrators gave lengthier and more face-saving accounts to friends than they did to acquaintances, and that they gave more face-saving accounts to high-status versus low-status victims.

In an effort to more directly assess the face implications of moves within the remedial interchange, researchers have assessed directly the extent to which various challenges, offerings, and evaluations are perceived to be relatively face-threatening or face-saving. Manusov, Kellas, and Trees (2004) observed friendship dyads in which one person elicited and the other person provided an account for a failure event experienced by the accounter. Both the accounter and the elicitor completed measures of the extent to which their own behavior was attentive to the other's face, and the other's behavior was attentive to their own face. Both elicitors and accounters perceived that offerings of concessions and refusals were less attentive to the elicitor's face than were excuses. When examining challenges, accounters perceived more face attentiveness when there was no verbal challenge than when there was a direct question or rebuke, or an indirect or open question.

We close this section by reviewing three studies that illustrate the diversity of interpersonal contexts, particularly romantic relationships and families, to which Goffman's concept of facework has been applied. First, although much of the research on face in close relationships tends to examine face threats between partners, Bell and Hastings (2011) remind us that a couple represents an identity or face that is confirmed or threatened by other members of the social network and larger society. In their thematic analysis of interviews with 38 interracial couples, Bell and Hastings found that stares and comments from strangers were the most common face-threatening acts. The types of corrective facework reported by interviewees included, for example, responding nonverbally (e.g., smile at the person who is staring so he or she gets embarrassed and looks away), ignoring the face threats, rationalizing face threats (the relationship is what matters, not others' opinions), and reframing the threats (e.g., people are simply not used to seeing interracial couples or "If someone thinks that I am a nigger, then he is the one who needs help").

A second study by McBride (2010) explored the interesting dilemma that arises when a person has broken up with a romantic partner or spouse and shared negative comments about that person with his or her family but then reconciles and reunites with the partner. Not only is it necessary to restore the face of the partner, but also to account for the decision to reconcile in a way that maintains one's own face. He found that persons used both active and passive corrective facework. For example, they actively updated the family, but set rules about discussing it or hedged on the details; they also provided accounts in the form of excuses (e.g., "he promises he is going to get alcoholism treatment") or justifications ("if it [counseling] doesn't work, I have shown my children that I tried"). Passive strategies included not updating the family and not providing an account or justification because of the perception that they would be unnecessary or they would be unsuccessful.

Finally, Cavanagh, Dobash, Dobash, and Lewis (2001) employed Goffman's conceptualization of remedial facework to investigate how men who were violent toward their intimate female partners made sense of and characterized their violence. The authors conducted in-depth interviews with Scottish men who had been convicted of violent domestic offenses, as well as with their victimized partners. They found that violent men employed remedial strategies to minimize the repercussions of morally offensive behavior. "In seeking to make the meaning of a violent act more 'acceptable,' men deploy strategies for managing the meanings they attach to violence. They also seek to impose these meanings upon the women they abuse" (p. 700). Men used various forms of accounts, including "denial" (e.g., "I wouldn't say I was violent," "I don't remember"), "shifting blame" (e.g., "It's her fault," "Everybody around here was brought up that way"), "minimization" (e.g., "It doesn't happen every week," "She only had a little bit of blood on her face"), and "reduced competence" ("I'm not violent when I'm sober," "I can't help it. I have a bad temper"). In addition, men "apologized; expressed remorse; sometimes cried; promised to change; assured their partner that the violence would never happen again; and offered gifts—sometimes very lavish" (p. 707). Finally, men used the remedial device of requests, which in this context could sometimes be considered demands (e.g., "I asked to her to stop nagging me, but she kept it up"). In this way, men shifted their responsibility for violence to the partner by rationalizing that the partner did not comply with their request. Cavanagh and colleagues (2001) contended that understanding this type of "exculpatory discourse" could be important in fashioning focused intervention designed to alter the meaning men ascribe to their violent behavior, and to modify their dysfunctional identity as a relational partner.

Evaluation of Face Theory

Undoubtedly, the most enduring contribution of Goffman's work, particularly his dramaturgical approach to face and facework, is his comprehensive analysis of the routine and ordinary traffic of social interaction. As Burns (1992) said of Goffman, "he made clear what was previously unclear, pointed to the significance of things that had been regarded as of little or no consequence, and disentangled what was previously an indiscriminate muddle" (p. 6).

Goffman's face theory meets the criteria of a good theory. First, it has a broad *scope* and explains phenomena that occur frequently or in a wide range of circumstances. In this chapter, we have focused only on the dramaturgical elements of Goffman's work, but even amid this selective range it is apparent that his work has implications for understanding virtually all aspects of interpersonal communication. We could never communicate unless the numerous, diverse, and complex aspects of our individual personalities were selectively organized into a coherent unit appropriate for the needs of the circumstances— i.e., the performance, role, or face that Goffman discussed. Moreover, we could never exchange the simplest greeting, let alone initiate or maintain personal relationships, without implicit (ritualized) rules to guide our understanding of the actions that we and others are performing.

A second strength of Goffman's dramaturgical perspective is its *heurism*. Goffman's influence on subsequent scholars interested in social interaction has been enduring and widespread. Space does not permit a description of these many applications, but they range from ritual teasing at coed wedding and baby showers (Braithwaite, 1995), to public use of cell phones (Humphreys, 2005), conflict management (Oetzel, Ting-Toomey, Yokochi, Masumoto, & Takai, 2000), maintaining post-divorce coparenting relationships (A. Miller, 2009), and negotiating identities when developing intercultural relationships (Imahori & Cupach, 2005). Indeed, a second-generation rendering of face and facework underlies a prominent theory of interaction known as politeness theory. As evident in Chapter 9 of this volume, the research in this area alone is extensive.

Paradoxically, however, sometimes the strengths of a theory are the source of its limitations. In the case of Goffman's work, his scope is so broad that it causes the theory to be weak on the criterion of *parsimony*. Specifically, Goffman's description of the elements and processes of social interaction is not concise. His initial rendering of his dramaturgical perspective, for example, required an entire book (Goffman, 1959).

Continuing the Conversation

Despite the broad heuristic power of Goffman's work, an area that has not received the attention we might expect from communication scholars is his notion of "social skill," which he also refers to as tact, savoir faire, or diplomacy. We believe that Goffman's ideas could be usefully employed to provide a fresh perspective on the construct of interpersonal communication competence. Given his focus on the ritual order of interaction, an individual's communication competence would be evidenced by the successful enactment of social roles and the facilitation of others' enactments. Drawing on the analogy of a card game, Goffman suggested that one aspect of our identity (our role or face) is like the hand we are dealt. The other aspect of our identity, however, is the skill with which we play that hand. Goffman (1967) illustrated the dilemmas with which each actor must grapple:

> Too little perceptiveness, too little savoir-faire, too little pride and considerateness, and the person ceases to be someone who can be trusted to take a hint about himself or give a hint that will save others embarrassment. . . . Too much perceptiveness or too much pride, and the person becomes someone who is thin-skinned, who must be treated with kid gloves, requiring more care on the part of others than he may be worth to them. Too much savoir-faire or too much considerateness, and he becomes someone who is too socialized, who leaves the others with the feeling that they do not know how they really stand with him. (p. 40)

We are not able to elaborate these ideas here, but we believe that they suggest a provocative alternative metaphor for interpersonal competence. Exploration of this approach could stimulate new conceptualization and measurement efforts in the area of interpersonal competence and social skills. Such efforts would hold promise not only for theory and research but ultimately for teaching and training individuals to develop perceptiveness, tact, effective facework, and aplomb at playing the ritual game.

References

Bell, G. C., & Hastings, S. O. (2011). Black and white interracial couples: Managing relational disapproval through facework. *The Howard Journal of Communication, 22,* 240–259.

Braithwaite, D. O. (1995). Ritualized embarrassment at "coed" wedding and baby showers. *Communication Reports, 8,* 145–157.

Burns, T. (1992). *Erving Goffman.* New York, NY: Routledge.

Cavanagh, K., Dobash, R. E., Dobash, R. P., & Lewis, R. (2001). "Remedial work": Men's strategic responses to their violence against intimate female partners. *Sociology, 35,* 695–714.

Cupach, W. R., & Metts, S. (1992). The effects of type of predicament and embarrassability on remedial responses to embarrassing situations. *Communication Quarterly, 40,* 149–161.

Cupach, W. R., & Metts, S. (1994). *Facework.* Thousand Oaks, CA: Sage.

Goffman, E. (1959). *The presentation of self in everyday life.* New York, NY: Doubleday.

Goffman, E. (1967). *Interaction ritual: Essays on face-to-face behavior.* New York, NY: Pantheon Books.

Hodgins, H. S., Liebeskind, E., & Schwartz, W. (1996). Getting out of hot water: Facework in social predicaments. *Journal of Personality and Social Psychology, 71,* 300–314.

Humphreys, L. (2005). Cellphones in public: Social interactions in a wireless era. *New Media & Society, 7,* 810–833.

Imahori, T. T., & Cupach, W. R. (2005). Identity management theory: Facework in intercultural relationships. In W. B. Gudykunst (Ed.), *Theorizing about communication and culture* (pp. 195–210). Thousand Oaks, CA: Sage.

Jourard, S. M. (1964). *The transparent self: Self-disclosure and well-being.* New York, NY: Van Nostrand Reinhold.

Manusov, V., Kellas, J. K., & Trees, A. R. (2004). Do unto others? Conversational moves and perceptions of attentiveness toward otherface in accounting sequences between friends. *Human Communication Research, 30,* 514–539.

McBride, M. C. (2010). Saving face with family members: Corrective facework after reconciling with a romantic partner. *Journal of Family Communication, 10,* 215–235.

Metts, S., & Cupach, W. R. (1989). Situational influence on the use of remedial strategies in embarrassing predicaments. *Communication Monographs, 56,* 151–162.

Miller, A. (2009). Face concerns and facework strategies in maintaining postdivorce coparenting and dating relationships. *Southern Journal of Communication, 74,* 157–173.

Miller, R. S. (1996). *Embarrassment: Poise and peril in everyday life.* New York, NY: Guilford.

Oetzel, J. G., Ting-Toomey, S., Yokochi, Y., Masumoto, T., & Takai, J. (2000). A typology of facework behaviors in conflicts with best friends and relative strangers. *Communication Quarterly, 48,* 397–419.

Semin, G. R., & Manstead, A. S. R. (1982). The social implications of embarrassment displays and restitution behavior. *European Journal of Social Psychology, 12,* 367–377.

18

Grounded Practical Theory

Theorizing Communicative Practices

Karen Tracy

- How does the small talk preceding a company's weekly staff meeting display the group to be both a mainstream American business and an especially health-and-fitness conscious community (Mirivel & Tracy, 2005)?
- What problems do students training to be psychics face in self-assessment discussions (Agne, 2010)?
- What dilemmas do graduate students face as they talk to departmental faculty and other graduate students about their research (Tracy, 1997a)?
- What are the interactional challenges faced by participants in online support groups (Aakhus & Rumsey, 2010)?
- How does cosmetic surgeons' talk manage tensions between selling elective surgeries (such as breast augmentation) and being good, patient-focused physicians (Mirivel, 2007)?
- What is a defensible communicative ideal for citizens speaking up in a public meeting about marriage between same-sex partners (Tracy & Hughes, in press)?

The above are examples of questions that grounded practical theory (GPT) has addressed. GPT is an approach to communication study that focuses on a small set of questions related to describing and cultivating interaction in existing communicative practices where a "communicative practice" is an activity in which talk is central to what people are doing. Communicative practices that GPT scholars have studied include physician-patient consultations, public meetings of a variety of types, crisis negotiations involving law enforcement officers, online support groups, academic brown bag discussions, and routine business meetings. While this theory has not yet been used explicitly to study communication in close relationships, it shows great promise and I will suggest applications to interpersonal communication in this chapter.

Intellectual Tradition of Grounded Practical Theory

Grounded practical theory was developed by Robert Craig and Karen Tracy in the 1990s (Craig, 1989; Craig & Tracy, 1995) and seeks to reconstruct communicative practices at three levels. The first and the most important level is that of a practice's problems. From studying the discourse of a practice, GPT aims to describe the web of problems that participants face in their different roles. The second level of reconstruction—the technical level—specifies the conversational moves that reflect problems and the interactional strategies that participants use to manage them. At the most abstract level—the philosophical level—a practice "can be reconstructed in the form of elaborated normative ideals and overarching principles that provide a rationale for the resolution of problems" (Craig & Tracy, 1995, p. 253). To develop normative ideals, GPT gives particular weight to participants' "situated ideals," ideals that can be inferred from comments of praise and blame that a practice's participants make about specific interactional moments. Often when people leave a practice, for example, a meeting, they make assessments. These remarks—"I know she's trying to be sensitive but she really let things drag"—cue how the multiple aims of a practice are expected to be put together.

GPT is an approach that blends an interpretive social science commitment to careful detailed description with the rhetorical interest in rendering judgment. Actually a meta-theory rather than a theory, GPT guides research by offering a set of questions to pose about particular communication practices. Although having a few features in common, grounded practical theory should not be confused with "grounded theory," a method developed by sociologists Barry Glaser and Anselm Strauss in the 1960s (Glaser & Strauss, 1967). Both GPT and grounded theory are primarily inductive research approaches committed to developing theory starting in the existing social world. Glaser and Strauss's method of grounded theory was concerned with spelling out how to arrive at interesting explanatory hypotheses about social life that could be tested quantitatively. In contrast, GPT's goal is "to create *practical* theories, situation-specific yet practice-general ideas to aid reflection. It is the interest in what is pragmatically useful—reasonable, effective, morally defensible—that distinguishes GPT from Grounded Theory" (Tracy, 2010, p. 218). A second difference, about which I will say more later, is the kind of data that GPT tends to use. Because GPT is focally interested in *communication* practices, recording, transcribing, and analyzing talk is essential.

If we frame GPT in terms of the most frequent way meta-theories are described, GPT would be identified as a hybrid critical-interpretive approach. It is an interpretive approach in that it is centrally involved in constructing a portrait of a communicative practice and its problems. It is a critical approach in that it recognizes that a researcher's values regarding what is good and right are part of the scholarly process. It differs from other critical approaches, though, because it is less focused on how power is shaping what goes on in situations. GPT builds proposals about what counts as good conduct drawing on Aristotle's idea of *phronesis,* which recognizes that what is a good way to act is a matter of careful judgment that must attend to the particulars of a situation.

Main Goals and Features of Grounded Practical Theory

A basic assumption of GPT is that most communicative practices are shaped by interactional dilemmas. In academic discussions, for instance, graduate students and faculty members want to appear intelligent but do not want to be seen as self-aggrandized (Tracy & Baratz, 1993). In school boards, the meeting chair wants to move the meeting along so that decisions can be made, but wants to do so in a way that ensures citizens feel they have had a fair chance to be heard (Potter & Hepburn, 2007). As a result of the dilemmas that are part of virtually all practices, a normative proposal about how participants ought to act needs to weigh the multiple goods to which a practice is committed. Thus we would evaluate this theory in its usefulness for understanding thought and action, rather than accuracy of predicting theorized relationships or showing how power is naturalized in a situation.

GPT developed simultaneously with action-implicative discourse analysis (Tracy, 1995; Tracy & Craig, 2010), a discourse analytic method designed to address GPT questions. Action-implicative discourse analysis spells out how to name and define a communicative practice and its problems; how to audio-record, transcribe, and analyze segments of talk; and it suggests what other kinds of data (institutional documents of a variety of types, interviews) could be collected to help build the kind of depth understanding that is needed by a researcher to arrive at good normative proposals.

To illustrate how the key theoretical concepts of GPT—(a) problems/dilemmas, (b) discourse strategies/moves, and (c) situated ideals—are worked out in the study of actual communicative practices, I focus on three different practices: academic colloquia, oral argument in appellate courts, and police/911 telephone calls. For academic colloquia, I describe the ideal for good discussion that was developed using participants' situated ideals as the starting point; for oral argument about same-sex marriage in appellate courts, I show how a discourse strategy makes apparent a key challenge of the speaking situation; and for the police calls, I describe the data and a few discourse strategies used to manage one of the problems. Following this, I describe how GPT can enlighten communication in close relationships.

ACADEMIC COLLOQUIA

A first practice that GPT has investigated is that of academic colloquia. Faculty and graduate students face a variety of problems in participating in research paper discussions. These problems include how to present oneself during the oral description of the research project so that the right level of expertise is established. If presenters hedge their experience and expertise too much, they set in motion implications that they are intellectually limited (i.e., not that smart). If, on the other hand, their talk suggests they possess a high level of expertise, they license especially difficult questions and the potential embarrassment of not having good answers (Tracy & Baratz, 1993).

Graduate students and faculty also face dilemmas as they pose questions to presenters (Tracy & Naughton, 1994), because questions imply how knowledgeable, interesting, and sophisticated a questioner sees a presenter to be, as well as how knowledgeable, interesting, and sophisticated the questioner is. Interviews with graduate students and faculty at two universities were used to identify the situated ideal for good intellectual discussion. Rather than a single ideal, two different ideals were identified. The first was constructive criticism and the second focused on the importance of ideas or "dialectic."

Constructive critics focused on avoiding hostility and creating positive outcomes. Within the constructive criticism ideal, high-status participants (i.e., faculty) were responsible for dealing with low-status participants (graduate students) in careful, supportive ways. The dialectic ideal, in contrast, emphasized faculty responsibility to create equality, focus on ideas, and minimize differences of status. For faculty to treat students in markedly different ways was to reify status and hinder the transformation of graduate students from novices into full-fledged colleagues. Interestingly, while faculty and graduate students generally favored one or the other ideal, traces of the other ideal could be found in just about everyone's talk. For example, one faculty member defined the purpose of academic discussion as needing to be idea focused and stated that participants should not concern themselves about how others were feeling. However, when this same faculty member focused on being a presenter she highlighted the importance of discussants saying something positive about a presenter's work because of how anxiety producing it is to present. The upshot of this, I argue, is the need for an ideal for intellectual discussion that recognizes that it is a communicative practice in which both ideas matter and people and their feelings need to be considered. When faculty and graduate students discuss ideas that are personally important to them, their competence and character are implicated. To do academic discussion well, participants need an ideal that keeps constructive criticism and the integrity and importance of ideas in an ongoing tension with each other.

ORAL ARGUMENT ABOUT
SAME-SEX MARRIAGE IN APPELLATE COURTS

Oral argument in state supreme courts is a particularly technical discourse practice involving a panel of judges (5–9 in most states) asking questions of opposing attorneys about an interpretive complexity related to a state's constitution or its statutes. The purpose of oral argument is to explore problems in each attorney's claims so that the judges can determine how they ought to vote in a case. Tracy (2011) studied the videotaped oral arguments in three state supreme courts that were considering whether each state's marriage law was unconstitutional. The parties that were central to the practice of oral argument in these same-sex marriage cases were (a) attorneys representing the gay and lesbian plaintiffs, (b) attorneys representing the state agencies responsible for officially legalizing marriages, and (c) the questioning judges from the three different courts.

This GPT study began by noticing (and documenting) variation in how parties used person-referencing terms for the gay and lesbian plaintiffs. Were these persons referred to in terms of their sexual orientation ("same-sex couples," "homosexuals," "gays and lesbians"), by the courtroom role ("plaintiffs"), or by some other term (e.g., "female couple," "second-class citizens," "person with whom you've brought children into the world")? Tracy (2011) argued that the outcome of these marriage law cases hinged on which of two competing principles of law were given priority: recognizing that law making was the responsibility of the legislative branch or a court exercising its responsibility to protect the rights of a discriminated-against minority.

A challenge that all parties faced within oral argument in these same-sex marriage cases was how they could recognize both principles as legitimate and yet treat one of them as deserving more weight. The ways parties did this, Tracy showed, was through the sheer number of person-referencing terms used. Plaintiffs' attorneys used far more than the attorneys defending state agencies did. In a situation, such as appellate court, that pitted individuals against a government agency, the number of person-terms used became a way to imply the reasonableness of giving weight to the principle of minority rights. In addition, parties who were against same-sex marriage used a greater number of the more negative terms to refer to parties ("homosexuals" versus "gays and lesbians") than did parties favoring same-sex marriage. Small differences in usage patterns of these discourse moves, then, reflected a strategy to argue for one principle of law in a context where several principles applied.

POLICE/911 TELEPHONE CALLS

The focal discourse data for studying citizen calls to 911 and the police were 650 calls in a major city's police department. Audiotaped copies of calls were downloaded from police archives, a log was made describing features of each call, and then a transcript was made of calls selected for detailed analysis. In addition to the discourse data, the researchers spent 10 months observing in the emergency center, sitting with call-takers and listening to conversations with citizens, attending training workshops, going on police ride-alongs, and studying the center's policy and training manuals. This immersion in a communicative practice, with particular attention given to the transcribing and analysis of discourse, is the first step of a GPT project. Then the researcher begins analysis, working to identify the interactional problems that faced participants and the discourse strategies they used.

In studying citizen-police exchanges, dilemmas were identified that confronted police call-takers answering calls and the citizens making them. Call-takers, for instance, need to deal with the fact that citizens usually brought a customer service frame to their requests for help, assuming that all they needed to do was name what they desired and help would be forthcoming (Tracy, 1997b). In reality, police departments have limited resources, necessitating careful screening of requests. Police departments also have concerns about officer safety that lead call-takers to seek information that citizens might believe delays the arrival of desired services. In addition, although the goal of the call-takers is to be as helpful as possible, their ability to accomplish this goal is constrained by institutional requirements not to give legal advice and to manage calls quickly so that they can be available for a next call (Tracy & Agne, 2002).

In initiating calls to the police, citizens, too, face problems. Consider one problem that callers sometimes faced (Tracy & Anderson, 1999):

> When citizens call the police to report a problem with (or caused by) another, they need not only to characterize the problematic action/event, but they must position themselves in relation to the complained-about person. This conversational work of positioning self, and describing the other's actions, is delicate business when the complained-about person is connected to the caller. Different constructions of the other and the problem affect whether callers get the help they are seeking. At the same time, alternate constructions offer different pictures of the other's blameworthiness and self's contribution to the problem. Furthermore, these verbal pictures become actions that others—call takers, police officers, the complained-about person, and additional people in the caller's web of connections—may interrogate for plausibility and evaluate as signs of a caller's character and moral fairness. (p. 202)

In a nutshell, a person calling the police to report a difficulty caused by someone with whom that person has a relationship is a "problem." On the one hand, the caller wants the trouble that the other person has caused resolved; on the other hand, it is generally regarded as inappropriate, unless the trouble is highly serious (e.g., violence), to cause a connected other to be in trouble with the police. How, then, did citizens manage this dilemma?

To minimize their closeness to another without explicitly lying, one strategy that citizens used was to describe the person causing the difficulty using generic terms such as "the man," "someone," and "the gentleman." Of note, while these terms are literally true—all males can be referred to as men, someones, or gentlemen—the terms are misleading. When a referred-to person is more closely linked to a speaker, these terms imply the absence of a closer relationship, such as being a friend, ex-boyfriend, or neighbor. Often, as the police call continued and the call-taker pursued particular pieces of information, the fact that "the man" was a family friend became apparent by virtue of the caller having information about the other that did not fit the frame of a stranger or a barely acquainted relationship.

A second strategy citizens used to mask the degree of closeness they had to another was to refer to the trouble causer as "a friend." Call number 167, below, offers an extended example of how a caller used the word "friend" as a relational distancing strategy. Through a variety of discourse specifics, identified in Tracy and Anderson (1999), the caller's term initially implied that the complained-about other was "just a friend" rather than a "boyfriend." As a second call-taker came on the phone to explore whether the police could help the caller retrieve her car, the ambiguity that the caller's use of the term "friend" was trading on became apparent. You will also see how the scholar using GPT notates the different ways people speak.

(Call 167, 3:30 p.m., female call-taker, female caller)

[transcript notations: (a) underline = vocal stress; caps = loud speech; (b) (.) = brief pause of 0.2 sec, and ((pause)) is a longer, untimed pause; (c) brackets = overlapping talk; (d) .hhh = inhalation; number of h's indicates length; (e) colons = prolonged sound]

CT1   Citywest Police?

C   Um, yeah, I need to file a complaint about my car being taken?

CT1   (.) It was *stolen?*

C   Well .hhhhh a friend borrowed it and h-he never brought it back.

. . .

C   Well, I didn't loan it, he *took* it.

CT1   ((pause)) I mean wh- are you saying that, you know did you *say* to him *at a:11,* and be honest with me, did you say, yeah go ahead borrow it but bring it right back?

C   Um no, I was in the hospital ((clear throat)) and (.) he was here staying with me, and he (.) took it while I was in the hospital, and then when I got out I couldn't reach him.

. . .

[several exchanges and transfer to a different call-taker]

CT2 Good afternoon auto theft, this is Ellen.

C   Um yeah I don't know what to do ((clearing throat)) A friend of mine uhmm was using my car while I was in the hospital? And he's been gone now for (.) well it's been, gosh about 36 hours. And I haven't been able to get in touch with him or (.) he doesn't have a local phone number, and I don't know what to do.

CT2 Okay a *friend* of yours, meaning an acquaintance friend? or a friend

    [a boyfriend?

C   [He was staying with me

CT2 Pardon?

CT2 A boyfriend?

C   Ye:ah.

CT2 Okay. So it's a boyfriend .

Citizens and call-takers face dilemmas that are affected by their positions in the practice of police/911 calls. As they confront problems, each party's talk reflects one or more problems, as well as attempts to manage the problems. GPT is interested in identifying the interactional problems and discourse strategies of existing communicative practices.

How Communication Is Conceptualized in Grounded Practical Theory

There are many ways to frame communication. Shepherd, St. John, and Striphas (2006) identified 27 different theoretical conceptualizations. As I described earlier with GPT, communication can be constructed as a practice. To conceive of communication as a practice is to recognize it as a connected, meaningful set of activities for people in particular cultural communities. A practice may be described at different levels of generality (e.g., emergency call taking versus questioning upset callers). Of note, practices are surrounded by larger discourses that include talk about desirable and problematic ways to participate in specific practices. It is this talk about practices that occurs among people as they go about their ordinary life activities that makes communicative practices socially significant: What should be standards of good conduct? What is or is not ethical? Does using a particular conversational technique have this positive or that negative effect? This everyday meta-discourse surrounding practices is a large part of how conduct in any particular practice is actually regulated.

In drawing on "practice" as the central concept, theorizing communication is taken to be a normative enterprise rather than an explanatory scientific one. As Craig (2006) puts it,

> A theory of a practice provides a particular way of *interpreting* [emphasis in original] practical knowledge, a way of focusing attention on important details of a situation and weaving them into a web of concepts that can give experience a new layer of meaning, reveal previously unnoticed connections, and suggest new lines of action. (p. 43)

For example, study of the 911 calls made visible the conflicting ways that callers and call-takers thought about what was required to get police help. To conceptualize communication as a practice is to work to develop communication theories that are useful for action. "Useful," however, is not a synonym for expedient and effective action. Rather, it is the morally serious judgments about action and consequences that pragmatist philosopher John Dewey (1910) advocated.

Research and Practical Applications of Grounded Practical Theory

GPT studies have tended to focus on institutional interaction, but even recognizing the issue of personal relationship uniqueness, explored in the next section, there are interpersonal practices that would benefit from adopting a GPT stance. For example, in friendship, it would be valuable to explore the discourse strategies used to manage the goals of being supportive to a friend while also honest and critical; it would also be useful to see how intimates navigate the problem of being honest about one's past conduct with a new partner while not revealing information that might be highly unflattering. Violation of relationship expectations is another area that GPT could inform. For example, responding appropriately to gifts a close other gives could be enlightened by GPT. As Robles (2012) shows, gift recipients are expected to show genuine appreciation for a gift even while it is recognized that some gifts are not much liked. Determining strategies and moving toward an ideal for managing the interactional trouble posed by gifts would be a valuable practice to understand better and is one GPT could help explicate.

Evaluation of Grounded Practical Theory

A first strength (and limitation) of GPT is that it "bridges" interpersonal and organizational communication theorizing. As a limitation, this strength would be described as "not fitting" into the major research interests in either interpersonal or organizational communication. With its primary focus on institutional practices, GPT finds itself reflecting about communicative practices in many of the same places as organizational scholars do. With its focus on interaction and its preference for practices in nonbusiness settings, it is different from most organizational communication. In the field of communication, a fairly sharp line is drawn between interpersonal communication and organizational communication theories. Drawing lines like this does not work well for GPT, because it reflects features of both interpersonal and organizational communication, and it also differs from each of them. The most typical choices of sites and practices, as I have noted, are the clearest features that distinguish GPT from other interpersonal communication research.

Second, GPT presupposes that a practice is meaningful at the sociocultural level, that it can be described in terms of multiple aims and purposes, and that the practice will be shaped by espoused institutional values and practical constraints related to time, money, and energy. It is this assumptive frame that grounds most GPT studies and enables an analyst to identify problems or dilemmas, as well as novel discourse strategies. For institutional practices, such as the ones I have mentioned throughout this chapter, it makes sense to ask what are better and worse ways for participants to conduct themselves as they juggle the multiple aims of the practice. For example, the relative uniformity of goals and ideals that can be assumed for police departments dealing with citizens, however, does not work as well with intimate relationships.

For communicative practices that are central to close relationships, there is less agreement about what constitutes right action. Strong cultural differences, as well as within-culture, social class, and value differences shape how people negotiate marrying or living together, parenting in blended families, and having (or not having) cross-cultural friendships. In American society, at least, there is a much stronger assumption that ideas as to what should count as better (and worse) ways to run a meeting, make a presentation, negotiate a contract, or give feedback to an employee are socially shared. In contrast, although close relationships are also cultural products (Fitch, 1998), there is a stronger expectation that there is not a single "best" way to "do" and communicate in close relationships. The ability of people to craft good, albeit idiosyncratic, relationships is one of the delights and challenges of intimate life. For this reason, posing normative questions about the best ways to participate in and structure communicative practices is more straightforward for institutional practices than it is for close relationship practices. However, as suggested in the previous section, GPT has potential, albeit more limited, for studying certain aspects of personal relationships.

Continuing the Conversation

I have referred to "communicative practice" throughout this chapter as if it were straightforward, an event we would all see and name the same way. This is not the case. The name for a practice frequently privileges the viewpoint of one category of participant over others, thereby making the analyst's task of naming a crucial one. For example, practices may be embedded in each other and conceptualized at different levels of abstraction. Consider how this issue applies to what I have referred to as the practice of school board meetings (Tracy, 2010). Other labels for this practice could be local governance, public meetings, or places of ordinary democracy. Alternatively, one could focus on smaller activities that are embedded in or related to one of these larger practices: One could study citizen participation, agenda setting meetings, candidate debates, board discussions, community discussions of controversial issues, or parent complaints to school districts. All of these are reasonable and valuable ways to frame talk in school governance sites, but each directs observation and analysis into different channels and makes likely the construction of different problems, discourse strategies, and ideals of conduct. What a practice (or problem) is named matters.

GPT is a meta-theoretical approach that advocates a set of questions to pose about a valued communication practice. As such, GPT could be used to reexamine communicative practices that have already been extensively studied, such as classroom teaching, divorce mediation, or therapy, as well as activities that are focal in personal relationships. To the degree that it is useful to have a firm grasp of the problems and dilemmas of a practice, its routine conversational strategies, and its situated ideals, GPT could bring fresh insights to reflection about conduct in communicative practices that society already assumes are important and it could shed light on previously unexamined practices. GPT enables understanding of the complexities of existing practices, and it helps a practice's participants reflect, plan, and act more wisely. This is the kind of theorizing communication scholars should be doing.

References

Aakhus, M., & Rumsey, E. (2010). Crafting supportive communication online: A communication design analysis of conflict in an online support group. *Journal of Applied Communication Research, 38,* 65–84.

Agne, R. (2010). Self-assessment as a dilemmatic communicative practice: Talk among psychics in training. *Southern Communication Journal, 75,* 306–327.

Craig, R. T. (1989). Communication as a practical discipline. In B. Dervin, L. Grossberg, B. J. O'Keefe, & E. Wartella (Eds.), *Rethinking communication; Volume 1; Paradigm issues* (pp. 97–122). Newbury Park, CA: Sage.

Craig, R. T. (2006). Communication as a practice. In G. J. Shepherd, G. St. John, & T. Striphas (Eds.), *Communication as . . .: Perspectives on theory* (pp. 38–47). Thousand Oaks, CA: Sage.

Craig, R. T., & Tracy, K. (1995). Grounded practical theory: The case of intellectual discussion. *Communication Theory, 5,* 248–272.

Dewey, J. (1910). *How we think.* Boston, MA: D. C. Heath and Company.

Fitch, K. L. (1998). *Speaking relationally: Culture, communication and interpersonal connection.* New York, NY: Guilford.

Glaser, B., & Strauss, A. (1967). *The discovery of grounded theory.* Chicago, IL: Aldine.

Mirivel, J. C. (2007). Managing poor surgical candidacy: Communication problems for plastic surgeons. *Discourse & Communication, 1,* 309–336.

Mirivel, J., & Tracy, K. (2005). Premeeting talk: An organizationally crucial form of talk. *Research on Language and Social Interaction, 38,* 1–34.

Potter, J., & Hepburn, A. (2007). Chairing democracy: Psychology, time, and negotiating the institution. In K. Tracy, J. P. McDaniel, & B. E. Gronbeck (Eds.), *The prettier doll: Rhetoric, discourse, and ordinary democracy* (pp. 176–202). Tuscaloosa: University of Alabama Press.

Robles, J. S. (2012). Troubles with assessments in gifting occasions. *Discourse Studies, 14,* 753–777.

Shepherd, G. J., St. John, G., & Striphas, T. (Eds.). (2006). *Communication as . . .: Perspectives on theory.* Thousand Oaks, CA: Sage.

Tracy, K. (1995) Action-implicative discourse analysis. *Journal of Language and Social Psychology, 14,* 195–215.

Tracy, K. (1997a). *Colloquium: Dilemmas of academic discourse.* Norwood, NJ: Ablex.

Tracy, K. (1997b). Interactional trouble in emergency service requests: A problem of frames. *Research on Language and Social Interaction, 30,* 315–343.

Tracy, K. (2010). *Challenges of ordinary democracy: A case study in deliberation and dissent.* University Park: Pennsylvania State University Press.

Tracy, K. (2011). What's in a name?: Stance markers in oral argument about marriage laws. *Discourse & Communication, 5,* 65–88.

Tracy, K., & Agne, R. R. (2002). "I just need to ask somebody some questions": Sensitivities in domestic dispute calls. In J. Cottrell (Ed.), *Language in the legal process* (pp. 75–89). Brunel, UK: Palgrave.

Tracy, K., & Anderson, D. L. (1999). Relational positioning strategies in calls to the police: A dilemma. *Discourse Studies, 1,* 201–226.

Tracy, K., & Baratz, S. (1993). Intellectual discussion in the academy as situated discourse. *Communication Monographs, 60,* 300–320.

Tracy, K., & Craig, R. T. (2010). Studying interaction in order to cultivate practice: Action-implicative discourse analysis. In J. Streeck (Ed.), *New adventures in language and interaction* (pp. 145–166). Amsterdam: John Benjamins.

Tracy, K., & Hughes, J. F. (in press). Democracy-appealing partisanship: A situated ideal of citizenship. *Journal of Applied Communication Research.*

Tracy, K., & Naughton, J. (1994). The identity work of questioning in intellectual discussion. *Communication Monographs, 61,* 281–302.

19

Narrative Theories

Making Sense of
Interpersonal Communication

Jody Koenig Kellas

Throughout the course of living everyday events, people build and communicate their relationships, cultures, and identities, in part through the stories they tell. Thus, narratives and storytelling are consequential sites for theorizing interpersonal communication. Research on personal narratives has merited and received a great deal of attention over the past two decades within a variety of disciplines including communication, psychology, sociology, sociolinguistics, English, folklore, and anthropology. Despite the growing interest in narratives and the common reference to narrative theory in interpersonal and family communication research, however, there is no single narrative theory that guides communication research generally or interpersonal communication research specifically. In fact, few narrative approaches are called narrative theories at all. Some scholars choose to use the term narrative theorizing instead as few narrative approaches have advanced into formal theories tested in particular communication contexts (P. Japp, personal communication, April 27, 2007). Despite this, there are several theoretically rich frameworks, perspectives, and bodies of research on narrative that are advanced in the interdisciplinary body of narrative research. Some communication scholars have begun to advance narrative theories specific to interpersonal contexts (see Langellier & Peterson's [2004] narrative performance theory), and the task of integrating the research on narrative has been approached elsewhere for various purposes (e.g., Bochner, 2002; Koenig Kellas & Trees, 2013; Ochs, 1997). Few attempts, however, have been made to integrate the vast and diverse literature on narrative and storytelling in ways that highlight the applicability of narrative theories to research on interpersonal communication and personal relationships (cf. Bochner, 2002; Langellier, 1989), nor in ways that represent a picture of narrative theories across paradigms (cf. Koenig Kellas, 2013). This chapter, therefore, offers a review of narrative theories, perspectives, and research traditions across paradigms that might enable a focus on communicating narratives and offer some clarity for how students and scholars of interpersonal communication may situate narrative in their research projects, their understanding of personal relationships, and their use and development of narrative theory.

Intellectual Tradition of Narrative Theories

Despite the diversity of narrative scholarship, most, if not all, research that grounds itself in narrative inquiry proposes to highlight the ways in which humans make sense of, construct, and socialize others about their identities, relationships, and lives (see Koenig Kellas & Trees, 2013). First, stories help us *make sense* of our lives. Narrative emplotment helps individuals organize lived events—many of which are messy, multivocal, complicated, or confusing—into more manageable packages that make sense in the context of their lives and relationships. For example, Lucy and Jake might tell and retell the story about the birth of their first child to friends and family. Although they experienced the joy of welcoming a healthy baby boy, Jesse, to the world, the birth itself was wrought with complications. Narrative theorizing would allow scholars to investigate the content of their story, how telling it helps them to make sense of the whirlwind of activities surrounding Jesse's birth, and how they might make sense of it in light of the sociohistorical and cultural context (i.e., master narratives) of childbirth in American society. Narrative sense-making often happens in the midst of difficulty, thus helping people to interpersonally cope with hardship by communicating stories of illness (Wittenberg-Lyles, Goldsmith, Ragan, & Sanchez-Reilly, 2010), stress (Koenig Kellas, Trees, Schrodt, LeClair-Underberg, & Willer, 2010), and other hardships to others.

A second purpose of narrative theories is to interrogate the ways in which stories *construct, confirm, reject, or negotiate individual and relational identities*. For example, Reese (1996) investigated the extent to which the story that a mother tells her child about his or her birth influences her child's self-understanding. When Lucy and Jake tell the story of Jesse's birth, they both narratively frame his identity and his entrance into the family system, and they also construct their own relationships by casting themselves as characters in and tellers of the story in relation to one another.

Narrative theorizing also concerns the process of *socialization* (Koenig Kellas & Trees, 2013). Family stories teach lessons about rules, rituals, and values inside and outside the family (Stone, 2004). For example, as Jesse grows up, Lucy tells stories about the importance of education in the Edwards family. She tells him the story of her great-grandfather at the turn of the century who, despite having 11 children, made sure he saved enough money to send every single one of them—including his daughters—to college.

Paradigmatically, the lion's share of research on narrative in communication grounds itself in interpretive and critical paradigms of research. Many of the scholars who have taken an interpretive or critical "narrative turn" (Bochner, 2002, p. 78) rejected the notion of narrative as a "fixed and stable communication phenomenon," as well as "the possibility of generalizing about the human condition" (Mumby, 1993, pp. 2–3), and thus positioned quantitative social science outside the narrative realm (Bochner, 2002). Over the last decade, more research has emerged from a post-positivist perspective on relational and family narratives. For example, Koenig Kellas and Kranstuber Horstman (in press) recently introduced the communicated narrative sense-making (CNSM) framework to organize research that examines the ways the rich qualitative nature of stories and storytelling can be linked in patterned ways to other interpersonal and relational phenomena, such as health and well-being.

Main Goals and Features of Narrative Theories

The main *features* of communication-based narrative theories are narratives, stories, and storytelling. The overarching *goals* of narrative theorizing are to better understand the content, process, functions, and outcomes of interpersonal narratives, stories, and storytelling. Based on the variety of narrative theories, the terminology used for their core concepts has become somewhat clouded. Often, the terms "narrative" and "story" are used interchangeably. Other scholars, however, provide distinct definitions for each concept (e.g., Ochs, 1997). In general, researchers view narrative more broadly than they view story. For example, scholars might use the term "master narrative" to situate Lucy and Jake's birth story in the larger narrative landscape of what it means to have a baby in American society. Alternatively, the term "narrative" might be used to encapsulate the many stories and chronicles of events surrounding Jesse's complicated birth.

The term "story" is used most generally to describe an individually constructed discourse unit that recounts a noteworthy event and may be seen as a genre of narrative (Ochs, 1997). Stories typically include plotlines with beginnings (e.g., "Lucy was three weeks away from her due date, so we were really surprised when her contractions started in the third inning of the baseball game we were watching!"), middles (e.g., "All of a sudden the whole mood of the room changed. When the doctors stopped smiling, I knew something was wrong."), and ends (e.g., "When I could finally wrap my arms around both of them, I knew everything would be OK."). Whereas stories summarize relational events and may act as representations of relational culture, "storytelling" is a process central to the construction and reflection of that culture. From an interpersonal perspective, researchers might be interested in "jointly told stories," that is, the collaborative constructions through which people recount events by assigning plot, character, and setting in a way that helps them make sense of and give meaning to the event(s) and to the relationship in which they are told. Lucy and Jake might jointly tell this story to family and friends, making the storytelling a collaborative effort that requires them to negotiate their meanings about the event and their relationship through the interactive accomplishment of the telling. Interpersonal researchers are also interested in "conversational storytelling" (Mandelbaum, 1987) or the ways in which stories emerge in interpersonal communication and how they are shaped and reshaped by both tellers and listeners' transactional meaning-making.

The main *goals* of communication-based narrative theories include illuminating the ways in which content and process reveal relationships, practices, meanings, and health as they are constructed interpersonally. The following sections outline the ways in which those goals are manifested across different theoretical and paradigmatic traditions.

How Communication Is Conceptualized in Narrative Theories

In his foundational article, David Maines (1993) positioned narrative, first and foremost, as a communicative phenomenon and one that deserves more attention and expertise from those who ground themselves in the study of symbolic meaning-making. In the highly interdisciplinary landscape of narrative scholarship, communication has much to add. To date, however, much extant research across disciplines focuses on master narratives or individual stories, rather than on the communicative features of storytelling. Communication-based narrative theorizing has and should continue to address this gap. The remainder of this section reviews how research from four different perspectives of narrative inquiry has and might further strengthen an understanding of communication-based theories of narrative.

NARRATIVE AS ONTOLOGY

At the broadest level of abstraction, scholars view narrative ontologically. That is, narrative constitutes our way of being in the world and is conceived as knowledge set against social and historical backgrounds. Fisher's (1989) narrative paradigm, for example, argued for the importance of studying narrative by asserting that people are inherently storytelling beings, or "authors and co-authors who creatively read and evaluate the texts of life and literature" (p. 18). He argued that all human communication and knowledge is interpretable and should be theorized as narrative. Others (e.g., Bruner, 1990) argued further that humans make sense of the things that happen to them in terms of narrative features (i.e., by mapping plot, sequence, agency onto the events in their lives so that they are easier to understand). Viewing narrative from this perspective would mean analyzing all of Jake and Lucy's interactions at the time of the birth as narratives themselves, or arguing that Lucy and Jake understand the disconnected set of complicated events better by assigning narrative properties to them. Importantly, narrative at this level does not focus on the story (e.g., Jesse's birth story), but rather focuses on the narrative nature of human interaction and cognition. By viewing humans as storytellers and human communication as narrative, interpretable, and assessed against a larger historical context, scholars like Fisher and Bruner established narrative as the way that humans exist within, and make sense of, the world.

Some scholars conceive of personal relationships, and the research about them, as narrative in nature. Bochner and his colleagues, for example, interpret research as narrative by introducing the concepts of evocative narrative and the autoethnography perspective. In this approach, researchers use their own personal experience as an interpretive story in which they make themselves and their experiences the subject of research. Combined, ontological approaches to narrative and storytelling provide theoretical backing for understanding narratives as inseparable from the ways in which we exist within, interpret, and understand personal relationships.

NARRATIVE AS EPISTEMOLOGY

Narrative as epistemology refers to theory and research that are concerned with narrative as the form of analysis. Orbuch (1997) distinguished among three types of narrative research in which storied accounts may be conceived: (a) the object of inquiry, (b) the means of inquiry, and (c) the product of inquiry. Approaches that adopt narrative as epistemology parallel in many ways the latter two types. First, some communication researchers invoke the term narrative theory when, in fact, they are using narrative methods to understand some other communication phenomenon; in other words, narrative is the means of collecting data about something beyond the story. For example, researchers might conduct in-depth semi-structured interviews in which many stories, such as Lucy and Jake's, about pregnancy and birth arise. Because of the rich, narrative descriptions that emerge during the interviews, the scholars might situate their research in narrative terms. For these scholars, narrative is the means of inquiry (Orbuch, 1997).

Other researchers reject the notion that narrative as epistemology constitutes narrative theory, arguing that in order to be called narrative inquiry or theorizing, the research must have narratives, stories, or storytelling as its primary focus or foci (see Reissman, 1993). For example, Koenig Kellas and Kranstuber Horstman's (in press) CNSM approach also situate narratives and storytelling as the *object* of inquiry by examining retrospective, interactional, and translational story*telling*. Moreover, narrative performance theory (Langellier & Peterson, 2006) focuses explicitly on the content, process, and identity construction in collaborative interpersonal storytelling performance. Ultimately, as Reissman pointed out, the possibilities for analyzing narrative are vast, and narrative analysis can attend to all three functions of language: (a) the ideational or referential meaning of what is said; (b) the textual, or the structure, syntax, and semantics of stories; or (c) the interpersonal, or the role of the relationship between speakers. Research that adopts these foci, including the content, structure, and interactive features of stories, are reviewed below.

NARRATIVE AS INDIVIDUAL CONSTRUCTION

Researchers who study narrative as individual construction collect and describe stories from individuals about themselves, their families, or their personal relationships. This research tends to examine either the structure or the content of personal relationship stories. Labov and Waletzky (1967), for example, developed a typology for characterizing a fully formed narrative. Such narratives include (a) an abstract that foregrounds the story with an overall summary, (b) an orientation that sets the scene and introduces characters, (c) complicating actions that describe the central events of the story, (d) a resolution that concludes the events, and (e) a coda that wraps the narrative up and often provides a moral to the story. In line with a structural perspective, Koenig Kellas and Manusov (2003) examined break-up stories for narrative completeness. Studies of narrative structure presume that the ability to organize a narrative according to socially acceptable criteria assumes importance. This is evidenced by the focus on "fully" and "complete" narratives and by the assertion that the absence of these narrative qualities may compromise the story coherence and the narrator's status as a storyteller and even as a competent person (Labov & Waletzky, 1967, although see Koenig Kellas, Willer, & Kranstuber, 2010 for a critique). The value-laden nature of story structure highlights the importance of the narrator's audience; however, research that focuses on narrative structure generally does little to analyze the audience's participation in the storytelling process.

Other narrative research focuses on the thematic content of stories in order to understand the ways in which individuals have constructed their individual and relational identities or made sense of relational events. For example, Kranstuber Horstman (2013) examined the themes that emerged in adult children's renditions of their parents' courtship stories in order to better understand the transmission of relational meanings across generations. Based on her findings, when Jesse grows up and recounts the story of his parents' courtship, it might be characterized as factual, romantic, tainted (with negative emotions or interactions), and/or as characterized by overcoming adversity.

Finally, inquiry on narrative as individual construction investigates the links between story structure and content, and the functions stories serve for individuals and relationships, such as individual and relational health. For example, researchers might analyze the themes associated with birth stories (like Lucy's and Jake's), how women communicate an emerging sense of mothering identity in these stories, or how the theme and organization of such stories helps to predict participants' satisfaction with their marriages and families. Individuals' recollection of important family storytelling (also known as retrospective storytelling) has been meaningfully linked to well-being (Koenig Kellas & Kranstuber Horstman, in press).

NARRATIVE AS RELATIONAL PROCESS

Finally, a growing body of narrative inquiry conceives of narrative relationally. The focus on storytelling at this level is on how audience members or relational partners negotiate the story itself or the history and "reality" of their relationship together, illuminating "storytelling," both as an act of performance, or way of "doing" relationships, and/or as a collaborative process of joint storytelling between relational partners. Scholars engaging in narrative theory as *performance* focus on the ways in which people tell stories and thereby "do" relationships. For example, in their narrative performance theory, Langellier and Peterson (2004) focused on collaborative storytelling among family members "as one of the many possible strategies for doing family and reproducing family culture" (p. 34). They concentrate on the dual sense in which storytelling is both performance (i.e., something a family does) and performative (the doing of storytelling that constitutes and forms the family). For example, Langellier and Peterson analyzed the division of narrative labor as three generations of Franco-American women jointly told family stories and found that women differed across generations in the ways that they told the stories, made sense of them, listened to each other, and facilitated the storytelling.

Conversation analysts also focus on the study of narrative and the accomplishments that narrators and audience members achieve when they negotiate the telling of a story. For example, Mandelbaum (1987) examined how "withs" (relationships) are interactively achieved in public through storytelling by examining the ways two potential tellers approach, forward, and ratify each other's versions of a shared story. More recently, Beach (2009) documented 61 recorded phone conversations between family members as they navigated one member's terminal cancer. Among the many discursive processes accomplished during these conversations, telling stories was a primary way of communicatively coping with cancer. As these examples illustrate, conversational storytelling as performance focuses on micro-analytic approaches to assessing narrative labor, how stories emerge naturally in conversation, how "problems" are dealt with in interaction, and how people "do" (accomplish) certain things in storytelling interaction.

Narrative inquiry also focuses on joint storytelling processes across relationships. Because of the focus on the ways in which relational members communicatively construct meaning, jointly told stories in and about relationships are significant processes of interpersonal and relational communication. A CNSM approach refers to this type of narrative research as *interactional storytelling* (Koenig Kellas & Kranstuber Horstman, in press). This line of scholarship examines the process of interactional sense-making (ISM) behaviors communicated during relational storytelling interactions including (a) "engagement" (involvement and warmth), (b) "turn-taking" (dynamism and distribution of turns), (c) "perspective-taking" (acknowledgment and confirmation of others' perspectives), and (d) "coherence" (organization and degree of collaboration or jointness) (Koenig Kellas & Trees, 2006). ISM behaviors have been examined in family triads about stories of difficulty (Trees & Koenig Kellas, 2009) and family identity (Koenig Kellas, 2005), as well as in married couples' stories of marital stress (Koenig Kellas et al., 2010). Overall this research suggests that spouses and families who engage in higher degrees of interactional sense-making, particularly perspective taking and coherence, also report higher levels of individual (e.g., husbands' mental health, Koenig Kellas et al., 2010) and relational (e.g., family cohesion, Trees & Koenig Kellas, 2009) well-being. In short, ISM research and other research about narrative as relational construction highlights the importance of links between storytelling and health for interpersonal communication theorizing.

Research and Practical Applications of Narrative Theories

The organizational typology of narrative literature advanced above acknowledges the potential for theories from different paradigms to inform our understanding of interpersonal communication. Research on the functions of narrative in and about personal relationships contributes to the growing portrait of theorizing relevant to the communication of narratives. Several studies reviewed below focus specifically on how individuals' stories lead to certain outcomes or accomplish general and particular functions such as communicating identity, coping with loss, and predicting psychological health and relational qualities.

(RE)STORYING IDENTITY AND LIVES

Theorizing on life stories and narrative therapy offer examples of how telling the stories of one's life may help to socially construct and revise identity in ways that benefit our psychological and relational well-being. Scholars (e.g., McAdams, 1997) have examined individuals' life stories to understand how people socially negotiate the coherence, or believability, of their identities through the stories they tell. McAdams's personal myth theory suggests that people have the ability to restory their lives when their current stories are unproductive or debilitating. This echoes narrative therapists' focus on "restorying," which is the belief that multiple interpretations exist for lived events, and that stories provide people with a means for creating new interpretations and for improving their understanding of their experiences. Although those who examine life stories and narrative therapy claim that story coherence must be socially negotiated, this body of research does little to examine the communicative processes associated with telling them. To address this, communication researchers have extended these theories by examining the significance of communicating one's myth. For example, Kranstuber Horstman (2012) examined experimentally the ways in which daughters' perceptions of their mothers' socially supportive behaviors predicted change in the framing and coherence of a story of difficulty they told over the course of three weeks. She found that daughters' narrative coherence decreased when mothers threatened their negative face, and narrative tone became more positive when mothers displayed empathy, social support, and positive facework. Thus, communication researchers are beginning to build on existing narrative theories to guide interpersonal research on the processes and outcomes of relational storytelling.

COPING WITH LOSS AND TRAUMA

The literature on the outcomes of accounts (stories) for failed relationships, loss, and trauma also attests to the potentially positive functions of stories. For example, Harvey, Orbuch, and Weber (1992) proposed a stress response model for account making and theorized that storytelling about relational loss allows account makers to achieve a better self-esteem, engage in emotional purging, establish a sense of control, and search for closure and understanding. Pennebaker's (1997) inhibition/confrontation framework and years of empirical research in the expressive writing paradigm suggested that ruminating about traumatic experiences is far less healthy than writing or telling stories about them. Koenig Kellas, Kranstuber Horstman, Willer, and Carr (in press) extended the expressive writing paradigm to interpersonal storytelling and found that when people told a friend a stressful story, their negative affect decreased over time. These studies indicate that stories can serve a healing function. In fact, Sedney, Baker, and Gross (1994) warned that the absence of stories may limit family communication and emotional relief from difficult events. At the same time, Koenig Kellas et al. (2014) found that tellers' perceptions of friends' communication effectiveness decreased over time, suggesting that communication may complicate the benefits of storytelling experienced at the individual level.

PREDICTING RELATIONAL QUALITIES
AND PSYCHOLOGICAL HEALTH

A growing line of communication research examines the relationships between narrative content, process, and individual and relational outcome variables. Because of the sense-making, identity construction, and socializing functions of storytelling, these processes often predict health and well-being. For example, Willer (2009) found that adolescent girls who had been victims of aggression from other girls and who engaged in a storytelling metaphor intervention about social aggression experienced decreases in negative affect and increases in forgiveness toward their aggressor over time.

Moreover, researchers have examined the ways in which couples' and families' joint storytelling helps to predict important relationship outcomes, such as satisfaction, functioning, and divorce. For example, Holmberg, Orbuch, and Veroff (2004) focused on newlyweds' storytelling processes and found that couples who differed in their joint storytelling style were less satisfied than couples who told the story in a similar style. CNSM research examines the implications of retrospective, interactional, and translational storytelling for individual and relational health. In this research, for example, the ISM behavior of perspective-taking significantly predicted higher levels of family satisfaction, cohesion, adaptability, and overall functioning in family triads telling a family identity story (Koenig Kellas, 2005) as well as lower levels of husbands' perceived stress (Koenig Kellas et al., 2010) and higher levels of wives' marital satisfaction (Koenig Kellas, Carr, Kranstuber Horstman, & DiLillo, 2013). These findings highlight the positive functions of narratives and storytelling in interpersonal interactions, further position narrative inquiry as consequential to our understanding of interpersonal communication, and have implications for theory building about narratives in interpersonal communication as discussed below.

Evaluation of Narrative Theories

Narrative theorizing has the potential to help us understand how people communicatively construct their individual and relational identities, make sense of the world and their interpersonal interactions, cope with loss, restore unproductive concepts of self and others, and explain relational qualities and outcomes such as satisfaction, well-being, and divorce. The breadth and diversity, however, function as both strengths and limitations of narrative theories. There is no one narrative theory to understand interpersonal communication, but most narrative research is based in theoretical traditions or developments. Further theory development, including theoretical conclusions which help explain, predict, and control communication behavior in post-positivist research, guide rich interpretations of individual or relational meaning-making in interpretive research, and reveal and evaluate injustice in critical research, will further strengthen communication-based approaches to narrative theory. Moreover, narrative theorizing and research operates under a positivity bias (Koenig Kellas et al., 2010). However, it is important to stress that stories have the potential to isolate individuals (e.g., Langellier & Peterson, 2004) as well as to reify traditional master narratives, making research on the dark side of storytelling a priority (see Koenig Kellas et al., 2010).

Continuing the Conversation

Narrative inquiry and theory building need to interrogate not only the positive functions of narrative and storytelling, but also examine the ways stories disconfirm, belittle, reject, reify stereotypes, or hurt individual and relational members. For example, we might investigate how master narratives for personal relationships, such as marriage, child-bearing, or family development, impact the interpersonal communication of individuals in marginalized relationships, such as homosexual couples, child-free couples, or stepfamilies. Additional research should focus on the potentially negative processes and functions of interpersonal storytelling, such as how partners manage the difficulties of narrative discrepancy or conflicting versions of a story.

Moreover, theories on narratives and storytelling need to be further developed and empirically confirmed. Within a CNSM framework (Koenig Kellas & Kranstuber Horstman, in press), for example, a theory of interactional narrative sense-making is developing based on empirical research that suggests that ISM behaviors predict individual and relational health. The pathways through which these relationships travel, however, deserve more empirical attention to further establish ISM as a theory. For example, ISM likely predicts health by helping to facilitate joint meaning making. In other words, the more relational partners can make meaning about narrative difficulty together, the more likely they are to feel satisfied and experience the health benefits of coherent, cathartic narrative meaning-making (see Figure 19.1).

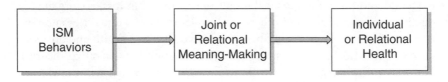

Figure 19.1   ISM Behaviors

These pathways may differ according to relationship type or topic, thus, ISM should be tested across contexts to confirm its theoretical features, axioms, and conclusions.

Building narrative theory in interpersonal communication research has implications in several applied settings, such as family therapy, couples counseling, doctor-patient communication, corporate training programs, textbooks on personal relationships, and other instructional approaches to understanding and improving interpersonal communication. The most exciting potential for building and testing narrative theories lies in the translational possibilities of research. For example, Wittenberg-Lyles and colleagues (2010) applied narrative theories to family stories in palliative care and translated their findings into communication curriculum for medical students receiving palliative care training. By building communication-based narrative theories, we may better understand the communicative processes by which we symbolically constitute our lives.

References

Beach, W. A. (2009). *A natural history of family cancer: Interactional resources for managing illness.* New York, NY: Hampton Press.

Bochner, A. P. (2002). Perspectives on inquiry III: The moral of stories. In M. L. Knapp & J. A. Daly (Eds.), *Handbook of interpersonal communication* (3rd ed., pp. 73–101). Thousand Oaks, CA: Sage.

Bruner, J. (1990). *Acts of meaning.* Cambridge, MA: Harvard University Press.

Fisher, W. R. (1989). *Human communication as narration: Toward a philosophy of reason, value, and action.* Columbia: University of South Carolina Press.

Harvey, J. H., Orbuch, T. L., & Weber, A. L. (1992). Introduction: Convergence of the attribution and accounts concepts in the study of close relationships. In J. H. Harvey, T. L. Orbuch, & A. L. Weber (Eds.), *Attributions, accounts, and close relationships* (pp. 1–18). New York, NY: Springer-Verlag.

Holmberg, D., Orbuch, T. L., & Veroff, J. (2004). *Thrice-told tales: Married couples tell their stories.* Mahwah, NJ: Lawrence Erlbaum.

Koenig Kellas, J. (2005). Family ties: Communicating identity through jointly told stories. *Communication Monographs, 72,* 365–389.

Koenig Kellas, J. (2013). Framing family: An introduction to narratives and storytelling in the family. In J. Koenig Kellas (Ed.), *Family storytelling: Negotiating identity, teaching lessons, and making meaning* (pp. 1–13). London: Routledge.

Koenig Kellas, J., Carr, K., Kranstuber, H., & DiLillo, D. (2013, November). *Communicated perspective-taking across contexts: Observational and other-report measures and their individual and relational correlates.* Paper presented to the Family Communication Division of the National Communication Association.

Koenig Kellas, J., & Kranstuber Horstman, H. (in press). Communicated narrative sense-making: Understanding family narratives, storytelling, and the construction of meaning through a communicative lens. In L. Turner & R. West (Eds.), *SAGE handbook of family communication.* Los Angeles, CA: Sage.

Koenig Kellas, J., Kranstuber, H., Willer, E. K., & Carr, K. (2014). The benefits and risks of storytelling and storylistening over time: Experimentally testing the expressive writing paradigm in the context of interpersonal communication. *Health Communication, 29,* 1–16.

Koenig Kellas, J., & Manusov, V. (2003). What's in a story? The relationship between narrative completeness and tellers' adjustment to relationship dissolution. *Journal of Social and Personal Relationships, 20,* 285–307.

Koenig Kellas, J., & Trees, A. R. (2006). Finding meaning in difficult family experiences: Sense-making and interaction processes during joint family storytelling. *Journal of Family Communication, 6,* 49–76.

Koenig Kellas, J., & Trees, A. (2013). Family stories and storytelling: Windows into the family soul. In A. L. Vangelisti (Ed.), *Handbook of family communication* (2nd ed., pp. 391–406). Mahwah, NJ: Lawrence Erlbaum.

Koenig Kellas, J., Trees, A. R., Schrodt, P., LeClair-Underberg, C., & Willer, E. K. (2010). Exploring links between well-being and interactional sense-making in married couples' jointly told stories of stress. *Journal of Family Communication, 10,* 174–193.

Koenig Kellas, J., Willer, E., & Kranstuber, H. (2010). Fairytales and tragedies: Narratively making sense of the dark side (and the dark side of making sense) of personal relationships. In W. Cupach & B. Spitzberg (Eds.), *The dark side of close relationships II* (pp. 63–93). New York, NY: Routledge.

Kranstuber Horstman, H. (2012). *How narrative sense-making changes over time: The role of mother-daughter communication during conversations about difficulty.* (Unpublished doctoral dissertation) University of Nebraska-Lincoln.

Kranstuber Horstman, H. (2013). "Love stories aren't always like the movies": The positive and negative relational implications of inherited parental courtship stories. In J. Koenig Kellas (Ed.), *Family storytelling: Negotiating identity, teaching lessons and making meaning.* New York, NY: Routledge.

Labov, W., & Waletzky, J. (1967). Narrative analysis: Oral versions of personal experience. In J. Helm (Ed.), *Essays on the verbal and visual arts: Proceedings of the 1966 annual spring meeting of the American Ethnological Society* (pp. 12–44). Seattle: University of Washington Press.

Langellier, K. M. (1989). Personal narratives: Perspectives on theory and research. *Text and Performance Quarterly, 9,* 243–276.

Langellier, K. M., & Peterson, E. E. (2004). *Storytelling in daily life: Performing narrative.* Philadelphia, PA: Temple University Press.

Langellier, K. M., & Peterson, E. E. (2006). Narrative performance theory: Telling stories, doing family. In D. O. Braithwaite, & L. A. Baxter (Eds.), *Engaging theories in family communication: Multiple perspectives* (pp. 99–114). Thousand Oaks, CA: Sage.

Maines, D. R. (1993). Narrative's moment and sociology's phenomena: Toward a narrative sociology. *Sociological Quarterly, 34,* 17–37.

Mandelbaum, J. (1987). Couples sharing stories. *Communication Quarterly, 35*(2), 144–170.

McAdams, D. P. (1997). *The stories we live by.* New York, NY: Guilford.

Mumby, D. K. (1993). Narrative and social control: Critical perspectives. Thousand Oaks, CA: Sage.

Ochs, E. (1997). Narrative. In T. van Dijk (Ed.), *Discourse as structure and process* (pp. 185–207). London, UK: Sage.

Orbuch, T. L. (1997). People's accounts count: The sociology of accounts. *Annual Review of Sociology, 23,* 455–478.

Pennebaker, J. W. (1997). *Opening up: The healing power of expressing emotions.* New York, NY: Guilford.

Reese, E. (1996). Conceptions of self in mother-child birth stories. *Journal of Narrative and Life History, 6,* 23–38.

Reissman, C. K. (1993). *Narrative analysis.* London, UK: Sage.

Sedney, M. A., Baker, J. E., & Gross, E. (1994). "The story" of a death: Therapeutic considerations with bereaved families. *Journal of Marriage and Family Therapy, 20,* 287–296.

Stone, E. (2004). *Black sheep and kissing cousins: How our family stories shape us.* New Brunswick, NJ: Transaction Publishers.

Trees, A. R., & Koenig Kellas, J. (2009). Telling tales: Enacting family relationships in joint storytelling about difficult family experiences. *Western Journal of Communication. 73,* 91–111.

Willer, E. K. (2009). *Experimentally testing a narrative sense-making metaphor intervention: Facilitating communicative coping about social aggression with adolescent girls.* (Unpublished doctoral dissertation) University of Nebraska-Lincoln.

Wittenberg-Lyles, E., Goldsmith, J., Ragan, S. L., & Sanchez-Reilly, S. (2010). *Dying with comfort: Family illness narratives and early palliative care.* Cresskill, NJ: Hampton Press.

20

Politeness Theory

How We Use Language to Save Face

Daena J. Goldsmith and Emily Lamb Normand

I n the 10 years they have been friends, Jean cannot recall a time when it was so difficult to know what to say to Pat. Six months ago, Pat's doctor told him to lose 20 pounds. Nothing has worked so far—crazy diets, contraptions purchased online, even hypnosis—and Pat is really frustrated. Pat's doctor said flat out, "Pat, get off the couch and into the gym!" Jean agrees and thinks Pat should join a nearby exercise club, but Jean knows weight is a sensitive topic, especially for Pat, and especially now. Giving advice could sound pushy, and Jean is not in much of a position to talk, not having set foot in a gym since high school.

Brown and Levinson's (1987) politeness theory helps answer several questions connected to this example. Why is it challenging for Jean to give advice to Pat in this situation? What features of Pat and Jean's relationship and of the particular situation might make it more or less difficult to give advice? Is there a way for Jean to advise Pat that will minimize some of the risks?

Intellectual Tradition of Politeness Theory

Brown and Levinson (1987) are sociolinguists who observed that we sometimes say what we mean directly, but frequently, we beat around the bush instead. For example, we could say, "Get me a drink" but often we make our request less bluntly (e.g., "Hey bud, could ya get me a cold one while you're up?") or we hint (e.g., "I'm parched!"). Brown and Levinson saw these patterns in three quite different languages (English, Tzeltal, and Tamil), and they proposed some basic principles to explain why people around the globe shared these linguistic features. Why don't we always just say what we mean, in the most direct, efficient way? How do you explain when and how we depart from directness and how those departures are interpreted? Politeness theory describes the various language forms we use and the social conditions related to their use and interpretation.

Politeness theory is a rational model (O'Keefe, 1992). It explains how features of language are interpreted in social contexts and why we see recurring patterns of language structure, use, and inference. The theory predicts how we use and interpret language (resembling a post-positivistic approach), but instead of explaining message production, it focuses on message design and interpretation in relation to social structure (resembling interpretive approaches).

Main Goals and Features of Politeness Theory

FACE AND FACE-THREATENING ACTIONS

Politeness theory begins with Goffman's (1967) concept of "face" (see Metts & Cupach, Chapter 17, in this volume). Brown and Levinson (1987, p. 61) defined "face" as "the public self-image that every member wants to claim for himself [or herself]." Several features of this concept are noteworthy. First, face is public. It is the identity we observe in your actions rather than your own mental self-concept. Second, face is social. Your success in performing an identity depends on others picking up on what you are doing and acting in ways that are more or less compatible. Third, face is claimed. It can be lost, saved, or sustained by how people act in an interaction. Finally, face is something we want. Brown and Levinson discuss positive and negative face wants. Positive face wants involve having our identity performance accepted by the others in the interaction. Negative face wants are the rights and respect that are due our image. We resent when people impose on us inappropriately or fail to show the proper deference.

Our face is on the line every time we interact—we are always enacting some public self-image. Many ordinary actions can threaten our own or another person's face. For example, questioning someone's actions, disagreeing, or interrupting can threaten positive face wants for approval, whereas making requests, asking favors, or reminding someone of an obligation can threaten negative face wants for respect and freedom of action.

In our earlier example, face wants may explain Jean's concerns about talking to Pat. Discussing weight is a reminder that Pat has a health problem. It threatens Pat's image as someone who can set a goal and meet it, and it may stir up insecurities about physical attractiveness. These are examples of positive face threats. Pat likely sees "healthy," "effective," and "attractive" as desirable social attributes and wants conversation with Jean to support that image. Pat is 20 pounds overweight whether they talk about it or not; the face threat comes from discussing it.

Advising Pat to join a health club illustrates negative face threats. The advice would recommend doing something effortful. In addition to the practical imposition on Pat's time and resources, the advice also threatens Pat's freedom to make up his own mind without others telling him what to do. Advice could also threaten positive face if Pat infers criticism of previous actions (diet, weight loss devices, hypnosis) or believes it implies that he had not already thought of this obvious solution.

If they end up talking about Pat's weight, each person's actions will be claiming face, threatening face, and/or saving face. What Jean says and how, and Pat's response and self-presentation, will shape the image each person performs. Will Jean come across as a concerned and caring friend, or as a bossy, hypocritical busybody? Will Pat seem like a pathetic couch potato or a confident, determined fighter in a battle shared by many other people?

POLITENESS STRATEGIES

Here are some ways Jean might advise Pat to join a gym:

1. "Pat, join Gym Sport."

2. "Hey, Pat, I know how hard you've been working at this weight loss thing and you got me thinkin' I should be doin' somethin' too. Let's join that gym that's on the way home from work. I'll pay for a trial pass if you'll go with me."

3. "Look, I know I'm about the last person to give health advice, but I wondered if maybe you'd considered possibly, you know, joining a gym? There's that one at 42nd and Taylor that's close and cheap. Up to you, of course, whatever you think."

4. "You won't believe who I saw coming out of Gym Sport—Chris Beason! Chris has lost so much weight that I almost didn't know who it was."

5. Jean could say nothing, and keep her advice to herself.

How do these options differ? As you read them, do you imagine different relationships between Jean and Pat? Are they close friends or not so close? Does one of them usually take the lead? Do some of these options sound more appropriate between women friends or between men? How does Jean seem— Confident? Careful? Concerned? How does Pat come off—Easy-going? Easily angered? Competent?

As Option 5 makes clear, we sometimes decide it is too risky to threaten another's face. However, when we need to commit a *face-threatening act* (FTA), politeness theory describes several ways our language can save the other person's face. Option 1 above illustrates the *bald on record* strategy. It states the FTA—in this case, advice to join the gym—explicitly or "on the record." Nothing else is said, which makes it "bald."

Options 2 and 3 are also on record because they explicitly state that Pat should join the gym. However, the way Jean words the advice and other things she says tone down the face threat. Option 2 uses *positive face redress,* compensating for face threat by playing up the solidarity between Jean and Pat. Jean claims common ground by using informal language, pointing out things they have in common, recognizing Pat's efforts, and assuming that Pat knows which gym it is. Jean is cooperative, offering to join the gym together, giving reasons to persuade Pat, and offering to pay for the trial offer. These strategies give approval and imply that the closeness and similarity between Jean and Pat makes it all right to give advice. Option 3 uses *negative face redress* to mitigate threat by being respectful. Jean apologizes, uses questions and hedges, gives Pat the option not to act, and minimizes how effortful it would be to join the gym. Jean explicitly says Pat does not have to do it and that it is Pat's decision. In contrast to positive face redress, these strategies are deferential, toning down forcefulness and keeping a careful distance.

Option 4 does not actually give advice. On record, Jean tells a story about Chris; if advising occurs, it is between the lines or "off record." Pat may nonetheless infer the advice—why else is Jean mentioning it—particularly if Jean has previously mentioned joining a gym, or if Chris has the same health condition as Pat, or if the statement comes up in a discussion of Pat's weight loss attempts. Going off record makes it possible for this to look like Pat's idea and not a directive from Jean (e.g., imagine Pat responding by saying, "You know, I've been thinking about joining that gym myself."). Alternatively, if Pat complains about being advised, Jean could always say, "I wasn't giving you advice. I was just talking about Chris." Off record strategies protect face by leaving room to maneuver. Face is public, so it matters whether or not the FTA is on the public record. However, there is a risk Pat will not take the hint. He might respond as if this is just a story about Chris and not consider joining the gym.

Politeness theory helps us hear how nuances of language create an overall impression—of the speaker, the hearer, the action, and the relationship. This shows how we reach interpretations, and it can help us identify our options in challenging situations.

SOCIAL CONDITIONS THAT SHAPE POLITENESS

Brown and Levinson (1987) claimed the five options range from least polite (bald on record) to most polite (do not do the FTA). Three features of social situations shape what strategy is the most appropriate. *Power (P)* refers to the degree to which one person can impose plans and self-evaluation on another (e.g., are you peers or does one person have more control or status than the other?). *Distance (D)* includes both closeness and social similarity (e.g., are you strangers from different walks of life or close friends of the same age, race, and sex?). *Rank (R)* refers to culturally defined understandings of how threatening different FTAs are (e.g., for many Americans, advice about weight loss is more sensitive than advice about good restaurants).

The combination of P, D, and R affects the *weight* (*W*, degree of face threat) in a situation. If W is large, choose a more polite strategy (Option 4 or 5); for small W, choose a less polite strategy (Option 1 or 2). You can seem rude and insensitive if you are not polite enough, but being too polite might not get your point across or might make your action seem more face threatening than it is. Imagine your best friend (equal P, low D) said to you, "Excuse me, I would never ask except that I'm in a horrible bind and I'll be grateful for life. Could I use your pen for a minute?" (low R). Using so much politeness when W is so small probably seems odd. You might wish your friend would just get to the point. You might think your friend is being sarcastic. You might wonder if your friend thinks you are unlikely to comply or thinks your relationship is fragile. Maybe your friend is just weird. Effective communication entails choosing the right amount of politeness for the situation. We use P, D, and R to *select face strategies and to figure out what others are trying to do and why.*

How can P, D, and R help us guess what Jean is likely to do or which option Pat would find most appropriate? Jean and Pat are friends, so D is probably low, and we could probe further how close and similar they are. American friends are often equal in power, but we could ask whether one person usually calls the shots, if one is more dependent on the other, or if they have different areas of expertise. Thinking about R means comparing advice to join a gym with other actions (e.g., ordering or requesting) as well as advice on different topics. P and D predict a friend would use a less polite strategy (e.g., Option 1 or 2) but because R is high, Jean might decide to handle this particular advice more carefully (e.g., Option 3 or 4). There is no precise calculus for determining which specific option Jean will choose, but P, D, and R are the social considerations she will use to choose and Pat will use to evaluate her choice. P, D, and R also help us to think comparatively. For example, how is Jean's choice likely to be different from what Pat's doctor said?

How Communication Is Conceptualized in Politeness Theory

Brown and Levinson (1987) view communication as a rational, social, cooperative activity. Although you might assume "rational" has to do with mental activities, we agree with O'Keefe (1992) that politeness theory tells us about linguistic and social structures rather than cognitive structures. By "rational" we mean it describes principles for reasoned judgment about communication.

These principles are socially shared. The theory explains why languages have these features and how people can arrive at shared understandings of the features. For example, Jean could have many motives for giving advice with positive redress: She may intend to help Pat, or promote the cause of physical fitness, or sound smart, or get Pat out of the house so she can have time alone, and so on. Positive redress could reflect sincere fellow feeling, but it could just be a manipulative way to persuade. Politeness theory is not useful for probing these personal, internal motivations. Instead, it helps us see how we recognize that advice has been given (i.e., that Jean intended to tell Pat to do something that he would not otherwise do) and why advice with positive redress presents different self-images and relationships than alternative ways of advising.

Brown and Levinson (1987) also presume we are motivated to cooperatively honor face in most of our mundane interactions. The kind of cooperation they assume involves co-participating in interaction (i.e., we assume that others desire to communicate information, that they are attempting to be relevant and not deceptive, and so on). As in a game of soccer or a court of law, there is agreement on the fundamental rules of the game, even though players may compete or oppose one another.

Research and Practical Applications of Politeness Theory

Politeness theory illuminates diverse issues of interest to scholars and laypeople alike, such as how crew politeness to a captain contributes to aviation accidents (Linde, 1988), how students talk with their instructors about a disappointing grade (Sabee & Wilson, 2005), how young people resist an undesired request for sex (Afifi & Lee, 2000), how elderly people respond to patronizing advice from younger people (Hummert & Mazloff, 2001), and how anesthesiologists handle workplace conflict (Jameson, 2004).

In communication and related disciplines, politeness theory has been interpreted in three distinct ways. Most communication scholars have used the theory to predict behavior. For example, Baxter (1984) asked students to imagine they were working on a group project and had to ask a group member to redo part of the project. Different versions of the scenario varied how well the students knew one another (D), whether the speaker was a group leader or just a member (P), and whether the rewrite involved much or little effort (R). Studies in this tradition have found partial support for the effects of P, D, and R on strategy choice. Most studies have examined requests and have found more polite requests from those with less power. The effects of distance are less consistent: In some studies, respondents are most polite with those they know least well, whereas in other studies, respondents are more polite to those they know best.

Other scholars have used politeness theory to predict how behavior will be evaluated. For example, Carson and Cupach (2000) found that managers who used redress to reprimand an employee were perceived as fairer and more competent than those who were bald on record. Studies of strategy interpretation have found partial support for the theory. The predicted order of politeness strategies (i.e., bald on record will be seen as less polite than redress, which will be less polite than off record) does not always hold. Under some circumstances, more direct strategies are seen as more polite, for example.

Some scholars find prediction problematic because our actions and evaluations are so dependent on who is interacting, their relationship, and the situation. These scholars use the theory heuristically to identify politeness phenomena and understand the processes that lead to our diverse, creative, situated, and often unpredictable use of politeness in specific situations. For example, Aronsson and Rundstrom (1989) showed how pediatricians were bald on record with children (e.g., "WHAT?! You SHOULD NOT do that") but polite to parents (e.g., "But then it's best to avoid cats, or what would you say?"). The doctor was appropriately polite to this mother of an allergic child, yet directing a bald on record statement *to the child with the mother present* ensured that neither missed the point.

Evaluation of Politeness Theory

One ongoing controversy concerns the cross-cultural relevance of the theory. Brown and Levinson (1987) proposed universal principles that underlie communication in particular cultures. They said that all humans have face wants and the capacity for rational choice to protect face. Cultural differences arise from differences in how P and D are distributed across social relationships and how R is distributed across social actions. If members of one culture seem to be "warm, easy-going, and friendly" (p. 243) compared to other cultures, it may be because they often use positive redress and that, in turn, may be because they do not recognize many power differences, or they value closeness and similarity, or they do not define very many actions as face threatening. Some say this explanation does not adequately represent diverse cultural beliefs and practices (e.g., Ting-Toomey, 1994; Watts, Ide, & Ehlich, 1992). For example, some cultures might understand politeness as normative behavior to fit into a social group instead of individual strategic choice. The negative face want for individual freedom and privacy might also be less valued in some cultures (Bargiela-Chiappini, 2003).

Another point of contention is how politeness strategies are conceptualized. Brown and Levinson (1987) said any of the politeness strategies can address either or both types of face threat. In contrast, Lim and Bowers (1991) distinguished between positive face wants for fellowship versus competence. They proposed that negative face concerns autonomy. Lim and Bowers believed different types of face work were needed to address each different type of face threat. Several scholars have taken issue with Brown and Levinson's emphasis on single speech acts done verbally. Goldsmith (2000) found the sequence of acts matters, so that when a friend asked for advice first, giving it bald-on-record was less face-threatening. If, in our example, Pat said, "Do you think I should join a gym?" then Option 1 ("Pat, join Gym Sport") becomes much more appropriate. Likewise, different nonverbal delivery can shape the potential for face-threat. Lamb Normand (2010) studied the face-threatening potential of emotional expressions between stepsiblings. She found that stepsiblings sometimes expressed emotions both verbally *and* nonverbally, and often they derived more relational meaning from the nonverbal message.

One of the theory's greatest strengths is its bold, ambitious scope. The theory draws together an incredibly wide range of language features into one comprehensive lens and also focuses our attention on these subtle features of talk. Brown and Levinson (1987) explained how these are responsible for fundamental concerns such as how we perceive others' images, how power and intimacy are negotiated in relationships, and how there come to be communication differences between genders, cultures, and other social groups. By proposing a parsimonious set of concepts, taking a strong stand on their interrelationships, and making explicit statements about what is and is not universal, the theory has prompted many tests and refinements. It has directed scholarly attention to studying how language forms build social life.

The theory is especially useful as a normative model of strategic communication (Goldsmith, 2007; O'Keefe, 1992; Wilson, Aleman, & Leatham, 1998). Rather than focusing on the frequency or likelihood of behaviors, the theory helps us understand how behaviors are interpreted and evaluated when they do occur. Many communication theories are variable analytic attempts to find the determinants of what people will say or do (and this has been a prominent interpretation of politeness theory, too). In contrast, politeness theory directs our attention to judgments of what people *should* say and do, *if* they wish to be seen as appropriate and effective. It focuses on dilemmas of interaction and on the creative and constructive ways people use language to enact identities and relationships as they pursue tasks such as requesting, advising, criticizing, or expressing emotion.

Continuing the Conversation

Scholars continue to extend and refine politeness theory, including new ways of thinking about face threat. For example, Tracy and Baratz (1994) suggested we focus on case studies that examine the relevance and form of face concerns in particular contexts and Wilson et al. (1998) modeled how we use contextual information to infer one another's goals and determine face threats. Johnson (2007) emphasized a more complex conceptualization of FTAs. She proposed expanding research to examine speech acts other than requests (in her study, refusals) and recognizing how one message can have multiple face threats for both the speaker and hearer. Knobloch, Satterlee, and DiDomenico (2010) demonstrated how integrating politeness theory with other communication theories (e.g., uncertainty reduction theory) can deepen our understanding of how we appraise face threats.

Given the controversy about the cross-cultural generalizability of the theory, we expect to see ongoing research comparing face concerns and face-work resources across cultures. For example, in their study of Chinese gift-giving exchanges, Feng, Chang, and Holt (2011) supported the theory's applicability in a non-Western culture. Attention to method will be especially important in continued study of cross-cultural politeness. In a study comparing face-work strategies used during requests among native-Japanese and native-English speakers, Gangé (2010) argued that linguistic politeness should be analyzed within context through both questionnaire *and* conversation. Gangé's participant interviews uncovered an important difference in how Japanese speakers understood negative face. Such methodological triangulation may allow researchers to better understand the intentions that motivate a speaker's polite and impolite behavior.

A final direction for future research concerns understanding the relationship between politeness and impoliteness and between researchers' concepts and judgments by laypeople. Bald on record strategies are still attempts to be polite, used when urgency or low W justifies a lack of politeness. In contrast, intentional efforts to be disagreeable, rude, and insulting entail a different, though perhaps parallel, set of strategies (e.g., Culpepper, Bousfield, & Wichmann, 2003). Furthermore, what we mean by politeness in everyday conversation does not correspond neatly to the definition of politeness in the theory. Watts (2003) developed an alternative framework for capturing these evaluations.

Let's return to Jean and Pat one last time. Does politeness theory offer them any help? It helps explain why the situation is challenging. We sometimes assume that if we are close to someone, we ought to be able to speak our minds. When we have difficulty being direct, we may doubt our own skill and psychological health or the strength of our relationship. Several theories and much research suggest this assumption is flawed, but nonetheless we sometimes feel bad when it is hard to say something to someone we care about. Politeness theory reminds us that directness is not always desirable and helps us pinpoint what is difficult about a situation: Pat's image as a socially desirable person capable of making changes and taking care of her own health, as well as Jean's image as someone who understands their relationship and does not overstep boundaries, who is sensitive to others, and who has certain rights and responsibilities in a relationship.

Politeness theory can also help us think of multiple ways to say something, and the relative advantages and disadvantages of each. If Jean is too direct, Pat may feel criticized and bossed around, but if Jean is too indirect, Pat may not grasp the suggestion. Using positive redress—the language of solidarity—could build on the closeness of their relationship to mute any possible criticism and to justify why Jean has an interest in directing Pat's behavior. Using negative redress—the language of deference—would acknowledge the sensitive nature of the topic and avoid sounding harsh or pushy. Hints and ambiguity could leave both friends with the option of ignoring the advice or of taking it without having to acknowledge that Jean told Pat what to do.

We conclude by encouraging you to observe how politeness theory may apply in your own life. First, it might explain recurring difficulties in some relationships. For example, it might help you figure out what it is about a rude coworker that you find so off-putting or how interactions with your instructor from a different culture create frustration for you both. Second, politeness theory might suggest alternative ways of pursuing your goals. Are you bald on record when it would be more effective to be more polite? Do you too often rely on off record strategies that do not get your point across? Does overreliance on negative redress strategies make you sound less powerful, or do positive redress strategies come across as too familiar? Politeness theory may also give you a way to explain communication differences and clarify your intentions if you decide to have a problem-solving conversation with someone you care about. Finally, even in the absence of communication problems, politeness theory can help you appreciate the finely tuned variations in our language that convey our images of self and other, construct our relationships, and conduct our interpersonal business.

References

Afifi, W. A., & Lee, J. W. (2000). Balancing instrumental and identity goals in relationships: The role of request directness and request persistence in the selection of sexual resistance strategies. *Communication Monographs, 67,* 284–305.

Aronsson, K., & Rundstrom, B. (1989). Cats, dogs, and sweets in the clinical negotiation of reality: On politeness and coherence in pediatric discourse. *Language and Society, 18,* 483–504.

Bargiela-Chiappini, F. (2003). Face and politeness: New (insights) for old (concepts). *Journal of Pragmatics, 35,* 1453–1469.

Baxter, L. A. (1984). An investigation of compliance-gaining as politeness. *Human Communication Research, 10,* 427–456.

Brown, P., & Levinson, S. C. (1987). *Politeness: Some universals in language usage.* New York, NY: Cambridge University Press.

Carson, C. L., & Cupach, W. R. (2000). Facing corrections in the workplace: The influence of perceived face threat on the consequences of managerial episodes. *Journal of Applied Communication Research, 28,* 215–234.

Culpepper, J., Bousfield, D., & Wichmann, A. (2003). Impoliteness revisited: With special reference to dynamic and prosodic aspects. *Journal of Pragmatics, 35,* 1545–1579.

Feng, H., Chang, H.-C., & Holt, R. (2011). Examining Chinese gift-giving behavior from the politeness theory perspective. *Asian Journal of Communication, 21,* 301–317.

Gangé, N. O. (2010). Reexamining the notion of negative face in the Japanese *Socio* linguistic politeness of request. *Language & Communication, 30,* 123–138.

Goffman, E. (1967). *Interaction ritual.* Garden City, NY: Anchor Books.

Goldsmith, D. J. (2000). Soliciting advice: The role of sequential placement in mitigating face threat. *Communication Monographs, 67,* 1–19.

Goldsmith, D. J. (2007). Brown and Levinson's politeness theory. In B. Whaley & W. Samter (Eds.), *Explaining communication: Contemporary theories and exemplars* (pp. 219–236). Mahwah, NJ: Erlbaum.

Hummert, M. L., & Mazloff, D. C. (2001). Older adults' responses to patronizing advice: Balancing politeness and identity in context. *Journal of Language and Social Psychology, 20,* 167–195.

Jameson, J. K. (2004). Negotiating autonomy and connection through politeness: A dialectical approach to organizational conflict management. *Western Journal of Communication, 68,* 257–277.

Johnson, D. I. (2007). Politeness theory and conversational refusals: Associations between various types of face threat and perceived competence. *Western Journal of Communication, 71,* 196–215.

Knobloch, L. K., Satterlee, K. L., & DiDomenico, S. M. (2010). Relational uncertainty predicting appraisals of face threat in courtship: Integrating uncertainty reduction theory and politeness theory. *Communication Research, 37,* 303–334.

Lamb Normand, E. (2010). *The experience and expression of emotion within stepsibling relationships: Politeness of expression and stepfamily functioning* (Doctoral dissertation). Retrieved from http://digitalcommons.unl.edu/commstuddiss/2/.

Lim, T., & Bowers, J. W. (1991). Facework: Solidarity, approbation, and tact. *Human Communication Research, 17,* 415–450.

Linde, C. (1988). The quantitative study of communicative success: Politeness and accidents in aviation discourse. *Language in Society, 17,* 375–399.

O'Keefe, B. J. (1992). Developing and testing rational models of message design. *Human Communication Research, 18,* 637–649.

Sabee, C. M., & Wilson, S. R. (2005). Students' primary goals, attributions, and facework during conversations about disappointing grades. *Communication Education, 54,* 185–204.

Ting-Toomey, S. (1994). *The challenge of facework: Cross-cultural and interpersonal issues.* Albany, NY: SUNY Press.

Tracy, K., & Baratz, S. (1994). The case for case studies of facework. In S. Ting-Toomey (Ed.), *The challenge of facework: Cross-cultural and interpersonal issues* (pp. 287–305). Albany, NY: SUNY Press.

Watts, R. J. (2003). *Politeness.* Cambridge, UK: Cambridge University Press.

Watts, R. J., Ide, S., & Ehlich, K. (1992). *Politeness in language: Studies in its history, theory, and practice.* Berlin, Germany: Mouton de Gruyter.

Wilson, S. J., Aleman, C. G., & Leatham, G. B. (1998). Identity implications of influence goals: A revised analysis of face-threatening acts and application to seeking compliance with same-sex friends. *Human Communication Research, 25,* 64–96.

21

Relational Dialectics Theory

Navigating Meaning From Competing Discourses

Leslie A. Baxter and Kristen M. Norwood

R elational dialectics theory (RDT) rests on the notion that relating is a complex process of meaning-making. The theory is meant to sensitize the researcher to certain processes and features of communication that facilitate understanding of the dialogic nature of relating. An analysis framed by RDT seeks to understand how meaning is constructed through the interpenetration of competing discourses. RDT takes a discourse to be a system of meaning or "a set of propositions that cohere around a given object of meaning," usually with an evaluative dimension (Baxter, 2011, p. 2). For example, many Americans value the discourse of individualism, which assumes, among other things, that the purpose of society is to serve the needs of individual selves. Like many theories of interpersonal communication, RDT has evolved over time, and this chapter traces its evolution.

Intellectual Tradition of Relational Dialectics Theory

Relational dialectics theory is a communication theory grounded in the work of Mikhail Bakhtin (1981, 1984, 1986, 1990; Voloshinov, 1986). While Bakhtin used literary texts to explicate his ideas, his central concern was the creation of meaning through dialogue, both literal and metaphorical. Baxter and Montgomery (1996) and Baxter (2004, 2006, 2011) built upon his work to create a theory that allows for an understanding of how we construct meaning for our relational experiences through the interplay of competing discourses. It is difficult to aptly situate RDT within one of the three commonly recognized meta-theoretical paradigms of our discipline (post-positive, interpretive, and critical, discussed in Chapter 1); since its first articulation (Baxter & Montgomery, 1996), RDT has been used by researchers in conjunction with each of these perspectives. Therefore, in describing the intellectual tradition of the theory we discuss RDT in relation to each framework and why it is a better or worse fit for the theory.

Particularly early on (and still, at times) RDT was used in quantitative, post-positivist research, wherein the theory's goal of understanding the competing forces that animate relational communication was only partially met by a focus on the presence and salience of mainly three dialectical tensions: autonomy-connection, openness-closedness, and novelty-predictability. While providing useful insights into what relational partners perceived as most significant among common relational tensions, this work offered a static understanding of discursive struggle. Furthermore, RDT is not a theory that strives for prediction or generalizability of findings, but rather intelligibility of situated communication within and about relationships. The benchmark of assessment for the theory is thus its heurism or ability to illuminate the meaning-making process. Hence, the post-positive paradigm is generally an ill fit for RDT.

More productively, RDT has been utilized in inductive, interpretive research, which better suits the goals of the initial articulation of the theory by Baxter and Montgomery (1996) (hereafter referred to as RDT 1.0). Like many interpretive theories, RDT 1.0 sought to understand how particular meanings are socially constructed and sustained through communication. The interpretive approach privileges participants' perspectives and the details of talk, providing a rich, evocative understanding of the meaning-making process. Also, it allows for context-specific discursive struggles to emerge. Rather than reducing a discursive struggle to a broad binary, it can account for various radiants of a discursive struggle that give specificity and texture to how meanings are created in different contexts. For example, the struggle between individualism and community has been found to manifest as, among other things, competition between dependence and independence as well as between self and other interests (Baxter, 2011). However, the interpretive paradigm also falls short as a framework for understanding discursive struggle because it not does account for the fragmented, contested nature of meaning or the power that resides in discourse.

The most recent articulation of RDT demonstrates how the theory has evolved to emphasize both the interplay of competing discourses (formerly referred to as the contradiction of united opposites) and the discursive inequality that characterizes this interplay. "RDT 2.0" (Baxter, 2011, p. 1) has evolved into a critical theory in that it directs our attention to issues of struggle and power. RDT in its current articulation provides us a way to examine the monologic *and* dialogic potential of communication: how some meanings get reproduced to the point of calcification as well as how new meanings can be created through dialogic struggle. In this, it accounts for culturally dominant systems of meaning that have the potential to become authoritative. Therefore, RDT 2.0 fits best within the postmodern critical project (see Baxter & Asbury, Chapter 14, in this volume).

Main Goals and Features of Relational Dialectics Theory

In articulating RDT 2.0, Baxter (2011) encourages researchers to move beyond identifying the presence of competing discourses in data to examine the way meaning is made from their intermingling. We present an abridged version of RDT 2.0 here by articulating three of its central propositions along with several key concepts. Although we present the propositions in list form, they must be understood as intertwined.

PROPOSITION 1: EVERY UTTERANCE IS EMBEDDED IN A LARGER UTTERANCE CHAIN.

One of Bakhtin's central arguments is that no utterance or turn at talk is socially isolated, but is in dialogue with utterances that circulate before it and those that might follow. First, each utterance responds to preceding utterances; it "refutes, affirms, supplements, and relies on the others, presupposes them to be known, and somehow takes them into account" (Bakhtin, 1986, p. 91). Second, an utterance is formed in anticipation of how it will be perceived by an immediate addressee as well as by others, more generally. Bakhtin says, "Both the composition and, particularly, the style of the utterance depend on those to whom the utterance is addressed, how the speaker (or writer) senses and imagines his addressees, and the force of their effect on the utterance" (1986, p. 95). Building on these arguments, Baxter and Montgomery (1996) presented a typology of links in the utterance chain that help us to locate our analyses: proximal already-spoken, proximal not-yet-spoken, distal already-spoken, and distal not-yet-spoken.

Relational partners interact on the basis of their relational history and in anticipation of their relational future. These are the proximal already-spoken and the proximal not-yet-spoken links in the utterance chain, respectively. At these sites, parties may reproduce their existing relational meaning or they may create a new one. For example, spouses might renew their marriage vows and re-establish the meaning of their marriage, or friends might renegotiate the meaning of their relationship to "friend with benefits."

In addition to relationship-specific meaning systems, utterances are also informed by shared cultural discourses. At the distal-already-spoken site, speakers call up systems of meaning to which they have access due to cultural membership in order to make sense of their experiences and to make their experiences intelligible to others. And, just as speakers anticipate the response of an immediate addressee, so too they anticipate how a more abstracted other or superaddressee (Bakhtin, 1986) might respond to their talk; therefore, they might show awareness of how theirs and others' relational experiences align with or are different from that which is considered normal or is idealized in a given culture. Although, theoretically, the proximal and distal sites are never isolated from one another, it is more manageable to focus an analysis at one or the other.

PROPOSITION 2: MEANING IS CONSTRUCTED THROUGH STRUGGLE AMONG DIFFERENT, OFTEN OPPOSING, DISCOURSES OF VARYING FORCE.

The central proposition of RDT is that meaning-making is a dialogic process characterized by the simultaneous fusion and differentiation of discourses. All speech communication is comprised of dialogue, whether it is a conversation between parties or a single utterance spoken by an individual because, according to Bakhtin (1981), language itself is "ideologically saturated" (p. 271). He elaborates:

> Every concrete utterance of a speaking subject serves as a point where centrifugal as well as centripetal forces are brought to bear. The processes of centralization and decentralization, of unification and disunification, intersect in the utterance. . . . [making it] a contradiction-ridden, tension-filled unity of two embattled tendencies. (p. 272)

While centripetal forces are those that "serve to unify and centralize the verbal-ideological world" (p. 271), centrifugal forces are those that decentralize or diversify meaning. For example, if a couple decides to sacrifice individual needs for what is good for the relationship, a discourse of community is functioning centripetally in contrast to the centrifugal discourse of individualism.

According to RDT, centripetal discourses are those that are dominant, often centered in relational talk, easily legitimated, and frequently taken for granted; therefore, these discourses hold more power in the meaning-making process. However, they are usually in concert with centrifugal discourses, which are more marginal symbolic systems. It is the struggle between these forces through which established meanings are reproduced or new meanings are made. Researchers should take seriously the power that is involved in the construction of meaning. RDT holds that power, "the discursive capacity to define social reality" (Baxter, 2011, p. 124), does not reside in individuals or social groups, but in discourse. Bakhtin (1984) was wary of the potential for centripetal discourses to become so dominant that alternative discourses are all but silenced, a condition of monologue. This can happen at the macro-level. For example, a discourse of anti-Semitism dominated Nazi Germany, leading to political oppression and genocide. We can also imagine a more micro-level monologic scenario in which a discourse of traditional patriarchy is so dominant in a relationship that reality is defined on the notion that a wife should be subservient to her husband and deserves punishment for offending him, resulting in intimate terrorism.

Wary of monologue, Bakhtin idealized transformative dialogue because it creates new meanings rather than reproducing existing ones. Most often, though, communication is characterized by something in between. Next, we discuss some types of interplay and their dialogic potential.

PROPOSITION 3: THE INTERPLAY OF DISCOURSES RESULTS IN VARIOUS ARRANGEMENTS OF MEANING THAT ARE NEVER FINALIZED, BUT ALWAYS IN FLUX.

RDT holds that speech communication is characterized by a continuum of interplay (see Figure 21.1) that ranges from instances of monologue to instances of transformative dialogue; types of interplay are more dialogic as we move from the left pole to the right pole of the spectrum.

Moving away from monologue, we can locate two overarching processes that characterize the middle of the spectrum, diachronic interplay and synchronic polemic interplay. In both processes, at least two discourses are at play, although differently so. "Diachronic" simply means occurring over time, whereas "synchronic" refers to one moment in time. Diachronic interplay is characterized by a privileging of one discourse at one juncture and a competing one at a later point in time or in another context. In both forms, a separation of discourses happens, making the interplay more difficult to identify without longitudinal data. Such ebb-and-flow inversions elide discursive struggles by constructing them in the form of either/or dilemmas. An example of dia-chronic interplay might be a romantic pair that alternates between privileging a discourse of individualism that legitimates their individual needs for time apart (for work, friends, or hobbies) and a discourse of community that legiti-mates "couple time."

Synchronic polemic interplay is characterized by the co-occurrence of mul-tiple discourses at a given time point. Synchronic interplay varies on at least four dimensions, two of which we will discuss here. In its antagonistic form, one speaker articulates one discourse and another speaker aligns with an opposing discourse. Imagine our romantic pair in an argument in which one

The Continuum of Dialogic Struggle

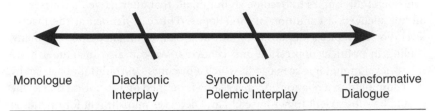

| Monologue | Diachronic Interplay | Synchronic Polemic Interplay | Transformative Dialogue |

Figure 21.1 The Continuum of Dialogic Struggle

partner wants to do her own thing but the other wants more time together. However, conflict between people is not necessary for synchronic polemic interplay. Competing discourses often are articulated in non-antagonistic forms wherein multiple discourses can be identified in even one speaker's talk. In its direct form, a speaker might entertain divergent perspectives, privilege one discourse and reject others, or construct *balance* (Baxter & Montgomery, 1996), wherein both discourses are partially legitimated yet still framed as opposing. For example, both parties in our romantic pair might honor both individualism and community by seeking a compromise ("Let's reserve Saturdays for our own thing and Sundays for us as a couple." "That's what I was thinking, too"). Alternatively, one or more discourses can be implicated only indirectly, which allows for more ambiguity of meaning. This indirectness can function to neutralize the struggle between competing discourses, to keep centrifugal discourses at the margins, or to temper the power of centripetal meanings.

Transformative dialogue, which anchors the continuum on its right, achieves a transformation of meaning such that discourses suspend an either/ or competition to create a new system of meaning. These new meanings can take the form of either a *hybrid* (Bakhtin, 1981, p. 358) or an *aesthetic moment* (Bakhtin, 1990, p. 67). A hybrid is a construction in which the formerly competing discourses are still identifiable yet are repositioned as compatible. Think of hybrids as salad dressing made by mixing oil and vinegar. The discourses (oil, vinegar) are distinct, yet they combine to form a new meaning—salad dressing. An aesthetic moment is a construction in which formerly competing discourses are merged in a way that profoundly alters each one. Think of this mixture as akin to a chemical reaction.[1] For example, two molecules of hydrogen combine with one molecule of oxygen to produce an entirely new entity— water. Bakhtin regarded this as aesthetic in that opposing discourses are transformed into a consummate whole.

To make these propositions and concepts of RDT more concrete, we provide the following sample conversation between sisters and a cursory analysis of it.[2]

1. Martha: Hey, Janie. I'm calling 'cause I need you to help me decide on a ring. James and

2. I are getting engaged. Check your e-mail, I sent you pictures.

3. Jane: Wait, you're getting engaged? You've been dating for what—three months?

4. Martha: Yeah, about that long.

5. Jane: That's not long enough to really know someone. Plus, you've both been divorced

6. and you rushed into an engagement just last year and that ended terribly! I guess I

7. thought you'd be more cautious. Please think of Leo—he's been through so much already.

8. Martha: What Leo needs is a happy mother and to have the things that other kids have—a

9. father, a house, a dog. I know people might think it impulsive, but this time is different.

10. Jane: How is it different?

11. Martha: I can't explain it. We just *know*. So, there's no reason to wait.

12. Jane: But, if you *know* then there's no reason to rush!

13. Martha: I appreciate your concern, but I just need your support as my sister, like always.

14. Jane: I'm *trying* to give you support—by keeping you from making the wrong decision!

15. I've been there for you through the highs and lows, and I kept quiet because I didn't

16. want to tell you how to run your life. But, I have to be honest now or I'll regret it.

17. Martha: Look, I'm not going to change my mind.

18. Jane: Well, it's obviously your decision and as sisters we have to stick together. So,

19. I'll be supportive by being happy for you without agreeing with you.

If we focus on the proximal sites of the utterance chain, we can interpret this as an antagonistic struggle of competing discourses of support, among others, through which Martha and Jane construct a new meaning for their relationship. Martha began the conversation by glossing over the "big news" of her impending engagement. Seemingly, she anticipates that Jane will not approve of this, and Martha's talk functions to narrow Jane's response to the topic of rings (lines 1–2). After Jane suggests Martha reconsider her decision, Martha's talk works to reproduce the past meaning of their relationship (line 13), which we learn in the next few lines rested on a discourse of sisterly support as agreement and unquestioned approval. Jane indicates that previously she had gone along with Martha's decisions even when she felt they were poor, comforted her when relationships went sour, and never chastised her for her bad judgment. However, in line 14, Jane puts forth a competing meaning of support, characterized by being a voice of reason that keeps Martha from repeating past mistakes. After Martha stands her ground, Jane's talk positions these discourses as compatible, reframing support to mean offering positive sentiment while being open about disagreement. This interplay constitutes a discursive hybrid.

If we focus on the distal sites in the utterance chain, we can see how cultural discourses are called up during, and make comprehensible, this relational meaning-making; specifically, the conversation is animated by a struggle between discourses of romanticism and rationality, individualism and community, and meanings of family. Upon learning of Martha's engagement, Jane immediately calls up a discourse of rationality. In fact, her question, "You've been dating for what—three months?" makes sense to us and to Martha because rationality is one discourse through which we understand love and relationships in our culture. The discourse of rationality holds that relationships should be pragmatic; in this instance it is invoked to imply that we cannot make sound relationship decisions when we do not fully know our partners, a process that takes a certain amount of time. In lines 9 and 11, Martha responds to both Jane and to a generalized other, whom she assumes will also judge the engagement as irresponsible against a discourse of rationality ("I know people might think it impulsive"), with a discourse of romanticism. The statement "We just *know*" makes sense to us and to Jane because a discourse of romanticism interplays with rationality in our symbolic landscape. This discourse holds that love transcends reason and that relationships should be about emotion, not pragmatism. In the next line, Jane's talk pacifies this discourse, allowing that one can have a reliable feeling that a relationship is right, but uses this to further legitimate the discourse of rationality by claiming that this sureness lends itself to patience.

Intertwined with these discourses is a struggle between individualism and community. In line 7, Jane implies that Martha is being selfish in her decision to become engaged so quickly, thinking of herself instead of her son and therefore centering individualism. Jane privileges the opposing discourse in asking Martha to shift her focus from self to other, in this case, Leo. Martha responds by pacifying (Baxter, 2011) the discourse of community, arguing that by fulfilling her interests she can fulfill Leo's, as her happiness will result in his happiness. To further rationalize her decision, Martha invokes a normative discourse (distal-not-yet-spoken) of traditional family, implying that a nuclear arrangement brings a child happiness and stability.

We also can see the discourses of individualism and community interplay in lines 15–19. Jane says that she withheld her opinions regarding Martha's romantic relationships in the past out of respect for her right to act autonomously, but now has decided to be more open for both of their sakes, indicating a shift toward a discourse of community. After Martha reasserts her right to make her own decisions, Jane constructs a balance between the centripetal discourse of individualism and the less powerful discourse of community. She partially affirms the former by acknowledging that the decision is Martha's to make, even if it is selfish, but also partially affirms the latter by privileging their sisterly bond over her own desire to influence Martha's decision. Hopefully, this somewhat superficial study of talk demonstrates how the sisters construct meaning for their relational experiences through the interplay of competing discourses.

How Communication Is Conceptualized in Relational Dialectics Theory

Following Bakhtin (1990), RDT takes communication to be constitutive of sociality, that is, both selves and relationships are constituted through it. RDT holds that experiences are given meaning through communication: "It is not experience that organizes expression, but the other way around—*expression organizes experience*" (Voloshinov, 1986, p. 85). Communication is not positioned as a representational tool that merely reflects or affects psychological or sociological phenomena; instead, those phenomena are constructed, that is, given meaning, through communicative practices. Additionally, communication is conceptualized as inherently tension-filled, and meaning is unfinalizable. Meaning emerges through struggle in interactional moments and, in this sense, is momentarily stable, but it is renegotiated with each ensuing interactional moment, whether the same meaning is recreated or a new one is constructed. Finally, RDT takes this process to be culturally specific; discourses that circulate in one culture or co-culture may not be recognized or relevant in another.

Research and Practical Applications of Relational Dialectics Theory

As mentioned, RDT has been used in a variety of ways. Researchers, in general, have provided us with a rich list of discursive oppositions across various relationship types, processes, and phenomena, but they have paid insufficient attention to how these oppositions interpenetrate and the meanings that are constituted from this interplay. Much research to date has emphasized only one goal of RDT, identifying competing discourses. Several researchers have asked "What are the oppositions that animate X?" where "X" can be a relationship type, an interpersonal process, or a given social phenomenon. This is an important undertaking, but researchers need to move beyond this task to focus on precisely *how* these discourses interpenetrate to construct meaning.

Some recent research focuses more on interplay, meaning-making, and power. For example, Harrigan and Braithwaite (2010) do well to move beyond the identification of competing discourses to analyze how their interplay constructs meaning. The authors show that through the interplay of discourses of legitimacy, expansion, similarity, and difference, families formed through visible adoption construct their families as legitimate by constructing most families as different in some way. Another example comes from Carr and Wang (2012), who examined forgiveness processes in families. The authors found, among other things, that family members' talk was characterized by opposing discourses of choice and obligation to forgive and that many participants centered obligation in the context of non-voluntary familial bonds. In a study of how family members make sense of a transgender relative's transition, Norwood (2013) found that interconnected competing discourses of selfhood (sovereign vs. social) and gender (biological essentialism vs. social construction) anchored family members' experiences of ambiguous loss. She moved beyond this, as well, to identify how various types of interplay facilitated different experiences of ambiguous loss. Finally, an example of recent research that focuses explicitly on power is Baxter, Scharp, Asbury, Jannusch, and Norwood's (2012) investigation of birthmothers' identity constructions articulated in their online adoption stories. Stories were characterized by two identity constructions, both of which resisted the dominant cultural discourse of intensive mothering that positions birthmothers as bad mothers.

Together, these studies and others can give us significant insight into the various relational contexts and circumstances in which we may find ourselves, but some might still be wondering, "so what?" Although the goal of RDT is not to predict relationships between variables or fix any particular communication problem, there are still practical applications that result from research guided by the theory. Most generally, RDT helps us to appreciate that the social world is rarely a cut-and-dried communicative site of stable and consistent meanings; it ought to be reassuring to appreciate that relating is a messy, tension-filled business rather than a sign that something is inherently wrong with the relationship. Other practical implications of RDT are more context-specific. For example, Thatcher (2011) provides suggestions for both members of Alcoholics Anonymous as well as for those who treat alcohol abuse regarding how to negotiate competing discourses of Christianity and spiritual pluralism within the AA doctrine. Norwood and Baxter (2011) argue that persons hoping to adopt must center and marginalize certain discourses in order to be optimally persuasive when writing "Dear Birthmother" letters. Suter, Reyes, and Ballard (2011) offer suggestions for changes to pre-adoptive education that would help families with visible adoptive ties discursively cope with the stigma they might face. And finally, Norwood (2013) argues that certain forms of interplay are helpful for family members in alleviating feelings of grief surrounding their loved ones' sex/gender transitions. Therefore, significant and concrete applications emerge from the deep understandings of relational phenomena that RDT directs us toward.

Evaluation of Relational Dialectics Theory

As a communication theory, RDT has several strengths. It is centered directly in communication, rather than in psychological or sociological constructs. Further, RDT theorizes about the process and products of communication rather than one or the other. Certainly, RDT succeeds in helping us understand the pushes and pulls inherent to relating.

However, RDT is composed of many interrelated, sophisticated concepts and therefore is not among the simplest of theoretical tools. One resulting challenge for a researcher is how to bracket an analysis; an attempt to focus on all of the theory's propositions and concepts can quickly become too complex an undertaking. Therefore, it might benefit researchers to focus on a subset of its concepts and propositions in a single study. Moreover, the act of bracketing the process of meaning-making is somewhat problematic against one of the theory's core principles, that meaning is unfinalizable. Nonetheless, doing so is our only means for understanding this process, and longitudinal data help to capture meaning-making as an ongoing process. To help navigate the theoretical complexity of RDT, Baxter (2011) articulates the method of contrapuntal analysis to direct focus to the centripetal-centrifugal struggle of discourses and the meanings that emerge from it.

A common criticism of RDT is that it has nothing new to add—researchers keep listing the same basic discursive tensions over and over. We think that this criticism holds merit for early RDT research (with the caveat that sometimes apparent similarity belies nuanced differences that are situation specific), but not for the theory itself. It is important for scholars to resist a "cookie-cutter" mentality in which contradictions identified in early work are simply overlaid onto a data set without attending to their nuances, additional or alternative discourses that might be animating meaning-making, and most importantly, how the discourses interpenetrate with one another. Recent work that emphasizes the process of meaning-making through discursive struggle is correcting this overreliance on listing a basic boilerplate of discourses without examining them in play with one another. Another common critique of RDT is that it does not predict anything about communication in relationships. This is true, but irrelevant as RDT is not a post-positivistic theory. We have also heard critics assert that RDT is imprecise and fuzzy. Our response is that RDT is not a post-positivist theory that endorses belief in a single, true objective reality; instead, it is a heuristic tool that obligates scholars to advance *an* interpretation rather than *the* interpretation of how meaning is made in utterances.

Continuing the Conversation

In addition to conducting more inductive research, we can continue and strengthen the conversation around RDT by shifting the language of RDT research to focus on competing discourses rather than competing desires. Desires are psychological constructs, and our meaning-making of a given need or desire is always embedded in a system of meaning or discourse, which ought to be the focus of attention according to RDT. Second, although researchers cannot always do full justice to each utterance site, researchers should strive to embed utterances in a "chain of speech communion" (Bakhtin, 1986, p. 93). This can be done by taking into account the discursive history of a given relationship, the broader cultural discourses that relationship parties jointly draw upon in making sense of their relationship, and the responses they anticipate to follow. Additionally, in order to better understand meaning as in flux, longitudinal work is needed that can examine both synchronic and diachronic forms of interplay. Finally, we can enrich our understanding of relational dialectics through a concentration on the power involved in the meaning-making process.

Notes

1. The authors thank Meryl Irwin for the chemical analogy.
2. We do not explain nor undertake a contrapuntal analysis here, but instead point to various features of the talk that illustrate tenants and concepts outlined above. For an explanation of contrapuntal analysis, see Baxter (2011).

References

Bakhtin, M. M. (1981). *The dialogic imagination: Four essays by M. M. Bakhtin* (M. Holquist, Ed.; C. Emerson & M. Holquist, Trans.). Austin: University of Texas Press.

Bakhtin, M. M. (1984). *Problems of Dostoevsky's poetics* (C. Emerson, Ed. and Trans.). Minneapolis: University of Minnesota Press.

Bakhtin, M. M. (1986). *Speech genres and other late essays* (C. Emerson & M. Holquist Eds.; V. McGee, Trans.). Austin: University of Texas Press.

Bakhtin, M. M. (1990). *Art and answerability: Early philosophical essays by M. M. Bakhtin* (M. Holquist & V. Liapunov, Eds.; V. Liapunov, Trans.). Austin: University of Texas Press.

Baxter, L. A. (2004). Distinguished scholar article: Relationships as dialogues. *Personal Relationships, 11,* 1–22.

Baxter, L. A. (2006). Communication as dialogue. In G. J. Shepherd, J. St. John, & T. Striphas (Eds.), *Communication as . . .: Perspectives on theory* (pp. 101–109). Thousand Oaks, CA: Sage.

Baxter, L. A. (2011). *Voicing relationships.* Thousand Oaks, CA: Sage.

Baxter, L. A., & Montgomery, B. M. (1996). *Relating: Dialogues & dialectics.* New York, NY: Guilford.

Baxter, L. A., Scharp, K., Asbury, A., Jannusch, A., & Norwood, K. (2012). "Birthmothers are not bad people": A dialogic analysis of online birthmother stories. *Qualitative Communication Research, 1,* 53–82.

Carr, K., & Wang, T. R. (2012): "Forgiveness isn't a simple process: It's a vast undertaking": Negotiating and communicating forgiveness in nonvoluntary family relationships. *Journal of Family Communication, 12,* 40 56.

Harrigan, M. M., & Braithwaite, D. O. (2010). Discursive struggles in families formed through visible adoption: An exploration of dialectical unity. *Journal of Applied Communication Research, 38,* 127–144.

Norwood, K. (2013). Grieving gender: Trans-identities, transition, and ambiguous loss. *Communication Monographs, 80,* 24–25.

Norwood, K. & Baxter, L. A. (2011). "Dear birth mother": Addressivity and meaning-making in online adoption-seeking parental letters. *Journal of Family Communication, 11,* 198–217.

Suter, E. A., Reyes, K. L., & Ballard, R. L. (2011). Adoptive parents' framing of laypersons' conceptions of family. *Qualitative Research Reports in Communication, 12,* 43–50.

Thatcher, M. S. (2011). Negotiating the tension between the discourses of Christianity and spiritual pluralism in Alcoholics Anonymous. *Journal of Applied Communication Research, 39,* 389–405.

Voloshinov, V. N. (1986). *Marxism and the philosophy of language* (L. Matejka & I. R. Titunik, Trans.). Cambridge, MA: Harvard University Press. (Original work published in 1929)

22

Speech Codes Theory

Traces of Culture in Interpersonal Communication

Gerry Philipsen

Intellectual Tradition of Speech Codes Theory

Speech codes theory was developed to apply to all contexts, modes, and settings of communicative conduct. In this chapter I explore its relevance to interpersonal communication. I define interpersonal communication as the production and interpretation of messages between or among two or more people, when those messages are concerned, explicitly or implicitly, with the people's selves and the people's relationships with each other.

The thesis I explore here is that whenever people engage in interpersonal communication there are traces of culture woven into their messages and into their interpretations of the meanings of those messages. These traces appear in many forms, verbal and otherwise. The traces I consider here are those that can be discerned in words that pertain to communicative conduct, and in premises that link two or more words that pertain to communicative conduct.

The following two vignettes illustrate what I mean by "interpersonal communication," "discern," "interpret," and "meaning and cultural traces."

A Norwegian woman complained to an interviewer that her husband won't stand up to his mother when she tries to interfere with the couple's independence. The husband says he believes in "peace at any price" (*fred for enhver pris*), but the wife says that sometimes the price is too high.

What does "peace" mean in this vignette? Why does the notion of peace at any price, usually used to talk about negotiations between nations over armed conflict, seem to have such importance to the Norwegian man, who uses it to justify his refusal to talk about important topics? What, for these interlocutors, is the meaning and force of the man's insistence on not talking bluntly with his mother?

This vignette is drawn from research by a Norwegian anthropologist, Marianne Gullestad, who studied words and expressions that were used "with frequency and intensity" (1992, p. 142) when some Norwegians talk about "interpersonal relations." Two Norwegian words that Gullestad focuses on are *fred* ("peace") and *ro* ("quiet"). She shows that when Norwegians use *fred* in talking about interpersonal relations, they do not express its primary meaning in Norwegian, "absence of war," but rather a secondary meaning, the sense of being "free from disturbances from others." In such contexts they use *ro* to refer to "a state of mind characterized by wholeness and control" (p. 146). To be free from disturbances from others, that is, to "find peace," is, according to a Norwegian logic, necessary to achieve the desired state of personal "wholeness and control." Thus "peace," Gullestad said, is often sought at any price, and is used as a justification for avoiding contact with others.

Gullestad (1992) used her study of *fred* and *ro* to construct a Norwegian "code" (pp. 103, 170) of "social relations" (p. 147), as follows:

1. "A certain social distance (peace) creates good social relations";

2. For an individual human being, "control of self is especially important" and is "especially connected to peace in its meaning of 'quiet' (*ro*)";

3. As "guidelines for action," one should strive to be "whole, balanced, and safe by not involving oneself too much and by avoiding open personal conflicts. People who do not understand a little hint ought to be avoided" (p. 147).

Because of Gullestad's references to "not involving oneself too much," "avoiding open personal conflicts," and the importance of understanding "a little hint," I regard her three points as a Norwegian speech code.

Now we return to the vignette, with some understanding of the meanings, of *fred* and *ro*, to the Norwegian husband and of the weight of the expression for him of *fred for enhver pris,* that some Norwegians consider "peace" crucial not just to "good social relations" but also to keeping oneself "whole, balanced, and safe" (p. 147). That is, some Norwegians speak about various ways of communicating as being crucial not only to interpersonal life, but also to their very sense of self.

In another example, an American university student recalls that when he was nine years old his parents divorced and his father was given weekly visiting rights. On the days that the boy spent with his father, the father insisted that they "communicate" about their "relationship." The father's efforts became burdensome to the boy, who wished his father had just taken him to a baseball game.

What do "communicate" and "relationship" mean to the people who participated in this second vignette? Why does the boy resist "communication," for which an American dictionary gives as the first sense, "the transfer of meaning"? Why would the father think that he and his son would have to communicate, over and over, about their "relationship," which presumably is a biological one of father and son? Is not the relationship of father and son immutable? What, for man and boy, is the force of the man's insistence that he and his son "communicate" about their "relationship"?

While Marianne Gullestad worked with Norwegian materials to formulate a Norwegian code of interpersonal relations, my colleagues and I in the United States, and other U.S. scholars, formulated an American code of interpersonal relations. Tamar Katriel and I began the process of constructing this code by tracing the appearance of "communication" in some American speech about interpersonal life. One of our earliest findings was that, as with the Norwegian usage of "peace" in speech about interpersonal relations, much American usage of "communication" in speech about interpersonal relations did not suggest its primary dictionary meaning, but rather something that carries more moral freight. We glossed the situated meaning of "communication" to be "close, open, supportive speech," with "close," "open," and "supportive" being terms that we also had to interpret (Katriel & Philipsen, 1981, p. 309). This definition was not in any dictionary, but warranted by the way people actually used the word "communication."

We also found (Katriel & Philipsen, 1981) that when Americans used the word "communication" in speech about interpersonal relations, they used it along with several other words we established as part of an American cultural vocabulary of interpersonal relations. Words we presented in 1981 include "relationship," "self," "work," and "feedback." Later studies provide detailed ethnographic interpretations of "commitment" (Quinn, 1982), "relationship" (Rosenthal, 1984), and "honest" (Carbaugh, 1988). You can find treatments of these words and their meanings as key words in this U.S. code of communicative conduct in the work of other scholars as well, for example, Bellah, Madsen, Sullivan, Swidler, and Tipton (1985); Philipsen (1992, 1997); Philipsen, Horkley, and Huhman (1999); and Swidler (2001). Just as Gullestad (1992) found evidence for a Norwegian premise that "a certain social distance (peace) creates good social relations" (p. 147), we found evidence for the widespread and significant use by Americans of a premise that communication is necessary for a relationship (Katriel & Philipsen, 1981). We used "What we need is communication" in the title of our article to represent an attitude expressed often by many of our respondents in discussing their relationships.

Here are two expressions of the premise we constructed. Hollandsworth (1995), a columnist in an American magazine, wrote about interpersonal relations in romantic situations: "Most women aren't satisfied in a relationship until they find a man who's truly communicative—a man who doesn't hesitate to discuss his feelings, desires, and anxieties" (p. 7). With regard to "relationship," the statement's use of "satisfied in" suggests that a "relationship" can be more or less satisfying, that is, "satisfaction" is a variable associated with "relationships." Two other popular writers wrote, "when communication breaks down, your relationship is headed for danger" (Bilicki & Goetz, 1995, p. 60), suggesting that a "relationship" is something that not only can vary, but that also is fragile, susceptible to "breakdown." With regard to the word "communicative," which is a form of the word "communication," Hollandsworth implied with his use of the word "truly" that there is a true (and false) variety of communication, and that in the true variant the "man" must "not hesitate" to engage in the speech activity of "discussion" (presumably a give and take of talk) about some specific topical areas—his "feelings," "desires," and "anxieties" (Hollandsworth, 1995, p. 7). These authors, writing in popular magazines, suggested a belief that "communication" and "relationship" are linked to each other in important ways; they thus echo Katriel and Philipsen's (1981) report of the widespread and significant American use of the premise that "communication is necessary for a relationship."

Now we can return to the American vignette, perhaps with a greater appreciation of the meanings of "communication" and "relationship" to the divorced father, and of the weight that the premise that "what we need is communication" (for "our relationship") carried for him. Although in some codes it would be unthinkable for a "relationship" to "break down" because one of the parties to it seems less than "satisfied" with it, this is the sort of talk that the American father was presumably exposed to, in his face-to-face interactions as well as in the popular media. (See, especially, Philipsen, 1992, Chapter 5, for a treatment of the correlation of face-to-face and mediated talk about "communication" and "relationships.")

Main Goals and Features of Speech Codes Theory

In interpreting the meanings and explaining the force in these vignettes of words and premises about communicative conduct, I suggested that the people mentioned in them used a code to produce, interpret, and evaluate their own and others' communicative conduct. I used my understanding of those codes to interpret and explain the communicative conduct of the people who used them. What sort of codes are these? I refer to them as "speech codes," which I define as follows: *Speech codes are historically situated and socially constructed systems of words, meanings, premises, and rules about communicative conduct.* The word "speech" in "speech codes" is a shorthand term, a figure of speech, standing here for all the possible means of communicative conduct that can be encountered in a given time and place. The word "code" in "speech codes" refers to a system of words, meanings, premises, and rules that people use as a resource to talk about, interpret, and shape communicative conduct. These senses of speech and of code, when placed together in the term speech code, establish a definition of a speech code as a historically situated and socially constructed system of words, meanings, premises, and rules that people use to talk about their own and others' communicative conduct.

In 1992, I set forth a prototypical version of speech codes theory, with four empirically grounded principles about their nature, their functioning in communicative conduct, and how to discover and describe them. In 1997, I made a formal statement of speech codes theory, with five empirically grounded propositions. In the latest version of the theory, Philipsen, Coutu, and Covarrubias (2005) expanded the theory to six propositions, responded to published criticisms of it, and clarified further the nature of the construct of code in it. In the paragraphs that follow I describe the main features of the theory, and the six speech codes propositions.

The first descriptive generalization is that *everywhere there is a distinctive culture, there will be found a distinctive speech code.* This was illustrated in the brief juxtaposition of (some elements of) Norwegian and American speech codes, with the suggestion that the Norwegian code gives greater endorsement than does the American to interpersonal communication that is indirect and respectful of personal boundaries, while the American code gives greater endorsement than does the Norwegian to directness of communication and a more changeable self. These are two among many accounts of speech codes that have been analyzed contrastively.

The second descriptive generalization is that *every individual will encounter multiple speech codes during a lifetime.* Thus, although a Norwegian or an American might use the codes I have described here, these individuals presumably can—and do—draw on other codes that are used in their social environments. Gullestad (1992) and Philipsen (1992) provided book-length treatments of the societies in which they studied the codes they reported; both cases showed evidence of more than one code being used in these societies.

The third descriptive generalization is that *in every speech code the words, meanings, premises, and rules pertaining to communicative conduct are systematically linked with words, meanings, premises, and rules pertaining to the nature of persons and the nature of social relationships.* This is illustrated here for the Norwegian code in the linkage between indirectness of communication and the preservation of the well-being of a bounded person. It is illustrated here for the American code in the linkage between openness and the strength of interpersonal relationships. The import of this generalization is that whenever people engage in interpersonal communication, and use words and premises pertaining to communicative conduct, they bring into the discussion words and premises that carry cultural traces that are always linked, for their meaning and significance, to words and meanings pertaining to notions of self or of interpersonal relations. These three generalizations are, respectively, Propositions 1, 2, and 3 of speech codes theory.

Speech codes theory posits a way to discover and describe traces of culture in communicative conduct. It does this through Proposition 5 of the theory, that *the words, rules, and premises of a speech code are inextricably woven into communicative conduct* (Philipsen, 2010; Philipsen et al., 2005). The import of Proposition 5 is that it tells one where to look (and listen) for traces of culture—that is, it tells one to look at (and listen to) communicative conduct, and to search therein for the use of a cultural code or codes. It also tells one what to look (and listen) for there, with a specification of a series of ways to discover traces of culture in speaking—for example, to search for the use of words or phrases about communicative conduct (e.g., "a little hint") and premises that include at least one word about communicative conduct (e.g., "communication is necessary for a relationship").

Speech codes theory posits a way to interpret and explain observed communicative conduct. In the presentation and examination of the two episodes presented above, I illustrated how speech codes, once discovered and described, can be used to interpret and explain communicative conduct, for example by showing the cultural meaning of the concept of peace and its importance to a Norwegian man in guiding his communicative conduct with his mother and his wife, and by showing the cultural meaning of the concepts of communication and relationship to an American man and the sense of imperative he felt to "communicate" so as to prevent a "breakdown" of the "relationship" with his son.

There are two propositions involved here. Proposition 4 of the theory says that *the significance of particular communicative acts is contingent on the speech codes that people use to interpret them*—that is, if someone observed a husband refusing to speak up to his mother in defense of the rights of his wife and himself as a couple, the not speaking up would be heard differently if interpreted in the terms of the Norwegian code than it would in the terms of the American code, as these codes were described above. Proposition 6 of speech codes theory says that *people use speech codes not only to interpret communicative conduct, but also to evaluate it (as good or bad) and to explain (that is, justify or account for) it.*

Speech codes theory is an empirical theory. Each of its six propositions was built on a foundation of empirical evidence. Most of that empirical evidence consists of ethnographic studies of speech codes in particular times and places and the comparative analysis of such studies. Gullestad's studies of Norwegian communicative conduct (1992) and the research of Katriel and Philipsen (1981), Philipsen (1975, 1976, 1986, 1992), Carbaugh (1988), Coutu (2000), and others into American communicative conduct are examples of such ethnographic work that provides an empirical account of a speech code in a particular time and place: Norway and the United States, respectively. Philipsen and Coutu (2005) cite a large body of speech codes research conducted in many societies and many languages throughout the world, a fund of research on which speech codes theory is based.

Speech codes theory is a dynamic theory. It is subject to change on the basis of new evidence or the rethinking of old evidence. For example, in the second and third published versions of the theory (Philipsen, 1997; Philipsen et al., 2005) one proposition was added based on a reconsideration of existing research or the consideration of new research, in each case leading to a data-based expansion of the number of propositions. (Coutu, 2000, was instrumental in driving the addition of Proposition 2.) Furthermore, each proposition in the theory is stated in such a way that it can be disconfirmed by new evidence or a rethinking of old evidence.

How Communication Is Conceptualized in Speech Codes Theory

I define "communication" as the production and interpretation of messages between or among two or more people. There is a commitment in the ethnographic research through which speech codes are discovered and described to pay attention to whatever the people one is studying take communication to be. This requires the researcher to listen carefully to the people she is observing and to be open to considering a variety of phenomena as falling within the domain of communication that the researcher might otherwise rule out (e.g., considering plants, trees, the wind, or other nonhuman and non-animal phenomena as potentially part of the communication process). At the same time, if there are no boundaries whatsoever as to what counts as communicative, it is difficult to say what precisely would or would not be included in a speech code, and it is in that spirit that in this exposition of speech codes theory I have presented working definitions of communication and of interpersonal communication.

Research and Practical Applications of Speech Codes Theory

Earlier in this chapter I presented two vignettes of interpersonal communication, one in Norway and one in America. These were interpreted by reference to what the people in the vignettes said and, by reference in each case, to a body of research into the cultural background of the people described in them. In each case, an illustration was provided of the idea that when people engage in interpersonal communication there are traces of culture in their messages about their selves and their relations to each other. The analysis showed that one place these traces appeared was in culturally distinctive words and premises pertaining to communicative conduct. And the analysis showed that culturally distinctive words and meanings pertaining to communicative conduct appeared in premises that link them to a culturally distinctive state of personal well-being and a culturally distinctive sense of interpersonal relations. The large body of speech codes research, conducted in many languages and many societies, shows that what I illustrated here for Norwegian and American interpersonal communication is true in many other places, including but not limited to Colombia, Finland, Germany, Israel, Mexico, Spain, Nicaragua, China, and Japan (see Philipsen, 2003). Speech codes theory takes these findings from many cultures and generalizes them to formulate a property of interpersonal communication in all times and places. That property is that *when words for and premises pertaining to communicative conduct appear in interpersonal communication there will be traces of culture present in them, and that these traces will bear culturally distinctive meanings and significance.*

Because of its demonstrated utility, across many languages and cultures, speech codes theory can help the participants in, or observers of, interpersonal communication, in any scene, situation, or human community, to understand the cultural significance of particular moments and milieu in which a person finds himself or herself. There are three ways the theory does this. First, it helps a person discern that a speech code is being used in someone's interpersonal messages, for example, by directing attention to words and premises about communicative conduct that are used in those messages. Second, it helps a person interpret the meanings of words about communicative conduct by tracing their use in relation to other words and meanings that co-occur with those words about communicative conduct. Third, it helps to explain why people say what they say in interpersonal messages by showing how, in the premises they use, they link their notions about ways of communicating to their notions about personal well-being and good social relations.

Evaluation of Speech Codes Theory

Speech codes theory has several strengths that help its users to interpret and explain culturally distinctive interpersonal communication. First, the theory specifies several propositions about the nature, discovery, and use of speech codes in interpersonal communication. Second, those propositions are grounded in a substantial fund of evidence gathered through experiment and experience in the study of speech codes. Third, speech codes theory provides several ways to help participants in interpersonal communication understand what they and their fellow interlocutors are saying about themselves and their relationships.

Speech codes theory is limited in that it applies to a narrow, albeit an important, dimension of interpersonal communication. That dimension is culture. The theory does not account for personal codes or for universal behavioral tendencies. Thus, it is a theory that is complementary to other theories that provide sharply focused ways to discern, interpret, and explain interpersonal communication.

Continuing the Conversation

I see four areas for future research and application of speech codes theory in interpersonal communication.

First, researchers should examine whether participants in interpersonal communication are aware of the use of speech codes by themselves and their interlocutors. As indicated above, we have a great deal of information, across many societies, that suggests that everywhere there is interpersonal communication the participants produce and interpret messages in part through the use of culturally distinctive words and premises pertaining to communicative conduct. When participants do the producing and interpreting, how aware are they that they are using a particular cultural code? For example, when someone talks with a friend, lover, spouse, or relative about their relation to each other, and uses such words as "peace," "quiet," "communication," or "relationship," is that person aware that he or she is speaking not naturally but culturally, that is, in the terms of a distinctive cultural code?

When someone repeats a version of the statement that "communication is necessary for a relationship," has that person considered whether things other than "communication" might be just as or more important to one's interlocutor of the moment, or in some particular situation? For example, is "communication" more important, or even as important, to a romantic or marital "relationship" as, say, carefulness in the making and keeping of romantic or marital vows, self-sacrifice in consideration of the other's well-being in the escalation of a romantic relationship, or fidelity to a partner? Textbooks in interpersonal communication tend to carry several pages, sometimes whole chapters, on the topics of self-disclosure and the negotiation of selves, but in many cases do not even mention such topics as the speech acts of promising or of making a vow. Additionally, can "relationships" end or break down? If so, what is the notion of relationship that is therefore implied? Cannot relationships be constituted on the basis of blood or the making of vows, and can blood be negotiated? Does awareness that one is using a particular code, say the American code discussed in this chapter, extend to the idea that in using this particular code one is emphasizing one set of moral and ethical commitments over others?

Second, researchers should examine the key terms and premises of the American code of "communication" that are referred to in this chapter. Several different key words in this code have been discerned and interpreted, including "communication," "close," "open," "supportive," "work," "self," "relationship," "commitment," and "honesty." What we do not know is how these and other words fit together into an American cultural system of symbols and meanings pertaining to communicative conduct. This American code is important to Americans and to anyone who wants to understand those Americans who use it, and yet there is little in the way of a systematic tying together of the diverse studies, each of which reveals something important about contemporary American life, but all of which, when put together into a comprehensive synthesis, would provide an important understanding of both America and the important speech code found in America.

Third, there is an emerged opportunity to study some new words and premises pertaining to communicative conduct that have appeared in online communication. There are many studies of online vocabulary, but there is little that discerns whether these new words and premises signal a major shift in understandings of the nature of person and interpersonal relations, or whether such already formulated codes as the Norwegian and U.S. examples illustrate continue, at their core, to have meaning and force in the lives of people. Speech codes theory gives a place to start such inquiries, for example, by holding up to a speech codes discernment exercise such emerged expressions as "bond-strengthening strategies," "relationship intel," the "communication handicap that comes with texting," "connect in person," "what he texts versus what he means," and the "'What Are We?' Talk," examples taken from 2013 editions of the popular magazine *Cosmopolitan*.

Fourth, researchers should examine what is the force, if any, that speech codes have on the thought and conduct of people who use those codes. Proposition 5 of speech codes theory implies that just because someone uses a speech code does not mean that the person's thought is restricted or shaped by that use, or that the person's communicative conduct is determined by the terms of the code. At the same time, there is a great deal of evidence that such codes indeed do have some shaping influence on the thought and conduct of those who use them. The question of cultural and linguistic determinism is a classic and enduring one. The more elaborated development elsewhere of Proposition 5 suggests several important lines of research that need to be pursued before we have a satisfactory understanding of the force of speech codes.

References

Bellah, R., Madsen R., Sullivan, W., Swidler, A., & Tipton, S. (1985). *Habits of the heart: Individualism and commitment in American life.* Berkeley: University of California Press.
Bilicki, B., & Goetz, M. (1995, April). What went wrong in the first place? *Woman's Own, 60.*
Carbaugh, D. (1988). *Talking American: Cultural discourses on DONAHUE.* Norwood, NJ: Ablex.
Coutu, L. M. (2000). Communication codes of rationality and spirituality in the discourse of and about Robert S. McNamara's In Retrospect. *Research on Language and Social Interaction, 33,* 179–211.
Gullestad, M. (1992). *The art of social relations: Essays on culture, social action and everyday life in modern Norway.* New York, NY: Oxford University Press.
Hollandsworth, S. (1995, May/June). 7 things you must know about a man before you get involved with him. *American Woman, 7,* 30.
Katriel, T., & Philipsen, G. (1981). "What we need is communication": "Communication" as a cultural category in some American speech. *Communication Monographs, 48,* 302–317.
Philipsen, G. (1975). Speaking "like a man" in Teamsterville: Culture patterns of role enactment in an urban neighborhood. *Quarterly Journal of Speech, 61,* 13–22.
Philipsen, G. (1976). Places for speaking in Teamsterville. *Quarterly Journal of Speech, 62,* 15–25.
Philipsen, G. (1986). Mayor Daley's council speech: A cultural analysis. *Quarterly Journal of Speech, 72,* 247–260.
Philipsen, G. (1992). *Speaking culturally: Explorations in social communication.* Albany, NY: SUNY Press.
Philipsen, G. (1997). A theory of speech codes. In G. Philipsen & T. L. Albrecht (Eds.), *Developing communication theories* (pp. 119–156). Albany, NY: SUNY Press.
Philipsen, G. (2003). Cultural communication. In W. Gudykunst (Ed.), *Cross-cultural and intercultural communication* (pp. 33–52).Thousand Oaks, CA: Sage.
Philipsen, G. (2010). Some thoughts on how to approach finding one's feet in unfamiliar cultural terrain. *Communication Monographs 77,* 160–168.
Philipsen, G., & Coutu, L. (2005). The ethnography of speaking. In K. Fitch & R. Sanders (Eds.), *Handbook of language and social interaction* (pp. 355–379). Mahwah, NJ: Erlbaum.
Philipsen, G., Coutu, L., & Covarrubias, P. (2005). Speech codes theory: Restatement, revisions, and response to criticisms. In W. Gudykunst (Ed.), *Theorizing about intercultural communication* (pp. 55–68). Thousand Oaks, CA: Sage.
Philipsen, G., Horkley, N., & Huhman, M. (1999). *"Communication" as a keyword in American culture.* Unpublished paper.
Quinn, N. (1982). "Commitment" in American marriage: A cultural analysis. *American Ethnologist, 9,* 775–798.
Rosenthal, P. (1984). *Words and values: Some leading words and where they lead us.* New York, NY: Oxford University Press.
Swidler, A. (2001). *Talk of love: How culture matters.* Chicago, IL: University of Chicago Press.

PART III

Relationship-Centered Theories of Interpersonal Communication

C hapters in the third and final part of the book share a relationship-centered approach to interpersonal communication, centered on understanding the role of communication in developing, enacting, sustaining, and terminating social and personal relationships. Communication scholars have been an integral part of an interdisciplinary and international group of researchers dedicated to the scientific study of personal relationships, an effort that kicked into gear in the late 1980s. Most of the scholars in this section of the book are active members of the International Association for Relationship Research (IARR), which includes members from disciplines including communication studies, family studies and child development, gerontology, psychology, and sociology (although we would note that many other scholars in the present volume are active in this association). What is unique about Part III is that the theories cohere around the context of personal relationships rather than around individual message production or processing, or discourse and interaction, as we saw in Parts I and II, respectively.

There are nine theories represented in this part of the book. Seven of the nine theories were developed by scholars who identify professionally with the communication discipline: Affection Exchange Theory, Communication Privacy Management Theory, Interpersonal Deception Theory, Media Multiplexity Theory, Relational Turbulence, Relationship Stages Theories, and Social Information Processing Theory. Two of the theories, Media Multiplexity and Relational Turbulence, are new to this edition of the book. The contributions of the communication discipline to the study of close relationships is evident from the development of these theories. Attachment Theory and Social Exchange Theories were developed in psychology and have been used extensively in that discipline and in several others.

Akin to the chapters in Part II, the chapters in Part III represent the breadth of meta-theoretical perspectives. Seven of the nine theories spring from post-positivism: Affection Exchange Theory, Attachment Theory, Interpersonal Deception Theory, Media Multiplexity Theory, Relational Turbulence, Social Exchange Theories, and Social Information Processing Theory. Common to these theories is the goal of explanation and prediction of patterns among communication variables. For those theories developed both from inside and from outside communication studies, the theorists presume an objective reality and cause-and-effect or functional patterns that can be discovered via scientific observation. In fact you will notice that some of these authors talk about their theories as scientific theories. For example, in their chapter on Affection Exchange Theory, Floyd, Judd, and Generous refer to the theory "as a scientific theory. Its principal purpose is to explain why human beings communicate affection to each other, and with what consequences." Clearly you can see the authors' goals fitting into the post-positivist paradigm.

Finally, as we saw in Part II of this volume, some theories defy categorization into one meta-theoretical discourse. Sometimes it is because theories originate in one paradigm and are adopted and studied by researchers in another tradition. We believe that is the case with Communication Privacy Management Theory. This theory originates from the communication studies discipline, which stems originally from research on self-disclosure begun in social psychology. The theory has been used by post-positivistic researchers interested in predicting and explaining boundaries and the regulation of revealing and concealing private information in dyadic, family, group, or organizational systems. Petronio and Durham rightly point out that the theory also has been used by interpretive scholars to understand the process of boundary regulation in various contexts. In terms of Relationship Stage Theories, the authors argue for their roots in post-positivism with more recent approaches also sharing assumptions of the interpretivist paradigm.

As with the chapters in Parts I and II of the book, the chapters in Part III also can be woven together with additional themes beyond paradigmatic membership. Several of the chapters emphasize how individuals produce and process messages, and thus could just as easily be grouped with the chapters in Part I were it not for their explicit focus on the context of personal relationships. Included in this grouping are Attachment Theory, Social Exchange Theory, Communication Privacy Management Theory, and Social Information Processing Theory. Other theories in this section display a focus on discourse and interaction patterns, including Relational Communication Theory, Relational Dialectics Theory, and Relationship Stage Theories.

Two of the theories—Affection Exchange Theory and Attachment Theory—provide examples of theories that draw on bioevolutionary arguments, although in different ways. Two of the chapters are explicitly focused on how relationships change over time: Relationship Stage Theories and Social Information Processing Theory. Relational Turbulence, while growing out of earlier work in uncertainty, focuses on messages and challenges during times of relational transition. Other theories focus on factors that motivate individuals to enter into, sustain, and terminate relationships, including Affection Exchange Theory, Attachment Theory, and Social Exchange Theory. Two of the theories, Media Multiplexity and Social Information Processing, help enlighten the central role of social media in interaction and the enactment of personal relationships.

Taken together, the chapters in this section of the book focus more narrowly than the chapters in the first two parts of the book. Whereas those chapters focus on face-to-face communication more generally, the chapters in this section share an interest in answering questions regarding why and how personal relationships form and function.

23

Affection Exchange Theory

A Bio-Evolutionary Look at Affectionate Communication

Kory Floyd, Colin Hesse,
and Mark Alan Generous

M any interpersonal relationships are initiated and maintained through
the exchange of affectionate behaviors, such as hugging, kissing, hand
holding, or saying "I love you." Indeed, expressions of affection often serve as
turning points that advance relational development. Affectionate communication contributes not only to the health of relationships, but also to the physical
health of the people in them. Why humans engage in affectionate behavior, and
why it is associated with these benefits, are among the questions addressed by
affection exchange theory (AET). This chapter will describe the purpose and
assumptions of AET and delineate its basic principles. It will also identify how
AET conceptually defines communication, and it will review some of the
research that has used AET to increase understanding of personal relationships. Finally, it will address the theory's strengths and limitations, and offer
suggestions for future research and applications.

Intellectual Tradition of AET

Affection exchange theory (AET) is a scientific communication theory that
most closely aligns with the paradigmatic assumptions of the post-positivist
tradition. Floyd originally proposed the theory in 2001 and articulated it more
fully in 2006. Its principal purpose is to explain why human beings communicate affection to each other, and with what consequences. AET's fundamental

assumptions are grounded in neo-Darwinian thought, particularly insofar as they suppose that (a) procreation and survival are superordinate human goals; (b) communicative behaviors can serve one or both of these superordinate goals, even in ways that aren't immediately apparent (such as by reinforcing close relationships with friends, who can contribute to survival by providing us with shelter and food during a crisis or contribute to procreation by introducing us to potential romantic partners); and (c) individuals need not be consciously aware of the evolutionary goals their behaviors serve.

Undergirding these are two even more fundamental assumptions. The first is that humans, like other living organisms, are subject to the principles of natural selection and sexual selection. As articulated by Darwin, these include the notion that heritable characteristics or tendencies that advantage an organism with respect to procreation or survival will be *selected for,* ensuring their greater representation in succeeding generations. For instance, any genetic characteristics that predispose people to be more affectionate will increase in frequency from generation to generation if affectionate behavior contributes to survival or procreation. The second fundamental assumption is that human communicative behavior is only partially subject to the willful control of the communicator. Evolved adaptive tendencies, as well as physiological influences (such as those of hormones), affect communicative behavior in ways that are not necessarily evident to the conscious self. As such, AET assumes that communication is affected not only by socially constructed influences (such as gender roles or cultural norms), but also by influences that are grounded in biology and evolutionary adaptation.

Main Goals and Features of AET

AET begins with the proposition that *the need and capacity for affection are inborn* (Proposition 1). That is, humans are born both with the ability and with the need to feel affection, which is defined as an internal state of fondness and intense positive feeling for a living target. This proposition has two important implications, the first of which is that humans need not learn to feel affection, but that both the ability and the need to experience affection are innate. The second implication is that the need for affection is fundamental in the human species, which implies benefits when it is met and negative consequences when it is unfulfilled.

The second proposition of AET is that *affectionate feelings and affectionate expressions are distinct experiences that often, but need not, covary* (Proposition 2). Here, the theory differentiates between the emotional experience of affection and the behaviors through which it is expressed. This distinction is consequential for two reasons. First, humans have the ability to experience affection without expressing it. One may have affectionate feelings for another, for instance, but fail to express them out of fear of rejection or out of deference to the social constraints of the context. Second, humans can express affection without feeling it, which is often done in the service of politeness norms but can also serve ulterior motives, such as acquisition of a favor.

The third, and perhaps most important, proposition is that *affectionate communication is adaptive with respect to human viability and fertility* (Proposition 3). This is the heart of AET, the proposal that receiving and conveying affectionate expressions contributes to survival and procreation success. Specifically, AET identifies two principal causal pathways through which affectionate communication serves these superordinate goals. One is that affectionate behavior promotes the establishment and maintenance of relationships, increasing access to material resources (such as food or shelter) and emotional resources (such as attention or social support) that help sustain life. The other is that engaging in affectionate communication portrays oneself to potential mating partners as a viable partner and a fit potential parent. The idea here is that conveying affection to a romantic partner can denote the emotional capacity and commitment necessary to be a loving mate and a responsible parent.

AET further provides that, because the motivations of survival and procreation are so fundamental, the experiences of feeling and exchanging affection covary with physiological characteristics governing immune system strength, stress, and reward. This sub-proposition addresses the question of why giving and receiving affection within a positive interpersonal relationship (such as a friendship or marriage) is so physically rewarding (and likewise, why failing to receive it is so physically aversive). Because these behaviors contribute to survival and procreation, it is adaptive that they would be physically pleasurable (much like eating, sleeping, or having sex are usually physically pleasurable experiences).

Not all affectionate behavior enhances survival and procreation, however. Within the wrong relationships or in the wrong contexts, affectionate communication can inhibit these motivations. AET thus proposes that *humans vary in their optimal tolerances for affection and affectionate behavior* (Proposition 4), and that *affectionate behaviors that violate the range of optimal tolerance are physiologically aversive* (Proposition 5). Floyd (1997; Floyd & Burgoon, 1999) was among the first to speculate that, although affectionate behavior is normatively positive, it can in fact produce quite negative outcomes under certain circumstances. Receiving an affectionate touch from a stranger, for instance, not only violates norms for appropriate social behavior but also can initiate a negative emotional and physiological response (i.e., a stress response). This is in contrast to the positivity typically associated with the exchange of affection, but is expected (according to AET) in situations in which the affectionate behavior may inhibit one's survival or procreation motivation.

How Communication Is Conceptualized in AET

AET conceptually defines only *affectionate* communication, rather than communication in general, although some broader concepts about communication can be derived from its approach. In the theory, affectionate communication is defined as encompassing those behaviors that encode feelings of fondness and intense positive regard and are generally decoded as such by their intended receivers. Although forms of affection display are largely shaped by cultural norms and constrained by contextual demands, it is the presentation (whether accurate or not) of an affectionate emotion that qualifies a behavioral expression as affectionate.

Floyd and Morman's (1998) tripartite model of affectionate behavior adds conceptual clarity by distinguishing between three forms of affection display: *verbal* communication of affection consists of spoken or written affectionate expressions such as "I love you," or "You mean so much to me"; *direct nonverbal,* which includes nonlinguistic or paralinguistic behaviors that denote affection within the relationship or speech community in which they are used (e.g., in North America, these include behaviors such as hugging, kissing, or holding hands); and *indirect nonverbal,* which is composed of behaviors that connote affection through the provision of social or material support (e.g., helping with a task or lending the use of a car). Unlike with verbal and direct nonverbal expressions, the affectionate message in indirect nonverbal expressions is ancillary to the behavior itself, and is consequently less overt.

As noted above, AET conceives of affectionate communication as a behavior that is affected by both socially constructed and evolutionarily derived influences, and that is only partially under the conscious control of the communicator. These assumptions are not necessarily limited to *affectionate* communication, per se, so although AET does not conceptualize other forms of communication, the theory would apply these conceptual principles to communicative behavior in general.

Research and Practical Applications of AET

Since AET was originally proposed in 2001 (Floyd, 2001), nearly 30 different tests of the theory have been conducted to help understand processes of interpersonal communication better. Many of these tests belong to one of two general categories: (1) those that have focused on which relationships are more affectionate than others (as well as the relational consequences of that affection), and (2) those that have focused on the mental and physical health benefits of being affectionate. Findings from both groups of studies are reviewed in this section.

AFFECTIONATE COMMUNICATION AND RELATIONSHIPS

AET proposes that affectionate communication serves as a resource that can contribute both to survival and reproductive success through the enhancement of relational bonds within various relationship types. As Hamilton (1964) originally proposed, reproductive success involves contributing one's genetic materials to future generations. Thus, individuals can achieve reproductive success not only by having children of their own, but also by ensuring the survival of others who carry their genes, such as nieces, nephews, grandchildren, and cousins. Importantly, personal relationships vary in terms of their level of genetic relatedness; humans share more genes in common with parents than grandparents, for instance, and more with siblings than with cousins. Consequently, some personal relationships are more important than others to genetic reproduction.

If this notion is true, and if affection is a resource that contributes to survival (as AET proposes), then certain relationships should be more affectionate than others. This hypothesis has been tested in several family relationships that vary systematically in their levels of genetic relatedness. For instance, Floyd and Morman (2002) found that men were more affectionate with biological sons than with stepsons, Floyd and Morr (2003) reported that adults were more affectionate with siblings than with siblings-in-law, and Mansson and Booth-Butterfield (2011) discovered that grandchildren received more direct and indirect nonverbal affection from biological grandparents than from nonbiological grandparents. These findings potentially support alternative, non-evolutionary explanations. For example, most fathers, siblings, and grandparents likely feel emotionally closer to, and have known their biological family members longer than, their nonbiological family members. As a result, variables such as closeness or relationship duration could account for the difference in affectionate behavior observed between these relationship types. The studies of father/son and sibling/sibling-in-law relationships ruled out numerous competing explanations, however. Specifically, the differences in affectionate behavior between biological sons and stepsons, and between siblings and siblings-in-law, could not be accounted for by differences in closeness, duration of the relationship, how far apart participants lived, how often they saw each other, or other plausible explanations. Even when all of these variables were controlled, the relationships still differed systematically in their levels of affectionate behavior in the ways that AET predicted.

In addition to genetic relatedness, reproductive viability can also influence how one gives affection within familial relationships. Although most parents would likely report being equally affectionate with all of their children, AET hypothesizes instead that parents give more affection to the children who are the most likely to produce offspring themselves (although the theory does not suggest that parents do this consciously). The explanation is that parents have greater reproductive success when their children reproduce than when they do not, making it evolutionarily adaptive to invest the greatest resources in children with the greatest reproductive potential. Several factors may inhibit reproductive probability, including sterility or the inability to attract a mate. Homosexuality also inhibits reproductive probability, and two studies have shown that fathers give more affection to their heterosexual sons than to their homosexual sons (Floyd, 2001; Floyd, Sargent, & Di Corcia, 2004).

Affectionate communication varies not only in familial relationships with respect to genetic relatedness and reproductive likelihood, but also in romantic relationships. Humans communicate affection in romantic relationships to demonstrate that they are invested in the relationship, as well as to enhance relational bonds with romantic partners. Enhancing relational bonds can benefit survival—via increased access to material and emotional resources—and reproductive probability—via availability of reproductive opportunity.

Romantic relationships vary in affection as a result of relational satisfaction and commitment—that is, amount of received affection can predict how satisfied one is in a romantic relationship, whereas expressed affection can predict how committed one feels in a romantic relationship (Horan & Booth-Butterfield, 2010). For example, Denes (2012) found that affectionate communication after sexual intercourse (i.e., "pillow talk") was not only more likely to occur in a committed relationship as opposed to a casual sexual relationship, but that this behavior was also positively related to relational trust, satisfaction, and closeness. Horan (2012) reported that affectionate communication is associated with perceptions of transgressions in romantic relationships, such that received affection is negatively associated with how partners assess the severity and hurt of relational transgressions. Finally, a new line of research seeks to examine how romantic couples implement deceptive affectionate messages (DAMs) within their relationships (Horan & Booth-Butterfield, 2011, 2013). DAMs provide an empirical test of Proposition 2 from AET, that humans can feel affection and not express it, or they can express affection but not really feel affectionate. Horan and Booth-Butterfield discovered that DAMs occur frequently in romantic relationships, and that they often do not make one feel emotionally or physiologically aroused like other, more serious forms of deception. In discussing their findings, these researchers concluded that DAMs are minor forms of deception that couples engage in to maintain positivity within the relationship. Collectively, these studies indicate that humans engage in affectionate behaviors, both genuinely and deceptively, within selective romantic relationships in order to increase relational trust, closeness, and satisfaction. These outcomes together can increase survival and reproductive viability for humans in romantic relationships, as well as improve their physiological health.

AFFECTIONATE COMMUNICATION AND HEALTH

A large body of research already shows that receiving affectionate behavior (especially affectionate touch) is beneficial to physical and mental health (for an extensive review, see Floyd, 2006a). One of the innovative aspects of AET, however, is its proposition that individuals can also reap health benefits by *giving* affection to others. Specifically, AET posits that expressing affection reduces the body's susceptibility to stress and activates its hormonal reward systems, which have sedative and analgesic effects.

Testing these ideas has involved two specific types of studies. The purpose of the first type has been to identify the health parameters that are reliably associated with affectionate behavior. These efforts began with Floyd's (2002) demonstration that highly affectionate people report higher self-esteem, general mental health, social engagement, and life satisfaction, as well as lower susceptibility to depression and stress, than less-affectionate people (see also Floyd, Hess et al., 2005). Floyd and his colleagues have also reported that trait affection level (i.e., how affectionate an individual typically is with others) is positively related to natural killer cell toxicity (Floyd et al., 2013) and 24-hour variation in the stress hormone cortisol (Floyd, 2006b; Floyd & Riforgiate, 2008), and is negatively related to resting heart rate (Floyd, Mikkelson et al., 2007b), resting blood pressure, and blood glucose (Floyd, Hesse, & Haynes, 2007). Whereas these studies have identified health benefits associated with affection, Floyd, Hesse, Boren, and Veksler (in press) recently discovered that trait affection predicts greater antibody activity among those seropositive for the Epstein-Barr virus, an indication of immune system suppression.

Working from these associations, the second type of study has sought to ascertain causal relationships between affectionate behavior and health outcomes. For instance, Floyd, Mikkelson et al. (2007a) demonstrated that affectionate communication accelerates physical recovery from elevated stress, although in a follow-up study, Floyd, Pauley, and Hesse (2010) showed that the pituitary hormone oxytocin plays a buffering role in that effect. Likewise, in a series of experiments, Floyd, Mikkelson, Hesse, and Pauley (2007) and Floyd, Boren, et al. (2009) demonstrated that increasing affectionate behavior can reduce blood lipid levels (which decreases the risk of heart attack and heart disease).

Evaluation of AET

Like all theories, AET enjoys certain strengths and endures certain liabilities. Among the most important strengths of AET is simply that it is the first comprehensive theory about affectionate communication. As a consequence, it is able to explain a wide range of findings identified by studies conducted within different theoretic traditions (see Floyd, 2006a). An additional strength is that AET answers higher-order questions about affectionate communication, such as why human beings are affectionate in the first place. Although other theories have been able to answer lower-order questions, such as when people are likely to reciprocate affectionate expressions, AET provides a conceptually broader and grander view of how affectionate communication contributes to important, enduring human motivations related to survival and procreation. A third strength, implied in the previous section, is that AET's hypotheses have enjoyed substantial empirical support, not only in the areas of family relationships and health, but also in nonverbal communication (Floyd & Ray, 2003) and persuasion (Floyd, Erbert, Davis, & Haynes, 2005).

The most consequential limitation of the theory is the lack of detail it presently offers regarding the pathways through which affectionate communication contributes to physical health. Generalized pathways are delineated, including the body's systems for reward and stress response, but these provide only broad bases for hypothesizing specific physiological effects. Researchers continue to discover, for instance, the particular hormones, chemical messengers, or immune system attributes that are most directly responsible for the benefits that affectionate behavior can bring, so the theory provides only general guidance on these questions. As research in this area continues to mature, it will facilitate greater precision in the theory's predictive ability.

Some may regard AET's relative lack of attention to social learning as an additional limitation, insofar as the theory fails to specify the cultural, political, economic, or environmental variables that account for the most variance in affectionate behavior. These omissions were intentional, not because AET conceives of these sources of variance as inconsequential, but because it adopts a bio-evolutionary approach that privileges the explication of evolutionary and physiological causes over socially constructed ones. This necessarily limits AET's predictive ability, however, just as exclusively social learning theories are similarly limited.

Continuing the Conversation

The exchange of affection is such a fundamental relational activity that its study offers much promise for understanding and improving the human condition. As noted above, one of the most important directions for future research and application relates to the improvement of mental and physical health. As experiments identify how affectionate communication is associated with immunocompetence, stress management, mental and emotional regulation, and other aspects of well-being, these findings may aid in the development of behavioral (nonpharmacological) interventions that could serve as ancillary treatments for physical and mental disorders.

A newly emerging line of empirical work addresses the genetic and neurological substrates of affectionate communication. Are highly affectionate and unaffectionate people "wired differently"? Using electroencephalography to examine neurological activity, Lewis, Heisel, Reinhart, and Tian (2011) predicted and found that high-affection communicators displayed greater relative electrical activity in the left anterior cortex versus the right anterior cortex, whereas the same asymmetry was not evident among low-affection communicators. This is noteworthy insofar as the left cortex mediates our tendency to approach and be friendly with others, which is an important context for affection. More recently, Floyd and Denes (2013) discovered that trait affection is higher for carriers of the GG allele (one of several possible forms of a gene) on the oxytocin receptor polymorphism rs53576 than for carriers of the AG or AA alleles, and that the genotype is more influential for those low in attachment security than for those high in attachment security. This was the first study to document a genetic association with the propensity for affectionate communication. As studies similar to these are conducted, they will begin to shed light on the question of innateness—how acquired or inborn is an individual's level of affectionate behavior? To what extent can we justifiably call it a trait?

These are two arenas in which AET provides testable predictions and useful guidance. Future research in these and other areas will further illuminate the many aspects of human life touched by the communication of affection.

References

Denes, A. (2012). Pillow talk: Exploring disclosures after sexual activity. *Western Journal of Communication, 76,* 91–108.

Floyd, K. (1997). Communicating affection in dyadic relationships: An assessment of behavior and expectancies. *Communication Quarterly, 45,* 68–80.

Floyd, K. (2001). Human affection exchange: I. Reproductive probability as a predictor of men's affection with their sons. *Journal of Men's Studies, 10,* 39–50.

Floyd, K. (2002). Human affection exchange: V. Attributes of the highly affectionate. *Communication Quarterly, 50,* 135–152.

Floyd, K. (2006a). *Communicating affection: Interpersonal behavior and social context.* Cambridge, UK: Cambridge University Press.

Floyd, K. (2006b). Human affection exchange: XII. Affectionate communication is associated with diurnal variation in salivary free cortisol. *Western Journal of Communication, 70,* 47–63.

Floyd, K., Boren, J. P., Hannawa, A. F., Hesse, C., McEwan, B., & Veksler, A. E. (2009). Kissing in marital and cohabiting relationships: Effects on blood lipids, stress, and relationship satisfaction. *Western Journal of Communication, 73,* 113–133.

Floyd, K., & Burgoon, J. K. (1999). Reacting to nonverbal expressions of liking: A test of interaction adaptation theory. *Communication Monographs, 66,* 219–239.

Floyd, K., & Denes, A. (2013, July). *Attachment security and oxytocin receptor gene polymorphism interact to influence affectionate communication.* Paper presented at the annual meeting of the International Communication Association, London, England.

Floyd, K., Erbert, L. A., Davis, K. L., & Haynes, M. T. (2005). *Human affection exchange: XVI. An exploratory study of affectionate expressions as manipulation attempts.* Unpublished manuscript, Arizona State University.

Floyd, K., Hess, J. A., Miczo, L. A., Halone, K. K., Mikkelson, A. C., & Tusing, K. J. (2005). Human affection exchange: VIII. Further evidence of the benefits of expressed affection. *Communication Quarterly, 53,* 285–303.

Floyd, K., Hesse, C., Boren, J. P., & Veksler, A. E. (in press). Affectionate communication can suppress immunity: Trait affection predicts antibody titers to latent Epstein-Barr virus. *Southern Communication Journal.*

Floyd, K., Hesse, C., & Haynes, M. T. (2007). Human affection exchange: XV. Metabolic and cardiovascular correlates of trait expressed affection. *Communication Quarterly, 55,* 79–94.

Floyd, K., Mikkelson, A. C., Hesse, C., & Pauley, P. M. (2007). Affectionate writing reduces total cholesterol: Two randomized, controlled trials. *Human Communication Research, 33,* 119–142.

Floyd, K., Mikkelson, A. C., Tafoya, M. A., Farinelli, L., La Valley, A. G., Judd, J. . . ., & Wilson, J. (2007a). Human affection exchange: XIII. Affectionate communication accelerates neuroendocrine stress recovery. *Health Communication, 22,* 123–132.

Floyd, K., Mikkelson, A. C., Tafoya, M. A., Farinelli, L., La Valley, A. G., Judd, J. . . ., & Wilson, J. (2007b). Human affection exchange: XIV. Relational affection predicts resting heart rate and free cortisol secretion during acute stress. *Behavioral Medicine, 32,* 151–156.

Floyd, K., & Morman, M. T. (1998). The measurement of affectionate communication. *Communication Quarterly, 46,* 144–162.

Floyd, K., & Morman, M. T. (2002). Human affection exchange: III. Discriminative parental solicitude in men's affection with their biological and non-biological sons. *Communication Quarterly, 49,* 310–327.

Floyd, K., & Morr, M. C. (2003). Human affection exchange: VII. Affectionate communication in the sibling/spouse/sibling-in-law triad. *Communication Quarterly, 51,* 247–261.

Floyd, K., Pauley, P. M., & Hesse, C. (2010). State and trait affectionate communication buffer adults' stress reactions. *Communication Monographs, 77,* 618–636.

Floyd, K., Pauley, P. M., Hesse, C., Veksler, A. E., Eden, J., & Mikkelson, A. C. (2013). *Affectionate communication is associated with immunologic and cardiologic health markers.* Manuscript submitted for publication.

Floyd, K., & Ray, G. B. (2003). Human affection exchange: IV. Vocalic predictors of perceived affection in initial interactions. *Western Journal of Communication, 67,* 56–73.

Floyd, K., & Riforgiate, S. (2008). Affectionate communication received from spouses predicts stress hormone levels in healthy adults. *Communication Monographs, 75,* 351–368.

Floyd, K., Sargent, J. E., & Di Corcia, M. (2004). Human affection exchange: VI. Further tests of reproductive probability as a predictor of men's affection with their sons. *Journal of Social Psychology, 144,* 191–206.

Hamilton, W. D. (1964). The genetical evolution of social behavior. I & II. *Journal of Theoretical Biology, 7,* 1–52.

Horan, S. M. (2012). Affection exchange theory and perceptions of relational transgressions. *Western Journal of Communication, 76,* 109–126.

Horan, S. M., & Booth-Butterfield, M. (2010). Investing in affection: An investigation of affection exchange theory and relational qualities. *Communication Quarterly, 58,* 394–413.

Horan, S. M., & Booth-Butterfield, M. (2011). Is it worth lying for? Physiological and emotional implications of recalling deceptive affection. *Human Communication Research, 37,* 78–106.

Horan, S. M., & Booth-Butterfield, M. (2013). Understanding the routine expression of deceptive affection in romantic relationships. *Communication Quarterly, 61,* 195–216.

Lewis, R. J., Heisel, A. D., Reinhart, A. M., & Tian, Y. (2011). Trait affection and asymmetry in the anterior brain. *Communication Research Reports, 28,* 347–355.

Mansson, D. H., & Booth-Butterfield, M. (2011). Grandparents' expressions of affection for their grandchildren: Examining grandchildren's relational attitudes and behaviors, *Southern Communication Journal, 76,* 424–442.

24

Attachment Theory

A Communication Perspective

Laura K. Guerrero

S arah, Elizabeth, and Maria get together to chat about life, love, and their divorces. As they talk, it becomes apparent that each woman is coping with her divorce differently. Sarah's divorce was finalized well over a year ago, yet she is not at all interested in dating. Instead, she throws herself into her career, wanting to prove to herself and her ex-husband that she is self-sufficient. Men who try to get to know Sarah describe her communication as aloof and dismissive. After trying to stop the inevitable, Elizabeth finally signed the divorce papers. She found herself clinging to her children and her sister, and wanting to find someone new because she hates being alone. Yet all of Elizabeth's relationships since the divorce have been short-lived, with her partners saying that Elizabeth wanted to get too close too soon. They describe her communication as overly affectionate and demanding. Maria also hopes for a new love interest, but she is too afraid of being hurt again to pursue any new romantic possibilities. She would rather be alone than risk rejection. Her communication style is passive and hesitant, and on the rare occasions when she does date, she puts a wall around herself so she does not get too attached to her date.

Why are Sarah, Elizabeth, and Maria reacting so differently to their divorces? Attachment theory provides a framework for understanding their reactions, as well as more general differences in people's communication. This chapter advances a communication perspective on attachment theory by showing that communication plays a central role in attachment theory—as a cause, consequence, and reinforcing agent of attachment, and as a mediator between attachment and relationship quality.

Intellectual Tradition of Attachment Theory

Attachment theory is a social scientific theory that crosses disciplinary and methodological boundaries. Attachment theorists have used various research methods, ranging from detailed observations and interviews to questionnaires and laboratory experiments. The theory has also been developed, extended, and tested using both inductive (or grounded) methods and reasoning, as well as deductive methods that involve testing hypotheses derived from the theory. Despite this diversity in approach and method, most scholars consider attachment theory to fall under the umbrella of post-positivism.

Attachment theory has its roots in John Bowlby's observations of maladjusted and hospitalized children. Based on these observations, Bowlby (1951) concluded that having a mutually close, caring, and stable relationship with a caregiver is necessary for a child's healthy mental, emotional, and social development. This basic idea was counter to Freudian psychoanalysis, which was popular at the time. Rather than seeing emotional problems as a product of fantasies and conflicting drives as psychoanalysts did, Bowlby believed that family interaction patterns—and by implication, communication—were critical for children's emotional health. Bowlby's ideas and observations are detailed in his trilogy of books (Bowlby, 1969, 1973, 1980) on attachment, separation, and loss.

Mary Ainsworth's research extended attachment theory, beginning with her observations of infant-mother communication in Uganda (Ainsworth, 1967). Next, Ainsworth conducted in-home observations of children in Baltimore and then compared those observations with findings from an experiment involving one-year-old children (Ainsworth, Blehar, Waters, & Wall, 1978). This experiment, referred to as the strange situation, exposed children to a sequence of events—including having the child and mother interact in a playroom, introducing a stranger into the environment, having the mother (and at some point, the stranger) leave and return—and noted the children's reactions. Three attachment styles emerged: secure, anxious-ambivalent, and avoidant. Secure children explored their environment the most freely, were somewhat upset when their mother left, and were happy when reunited with her. Anxious-ambivalent children were hesitant to explore the environment without their mother present, became extremely anxious when she left, and ambivalent (relieved and angry) when she returned. Avoidant children showed little reaction when their mothers or strangers left or returned. Importantly, observations revealed that secure, anxious-ambivalent, and avoidant children experienced different communication with their caregivers at home.

Another major advancement in attachment theory occurred in the 1980s when psychologists began applying attachment to adult love relationships (e.g., Hazan & Shaver, 1987). Since then, the theory has been applied to various relationships, including those between friends, romantic partners, and siblings. Initially, most scholars theorized that the attachment style a person develops as a child persists into adulthood. However, most scholars now believe that although attachment styles are relatively stable, they can be modified. Around 70% of adults perceive themselves to have a consistent attachment style, while 30% perceive that it has fluctuated (e.g., Davila, Burge, & Hammen, 1997). Attachment styles are stable because the foundation for personality development laid during childhood is strong. In addition, attachment styles are reinforced when people engage in social behaviors consistent with those styles. Changes in attachment style are often precipitated by critical events, such as divorce, death, or developing a healthy relationship. So Elizabeth may have been more secure before her divorce than after her divorce, and Maria might become more secure if she meets someone who patiently waits for her to get over her fear of rejection. Attachment style can also vary as a function of relationship type and relational partner (Pierce & Lydon, 2001). So Sarah might avoid getting close to most people following her divorce, but she may still be close to her mother and daughter.

Although many consider attachment theory to be primarily a psychological theory, Ainsworth and Bowlby (1991) noted that it has always "been eclectic, drawing on a number of scientific disciplines, including developmental, cognitive, social, and personality psychology, systems theory, and various branches of biological science, including genetics" (p. 340). The theory has been used by psychologists, family scholars and clinicians and, to a lesser extent, by communication researchers. Thus, while attachment theory was developed by psychologists it has been applied by scholars from different disciplines, including communication. The vast majority of communication research has focused on adult attachment. Therefore, the remainder of this chapter emphasizes attachment theory as applied to adult relationships.

Main Goals and Features of Attachment Theory

Initially, the main goal of attachment theory was to determine how social interaction between infants and caregivers affects personality development, including emotional health (Ainsworth & Bowlby, 1991). Presently the theory focuses more broadly on how attachment styles function within various types of close relationships. Most research on adult attachment has focused on uncovering attachment-style differences in cognition, emotion, and communication. Indeed, one feature that sets attachment theory apart from other theories is that it is designed to explain and predict cohesive patterns of cognition, emotion, and behavior across the life span.

Attachment styles are based on models of self and others (see Figure 24.1). The model of self reflects the degree to which a person has a positive versus a negative image of self as worthwhile, lovable, and self-sufficient. People with negative models of self have high levels of *attachment anxiety* because they fear rejection or abandonment. The model of others reflects how responsive, caring, and rewarding people expect others to be toward them. People with negative models of others experience high levels of *attachment avoidance* and tend to be uncomfortable with closeness.

Bartholomew and Horowitz (1991) described four distinct attachment styles for adults: *secure* (positive model of self and others), *dismissive* (positive model of self, negative model of others), *preoccupied* (negative model of self, positive model of others), and *fearful* (negative model of self and others). Secure individuals desire a balance of autonomy and closeness within their relationships. Dismissive individuals are fiercely independent, sometimes to the point of distancing others to prove they can cope on their own. They dislike relying on others, and prioritize personal goals and activities over relationships. Preoccupied individuals are exactly the opposite—they crave intimacy and put a much higher premium on close relationships than personal activities.

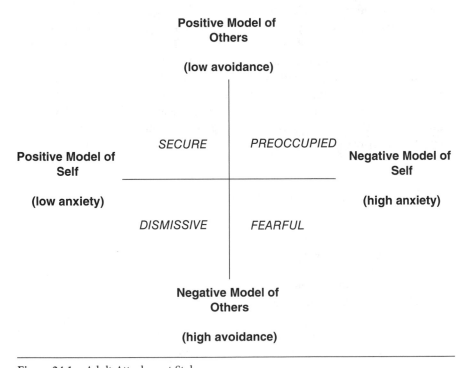

Figure 24.1   Adult Attachment Styles

They cling to their relationships because they worry that their partners will abandon them. Fearful individuals have usually been hurt or rejected in past relationships, so they are afraid of getting close to others even though they would like the security of a close relationship. Take another look at the scenario at the beginning of this chapter. Can you deduce each woman's attachment style? Based on the brief descriptions given, it is likely that Sarah is dismissive, Elizabeth is preoccupied, and Maria is fearful.

Research on adult attachment has focused primarily on two issues: (1) how people with different attachment styles vary in terms of perceptions, emotional experiences, and communication; and (2) how attachment is related to relationship outcomes, such as satisfaction, trust, and stability. For example, Jang, Smith, and Levine (2002) examined how people react upon discovering deception by a relational partner. Secure individuals were most likely to talk about the issue; dismissive individuals were most likely to terminate the relationship. A main tenet of attachment theory is that individuals with secure attachments have more positive thoughts and emotions, communicate in more constructive ways, and have healthier relationships than individuals with insecure attachments. Attachment theorists also seek to identify the types of thoughts, emotions, and communication that are characteristic of people with preoccupied, dismissive, and fearful attachment.

How Communication Is Conceptualized in Attachment Theory

Communication occupies a central position in attachment theory. In fact, communication plays at least four roles in the attachment process, as shown in Figure 24.2 and described next.

COMMUNICATION AS A CAUSE OF ATTACHMENT STYLE

Communication causes attachment styles to develop and change (see Line 1 in Figure 24.2). As discussed previously, young children tend to develop different attachment styles based on communication with caregivers. Communication continues to function as a causal agent of attachment throughout one's life (Ainsworth & Bowlby, 1991). New social interactions with significant others modify existing models of self and others, and, consequently, one's attachment style. A young child who has been neglected by her parents may become more secure after making a few good friends. Conversely, a young man may have wonderful interactions with his family, but if he is criticized and hurt by dating partners, he might develop a fearful attachment in romantic relationships.

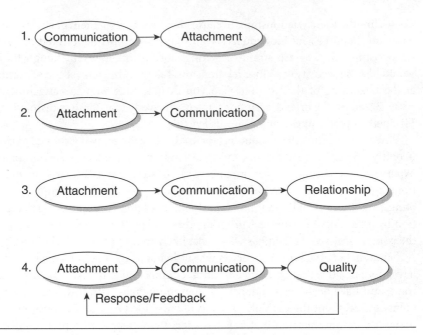

Figure 24.2 Connections Between Communication and Attachment

COMMUNICATION AS A CONSEQUENCE OF ATTACHMENT STYLE

Once an attachment style has developed, communication reflects a person's perceptions of both self and others (see Line 2, Figure 24.2). Take Sarah, Elizabeth, and Maria as examples. Sarah might turn down opportunities to date new men by saying, "I'm too busy with my career to get involved with anyone right now." Such a statement indicates that Sarah sees her personal ambitions as more important than establishing new relationships. Elizabeth might complain to her sister and children that they are not "there for her" when she needs them, or tell dating partners that they do not "spend enough time" with her. These are classic preoccupied statements that reflect Elizabeth's need for self-validation and her fear of being alone. Finally, if Maria's friends manage to talk her into attending a social gathering, she might sit in the corner watching people rather than initiating conversation with someone she finds attractive. In each of these cases, the woman's communication (or in Maria's case, her lack of communication) is a "consequence" of her attachment style.

COMMUNICATION AS A MEDIATOR OF ATTACHMENT AND RELATIONSHIP QUALITY

Research suggests that secure individuals have a communication style that promotes healthy relationships (see Line 3, Figure 24.2). Secure individuals report more relationship satisfaction and stability than individuals with other attachment styles (Feeney, Noller, & Roberts, 2000). Feeney and her colleagues theorized that attachment style differences in communication help explain why secure individuals have more satisfying relationships. Specifically, the use of constructive conflict behavior (Feeney, 1994), self-disclosure (Keelan, Dion, & Dion, 1998), and positive forms of emotional expression (Guerrero, Farinelli, & McEwan, 2009) help explain why secure couples report more relational satisfaction. Thus, communication is a vehicle through which secure individuals develop and maintain successful relationships.

COMMUNICATION AS REINFORCING OF ATTACHMENT STYLE

Attachment styles are self-reinforcing. People tend to communicate in ways that are consistent with their attachment styles, which then leads people to treat them in ways that reinforce their models of self and others (Bartholomew, 1993; see Line 4, Figure 24.2). Secure individuals display communication that reflects self-confidence and positive feelings toward others, leading people to respond positively to them. Interaction with an insecure person is often less enjoyable. Imagine being a friend of Sarah, Elizabeth, or Maria. How might you respond to their behavior? If Sarah rarely returned your phone calls because she was busy with work, you would probably stop calling her. As a result, Sarah might learn to cope without her friends, reinforcing the dismissive notion that relationships are not as important as her own personal goals. If Elizabeth constantly called you to complain about her ex-husband and ask about any single men you know, you would probably start to pull away, which would fuel her preoccupied perception that other people do not value her as much as she values them. With Maria, you might get frustrated that she never wants to go new places and meet people. Eventually Maria's behavior might isolate her from you and her other friends (who would probably stop inviting her to go out with them), and also prevent her from meeting any interesting new men.

Research and Practical Applications of Attachment Theory

People communicate in different ways. Some people are more aggressive than others during conflict. Some people show emotions readily, whereas others are more guarded. Similarly, some individuals are more comfortable giving and receiving affection than others. Attachment theory helps explain these types of individual differences in communication. Specifically, people with different attachment styles vary in terms of relational maintenance behavior, conflict behavior, expressions of intimacy and emotion, and social skill.

MAINTENANCE BEHAVIOR

Secure individuals report using more prosocial maintenance behaviors, such as being romantic, sharing activities, assuring one another of commitment, and acting cheerful and optimistic, than do individuals with insecure attachment styles (Bippus & Rollin, 2003; Guerrero & Bachman, 2006; Simon & Baxter, 1993). Secure individuals also interpret their partners' attempts to repair a relationship more positively by viewing those messages as more polite and honest (Bello, Brandau-Brown, & Ragsdale, 2008). Furthermore, people with insecure attachment styles report using more antisocial behavior to try to maintain their relationships. For example, compared to secure individuals, dismissive and fearful individuals are more likely to report inducing jealousy as a way to maintain their relationships, whereas preoccupied individuals are more likely to report using spying (Goodboy & Bolkan, 2011).

CONFLICT BEHAVIOR

Secure individuals also engage in more constructive conflict behavior than do insecure individuals. Pietromonaco, Greenwood, and Feldman Barrett (2004) explained that because secure individuals feel less threatened by conflict, they are better able to focus on problem solving. Preoccupied individuals see conflict as a threat because they fear abandonment, dismissive individuals see conflict as a threat because managing conflict requires disclosure and shows interdependence, and fearful individuals see conflict as a threat for all these reasons (Pietromonaco et al., 2004). People with avoidant attachment styles (dismissive and fearful) are most likely to use withdrawal and defensiveness in response to conflict, whereas preoccupied individuals are most likely to engage in demanding behavior, nagging, and whining (e.g., O'Connell-Corcoran & Mallinckrodt, 2000). Secure individuals, in contrast, engage more problem solving and compromise during conflict (Bippus & Rollin, 2003; Pistole, 1989). Couples comprised of a preoccupied and a dismissive partner may be especially likely to engage in demand-withdraw conflict patterns, with the preoccupied partner demanding more intimacy and the dismissive partner withdrawing (Millwood & Waltz, 2008). Couples containing two secure partners report engaging in the least demand-withdrawal (Domingue & Mollen, 2009). Men with a preoccupied (or anxious) attachment style are also more likely to engage in aggressive communication, especially if their relationship is characterized by demand-withdraw (Fournier, Brassard, & Shaver, 2011).

EXPRESSIONS OF INTIMACY

Individuals with positive models of others (secures and preoccupieds) exhibit more nonverbal and verbal intimacy than those with negative models of others (dismissives and fearfuls). Two studies looked at nonverbal communication during conversations between romantic partners. In the first study (Guerrero, 1996), secure and preoccupied individuals displayed more facial and vocal pleasantness, interest, and attentiveness than did dismissive and fearful individuals. In the second study (Tucker & Anders, 1998), secure individuals displayed more laughter, touch, smiling, expressiveness, and enjoyment than did people with insecure attachment styles. Findings for self-disclosure follow a similar pattern. Secure individuals engage in the most "appropriate and flexible patterns of self-disclosure" (Feeney et al., 2000, p. 198). Preoccupied individuals also engage in high levels of self-disclosure; however, their disclosure is sometimes inappropriate or indiscriminate (Mikulincer & Nachshon, 1991). The two avoidant styles of attachment—dismissive and fearful—are characterized by lower levels of disclosure (Feeney et al., 2000).

EMOTIONAL EXPRESSION

Attachment style is also related to how people express emotion. Compared to secure spouses, anxious spouses are less likely to express love, and avoidant husbands are less likely to express love, pride, or happiness (Feeney, 1999). Secure individuals respond to jealousy in constructive ways that help maintain relationships, whereas preoccupied individuals report relatively high levels of surveillance behavior (such as checking up on the partner), and fearful and dismissive individuals tend to deny jealous feelings (Guerrero, 1998). While angry, secure individuals are likely to use negotiation or assertive communication, preoccupied individuals are likely to use aggressive or passive aggressive behavior, and fearful individuals are likely to use passive behavior (Feeney, 1995; Guerrero et al., 2009). Of the four styles, secure individuals are most likely to cope with sadness by seeking social support from others and engaging in positive activity that distracts them from their problems (Guerrero et al., 2009).

SOCIAL SKILL

Secure individuals are the most socially skilled in terms of expressing themselves, responding appropriately to others, and providing comfort to others (Kunce & Shaver, 1994; Weger & Polcar, 2002). Dismissive and fearful individuals are especially likely to have trouble expressing themselves and comforting others, preoccupied individuals are especially likely to be overly sensitive and anxious, and fearful individuals are especially likely to lack assertiveness (Guerrero & Jones, 2005). Fearful individuals may be the least socially skilled of the four styles because their high levels of avoidance and anxiety keep them from initiating social interaction and developing interpersonal skills. In conversations with romantic partners, fearful individuals show signs of anxiety (e.g., a lack of fluency, long response latencies, and a lack of composure) as well as signs of avoidance (e.g., relatively far proxemic distancing and low levels of focus on the partner; Guerrero, 1996; Guerrero & Jones, 2005), suggesting that their negative models of self and others are indeed reflected in behavior.

Evaluation of Attachment Theory

Attachment theory's strengths include its intuitive appeal, parsimony, applicability, generalizability, multidisciplinary nature, and ability to generate research. Attachment theory is intuitively appealing. People can relate to the four attachment styles and see themselves and others fitting into certain styles. The theory is parsimonious as the concept of attachment style represents the intersection of working models of self and others while also explaining coherent patterns of cognition, emotion, and behavior. Attachment-style differences have been found for a variety of perceptions, emotions, and behaviors, making the theory applicable to many aspects of relationship functioning. Attachment theory is also generalizable to various relationships that occur throughout the life span. Another important strength of attachment theory is that it crosses disciplinary and methodological boundaries, which has promoted dialogue among scholars from different fields, leading to a more comprehensive understanding of attachment processes. Perhaps the most impressive strength of attachment theory is its ability to generate research. As of 2013, Bowlby's trilogy of attachment books was cited over 26,000 times in Google Scholar, Ainsworth et al.'s (1978) book was cited nearly 13,000 times, and over 59,000 results emerged in a Google Scholar search for the phrase "attachment theory."

In some ways, attachment theory has also been plagued by its popularity. When a theory becomes popular, it can attain a kind of "fad" status, with everyone attempting to undertake research and publish research on that topic. This leads to a surge of research, but sometimes the research varies greatly in quality. This is the case in some research involving attachment, where it appears that attachment was thrown in as a variable without much theoretical justification. A related limitation is that attachment style is often treated solely as a personality variable. This has led some communication scholars to argue that attachment theory is not a theory at all, but rather a glorified individual-difference variable. However, the best studies on attachment are usually grounded in theoretical principles focused on the underlying mechanisms of attachment—such as models of self and others and the accumulated experiences that people have in relationships. As research on adult attachment has progressed, studies have generally become more sophisticated and nuanced.

Another common critique focuses on how attachment styles are measured. Research exploring differences based on adult attachment styles progressed more rapidly than work aimed at developing reliable and valid measures of attachment. As a result, researchers measure attachment using a variety of methods, which makes it difficult to compare, contrast, and generalize findings from different studies. Currently, many attachment researchers examine two dimensions, anxiety and avoidance, which are thought to tap into working models of self and others, respectively. While these dimensions are important, they do not capture the unique features that characterize the four attachment styles. For example, knowing Elizabeth is high in anxiety and low in avoidance fails to provide information about how much she craves closeness and obsesses over her relationships. Knowing Maria is high in both anxiety and avoidance does not tell researchers how much she fears intimacy. Thus, the best system for measuring attachment may include gauging anxiety and avoidance, as well as characteristics unique to each style (such as preoccupation and fear of intimacy).

Continuing the Conversation

From a communication perspective, it would be helpful for researchers to better understand the practical role that communication plays in attachment theory. Bowlby hoped clinicians would use principles of attachment theory to help insecure people develop more positive models of themselves and others (Ainsworth & Bowlby, 1991). Counselors and clinicians can apply attachment theory to help people develop the types of social skills that improve their models of self and others and, ultimately, promote healthier relationships. Knowing partners' attachment styles may uncover potential problem areas. For instance, if a dismissive is paired with a preoccupied, these individuals are likely to have different needs regarding how close or interdependent they want to be. The preoccupied person needs to give the dismissive person space, and the dismissive person needs to remember to show affection once in a while. Imagine how you could help Sarah, Elizabeth, and Maria develop more secure styles. You might entice Sarah to engage in interesting social activities that complement her personal goals. With Elizabeth, you might resist the impulse to pull away and instead listen to her problems and bolster her self-esteem. Finally, you might gradually introduce Maria to a wider circle of friends who may help her feel comfortable in new social situations.

Although attachment theory is highly developed, questions still remain. From a communication perspective, it is critical to learn more about how communication modifies and reinforces attachment styles, as well as how communication helps explain why secure people generally have healthier relationships than insecure people. Longitudinal studies could involve instructing one partner to engage in behaviors that might help bolster the other partner's model of self or others, perhaps by increasing affection, providing the partner more space, or complimenting the partner more often. Over time, these behaviors could improve an insecure person's model of self or others. Communication researchers should also try to uncover patterns of behavior that reinforce attachment styles by looking at how people respond to preoccupied, fearful, and dismissive behavior. Finally, research has determined that attachment-style differences in self-disclosure, conflict behavior, and emotional communication influence relational satisfaction; there are likely other types of communication that help explain why secure attachment is related to satisfaction. Pinpointing these behaviors may help people build and sustain better relationships.

In sum, communication scholars have been slower than researchers from other disciplines to use attachment theory in their work. Yet communication research could highlight and extend some of the key ideas in the theory, as well as provide explanations for why attachment styles are relatively stable yet changeable, and how attachment-related behavior influences the development, maintenance, and satisfaction level of relationships. As such, communication researchers are poised to make important contributions to the further refinement and extension of attachment theory.

References

Ainsworth, M. D. S. (1967). *Infancy in Uganda: Infant care and the growth of love.* Baltimore, MD: Johns Hopkins University Press.

Ainsworth, M. D. S., Blehar, M. C., Waters, E., & Wall, S. (1978). *Patterns of attachment: A psychological study of the strange situation.* Hillsdale, NJ: Erlbaum.

Ainsworth, M. D. S., & Bowlby, J. (1991). An ethological approach to personality development. *American Psychologist, 46,* 333–341.

Bartholomew, K. (1993). From childhood to adult relationships: Attachment theory and research. In S. Duck (Ed.), *Understanding relationship processes: Vol. 2. Learning about relationships* (pp. 30–62). Newbury Park, CA: Sage.

Bartholomew, K., & Horowitz, L. M. (1991). Attachment styles among young adults: A test of a four-category model. *Journal of Personality and Social Psychology, 61,* 226–244.

Bello, R. S., Brandau-Brown, F. E., & Ragsdale, J. D. (2008). Attachment style, marital satisfaction, commitment, and communal strength effects on relational repair message interpretation among remarrieds. *Communication Quarterly, 56,* 1–16

Bippus, A. M., & Rollin, E. (2003). Attachment style differences in relational maintenance and conflict behaviors: Friends' perceptions. *Communication Reports, 16,* 113–123.

Bowlby, J. (1951). *Maternal care and mental health.* Geneva, Switzerland: World Health Organization.

Bowlby, J. (1969). *Attachment and loss: Vol. 1. Attachment.* New York, NY: Basic Books.

Bowlby, J. (1973). *Attachment and loss: Vol. 2. Separation.* New York, NY: Basic Books.

Bowlby, J. (1980). *Attachment and loss, Vol. 3: Loss, sadness and depression.* New York, NY: Basic Books.

Davila, J., Burge, D., & Hammen, C. (1997). Why does attachment style change? *Journal of Personality and Social Psychology, 73,* 826–838.

Domingue, R., & Mollen, D. (2009). Attachment and conflict communication in adult romantic relationships. *Journal of Social and Personal Relationships, 26,* 678–696.

Feeney, J. A. (1994). Attachment style, communication patterns, and satisfaction across the life cycle of marriage. *Personal Relationships, 1,* 333–348.

Feeney, J. A. (1995). Adult attachment and emotional control. *Personal Relationships, 2,* 143–159.

Feeney, J. A. (1999). Adult attachment, emotional control, and marital satisfaction. *Personal Relationships, 6,* 169–185.

Feeney, J. A., Noller, P., & Roberts, N. (2000). Attachment and close relationships. In C. Hendrick & S. S. Hendrick (Eds.), *Close relationships: A sourcebook* (pp. 185–201). Thousand Oaks, CA: Sage.

Fournier, B., Brassard, A., & Shaver, P. R. (2011). Adult attachment and male aggression in couple relationships: The demand-withdraw communication pattern and relationship satisfaction as mediators. *Journal of Interpersonal Violence, 26,* 1982–2003.

Goodboy, A. K., & Bolkan, S. (2011). Attachment and the use of negative relational maintenance behaviors in romantic relationships. *Communication Research Reports, 28,* 327–336.

Guerrero, L. K. (1996). Attachment-style differences in intimacy and involvement: A test of the four-category model. *Communication Monographs, 63,* 269–292.

Guerrero, L. K. (1998). Attachment-style differences in the experience and expression of romantic jealousy. *Personal Relationships, 5,* 273–291.

Guerrero, L. K., & Bachman, G. F. (2006). Associations among relational maintenance behaviors, attachment-style categories, and attachment dimensions. *Communication Studies, 57,* 341–361.

Guerrero, L. K., Farinelli, L., & McEwan, B. (2009). Attachment and relational satisfaction: The mediating effect of emotional communication. *Communication Monographs, 76,* 487–514.

Guerrero, L. K., & Jones, S. M. (2005). Differences in conversational skills as a function of attachment style: A follow-up study. *Communication Quarterly, 53,* 305–321.

Hazan, C., & Shaver, P. (1987). Conceptualizing romantic love as an attachment process. *Journal of Personality and Social Psychology, 52,* 511–524.

Jang, S. A., Smith, S. W., & Levine, T. R. (2002). To stay or to leave? The role of attachment styles in communication patterns and potential termination of romantic relationships following discovery of deception. *Communication Monographs, 69,* 236–252.

Keelan, J. P. R., Dion, K. K., & Dion, K. L. (1998). Attachment style and relationship satisfaction: Test of a self-disclosure explanation. *Canadian Journal of Behavioural Science, 30,* 24–35.

Kunce, L. J., & Shaver, P. R. (1994). An attachment-theoretical approach to caregiving in romantic relationships. In K. Bartholomew & D. Perlman (Eds.), *Advances in personal relationships: Vol. 5. Attachment processes in adulthood* (pp. 205–237). Bristol, PA: Kingsley.

Mikulincer, M., & Nachshon, O. (1991). Attachment styles and patterns of self-disclosure. *Journal of Personality and Social Psychology, 61,* 321–331.

Millwood, M., & Waltz, J. (2008). Demand-withdraw communication in couples: An attachment perspective. *Journal of Couple and Relationship Therapy, 7,* 297–320.

O'Connell-Corcoran, K., & Mallinckrodt, B. (2000). Adult attachment, self-efficacy, perspective taking, and conflict resolution. *Journal of Counseling and Development, 78*, 473–483.

Pierce, T., & Lydon, J. E. (2001). Global and specific relational models in the experience of social interactions. *Journal of Personality and Social Psychology, 80*, 613–631.

Pietromonaco, P. R., Greenwood, D., & Feldman Barrett, L. (2004). Conflict in adult close relationships: An attachment perspective. In W. S. Rholes & J. A. Simpson (Eds.), *Adult attachment: New directions and emerging issues* (pp. 267–299). New York, NY: Guilford.

Pistole, M. C. (1989). Attachment in adult romantic relationships: Style of conflict resolution and relationship satisfaction. *Journal of Social and Personal Relationships, 6*, 505–510.

Simon, E. P., & Baxter, L. A. (1993). Attachment-style differences in relationship maintenance strategies. *Western Journal of Communication, 57*, 416–430.

Tucker, J. S., & Anders, S. L. (1998). Adult attachment style and nonverbal closeness in dating couples. *Journal of Nonverbal Behavior, 22*, 109–124.

Weger, H., & Polcar, L. E. (2002). Attachment style and person-centered comforting. *Western Journal of Communication, 66*, 64–103.

25

Communication Privacy Management Theory

Significance for Interpersonal Communication

Sandra Petronio and Wesley T. Durham

L auren was a 20-year-old college student who seemingly had everything. She was voted football Homecoming Queen, her grades were exceptional, and she had a full-ride scholarship. Life was good. However, during the summer between her junior and senior year, Lauren's dreams were altered. Immediately following her junior year, her college sweetheart broke off their romantic relationship. Surprised and brokenhearted, Lauren began drinking and partying heavily, finding herself having a string of regrettable sexual encounters.

At the beginning of senior year, Lauren and her college sweetheart rekindled their relationship. Lauren was as happy as she had ever been. However, as she did every fall, Lauren donated blood during the university's blood drive. Four weeks after donating, Lauren was notified that her blood had tested positive for HIV. The counselor told her that she needed to notify all individuals with whom she had intercourse because they might have been exposed to the virus. Immediately, Lauren began to panic. She wondered how to tell her previous sexual partners, her parents, her friends, and more importantly her boyfriend.

Lauren's story indicates the tensions and decisions that can accompany managing private information. In our everyday lives, there is a complexity to privacy management. We need a road map to find the right path so we do not feel embarrassed, hurt someone's feelings, or reveal more than we want to others. Theoretical frameworks and research generated from theories can give insights into why we make certain decisions. They help us see potential mistakes, and assist in understanding ways we think about privacy and how we cope with privacy infractions. This chapter gives a brief introduction to a theory called communication privacy management (CPM), developed by one of the authors, Petronio (2002, 2013). In this chapter, we discuss the purpose, principles, and value of CPM. CPM is a theory that assists researchers, students, and practitioners to grasp how individuals reveal and conceal private information.

Intellectual Tradition of Communication Privacy Management Theory

CPM is a "homegrown" communication theory based on systematic research designed to develop an evidence-based understanding of the way people regulate revealing and concealing. On initially encountering CPM, it is helpful to leave previously held beliefs about disclosure behind. Unlike earlier theories, CPM views "disclosure" as the process of revealing private information, yet always in relation to concealing private information. Since these two concepts are in a dialectical tension with each other, the way revealing and concealing take place is through a rule management system. This notion shifts the frame from focusing only on "self-disclosure" to a broader, more comprehensive view that includes "private disclosures" capturing both the elements of privacy and the process of disclosure. Petronio (2002) argued that "CPM makes private information, as the content of what is disclosed, a primary focal point" (p. 3). CPM also depends on the notion of boundaries to give us a way to conceptualize how the management process works.

Unlike many theories fitting neatly within one particular methodological paradigm, CPM has proven to be a useful theoretical tool for interpretivists and post-positivists alike. This is largely because CPM was not developed as a methodology. An interpretivist's research methods capture human action that is purposive and socially embedded to determine meaning attributed by others who interact from within that same web of meaning (Baxter & Babbie, 2004). Thus, CPM can be used within an interpretivist's methodological frame insofar as human action, such as the disclosure of private information, is purposive, rule driven, and interpreted by those participating in the disclosure event. On the other hand, CPM has also been used successfully to guide post-positivist research. According to Baxter and Babbie (2004), post-positivist research attempts to explain, predict, and control human behavior. For instance, Caughlin and his colleagues have effectively used CPM to guide post-positivist research on the correlation between topic avoidance and relational (dis)satisfaction (e.g., Caughlin & Afifi, 2004). This theory gives versatility of methodology because it was not developed with a methodological objective as its guide.

Instead, CPM theory offers principles and a prospective that allow researchers to use different methodologies.

Main Goals and Features of Communication Privacy Management Theory

CPM is organized around three guiding maxims. First, we discuss *assumption maxims* that underlie CPM theory. Next, we introduce *axiomatic maxims* that represent main principles defining privacy management according to CPM theory. Last, we discuss *interaction maxims* found in CPM theory that guide communicative actions in regulating privacy.

The assumption maxims include: (1) public-private dialectical assumptions, (2) privacy management assumptions, and (3) boundary metaphor assumptions.

PUBLIC-PRIVATE DIALECTICAL ASSUMPTIONS

CPM views the process of disclosure as inherently dialectical, meaning when people disclose, they manage a friction—a push and pull—of wanting to reveal and conceal private information. In Lauren's story, we see that she feels conflicted about revealing, knowing she has to and wanting to conceal her diagnosis to avoid humiliation, relational trauma, and coping with the outcome. The simultaneous nature of wanting to tell and also wanting to conceal makes CPM's theoretical map necessary to understand how people navigate privacy.

PRIVACY MANAGEMENT ASSUMPTIONS

CPM posits three validated assumptions about privacy management. First, people believe they rightfully own their private information, even when they might tell their information to someone. Second, because information is defined as private, with potential vulnerabilities, people believe they have the right to control the flow of information to others. CPM argues the best way to understand management ownership and control is through "privacy rules." These are not rigid rules. Rather, think about them as *rules* with a little "r" instead of unbending rules with a big "R" given the possibility of needed rule change. Privacy rules have to be flexible in order to be effective. If you break up with your relational partner you will no longer want to confide in him or her the same way you did when you were together, thus you change your privacy rules, similar to the way you might change your Facebook privacy setting when you unfriend someone. CPM accounts for the need to shift and change these rules. Third, since we do not live in a perfect world, managing private information can break down as a result of unsuccessful management of private information.

BOUNDARY METAPHOR ASSUMPTIONS

CPM uses a boundary metaphor to mark borders of ownership surrounding private information, and boundaries illustrate the transactional nature of how that information is managed with others. The boundaries can be "thick" when we are less likely to reveal information, the boundaries can be "thin" with higher likelihood of disclosure, and there can be fluctuations where disclosure or concealing is incremental, or shifts back and forth from openness to denying access. The boundaries represent symbolic lines denoting information with potential vulnerabilities considered private (Petronio, 2002).

Three axiomatic maxims define CPM theory: (1) conceptualizing private information ownership, (2) conceptualizing private information control, and (3) conceptualizing private information turbulence.

CONCEPTUALIZING PRIVATE INFORMATION OWNERSHIP

Private information is defined by CPM as information individuals believe they own and control because if it is known there would be potential for vulnerabilities. Hence, private information is something people believe is rightfully theirs to protect or disclose. Persons selected to know are considered "authorized" to become co-owners of the information. This is in opposition to being *unauthorized,* where private information is taken without the owner's permission, for example, having personal information sold without the owner's authorization. This particular CPM assumption has extended how the process of disclosure and privacy are understood and illustrates the assumption of boundaries regulation discussed above.

CONCEPTUALIZING PRIVATE INFORMATION CONTROL

Since individuals believe they own their private information and assume the right to control third-party disclosure, they need a means of regulating control over the flow of private information. CPM uses the concept of "privacy rules" to represent how people make choices about retaining control or permitting access to others. Privacy rules are developed and applied using two types of criteria, (1) *core* and (2) *catalyst* (Petronio, 2013). *Core criteria* are more durable, at times, functioning in the background and include criteria such as culture, gender, and privacy orientations. Cultural criteria are important because privacy can be defined as a societal or group value. If a culture values openness as important to societal functioning, people from that culture tend to embrace openness rather than secrecy. Men and women differ in the kind of privacy rules they use, leading to divergent requirements for revealing or concealing. Women need to feel confident in recipients they select, whereas men often focus on whether the situation is appropriate (Petronio, 2002). Families develop and socialize members to have privacy orientations guiding the degree of family information openness or protection (Serewicz & Canary, 2008).

Catalyst criteria account for times when privacy rules are responsive to needed change. Rule change occurs when the risk-benefit ratios fluctuate, when motivations for telling or concealing are altered, or when situations occur that call for different privacy rules, such as in divorce or relational breakdowns such as the issues Lauren faced. Both core and catalyst criteria serve to guide the development and application of privacy rules people use to manage their boundaries.

CONCEPTUALIZING PRIVACY INFORMATION TURBULENCE

There are many ways privacy management breaks down, and we also know that there are levels of turbulence from minor ripples to full breakdowns like snooping or intentionally stealing identity information. When privacy rules do not work, people typically need to recalibrate them to fit their needs. If you disclosed private information to someone in confidence but, nevertheless, that person gossips, repeating the information without permission, you probably will not disclose personal information to that person again. Gossip, by definition, violates how a person wants their private information managed. Once the violations are discovered, trust is breached and access rules tend to change.

How Communication Is Conceptualized in Communication Privacy Management Theory

In the previous section we discussed assumption maxims that underlie CPM theory. These axiomatic maxims represent CPM operating principles. This section illustrates why CPM is considered a communication theory. CPM is born out of a communication perspective and is wholly *communication* theory. Fundamentals of the theory and tests of the principles are predicated on seeking an understanding of a communication phenomenon and as such, CPM is one of the first solidly positioned communication theories. Unlike earlier perspectives on disclosure, CPM makes the communicative process the central feature by taking into account both the recipient and the discloser (Petronio & Reierson, 2009).

Three interaction maxims represent how CPM is, at its heart, a communication theory, born and bred. These include: (1) shared privacy boundaries, (2) coordinating privacy boundaries, and (3) ramifications of privacy boundary turbulence.

SHARED PRIVACY BOUNDARIES

One of the most innovative and attractive features of CPM theory is the argument for a different way to think about the aftermath of disclosure. As Petronio (2002, 2013) points out, once a person discloses private information, this action fundamentally changes the nature of the information. Accordingly, the information is no longer solely owned by the discloser (aka, "original owner"). "Sharing" was once used as a substitute phrase for disclosure, but in many ways Petronio's conceptualization of sharing is more accurate. Thus, when you tell someone private information, you are making that person a co-owner or shareholder of the information. Together you create one mutual boundary around the information.

CPM explains that you can have many layers of privacy boundaries where shared information resides. For example, you can have dyadic privacy boundaries when only two people are co-owners, group privacy boundaries, family privacy boundaries, organizationally private boundaries (i.e., proprietary information), and even societal private boundaries (i.e., information in the United States protected by the Department of Homeland Security). Because shared privacy boundaries make the calculus for privacy regulation more complex, Petronio (2002) proposed three operations that regulate privacy boundary coordination for the mutually held private information.

COORDINATING SHARED PRIVACY BOUNDARIES

Operations used to coordinate shared privacy boundaries refer to how individuals co-own and co-manage private information. As mentioned, CPM does not view disclosure as a unidirectional or one-dimensional communication process. Instead, disclosed private information affects both the discloser and the recipient of disclosure. After people reveal private information, all recipients are considered responsible for co-managing the information. Petronio (2002, 2013) argues boundaries must be coordinated through negotiations of privacy rules to have synchronized and effective management. Coordination of privacy boundaries uses three operations: privacy boundary linkages, private information co-ownership rights, and privacy boundary permeability.

Privacy boundary linkages represent alliances formed between a discloser and recipients. Boundary linkages occur in numerous ways. A discloser can target a particular recipient in order to intentionally reveal private information, the information can be solicited, such as during a doctor's visit, or the original owner can grant access, for example, to their medical records. Sometimes, an unintended recipient can receive private information accidentally (Petronio, Jones, & Morr, 2003). For instance, a roommate may have overheard Lauren tell her boyfriend that she is HIV positive. While Lauren might have intended to link her boyfriend into the privacy boundary around her status, she did not plan on the roommate finding out.

Private information co-ownership rights refers to privileges and amount of expected responsibility for co-owners of private information. In the example above, Lauren discloses her HIV status intentionally to her boyfriend. Her boyfriend becomes a shareholder or stakeholder of the information. The complication of knowing is, no doubt, dramatic for him. Although he may think it is important to know, knowing about her status may also prove dilemmatic (Greene, Derlega, Yep, & Petronio, 2003). This example illustrates that, although the role of recipient, as a co-owner, may be positive, it also may cause the confidant to experience conflict, particularly if he or she is not able to cope with the information disclosed. With disclosures, confidants also frequently receive privacy rules for how the information should be handled. In our example, Lauren is likely to ask her boyfriend to keep her status confidential, perhaps even pleading with him to have the information remain between the two of them. Petronio (2002) argued that if the parameters for dealing with private information are clear between the parties, then co-owners more aptly regulate access to the private information in a similar way. However, when these parameters are not clear, it is more likely that a co-owner will breach a rule about how the information should be co-managed. This discussion illustrates an underlying condition of smooth boundary coordination. In other words, when involved parties are intentionally privileged and negotiate rules this allows for efficient and effective regulation of the information with fewer complications.

Privacy boundary permeability refers to the amount of access to or openness within a privacy boundary. As access to private information increases, boundaries become more permeable. Since boundary permeability signifies the level of access, thinner walls represent more openness so private information flows more easily. In opposition to this, thicker boundary walls represent less access or no access, as with secrets (Petronio, 2002). No doubt, Lauren intended for the information about her HIV status to remain within an impermeable privacy boundary with her boyfriend.

When boundaries are jointly coordinated, CPM describes three ways that they are managed. First, collective boundaries can be managed in a "disproportionate" way: one person in the boundary discloses more private information than other recipients. For example, when people are in need of health care they willingly disclose a great deal of private information, yet information is not typically reciprocated by the health care worker (Petronio & Kovach, 1997). Second, collective boundaries can be managed in an "intersected" fashion: Each member shares and co-owns information in equitable ways. Third, collective boundaries can be managed in a "unified" way: Everyone is responsible for jointly held information. Unified boundaries are most often found in families, where personal information affects the group as well as the individual family member (Petronio, 2002).

RAMIFICATIONS OF PRIVACY BOUNDARY TURBULENCE

As mentioned earlier, smooth management when private information is co-owned requires coordinated actions. Often, due to incongruent expectations, misunderstanding privacy parameters, or conflicted access rules for handling private information, boundary turbulence ensues. Suppose the roommate of Lauren's boyfriend heard Lauren disclosing she was HIV positive. Even if Lauren and her boyfriend keep her HIV-positive status private, her boyfriend's roommate may not understand how the couple wants to manage that information. Ramifications such as recalibrating privacy rules may result if the roommate reveals Lauren's HIV-positive status to someone else without her permission. There are many cases where turbulence occurs: In particular, privacy violations, dilemmas, and misconceptions about ownership contribute to boundary turbulence. In each case, there are potential negative relational ramifications when privacy boundaries become turbulent.

Research and Practical Applications of Communication Privacy Management Theory

CPM is a dynamic theory that has been applied to explore a number of interpersonal communication issues. As examples, researchers using CPM have studied: (a) use of social media (Child, Haridakis, & Petronio, 2012; Kanter, Afifi, & Robbins, 2012), (b) stepfamily communication (Afifi, 2003), (c) marital communication (Petronio & Jones, 2006; Steuber & Solomon, 2012;), (d) interpersonal health issues (Bylund, Peterson, & Cameron, 2010; Petronio & Lewis, 2010), (e) child sexual abuse (Petronio, Reeder, Hecht, & Mon't Ros-Mendoza, 1996), and (f) family interactions (Docan-Morgan 2011; Durham, 2008).

Turbulent conditions, such as privacy dilemmas and breakdowns in disclosure processes, represent important areas of research in interpersonal communication because of the intrinsically complex nature of privacy management within relational systems. Studying privacy turbulence gives a way to decipher the unevenness of human interaction. Besides helping to understand the dynamics of relational systems, privacy turbulence also highlights the recipient of disclosures. While emphasis of the confidant has been sparse, researchers using CPM have begun to examine such issues as pregnant women and the unsolicited disclosive advice they receive from others (Petronio & Jones, 2006). CPM theory has also provided insights into how stepchildren feel caught between two families. They must manage information that they receive differently depending on which privacy rules prevail in different households, and they are concerned about regulating issues of loyalty (Afifi, 2003). Similar issues are found with academic athletic advisors and keeping confidence of student-athletes while also balancing loyalties to their university employer (Thompson, Petronio, & Braithwaite, 2012). Through CPM, we can better understand the dilemmas physicians and their families face when involved in medical errors as well as clinicians with patients (Petronio, 2006; Petronio, Helft, & Child, 2013). Furthermore, bereavement researchers have commented on the confusion that many recipients feel after an individual discloses information pertaining to the death of a child (Hastings, 2000; Toller & McBride, 2013). According to Hastings, although the recipients of particular disclosures may wish to provide support to bereaved parents, they might not know how to provide it. Some disclosures might thus be perceived by recipients as burdensome and those recipients take on the role of the reluctant confidant for the discloser (Bergen & McBride, 2008).

The privacy rules that guide disclosures in marital interactions characterize a burgeoning area of privacy (Durham, 2008). Petronio (2002, 2011) suggested that newlyweds often struggle with determining what private information they should disclose to one another as they develop privacy rules. As Serewicz and Canary (2008) pointed out, newlyweds go through a process of formulating acceptable levels of openness and closedness in their marriages; privacy rules are created through this process. Roloff and Ifert (2000) suggested that one of the most important determinants of successful boundary management might be how marital couples negotiate the disclosure of partner criticism. Withholding complaints has both positive and negative outcomes for marriages. By resisting the urge to criticize one's spouse, the individual may successfully avoid marital conflict; however, if spouses never verbalize criticism toward each other, then both spouses are unlikely to confront the undesirable or damaging behavior of the other. Because CPM provides a frame for the interface of privacy and disclosure, it encourages thinking about the conditions of both revealing and concealing. The research on topic avoidance illustrates a privacy rule strategy that is used when individuals feel compelled to keep information protected within the privacy boundary. For instance, researchers have studied (a) topic avoidance and the role of the reluctant confidant within friendships (Afifi & Guerrero, 1998, 2000), (b) privacy management on Facebook (Waters & Ackerman, 2011), and (c) explaining privacy turbulence erupting from spousal discrepancies in disclosures about infertility (Steuber & Solomon, 2012).

People with all kinds of relational connections are linked into privacy boundaries or isolated from information (Petronio, 2002, 2013). Research by Caughlin (2002) shows the way people regulate privacy rules in voluntary relationships like friendships. Friendship relationships tend to have more lenient rules that guide disclosures than exist in involuntary, familial relationships. In some cases, however, individuals experience boundary turbulence when they mistakenly reveal too much information or withhold information from their friends. Consequently, relational problems can erupt because of turbulence in privacy management when individuals do not disclose enough (Afifi & Steuber, 2010) or when they disclose too much.

CPM argues that one of the criteria on which privacy rules are predicated is the motivation for revealing or concealing private information. Some research has begun to understand the ways in which motivations impact the choice to reveal or conceal. Afifi and her colleagues have directly studied the link between motivations and privacy management within a CPM framework (e.g., Afifi, 2003; Caughlin & Afifi, 2004). For instance, they found that relational dissatisfaction was moderated by an individual's motivations for avoiding disclosure of a topic, suggesting that motivational criteria for decision making regarding revealing and concealing is a robust theoretical assumption. An interesting study examined the relational impact of "punitive secrets," where one partner is motivated to conceal knowing that the other partner is keeping a secret, yet already knowing the content (Caughlin, Scott, Miller, & Hefner, 2009). As seems logical, when the secret was about betrayals of confidence or personal gain, for example, they were more hurtful to the relationship. Looking at disclosure patterns for child sexual abuse victims, Petronio and colleagues (1996) found that some of these children did not disclose information because they had been threatened by the perpetrators and were afraid to tell. Consequently, the children constructed a set of rules that were largely dependent on carefully managing their privacy boundaries. Such children told only after they "hint around," testing to see if they could trust the confidant, or they only told if someone gently inquired whether there might have been abuse. In other words, the children waited to be given permission, and they selected a setting where they felt safe. As CPM continues to be used to study a wide variety of issues, the verification of CPM principles continues to confirm the viability of the ideas and can judge its theoretical weight.

Evaluation of Communication Privacy Management Theory

CPM is a valuable theory containing significant strength. Unlike many previous theories adopted from other disciplines, CPM represents a theory explicitly grounded in and derived from "communication." CPM is a theory of communication that helps us to understand how and why we reveal and conceal private information. In its short life, CPM has generated a plethora of research in a multitude of contexts across disciplines such as computer science, health, psychology, sociology, business, and government. In communication, CPM has been used primarily by researchers in interpersonal, family, and health communication. However, as the other disciplines show us, CPM can be used to understand privacy and disclosure in contexts such as health care, education, social media, business, economics, and organizations. The greatest strength of CPM is its utility and heuristic value in both basic and applied research. CPM's flexibility as a theory both aids researchers in fully understanding the privacy expressiveness dialectic and its applicability to real-world problems. Although there is much strength, we also recognize that CPM theory is very new. More work is needed in developing measures to capture the full complement of ways CPM can help us understand how people manage private information.

Continuing the Conversation

The directions for future research using CPM theory are numerous. Balancing privacy and disclosure is not only a task found in close personal relationships. The theory is applicable to address questions about social media and making choices about revealing information in online social networking. In health care, providers must both keep patient confidentiality and disclose their health information appropriately, for example, to another health care clinician. In the workplace CPM can help us understand how coworkers share personal information to be held in confidence. CPM can shed light on how educators attempt to balance immediacy with professional distance and make wise choices about how much they reveal about themselves to their students. CPM represents a theoretical perspective that allows us to better understand what individuals disclose, what they keep private, and how private information is handled among groups of people. Future research needs to continue testing the viability of applying the theory. In addition, it is necessary to develop a diagnostic tool to help us understand the reasons turbulence occurs and a repair mechanism to teach us how to mend privacy breakdowns. As we have seen, the heuristic value of CPM, for not only communication, but also many different contexts and disciplines, is very promising.

References

Afifi, T. (2003). "Feeling caught" in stepfamilies: Managing boundary turbulence through appropriate communication privacy rules. *Journal of Social and Personal Relationships, 20*, 729–755.

Afifi, T., & Steuber, K. (2010). The cycle of concealment model. *Journal of Social and Personal Relationships, 27*, 1019–1034.

Afifi, W. A., & Guerrero, L. K. (1998). Some things are better left unsaid II: Topic avoidance in friendships. *Communication Quarterly, 46*(3), 231–249.

Afifi, W. A., & Guerrero, L. K. (2000). Motivations underlying topic avoidance in close relationships. In S. Petronio (Ed.), *Balancing the secrets of private disclosures* (pp. 165–179). Mahwah, NJ: Erlbaum.

Baxter, L. A., & Babbie, E. (2004). *The basics of communication research*. Belmont, CA: Wadsworth.

Bergen, K. J., & McBride, M. C. (2008). Becoming a reluctant confidant: Communication boundary management in close friendships. *Texas Speech Communication Journal, 33*, 50–61.

Bylund, C. L., Peterson, E. B., & Cameron, K. A. (2010). A practitioner's guide to interpersonal communication theory. An overview and exploration of selected theories. *Patient Education and Counseling, 87*, 261–267.

Caughlin, J. (2002). The demand/withdraw pattern of communication as a predictor of marital satisfaction over time. *Human Communication Research, 28*, 49–86.

Caughlin, J., & Afifi, T. D. (2004). When is topic avoidance unsatisfying? Examining moderators of the association between avoidance and dissatisfaction. *Human Communication Research, 30*, 479–513.

Caughlin, J., Scott, A. M., Miller, L. E., & Hefner, V. (2009). Putative secrets: When information is supposedly a secret. *Journal of Social and Personal Relationships, 26*, 713–742.

Child, J., Haridakis, P., & Petronio, S. (2012). Blogging privacy rule orientations, privacy management, and content deletion practices: the variability of online privacy management activity at different stages of social media use. *Computers and Human Behavior, 28*, 1859–1872.

Docan-Morgan, S. (2011). "They don't know what it's like to be in my shoes": Topic avoidance about race in transracially adoptive families. *Journal of Social and Personal Relationships, 28*, 336–355.

Durham, W. T. (2008). The rule-based process of revealing and concealing family planning decisions of voluntarily child-free couples: A communication privacy management perspective. *Communication Studies, 59*, 132–147.

Greene, K., Derlega, V. J., Yep, G., & Petronio, S. (2003). *Privacy and disclosure of HIV interpersonal relationships*. Mahwah, NJ: Erlbaum.

Hastings, S. O. (2000). Self-disclosure and identity management by bereaved parents. *Communication Studies, 51*, 352–369.

Kanter, M., Afifi, T., & Robbins, S. (2012). The impact of parents "friending" their young adult child on Facebook on perceptions of parental privacy invasions and parent-child relationship quality. *Journal of Communication, 62*, 900–917.

Petronio, S. (2002). *Boundaries of privacy: Dialectics of disclosure*. Albany, NY: SUNY Press.

Petronio, S. (2006). Impact of medical mistakes: Navigating work-family boundaries for physicians and their families. *Communication Monographs, 73*, 462–467.

Petronio, S. (2011). The embarrassment of private disclosures: A case study of newly married couples. In D. Braithwaite & J. T. Wood (Eds.), *Casing interpersonal communication: Case studies in personal and social relationships* (pp. 93–101). Dubuque, IA: Kendall Hunt Publishing.

Petronio, S. (2013). Brief status report on communication privacy management theory. *Journal of Family Communication, 13*, 6–14.

Petronio, S., Helft, P. R., & Child, J. T. (2013). A case of error disclosure: A communication privacy management analysis. *Journal of Public Health Research, 2,* 175–181.

Petronio, S., & Jones, S. S. (2006). When "friendly advice" becomes privacy dilemma for pregnant couples: Applying CPM theory. In L. Turner & R. West (Eds.), *The family communication sourcebook* (pp. 201–208). Thousand Oaks, CA: Sage.

Petronio, S., Jones, S. S., & Morr, M. (2003). Family privacy dilemmas: A communication privacy management perspective. In L. Frey (Ed.), *Bona fide groups* (pp. 23–56). Mahwah, NJ: Erlbaum.

Petronio, S., & Kovach, S. (1997). Managing privacy boundaries: Health providers' perceptions of resident care in Scottish nursing homes. *Journal of Applied Communication Research, 25,* 115–131.

Petronio, S., & Lewis, S. S. (2010). Medical disclosure in oncology: Families, patients, and providers. In M. Miller-Day (Ed.). *Family communication and health transitions* (pp. 269–296). New York, NY: Peter Lang.

Petronio, S., & Reierson, J. (2009). Regulating the privacy of confidentiality: Grasping the complexities through communication privacy management. In T. Afifi & W. Afifi (Eds.), *Uncertainty, information management, and disclosure decisions: Theories and applications* (pp. 365–383). New York, NY: Routledge.

Petronio, S., Reeder, H., Hecht, M., & Mon't Ros-Mendoza, T. (1996). Disclosure of sexual abuse by children and adolescents. *Journal of Applied Communication Research, 24,* 181–199.

Roloff, M. E., & Ifert, D. E. (2000). Conflict management through avoidance: Withholding complaints, suppressing arguments, and declaring topics taboo. In S. Petronio (Ed.), *Balancing the secrets of private disclosures* (pp. 151–163). Mahwah, NJ: Erlbaum.

Serewicz, M. C. M., & Canary, D. J. (2008). Assessments of disclosure from the in-laws: Links among disclosure topics, family privacy orientations, and relational quality. *Journal of Social and Personal Relationships, 25,* 333–357.

Steuber, K. R., & Solomon, D. H. (2012). Relational uncertainty, partner interference, and privacy boundary turbulence: Explaining spousal discrepancies in infertility disclosures. *Journal of Social and Personal Relationships, 29,* 3–27.

Thompson, J., Petronio, S., & Braithwaite, D. O. (2012). An examination of privacy rules for athletic/academic advisors and college student-athletes: A communication privacy management perspective. *Communication Studies, 63,* 54–76.

Toller, P. W., & McBride, M. C. (2013). Enacting privacy rules and protecting disclosure recipients: Parents' communication with children following the death of a family member. *Journal of Family Communication, 13,* 32–45.

Waters, S., & Ackerman, J. (2011). Exploring privacy management on Facebook: Motivations and perceived consequences of voluntary disclosure. *Journal of Computer-Mediated Communication, 17,* 101–115.

26

Interpersonal Deception Theory

Purposive and Interdependent Behavior During Deceptive Interpersonal Interactions

Judee K. Burgoon and David B. Buller

D eception is ubiquitous. Humans dissemble about everything, from whether they are irritated with their partner, to how qualified they are for a job, to their intentions to exercise. When construed broadly to include not just bald-faced lies but also white lies, omissions, equivocations, and hedges, deception is commonplace and produces important consequences (Hancock, Thom-Santelli, & Ritchie, 2004). This state of affairs stands in contrast to the presumption in most encounters that others will be truthful (Grice, 1989).

In this chapter, we present a theory that examines deception through the lens of interpersonal communication. Interpersonal deception theory (IDT) (Buller & Burgoon, 1996; Burgoon & Buller, 2004) can be contrasted with more psychologically oriented models, such as the leakage hypothesis (Ekman & Friesen, 1969) or four-factor theory (Zuckerman, DePaulo, & Rosenthal, 1981). It focuses less on inward psychological and involuntary autonomic responses (e.g., fear reactions) and more on outward social factors such as the communicative interplay between sender and receiver. IDT emphasizes aspects of deception that are voluntary and intentional, as well as the individual and social factors that influence deception and suspicion displays, interaction patterns between deceiver and deceived, and outcomes of credibility and detection accuracy. IDT is comprised of a number of assumptions and propositions (empirically based, testable statements). An abbreviated and updated overview of them is presented here.

Intellectual Tradition of
Interpersonal Deception Theory

IDT was developed by Judee Burgoon and David Buller in 1996. It is a post-positivist theory, with an interconnected set of general statements predicting and explaining the background circumstances, processes, and outcomes of interpersonal deception. It is based on assumptions about the strategic, interactive, and evolving nature of interpersonal communication and deception that underpin the theory's propositions. IDT takes a bird's eye view, attempting to explain the most important features of a deceptive episode. It does not ignore individual concerns such as fear of detection, but it elevates the importance of the communication process between interlocutors. For example, it considers communicators' natural tendencies to synchronize conversational patterns and how deception might alter that. Many communication features are neither original with IDT nor limited solely to deception. IDT's macro-level, systems perspective also means that it does not present a single, micro-level causal mechanism but rather attempts to model the entire deception process as a communication episode. What happens outside interpersonal interactions (e.g., investigating a cheating spouse) is outside its scope.

A core assumption of IDT is that deception is no different from other forms of communication in that humans are goal-oriented, adaptive creatures. Their communication—whether truthful or deceptive—is intended to satisfy a host of goals such as presenting oneself favorably to others, managing expressions of feelings and emotions in an acceptable way, maintaining relational harmony, easing conversational flow, and persuading others to accept one's assertions and requests. Both sender and receiver in any communicative exchange have multiple goals, which means that communication is naturally an adaptive give-and-take as interlocutors each seek to achieve their own goals. Although many of the functions of human communication become routinized early on and operate at a low level of awareness, they still represent deliberate action. Because deception is by definition an intentional act, IDT underscores that it should be characterized as strategic: Perpetrators pursue various tactics to achieve their deception goals, to be seen as credible, to have their duplicity accepted as truth, and to evade detection.

Another core assumption is that information management is fundamental to communication. People choose to hide, distort, misrepresent, obfuscate, or avoid transmitting information in their communication by manipulating veracity, completeness, directness, relevance, and personalization of messages. Deceivers manage not only the central message, which is usually verbal and conveys the deceptive content, but also the accompanying language style and nonverbal behaviors that are intended to put forward a credible self-presentation.

Notwithstanding the assumption that deceptive episodes are fraught with intentional actions, another assumption is that deception may include unintended actions (e.g., nonverbal cues) that inadvertently reveal the sender's deceptive intent or the true state of affairs. These include cognitive and emotional responses (e.g., heightened arousal, negative affect, and cognitive effort) that differ from truth tellers (Johnson, Barnhardt, & Zhu, 2004; Vrij, Fisher, Mann, & Leal, 2006).

A third key assumption in IDT is that receivers, as active participants in deceptive episodes, influence the time course and ultimate outcomes of those episodes. Receivers are information processors who may have their "antenna" tuned into the senders' actions; who experience greater cognitive difficulty, unpleasantness, and vigilance when their suspicions are aroused; who provide various forms of feedback to senders that can range from acceptance to skepticism to outright disbelief; and who themselves may strategically adapt their own communication style as their suspicions wax and wane.

These assumptions (and several others) are the "drivers" for IDT. They answer many of the "why" questions regarding what deceivers and their targets think and do.

Main Goals and Features of Interpersonal Deception Theory

Deception is a case in which the goals of interlocutors are in conflict with one another. IDT endeavors to explain how both sender and receiver navigate such episodes. Consider, for instance, a married couple arguing about a husband's penchant for gambling. In response to his denials that he has a gambling problem, the wife may take a new tack on how she questions him about his whereabouts. In turn, he may become more evasive in how he answers. Ultimately, whether she uncovers the truth, and whether each party regards the conversation as successful, will be governed by the combination of senders' actions, receivers' reactions, and the interplay between them. (Note that if she chooses to follow him to a casino, this kind of investigative action is outside the scope of IDT; when and how she confronts him is, however, within its scope.)

The propositions in IDT cover the entire process of deceptive communication and must be understood in conjunction with one another and with the assumptions. The first two propositions are general statements intended to identify key contextual and relationship factors in which all deceptive episodes are enmeshed. The first proposition originated from a desire to highlight how features of the communication context have a substantial influence on how a deceptive communication episode unfolds. Two that are singled out are interactivity and task demands. *Interactivity* refers to whether the message exchange is interdependent and contingent (a given message is connected to prior messages), takes place in real time (synchronous rather than asynchronous), and has a rich array of interrelated verbal and nonverbal channels available through which interaction takes place. An e-mail breaking off a relationship is quite different from a face-to-face breakup. The first is low on interactivity; the second is highly interactive (including contingent turns at talk in real-time and a multiplicity of channels).

Task demands concern whether or not participants are engaged in a conversation that is mentally or emotionally difficult to conduct. Telling a hard truth can be even more challenging than telling a facile white lie, but more often than not, deception is more challenging than telling the truth, especially if it must be done on the spot.

The second proposition calls attention to the relationship between sender and receiver as a significant influence on what participants think and do. Interactions must be interpreted within the context of that relationship. Lying to a police officer will differ from lying to a loved one because of such factors as familiarity and positive or negative valence of the relationship.

Proposition 1: Context features of deceptive interchanges systematically affect sender and receiver cognitions and behaviors; two of special importance are the interactivity of the communication medium and the demands of the conversational task.

Proposition 2: Relational features of deceptive interchanges systematically affect sender and receiver cognitions and behaviors; two of special importance are familiarity and relationship valence.

The husband, should he choose to deceive his wife about his gambling, can capitalize on the availability of social cues in full audiovisual contexts (e.g., face-to-face conversations between the couple) to present himself in the most appealing fashion and keep telltale indicators of deceit in check. Comparatively, more telltale signs might be available for her to detect if the couple just exchanged e-mails. The husband might also choose a real-time (synchronous) form of communication such as the telephone to foster a sense of closeness and trust with his wife, while reducing the availability of telltale visual signs and the persistent record that e-mails create. However, synchronous communication has its drawbacks. The husband has to produce messages on the fly, with less time to prepare or edit them, so he risks greater detectability. The demands of the task and the wife's familiarity with how her husband dissembles must also be considered. Telling a white lie about whether the wife's new hairstyle is becoming is an easy task. Trying to hide substantial gambling losses is much more challenging. Plus, more is at stake if the couple values their marriage. As for the matter of familiarity, people in close relationships know each other's history, values, daily routines, and usual communication style. Deceivers can capitalize on this knowledge to construct plausible messages. Detectors can also use this information to unmask lies. However, the advantage in this "cat and mouse" game typically goes to deceivers (Burgoon, Buller, & Floyd, 2002).

Context and relationship factors not only influence how a deceptive episode unfolds and with what consequences, but also receivers' and deceivers' cognitive-affective states. People give each other the benefit of the doubt more often when communicating face-to-face, and with someone they like and trust, than when using an electronic medium. Knowing this, deceivers may be less fearful that their loved ones will suspect them.

> Proposition 3: Interactive contexts and positively toned relationships are associated with higher expectations that a sender is truthful.

> Proposition 4: Deceivers' fear of detection is positively influenced by how familiar receivers are with general deceptive behavior or knowledge of the sender; it is inversely related to receivers' expectations for truthfulness and how relationally familiar (acquainted) they are with the deceiver.

Because of their strong attachments and positive feelings for one another, marital partners often give each other the benefit of the doubt. Thus, the wife may accept as truthful the husband's claims that he gambles only infrequently or loses only small amounts. This propensity to "look the other way," which draws on their relational closeness, may alleviate his fear of being detected. However, two other forms of familiarity—behavioral and informational—may have opposite effects. Just as people become nervous about interacting with deception experts, who know a lot about what deception looks like, and with people who know a lot about their history, so do relational partners who have a great deal of autobiographical knowledge about each other and know each other's routines. The husband may become anxious when deceiving if he fears that his wife knows his communication patterns well enough to recognize irregularities in them.

The next set of propositions concerns behavioral displays. They are grounded in what was formerly a proposition but is better regarded as an assumption that deception, like other forms of communication, includes not only involuntary and inadvertent (nonstrategic) behavior, but also intentional and deliberate (strategic) elements. Nonstrategic activity includes behaviors that display arousal, negative or dampened affect, depressed involvement, and/or impaired speech. Strategic activity includes managing the informational content of messages, associated nonverbal behaviors, and overall image. Propositions 5 through 7 predict how these displays are affected by context, relationship, the deceiver's motives and social skills, and the receiver's expectations and suspicions. The full reasoning behind these and subsequent propositions can be found in Burgoon and Buller (2004).

> Proposition 5: Interactive contexts heighten strategic activity and lessen nonstrategic activity over time.
>
> Proposition 6: Target benefit alters strategic and nonstrategic activity during deception such that:
>
> (a) Deceiving for self-gain prompts more, and qualitatively different, strategic activity than deceiving for the benefit of others; and
>
> (b) Deceiving for self-gain prompts more nonstrategic behavior associated with concerns over detection and increased strategic activity to avoid detection than deceiving for the benefit of others.
>
> Proposition 7: Deceiver motivation to behave strategically is
>
> (a) inversely related to receiver expectations for truthfulness,
>
> (b) positively related to relational familiarity with the target, and
>
> (c) positively related to communicator skill.

To illustrate, and contrary to what might seem intuitive, the gambling husband will have an easier time bringing any nervousness and speech disfluencies under control if he dupes his wife during face-to-face conversation than through an exchange of voice mail messages (Proposition 5). His choice of strategies will also be affected by whether he is deceiving primarily for his own benefit, such as preserving his reputation (an identity goal), escaping marital conflict (a relational goal), and continuing his gambling (an instrumental goal), than for his wife's benefit (Proposition 6a). It is easier, for example, to tell a lie if the purpose is to protect the other person rather than the self. When deceiving for his own gain, the husband's likely first gambit will be concealment—omitting any reference to his gambling in accounts of his whereabouts—rather than outright lying because lies are more difficult to keep straight, are more easily uncovered by those familiar with his history and day-to-day routines (e.g., the wife rather than a neighbor; Proposition 6b), and will have more devastating impact on his image and relationships if found out. He will take advantage of family and coworkers' expectations for truthfulness to accept whatever he says (Proposition 7a). He will also do better at keeping nonstrategic behavior in check if he is a skilled communicator and if his targets are trusting, unfamiliar with him, and unschooled in deception (Propositions 7b and 7c).

Propositions 8 and 9 call attention to factors that should influence judgments of a sender's credibility and deception detection. The aforementioned factors of interactivity and communicator skill that motivate senders to engage in strategic activity should enhance their credibility and aid them in evading detection. Two other salient factors are truth bias and communication normalcy. *Truth bias* refers to the tendency to overestimate the truthfulness of others when making judgments of their veracity, and in some quarters, may be viewed as synonymous with a priori expectations that others are truthful. Truth bias elevates judgments of credibility and lowers detection accuracy. Adhering to "normal," expected communication patterns rather than displaying anomalous behavior should also enhance sender credibility and contribute to the individual's deceit going undetected.

Proposition 8: Receivers are more likely to judge senders as credible when

(a) the context is interactive,

(b) senders are skilled communicators,

(c) receivers are truth biased, and

(d) sender communication adheres to the receiver's expectations for normality.

Proposition 9: Receivers are less likely to detect deception when

(a) the context is interactive,

(b) senders are skilled communicators,

(c) receivers are truth biased,

(d) sender communication follows expected patterns, and

(e) receivers are unfamiliar with sender information and behavior.

These propositions suggest that the deck is stacked against the wife discovering her husband's duplicity about gambling, because she is likely to be predisposed toward believing him, especially if she has no cause to suspect a problem and he is skilled at communicating (Propositions 8b, 9b, 8c, and 9c). The husband will do well if he conforms to normal conversational patterns typical of the couple's interaction styles (Propositions 8d and 9d). If he strays from his usual communication demeanor, say, by becoming withdrawn or overly talkative, she is bound to become suspicious. If she has verifiable information, such as receipts from the casino, and she knows he has begun deviating from his normal routine of arriving home for dinner at 7 p.m., she will also be more successful in catching him in his lies.

Suspicion is a critical component of deceptive episodes. The next propositions speak directly to its role, positing that suspicious receivers adjust their communication patterns, which often alert senders to their skepticism. And, just as truthful communication entails senders attending and adapting to feedback from the receivers, deceivers also attune to signs that receivers are suspicious (such as atypical behavior or probing questions) and modify their verbal and nonverbal messages accordingly to be more believable.

Proposition 10: Receiver suspicion prompts changes in receiver strategic and nonstrategic behavior.

Proposition 11: Senders attune to receiver suspicion.

Proposition 12: Sender perception of suspicion is positively related to

(a) receiver deviations from expected behavior, and

(b) receiver behavior signaling disbelief, uncertainty, or the need for additional information.

Proposition 13: Receiver suspicion (perceived or actual) evokes changes in the sender's strategic and nonstrategic behavior.

These propositions are probabilistic. Some receivers are skilled at keeping their suspicions hidden, and some deceivers are oblivious to signs that their target disbelieves them. The main point is that suspicion also has associated changes that can be "read" by deceivers, who then try to allay those suspicions. According to these propositions, then, the wife's suspicions can backfire, making it even more difficult to detect her husband's deceptions if she reveals her suspicions by probing or appearing surprised or incredulous (Proposition 12) because he may pick up on her signals of disbelief (Proposition 11) and make strategic adjustments to bolster his believability (Proposition 13).

It is important to remember that conversations are not static; sender and receiver cognitions and behavioral patterns fluctuate in response to each other's behaviors. The next two propositions underscore that this process is dynamic and adaptive.

Proposition 14: Deception and suspicion displays change over time.

Proposition 15: Reciprocity is the dominant interaction adaptation pattern between senders and receivers during interpersonal deception.

Consider what happens if the suspicious wife indirectly questions her husband about the work he was purportedly doing at the office last night when he was actually at a local casino. He may evade by talking instead about what other people were doing. Suppose she then shifts to a more direct approach, asking if he stopped at the casino last night. He may try to stonewall about his whereabouts by omitting the critical detail of being at the casino. If she escalates to a more direct accusation, he may reciprocate with a stronger assertion that he has not been gambling. If she persists, he may fabricate a story about his whereabouts. If she doesn't buy that story, she may respond with anger, to which he may respond in kind with angry indignation. Thus, the deceptive exchange will change in character over the conversation's time course (Proposition 14). Because a deceptive exchange is embedded within normal conversational patterns, one of the most prevalent being the tendency for relational partners to reciprocate one another's interaction patterns, each person's manner of communicating typically will beget similar (reciprocal) verbal and nonverbal behaviors from the conversational partner (Proposition 15).

The last set of propositions concerns the outcomes of a deceptive episode—for the receiver, credibility attributions and detection success; for the sender, perception of success. Both are affected by recency effects, including the most recent receiver cognitions and the sender's most recent communication demeanor.

Proposition 16: Terminal judgments of sender credibility and receiver detection accuracy are a function of:

(a) last receiver cognitions (suspicion, truth biases), and

(b) last sender behavioral displays.

Proposition 17: Senders' perceptions of deception success are a function of

(a) perceived suspicion and

(b) last receiver behavioral displays.

With the ongoing interplay between husband and wife, it follows that judgments should also change. Credibility judgments and detection accuracy depend more on what happens at the end than the beginning or middle of an interaction (Propositions 16 and 17). If a wife is not very good at reading nonverbal signals, or if the husband has put forth a believable demeanor by interaction's end, she will not detect his deception and he will be successful. For instance, the husband could capitalize on the tendency to reciprocate by resorting to affectionate teasing rather than anger when confronted, cajoling his wife into responding with similar shows of affection that would reestablish her trust and thus mislead her, even if she was unsure of his truthfulness at earlier times in the conversation.

We have tested these propositions in a 20-year series of studies. Our program of research has supported many of the propositions of IDT, including differential displays and judgments due to interactivity and medium of communication (Buller, Strzyewski, & Hunsaker, 1991; Burgoon, Bonito, et al., 2002; Burgoon, Buller, & Floyd, 2002; Zhou, Burgoon, Twitchell, & Nunamaker, 2004), interpersonal relationship effects (Buller, Burgoon, White, & Ebesu, 1994), strategic and nonstrategic behavior by senders and receivers (Burgoon & Buller, 1994), motivation by senders (Burgoon & Floyd, 2000), senders' social skills (Burgoon, Buller, Guerrero, Afifi, & Feldman,

1996), suspicion by receivers and senders' reactions (Burgoon, Buller, Dillman, & Walther, 1995; Burgoon, Buller, Ebesu, Rockwell, & White, 1996), evolution in behavioral displays over time (Burgoon, Buller, White, Afifi, & Buslig, 1999), reciprocity between senders and receivers (Burgoon, Stern, & Dillman, 1995), and senders' and receivers' judgments at the end of an interaction (Burgoon, Buller, & Guerrero, 1995).

How Communication Is Conceptualized in Interpersonal Deception Theory

Our repeated emphasis on conceptualizing communication as a joint creation of sender and receiver that is dynamic and achieves multiple aims simultaneously may seem strange to communication students who consider these qualities to be axiomatic. But, many other models of deception at least implicitly consider communication to be unidirectional—a sender delivers a message to a receiver who passively judges its veracity (e.g., the husband answers questions about his gambling habit and the wife simply decides if he is believable). People may not always be fully cognizant of their actions, but they are not just reactive organisms. Conversations introduce numerous cognitive, affective, and behavioral demands. Deception can ratchet up those demands. As demands ebb and flow, participants will necessarily conserve and channel their resources. Thus, husband and wife will not remain fully vigilant about each other's behaviors. Normative expectations for honesty and reciprocity will influence interpretations, credibility assessments, and behavioral responses, especially if behaviors deviate from normal patterns.

Research and Practical Applications of Interpersonal Deception Theory

IDT can serve as a lens for modeling interpersonal communication more generally. Its principles related to the dynamic, interdependent, evolutionary, and context-dependent character of deceptive interchanges pertain equally to truthful exchanges. Deceivers and truth-tellers alike usually manage their self-presentations so as to appear normal and credible. They create reciprocal interaction patterns, adapt to one another's feedback, and can capitalize on truth biases to build a believable story line with interlocutors' unwitting assistance. IDT underscores the importance of understanding any interpersonal encounter as one of mutual influence and change. Investigations of IDT's principle of interactivity aimed to understand how mediated forms of dissembling (e.g., chat, teleconferencing) might differ from face-to-face interaction in terms of involvement, connection, common ground, believ-ability, and behavioral patterns (e.g., Burgoon, Bonito, et al., 2002). Those characteristics are relevant to all forms of interpersonal interactions (see Burgoon, Chen, & Twitchell, 2010).

Evaluation of Interpersonal Deception Theory

IDT has not been immune to criticism. Stiff (1996) raised definitional issues regarding "interpersonal" and "interactive" and advocated that deception be approached as a persuasive activity, a proposal consistent with the IDT premise that deception is strategic. Others have questioned whether deceivers adapt their behaviors (although this tenet has been tested and supported, see Stiff, Corman, Krizek, & Snider, 1994; White & Burgoon, 2001). DePaulo, Ansfield, and Bell (1996) faulted IDT for failing to advance a solitary causal mechanism. In our opinion, incorporating multiple interrelated processes is a strength of IDT in that they systematically connect assumptions and propositions to pro-mote macro-level understanding of communicative phenomena. Theories such as IDT are useful if higher-order generalizations (propositions) generate multiple testable hypotheses that, in principle, can be empirically discon-firmed. IDT makes testable claims and ones for which the evidence could turn out to be non-supportive. For instance, a prediction such as "deceptive displays change over time" can be falsified by evidence that deception displays remain stable over time.

That said, some of the initial IDT propositions were pitched at too abstract a level and warranted revisions to achieve greater precision. For example, the original proposition of how suspicion is manifested in behavior could not generate a falsifiable prediction. Our reworded version (Proposition 13) implies that suspicious receivers will differ from non-suspicious ones by exhibiting both strategic responses (e.g., adoption of various questioning strategies) and inadvertent ones that betray their suspicion. Also, some of the propositions (e.g., 1 and 2) were worded as generic functional statements about variables important in the communication process, but they did not specify directionality.

The substance of other propositions deserves further scrutiny, and we our-selves now take issue with some. Case in point is a meta-analysis by Bond and DePaulo (2008) that disputes the claim that receivers vary in their ability to detect deception. Their analysis shows strong homogeneity in detection accu-racy across individuals and studies. Thus, skill may only exert substantial impact on the production, but not the interpretation, of deceptive messages. With this in mind, we welcome further critiques, tests, and discussion of IDT so that our collective understanding of interpersonal deception advances.

Continuing the Conversation

Apart from evaluating specific propositions, one recent direction for IDT research has been extension to new technologies and media. For example, IDT is being used to guide the development of technologies for automatically detecting deception and hostile intent (Jensen, Meservy, Burgoon & Nunamaker, 2009). Many language features can be automatically extracted from transcribed text using parsers, data mining, and classification software. Many nonverbal visual features can be automatically identified from video-taped images using computer vision techniques. These are being tested for their ability to discriminate truth from deception or suspicious from trust-worthy conduct, with an eye toward uses by law enforcement and security screeners. The same behavioral signatures are being incorporated into train-ing on deception detection in such contexts as forensic auditing, border pro-tection, and criminal investigations. As more insights emerge into how deception is conducted under different circumstances, precision in detecting deception should improve.

References

Bond, C. F., Jr., & DePaulo, B. M. (2008). Individual differences in detecting deception: Accuracy and bias. *Psychological Bulletin, 134,* 477–492.

Buller, D. B., & Burgoon, J. K. (1996). Interpersonal deception theory. *Communication Theory, 6,* 203–242.

Buller, D. B., Burgoon, J. K., White, C., & Ebesu, A. S. (1994). Interpersonal deception: VII. Behavioral profiles of falsification, equivocation, and concealment. *Journal of Language and Social Psychology, 13,* 366–396.

Buller, D. B., Strzyzewski, K. D., & Hunsaker, F. G. (1991). Interpersonal deception: II. The inferiority of conversational participants as deception detectors. *Communication Monographs, 58,* 25–40.

Burgoon, J. K., Bonito, J. A., Ramirez, A., Kam, K., Dunbar, N., & Fischer, J. (2002). Testing the interactivity principle: Effects of mediation, propinquity, and verbal and nonverbal modalities in interpersonal interaction. *Journal of Communication, 52,* 657–677.

Burgoon, J. K., & Buller, D. B. (1994). Interpersonal deception: III. Effects of deceit on perceived communication and nonverbal behavior dynamics. *Journal of Nonverbal Behavior, 18,* 155–284.

Burgoon, J. K., & Buller, D. B. (2004). Interpersonal deception theory. In S. Seiter & R. H. Gass (Eds.), *Perspectives on persuasion, social influence, and compliance gaining* (pp. 239–264). Boston, MA: Allyn & Bacon.

Burgoon, J. K., Buller, D. B., Dillman, L., & Walther, J. (1995). Interpersonal deception: IV. Effects of suspicion on perceived communication and nonverbal behavior dynamics. *Human Communication Research, 22,* 196.

Burgoon, J. K., Buller, D. B., Ebesu, A., Rockwell, P., & White, C. (1996). Testing interpersonal deception theory: Effects of suspicion on nonverbal behavior and relational messages. *Communication Theory, 6,* 243–267.

Burgoon, J. K., Buller, D. B., & Floyd, K. (2002). Does participation affect deception success? A test of the inter-activity effect. *Human Communication Research, 27,* 503–534.

Burgoon, J. K., Buller, D. B., & Guerrero, L. K. (1995). Interpersonal deception: IX. Effects of social skill and nonverbal communication on deception success and detection accuracy. *Journal of Language and Social Psychology, 14,* 289–311.

Burgoon, J. K., Buller, D. B., Guerrero, L. K., Afifi, W., & Feldman, C. (1996). Interpersonal deception: XII. Information management dimensions underlying deceptive and truthful messages. *Communication Monographs, 63,* 50–69.

Burgoon, J. K., Buller, D. B., White, C. H., Afifi, W. A., & Buslig, A. L. S. (1999). The role of conversational involvement in deceptive interpersonal communication. *Personality and Social Psychology Bulletin, 25,* 669–685.

Burgoon, J. K., Chen, F., & Twitchell, D. (2010). Deception and its detection under synchronous and asynchronous computer-mediated communication. *Group Decision and Negotiation, 19,* 346–366.

Burgoon, J. K., & Floyd, K. (2000). Testing for the motivation impairment effect during deceptive and truthful interaction. *Western Journal of Communication, 64,* 243–267.

Burgoon, J. K., Stern, L. A., & Dillman, L. (1995). *Interpersonal adaptation: Dyadic interaction patterns.* New York, NY: Cambridge University Press.

DePaulo, B. M., Ansfield, M. E., & Bell, K. L. (1996). Theories about deception and paradigms for studying it: A critical appraisal of Buller and Burgoon's interpersonal deception theory and research. *Communication Theory, 6,* 297–296.

Ekman, P. & Friesen, W. V. (1969). Nonverbal leakage and clues to deception. *Psychiatry, 32,* 88–106.

Grice, H. P. (1989). *Studies in the ways of words.* Cambridge, MA: Harvard University Press.

Hancock, J. T., Thom-Santelli, J., & Ritchie, T. (2004). Deception and design: The impact of communication technology on lying behavior. In, *Proceedings of the SIGCHI conference on Human factors in computing systems* (pp. 129–134). New York, NY: ACM.

Jensen, M. L., Meservy, T., Burgoon, J. K., & Nunamaker, J. F. (2009). Automatic, multimodal evaluation of human interaction. *Group Decision & Negotiation, 19,* 367–389.

Johnson, R., Jr., Barnhardt, J., & Zhu, J. (2004). The contribution of executive processes to deceptive responding. *Neuropsychologia, 42,* 878–901.

Stiff, J. B. (1996). Theoretical approaches to the study of deceptive communication: Comments on interpersonal deception theory. *Communication Theory, 6,* 289–296.

Stiff, J. B., Corman, S., Krizek, B., & Snider, E. (1994). Individual differences and changes in nonverbal behavior: Unmasking the changing faces of deception. *Communication Research, 21,* 555–581.

Vrij, A., Fisher, R., Mann, S., & Leal, S. (2006). Detecting deception by manipulating cognitive load. *Trends in Cognitive Sciences, 10,* 141–142.

White, C. H., & Burgoon, J. K. (2001). Adaptation and communicative design: Patterns of interaction in truthful and deceptive conversations. *Human Communication Research, 27,* 9–37.

Zhou, L., Burgoon, J. K., Twitchell, D., & Nunamaker, J. F., Jr. (2004). Automating linguistics-based cues for detecting deception in text-based asynchronous computer-mediated communication. *Group Decision and Negotiation, 13,* 81–106.

Zuckerman, M., DePaulo, B. M., & Rosenthal, R. (1981). Verbal and nonverbal communication of deception. In L. Berkowitz (Ed.), *Advances in experimental social psychology* (pp. 1–59). New York, NY: Academic Press.

27

Media Multiplexity Theory

Technology Use and Interpersonal Tie Strength

Andrew M. Ledbetter

During the last 24 hours, I have instant messaged with a high school friend, spoken on the phone with my grandmother, given my kids a hug, e-mailed one of the editors of this book, Facebooked with acquaintances across the nation, and played a popular word game app with friends. My strong guess is that nearly every reader of this chapter could provide a similar account of their previous day. Without question, many people's lives have become relentlessly multimodal; in other words, we employ many different media to maintain our interpersonal relationships. Although we conduct our relationships multimodally, we do not allocate media to relationships at random. After all, media choices convey metamessages about the relationship (Sitkin, Sutcliffe, & Barrios-Choplin, 1992), as anyone who has been fired via e-mail or dumped via text message can attest. Moreover, the *number* of media chosen also says something about the state of our relationship. It would be odd to communicate with a spouse through only one communication medium, just as it may be strange to communicate with an acquaintance through many channels.

Media multiplexity theory (MMT) seeks to explain how and why the strength of an interpersonal bond is associated with the number of media used to maintain the relationship. Specifically, the theory asserts that dyads with stronger ties use more media to maintain their relationships and, simultaneously, employing more media in relationships may strengthen relational ties. To date, MMT represents the most comprehensive and systematic attempt to explain how the multimodality of social life influences, and is influenced by, the characteristics of interpersonal relationships. This chapter will explore both the historical development of MMT and its current application by interpersonal communication researchers.

Intellectual Tradition of Media Multiplexity Theory

MMT's roots lie in the interdisciplinary study of communication technology, incorporating concepts from information sciences, sociology, and communication. Most chiefly, Haythornthwaite (2000, 2001, 2005) developed MMT from Granovetter's (1973) classic work on social network ties. Granovetter identified *tie strength* as a "combination of the amount of time, the emotional intensity, the intimacy (mutual confidence), and the reciprocal services" exchanged in the relationship (p. 1361). He argued that both *strong ties* and *weak ties* yield psychosocial benefits. Although strong ties meet needs for belonging and emotional fulfillment, they cost much time and energy, and the small size of a person's strong tie network only allows access to a prescribed set of resources. Weak ties bear no such costs (nor such emotional benefits), but do provide access to a wider set of information and resources through the social network. Social networking sites such as Facebook often facilitate the formation of such weak ties (Ellison, Steinfield, & Lampe, 2007). For example, when I moved to Texas, I found my real estate agent through asking my Facebook network for help. In the end, I made contact with a great realtor through the friend of a sister of a former graduate student—the power of weak ties in action.

Haythornthwaite (2005) extended Granovetter's (1973) work by identifying an additional indicant of tie strength: the number of media used in a dyad. She initially discovered this association serendipitously: "Asking 'who talks to whom about what and via which media' revealed the unexpected result that more strongly tied pairs make use of more of the available media, a phenomenon I have termed *media multiplexity*" (Haythornthwaite, 2005, p. 130, emphasis added). Although her initial MMT research focused on communicative effectiveness in organizational (Haythornthwaite, 2001) and educational (Haythornthwaite, 2000) settings, she also sought to explain conflicting findings about the effect of communication technology on interpersonal relationship quality (Haythornthwaite, 2002).

MMT adopts post-positivist metatheoretical assumptions and has developed via quantitative research, although the approach of MMT scholars sometimes differs from other post-positivist interpersonal communication theories. In contrast to the socio-psychological approach adopted by theories such as the theory of motivated information management (W. Afifi & Robbins, Chapter 11, this volume) or social information processing theory (SIPT; Walther, Chapter 31, this volume), early MMT research identified more closely with the cybernetic metatheoretical tradition (Craig, 1999). Following its roots in Granovetter (1973), the first wave of MMT research employed social network analysis to explain patterns among work and educational groups (e.g., Haythornthwaite, 2000). The second wave of research has moved MMT toward a more socio-psychological approach, employing survey methods to examine associations between media use and relational outcomes in interpersonal dyads without regard to their membership in an overarching organizational structure (e.g., Ledbetter & Kuznekoff, 2012).

Main Goals and Features of Media Multiplexity Theory

MMT offers three interrelated claims regarding the use of communication media in interpersonal relationships: (a) Communication content differs by tie strength rather than by medium, (b) across time, tie strength and media use cause each other, and (c) the addition or subtraction of a medium alters the nature of ties within a social network. This section will explore each of these claims in turn.

COMMUNICATION CONTENT DIFFERS BY TIE RATHER THAN MEDIUM

Earlier online communication theory argued that a medium's characteristics determine the communication content that can move effectively across it. For example, the reduced social context cues perspective (Sproull & Kiesler, 1986) argued that text-only exchanges obscure cues to appropriate behavior, thus generating disinhibited (and sometimes hostile) communication. Like SIPT, MMT contends this is not the case. Whereas SIPT identifies time as a moderating factor (such that online relationship development can equal face-to-face exchanges given sufficient time), MMT instead locates tie strength as a driving theoretical mechanism that explains why any medium can facilitate interpersonal relationships.

Strong ties frequently exchange resources (e.g., information, services, or social support), and will continue to do so regardless of the medium through which partners communicate. Indeed, because such ties possess greater interdependence and intimacy, they may find multiple media necessary to sustain the bond. A married couple is a prototype of such a strong tie. During a typical workday, a couple may see each other in the morning and evening, exchange e-mails and instant messages about whether to sign the kids up for swimming lessons, text about the need to pick up milk on the way home, and perhaps talk on the phone during the commute. The nature of the tie—and specifically, the large amount of resources exchanged within it—drives their choice to use multiple media. In contrast, an acquaintance from church does not require so many media to sustain the relationship, with the weak tie sustained through face-to-face hallway greetings and, perhaps, the occasional short note on the congregation's Facebook page. Although Haythornthwaite (2002) is careful to note that the characteristics of a communication medium may alter a message's meaning in some cases, her overarching claim is that "online exchanges are as real in terms of their impact on the tie as are offline exchanges" (p. 388). As such, the theory foregrounds relationship characteristics and goals as determining forces in interpersonal media choice.

To Granovetter's (1973) identification of strong and weak ties, Haythornthwaite (2005) added a third type of tie: the *latent tie,* or "a connection available technically, even if not yet activated socially" by virtue of the medium's availability (p. 137). At my university, our course management software allows a student to e-mail any other student in the course. Most students do not send such messages, but the software forges a latent tie that, through communication, could become a weak tie. Likewise, Facebook creates a latent tie between any two unconnected users of the site, with those latent ties (potentially) becoming weak ties through communication on the site (Ellison, Steinfield, & Lampe, 2011). Similarly, Baym and Ledbetter's (2009) investigation of a music-based social networking site found evidence of weak ties forged through shared musical interests, but those weak ties rarely became strong.

TIE STRENGTH AND MEDIA USE
CAUSE EACH OTHER ACROSS TIME

Although MMT locates tie strength as a cause of media use, the theory also acknowledges that media use, over time, influences tie strength. As Haythornthwaite (2002) noted, additional chances to communicate via any means increase the chance that a relationship will become a strong tie. In contrast to early MMT research, communication scholars have devoted attention to this direction of causation. It is worth noting that although the mutually causal association between tie strength and media use has been elaborated theoretically, it has yet to receive clear empirical validation. Most studies employ cross-sectional survey methods, and thus offer only weak evidence of causation.

Whereas Haythornthwaite (2002, 2005) measured media multiplexity by summing the number of media used in a relationship, other scholars have assessed the use (or frequency) of each medium separately. For example, Baym and Ledbetter (2009) found that a host of communication media predicted close friendship among social networking site users, including face-to-face visits, telephone calls, and communication through the social networking site itself. Ledbetter (2009b) obtained similar findings, with face-to-face, phone calls, instant messaging, and social networking site use all positively associated with tie strength. Likewise, other researchers have found independent contributions to relational quality for Facebook use (Ledbetter et al., 2011) and video game communication (Ledbetter & Kuznekoff, 2012) as compared to offline communication, as well as for texting and voice phone calls (Hall & Baym, 2012) when controlling for both in a single model.

ADDING OR SUBTRACTING A MEDIUM ALTERS TIES

MMT adopts a broader definition of *media* than other online communication theories. Rather than defining a medium as a communication channel (e.g., e-mail), Haythornthwaite (2002) considers a medium as the intersection of channel and social context. For example, both the weekly strategy meeting and the quarterly company picnic occur face-to-face, but their differing social goals and context would qualify each as different media. Although Baym and Ledbetter (2009) noted that such distinctions in media use may eventually cease to be meaningful, including social context in the definition of media is a unique contribution of the theory.

When comparing educational and task groups, Haythornthwaite (2005) observed that media use occurred on a *unidimensional scale,* such that "those who use only one medium, use the same one medium; those who use two, tend to use the same second medium, etc." (p. 130). Each workgroup tended to adopt one or two media as "base" media used for communication across the membership, and then tailored other media for use only with strong ties. Although researchers have yet to extend MMT to families, they serve as an example of this phenomenon. For instance, the geographically dispersed Smith family may use a private Facebook group to communicate across all extended family members. Beyond this base, stronger family ties may exchange private e-mails to share more personalized information, with particularly strong ties engaging in voice phone calls. In contrast, the Johnsons may use an e-mail listserv as their base medium, with stronger ties occasionally posting on each other's Facebook walls and the strongest ties constantly texting. Although the Smith and Johnson families differ in how they use media, the families exhibit similarity by organizing their available media in a hierarchy from those used with all ties to those devoted to stronger ties.

Consistent with the cybernetic grounding of the theory, MMT recognizes that forces beyond the dyad's control—such as a distant relative's creation of a family e-mail listserv—often shape the dyad's media environment. A central thesis of MMT is that the effect of adding or subtracting an available medium depends on the strength of a tie. Specifically, changes to the media landscape alter strong ties only minimally, but may change the nature of weak ties considerably (Haythornthwaite, 2005). Consider an extended family that begins a new tradition of yearly family reunions. Those reunions may create new latent ties by allowing distal members of the extended family network to forge new relationships. For extended family members who are weak ties, such as second and third cousins, the reunion provides a space for communication that may powerfully build their bond, perhaps transforming some weak ties into strong ties. The reunion may also strengthen strong ties, but given that such ties already communicate via several media, the reunion exerts less potent influence on them versus weaker ties.

A similar pattern emerges when a medium becomes unavailable—say, the aunt who planned the reunion passes away and no one picks up the task. This eliminates one venue for latent ties among family members, and weak tie family relationships may fade without the opportunity to rekindle bonds face-to-face each year. Although strong ties may suffer some loss of contact, MMT predicts strong ties will generally continue unabated because they employ several other media for relational maintenance. Although this example addresses face-to-face contact specifically, the same phenomena would apply for any gain or loss of medium—Grandpa finally getting a text messaging plan, a friend shutting down his Facebook page, or an organization removing phones to save money.

How Communication Is Conceptualized in Media Multiplexity Theory

Consistent with Granovetter's (1973) view that interpersonal relationships be defined by the exchange of resources, MMT conceptualizes communication as the means by which such exchanges occur and connect people in an overarching network structure (Haythornthwaite, 2002). In contrast to several other theories of communication media (e.g., media richness theory; Daft & Lengel, 1986), MMT argues that medium properties shape communication content far less than the nature of the relational tie. Following this claim, MMT conceptualizes communication as a union of the *medium* of connection and the *content* expressed via that medium (Haythornthwaite, 2005).

This approach echoes the classic Shannon and Weaver (1949) model of communication as a *message* transmitted through a *channel*. Although early MMT research foregrounded the latter, Haythornthwaite (2001) also examined communicative content such as work collaboration, socializing, and emotional support, finding similar network configurations across content types. What such a network approach cannot do is separate content and media effects into statistically distinguishable components. My own work using MMT has focused, in part, on accomplishing this separation. In one study (Ledbetter, 2010), participants completed Canary and Stafford's (1992) relational mainte-nance scale twice, once for face-to-face communication and once for online communication with a same-sex friend. Advanced statistical techniques can separate these survey responses into variance representing the maintenance behavior (e.g., positivity, openness) without regard to medium, and variance representing use of each medium for maintenance regardless of content. Using this technique, I demonstrated that positivity and social networks positively predicted *equality* of mutual influence (i.e., the extent to which partners find their mutual influence agreeable; Canary, Weger, & Stafford, 1991), whereas, consistent with MMT, both the face-to-face and online medium-specific constructs positively predicted *strength* of mutual influence (i.e., the degree and diversity of influence; Berscheid, Snyder, & Omoto, 1989). In another similar study (Ledbetter, Broeckelman-Post, & Krawsczyn, 2011), we decomposed a measure of everyday talk (Goldsmith & Baxter, 1996), finding that online communication attitudes were associated with the medium-specific constructs.

Research and Practical Applications of Media Multiplexity Theory

Broadly, application of MMT rests in two domains: applications in bounded or semi-bounded groups versus applications apart from a group structure. Haythornthwaite focused on the former, using the theory to address how communication patterns change over time in educational and organizational workgroups (Haythornthwaite, 2000, 2001, 2002, 2005). By collecting longitudinal data from such clearly bounded networks, her findings identified the establishment of a base medium used for interaction across the group and more specialized media used for stronger ties within the group (i.e., the unidimensional scale). Although, traditionally, interpersonal communication scholars have devoted more attention to relationally oriented contexts versus such task-oriented contexts, certainly the "person to person" communication that is the focus of this book often occurs within a broader organizational structure. In other words, friendships occur in workplace and school settings, as well as in units such as neighborhoods, religious congregations, and social clubs. MMT offers a useful framework for investigating interpersonal relationships in such contexts.

As an example of one MMT application to interpersonal relationships within a bounded organizational structure, Van Cleemput (2012) employed insights from MMT to examine clique formation among Belgian high school students. She noted that cliques are an inherently network-level phenomenon, because they arise from both individual- and group-level processes. As nearly any high school student can attest, this clique structure possesses tremendous social and interpersonal importance. Her study examined how communication technologies enable and constrain friendship and clique maintenance. Following media multiplexity theory, Van Cleemput reasoned that characteristics of the dyad (i.e., tie strength, network embeddedness, and sex composition) and characteristics of the social context (i.e., shared classes and shared neighborhood) would predict media use within the network.

After obtaining data from 97.5% of the students in the grade level under investigation, her social network analysis revealed that tie strength and embeddedness served as the strongest predictors of several types of media use. Among the high school students, face-to-face and instant messaging served as "base" media that crossed across cliques, whereas students reserved voice telephone, text messaging, and e-mail for stronger ties within a clique. These results highlight how school peer networks exist even when not in the school context, perhaps with implications for adolescent health. For instance, although communication technologies can foster the development of healthy peer relationships, the demands of constant peer contact may generate stress in the teenager.

The peril of constant connection also served as a starting point for Hall and Baym's (2012) investigation of mobile phone contact among friends. In contrast to Van Cleemput (2012), Hall and Baym did not investigate a bounded social network, but instead employed survey methods to examine a relationship of the participant's choosing. Borrowing insights from relational dialectics theory (Baxter & Norwood, Chapter 21, this volume), Hall and Baym noted that cell phones can foster increased connectedness, yet their ubiquity also threatens autonomy. Specifically, "the expectations of friends to inform, share, and maintain relationships via text messaging and cell phone calls can also lead to feelings of imprisonment and entrapment" (Hall & Baym, 2012, p. 317). Their results indicated that both phone calls and text messaging are associated with the expectation that friends will maintain their relationship using mobile phones, and such expectations, in turn, are associated with feelings of overdependence, entrapment, and reduced friendship satisfaction. Although consistent with MMT, their results also extend the theory by highlighting one "dark side" of tie strength.

One possible avenue for practical application involves the maintenance of family relationships. The family represents an attractive site for MMT research, given that a family possesses different patterns of tie strength and interdependence among members, a network structure, and boundaries commonly defined by biological and legal ties (Stamp, 2004). Moreover, Kennedy and Wellman (2007) noted that family ties vary in their degree of media multiplexity. Leach and Braithwaite's (1996) examination of *family kinkeepers,* or family members that spread information and maintain relationships throughout an extended family network, provides an intriguing starting point for such investigation. Their study found kinkeepers were most often older women who maintained family ties through telephone, postal mail, and face-to-face meetings (e.g., family reunions). MMT is well-positioned to explain how kinkeepers employ newer media to maintain family relationships and how such media use is associated with family cohesion and satisfaction. Such insights would not only help families maintain healthy relationships, but would also help families adjust their kinkeeping behaviors when the kinkeeper becomes unavailable (e.g., through death, disability, or fatigue with the role).

Evaluation of Media Multiplexity Theory

Although much younger than most of the theories addressed in this book, MMT has achieved an impressive amount of popularity among new media scholars both within and outside the communication discipline. For many, the theory's appeal lies in its relatively parsimonious account of multimodality, a phenomenon which theorists have often observed but seldom elaborated in a systematic fashion. By abstracting ties away from specific media properties and individual communicator characteristics, MMT highlights how mediated ties reshape relationships and the networks in which they exist. Interpersonal communication scholars should also appreciate the theoretical centrality afforded to the relationship; arguably, the strength of the relational tie is the mechanism that drives the theory.

Despite the primacy of relationships in the theory, some interpersonal communication scholars will be dissatisfied with MMT's undifferentiated articulation of relationship characteristics relevant to media use. By collapsing nearly all properties of an interpersonal relationship into the construct of tie strength, MMT ignores how constructs such as emotional closeness, interdependence, commitment, communication satisfaction, and equity may differentially predict media use. One notable exception, however, is Ledbetter's (2010) attempt to compare the effect of different relationship characteristics by identifying separate effects associated with control mutuality and interdependence. Clearly, interpersonal communication scholars possess the opportunity to advance the theory by providing a more complete picture of interpersonal bonds.

A second criticism concerns the failure to incorporate individual cognitions into the theory. Haythornthwaite (2005) claimed such cognitions are of little importance in a network-oriented theory, because "it is the interaction between people that matters, rather than what individuals think or do on their own" (Haythornthwaite, 2005, p. 127). In contrast, Ledbetter and Mazer (in press) argued that communicator cognitions might elaborate the theoretical mechanism for why media use predicts tie strength. Their results indicated that attitudes toward communicating online (specifically, toward online self-disclosure and social connection; Ledbetter, 2009a) moderated the association between frequency of Facebook communication and relational interdependence. Specifically, Facebook communication frequency was a positive predictor of interdependence only in the presence of positive attitudes toward online communication. Thus, they concluded that interpersonal partners will choose communication media they both perceive positively when outside forces do not limit media choice.

A third criticism concerns the measurement of media use in research invoking the theory. A cursory glance at the literature reveals several disparate measurement strategies, including summing the number of media used in a relationship, binary assessment of individual media (e.g., simple "yes/no" measures of use of each media in the relationship), scale questions about number of messages in a given period of time, more subjective scale questions about perception of frequency, and calculation of each medium's proportion of the total communication in the relationship. Ledbetter (2009b) tackled this issue most directly when he demonstrated that perceived frequency predicted interdependence but proportion of media use did not. Nevertheless, which method of measurement is best for which contexts and theoretical/practical purposes awaits elaboration.

Continuing the Conversation

Perhaps the most pressing question for MMT researchers concerns the direction of causation in the theory. Currently, the theory treats media use and tie strength as mutually causal, yet researchers have tended to look at either causal direction in isolation (depending on the aim of the particular study). What remains is to examine both together. A sophisticated longitudinal panel study could redress this concern powerfully; given the aims of the theory, the best longitudinal design would include both members of a dyad. Of course, longitudinal designs are complex, and dyadic longitudinal designs especially so (Kenny, Kashy, & Cook, 2006); but until researchers conduct such longitudinal research, our understanding of the chief theoretical associations in the theory will remain less than clear.

A second direction for future theoretical development concerns the role of organizational and group norms. Ledbetter and Mazer (in press) noted that such norms exist in some circumstances (e.g., the school setting observed by Van Cleemput, 2012), yet remain absent in others (e.g., voluntary friendships; Rawlins, 1992). Furthermore, Ledbetter and Mazer recasted this difference in terms of individual versus group identity, a key concern in the social identity theory tradition (see Giles & Soliz, Chapter 12, this volume). Thus, they argued that identity orientation may alter the extent to which individual attitudes predict media use, with such attitudes predicting media use when *individual* identity is salient but exerting less (or no) influence when *group* identity is salient. An alternative possibility, yet not necessarily a contradictory one, is that broader cultural contexts offer norms for media use. For instance, Kim, Kim, Park, and Rice (2007) found that face-to-face and telephone functioned as base media across many relationship types in Korea, with other media serving more specialized relationship functions. Intuitively, it is likely both individual and cultural concerns dictate media choice to an extent, and future work could extend MMT to account for such factors alongside the network/dyadic predictors already identified in the theory.

Third and finally, unlike other popular theories of online communication (e.g., Walther, Chapter 31, this volume), MMT does not incorporate medium properties as a central (or even peripheral) element of the theory. Yet, we know from theories such as SIPT that channel characteristics shape relational development in predictable and powerful ways. A more complete account of multimodality probably needs to include medium properties (such as synchronicity and textuality) as a component.

Although multimodality is not difficult to find, it is frustratingly difficult to research and theorize its essential nature, antecedents, and consequences. MMT's network-based approach has served as one heuristic starting point for understanding this potent aspect of interpersonal communication in the early 21st century. The more recent incorporation of socio-psychological approaches—often by interpersonal communication scholars—has further broadened and strengthened the theory. Addressing causation, group norms, and medium characteristics are three exciting directions for interpersonal communication scholars to continue the conversation—and given the increasing centrality of technology in interpersonal relationships, it is a conversation well worth continuing.

References

Baym, N. K., & Ledbetter, A. M. (2009). Tunes that bind?: Predicting friendship strength in a music-based social network. *Information, Communication & Society, 12*, 408–427.

Berscheid, E., Snyder, M., & Omoto, A. M. (1989). The relationship closeness inventory: Assessing the closeness of interpersonal relationships. *Journal of Personality and Social Psychology, 57*, 792–807.

Canary, D. J., & Stafford, L. (1992). Relational maintenance strategies and equity in marriage. *Communication Monographs, 59*, 239–267.

Canary, D. J., Weger, H., & Stafford, L. (1991). Couples' argument sequences and their associations with relational characteristics. *Western Journal of Speech Communication, 55*, 159–179.

Craig, R. T. (1999). Communication theory as a field. *Communication Theory, 9*, 119–161.

Daft, R. L., & Lengel, R. H. (1986). Organizational information requirements, media richness and structural design. *Management Science, 32*, 554–571.

Ellison, N. B., Steinfield, C., & Lampe, C. (2007). The benefits of Facebook "friends": Social capital and college students' use of online social network sites. *Journal of Computer-Mediated Communication, 12*, 1143–1168.

Ellison, N. B., Steinfield, C., & Lampe, C. (2011). Connection strategies: Social capital implications of Facebook-enabled communication practices. *New Media & Society, 13,* 873–892.

Goldsmith, D. J., & Baxter, L. A. (1996). Constituting relationships in talk: A taxonomy of speech events in social and personal relationships. *Human Communication Research, 23,* 87–114.

Granovetter, M. S. (1973). The strength of weak ties. *American Journal of Sociology, 78,* 1360–1380.

Hall, J. A., & Baym, N. K. (2012). Calling and texting (too much): Mobile maintenance expectations, (over)dependence, entrapment, and friendship satisfaction. *New Media & Society, 14,* 316–331.

Haythornthwaite, C. (2000). Online personal networks: Size, composition and media use among distance learners. *New Media & Society, 2,* 195–226.

Haythornthwaite, C. (2001). Exploring multiplexity: Social network structures in a computer-supported distance learning class. *The Information Society, 17,* 211–226.

Haythornthwaite, C. (2002). Strong, weak, and latent ties and the impact of new media. *The Information Society, 18,* 385–401.

Haythornthwaite, C. (2005). Social networks and Internet connectivity effects. *Information, Communication & Society, 8,* 125–147.

Kennedy, T. L. M., & Wellman, B. (2007). The networked household. *Information, Communication & Society, 10,* 645–670.

Kenny, D. A., Kashy, D. A., & Cook, W. L. (2006). *Dyadic data analysis.* New York, NY: Guilford.

Kim, H., Kim, G. J., Park, H. W., & Rice, R. E. (2007). Configurations of relationships in different media: FtF, email, instant messenger, mobile phone, and SMS. *Journal of Computer-Mediated Communication, 12,* 1183–1207.

Leach, M. S., & Braithwaite, D. O. (1996). A binding tie: Supportive communication of family kinkeepers. *Journal of Applied Communication Research, 24,* 200–216.

Ledbetter, A. M. (2009a). Measuring online communication attitude: Instrument development and validation. *Communication Monographs, 76,* 463–486.

Ledbetter, A. M. (2009b). Patterns of media use and multiplexity: Associations with sex, geographic distance and friendship interdependence. *New Media & Society, 11,* 1187–1208.

Ledbetter, A. M. (2010). Content- and medium-specific decomposition of relational maintenance behaviors in friendships: Integrating equity and media multiplexity approaches. *Journal of Social and Personal Relationships, 27,* 938–955.

Ledbetter, A. M., Broeckelman-Post, M. A., & Krawczyn, A. M. (2011). Modeling everyday talk: Differences across communication media and sex composition of friendship dyads. *Journal of Social and Personal Relationships, 28,* 223–241.

Ledbetter, A. M., & Kuznekoff, J. H. (2012). More than a game: Friendship relational maintenance and attitudes toward Xbox LIVE communication. *Communication Research, 39,* 269–290.

Ledbetter, A. M., & Mazer, J. P. (in press). Do online communication attitudes mitigate the association between Facebook use and relational interdependence?: An extension of media multiplexity theory. *New Media & Society.*

Ledbetter, A. M., Mazer, J. P., DeGroot, J. M., Mao, Y., Meyer, K. R., & Swafford, B. (2011). Attitudes toward online social connection and self-disclosure as predictors of Facebook communication and relational closeness. *Communication Research, 38,* 27–53.

Rawlins, W. K. (1992). *Friendship matters: Communication, dialectics, and the life course.* New York, NY: Aldine de Gruyter.

Sitkin, S. B., Sutcliffe, K. M., & Barrios-Choplin, J. R. (1992). A dual-capacity model of communication media choice in organizations. *Human Communication Research, 18,* 563–598.

Shannon, C., & Weaver, W. (1949). *The mathematical theory of communication.* Urbana: University of Illinois.

Sproull, L., & Kiesler, S. (1986). Reducing social context cues: Electronic mail in organizational communication. *Management Science, 32,* 1492–1511.

Stamp, G. H. (2004). Theories of family relationships and a family relationships theoretical model. In A. L. Vangelisti (Ed.), *Handbook of family communication* (pp. 1–30). Mahwah, NJ: Lawrence Erlbaum Associates.

Van Cleemput, K. (2012). Friendship type, clique formation and the everyday use of communication technologies in a peer group. *Information, Communication & Society, 15,* 1258–1277.

28

The Relational Turbulence Model

Communicating During Times of Transition

Leanne K. Knobloch

I magine two adventurers canoeing down a river. For much of the trip, the water is calm and smooth, the weather is peaceful, and the canoe glides effortlessly downstream with the current. The passengers are free to enjoy the sights and sounds of the great outdoors. When a rocky stretch of river bed is accompanied by stronger winds, however, the canoers discover that their previously relaxed paddling methods are no longer effective. The canoe bounces around unpredictably from the momentum of the white-capped eddies, which escalates the difficulty of accomplishing even simple tasks, such as reaching for sunglasses or adjusting a hat. The passengers may shake with fear, shout with exuberance, or tip the canoe with an ill-timed move. Their thoughts, feelings, and behaviors amidst the turbulence provide a foundation for what lies ahead: They may reach calm waters exhilarated and unscathed, frightened and apprehensive, or frustrated and soaking wet.

The *relational turbulence model* suggests that the pandemonium the canoers encounter on the rugged patch of water is akin to the upheaval that romantic partners experience during times of transition. According to the model, the progression of a romantic relationship is punctuated by unique periods of intense relating similar to a peaceful stretch of river giving way to suddenly turbulent conditions (Knobloch & Theiss, 2010; Solomon & Theiss, 2008; Solomon, Weber, & Steuber, 2010). Just as the trajectory of the canoe depends on the paddlers' ability to alter their prior techniques for navigating the river, the trajectory of romantic relationships depends on what people say and do during times of transition. Indeed, transitions are decisive moments that can lead to dyadic growth or decline (Solomon & Theiss, 2011).

The twin goals of this chapter are to explicate the relational turbulence model and to synthesize research evaluating the model's claims. I begin by describing the scholarly roots of the model. Then, I explain the model's key objectives, claims, and tenets. After defining how the model portrays communication, I summarize recent studies and practical applications stemming from the model. I conclude by evaluating the strengths and weaknesses of the model and proposing ideas for future expansion.

Intellectual Tradition of the Relational Turbulence Model

Theories of relationship development traditionally characterize progression in one of two ways (Baxter & Montgomery, 1996, pp. 57–58). *Qualitative change perspectives* assume that relationships exist in a relatively static form until they are transformed by a sudden, major change. Accordingly, qualitative change perspectives portray relationship development as a series of demarcated stages containing unique features (e.g., Aldous, 1996; Knapp, 1984; Rodgers & White, 1993). In contrast, *quantitative change perspectives* contend that relationships change in degree, but not in kind, as they progress. Quantitative change perspectives depict relationship development as incremental shifts in key characteristics such as intimacy, self-disclosure, uncertainty, and commitment (e.g., Altman & Taylor, 1973; Berger & Calabrese, 1975; Rusbult, Drigotas, & Verette, 1994).

The relational turbulence model integrates these two approaches to conceptualizing relationship development. The model defines a *transition* as a discontinuous phase in the progression of a relationship that corresponds with changes in how partners think, feel, and behave (Knobloch, 2007). Accordingly, the model incorporates qualitative change principles by proposing that transitions transform how individuals define their relationship and behave toward each other (Solomon & Theiss, 2011). The model also argues that transitions are critical junctures during which individuals become vigilant about their partnership and react intensely to even minor occurrences (Knobloch & Theiss, 2010; Solomon et al., 2010). *Relational turbulence* encompasses the tumult, upheaval, and turmoil that people experience when relationships are in flux (Knobloch, 2007; McLaren, Solomon, & Priem, 2011; Solomon & Theiss, 2011). The model proposes that individuals are cognitively, emotionally, and behaviorally reactive to dyadic circumstances during times of transition (e.g., happy events are more joyous, unexpected events are more uncertainty-provoking, unpleasant events are more distressing, exciting events are more thrilling). The model embraces quantitative change principles, then, by positing that transitions coincide with escalated volatility.

Although the relational turbulence model draws on interdisciplinary theorizing from both qualitative and quantitative change perspectives, it is situated squarely in the field of interpersonal communication. It employs a post-positivist theoretical orientation by distinguishing two mechanisms that give rise to relational turbulence during times of transition: relational uncertainty and interference from partners. Whereas the relational uncertainty explanation has its roots in uncertainty reduction theory from the field of interpersonal communication (Berger & Bradac, 1982; Berger & Calabrese, 1975), the interference from partners explanation has its roots in the emotion-in-relationships model from the field of social psychology (Berscheid, 1983, 1991).

Main Goals and Features of the Relational Turbulence Model

The model identifies relational uncertainty as an intrapersonal foundation underlying turmoil when relationships are in flux (Solomon & Knobloch, 2001, 2004; Solomon & Theiss, 2008). *Relational uncertainty* refers to the degree of confidence (or lack of confidence) that individuals have in their judgments about the nature of their relationship (Knobloch, 2010; Knobloch & Solomon, 2002a). It exists in three forms (Berger & Bradac, 1982; Knobloch & Solomon, 1999). *Self uncertainty* indexes people's questions about their own investment in the relationship ("How certain am I about how important this relationship is to me?"). *Partner uncertainty* denotes how unsure individuals are about their partner's participation in the relationship ("How certain am I about how important this relationship is to my partner?"). Finally, *relationship uncertainty* entails ambiguity about the nature of the relationship itself ("How certain am I about the current status of this relationship?"). All three sources of relational uncertainty contribute to the overarching construct (Knobloch, 2010).

The model argues that relational uncertainty sparks reactivity because people lack information to guide the sense-making process. Indeed, when individuals are confronted with questions about their relationship, they have difficulty both producing and processing messages (e.g., Knobloch, Miller, Bond, & Mannone, 2007; Priem & Solomon, 2011), which may pave the way for hypervigilance. For example, people experiencing relational uncertainty appraise unexpected events to be more upsetting (Knobloch & Solomon, 2002b), irritations to be more severe (Solomon & Knobloch, 2004; Theiss & Knobloch, 2009; Theiss & Solomon, 2006b), hurtful episodes to be more distressing (Theiss, Knobloch, Checton, & Magsamen-Conrad, 2009), sexual intimacy to be less fulfilling (Theiss & Nagy, 2010), and social network members to be less supportive of their partnership (Knobloch & Donovan-Kicken, 2006). With respect to emotion, individuals grappling with relational uncertainty are more prone to anger, sadness, fear, and jealousy (Knobloch, Miller, & Carpenter, 2007; Knobloch & Theiss, 2010; Theiss & Solomon, 2006a). Most broadly, romantic partners who are unsure about involvement view their relationship as more turbulent (Knobloch & Theiss, 2010; McLaren, Solomon, & Priem, 2012). This evidence is consistent with the model's premise that relational uncertainty may underlie tumult during times of transition.

The model designates interference from partners as an interpersonal foundation of upheaval (Solomon & Knobloch, 2001, 2004; Solomon & Theiss, 2008). The model's reasoning about interference from partners is grounded in Berscheid's (1983, 1991) theorizing about how dyads establish and re-establish interdependence in relationships over time (Knobloch & Solomon, 2004). Berscheid (1983, 1991) argued that relationship development occurs as people intertwine their lives—first during the acquaintance process and again whenever major changes arise. Disturbances inevitably transpire as individuals insert and re-insert themselves into each other's daily routines. *Interference from partners* occurs when a partner's interruption disrupts a person's ability to accomplish a goal ("How am I supposed to lose weight when you keep making cookies?" "You didn't really rent another action movie, did you?"). *Facilitation from partners* arises when a partner's interruption helps a person achieve a goal ("Bike ride—good idea!" "Shrimp stir fry? What an awesome surprise!").

According to the relational turbulence model, people who encounter frequent disruptions from their partner are vulnerable to reactivity. Researchers using the model have linked interference from partners to both cognitive and emotional markers of turmoil. For example, individuals experiencing interference from partners judge irritations to be more threatening to their relationship (Solomon & Knobloch, 2004; Theiss & Knobloch, 2009; Theiss & Solomon, 2006b); they consider hurtful events to be more intentional and more damaging to their relationship as well (Theiss et al., 2009). They perceive sexual activity to be less satisfying (Theiss & Nagy, 2010), and view friends and family members to be less encouraging of their relationship (Knobloch & Donovan-Kicken, 2006). They experience more negative emotions, including anger, sadness, fear, and jealousy (Knobloch, Miller, & Carpenter, 2007; Knobloch & Theiss, 2010; Theiss & Solomon, 2006a). They also characterize their relationship, in general, as more tumultuous (Knobloch, 2007; Knobloch & Theiss, 2010; McLaren et al., 2011). Collectively, this evidence coheres with the model's theorizing that interference from partners may be a basis of volatility during times of transition.

As an illustration of these ideas, consider the upheaval that Enrique and Ella experience when they welcome their first child into their lives. No matter how many books they read or how much advice is heaped on them, nothing can fully prepare them for the transition. Enrique feels left out by Ella's around-the-clock focus on the baby, Ella gets upset when Enrique does not pitch in cheerfully to help with chores, and both partners feel less connected to each other. They experience plenty of questions about their relationship: How committed is each partner to caring for their family? How will they maintain a romantic bond in the midst of night feedings, mounds of laundry, and streams of well-wishers invading their home? They also disrupt each other's daily routines: Enrique's tendency to get distracted photographing the baby's every smile often results in charred meals, Ella's sunrise gym sessions wake Enrique up early after long nights comforting the baby, and both are guilty of overstuffing the dirty diaper bin so the other person has to empty it. According to the model, the relational uncertainty and interference from partners that Enrique and Ella experience lead them to overreact with anger to thoughtless remarks, on one hand, and with joy to unexpected compliments, on the other. They find themselves jumping to conclusions, experiencing strong emotions, and simultaneously shying away from conflict-inducing topics but getting carried away during the arguments that do arise. Ultimately, the transition furnishes mixed outcomes for their partnership: They spend less quality time together but learn to appreciate each other more.

How Communication Is Conceptualized in the Relational Turbulence Model

Communication has a central place in the relational turbulence model (Solomon et al., 2010; Theiss & Knobloch, 2013). Of course, people's communication can initiate transitions (e.g., "Will you marry me?"), but to date the model has focused on how the mechanisms of relational turbulence predict communication outcomes via both message production and message processing (Solomon & Theiss, 2011). With respect to message production, the model argues that people's reactivity during times of transition is reflected not only in extreme cognitions and emotions, but also in extreme communication behaviors. More specifically, the model proposes that individuals experiencing relational uncertainty and interference from partners rely on both indirect and assertive messages.

Researchers have documented evidence compatible with the model's claim that relational uncertainty coincides with both avoidant and aggressive messages. On one hand, individuals experiencing relational uncertainty are reluctant to express feelings of jealousy (Theiss & Solomon, 2006a), to discuss their partner's irritating behavior (Theiss & Knobloch, 2009; Theiss & Solomon, 2006b) or hurtful actions (Theiss et al., 2009), to communicate directly about sexual intimacy (Theiss, 2011), and to talk openly about sensitive topics (Knobloch & Carpenter-Theune, 2004; Knobloch, Ebata, McGlaughlin, & Theiss, 2013), including the nature of their relationship (Knobloch & Theiss, 2011b). On the other hand, people grappling with questions about their own involvement in a relationship (i.e., self uncertainty) are more likely to confront partners about irritations (Theiss & Solomon, 2006b) and less likely to manage conflict constructively (Theiss & Knobloch, in press). In a study examining both halves of the model's logic about polarized communication, Theiss and Knobloch (2013) found that military personnel returning home from deployment report more closed yet more aggressive communication with their romantic partner under conditions of relational uncertainty. This work, viewed as a set, implies that relational uncertainty may be a foundation of reactivity in message production.

Interference from partners, too, may correspond with both passive and assertive messages. With respect to avoidance, military service members experiencing interference from partners are less likely to engage in open communication (Theiss & Knobloch, 2013) and to maintain their relationship through assurances (Theiss & Knobloch, in press) during the post-deployment transition. With respect to aggression, individuals encountering interference from partners display less affiliation in conversation (Knobloch, 2008), behave more argumentatively (Theiss & Knobloch, 2013), and employ less constructive conflict management strategies (Theiss & Knobloch, in press). These findings hint that disruptions to everyday routines may be a harbinger of polarized message production.

The model posits that the mechanisms of relational turbulence have implications for message processing as well. On this point, the model imports logic from relational framing theory (Dillard, Solomon, & Samp, 1996; McLaren & Solomon, Chapter 9, this volume) to describe how relational uncertainty and interference from partners may guide the inferences people draw from each other's utterances. Relational framing theory proposes that individuals glean information about the nature of a relationship by interpreting their partner's messages through the frames of dominance-submissiveness and affiliation-disaffiliation. Further, the theory contends that characteristics of relationships (such as relational uncertainty and interference from partners) constitute one set of cues that shape people's judgments of dominance-submissiveness and affiliation-disaffiliation. A combination of the two perspectives implies that individuals experiencing questions and disruptions may view their partner's messages as dominating and disaffiliative. Initial evidence is consistent with this claim. Among husbands and wives in conversation, relational uncertainty corresponds with perceptions that a spouse's messages are more dominating and less affiliative (Knobloch, Miller, Bond, & Mannone, 2007), and interference from partners corresponds with perceptions that a spouse's messages are less affiliative (Knobloch, 2008). In the context of hurtful episodes, women experiencing interference from partners and men experiencing relational turbulence see their partner's messages as more dominating (McLaren et al., 2012). Taken together, these studies indicate that relational uncertainty and interference from partners may play a role in message processing.

Research and Practical Applications of the Relational Turbulence Model

The relational turbulence model originated in the context of dating partners navigating the transition from causal dating to serious involvement (Solomon & Knobloch, 2001, 2004; Solomon & Theiss, 2008), but shortly thereafter, scholars began broadening the model's scope to other transitions. For example, investigators have focused on normative shifts within romantic relationships, such as couples becoming parents (Theiss, Estlein, & Weber, 2013) or launching children from their home (Nagy & Theiss, 2013). Researchers also have considered transitions sparked by health challenges, such as romantic partners battling breast cancer (Weber & Solomon, 2008), grappling with infertility (Steuber & Solomon, 2008, 2012), or managing depressive symptoms (Knobloch & Delaney, 2012). In addition, scholars have investigated transitions relevant to particular cohorts, such as military couples (Knobloch & Theiss, 2011a; Theiss & Knobloch, 2013) and military adolescents (Knobloch, Pusateri, Ebata, & McGlaughlin, in press) negotiating a service member's return home from deployment. Collectively, this work spotlights the model's versatility.

For a flavor of the model in action, consider a pair of studies on infertility and relational turbulence. In a first investigation, Steuber and Solomon (2008) analyzed online forums, message boards, and blogs containing personal testimony from individuals grappling with infertility. Themes of relational uncertainty included questions about (a) the importance of the romantic relationship relative to achieving pregnancy, and (b) who is to blame for the inability to reproduce. Issues of interference from partners included disruptions tied to (a) privileging fertility above all other commitments, and (b) being overinvolved or underinvolved in treatment procedures. In a second study, Steuber and Solomon (2012) evaluated the mechanisms of relational turbulence as predictors of couples' difficulty managing private information. They collected survey responses from 50 infertile couples who reported on disclosures to a total of 250 social network members. Interference from partners did not predict problems coordinating disclosures, but when husbands reported that they or their wives were experiencing relational uncertainty, husbands viewed their wives as less accepting of their disclosures to social network members. In sum, both studies suggest that the relational turbulence model may have relevance to the context of infertility.

Another example is research on military couples during homecoming following deployment (Knobloch & Theiss, 2014). As a first step, Knobloch and Theiss (2012) collected open-ended survey responses from 259 recently reunited individuals (137 service members, 122 at-home partners) to identify themes of relational uncertainty and interference from partners salient during the transition. Issues of relational uncertainty included questions about how to (a) sustain commitment, (b) integrate daily routines, (c) divide household chores, (d) adapt to personality shifts, (e) negotiate sexual intimacy, (f) protect the service member's physical and emotional health, and (g) communicate well. Sources of interference from partners included disruptions related to (a) managing everyday routines, (b) completing domestic tasks, (c) distributing control, (d) feeling smothered, (e) parenting, (f) negotiating differences between partners, (g) coordinating social activities, and (h) prioritizing time together. As a second step, Knobloch and Theiss (2011a) and Theiss and Knobloch (in press) collected closed-ended data from returning service members and at-home partners reunited within the past six months. Their results documented both relational uncertainty and interference from partners as predictors of upheaval. Most recently, Knobloch, Ebata, McGlaughlin, and Ogolsky (2013) tracked 118 military couples once per month during the first three months after homecoming. Their findings identified relational uncertainty and interference from partners as predictors of people's reintegration difficulty during the transition. Together, this scholarship showcases the applicability of the relational turbulence model to military couples reunited following deployment.

Evaluation of the Relational Turbulence Model

Just as the best interpersonal relationships blossom when partners build on their strengths and shore up their weaknesses, theories of interpersonal communication improve when scholars hone and refine their ideas. One strength of the relational turbulence model is that it integrates both qualitative and quantitative change perspectives of relationship development. Moreover, by melding theorizing about relational uncertainty and interference from partners, the model assimilates both intrapersonal and interpersonal explanations for upheaval during times of transition. A third strength is that the model lends itself to investigation via diverse research designs (e.g., questionnaires, interviews, content analyses, observational coding) and forms of inquiry (e.g., qualitative and quantitative methods). Perhaps most notably, the model has considerable heuristic value for illuminating a variety of transitions.

Questions yet to be answered by the model represent limitations to address in future research. First, when does a transition begin and end? To date, the model has not explicated the conditions that mark the start and finish of a transition. Scholars have begun testing the model over time (Knobloch, Ebata, McGlaughlin, & Ogolsky, 2013; Solomon & Theiss, 2008; Theiss et al., 2009), but the elusive gold standard is prospective longitudinal data across the full trajectory of a transition (e.g., Theiss et al., 2013). Second, how is relational turbulence manifest in conversation? Much more is known about people's global communication strategies than micro features of their conversations during times of transition, which is unfortunate because conversations are the building blocks of relationship trajectories (e.g., Goldsmith & Baxter, 1996). Finally, scholars have started to examine the interplay within dyads, and this work demonstrates that individuals are responsive to each other's experiences of relational uncertainty and interference from partners (Knobloch & Theiss, 2011b; Theiss & Knobloch, 2009). Future research is needed to theorize more explicitly about mutual influence within couples when relationships are in flux (Knobloch, Ebata, McGlaughlin, & Theiss, 2013).

Continuing the Conversation

The relational turbulence model is maturing to the point that practical applications are plausible. A key question kicks off this conversation: How could the model be used to help people navigate times of transition more constructively? Perhaps infertile couples, for example, could benefit from recognizing the issues of relational uncertainty and interference from partners that are likely to surface during treatment (e.g., Steuber & Solomon, 2008). Perhaps military couples, as another example, could fare better upon reunion following deployment if they learned how to anticipate questions about involvement and troubleshoot routines prone to hindrance (e.g., Knobloch & Theiss, 2011a, 2012). Perhaps empty-nest couples could navigate the transition more effectively if they were knowledgeable about the changes to their relationship, issues of relational uncertainty, and sources of interference from partners that are likely to transpire (Nagy & Theiss, 2013). As a final example, perhaps individuals grappling with depression could enhance the well-being of their romantic relationship if they understood how to handle dyadic ambiguity and manage disruptions from partners (Knobloch & Delaney, 2012; Knobloch & Knobloch-Fedders, 2010). Translating the model into evidence-based programming will require researchers to collaborate with clinicians, practitioners, and educators united by the goal of helping individuals communicate effectively in the midst of changing circumstances.

References

Aldous, J. (1996). *Family careers: Rethinking the developmental perspective.* Thousand Oaks, CA: Sage.

Altman, I., & Taylor, D. (1973). *Social penetration: The development of interpersonal relationships.* New York, NY: Holt, Rinehart, & Winston.

Baxter, L. A., & Montgomery, B. M. (1996). *Relating: Dialogues and dialectics.* New York, NY: Guilford.

Berger, C. R., & Bradac, J. J. (1982). *Language and social knowledge: Uncertainty in inter-personal relationships*. London, UK: Edward Arnold.

Berger, C. R., & Calabrese, R. J. (1975). Some explorations in initial interaction and beyond: Toward a developmental theory of interpersonal communication. *Human Communication Research, 1,* 99–112.

Berscheid, E. (1983). Emotion. In H. H. Kelley, E. Berscheid, A. Christensen, J. H. Harvey, T. L. Huston, G. Levinger, E. McClintock, L. A. Peplau, & D. R. Peterson (Eds.), *Close relationships* (pp. 110–168). New York, NY: Freeman.

Berscheid, E. (1991). The emotion-in-relationships model: Reflections and update. In W. Kessen, A. Ortony, & F. Craik (Eds.), *Memories, thoughts, and emotions: Essays in honor of George Mandler* (pp. 323–335). Hillsdale, NJ: Erlbaum.

Dillard, J. P., Solomon, D. H., & Samp, J. A. (1996). Framing social reality: The relevance of relational judgments. *Communication Research, 23,* 703–723.

Goldsmith, D. J., & Baxter, L. A. (1996). Constituting relationships in talk: A taxonomy of speech events in social and personal relationships. *Human Communication Research, 23,* 87–114.

Knapp, M. L. (1984). *Interpersonal communication and human relationships*. Boston, MA: Allyn & Bacon.

Knobloch, L. K. (2007). Perceptions of turmoil within courtship: Associations with intimacy, relational uncertainty, and interference from partners. *Journal of Social and Personal Relationships, 24,* 363–384.

Knobloch, L. K. (2008). Extending the Emotion-in-Relationships Model to conversation. *Communication Research, 35,* 822–848.

Knobloch, L. K. (2010). Relational uncertainty and interpersonal communication. In S. W. Smith & S. R. Wilson (Eds.), *New directions in interpersonal communication research* (pp. 69–93). Thousand Oaks, CA: Sage.

Knobloch, L. K., & Carpenter-Theune, K. E. (2004). Topic avoidance in developing romantic relationships: Associations with intimacy and relational uncertainty. *Communication Research, 31,* 173–205.

Knobloch, L. K., & Delaney, A. L. (2012). Themes of relational uncertainty and interference from partners in depression. *Health Communication, 27,* 750–765.

Knobloch, L. K., & Donovan-Kicken, E. (2006). Perceived involvement of network members in courtships: A test of the relational turbulence model. *Personal Relationships, 13,* 281–302.

Knobloch, L. K., Ebata, A. T., McGlaughlin, P. C., & Ogolsky, B. (2013). Depressive symptoms, relational turbulence, and the reintegration difficulty of military couples following wartime deployment. *Health Communication, 28,* 754–766.

Knobloch, L. K., Ebata, A. T., McGlaughlin, P. C., & Theiss, J. A. (2013). Generalized anxiety and relational uncertainty as predictors of topic avoidance during reintegration following military deployment. *Communication Monographs, 80,* 452–477.

Knobloch, L. K., & Knobloch-Fedders, L. M. (2010). The role of relational uncertainty in depressive symptoms and relationship quality: An actor-partner interdependence model. *Journal of Social and Personal Relationships, 27,* 137–159.

Knobloch, L. K., Miller, L. E., Bond, B. J., & Mannone, S. E. (2007). Relational uncertainty and message processing in marriage. *Communication Monographs, 74,* 154–180.

Knobloch, L. K., Miller, L. E., & Carpenter, K. E. (2007). Using the relational turbulence model to understand negative emotion within courtship. *Personal Relationships, 14,* 91–112.

Knobloch, L. K., Pusateri, K. B., Ebata, A. T., & McGlaughlin, P. C. (in press). Communicative experiences of military youth during a parent's return home from deployment. *Journal of Family Communication.*

Knobloch, L. K., & Solomon, D. H. (1999). Measuring the sources and content of relational uncertainty. *Communication Studies, 50,* 261–278.

Knobloch, L. K., & Solomon, D. H. (2002a). Information seeking beyond initial interaction: Negotiating relational uncertainty within close relationships. *Human Communication Research, 28,* 243–257.

Knobloch, L. K., & Solomon, D. H. (2002b). Intimacy and the magnitude and experience of episodic relational uncertainty within romantic relationships. *Personal Relationships, 9,* 457–478.

Knobloch, L. K., & Solomon, D. H. (2004). Interference and facilitation from partners in the development of interdependence within romantic relationships. *Personal Relationships, 11,* 115–130.

Knobloch, L. K., & Theiss, J. A. (2010). An actor-partner interdependence model of relational turbulence: Cognitions and emotions. *Journal of Social and Personal Relationships, 27,* 595–619.

Knobloch, L. K., & Theiss, J. A. (2011a). Depressive symptoms and mechanisms of relational turbulence as predictors of relationship satisfaction among returning service members. *Journal of Family Psychology, 25,* 470–478.

Knobloch, L. K., & Theiss, J. A. (2011b). Relational uncertainty and relationship talk within courtship: A longitudinal actor-partner interdependence model. *Communication Monographs, 78,* 3–26.

Knobloch, L. K., & Theiss, J. A. (2012). Experiences of U.S. military couples during the post-deployment transition: Applying the relational turbulence model. *Journal of Social and Personal Relationships, 29,* 423–450.

Knobloch, L. K., & Theiss, J. A. (2014). Relational turbulence within military couples during reintegration following deployment. In S. MacDermid Wadsworth & D. S. Riggs (Eds.), *Military deployment and its consequences for families* (pp. 37–59). New York, NY: Springer.

McLaren, R. M., Solomon, D. H., & Priem, J. S. (2011). Explaining variation in contemporaneous responses to hurt in premarital romantic relationships: A relational turbulence model perspective. *Communication Research, 38,* 543–564.

McLaren, R. M., Solomon, D. H., & Priem, J. S. (2012). The effect of relationship characteristics and relational communication on experiences of hurt from romantic partners. *Journal of Communication, 62,* 950–971.

Nagy, M. E., & Theiss, J. A. (2013). Applying the relational turbulence model to the empty-nest transition: Sources of relationship change, relational uncertainty, and interference from partners. *Journal of Family Communication, 13,* 280–300.

Priem, J. S., & Solomon, D. H. (2011). Relational uncertainty and cortisol responses to hurtful and supportive messages from a dating partner. *Personal Relationships, 18,* 198–223.

Rodgers, R. H., & White, J. M. (1993). Family development theory. In P. G. Boss, W. J. Doherty, R. LaRossa, W. R. Schumm, & S. K. Steinmetz (Eds.), *Sourcebook of family theories and methods: A contextual approach* (pp. 225–254). New York, NY: Plenum.

Rusbult, C. E., Drigotas, S. M., & Verette, J. (1994). The investment model: An interdependence analysis of commitment processes and relationship maintenance phenomena. In D. J. Canary & L. Stafford (Eds.), *Communication and relational maintenance* (pp. 115–140). New York, NY: Academic.

Solomon, D. H., & Knobloch, L. K. (2001). Relationship uncertainty, partner interference, and intimacy within dating relationships. *Journal of Social and Personal Relationships, 18,* 804–820.

Solomon, D. H., & Knobloch, L. K. (2004). A model of relational turbulence: The role of intimacy, relational uncertainty, and interference from partners in appraisals of irritations. *Journal of Social and Personal Relationships, 21,* 795–816.

Solomon, D. H., & Theiss, J. A. (2008). A longitudinal test of the relational turbulence model of romantic relationship development. *Personal Relationships, 15,* 339–357.

Solomon, D. H., & Theiss, J. A. (2011). Relational turbulence: What doesn't kill us makes us stronger. In W. R. Cupach & B. H. Spitzberg (Eds.), *The dark side of close relationships II* (pp. 197–216). New York, NY: Routledge.

Solomon, D. H., Weber, K. M., & Steuber, K. R. (2010). Turbulence in relational transitions. In S. W. Smith & S. R. Wilson (Eds.), *New directions in interpersonal communication research* (pp. 115–134). Thousand Oaks, CA: Sage.

Steuber, K. R., & Solomon, D. H. (2008). Relational uncertainty, partner interference, and infertility: A qualitative study of discourse within online forums. *Journal of Social and Personal Relationships, 25,* 831–855.

Steuber, K. R., & Solomon, D. H. (2012). Relational uncertainty, partner interference, and privacy boundary turbulence: Explaining spousal discrepancies in infertility disclosures. *Journal of Social and Personal Relationships, 29,* 3–27.

Theiss, J. A. (2011). Modeling dyadic effects in the associations between relational uncertainty, sexual communication, and sexual satisfaction for husbands and wives. *Communication Research, 38,* 565–584.

Theiss, J. A., Estlein, R., & Weber, K. M. (2013). A longitudinal assessment of relationship characteristics that predict new parents' relationship satisfaction. *Personal Relationships, 20,* 216–235.

Theiss, J. A., & Knobloch, L. K. (2009). An actor-partner interdependence model of irritations in romantic relationships. *Communication Research, 36,* 510–537.

Theiss, J. A., & Knobloch, L. K. (2013). A relational turbulence model of military service members' relational communication during reintegration. *Journal of Communication, 63,* 1109–1129.

Theiss, J. A., & Knobloch, L. K. (in press). Relational turbulence and the post-deployment transition: Self, partner, and relationship focused turbulence. *Communication Research.*

Theiss, J. A., Knobloch, L. K., Checton, M. G., & Magsamen-Conrad, K. (2009). Relationship characteristics associated with the experience of hurt in romantic relationships: A test of the relational turbulence model. *Human Communication Research, 35,* 588–615.

Theiss, J. A., & Nagy, M. E. (2010). Actor-partner effects in the associations between relationship characteristics and reactions to marital sexual intimacy. *Journal of Social and Personal Relationships, 27,* 1089–1109.

Theiss, J. A., & Solomon, D. H. (2006a). Coupling longitudinal data and multilevel modeling to examine the antecedents and consequences of jealousy experiences in romantic relationships: A test of the relational turbulence model. *Human Communication Research, 32,* 469–503.

Theiss, J. A., & Solomon, D. H. (2006b). A relational turbulence model of communication about irritations in romantic relationships. *Communication Research, 33,* 391–418.

Weber, K. M., & Solomon, D. H. (2008). Locating relationship and communication issues among stressors associated with breast cancer. *Health Communication, 23,* 548–559.

29

Stage Theories of Relationship Development

Charting the Course of Interpersonal Communication

Paul A. Mongeau and Mary Lynn Miller Henningsen

Shrek: [Yelling] Layers! Onions have layers. Ogres have layers. Onions have layers. Ogres have layers. You get it? We both have layers.

Donkey: Oh, you both have layers. You know, not everybody likes onions.

(Warner, Williams, Katzenberg, Adamson, & Jenson, 2001)

Close personal relationships with friends, coworkers, and lovers change over time. This chapter focuses on two stage theories that attempt to describe how people initiate, escalate, and dissolve relationships. These theories explain how and why interpersonal communication evolves as relationships move from strangers or acquaintances to close friends or romantic partners and, perhaps, back again. In this chapter, we describe the functions of stage theories, the stages proposed in two theories, and the role of communication in these theories. We also evaluate stage theories and offer future suggestions.

This chapter describes two stage theories: social penetration theory and the staircase model. Before describing the theories, we want to explain why we call social penetration a theory but refer to the staircase as a model. In most post-positivistic scholarship, theories provide descriptions, explanations, and predictions about a phenomenon. Social penetration theory does all these things as it describes relationship development through stages, provides an explanation for movement through those stages (framed as rewards and costs), and posits a number of predictions about that movement. Conversely, the staircase model describes relationship stages and how they differ, but it does not develop an explanation for, nor clear predictions concerning, movement among those stages. Thus, we will refer to social penetration "theory" and the staircase "model," but we will use the term "theories" when referring to the two together.

Intellectual Traditions of Stage Theories

Stage theories (Altman & Taylor, 1973; Knapp & Vangelisti, 2009; see also Knapp, 1978) have post-positivistic roots, but they also have both dialectic and social constructionist elements. Stage theories' post-positivistic roots stem from social penetration theory (Altman & Taylor, 1973), which included a series of broad, a priori hypotheses about the causes and effects of interpersonal communication. Researchers could observe social penetration and compare those observations to the theory's predictions. On the other hand, stage theories are social constructionist as they describe relationships, their development, and their de-escalation as communicative processes. Specifically, stage theories assume that people construct, reconstruct, and deconstruct their relationships through verbal and nonverbal communication. Furthermore, Altman, Vinsel, and Brown (1981) cast social penetration and relationship development in dialectical terms, suggesting that relational development is not a one-way street toward greater openness, intimacy, and understanding. Instead, a number of contradictory forces simultaneously draw partners toward both greater openness and greater privacy (see also Chapter 21, this volume).

Main Goals and Features of Stage Theories

The three primary features of stage theories of relationship development are (a) the stages, (b) the rules concerning movement through stages, and (c) how interpersonal communication differs or changes across stages. We focus on the first two features in the upcoming section and discuss the role of communication in the next.

RELATIONSHIP STAGES

Stage theories of relationship development (i.e., Altman & Taylor, 1973; Knapp & Vangelisti, 2009) share several important assumptions and characteristics. This is true, in large part, because Knapp (1978) relied on social penetration theory's intellectual contribution when initially developing his model. First, both stage theories presume that relationship development is characterized by changes in interpersonal communication. As relationships develop, communication shifts from superficial and impersonal to intimate and personal (G. Miller & Steinberg, 1975). Second, both theories focus on the development and deterioration of relationships. Third, both theories use a similar organizing metaphor (i.e., social penetration or what Knapp [1978] originally referred to as social intercourse).

Although there are important similarities between the theories, there are also two basic differences (for a detailed comparison, see K. Miller, 2005). First, Knapp and Vangelisti's (2009) model presents separate sets of stages for escalation and de-escalation. On the other hand, Altman and Taylor (1973) argued that relationship de-escalation and relational escalation stages are the same, but occur in the opposite direction (i.e., like a video clip shown in reverse). Second, Knapp and Vangelisti focus almost exclusively on communication between partners, although Altman and Taylor (1973) balance communicative and psychological processes (e.g., assessments of rewards and costs associated with growing closer).

STAGES OF SOCIAL PENETRATION

According to social penetration theory (Altman & Taylor, 1973), relationships develop and de-escalate via changes in verbal, nonverbal, and environmentally oriented behaviors (e.g., access to special possessions or places). Changes in verbal communication focus on self-disclosure (i.e., communicating private information to the other person). Altman and Taylor, social psychologists by training and assumptions, described the development of self-disclosure using an onion metaphor (thus, our opening line from *Shrek*). Imagine that all the information about yourself is somewhere inside an onion. The onion has four layers: the surface, the periphery, the intermediate, and the central layers. As information is disclosed, the layers of the onion are peeled back, signifying the development of the relationship.

Information on the *surface* includes things that others can learn just by looking at you (e.g., sex, race, and approximate age). Just below the surface is the *peripheral* layer. This layer includes information that you would share in just about any social circumstance (e.g., your first name, college major, or hometown). Peeling peripheral layers leads to the *intermediate* layer. This layer contains information that you share infrequently, but that you do not keep hidden per se. For example, Paul jokingly says that he does not tell just anyone that his freshman year in college were the four happiest years of his life, and Min does not often share that she loved the "History of Concrete" episode of *Modern Marvels*. (OK, we told everyone reading this book, but we are all good friends now, right?) Finally, peeling layers beyond the intermediate layer leads to the *central* layer where information is extremely private and is disclosed only when the relationship is very close and the communicator is certain the receiver is trustworthy (Altman & Taylor, 1973).

Altman and Taylor (1973) defined four relationship development stages in terms of depth (i.e., how personal the information communicated is) and breadth (i.e., the number of topics discussed) of self-disclosure (see Table 29.1). An initial interaction between strangers would be a typical example of Altman and Taylor's first stage, *orientation*. These interactions typically involve little personal sharing. New coworkers, for example, might share a broad range of surface and peripheral information such as where they went to school or their hometowns, but no information past the periphery.

The second stage, *exploratory affective exchange,* includes casual relationships, for example, between people known only through work or school, and involves mutual disclosure of a wider array of information. Disclosure continues and broadens at the periphery and, on certain topics, may include information from the intermediate levels. Partners exhibit nonverbal cues (e.g., eye contact, facial expressions, touch, and body movements) that reflect a desire to get to know the partner and correspond to the depth of verbal disclosures. At this stage, information at the central level remains closely guarded and private.

Altman and Taylor's (1973) third stage, *affective exchange,* includes close friendships or romantic relationships "in which people know one another well and have had a fairly extensive history of escalation" (p. 139). In this stage, communication at the peripheral layers is open and broad. Important to this stage, though, is heightened activity at the intermediate and central levels. Partners have removed barriers that inhibited communication on private issues. Unlike earlier stages, communication at the central level does occur, but it remains guarded and is not provided as freely as communication at the peripheral and intermediate levels.

Few relationships reach the final level of *stable exchange*. At this level, partners are granted access to nearly all information on all topics at all levels (i.e., surface, peripheral, intermediate, and central). Consequently, partners know each other extremely well. Altman and Taylor (1973) cautioned, however, that social penetration is never total, and despite considerable verbal, nonverbal, and environmentally oriented exchanges, partners remain somewhat of a mystery to each other. Thus, our predictive and explanatory abilities with each other, although likely increasingly accurate in long-term relationships, are never perfect.

Table 29.1 Social Penetration Theory Stages, Definitions, and Examples From the Movie *Shrek*

Stage	Definition	Example From Shrek
Orientation	Initial interactions between strangers that involve very little personal sharing	*When Shrek and Fiona initially meet* . . . Fiona: You're an ogre. Shrek: Oh, you're expecting Prince Charming? Fiona: Well, yes, actually. This is all wrong. You are not supposed to be an ogre.
Exploratory affective exchange	Mutual disclosure between the dyad on a wider range of topics (though the topics largely remain at the periphery and occasionally intermediate levels)	*Shrek and Fiona are eating rotisserie-style swamp rat* . . . Shrek: Maybe you can come and visit me in the swamp sometime. I'll cook all kinds of stuff for you—swamp toad soup, fish eye tartar. You name it. Fiona: I'd like that.
Affective exchange	Communication between the members of the dyad: open at the periphery with increasing disclosure at the intermediate and central levels	*Just after Fiona turns into an ogre* . . . Shrek: Fiona, [He pulls Fiona closer] I love you. Fiona: Do you really? Shrek: Really, really. Fiona: [Sighs] I love you, too.
Stable exchange	Communication open at all levels (i.e., surface, peripheral, intermediate, and central)	*Fiona is permanently transformed into an ogre and passes out on the floor. Shrek pulls her to her feet* . . . Shrek: Fiona? Are you all right? Fiona: Well, yes . . . But I don't understand. I was supposed to be beautiful. Shrek: [Smiling] But you are beautiful.

Source: Warner et al., 2001.

In social penetration theory, Altman and Taylor (1973) referred to relationship deterioration and dissolution as *social depenetration,* and claimed that it was the mirror of the penetration process. In the theory, relationships deteriorate because partners decrease intimate self-disclosure on an increasing number of topics over time.

KNAPP AND VANGELISTI'S STAGES OF DEVELOPMENT AND DETERIORATION

Knapp (1978), a communication scholar, also developed a stage model of relationship development and deterioration (in part based on the social penetration stages). The metaphor Knapp (1978; Knapp & Vangelisti, 2009) chose was a staircase, where each relational stage represented a different step. Relational development was represented by movement up the steps along the left-hand side of the staircase, while deterioration was represented by movement down the steps along the staircase's right-hand side (see Figure 29.1). Between the two sets of stages is a stabilizing section where partners can remain if both agree.

Knapp and Vangelisti (2009) proposed five stages of coming together. First, *initiating* involves opening channels of communication and initial contact between partners. Second, *experimenting* allows partners to get to know each other better by moving from superficial to more personal communication. Third, in the *intensifying* stage, partners acknowledge the special nature of their relational connection. The fourth stage of relationship development is *integrating*, when the two partners figuratively become a single entity. In this stage, communication is easy between partners as they share nearly everything. Through the integrating phase, Knapp and Vangelisti's stages are similar to Altman and Taylor's (1973). The final stage of relational development in Knapp and Vangelisti's model, *bonding*, has no analogue in Altman and Taylor's theory. Bonding, such as a marriage ceremony, represents the public formalization of the couple and cements a legal, personal, and social commitment between partners.

Knapp and Vangelisti (2009) also described five stages of relationship dissolution that mirror, for the most part, their stages of development. First, *differentiating* involves partners separating themselves from the couple and focusing on their uniqueness. The next stage of dissolution is *circumscribing*, where partners engage in less frequent, and less personal, communication. In the third dissolution stage, *stagnating*, partners communicate negative feelings nonverbally and tend to imagine interaction (e.g., "I'll say this and then she'll say that and then she'll slam the door and then I'll go drink with my buddies") rather than repeat fights. In the fourth stage, *avoiding*, partners attempt to increase physical and psychological space to prepare themselves for life without their partner. The final dissolution stage is *termination* or the actual ending of the relationship (i.e., couple or friendship). Termination can occur during an initial interaction, after a long relationship, or anyplace between those points.

MOVEMENT ACROSS AND BETWEEN STAGES

Social penetration theory (Altman & Taylor, 1973) predicts that the *minimax* principle drives relationship development and deterioration. The minimax principle suggests that people seek relationships that maximize rewards (e.g., time, affection, trust, and loyalty) and minimize costs (e.g., frustrations, conflicts, and lost opportunities) in current, and projected future, interactions. Altman and Taylor's definitions of rewards and costs are similar to those described in social exchange theories (see Chapter 30). Essentially, relational development depends on the relative ordering of rewards and costs (i.e., outcomes, or *O*), general expectations for relationships (i.e., comparison level, or *CL*), and perceived outcomes from the next best alternative, which might involve being alone (i.e., comparison level for alternatives, or *CLalt*).

Knapp and Vangelisti (2009) also provided a number of guidelines for movement between stages. They argued, "Movement is generally systematic and sequential. Movement may be forward. Movement may be backward. Movement occurs within stages. Movement is always to a new place" (p. 47). In addition, they claim that partners should not skip stages because they might miss important information concerning their partner.

Both stage theories (Altman & Taylor, 1973; Knapp & Vangelisti, 2009) appear to describe relationship development and dissolution as linear (i.e., a progression toward increased or decreased intimacy), but closer inspection suggests that movement through stages may not be linear. For example, Altman and Taylor claimed that relationship development "ebbs and flows, does not follow a linear course, and cycles and recycles through levels of exchange" (p. 135). The staircase model indicates that movement through the model can be unpredictable. Just because a couple advances to intensifying does not mean that integrating is, inevitably, the next stage. Instead, they could move back to experimenting, slide to circumscribing, or terminate. We describe the linear nature of these theories in the evaluation section below.

How Communication Is Conceptualized in Stage Theories

"Communication is critical in developing and maintaining interpersonal relationships" (Taylor & Altman, 1987, p. 257). In stage theories, communication is represented as not only the mechanism through which relationships develop (and dissolve) but also as an important marker for the movement through stages. Both stage theories differentiate stages primarily using verbal and nonverbal communication. As relationships develop and dissolve, a number of important changes occur in the nature of interpersonal communication. These changes both reflect and signal how the individuals value, nurture, and identify the relationship in their lives.

Social penetration theory (Altman & Taylor, 1973) conceptualizes communication primarily as the breadth and depth of self-disclosure. The onion model describes relationship development as increases in (and relationship deterioration as decreases in) the intimacy of self-disclosures. Moreover, as self-disclosures become more (or less) personal, nonverbal messages and environmentally oriented behaviors exchanged between partners shift to match the nature of the verbal messages.

The staircase model (Knapp & Vangelisti, 2009) posits dimensions along which communication varies. Knapp and Vangelisti suggest that communication varies along several dimensions: stylized-unique, difficult-efficient, rigid-flexible, awkward-smooth, public-personal, hesitant-spontaneous, and overt judgment suspended-overt judgment given. As relationships develop, communication becomes more idiosyncratic as it takes on a style of its own. Partners gain an ability to say things their own way (i.e., unique), in few words (i.e., efficient), in multiple ways (i.e., flexible), easily (i.e., smooth), utilizing assumptions about the hearer and the relationship (i.e., personal), without delay or forethought (i.e., spontaneous), and providing explicit (i.e., on record) information about their own feelings and perceptions (i.e., overt judgment given). Communication in relationships varies based on the particular developmental stage.

Research and Practical Applications of Stage Theories

The use of stage theories is a bit of a contradiction. Even though they have been credited with generating scholarly interest in a wide variety of communication topics, there have been few direct tests of these theories (for reasons described in the next section). For example, Welch and Rubin (2002) argued that Knapp's (1978) explication of relationship dimensions (e.g., narrow-broad, and public-personal) contributed to scholarly interest in the way relationships are defined (often implicitly) through communication (e.g., Burgoon & Hale, 1987). Researchers still study the dimensions underlying the relational meaning of communication (e.g., Dillard, Solomon, & Palmer, 1999; see also Chapter 9, this volume).

K. Miller (2005) argued that research on self-disclosure in a variety of contexts also owes an intellectual debt to social penetration theory. Reviews of self-disclosure research (e.g., Dindia, 2000) remain supportive of many of the roles and functions of communication in relationship development as outlined within social penetration theory. Recent research on self-disclosure in specific contexts such as online dating (Ledbetter et al., 2011), same-sex friendships (e.g., Hall, 2011), and topic avoidance in families (e.g., Merrill & Afifi, 2012) reaffirm the importance of the stage theories of relationship development.

Other research owes an intellectual debt to the stage theories and deepened the descriptions of the stages provided in the initial model. For example, Duck (1982) developed a model of relationship dissolution (without a corresponding set of development stages) that focused as much on the social network as it does the couple involved. Moreover, Duck contended that the disengagement process lasts far beyond termination. Even our own research on date initiation and romantic relationship transitions—how relationships make the shift from platonic to romantic—stems in important ways from these stage theories (Mongeau, Serewicz, Henningsen, & Davis, 2006). For example, the nature of the transition differs strongly depending on the couple's developmental history.

Despite the heuristic value and the role of stage theories in generating scholarship, the theories are not without problematic elements. In the next section, we briefly discuss the strengths and limitations of stage theories.

Evaluation of Stage Theories

The breadth and range of stage theories represents a double-edged sword. On the one hand, few communication theories can boast the scope or influence of social penetration theory. Specifically, it "has been widely used as a model in teaching about interpersonal relationships and as an overarching framework for considering relational development" (K. Miller, 2005, p. 175). Understanding relationship progression from stage to stage, the mechanisms for moving forward and backward, and the stabilization of relationships are important, parsimonious, devices for students of relationship research.

On the other hand, the breadth and scope of social penetration theory makes it difficult to adequately test as a whole (see also K. Miller, 2005). Few studies have followed relationships from initial interaction to termination. Indeed, the logistical and ethical implications of investigating relationships for such an extended period make the process difficult at best. Even Welch and Rubin (2002), who created a scale to measure Knapp's (1978) stages, used cross-sectional rather than longitudinal data in their study. Rather than follow relationships over time, they investigated a large number of relationships (at all points of development) at a single point in time.

As we noted previously, a second limitation of the stage theories concerns confusion regarding the linear nature of the stages. Although both Altman and Taylor (1973) and Knapp and Vangelisti (2009) noted that relationships may not follow a linear progression, the vocabulary used to describe relationship development and deterioration—as well as the rules for moving between stages—implies a linear path. For example, Knapp and Vangelisti argued that the process of relational development may not be linear, but later stated,

> Many people experience a general sequencing effect because (1) each stage contains important presuppositions for the following stage, (2) sequencing makes forecasting adjacent stages easier, and (3) skipping steps is a gamble on the uncertainties presented by the lack of information that could have been learned in the skipped step. (p. 48)

This clearly implies that relationships either do, or should, follow a linear developmental path. Along similar lines, Altman and colleagues (1981) provided a dialectical view of social penetration processes (which presumes that neither openness nor privacy is preferred), but later equated good communication with openness: "Communication and disclosure intimacy appear to be the sine qua non of developing satisfying interpersonal relationships" (Taylor & Altman, 1987, p. 257), suggesting a linear view of relationship development.

Baxter and Montgomery (1996) provided a stinging critique of the linear nature of stage theories. In part, they took aim at the assumption that relationships progress in a one-way manner toward greater intimacy, closeness, and certainty. According to the linear view, healthy relationships grow while sick relationships decline. Baxter and Montgomery, instead, presented a dialectical view where "relationships change in fluid patterns of more or less openness, more or less intimacy, more or less certainty and so forth" (pp. 58–59). Moreover, they argued that relationships do not reach a balance or stabilize. Instead, relationships are constantly changing because they are buffeted by opposing forces (e.g., the simultaneous need for certainty and the desire for spontaneity; see Chapter 21, this volume).

An example of a nonlinear relationship trajectory is highlighted in Dailey, Rossetto, Pfiester, and Surra's (2009) recent investigation of on-again/off-again (i.e., OAOA) dating relationships. In OAOA relationships, partners date and break up only to later reconcile and return to a romantic dating relationship. In their study, some relationships went through several breakups and renewals (Dailey et al., 2009). Consistent with stage theories, reasons for breakups include conflict between partners, stagnation, and a desire to pursue relational alternatives. Also consistent with the theories, reasons for renewal included more effective communicating between partners, renewed effort to maintain the relationship, and increased intimacy (Dailey et al., 2009). From these data, it seems clear that the nature of communication (including the breadth and depth of self-disclosures) in the relationship sparks both breakups and the renewals.

Complicating the (non)linear nature of relationships further, the amount of time a couple spends at a particular stage, and the forward or backward movement between stages, depends on the partners and their unique circumstances. For example, while Shrek and Fiona develop a romantic relationship through a reasonably linear path, Shrek and Donkey's friendship jumps among stages of development and dissolution as they bicker. In many cases, rather than a staircase, a better metaphor for relationship development might be a rollercoaster in near total darkness. There are twists and turns, steep climbs, and perilous falls that, for the most part, we cannot see coming.

A third limitation of stage theories is that they are not described specifically enough. Both Altman and Taylor (1973) and Knapp and Vangelisti (2009) described their stages relatively briefly. In fairness, the stages represent only a small part of social penetration theory. Moreover, Knapp and Vangelisti never presented the staircase model as theoretical (thus, our reticence to call it a *theory*). Moreover, neither theory was meant to be taken as the only way that relationships develop. Altman and Taylor claimed that "to speak of a set number of stages of the social penetration process is artificial" (p. 135), while Knapp and Vangelisti indicated that any direction of movement is possible from any point of the model.

A fourth criticism is that stage theories (particularly the staircase model) do not effectively describe the development of couples who are not in heterosexual romantic relationships. In heterosexual dating, the script from initiating to bonding is largely known and shared. On the other hand, it is difficult to know how to map other, particularly nontraditional or nonromantic, relationships (e.g., friendships and GLBT romantic relationships) where legally sanctioned bonding ceremonies are not always available to partners.

Finally, an important point of controversy concerning social penetration theories is Altman and Taylor's (1973) use of economic concepts (e.g., rewards and costs) from social exchange theories (see Chapter 30, this volume). People feel strongly about the utility of resource exchange in evaluating close personal relationships. Most of our students (and most communication scholars, for that matter) either love or absolutely hate (with little middle ground) using rewards and costs to explain relationship development and dissolution. Some people find using rewards and costs to assess the attractiveness of relationships to be both natural and useful. Research indicates that including rewards and costs increases the accuracy of explanations of relationship development (e.g., Sunnafrank, 1990). On the other hand, others argue that there is something unique about close relationships that make trying to reduce them to calculating rewards and costs totally inappropriate. For example, Wood (1997) claimed that "relationships are not governed by and cannot be explained by economic principles or cost-benefit considerations" (p. 234). Knapp and Vangelisti (2009) and other scholars (e.g., Berger & Calabrese, 1975) circumnavigated this controversy by focusing on the role of communication (rather than reward-cost notions) in relationship development.

In sum, even though they have been cited widely, stage theories fall short in terms of theoretical clarity and specificity. In order to develop into a strong "theory" of relationship development, these stage theories need to be explicated much more completely and studied. As metaphors spurring our scholarly imaginations, however, they have been overwhelming successes.

Continuing the Conversation

From our analysis of their strengths and weaknesses, continuing the conversation concerning stage theories should focus on three issues. The first two issues stem from the fact that stage theories were first developed 40 years ago and should be (re)considered given the dramatic social and relational changes that occurred since then (e.g., Bogle, 2008). Therefore, first, communication scholars should investigate how and why communication differs as relationships change *over time*. For example, current campus sexual norms suggest that in many cases, sexual activity (e.g., a hookup) precedes significant self-disclosure and other intimate nonverbal message behaviors (e.g., Bogle, 2008). Scholars need to investigate how the early initiation of sexual behavior influences relationship development dynamics.

Second, stage theories should be reconsidered to incorporate the influence of technology (e.g., social networking sites such as Facebook, Twitter, and other social media) on relationship development. Stage theories assume that as partners progress through relationship stages, uncertainty decreases and communication between partners becomes more personal and private. Fox, Warber, and Makstaller (2013) indicated that a Facebook-rich environment violates these assumptions. In early relationship stages (e.g., initiating and experimenting), Facebook provides considerable information about the partner that was once revealed through intentional self-disclosure. This finding suggests a need to revise and rethink the role of information sharing in early relationship development stages. In later stages, Fox et al. suggest that becoming "Facebook official" may mark a new developmental stage that goes beyond serious and exclusive dating. Relationship status changes that appear on Facebook allow social network members to learn, and comment upon, new pairings. Before Facebook, this information was spread in more limited and purposeful ways. Thus, Fox et al. demonstrate that Facebook adds complexity to an already complicated relational development process.

Finally, researchers should investigate communication in the development and dissolution of different relationship types. The notion that stages should apply to all relationship types has not been widely considered. Characteristics such as the voluntary (e.g., dating partners and friends) or involuntary (e.g., in-laws and coworkers) nature of the relationship, the partners' culture (e.g., Japan versus Afghanistan versus the United States), or individual differences (e.g., age, relational experience, or sexual orientation) could influence communication and relational development processes.

References

Altman, I., & Taylor, D. A. (1973). *Social penetration: The development of interpersonal relationships*. New York, NY: Holt, Rinehart, & Winston.

Altman, I., Vinsel, A., & Brown, B. B. (1981). Dialectic conception in social psychology: An application to social penetration and privacy regulation. In L. Berkowitz (Ed.), *Advances in experimental social psychology* (vol. 14, pp. 107–160). New York, NY: Academic Press.

Baxter, L. A., & Montgomery, B. M. (1996). *Relating: Dialogues and dialectics.* New York, NY: Guilford.

Berger, C. R., & Calabrese, R. J. (1975). Some explorations in initial interaction and beyond: Toward a development of theory of interpersonal communication. *Human Communication Research, 1,* 99–112.

Bogle, K. A. (2008). *Hooking up: Sex, dating, and relationships on campus.* New York, NY: New York University Press.

Burgoon, J. K., & Hale, J. L. (1987). Validation and measurement of the fundamental themes of relational communication. *Communication Monographs, 54,* 19–41.

Dailey, R. M., Rossetto, K. R., Pfiester, A., & Surra, C. A. (2009). A qualitative analysis of on-again/off-again romantic relationships: "It's up and down, all around." *Journal of Social and Personal Relationships, 26,* 443–466.

Dillard, J. P., Solomon, D. H., & Palmer, M. T. (1999). Structuring the concept of relational communication. *Communication Monographs, 66,* 49–65.

Dindia, K. (2000). Sex differences in self-disclosure, reciprocity of self-disclosure, and self-disclosure and liking: Three meta-analyses reviewed. In S. Petronio (Ed.), *Balancing the secrets of private disclosures* (pp. 21–35). Mahwah, NJ: Erlbaum.

Duck, S. W. (1982). A topography of relationship disengagement and dissolution. In S. W. Duck (Ed.), *Personal relationships 4: Dissolving personal relationships* (pp. 1–30). New York, NY: Academic Press.

Fox, J., Warber, K. M., & Makstaller, D. C. (2013). The role of Facebook in romantic relationship development: An exploration of Knapp's relational stage model. *Journal of Social and Personal Relationships. 30,* 771–794.

Hall, J. A. (2011). Sex differences in friendship expectations: A meta-analysis. *Journal of Social and Personal Relationships, 28,* 723–747.

Knapp, M. L. (1978). *Social intercourse: From greeting to goodbye.* Needham Heights, MA: Allyn & Bacon.

Knapp, M. L., & Vangelisti, A. (2009). *Interpersonal communication and human relationships* (6th ed.). Boston, MA: Allyn & Bacon.

Ledbetter, A. M., Mazer, J. P., DeGroot, J. M., Meyer, K. R., Mao, Y., & Swafford, B. (2011). Attitudes toward online social connection and self-disclosure as predictors of Facebook communication and relational closeness. *Communication Research, 38,* 27–53.

Merrill, A. F., & Afifi, T. D. (2012). Examining the bidirectional nature of topic avoidance and relationship dissatisfaction: The moderating role of communication skills. *Communication Monographs, 79,* 499–521.

Miller, G. R., & Steinberg, M. (1975). *Between people: A new analysis of interpersonal communication.* Chicago, IL: Science Research Associates.

Miller, K. (2005). *Communication theories: Perspectives, processes, and contexts* (2nd ed.). Boston, MA: McGraw Hill.

Mongeau, P. A., Serewicz, M. C. M., Henningsen, M. L. M., & Davis, K. L. (2006). Sex differences in the transition to a heterosexual romantic relationship. In D. J. Canary & K. Dindia (Eds.), *Sex differences and similarities in communication: Critical investigations of sex and gender in interaction* (2nd ed., pp. 337–358). Mahwah, NJ: Erlbaum.

Sunnafrank, M. (1990). Predicted outcome value and uncertainty reduction theories: A test of competing perspectives: *Human Communication Research, 17,* 76–103.

Taylor, D. A., & Altman, I. (1987). Communication in interpersonal relationships: Social penetration processes. In M. E. Roloff & G. R. Miller (Eds.), *Interpersonal processes: New directions in communication research* (pp. 257–277). Newbury Park, CA: Sage.

Warner, A., Williams, J. H., Katzenberg, J. (Producers), Adamson, A., & Jenson, V. (Directors). (2001). *Shrek* [Motion picture]. United States: DreamWorks SKG.

Welch, S. A., & Rubin, R. B. (2002). Development of relationship stage measures. *Communication Quarterly, 50*, 24–40.

Wood, J. T. (1997). *Communication theories in action: An introduction.* Belmont, CA: Wadsworth.

30

Social Exchange Theories

Calculating the Rewards and Costs of Personal Relationships

Laura Stafford

// **I** just wasn't getting anything out of that relationship." "She was too high maintenance." We hear people give reasons like these for ending a romantic involvement. Such reasons indicate decisions and actions based on perceptions of costs (what we are putting into a relationship) versus rewards (what we are getting out of a relationship). The idea that interpersonal interaction is guided by calculations of costs and rewards is central to theories of social exchange. This chapter presents the major premises and concepts common among these social exchange theories. In doing so, three variations of social exchange theories—resource theory, interdependence theory, and equity theory—are highlighted.

Intellectual Tradition of Social Exchange Theory

Exchange theories can be traced to psychologists Thibaut and Kelley (1959) or sociologists Homans (1961) and Blau (1964), and have roots in economics (rewards and costs) or behaviorist psychology (rewards and punishments). The common thread among these theories is the analogous connection to economic exchange. Just as in a profit-motivated economic exchange, in social exchange, decisions are based on projections of the rewards and costs of a particular course of action. We decide to invest money in one stock as opposed to another because of our expectations of the dividends we will earn. Similarly, we make decisions about and engage in behaviors we expect to be rewarding. In both arenas, we act in a manner we believe will be profitable. Exchange theory does not presume that we always seek to maximize our rewards and minimize our costs, nor that we are only interested in maximizing our own profits at the expense of others: Reciprocity and fairness are also part of exchange theory.

Social exchange theories are post-positivist in orientation; they largely rest on propositions that can be tested. Humans are seen as rational creatures who, on some level, engage in a cost-benefit analysis: a weighing of the pros and cons of interpersonal interaction and relationships.

Main Goals and Features of Social Exchange Theory

Like other social scientific approaches, the primary goal of social exchange theories is to predict and explain behavior. According to social exchange theories, we can predict and explain behavior through an understanding of the factors that individuals take into account (rewards and costs) in making decisions.

Social exchange theories share basic assumptions: Social behavior is a series of transactions. Individuals attempt to maximize their rewards and minimize their costs. When individuals receive rewards from others, they feel a sense of obligation. Embedded within these assumptions are two main concepts: self-interests and interdependence. Self-interests drive individuals to act in accordance with perceptions and projections of rewards and costs associated with an exchange, or potential exchange, of resources. Interdependence refers to the extent to which one person's outcomes depend on another person's outcomes. Before delving further, we must understand the "social" aspects of social exchange, as well as consider what constitutes rewards and costs.

THE SOCIAL IN SOCIAL EXCHANGE

An exchange is a transfer of something in return for something else (Roloff, 1981). This can occur between an individual and the environment. However, "social" exchange requires a connection with another human. Social exchange is somewhat different from economic exchange. Economic exchange typically involves legal obligations, whereas social exchange relies on trust or goodwill; social exchange is voluntary. Economic exchange demands an exact specification of the rewards and costs of both parties; social exchange leaves the rewards and costs open. Economic exchange involves a set, and often short, time frame for the exchange to occur. Economic exchange frequently involves negotiating and is similar from person to person. In social exchange the time frame is more likely to be undetermined and flexible. It seldom involves explicit bargaining and is more likely to be individualized. Consider the following conversation between friends:

"I need a ride home."

"What's in it for me?"

"I'll bake you two dozen homemade brownies."

"Make it three dozen."

"Okay, three dozen. Let's go."

"Not so fast. We need to specify the terms. I want them this weekend and you bring them to my house."

"I'm the one without a car. You pick them up, and it will have to be next weekend. But I will make them double chocolate chip."

"All right, double chocolate chips are worth the wait. Deal."

"Okay. Let's go."

"Hold on. We need to draw up a contract. How do I know you will bake the brownies if I don't have it in writing?"

Likely this conversation feels quite odd, and a friend who negotiates how many brownies a ride is worth is probably not someone we'd want to keep as a close friend. The reason the interaction sounds peculiar is because it is more akin to economic exchange than social exchange.

Though different, it is debatable as to how distinct social and economic exchanges are. Friends *could* have a conversation like the one of above. And squabbling siblings may retort to a request with, "What's in it for me?" Partners do sometimes negotiate: "I walked the dog last time. It's your turn." Not all economic exchanges involve bargaining. In the United States, we seldom negotiate with the grocer how much we should pay for milk or bread, but we expect to "haggle" over the price of a car. Also obligations, though seldom legally enforceable, do exist among family members, friends, and romantic partners, and thus may not feel voluntary: "My brother let me crash on his couch for a week last summer. Now I have to let him spend the night at my place."

SELF-INTERESTS AND INTERDEPENDENCE

Social exchange theories are based on the concepts of self-interests and interdependence. Individuals are motivated to interact with others in ways that serve their self-interests. Though this might mean we seek to maximize our profits at the cost of others, this is not always the case. Often it is in our best interests to cooperate so that both parties' profits are maximized. In addition, considerations of fairness or justice come into play.

To understand "interdependence," it is useful to think about independence and dependence. Total independence occurs when one's outcomes are based solely on one's own efforts, and complete dependence occurs when one's outcomes are based solely on the efforts of another. The enjoyment (reward) of thriving plants in your apartment is based on your own efforts to water and care for them. Complete dependence is exemplified by a parent-infant relationship: A baby is entirely dependent on a caregiver for rewards.

Interdependence means that each person's outcomes are influenced by the other's efforts. In a long-term relationship each person's satisfaction (a reward) is influenced by the efforts of the other person. If within a particular marriage the husband enjoys being home with the children while the wife pursues her career, and she enjoys pursuing her career, both are receiving their desired rewards with the aid of the other. If she did not earn enough income, he could not afford to stay home with the children; if he did not care for the children, she would not be able to pursue her career. Such interdependence (or degree of dependence) is subject to the availability of alternative sources to satisfactorily meet needs. If the wife has other equally suitable child care options, her reward of pursuing her career is less dependent on her husband.

Obviously this example is oversimplified. A partner might meet needs in one arena and not in another. In a long-term relationship, the level of dependence or interdependence, overall, refers to the "extent to which an individual 'needs' a relationship and relies primarily on a given partner and relationship for the fulfillment of important needs" (Rusbult, Drigotas, & Verette, 1994, p. 117), needs an individual believes cannot be acceptably met elsewhere.

COSTS, REWARDS, AND RESOURCES

Resources constitute rewards when they provide pleasure and costs when they provoke pain, anxiety, embarrassment, or mental and physical effort. Resource theory, an exchange theory developed by Foa and Foa (1976, 2012) identifies types of resources: money, goods, status, love, services, and information. These resources vary in how concrete they are. Fudge brownies (a good) are tangible; popularity (status) is not. Resources also vary in how unique they are to a particular individual. Consider love: Love is abstract. It is difficult to quantify or even define. It is highly individualized. No matter how fuzzy, abstract, and unquantifiable love may be, it is given specifically and uniquely to another. Money, on the other hand, is quite concrete. It is also universal. We know what a dollar is and how much it is worth. One $10 bill is as good as another, and can be given to many different people in the same way, with no particular individual or unique qualities attached.

We are more satisfied when similar resources are exchanged (Foa & Foa, 1976). Goods, like groceries, cars, or clothes, are more similar to money than they are to love. Therefore an exchange involving money for money (exchanging a $10 bill for two $5 bills) or money for goods (money for groceries) is more likely to be gratifying than an exchange of money for love.

Relationship type also influences the exchange of resources. Money for services is expected between a mechanic and a customer. The next time you need an oil change your offer of love is unlikely to been seen as an acceptable exchange. Among friends, on the other hand, exchanging money for services is not generally appropriate. If your friend covers for you at work, you are more likely to reciprocate with—and it is more likely for both of you be content with—not an exchange of money, but rather with an understanding that "I owe you one."

How Communication Is Conceptualized in Social Exchange Theory[1]

Communication can serve social exchange in three ways: (a) Communication is the means through which bargaining about the exchange occurs, that is, communication is the tool of negotiation, (b) At other times, however, communication itself is the resource to be exchanged, the reward or cost. A hurtful comment from a friend may be a cost of that friendship, and a compliment might be a reward, (c) In addition, the exchange may have symbolic or communicative value (Molm, Schaefer, & Collett, 2007).

Though Roloff (1981) conceived of exchange as a transfer, implying a loss by one party, he later contended that one might give away a resource, thus rewarding another, and keep the resource. Consider someone who has a juicy piece of gossip. That person can give this gossip to many other people, and that person might also receive rewards (more gossip from others). But the traders of the gossip do not lose the information. Similarly, you might compliment several different individuals. Such a compliment may be a reward for the other, but to what extent it is traded, exchanged, or a cost to the giver is more questionable. Though this is especially noticeable in communication, this holds true for many resources. You can give affection or love without giving love away.

Communication can also be misconstrued. Communication intended to be a reward for another (praise) could be interpreted as sarcastic and insincere, and the recipient could believe that a punishment or cost has been incurred instead. Interpersonal conflict is often the result of different meanings or values placed on the resources exchanged. If you give your partner advice or offer help (in your mind a reward) your partner might think you are implying they are incompetent, and thus perceive your advice as a punishment or cost.

Finally, simply engaging in the exchange can serve a symbolic function for the relationship. That you are willing to give me a ride home, no brownies required, both symbolizes and reinforces (communicates to me) that we are friends.

Research and Practical Applications of Social Exchange Theory

Two variations of social exchange theory are particularly well known in the field of interpersonal communication and relationships: interdependence theory and equity theory.

INTERDEPENDENCE THEORY: ALTERNATIVES AND COMPARISON LEVELS

Interdependence theory, developed by Thibaut and Kelly (1959; Kelley, 1979; Kelley & Thibaut, 1978), has at its core the control of resources. Individuals assess the rewards of their relationships through comparison levels (*CL*) and alternatives (comparison levels of alternatives, or *CLalt*). The *CL* can be thought of as what one believes one *should* be receiving and the *CLalt* as what one believes one *could* be receiving.

The *CL* is the standard an individual uses to judge how attractive or satisfactory a particular relationship is. Individuals contemplate how well the outcome of a current situation meets the standards or expectations of what they believe they deserve. If your girlfriend forgets your birthday *again*, you might find yourself contemplating, "Why am I still with this loser? I deserve so much better!" If so, you are thinking about or comparing the rewards of your current situation to what you believe you *should* be receiving from a romantic partner, one who appreciates you enough to remember your birthday.

The *CLalt* is the lowest level of rewards deemed acceptable when considering possible alternative relationships. Just because we think romantic partners should remember our birthday, doesn't mean we actually believe that a relationship with someone who meets all of our expectations is possible. We might continue a relationship because we believe that the relationship is better than any alternatives open to us. It is your *CLalt* you are considering when a relationship does meet your minimum standards. Even though you believe you *deserve* better, you do not believe you can *do* better.

Interdependence theory remains a theoretical framework used often to help understand communication and relationships. For example, it has been used to explore why someone discloses, or choses, not to disclose personal information to others (e.g., Derlega, Winstead, Mathews, & Braitman, 2008). You might disclose a financial problem to a parent in hopes of receiving help (a reward).

However, you might choose not to disclose your money woes to your parents out of concern they might not respect you as an adult (a cost). This theory has been used to help understand why people stay in abusive relationships (Rusbult & Martz, 1995). When considering their comparison level of alternatives, women who have few or no economic alternatives to their current situation might decide they have little choice but to remain in the abusive relationship because they are highly dependent upon that partner.

In sum, interdependence theory makes the point that satisfaction—and thus decision making and action—is based on how much above or below one's comparison level the outcomes of a particular situation are, as well as how much above or below the projected outcomes the outcomes from alternatives are perceived to be. We consider to what extent our outcomes are controlled by a particular partner or relationship. We contemplate what we believe we *should* receive as well as what we believe we *could* receive, and we act accordingly. This does not mean that our projections are accurate. Research suggests that the more committed we are to a partner and the more we have invested in a relationship, the more likely we are to mentally downplay possible alternatives and perceive our current relationship as superior to others' relationships (Rusbult & Agnew, 2010).

EQUITY THEORY

Theories of social exchange do not assume that humans will seek to gain the most from others regardless of the costs to others. Equity theory holds that we consider fairness.

Fairness can be thought of as equity in the distribution of costs and rewards. It can be considered in the short run: "I cooked dinner. You do the dishes." It is also considered in the long run: "I'll finish my degree first while you put me through college, then it will be your turn." A sense of equity or inequity accumulates over the course of a relationship. Though the time of reciprocity may be elongated, equity theorists propose that inequity will catch up to us at some point.

Whereas interdependence theory emphasizes dependence on or control of resources, equity theory emphasizes fairness. Adams's (1965) notion of "distributive justice" contends that people think and act so that rewards are distributed in accordance with their efforts. Three types of (in)equity might occur: (a) You consider whether the ratio of your rewards to costs is equal to your partner's ratio, (b) you consider the exchange relationship you and your partner have with a third individual, or (c) you compare your relationship to others in similar circumstances.

First, think about a situation wherein neither relational partner is putting much into the romantic relationship, and neither is getting much out of it; the ratio of inputs to outcomes is the same. Both may desire a casual, friends-with-benefits relationship, requiring little romantic effort on either part. Equity exists and both are satisfied. If one person contributes a great deal to the relationship and the other contributes little, then even though the first person may feel the relationship is rewarding, inequity occurs if the second person is reaping the same benefits without the same efforts.

In the second type of (in)equity when we perceive our efforts to be on par with another person's efforts with the same exchange partner (a third party), we again perceive equity. When you and a classmate engage in a joint project, if you share the workload and the instructor gives you the same grade, the ratio of input (work on the project) to outcome (the grade) is equal. Conversely, if you do most of the work and your partner does little but you receive the same grade, you likely will perceive the distribution of rewards as unfair.

To understand the third type of inequity, suppose I work hard at a relationship and my partner doesn't, yet all of my friends also work just as hard as I in their relationships and none of their partners contribute to their relationships either. If my ratio of inputs to outputs in my romantic involvement is the same as my perception of the ratio of inputs to outputs of others in the same circumstance, I may then perceive my arrangement to be fair.

If partners perceive that their relative contributions are unequal then the relationship is inequitable. This inequity results in emotional distress—and the greater the inequity the greater the distress (Sprecher, 2001). The one who is "underbenefitted" often experiences anger. Alternatively, feelings of guilt may emerge if we are the "overbenefitted party" who perceives that we are getting more out of a relationship than we are giving. If people prefer fairness to profits, then feeling guilty about our profitable relationship makes sense.

Research on relational maintenance does indicate, for example, that individuals who believe they are in equitable marriages are both likely to be more satisfied with those marriages and to engage in behaviors such as sharing household tasks and being positive and reassuring, to help maintain those relationships (Canary & Stafford, 1992; Stafford & Canary, 2006).

Given that inequity causes distress, we attempt to restore equity through changing our outcomes or inputs. We attempt to maintain equity by changing our actions or our perceptions. You might equalize the balance by not putting so much effort into your relationship, convincing your partner to put more into the relationship, or ending the relationship. Another course is to distort your perceptions of rewards and costs: "I'm really not working any harder than my roommate. I enjoy mowing the lawn; it's good exercise. I'm outside in the fresh air. It's not really work." If you change your perception of a cost into a reward, equity is restored. In short, equity theory poses that rules of fairness or justice outweigh our desire to get the most we can.

Evaluation of Social Exchange Theory

Most criticisms have been aimed at the primary premises of exchange perspectives. Three are offered here. Some relationships transcend social exchange. People are not necessarily "self-serving." People are not as rational as social exchange theories seem to portray them.

Critics contend that some relationships cannot be explained by social exchange theories. Relationships based in "true love" simply are not subject to an exchange perspective; love in its pure form is selfless as opposed to self-serving (Fromm, 1956). Long-term intimate relationships, it has been argued, are, or become, communal relationships wherein each person's concern is primarily for the other's welfare (Mills & Clark, 2001).

Similarly, social exchange does not allow for altruism; some proponents of social exchange agree with this criticism. Blau (1964) considered altruism as "beyond the scope" of social exchange. Others (e.g., Homans, 1961), however, contended that altruism is a reward because the negative feelings that come with inequity, such as anger or guilt, are themselves costs: When we act in ways to eliminate these feelings, we are ultimately acting in our own self-interest, not out of concern for others.

Continuing with the second criticism—that people are not necessarily self-serving—it has been argued that individuals differ in the degree to which they feel they ought to repay or be repaid. Some individuals may have more of an "exchange orientation" than others (Murstein, 1971). Those high in exchange orientation more actively keep score, whereas those low in exchange orientation care little about equity. Also, some cultures seem to value and foster exchange orientations more than other cultures do (Van Yperen & Buunk, 1990).

A third critique is that people simply do not think or behave in a rational manner. Yet many supporters of social exchange tend to agree that people are not always rational. We might go for long periods without considering our rewards and costs. At some point, though, perhaps a critical incident transpires (your partner has an affair), or a mundane one happens just one too many times (your partner didn't come home for dinner again) and we take notice of (in)equity. It is unclear as to how long one waits for the scales to be balanced, or even before one realizes that they are not balanced, before computations begin. Yet equity theorists contend that at some point inequities will be recognized and dealt with.

Social exchange theories also have a number of strengths. Theories are often evaluated as to their parsimony, heuristic value, predictive value, and falsifiability. Parsimony refers to how simple or complex a theory is. If one explanation is complicated and another equally good explanation is simple, the more parsimonious (simpler) explanation (theory) is preferred. In spite of the numerous variations of social exchange theories, the central premises are few and simple, making social exchange theories as a group parsimonious.

Theories that prompt further investigation are considered heuristic. Social exchange theories have generated a significant amount of research, which demonstrates their heuristic value. Within the confines of interpersonal communication and close relationships alone, social exchange theories have been applied to self-disclosure (Altman & Taylor, 1973), relationship initiation and development (Cate, Lloyd, & Long, 1988), sexual activity (Sprecher, 1998), conflict (Roloff, 1981), and the maintenance of romantic, friend, and family relationships (Canary & Stafford, 2001; Vogl-Bauer, Kalbfleisch, & Beatty, 1999), to give only a few examples.

Theories are also judged on their "falsifiability." Can the ideas be tested? Some abstract ideas are difficult to test. It is likely impossible to determine if altruism is enacted—not out of the desire to serve or help others, but because it makes us feel good about ourselves, leaving these theories open to criticism on this front.

In terms of its primary goal given its characterization as a post-positivist theory, overall, exchange theory also does fairly well in terms of predictive value. In summarizing research based in interdependence theory, Rusbult and colleagues (1994) reported that

> abundant evidence suggests that when individuals are more dependent on their relationships—that is, when they are more committed, more satisfied, more heavily invested, and perceive that their alternatives are poor—their relationships are more likely to persist over time. (p. 132)

The work of Hatfield (formerly Walster), with main focus on the comparison of one's ratio to one's partner's ratio wherein interdependence is presumed, supports social exchange assumptions (Hatfield, Traupmann, Sprecher, Utne, & Hay, 1985; Walster, Berscheid, & Walster, 1973; Walster, Walster, & Berscheid, 1978).

Continuing the Conversation

Debate continues about the degree to which social exchange theories can account for human behavior, if exchange principles apply to everyone in all cultures, and—if not—under which conditions and in which relationships what individuals consider and act on social exchange. Some argue that equity theories are not universal but rather are a product of individualistic, capitalistic societies.

Though some research has indicated that individuals might vary in their exchange orientation, there is little understanding of what might account for being more or less exchange oriented. For example, research is beginning to explore whether those who hold religious views about their marriage (the belief that their marriage is sacred) might be more protective of their relationship and thus less vulnerable to inequities in the relationship (DeMaris, Mahoney, & Pargament, 2010).

Though research focuses on an individual's perceptions of one's own costs and rewards, we might apply social exchange in our efforts to understand others' choices. Of course, we do apply social exchange ideas when we cynically believe an attractive young man cannot genuinely be in love with a significantly older and less attractive, wealthy woman. We think we fully understand the exchange in that relationship. However what might seem completely irrational to us, for example, when a friend remains involved in a harmful relationship, we might be able to be more understanding, supportive, or act in ways to provide instrumental help, if we considered the rewards and costs of staying and leaving the relationship from the perspective of our friend. Perhaps most importantly for communication scholars, a profitable direction for research would be greater consideration of communication as the resource of exchange itself as well as the symbolic function of exchange, and not simply the means to broker exchanges.

Note

1. I would like to acknowledge Michael Roloff's contribution, through discussion, to the ideas offered regarding the role of communication in social exchange.

References

Adams, J. (1965). Inequity in social exchange. In L. Berkowitz (Ed.), *Advances in experimental social psychology: Vol. 2* (pp. 267–299). New York, NY: Academic Press.

Altman, I., & Taylor, D. (1973). *Social penetration: The development of interpersonal relationships.* New York, NY: Holt, Rinehart, & Winston.

Blau, P. (1964). *Exchange and power in social life.* New York, NY: John Wiley.

Canary, D. J., & Stafford, L. (1992). Relational maintenance strategies and equity in marriage. *Communication Monographs, 59,* 243–267.

Canary, D. J., & Stafford, L. (2001). Equity in the preservation of personal relationships. In J. Harvey & A. Wenzel (Eds.), *Close romantic relationships: Preservation and enhancement* (pp. 133–151). Mahwah, NJ: Erlbaum.

Cate, R. M., Lloyd, S. A., & Long, E. (1988). The role of rewards and fairness in developing premarital relationships. *Journal of Marriage and the Family, 50,* 443–452.

DeMaris, A., Mahoney, A., & Pargament, K. I. (2010). Sanctification of marriage and general religiousness as buffers of the effects of marital inequity. *Journal of Family Issues, 31,* 1255–1278.

Derlega, V. J., Winstead, B. A., Mathews, A., & Braitman, A. L. (2008). Why does someone reveal highly personal information? Attributions for and against self-disclosure in close relationships. *Communication Research Reports, 25,* 115–130

Foa, E. B, & Foa, U. G. (1976). Resource theory of social exchange. In J. W. Thibaut, J. T. Spence, & R. C. Carson (Eds.), *Contemporary topics in social psychology* (pp. 99–131). Morristown, NJ: General Learning Press.

Foa, E. B, & Foa, U. G. (2012). Resource theory of social exchange. In K. Törnblom & A. Kazemi (Eds.), *Handbook of Social Resource Theory: Theoretical extensions, empirical insights and social applications* (pp. 15–32). New York, NY: Springer.

Fromm, E. (1956). *The art of loving.* New York, NY: Harper & Row.

Hatfield, E., Traupmann, J., Sprecher, S., Utne, M., & Hay, M. (1985). Equity in close relationships. In W. Ickes (Ed.), *Compatible and incompatible relationships* (pp. 91–117). New York, NY: Springer-Verlag.

Homans, G. (1961). *Social behavior: Its elementary forms.* New York, NY: Harcourt Brace Jovanovich.

Kelley, H. H. (1979). *Personal relationships: Their structures and processes.* Hillsdale, NJ: Erlbaum.

Kelley, H. H., & Thibaut, J. W. (1978). *Interpersonal relations: A theory of interdependence.* New York, NY: Wiley.

Mills, J., & Clark, M. S. (2001). Viewing close romantic relationships as communal relationships: Implications for maintenance and enhancement. In J. Harvey & A. Wenzel (Eds.), *Close romantic relationships: Maintenance and enhancement* (pp. 13–25). Hillsdale, NJ: Erlbaum.

Molm, L. D., Schaefer, D. R., & Collett, J. L. (2007). The value of reciprocity. *Social Psychology Quarterly, 70,* 199–217.

Murstein, B. K. (1971). A theory of marital choice and its applicability to marriage adjustment. In B. I. Murstein (Ed.), *Theories of attraction and love* (pp. 100–151). New York, NY: Springer.

Roloff, M. E. (1981). *Interpersonal communication: The social exchange approach.* Beverly Hills, CA: Sage.

Rusbult, C. E., & Agnew, C. R. (2010). Prosocial motivation and behavior in close relationships. In M. Mikulincer & P. R. Shaver (Eds.), *Prosocial motives, emotions, and behavior: The better angels of our nature* (pp. 327–345). Washington, DC: American Psychological Association.

Rusbult, C. E., Drigotas, S. M., & Verette, J. (1994). The investment model: An interdependence analysis of commitment processes and relationship maintenance phenomena. In D. J. Canary & L. Stafford (Eds.), *Communication and relational maintenance* (pp. 115–140). New York, NY: Academic Press.

Rusbult, C. E., & Martz, J. M. (1995). Remaining in an abusive relationship: An investment model analysis of nonvoluntary dependence. *Personality and Social Psychology Bulletin,* 558–571.

Sprecher, S. (1998). Social exchange theories and sexuality. *Journal of Sex Research, 35,* 32–43.

Sprecher, S. (2001). Comparison of emotional consequences of and changes in equity over time using global and domain-specific measures of equity. *Journal of Social and Personal Relationships, 18,* 477–501.

Stafford, L., & Canary, D. J. (2006). Equity and interdependence as predictors of relational maintenance strategies. *Journal of Family Communication, 6,* 227–254.

Thibaut, J. W., & Kelley, H. H. (1959). *The social psychology of groups.* New York, NY: Wiley.

Van Yperen, N. W., & Buunk, B. P. (1990). A longitudinal study of equity and satisfaction in intimate relationships. *European Journal of Social Psychology, 20,* 287–309.

Vogl-Bauer, S., Kalbfleisch, P. J., & Beatty, M. J. (1999). Perceived equity, satisfaction, and relational maintenance strategies in parent-adolescent dyads. *Journal of Youth and Adolescence, 28,* 27–49.

Walster, E., Berscheid, E., & Walster, G. W. (1973). New directions in equity research. *Journal of Personality and Social Psychology, 25,* 151–176.

Walster, E., Walster, G., & Berscheid, E. (1978). *Equity: Theory and research.* Boston, MA: Allyn & Bacon.

31

Social Information Processing Theory

Impressions and Relationship Development Online

Joseph B. Walther

For partners who first meet each other through an online dating site, or students who undertake group projects in online courses, or those who work in their organizations' globally distributed teams, there is often considerable concern about what those distant partners are like: whether they are reliable, hard-working, enjoyable, and if they have a good sense of humor. We might think that with only e-mail or text-based messaging to connect us, learning the answers to these questions is impossible. And yet, a matter of weeks (or several late nights of chatting) later, people are grinning at each other's messages, developing rapport, and often becoming friends, sometimes to their great surprise. From the perspective of the social information processing theory (SIPT) of computer-mediated communication (CMC), this transition is not surprising. This theory explains how people get to know one another online, without nonverbal cues, and how they develop and manage relationships in the computer-mediated environment (Walther, 1992).

Intellectual Tradition of SIPT

The SIPT developed as a response to theories and research in social psychology, management science, and information theory that lacked certain assumptions from communication theory about the relationships between verbal and nonverbal cues, as well as the developmental nature of relationships over time. It is worth reviewing the short history of CMC research to see how a communication-oriented view came to contribute to things.

In the late 1970s and the 1980s, when the digital communication systems we now know as the Internet first came into relatively widespread use (in business, military, and academic organizations), several theories were imported from other domains to try to predict and explain what happens when people communicate online rather than by phone or face-to-face. When people encounter each other for the first time in a face-to-face setting, there is abundant information immediately about who each person is. People quickly form first impressions based on others' physical features, such as body type, attractiveness, and the slogan on someone's T-shirt, as well as the quality of their voices, the distance at which they approach or to which they retreat, and other cues. An individual makes initial "hypotheses" about who others are based on these cues, and then tests those hunches through conversations, in which one senses what they say and how they say it, their conversation style, and their other behaviors such as vocal cues, posture, facial expression, and gestures (Snyder & Stukas, 1999).

When we encounter other people in CMC, we frequently do not have the variety, abundance, and relatively effortless means to size up others and to signal the characteristics we want them to perceive about us. Theories from other fields suggested that the lack of nonverbal cues prevents us from making inferences about other people (e.g., Short, Williams, & Christie, 1976). These theories were used to predict that the absence of nonverbal cues from CMC either (a) thwarts users' abilities to tell who they are and what they are like, (b) causes users to lose interest in one another as real individuals, and/or (c) deters the expression of emotional, personal, or relational messages (Siegel, Dubrovsky, Kiesler, & McGuire, 1986).

Yet other theories argued that, in the absence of nonverbal cues that individuate one person from another when we interact online, we respond to others based on what social groups we believe they belong to using categorizations that are obvious to us at the moment (e.g., sophomores vs. seniors, Wolverines vs. Spartans). When those frames of mind are activated, we relate to others either as members of an in-group, in which case we assume they are similar to us and treat them favorably, or as members of an out-group, in which case we reject them through dislikable responses. The tendency to "see" others this way is raised when, as is the case in CMC, we cannot literally see them (Reicher, Spears, & Postmes, 1995).

The SIPT differs from either of these positions in two important respects. First, the SIPT approach draws on a "functional" approach to the relationship of verbal and nonverbal cues. A functional view of communication assumes that social information (such as information about one's personality and demeanor, or emotion and interpersonal regard) can be expressed through nonverbal and/or through verbal means, that is, through language (Burgoon, Buller, & Woodall, 1989). Although this argument is simple enough, it contradicts many people's intuition as well as other theories about nonverbal communication. Many assume that a person needs to see someone to tell who he or she really is; that it is not possible to get an accurate impression of others until they are together, in person, to be seen and heard. Many theorists also equate nonverbal information as being the only set of channels by which we accomplish the functions that nonverbal information *usually* performs. Of course, there is no doubt that facial expressions express emotions, for instance, or that invading another person's personal space can convey dominance or threat. Expressing emotions and conveying dominance are both social functions, and nonverbal cues are natural and generally effective means of performing them.

If we distinguish between the functions and the symbols used to achieve those functions, however, a different view arises. A variety of cues or cue combinations can convey a particular function. Language cues, including the style and the verbal content of the articulated message, can also convey social information. Brevity vs. verbosity, formality vs. informality, and uncertainty vs. confidence are familiar examples of language style. Likewise, expressions of similarity and affection, or stern reprisals, are content-level examples of liking, emotion, or dominance. People use these forms of language in speech and in writing, in addition to or instead of nonverbal cues. Nevertheless, the interchangeability of verbal and nonverbal cues has been ignored in most of the early social psychological thinking about CMC, which focused primarily on the expected impersonal effects of a medium with no nonverbal behaviors (e.g., Siegel et al., 1986). The assumption that people can convey similar social meanings using either nonverbal or verbal cue systems is most widely recognized in the field of communication studies (although even there, it is often neglected), and because it is a foundational assumption of SIPT, it is one of the characteristics that makes SIPT a theory rooted in the communication discipline.

There are two more, somewhat related, underpinnings of SIPT. The theory assumes that relationships develop over time (a notion first developed in social and group psychology). It also assumes that the process of communication is slower in CMC than it is in face-to-face communication (similar to information-theory's notions of *bandwidth*). Put these two contentions together, and add the previous assumption that social information can, in principle, traverse language cues, and it leads to the proposition that people can get to know one another and develop relationships online, albeit more slowly and through different means than through face-to-face interaction. In this sense, although SIPT recognizes certain axioms from other disciplines' theories, their unique combination in SIPT can be said to constitute an original, communication-oriented theoretical framework.

As may be coming into focus, SIPT offers several preliminary assumptions about the comparability of verbal and nonverbal communication, the qualities of mediated channels that affect the rate of the exchange of information that we use in relating to others, and human motivations in encounters with other people. This framework, and the way the assumptions are articulated and combined, reflects a post-positivist theory. Its limited and well-defined set of assumptions leads to the derivation of certain propositions, from which a number of researchable hypotheses can (and have been) tested empirically in various contexts and relationships in which CMC takes place. These assumptions, propositions, and several hypothesis tests will be described more fully in the discussion to follow.

Main Goals and Features of SIPT

SIPT explains how we develop impressions and social relationships with one another, over time, online, without recourse to nonverbal cues. The central arguments of the theory pertain to (a) the alteration of impression-bearing, emotional, and relation-managing information (i.e., social information rather than task-related information); (b) how it is translated into verbal and textual symbols online; and (c) the process by which the translation produces message exchanges that are not as quick as face-to-face conversations. Each of these features warrant more thorough description below, but they combine to render a core prediction of the theory: When sufficient time elapses so that ample communicative exchanges are made, CMC facilitates an exchange of personal and relational information sufficient for developing impressions and managing interpersonal relations no less so than face-to-face communication, albeit more slowly (Walther, 1992).

TRANSLATION OF CUES

SIPT differs from other theories of CMC regarding the functions of impression-bearing and relational cues, and the degree to which nonverbal and verbal or textual cues may perform them. SIPT explicitly assumes that individuals are motivated to form impressions and develop relationships of some kind, no matter what medium they are using. Therefore, according to SIPT, when nonverbal cues are unavailable—as they are in text-only e-mail or online chat—the remaining communication systems are employed to do the work of those that are missing. In other words, that which is typically nonverbal elsewhere is verbal (and typed) in CMC. Language and writing are held to be virtually interchangeable with, and are no less useful than, nonverbal cues in the management of impressions and relationships.

TIME AND RATE

SIPT considers how the use of language, and a typed medium, affects communication rate, and therefore, how the rate of information exchange differs in CMC from face-to-face communication. Because the rate of information exchange is slower in CMC than face-to-face interaction, CMC expands the time frame required to be effective in social situations.

In face-to-face communication, the concurrent exchange of verbal messages along with appearance, kinesics (body movement and facial expression), vocalics (quality and use of the voice), proxemics (increases, decreases, and uses of space), and haptics (touch) provide an abundance of information all at once. The various cues do not always duplicate one another in terms of meaning; they complement, contradict, accentuate, or minimize verbal cues and other nonverbal expressions (Ekman & Friesen, 1969). These simultaneous expressive systems allow us to process, rapidly and intuitively (although imperfectly), a great deal of social information.

When one code system alone must do the work of all possible code systems—in this case, language performing all expressive functions—we expect that less information may traverse a single message than if more numerous cues were involved. For this reason, according to SIPT, the rate of social information is slower in CMC relative to face-to-face communication. Because less information travels in every message exchange, it requires more exchanges to reach the same level of impressions and relationship development as would generally occur more quickly in face-to-face interaction. When we also recognize that asynchronous CMC (such as e-mail or Facebook comments) does not take place in real time, and that a single question-and-answer turn may take hours or days to complete, we start to appreciate how the rate of information interacts with time. Indeed, research has shown that CMC takes longer to facilitate impressions (Walther, 1993) and to develop more levels of relational communication (Walther & Burgoon, 1992).

How Communication Is Conceptualized in SIPT

The theory differs from most other theories of CMC because of its central and explicit conceptualizations of communication. In a sense, SIPT offers a somewhat mechanistic view of communication. That does not mean that the tone of communication is machine-like. Rather, it appreciates certain qualities of interpersonal communication—nonverbal and verbal—without any mystique.

It does not privilege nonverbal communication as better or more potent on some primal or intuitive basis. Rather, it looks at message symbols as being transmitted through various codes, codes that have different carrying capacities. Within SIPT, communication symbols are functionally interchangeable, communication is a process, and the accretion and interpretation of social information exchanges through this process defines relationship development over time. It treats the relative potential of verbal and nonverbal exchanges to create meaning as though they are subject to some sort of mathematical formulae (although the equivalencies are implicit and not specified).

The SIPT is a *process* theory in the sense that it views interpersonal meanings as accumulating iteratively—that is, in association with a build-up of information over a series of communicative interactions in order to build a psychological model of one's online partners (see Miller & Steinberg, 1975). At first glance, this view may seem at odds with the functional interchangeability view above. After all, if a person can achieve the same thing using words as by using gestures, why does he or she need many exchanges to transfer meanings? The SIPT view is that some information channels (such as face-to-face interaction) transmit many types of symbols quickly, whereas other channels move fewer types of symbols slowly. The symbols that CMC carries move slowly and need more exchanges to accrue functional utility.

Research and Practical Applications of SIPT

A good deal of research employing SIPT has focused on testing the theory's basic claims and underlying mechanisms, whereas other studies have tried to apply it to many of the ever-growing contexts of CMC that it may help to explain.

Walther, Loh, and Granka's (2005) study in particular illustrated basic research on SIPT and whether and how it works. Their experiment sought to demonstrate the exchangeability of verbal and nonverbal cues between CMC and face-to-face settings explicitly. In their experiment, a number of unacquainted people had two-person conversations about a moral dilemma. Half the conversations took place face-to-face, and the other half of the conversations took place with the two people each in a different room, using a popular CMC chat program. Unbeknownst to one partner, the researchers asked the other partner to adopt one of two social attitudes after the first minute of interaction. In half the dyads, the individuals were to act as if they really liked their partner and wanted to make that person like them, too, and to convey this by whatever techniques they wished. In the other half of the dyads, the individuals were asked to behave as if they grew to dislike the partner strongly, and wanted the person never to contact them again. After the conversations, the couples were separated. The naïve individuals who had not been prompted to behave one way or another rated how affectionate their partners' communication was.

The results of their study provided clear support of SIPT hypotheses. First, there was no difference between CMC and face-to-face in terms of how affectionate the partners were; the only significant difference was due to whether the partner was asked to be nice or be mean. The results of the analyses of face-to-face audio and video recordings and CMC transcripts showed a number of specific cues that are associated with variations in liking. As expected, the face-to-face participants conveyed liking and disliking primarily through variations in vocalics (e.g., vocal pleasantness and pauses during speech), followed by kinesics (e.g., body relaxation, smiling, and gaze). No language effects in the face-to-face conversations were associated with liking judgments. In CMC, on the other hand, a good variety of verbal cues were associated with liking or disliking. These included outright statements of affection (e.g., "I like you"), as well as the ways that people expressed disagreement with one another. For example, ignoring a partner's idea and flatly offering an alternative in response was associated with decrements in liking. All in all, the amount of attitude conveyed through language in CMC was no less than the amount conveyed through voice, movement, and facial expression face-to-face.

Prior to Walther et al.'s (2005) experiment, early SIPT studies addressed contradictions in the research about online groups and virtual communities. Many previous experiments using synchronous CMC and face-to-face groups that took place in the 1980s and 1990s depicted CMC as reducing social information and leading to hostility and negativity. These results formerly were attributed to the CMC medium, and its lack of nonverbal cues was characterized as a source of uncertainty and discomfort (Hiltz, Johnson, & Turoff, 1986). At nearly the same time, anecdotal reports accumulated that portrayed CMC much more favorably in "virtual communities" where people exchanged information, advice, and friendly chatter (Rheingold, 1993). These reports challenged the idea that the lack of nonverbal cues alone could be a defining characteristic of CMC.

The SIPT research found a way to resolve these conflicts, however. From SIPT's perspective, the short time limits provided to CMC groups in the early experiments did not provide enough time for users to exchange messages, develop impressions, and relate to one another. SIPT research showed that CMC groups required more time to exchange an equivalent amount of information as in face-to-face groups, and when CMC groups had ample time, they developed the level of affection and sociability seen in face-to-face groups (Walther & Burgoon, 1992).

Although SIPT's assumptions and derived propositions suggest a certain abstraction and formality to the theory, these structural qualities have allowed the theory to be applied rather broadly to several contexts of CMC, including virtual groups, online friendships, distance education, and online dating, to name a few. For instance, even though e-mail and bulletin boards were the dominant forms of CMC when the theory was first articulated in the early 1990s, it has been useful in understanding new, synchronous (real-time) CMC platforms such as chat rooms and instant messaging systems. It has also helped distinguish the interpersonal effects of such new tools as videoconferencing from older, asynchronous ("store-and-forward") channels (Nowak, Watt, & Walther, 2005). It has been applied to online work groups and virtual teams (Walther & Bunz, 2005; Wilson, Straus, & McEvily, 2006), how people develop friendships and romantic relationships online (Parks & Floyd, 1996), electronic classrooms and distance education (Schweizer, Paechter, & Weidenmann, 2001), chat rooms (Henderson & Gilding, 2004), and online dating (Gibbs, Ellison, & Heino, 2006), among others.

As newer Internet platforms (e.g., online games) and social network sites (e.g., Facebook) have become popular, SIPT has been applied successfully in many of them. Even in an avatar-based online swordfight game (in which players control cartoon representations who chat and fight on the screen), time online is associated with greater levels of socio-emotional comments (Peña & Hancock, 2006). It is important to note, however, that these studies assessed time online as a player's history, or the amount of time since she or he joined that game. This is not exactly the way SIPT conceptualizes time; in SIPT, time is an interval in which a number of messages accrue, regardless of an individual's personal history with a medium. More recent research has shown that individuals who try to learn about others using the pictures and self-descriptions that others post on a site like Facebook reduce their uncertainty about others more effectively through interactive text-based chat than by looking at photos or the biographical information people place in their profiles (Antheunis, Valkenburg, & Peter, 2010). This suggests that the processes described by SIPT are robust even in the face of new, multi-channel communication systems.

Evaluation of SIPT

SIPT has become a popular theory of CMC, which may be based on two contrasting qualities: (a) its intuitive application, on the one hand, and (b) its formal articulation of assumptions and propositions, on the other. Many individuals have encountered each other for the first time online, and although many new networking systems promote picture exchanges, many do not. It is still quite common, as it became through the 1990s, for people to have first contact with others in a text-based online hobby discussion, technology discussion, or other kinds of chat rooms, bulletin boards, games, and other venues. People grow to recognize one another and attribute characteristics to one another, liking develops, and ongoing relationships take shape. These developments were theoretically unaccounted for before SIPT's introduction, both for academic researchers and for other people who become ensconced within the Internet.

The formal articulation of SIPT's five underlying assumptions and six propositions make it a well-defined and relatively parsimonious theory. When theories formally identify a limited and clearly related set of assumptions and propositions, it is easier for researchers to see precisely which aspect of a theory is being tested, extended, or challenged by any particular study or set of observations. These characteristics, as well as its open-ended applicability to new and emerging social media systems, add to its considerable heuristic value. Its clear structure makes it relatively easy for scholars to assess what part of the theory, specifically, is being supported or challenged by empirical research. For instance, Roberts, Smith, and Pollock (1996) found a rapid progression from no familiarity to intimate relating among some users of an online synchronous chat facility. Roberts and colleagues suggested that this challenges the proposition in SIPT about CMC requiring a longer time in order to achieve a relatively high level of intimacy (although it fails to challenge SIPT's proposition regarding the conversion of social information from nonverbal cues into verbal cues). Such assertions challenge researchers to extend their thinking: Can the interaction goals or context modify the rate of relationship development in CMC? Or does synchronous online chat approach the rapidity of face-to-face communication and thus provide a similar amount of message exchanges in a limited amount of time than we would see over a much longer time in e-mail or bulletin boards (despite the absence of nonverbal cues)? Whichever of these two possibilities turns out to be the case, it will have subtle implications for the understanding of the rate/time aspect of SIPT.

In terms of falsifiability, researchers have challenged aspects of SIPT's underlying assumption that people are generally motivated to develop impressions and relationships with one another. Prior to the recognition that this assumption was questionable, cases in which the online behavior predicted by SIPT did not accrue made it unclear whether the theory as a whole was false or if it pertained some times and not others, that is, if boundaries needed to be articulated. By testing systematic variations in people's motivation to impress or relate with others online, by testing factors that heighten or dampen this motivation, and by finding corresponding changes in online affinity, the boundaries of the theory will become narrower, but the theory will become more precise and useful. For instance, one study (Walther, 1994) drew on previous offline research on the effect of anticipated future interaction as a factor that propels greater uncertainty reduction and liking. In a CMC setting, strangers were brought together and either led to anticipate more future interaction with one another doing several online tasks, or led to anticipate interaction on a single online task. Indeed, the degree of anticipated future interaction affected the positivity of online relational development quickly and powerfully enough that relational levels among those with greater anticipated future interaction were no different from an offline comparison condition. As a result of these refinements, we no longer suggest that SIPT dynamics will happen in every CMC encounter. However, within the boundary condition of instances when longer-term online interaction is expected, SIPT is more likely to take effect, and we know a bit more precisely that anticipating ongoing interaction is one of the motivating theoretical mechanisms.

Examples of SIPT's application to a variety of social media platforms and contexts, as well as its applicability to face-to-face comparison conditions (as suggested earlier in this chapter), indicate that the theory has broad scope. The scope, testability, and heuristic value of the theory may be among the factors that has led other researchers to draw frequently on SIPT in their own studies, as reflected by over 1,750 published citations to the original SIPT article to date, according to the Google Scholar database.

Continuing the Conversation

Like any theory, SIPT is subject to continued modification, extension, and refinement. Unlike most theories of interpersonal communication, SIPT includes as a central construct aspects of communication technology, and the ways these technologies develop are in rapid flux. The Internet was not originally developed with human communication as its central purpose. However, its contemporary use as a communication medium seems to eclipse any other function to most people. As new Internet communication tools develop, we are forced to ask how SIPT can account for the most modern applications, if it can do so at all. We have already discussed Antheunis et al's (2010) study of SIPT in a social network site environment, which expected to find users drawing on the photos and bios of others' profiles. Instead, they found that users rely on text-based interaction to reduce uncertainty about others. Blogs, Twitter, and mobile texting continue to make text-based messaging a primary communication modality, suggesting that SIPT's utility as a theory of text-based interaction may be growing rather than waning.

The main challenge for SIPT arises as many of the uses to which CMC is put nowadays are in "hybrid" relationships, as opposed to strictly online or offline relationships. It is probably the case that we communicate with most of the people with whom we have face-to-face relationships by some electronic means as well. There are the high school friends we no longer see face-to-face but with whom we keep up via Facebook exclusively, and of course there are grocery store clerks with whom we have face-to-face encounters but nothing online. But our mainstay relationships are probably, for the most part, multi-modal (i.e., online and offline, both). How the dynamics of online and offline communication complement each other is a question that SIPT may need some adjustment to address. At the same time, the fact that we continue to learn about each other from online postings, that we prefer to disclose some things online than in person, and that we do send text messages via our mobile phones rather than just call and talk or leave voice mail, suggests that there remains something special about textual CMC's appeal and utility. It is that something that SIPT may help us to capture even as relationships occur across more media, and the choices of media with which to manage them continue to advance.

References

Antheunis, M., Valkenburg, P. M., & Peter, J. (2010). Getting acquainted through social network sites: Testing a model of online uncertainty reduction and social attraction. *Computers in Human Behavior, 26,* 100–109.

Burgoon, J. K., Buller, D. B., & Woodall, W. G. (1989). *Nonverbal communication: The unspoken dialogue.* New York, NY: Harper & Row.

Ekman, P., & Friesen, W. V. (1969). The repertoire of nonverbal behavior: Categories, origins, usage, and coding. *Semiotica, 1,* 49–98.

Gibbs, J. L., Ellison, N. B., & Heino, R. D. (2006). Self-presentation in online personals: The role of anticipated future interaction, self-disclosure, and perceived success in Internet dating. *Communication Research, 33,* 1–26.

Henderson, S., & Gilding, M. (2004). "I've never clicked this much with anyone in my life": Trust and hyperpersonal communication in online friendships. *New Media & Society, 6,* 487–506.

Hiltz, S. R., Johnson, K., & Turoff, M. (1986). Experiments in group decision making: Communication process and outcome in face-to-face versus computerized conferences. *Human Communication Research, 13,* 225–252.

Miller, G. R., & Steinberg, M. (1975). *Between people: A new analysis of interpersonal communication.* Palo Alto, CA: Science Research Associates.

Nowak, K. L., Watt, J., & Walther, J. B. (2005). The influence of synchrony and sensory modality on the person perception process in computer-mediated groups. *Journal of Computer-Mediated Communication, 10*(3). Retrieved June 1, 2006, from http://jcmc.indiana.edu/v0l10/issue3/nowak.html.

Parks, M. R., & Floyd, K. (1996). Making friends in cyberspace. *Journal of Communication, 46,* 80–97.

Peña, J., & Hancock, J. T. (2006). An analysis of socioemotional and task communication in online multiplayer video games. *Communication Research, 33,* 92–109.

Reicher, S., Spears, R., & Postmes, T. (1995). A social identity model of deindividuation phenomena. *European Review of Social Psychology, 6,* 161–198.

Rheingold, H. (1993). *The virtual community: Homesteading on the electronic frontier.* Reading, MA: Addison-Wesley.

Roberts, L. D., Smith, L. M., & Pollock, C. (1996, September). *A model of social interaction via computer-mediated communication in real-time text-based virtual environments.* Paper presented at the annual conference of the Australian Psychological Society, Sydney, Australia.

Schweizer, K., Paechter, M., & Weidenmann, B. (2001). A field study on distance education and communication: Experiences of a virtual tutor. *Journal of Computer-Mediated Communication, 6*(2). Retrieved June 1, 2006, from http://jcmc.indiana .edu/v016/issue2/schweizer.html.

Short, J., Williams, E., & Christie, B. (1976). *The social psychology of telecommunications.* London, UK: John Wiley.

Siegel, J., Dubrovsky, V., Kiesler, S., & McGuire, T. W. (1986). Group processes in computer-mediated communication. *Organizational Behavior and Human Decision Processes, 37,* 157–187.

Snyder, M., & Stukas, A. A. (1999). Interpersonal processes: The interplay of cognitive, motivational, and behavioral activities in social interaction. *Annual Review of Psychology, 50,* 273–303.

Walther, J. B. (1992). Interpersonal effects in computer-mediated interaction: A relational perspective. *Communication Research, 19,* 52–90.

Walther, J. B. (1993). Impression development in computer-mediated interaction. *Western Journal of Communication, 57,* 381–398.

Walther, J. B. (1994). Anticipated ongoing interaction versus channel effects on relational communication in computer-mediated interaction. *Human Communication Research, 20,* 473–501.

Walther, J. B., & Bunz, U. (2005). The rules of virtual groups: Trust, liking, and performance in computer-mediated communication. *Journal of Communication, 55,* 828–846.

Walther, J. B., & Burgoon, J. K. (1992). Relational communication in computer-mediated interaction. *Human Communication Research, 19,* 50–88.

Walther, J. B., Loh, T., & Granka, L. (2005). Let me count the ways: The interchange of verbal and nonverbal cues in computer-mediated and face-to-face affinity. *Journal of Language and Social Psychology, 24,* 36–65.

Wilson, J. M., Straus, S. G., & McEvily, B. (2006). All in due time: The development of trust in computer-mediated and face-to-face teams. *Organizational Behavior and Human Decision Processes, 99,* 16–33.

Index

NOTE: Figures and tables are indicated as (fig.) and (table).

About the Editors

Dawn O. Braithwaite (PhD, University of Minnesota) is a Willa Cather Professor and Chair of Communication Studies at the University of Nebraska–Lincoln. She studies communication in discourse-dependent families, rituals, and dialectics of relating, authoring over 100 articles and five books. She received the National Communication Association (NCA) Brommel Award for Family Communication, UNL College of Arts & Sciences Social Science Research Award, and is a Western States Communication Association Distinguished Scholar. She is a senior fellow with the Council on Contemporary Families and a past president of the NCA.

Paul Schrodt (PhD, University of Nebraska–Lincoln) is the Philip J. and Cheryl C. Burguières Professor and Graduate Director in the Department of Communication Studies at Texas Christian University. He studies the communicative cognitions and behaviors that facilitate family relationships, with a particular interest in stepfamily functioning. He has authored more than 80 journal articles and book chapters, and he is the recipient of the NCA Brommel Award for Family Communication, the Early Career Award in Interpersonal Communication, and the Dean's Research Award from TCU.

About the Contributors

Tamara Afifi (PhD, University of Nebraska–Lincoln) is a professor in the Department of Communication Studies at the University of Iowa. Her research focuses on (1) information regulation (privacy, secrets, disclosure, avoidance) in parent-child and dating relationships, and (2) communication processes related to uncertainty, loss, stress, and coping in families, with particular emphasis on post-divorce families. Her current research examines the impact of parents' conflict and other communication skills on adolescents' physiological stress responses.

Walid A. Afifi (PhD, University of Arizona) is a professor in the Department of Communication Studies at the University of Iowa. He has published over 60 articles and chapters, and he is an author on two books. His program of research revolves around uncertainty and information-management decisions and has led to the development of the theory of motivated information management.

Austin S. Babrow (PhD, University of Illinois) is professor of communication studies at Ohio University. He studies the intersection of communication, uncertainty, and values, and particularly the social construction of uncertainties and profound values associated with health, illness, and risk. He is also exploring environmental, spiritual, and ethical communication. He is past chair of the Health Communication and Communication as Social Construction Divisions of the National Communication Association.

Leslie A. Baxter (PhD, University of Oregon) is a professor of communication studies and collegiate fellow in the College of Liberal Arts and Sciences at the University of Iowa. She is interested in the relational dialectics of relating, especially in nontraditional families. She has published over 165 articles, contributed chapters, and books. She has been honored with numerous awards for her scholarship throughout her career, including the NCA Distinguished Scholar Award.

Charles R. Berger (PhD, Michigan State University) is professor emeritus at the University of California, Davis. In addition to developing uncertainty reduction theory and planning theory, he is currently working on story appraisal theory, a framework for explaining narrative impact. He is author of *Language and Social Knowledge* (with James J. Bradac) and *Planning Strategic Interaction.* He is a past president and a fellow of the International Communication Association and a National Communication Association Distinguished Scholar.

Graham D. Bodie (PhD, Purdue University) is associate professor of communication theory at Louisiana State University. He studies the role of listening in various relationships, especially during troubles talk, publishing over 60 articles and chapters on these topics. Graham is a recipient of several Early Career Awards (National Communication Association, Southern States Communication Association, International Listening Association), and his research has been funded by the Louisiana Board of Regents and the LSU Council on Research.

David B. Buller (PhD, Michigan State University) is senior scientist and director of Research at Klein Buendel, Inc. in Golden, Colorado. He studies health communication strategies, including technologies such as the Internet and mobile computing, for improving health behavior to prevent chronic disease. He has published over 150 books, chapters, and articles. His research has been supported by the Army Research Institute and Office, National Institutes of Health, and Centers for Disease Control and Prevention.

Judee K. Burgoon (EdD, West Virginia University) is professor and director of Human Communication Research for the Center for the Management of Information, University of Arizona. She has authored or edited 15 volumes and nearly 300 articles and chapters related to deception and nonverbal and verbal communication. Her scholarship has been funded by numerous agencies, including the National Science Foundation, and she has received the highest honors given by the International Communication Association and National Communication Association.

Kristen Carr (PhD, University of Nebraska–Lincoln) is an assistant professor in the Department of Communication Studies at Texas Christian University. Her research focuses on the communicative development of resilience to adversity as well as the individual and relational outcomes of supportive communication while negotiating stressful and non-normative experiences.

William R. Cupach (PhD, University of Southern California) is professor emeritus in the School of Communication at Illinois State University. His research pertains to problematic interactions in interpersonal relationships, including such contexts as embarrassing predicaments, relational transgressions, interpersonal conflict, social and relational aggression, obsessive relational pursuit, and stalking. He previously served as associate editor for the *Journal of Social and Personal Relationships* and is a past president of the International Association for Relationship Research.

Shardé Davis (MA, University of California, Santa Barbara) is a doctoral student in the Department of Communication Studies at the University of Iowa. Her interdisciplinary research program uses theories and approaches from communication, feminist studies, and ethnic studies to investigate how ethnicity and gender shape relational dynamics and communication processes.

Amanda Denes (PhD, University of California, Santa Barbara) is an assistant professor in the Department of Communication at the University of Connecticut. She received her MA from UCSB in 2009 and her BA from Boston College in 2007. She broadly studies interpersonal communication, physiology, disclosure, identity, and health.

James Price Dillard (PhD, Michigan State University) is Liberal Arts Research Professor of Communication Arts & Sciences at The Pennsylvania State University. He studies how people create influence messages and the processes by which they create change in others, with an emphasis on the role of emotion. He was an editor of the journal *Human Communication Research*.

Wesley T. Durham (PhD, University of Nebraska–Lincoln) is an associate professor of communication studies at the University of Southern Indiana. His research agenda focuses on how individuals disclose health-related topics and issues to other family members. His primary research interests include disclosure and privacy processes in the contexts of family planning and sexual health.

Kory Floyd (PhD, University of Arizona) is a professor and associate director of the Hugh Downs School of Human Communication at Arizona State University. His research focuses on the communication of affection in close relationships and its relation to physiological markers of health. He has written or edited a dozen books and nearly 100 journal articles and book chapters and is the current editor of *Communication Monographs*.

Mark Alan Generous (MA, Texas State University) is a doctoral student in the Hugh Downs School of Human Communication at Arizona State University. His research focuses primarily on the effects of messages on relationship development and dissolution in intimate, familial, student-teacher, and professional relationships. His work has appeared in journals such as *The Journal of Family Communication* and *Death Studies*.

Howard Giles (PhD, DSc, University of Bristol) is professor of communication at the University of California, Santa Barbara. He is founding editor of the *Journal of Language and Social Psychology*. Giles was past president of both the International Communication Association and the International Association of Language and Social Psychology. His research interests encompass interpersonal and intergroup communication processes in intergenerational, police-civilian, and other settings, and he is the editor of the *Handbook of Intergroup Communication*.

Daena J. Goldsmith (PhD, University of Washington) is professor of Rhetoric & Media Studies at Lewis & Clark College. She studies how people enact identities and relationships in everyday interactions, including conversations between spouses or partners, advice-giving amongst friends and family, and storytelling face-to-face and online. Her two books and many of her recent articles focus on how couples or families talk about illnesses, including heart disease, cancer, HIV/AIDS, and autism.

John O. Greene (PhD, University of Wisconsin–Madison) is a professor in the Brian Lamb School of Communication at Purdue University. He has been identified as one of the top 100 most productive researchers in the history of the communication discipline (*Communication Monographs*, 1999; *Communication Quarterly*, 2004). He is a two-time recipient of the Gerald R. Miller Book Award (2002, 2004), and in 1994 received the National Communication Association's Charles H. Woolbert Research Award.

Laura K. Guerrero (PhD, University of Arizona) is a professor in the Hugh Downs School of Human Communication at Arizona State University. Her research focuses on relational, nonverbal, and emotional communication. She has published over 100 articles and chapters on these topics, as well as several books, including *Close Encounters: Communication in Relationships, Nonverbal Communication in Close Relationships,* and *The Nonverbal Communication Reader,* among others.

Michael L. Hecht (PhD, University of Illinois) is a Distinguished Professor of communication arts and sciences at The Pennsylvania State University and president of REAL Prevention, LLC. Dr. Hecht specializes in health, intercultural, and interpersonal communication. His current research studies the social processes of drug offers as well as narrative and culturally grounded health message design. This research helped form *keepin' it REAL,* a substance use prevention curriculum for elementary and middle school students.

Mary Lynn Miller Henningsen (PhD, University of Wisconsin) is an associate professor in the Department of Communication at Northern Illinois University. She studies interpersonal goals in romantic, group, and academic contexts. She has published over 25 articles and book chapters in a variety of publications.

Colin Hesse (PhD, Arizona State University) is an assistant professor of speech communication at Oregon State University. His research focuses on the importance of emotional communication and affectionate communication in close relationships. He has published several journal articles and book chapters, and he is the incoming vice-chair of the interpersonal interest group for the Western States Communication Association.

James M. Honeycutt (PhD, University of Illinois) is an LSU Distinguished Professor of Communication Studies and has published five books and over 100 articles and chapters while being the winner of numerous research awards. He is the founder of the Matchbox Interaction Lab at LSU and has shaped research in interdisciplinary fields including communication, psychology, and family studies. He is internationally known for his work in relationship scripts, imagined interaction, personality, and cognition.

Jody Koenig Kellas (PhD, University of Washington) is an associate professor in the Department of Communication Studies at the University of Nebraska–Lincoln. Her research concerns links between communicated sense-making and health. She has over 35 publications including an edited volume on family storytelling. Her research has been honored with the Family Communication Division's Outstanding Article Award, the *Journal of Family Communication* Article of the Year Award, and the GLBTQ Monograph of the Year Award.

Leanne K. Knobloch (PhD, University of Wisconsin–Madison) is an associate professor in the Department of Communication at the University of Illinois. Her research addresses how people communicate during times of transitions. Her scholarship has been honored by the Franklin H. Knower Article Award from the Interpersonal Communication Division of the National Communication Association, the Article Award from the International Association for Relationship Research, and the Golden Anniversary Monograph Award from the National Communication Association.

Andrew M. Ledbetter (PhD, University of Kansas) is an associate professor in the Department of Communication Studies at Texas Christian University. His research addresses how people use communication technology to maintain their interpersonal relationships. A related interest concerns parent-child communication and psychosocial outcomes, including technology use. He has published over 35 articles and has served in leadership roles in the National Communication Association and Central States Communication Association.

Erina L. MacGeorge (PhD, University of Illinois) is associate professor in communication arts and sciences at The Pennsylvania State University. She studies how communication contributes to effective problem-solving, decision-making, and coping, with a focus on advice. Her work has been funded by the National Science Foundation, and appears in outlets that include *Communication Research, Communication Monographs, Human Communication Research,* and the *SAGE Handbook of Interpersonal Communication.*

Valerie Manusov (PhD, University of Southern California) is a professor in the Department of Communication at the University of Washington. She is currently their director of graduate studies and a member of the Arts & Sciences College Council. Her research focuses largely on the interpretation of nonverbal behavior, often using attribution theories as a framework for doing so.

Rachel M. McLaren (PhD, The Pennsylvania State University) is an assistant professor in the Communication Studies Department at the University of Iowa. Her research seeks to clarify the interplay of communication, cognition, and emotion in responses to significant experiences, such as hurtful interactions, within personal relationships.

Sandra Metts (PhD, University of Iowa) is professor emeritus in the School of Communication at Illinois State University. Her research interests include sexual communication, forgiveness following relational transgressions, and the experience and expression of emotions in close relationships and stepfamilies. She has served as the editor of *Communication Reports,* associate editor for *Journal of Social and Personal Relationships* and *Personal Relationships,* and as president of the Central States Communication Association.

Paul A. Mongeau (PhD, Michigan State University) is professor and associate chair of the Hugh Downs School of Human Communication at Arizona State University. He studies communication in the initiation of romantic and quasi-romantic relationships (e.g., friends with benefits) and social influence processes in a number of contexts. He has published one book and over 50 articles and book chapters. He is currently first vice president of the Western States Communication Association.

Emily Lamb Normand (PhD, University of Nebraska–Lincoln) is an assistant professor at Lewis University. In her research she explores how emotional discourse creates, negotiates, and sustains personal and relational identities across a variety of relationship types. Her primary research agenda on emotional communication has been in the context of the stepsibling relationship.

Kristen M. Norwood (PhD, University of Iowa) is assistant professor of communication in the Department of English and Communication at Fontbonne University. She is interested in relational, family, and gender communication, particularly the connections between relational and cultural communication in the contexts of adoption, transgender identity transitions, and the negotiation of motherhood and work. Her research has been published in journals such as *Communication Monographs, Journal of Family Communication,* and *Management Communication Quarterly.*

Sandra Petronio (PhD, University of Michigan) is a professor in the Department of Communication Studies and the Fairbanks Center for Medical Ethics at Indiana University–Purdue University, Indianapolis. Her areas of expertise include health, interpersonal, and family communication. She has published five books, over 100 scholarly articles on privacy and disclosure, and received the National Communication Association's Knapp Award in Interpersonal Communication and Brommel Award in Family Communication. Petronio created and authored communication privacy management theory.

Gerry Philipsen (PhD, Northwestern University) is a professor of communication at the University of Washington. He studies culturally distinctive ways of communicating, communication in small task-oriented groups, and the modern history of the communication discipline. He is a recipient of numerous awards for distinction in research and teaching. He has served as department chair and as chair of the University of Washington faculty. He was named a Distinguished Scholar of the National Communication Association.

Stephanie Robbins (PhD, University of California, Santa Barbara) is an assistant professor in the School of Communication Studies at Ohio University. Her research focuses on the intersection of interpersonal communication and new media, particularly the factors which affect individuals' responses to disclosures in both online and offline contexts. She enjoys both research and teaching, but spends the rest of her time baking, reading, and secretly analyzing all of her friends' posts on Facebook.

Jordan Soliz (PhD, University of Kansas) is an associate professor of communication studies at the University of Nebraska–Lincoln. His research investigates communication and intergroup processes primarily in personal and family relationships, with an emphasis on multiethnic families, interfaith families, and grandparent-grandchild relationships. In addition to various edited volumes, his work has been published in *Communication Monographs, Communication Quarterly, Journal of Family Communication, Journal of Marriage and Family,* and the *Journal of Language and Social Psychology.*

Denise Haunani Solomon (PhD, Northwestern University) is a professor of communication arts and sciences at The Pennsylvania State University. She studies the role of communication in relationship transitions and how interpersonal communication both threatens and bolsters well-being. Her work appears in journals devoted to both communication and personal relationships research, and she is the author of the textbook *Interpersonal Communication: Putting Theory into Practice.*

Brian H. Spitzberg (PhD, University of Southern California) is Senate Distinguished Professor in the School of Communication at San Diego State University. His areas of research include communication assessment, interpersonal communication skills, conflict, jealousy, infidelity, intimate violence, sexual coercion, stalking, and meme diffusion in society. He is (co)author or co-editor of seven scholarly books, and (co)author of over 100 scholarly articles and chapters.

Laura Stafford (PhD, University of Texas) is a professor and director of the School of Media and Media and Communication at Bowling Green State University. She studies long-distance relationships and relational maintenance, and her recent work has considered the role of religion in marriage. She is a past editor of the *Journal of Applied Communication* and a past chair of the Interpersonal Communication Divisions of NCA and ICA.

Katie M. Striley (MA, Ohio University) is a doctoral candidate in the Department of Communication Studies at Ohio University. Her primary research interest is the communicative construction of systems of inclusion and exclusion. She studies exclusive communication, such as ostracism, bullying, and social rejection. She also explores inclusive communication like dialogue and deliberation. Recently, she has begun researching the intersection of risk discourse and exclusive communication.

Karen Tracy (PhD, University of Wisconsin–Madison) is professor and chair of communication at the University of Colorado, Boulder. She is a discourse analyst who studies communication problems in a range of institutional contexts, including law and policing, governance groups, and mediation. She is a Distinguished Scholar at the National Communication Association, a fellow in the International Communication Association, and the author of four books, four edited volumes, and over 80 journal articles and chapters.

Joseph B. Walther (PhD, University of Arizona) is Wee Kim Wee Professor in Communication Studies in the Wee Kim Wee School of Communication and Information at Nanyang Technological University. His work focuses on computer-mediated communication in personal relationships, groups, educational, and organizational contexts. He has chaired the Organizational Communication and Information System division of the Academy of Management, and the Communication and Technology division of the International Communication Association (ICA). He is a fellow of the ICA.

Cindy H. White (PhD, University of Arizona) is associate professor of communication at the University of Colorado, Boulder. She has published work on deception, relational loss, social support, and health communication, and she is co-editor of *Together Alone: Personal Relationships in Public Places*. Her current research explores expectations for communication between young adults and their parents about purchasing/consumption and the communicative challenges young adults face when they intervene to reduce peers' risky behavior.

Julia T. Wood (PhD, The Pennsylvania State University) is Lineberger Distinguished Professor of Humanities Emerita at the University of North Carolina at Chapel Hill. She studies and teaches about personal relationships and gender, communication, and culture. During her career, she has published 25 books and over 100 articles and chapters and has been honored with awards for teaching and research, including the Francine Merritt Award for Contributions to the Lives of Women and induction into the National Communication Association's Distinguished Scholars.

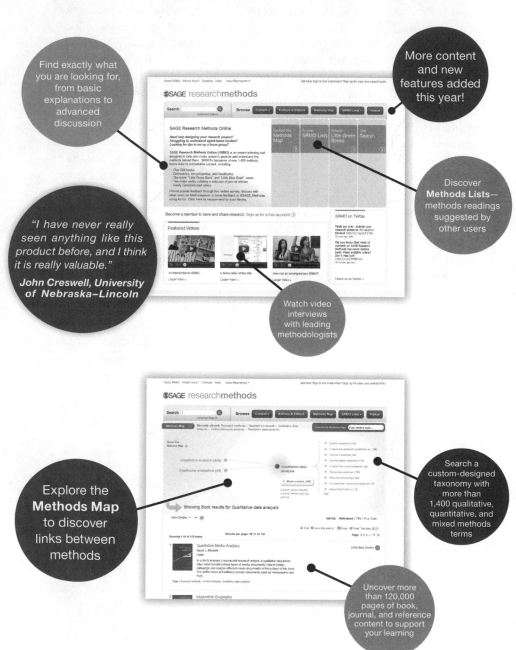

⑨SAGE researchmethods

The essential online tool for researchers from the world's leading methods publisher

Find exactly what you are looking for, from basic explanations to advanced discussion

More content and new features added this year!

"I have never really seen anything like this product before, and I think it is really valuable."

John Creswell, University of Nebraska–Lincoln

Discover **Methods Lists**— methods readings suggested by other users

Watch video interviews with leading methodologists

Explore the **Methods Map** to discover links between methods

Search a custom-designed taxonomy with more than 1,400 qualitative, quantitative, and mixed methods terms

Uncover more than 120,000 pages of book, journal, and reference content to support your learning

Find out more at
www.sageresearchmethods.com